# THE ANNOTATED LINCOLN

Painted from Life
by Thomas Hicks. Springfield, Illinois.
June 14th 1860.

THE ANNOTATED

# Lincoln

## ABRAHAM LINCOLN

EDITED BY
Harold Holzer and Thomas A. Horrocks

THE BELKNAP PRESS *of* HARVARD UNIVERSITY PRESS
*Cambridge, Massachusetts · London, England*
2016

First printing

Frontispiece: Thomas Hicks, portrait of Abraham Lincoln, oil on canvas (Springfield, 1860). This is the first life painting of Abraham Lincoln, painted shortly after he became the Republican candidate for president.

Library of Congress Cataloging-in-Publication Data
Lincoln, Abraham, 1809–1865.
  [Works. Selections]
  The annotated Lincoln / Abraham Lincoln ; edited by Harold Holzer
  and Thomas A. Horrocks.
       pages cm
  Includes bibliographical references.
  ISBN 978-0-674-50483-7 (alk. paper)
  1. Lincoln, Abraham, 1809-1865.   2. Presidents—United States—
Biography. 3. United States—Politics and government—1815–1861.
4. United States—Politics and government—1861–1865. 5. Speeches,
addresses, etc., American—19th century.
I. Holzer, Harold. II. Horrocks, Thomas A. III. Title.
      E457.92 2015b
      973.7092—dc23
      [B]
        2015019302

*To the memory of our parents*

CHARLES HOLZER (1910–1994)

ROSE LAST HOLZER (1916–2015)

AUGUSTA FOX HORROCKS (1910–1984)

CHARLES A. HORROCKS (1917–1996)

# Contents

# Lincoln Chronology

1809
February 12           Born in Hardin County, Kentucky

1811
Spring           Family moves to Knob Creek Farm in Kentucky

1815
Autumn           Attends school for the first time, and only for a few weeks

1816
December           Family moves from Kentucky to Indiana

1818
October 5           Mother, Nancy Hanks Lincoln, dies of "milk sick," the result of drinking milk from a cow that has eaten the poisonous snakeroot plant

1819
December 2           Father, Thomas Lincoln, marries widow Sarah Bush Johnston

1824           Formal schooling ends

1827           Operates a passenger ferry on the Ohio River

1828
January 20                    Sister Sarah Lincoln Grigsby dies in childbirth

1828
Spring–summer                 Travels to New Orleans by flatboat

1830
March                         Family moves from Indiana to Illinois

1831
April–July                    Takes flatboat with cargo to New Orleans for Denton
                              Offutt

1831
July                          Settles in New Salem, Illinois

1831
August 1                      Becomes clerk in Denton Offutt's New Salem store

1832
March 9                       Announces candidacy for the Illinois House of Repre-
                              sentatives

1832
April–July                    Serves in the Black Hawk War

1832
August 6                      Loses election for the Illinois House of Representa-
                              tives, his first political campaign, though he wins near-
                              unanimous vote from New Salem

1833
January 15                    With William F. Berry, purchases a store in New Salem
                              for $750

1833
May 7            Appointed postmaster of New Salem (serves until May 1836); also works as "agent" for pro-Whig *Sangamo Journal*

1834
January 6            Makes his first known land survey

1834
August 4            Wins election to Illinois House of Representatives

1834
Autumn            Begins studying law

1834
December 1            Takes seat in Illinois House of Representatives

1835
March 7            Creditors auction off his personal possessions to cover his debts

1835
August 25            Ann Rutledge dies

1836
August 1            Wins election to a second term in the Illinois House of Representatives

1836
September 9            Admitted to the Illinois bar by the Illinois Supreme Court

1837
March 3            With fellow legislator Dan Stone, presents an antislavery resolution in the Illinois House of Representatives. This is Lincoln's first public statement against slavery.

1837
April 15                        Moves to Springfield, the new capital of Illinois, and
                                becomes John T. Stuart's junior law partner

1838
January 27                      Delivers antiviolence address to the Young Men's Ly-
                                ceum of Springfield, Illinois

1838
August 6                        Reelected to third term in the Illinois House of Repre-
                                sentatives

1839
October 8                       Named a Whig presidential elector

1840
August 3                        Wins reelection to fourth term in Illinois House of
                                Representatives

1840
Fall–winter                     Engaged to Mary Todd; breaks engagement

1841
April 14                        Forms a new law partnership with Stephen T. Logan

1842
September 22                    Duel with Illinois state auditor James Shields is called
                                off at the last moment, by mutual agreement

1842
November 4                      Marries Mary Todd in a small ceremony at the Spring-
                                field home of the bride's sister, the same day the couple
                                announced their intention to marry

1843
August 1                        The Lincolns' first child, Robert Todd Lincoln, is born

1844
May 1

The Lincolns move from the Globe Tavern, where they had been living since their marriage, to their first and only home in Springfield, located at the corner of Eighth and Jackson Streets

1844
October–November

Campaigns actively for Whig presidential candidate Henry Clay

1844
December

Dissolves partnership with Logan and forms new law partnership with William Henry Herndon

1846
March 10

The Lincolns' second child, Edward Baker (Eddy) Lincoln, is born

1846
August 3

Elected to Congress, representing Illinois's Seventh District in the U.S. House of Representatives

1847
December 6

Begins his service in the Thirtieth U.S. Congress; term will end March 4, 1849

1847
December 22

In House of Representatives, introduces his "Spot" Resolutions against the Mexican War

1848
September 12–22

Campaigns in New England for Whig presidential candidate Zachary Taylor

1849
May 22

Receives patent for a device for refloating vessels that have run aground

1850
February 1                          Three-year-old son Edward (Eddy) dies from pulmo-
                                    nary tuberculosis

1850
December 21                         The Lincolns' third son, William Wallace (Willie)
                                    Lincoln, is born

1851
January 17                          Father Thomas dies in Coles County, Illinois

1853
April 4                             The Lincolns' fourth son, Thomas (Tad) Lincoln, is
                                    born

1854
September 12–October                Delivers speeches in several Illinois towns against
16                                  Illinois senator Stephen A. Douglas and his Kansas-
                                    Nebraska Act, which was signed into law by President
                                    Franklin Pierce the previous May

1854
November 7                          Elected to the Illinois House of Representatives on a
                                    fusion ticket comprising several groups opposed to the
                                    Kansas-Nebraska Act

1854
November 27                         Resigns from the Illinois House of Representatives to
                                    become a candidate for the U.S. Senate

1855
February 8                          Loses election to the U.S. Senate and ends up support-
                                    ing antislavery Democrat Lyman Trumbull

1856
February 22                         Joins movement to form the Illinois Republican Party

1856
June 19

Comes in second in balloting for vice president at the Republican National Convention in Philadelphia

1856
Summer–fall

Campaigns actively for Republican ticket in the presidential contest

1857
June 26

Delivers speech against the Supreme Court's *Dred Scott* decision in the Illinois House of Representatives

1858
June 16

Illinois Republican Party nominates Lincoln for the U.S. Senate against Democrat Stephen A. Douglas. Lincoln accepts nomination and delivers his "House Divided" speech in Springfield.

1858
August 21–October 15

Lincoln and Douglas hold seven debates across Illinois

1858
November 2

State elections give Senator Douglas a majority in the state legislature, ensuring his reelection over Lincoln

1859
December 20

Writes brief autobiographical sketch at the request of Illinois newspaper publisher Jesse Fell

1860
February 27

Delivers address at Cooper Union in New York City, establishing himself as a major contender for the Republican presidential nomination

1860
May 10

Illinois Republican Party chooses Lincoln as its presidential nominee at state convention in Decatur

1860
May 18

Republican National Convention meets in Chicago and nominates Lincoln for president on the third ballot

1860
November 6

Elected president, receiving nearly 40 percent of the popular vote and 60 percent of the electoral vote against three opponents

1860
December 20

In response to Lincoln's election, South Carolina secedes from the Union

1861
January 9–February 1

Mississippi, Florida, Alabama, Georgia, Louisiana, and Texas secede from the Union

1861
February 4

Delegates from six of the seven states that seceded from the Union meet in Montgomery, Alabama, and form the Confederate States of America

1861
March 4

Inaugurated as sixteenth president of the United States. In his inaugural address Lincoln assures Southerners that he has no intention of abolishing slavery where it exists, but vows "to hold, occupy, and possess" federal property within the seceded states.

1861
March 29

Orders relief expeditions to provision two federal forts in the South, Fort Sumter in South Carolina and Fort Pickens in Florida

1861
April 12–13            The Civil War begins when rebel troops, respond-
                       ing to Lincoln's attempt to resupply Fort Sumter in
                       Charleston, South Carolina, bombard the fort and
                       force its surrender and evacuation

1861
April 15               Issues proclamation calling for states to send 75,000
                       militia troops to Washington

1861
April 17–June 8        Virginia, Arkansas, North Carolina, and Tennessee
                       secede from the Union

1861
April 19               Orders blockade of coastline of the Confederacy

1861
April 27               Temporarily suspends writ of habeas corpus along the
                       line of troop movements between Philadelphia and
                       Washington

1861
July 21                Confederate forces defeat Union forces at the Battle of
                       Bull Run (Manassas, Virginia), the first major military
                       action of the Civil War

1861
July 27                Appoints General George B. McClellan commander
                       of all federal troops in the Washington area, soon to be
                       organized as the Army of the Potomac

1861
August 6               Signs First Confiscation Act, which nullifies owners'
                       claims on any fugitive or confiscated slaves who had
                       been employed in the Confederate war effort

1861
August 30

Concerned about maintaining loyalty of the Border States, Lincoln reverses orders of Union general John C. Frémont that established martial law in Missouri and emancipated slaves of Confederate sympathizers

1861
November 8

Captain Charles Wilkes of the *U.S.S. San Jacinto* stops the British mail ship *Trent* and removes Confederate emissaries James M. Mason and John Slidell, precipitating an international crisis. On December 26, Lincoln releases Mason and Slidell to defuse the crisis and prevent Great Britain from possibly siding with the Confederacy.

1861
December 3

Sends his first annual message to Congress, recommending a program of compensated emancipation and the colonization of freed slaves outside the United States

1862
January 11

Appoints Edwin M. Stanton secretary of war to replace the incompetent Simon Cameron

1862
February 6–16

General Ulysses S. Grant captures Forts Henry and Donelson in Tennessee

1862
February 20

Son William (Willie) Lincoln dies of typhoid fever

1862
March 6

Sends message to Congress calling for financial assistance for states that adopt plans for gradual, compensated emancipation

1862
March 9

The first encounter between two ironclad warships, the *U.S.S. Monitor* and the *C.S.S. Virginia* [*Merrimack*], takes place at Hampton Roads, Virginia, and results in a draw

1862
March 11

Removes General McClellan as general in chief of the Union armies; McClellan remains commander of the Army of the Potomac

1862
April 6–7

Union forces under General Grant are victorious in the Battle of Shiloh (Pittsburg Landing, Tennessee), one of the bloodiest battles of the war

1862
April 16

Signs legislation for immediate abolition of slavery in the District of Columbia. The legislation includes compensation for loyal slave owners as well as funds for colonization.

1862
April 25

Union admiral David G. Farragut and his naval forces capture the city of New Orleans

1862
May 19

Nullifies order of Major General David Hunter emancipating slaves in South Carolina, Georgia, and Florida

1862
May 20

Signs Homestead Act, which provides land grants of up to 160 acres on the Western plains, at reduced rates

1862
June 19

Signs law prohibiting slavery in the territories

1862
July 1

Signs Pacific Railway Act, authorizing construction of the nation's first transcontinental railroad

1862
July 2

Signs the Morrill Land Grant College Act, which provides federal land grants to states and territories for the establishment of agricultural and mechanical colleges

1862
July 11

Appoints General Henry W. Halleck as general in chief of the Union armies, the position held by General McClellan until he was removed the previous March

1862
July 17

Signs the Second Confiscation Act, imposing severe penalties on Southern rebels, including the seizure of property and slaves, and the Militia Act, which authorizes the enrollment of blacks in the war effort

1862
July 22

Presents to his cabinet a draft of the Emancipation Proclamation. Secretary of State William H. Seward convinces Lincoln to delay its announcement until the Union armies have achieved a decisive victory on the battlefield.

1862
August 17–September 23

A Sioux uprising takes place in Minnesota

1862
September 17

Union forces under General McClellan halt the Confederate advance into Northern territory at the Battle of Antietam (near Sharpsburg, Maryland), the bloodiest single day of the Civil War

1862
September 22

Issues preliminary Emancipation Proclamation, which declares that all slaves in Confederate territories will be considered "forever free" on January 1, 1863, and promises aid to states that adopt plans for gradual, compensated emancipation

1862
September 24

Orders a general suspension of the writ of habeas corpus for "all Rebels and insurgents" and their supporters

1862
November 5

Having failed to pursue General Robert E. Lee's defeated troops after the Battle of Antietam, General McClellan is removed from his command of the Army of the Potomac by Lincoln, who replaces him with General Ambrose E. Burnside

1862
December 1

In second annual message to Congress, reaffirms his support for gradual, compensated emancipation with colonization

1862
December 13

Union forces, under command of General Burnside, are soundly defeated at the Battle of Fredericksburg (Virginia)

1863
January 1

Signs final Emancipation Proclamation, which frees all slaves in territories under Confederate control, except in certain exempted areas, and authorizes the enlistment of black soldiers in the Union army

1863
January 25                          Relieves General Burnside of command of the Army
                                    of the Potomac and replaces him with General Joseph
                                    Hooker

1863
March 3                             Congress passes first military draft legislation. The law
                                    allows men to pay substitutes to serve for them.

1863
May 2–May 4                         The Army of the Potomac, under command of General Hooker, suffers another major defeat at the hands of
                                    General Lee's Army of Northern Virginia at the Battle
                                    of Chancellorsville (Virginia)

1863
June 24                             General Lee's Army of Northern Virginia commences
                                    its second invasion of Northern territory

1863
June 27                             Replaces General Hooker as commander of the Army
                                    of the Potomac with General George Gordon Meade

1863
July 1–3                            Union forces defeat Lee's army at the Battle of Gettysburg (Pennsylvania)

1863
July 4                              Union forces under General Grant capture Vicksburg,
                                    Mississippi, along with nearly 30,000 Confederate
                                    soldiers

1863
July 8                              Union forces capture Port Hudson, Mississippi, the
                                    last significant garrison on the Mississippi River

1863
July 13–16                          Draft riots roil New York City

1863
September 20                 Union forces suffer defeat at the Battle of Chickam-
                            auga, Georgia

1863
October 3                   Proclaims November 26, 1863, as the first national ob-
                            servance of Thanksgiving

1863
November 19                 Delivers the Gettysburg Address at ceremonies dedi-
                            cating a new military cemetery at the battlefield

1863
November 23–26              Union forces under General Grant drive Confederate
                            forces away from Chattanooga, Tennessee
1863
December 8                  Sends third annual message to Congress. It includes a
                            Ten Percent Plan for Reconstruction and the Procla-
                            mation of Amnesty and Reconstruction, which of-
                            fers lenient terms for Southerners who return to the
                            Union, including pardons for Confederates who take
                            the oath of allegiance to the United States.

1864
March 10                    Names Ulysses S. Grant general in chief of the Union
                            armies

1864
March 13                    In a letter to Governor Michael Hahn of Louisiana,
                            declares that he favors limited black suffrage

1864
May 5–6                     In the Battle of the Wilderness (Virginia), forces under
                            General Grant and General Lee meet for the first time
                            and fight to a draw

1864
May 8–12

In the Battle of Spotsylvania Courthouse (Virginia), Union and Confederate forces again fight to a draw. General Grant declares that he intends to "fight it out on this line if it takes all summer."

1864
May 31

A group of Radical Republicans meet in Cleveland and nominate former Republican presidential candidate and Union general John C. Frémont as a third-party candidate for president. (Frémont will withdraw from race on September 17.)

1864
June 3–4

At the Battle of Cold Harbor (Virginia), General Grant's assault on the Confederate positions produces enormous casualties but no victory. The Northern public is appalled at the mounting casualties in Grant's campaign.

1864
June 8

The Republican Party holds its national convention in Baltimore and nominates Lincoln for a second term as president and Andrew Johnson, a war Democrat from Tennessee, for vice president, over Hannibal Hamlin; party changes its name to the Union Party

1864
June 28

Approves legislation repealing the Fugitive Slave Law

1864
June 30

Accepts the resignation of Secretary of the Treasury Salmon P. Chase; the next day, names William P. Fessenden of Maine as Chase's successor

1864
July 2                          Pocket vetoes the Wade-Davis Bill, which would have
                                given Congress control of Reconstruction

1864
July 11–12                      Confederate troops under General Jubal Early threaten
                                Washington, D.C., after they raid Maryland, causing
                                panic in the nation's capital. Lincoln himself comes
                                under fire while observing the fighting at Fort Stevens,
                                Maryland.

1864
July 18                         Issues call for an additional 500,000 enlistments; also
                                announces that the "abandonment of slavery" should
                                be considered a precondition for any negotiations on
                                ending the war

1864
August 31                       The Democratic Party, meeting in Chicago, nominates
                                George B. McClellan for president and George H.
                                Pendleton of Ohio for vice president on a platform
                                calling for an end to the war

1864
September 2                     General William Tecumseh Sherman and his Union
                                forces capture the city of Atlanta

1864
November 8                      Reelected president, with 55 percent of the popular
                                vote and 212 electoral votes to McClellan's 21

1864
November 16                     General Sherman begins his "March to the Sea" from
                                Atlanta to Savannah, Georgia

1864
December 6            Presents fourth annual address to Congress

                     Nominates Salmon Chase, his former secretary of the
                     treasury, to succeed Roger B. Taney as chief justice of
                     the Supreme Court

1865
January 31           The U.S. House of Representatives follows the U.S.
                     Senate and passes theThirteenth Amendment to the
                     Constitution, abolishing slavery. Lincoln had strongly
                     lobbied for this measure, against the wishes of his
                     advisers. Two-thirds of the states would ratify it by
                     December 1865 and it would become law.

1865
February 3           With Secretary of State William H. Seward, meets
                     with Confederate peace commissioners on a steam-
                     boat near Hampton Roads, Virginia, to discuss pos-
                     sible cessation of fighting; meeting ends without any
                     progress

1865
February 17          General Sherman's army captures Columbia, South
                     Carolina

1865
March 3              Signs legislation establishing the Freedmen's Bureau
                     to aid former slaves in their adjustment to impending
                     freedom

1865
March 4              Inaugurated for a second term; delivers an address call-
                     ing for reconciliation, with "malice toward none, with
                     charity for all"

1865
March 27–28

Meets with General Grant, Admiral David D. Porter, and General Sherman on the *River Queen* at City Point, Virginia, and directs them to offer terms of surrender to their Southern counterparts

1865
April 2

General Lee and his army evacuate Petersburg, Virginia, and the Confederate government flees from Richmond. Union forces take control of the Confederate capital city as jubilation spreads throughout the North.

1865
April 5

Visits Richmond with his son Tad and is warmly welcomed by hundreds of freed blacks

1865
April 9

General Lee surrenders his Army of Northern Virginia to General Grant at Appomattox Court House in Virginia

1865
April 11

At the White House, delivers what turns out to be his last speech, calling, as he did in his second inaugural address, for reconciliation with the defeated South, and also voicing support for limited black suffrage in the South

1865
April 12

Mobile, Alabama, falls to Union troops

1865
April 14

Assassinated by actor, white supremacist, and Confederate sympathizer John Wilkes Booth while attending a play at Ford's Theatre in Washington with his wife and another couple

1865
April 15                          Dies at 7:22 in the morning

1865
April 19                          Funeral held in the East Room of the White House

1865
April 19–20                       Body lies in state in the U.S. Capitol

1865
April 12–May 3                    Lincoln funeral train travels from Washington, D.C.,
                                  to Springfield, Illinois. More than a million admirers
                                  view the late president's remains along the route.

1865
May 4                             Funeral in Springfield; Lincoln's remains placed tem-
                                  porarily in receiving vault at Oak Ridge Cemetery

THE ANNOTATED LINCOLN

# Introduction

"*Writing*—the art of communicating thoughts to the mind, through the eye—is the great invention of the world."

So Abraham Lincoln once eloquently put the matter in a declaration that offers itself as evidence of its truth, in one of his most curious and least remembered public addresses: a lengthy lecture on discoveries and inventions ranging from "the fig-leaf apron" in the Garden of Eden to America's "steamboats and railroads."[1]

Mundane the speech may have otherwise been, but when its subject turned to writing—embracing everything from Webster's dictionary to the "five books of Moses"—Lincoln proved positively inspired. Writing remained the greatest of discoveries, he emphatically insisted, "great in enabling us to converse with the dead, the absent, and the unborn, at all distances of time and of space."

Lincoln spoke not only from conviction but also from personal experience. In regard to writing—even writing about writing—Lincoln stands as one of its most inspired practitioners. From his earliest scribblings as a teenager to his final memoranda on the day he went to Ford's Theatre, Abraham Lincoln may have spent more time writing—most of it wisely and memorably—than performing any other task. We think of him perhaps first as a rail splitter, an attorney, a debater, a stump speaker, a commander in chief, an emancipator, or a pardoner—but nearly all of those roles required mastery of the art of writing, and over the years Lincoln's compositions, the most significant of which are featured in this volume, included legal documents, letters, and orations as long as 10,000-word stem-winders and as succinct as the 272 words he spoke at Gettysburg, along with presidential proclamations, dispatches, and declarations. With such a huge archive to his credit, it remains difficult to imagine how Lincoln ever found the time to do much

House in which Abraham Lincoln was born. Photograph (ca. late 19th century?). This is the traditional log cabin birthplace. The cabin was reassembled with what were alleged to be the original logs from Lincoln's birthplace.

else. Using the crude implements of the day—at the end of his life, no better than steel-nib pens and ink dipped regularly from inkwells and blotted once applied to paper—Lincoln created an American treasure trove of definitive thoughts on freedom, opportunity, and nationhood.

That Lincoln would come to be celebrated after his death as one of this nation's greatest writers would have surprised and perhaps shocked some of the well-educated contemporaries who saw the living Lincoln as a man lacking the accoutrements of refinement, as nothing more than a country bumpkin who spoke like a hayseed and wrote like a yokel completely ignorant of the fundamentals of grammar. Lincoln, of course, was always aware of those who underestimated his intelligence and talents. As a young man, painfully conscious of his intellectual deficiencies, Lincoln committed himself to a rigorous course of self-education, so that by the time he reached middle age he possessed a steely inner confidence in his ability to hold his own intellectually with his more refined and better-educated peers. Behind the folksy nineteenth- and early twentieth-century images of Lincoln reading and writing by the hearth fire in a log cabin isolated on the prairie lies a real story of a

Lincoln's stepmother, Sarah Bush Lincoln, at age seventy-seven. Photograph (ca. 1865).

man whose life was, in many ways, a constant act of becoming, including becoming a great writer.

Born on February 12, 1809, in a log cabin near Hodgenville, Kentucky, Abraham Lincoln was the second of Thomas and Nancy Hanks Lincoln's three children. Lincoln's Virginia-born parents named their first son in honor of his paternal grandfather, Abraham, who was killed by Indians in 1786. Within two years of Lincoln's birth, his parents, in search of more fertile land, moved the family seven miles away to Knob Creek, where a third child, Thomas, was born, only to die shortly after birth. When Lincoln was seven years old, the family made another move, instigated primarily by Thomas Lincoln's problems with land titles, this time across the Ohio River to the southern Indiana frontier.

In 1818, two years after arriving in Indiana, Lincoln's mother died from a disease called "milk sick," probably caused by drinking milk from cows that had ingested poisonous snakeroot. A year later, ten-year-old Abraham and his older sister, Sarah (who would die in childbirth in 1826), gained a stepmother when Thomas Lincoln married Sarah Bush John-ston, a widow with three children of her own. Although Lincoln deeply mourned the death

Louis Prang, after Eastman Johnson, *The Boyhood of Lincoln (An Evening in a Log Hut)*. Chromolithograph (Boston, 1868). This version of Eastman Johnson's iconic rendering of Lincoln's youthful attempt at self-improvement was included in "Prang's American Chromos," a series issued by the popular printmaking firm.

of his mother, he developed a warm affection for his stepmother, who, unlike Lincoln's father, encouraged and supported her stepson's tireless pursuit of knowledge. After thirteen years in Indiana, the Lincoln family, searching for better economic opportunities, moved again, this time to Macon County, Illinois.

An exemplar of the self-made man, Lincoln worked tenaciously to overcome his humble beginnings. Self-conscious about the primitive environment into which he was born, the illiteracy of his parents, and a formal education limited to less than a year, Lincoln embarked on a vigorous regimen of self-improvement, spending as much time as he could enhancing his reading and writing skills. His limited exposure to formal schooling was not an unusual circumstance in early nineteenth-century America; it was an experience shared by many of his generation, especially those residing in the western and southern regions of the country. What was extraordinary about Lincoln's experience, however, was the remarkable trajectory of his career, which culminated in his election and reelection as president of the United States and his emergence as one of this country's greatest writers of nonfiction, despite what he referred to as his "defective" education and the fact that he did not master the fundamentals of grammar until he reached his early twenties.[2]

Lincoln's writing skills in his mature years were primarily influenced by his youthful reading habits. His early reading tended to be intensive rather than extensive. Since books were scarce on the frontier, he would have read a few books more than once, memorizing much of what he read. The King James Bible, for example, was one such book that Lincoln, as well as many Americans of the time, read, reread, and memorized. As shown in several of the documents presented in this volume, Lincoln possessed a fluent knowledge of the Bible.[3] An increasingly voracious reader, he devoured other books belonging to his stepmother or borrowed from neighbors, such titles as *Aesop's Fables,* John Bunyan's *The Pilgrim's Progress,* Daniel Defoe's *Robinson Crusoe,* Benjamin Franklin's *Autobiography,* and Mason Locke Weems's and David Ramsay's biographies of George Washington.[4]

Other books integral to Lincoln's development as a writer—and speaker—were Thomas Dilworth's *New Guide to the English Tongue* (1740), William Scott's *Lessons in Elocution* (1779), Lindley Murray's *English Reader* (1795), and Samuel Kirkham's *English Grammar* (1823). Lincoln was introduced to Dilworth's work (popularly known as Dilworth's *Spelling-Book*) during his time in Indiana or later in New Salem, Illinois. In addition to lessons in spelling, pronunciation, and grammar, the *Spelling-Book* contained selections of prose and verse by leading eighteenth-century British authors. Lincoln copied out and memorized sections of Scott's *Lessons in Elocution,* especially those passages meant to improve reading and speaking skills. Murray's popular *English Reader,* which Lincoln believed was the best schoolbook of its time, also offered for its various exercises poetry and prose selections from British authors of the same period. After Lincoln left the family farm and moved to New Salem, he embarked on a study of Kirkham's *English Grammar* to further improve his writing skills, walking several miles to borrow the book from an acquaintance.[5]

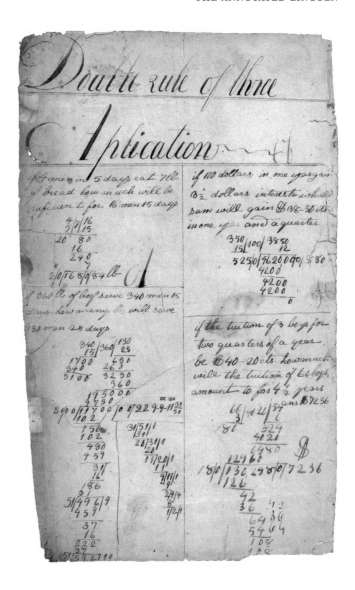

Abraham Lincoln, exercise book fragment.
Manuscript (ca. 1825). This scrapbook page
contains mathematical exercises in the hand of
the teenage Lincoln.

Lincoln's ability to write the eloquent prose for which he became famous developed over time, gradually enhanced through strenuous practice and constantly reinforced through his active reading habits. After Lincoln's death, his stepmother recalled Lincoln's fascination with words and their meaning when he was young: "Abe read all the books he could lay his hands on—and when he came across a passage that Struck him he would write it down on boards if he had no paper & keep it there till he did get paper—then he would re-write it— look at it repeat it—He had a copy book—a kind of scrap book in which he would put down all things and this preserved them."[6]

Lincoln's schoolhouse in Knob Creek, Kentucky. Photograph (1932). Lincoln's formal education lasted no more than one year in total. This windowless building housed the first school Lincoln attended.

Ernest F. Hubbard, after Morgan J. Rhees, *Youth of Abraham Lincoln.* Engraving (1889). This print depicts a young Lincoln reading a book, taking a break from splitting rails.

While Lincoln appeared to have minimal interest in fiction, he did enjoy reading works of biography, history, and, especially, humor and poetry.[7] As a young man, he was known for his skill as a storyteller. Habitually turning to a seemingly endless supply of jokes and witty anecdotes (some of which were of the off-color, barnyard variety intended solely for male listeners) to make a point or merely to add levity to a conversation, Lincoln throughout his life used homespun, humorous stories in a variety of situations, to connect with members of a jury, fellow lawyers and politicians, and ordinary folks he met in his travels across Illinois or in the White House. Thus it is not surprising that Lincoln was attracted to works of humor, ranging from the various jest books that circulated on the frontier to writings of contemporary humorists and satirists who published under the names Artemus Ward (Charles Farrar Browne), Petroleum V. Nasby (David Ross Locke), and Orpheus C. Kerr (Robert Henry Newell, his pen name a play on "office seeker"). Even during the darkest days of his presidency, Lincoln turned frequently to the works of Ward, Nasby, and Kerr for entertainment and to escape from the burdens of office and the horrors of war.[8]

As a young man, Lincoln developed a particular love for poetry, becoming an avid reader and an occasional writer of verse, ranging from his adolescent satirical jottings, such as "Abraham Lincoln is my name / And with my pen I wrote the same / I wrote in both hast [sic] and speed / And left it here for fools to read," to his melancholic and sentimental poems from his twenties and thirties (his 1846 "My Childhood-Home I See Again" is featured in this book).[9] His favorite poets, some of whose works he would have initially encountered in the texts of Dilworth, Scott, and Murray, included Robert Burns, Lord Byron, William Knox, Alexander Pope, and, of course, William Shakespeare. Numerous friends and acquaintances spoke of Lincoln's early and profound admiration for Shakespeare. Ninian Wirt Edwards for one, brother-in-law of Mary Lincoln, claimed that Lincoln read the Bard "Every Evening," while Lincoln's law partner William Henry Herndon asserted that his fellow attorney carried a "well-worn copy of Shakespeare, in which he read no little in his leisure moments." Several documents presented in this collection contain quotes from Shakespeare, and Lincoln wrote a fascinating defense of his own favorite plays and soliloquies in an exchange of letters with the eminent Shakespearian actor James H. Hackett.[10]

Up until the age of twenty-one, Lincoln worked on the family farms, assisting his father in planting crops, clearing trees, and splitting rails for fences. When his labor was not required at home, he performed a variety of odd jobs on other farms and as a ferryman and flatboat operator. Lincoln's quest for self-improvement at the expense of the farm work he despised, however, strained his relationship with his father, who, in the view of his ambitious son, lacked the desire to better himself or his family. In an 1860 autobiographical sketch presented in this volume, Lincoln dismissively referred to his father's illiteracy, claiming that Thomas Lincoln "never did more in the way of writing than to bunglingly sign his own name." Once he reached the age of twenty-one Lincoln struck out on his own, anxious to leave behind the physical work associated with the soil to pursue a career requiring more

Harriet Putnam, *Lover of Books and Study*. Print (1900–1910). A romanticized image of Lincoln as a boy reading by the hearth fire in a log cabin.

brains than brawn. After settling in New Salem, a small village on the Sangamon River near Springfield, Illinois, Lincoln remained in only infrequent contact with his parents. In 1851 he refused to visit his father on his deathbed, and he did not attend the funeral. Although he did pay a visit to his stepmother before he left for Washington to assume the presidency, there is no evidence that she or his father ever met Lincoln's wife or children. He had moved up in the world, and there would be no sentimental glancing back.

During his six years in New Salem, Lincoln tried his hand at various occupations, including store clerk, mill hand, postmaster, and surveyor. In 1832, when the Black Hawk War broke out, he was named captain of the local militia, although he did not engage in combat. That same year he ran for his first political office, a seat in the Illinois legislature. Lincoln favored the Whig Party because of his admiration for its leader, Henry Clay, and his enthusiasm for its program of government support for education, internal improvements, a centralized banking system, and domestic manufacturing through protective tariffs. Although Lincoln lost his first bid for public office (despite garnering more than 90 percent of the New Salem vote), his political ambition was not in the least dampened. Two years later his second campaign was successful, and he went on to serve four consecutive terms in the state legislature.

During his New Salem years, when he developed interests in surveying, law, and politics, Lincoln became an avid reader of works in all those subjects. For example, when he began to consider a legal career, Lincoln studied several of the standard legal textbooks he borrowed from a lawyer friend, teaching himself enough to obtain a license in 1836 to practice law in Illinois. Over the next twenty-five years he developed a successful practice that provided his family with a comfortable middle-class living. His practice also allowed him to pursue a political career.

Lincoln had abandoned the intensive reading habits of his youth by the time he achieved success as a lawyer and politician in Springfield. In fact, according to one historian, Lincoln appeared at the time to have read "little more . . . than his professional and political interests required."[11] Lincoln's political interests demanded not only that he be well read on the issues of the day, but also that he communicate effectively through the spoken and written word. When it came to politics, Lincoln's voracious reading habits shaped and were shaped by his burning ambition to achieve success as a statesman. Acutely aware of the power of print in influencing public opinion, Lincoln, from the beginning of his political career in New Salem and Springfield, and through his years as president, devoured a variety of political publications, especially newspapers. A shrewd politician, Lincoln used print to further his own and his party's agenda, contributing hundreds of anonymous editorials to Springfield's *Sangamo Journal* (later called the *Illinois State Journal*) and courting and cultivating newspaper editors and journalists. When serving in the United States Congress, Lincoln took full advantage of his franking privileges to mail printed versions of his speeches to constituents back home in Illinois. In the 1840 presidential campaign Lincoln undertook a number of initiatives in Illinois on behalf of fellow Whig William Henry Harrison, including serving as one of the editors of the *Old Soldier,* a pro-Harrison campaign newspaper. When running for president himself twenty years later, seeking support from the key swing-vote German American community, Lincoln secretly invested in a Springfield German-language newspaper, the *Illinois Staats-Anzeiger,* to promote the Republican cause.[12]

Lincoln's initial efforts at political speaking and writing are examples of a self-taught man struggling to achieve the most effective style and voice. For Lincoln, speaking and writing were often linked; he understood that in many cases more people would read one of his speeches, most likely in a newspaper, than would hear it. In composing his early speeches, Lincoln followed the conventions of the time, producing prose that tended to be formal and ponderous, occasionally sprinkled with florid and verbose passages he would avoid in his later writings. Early in his career, Lincoln, who relished the rough-and-tumble give-and-take of the political arena, also made use of his humorous storytelling skills and canny ability to imitate various styles of vernacular speech to mock opponents. The most famous example (or infamous, considering that it almost led to a duel, an experience Lincoln regretted for the rest of his life) is the 1842 "Rebecca" letter included in this work. Two years before, a Lincoln stump speech included such a brutally hilarious and scathing imitation—popularly known as a "skinning"—of Democrat Jesse B. Thomas that it brought his opponent to tears.[13] As is apparent in successive entries in *The Annotated Lincoln,* Lincoln always retained his sharp humor, but over time he dispensed with the hard-edged ridicule that peppered his earlier speeches and writings.

In 1837 Lincoln moved to Springfield, Illinois's capital city, where he established himself as a lawyer and politician and also met, courted, and married Kentucky-born Mary Todd, with whom he commenced raising a family that eventually included four boys. His two terms and eight years in the state legislature provided him with an education in the art of politics. He developed shrewd political skills and leadership abilities, becoming adept at forming coalitions, drafting legislation, and debating policy. In his years in the legislature, Lincoln became a leader of the Illinois Whig Party and was actively involved in passing legislation for massive internal improvement projects to build canals and railroads across the state. Also in 1837, during his second term, Lincoln issued his first public statement on slavery (included in this collection) when he voted against a resolution that condemned antislavery societies. Although not an abolitionist, he strongly opposed slavery, claiming that the institution was "founded on both injustice and bad policy." In addition to his legal and political activities, Lincoln presented several public lectures, speaking on such topics as temperance and agriculture, as well as discoveries and inventions.

Lincoln's career in the Illinois state legislature ended in 1842 when he decided not to seek reelection. He was ready to fish in a bigger pond, and soon set his eyes eastward toward the U.S. Congress. His chance came in August 1846 when, after gaining the Whig nomination to represent Illinois's Seventh Congressional District, he defeated his Democratic opponent. When he arrived in the nation's capital to take his seat in Congress, Lincoln was anxious to make his mark on the national stage, choosing opposition to the Mexican War as one of his signature issues. Although the war was popular in his own district, Lincoln, like many Whigs, opposed the conflict that began in 1846, claiming that it was initiated by Democratic president James K. Polk under the false premise that U.S. territory had been invaded by Mexican soldiers. Despite his belief that the war was unnecessary and unconsti-

*Abraham Lincoln's Residence, Springfield, Illinois, 1860.* Hand-colored lithograph, based on a photograph taken by J. A. Whipple in the summer of 1860. Lincoln and his sons Willie and Tad stand with their father inside the front fence.

tutional, Lincoln did support legislation aiding the troops. Nevertheless, Democrats fiercely questioned his patriotism. In addition to his Mexican War stance, Lincoln voted several times for the Wilmot Proviso, which would have prohibited slavery in territories acquired from Mexico, and drafted a bill to end slavery—gradually—in the nation's capital. The latter measure, which stipulated a referendum on slavery and compensation for slave owners, was never submitted for a vote.

After serving one term in Congress, adhering to a rotation-in-office agreement with fellow Whigs back in Illinois, Lincoln reluctantly did not seek reelection. Returning to Springfield with his political career seemingly at a dead end, he resumed his legal practice, suffered the death of his three-year-old son Edward (Eddy) from pulmonary tuberculosis, and kept up with state and national politics despite his own bleak prospects. Lincoln's formal reentry into the political arena came about in 1854 with the passage of the Kansas-Nebraska Act, written largely by Stephen A. Douglas, Democratic senator from Illinois, who had achieved a level of political success that Lincoln craved.

Currier & Ives, after Louis Ransom, *John Brown meeting the slave mother and her child on the steps of Charlestown jail on his way to execution.* Lithograph (New York, 1863). This print, issued for Northern customers during the Civil War, is a melodramatic portrayal of an apocryphal incident in the life of antislavery hero John Brown.

By repealing the Missouri Compromise of 1820, which banned slavery above the Mason-Dixon Line, and thus shifting decisions about slavery from Congress to the residents of territories in what remained of the Louisiana Purchase, Douglas's Kansas-Nebraska Act sent shock waves through the American political system, destroying the Whig Party, dividing

Democrats (leading to the birth of the Republican Party), and fueling sectional tensions as slavery once again emerged as the predominant political issue. Lincoln believed that the Constitution prevented congressional interference with slavery in those states where it already existed but saw no such protection in the territories, claiming that allowing slavery's expansion into the West contradicted the wishes of the Founding Fathers, who, according to Lincoln, adopted the Declaration of Independence and the Northwest Ordinance of 1787 with the purpose of assisting the institution's eventual demise. Over the next several years Lincoln emerged as a leading critic of the Kansas-Nebraska bill—and Douglas—and of slavery's expansion into the territories, becoming a leader of an anti-Nebraska coalition in Illinois, first as a Whig and then as an active member of the new Republican Party, an organization founded primarily to fight the spread of slavery outside of the Southern states where it already existed. His influence expanding, Lincoln worked to unite various factions of Illinois's Republican coalition, giving speeches, raising money, recruiting candidates, and devising strategy. In 1856, at the Republican Party's first national convention, he came in second in the balloting for the vice presidential nomination.

It was during the 1850s that Lincoln not only returned to the political battlefield but also emerged as the leading spokesman for the nascent Republican organization in Illinois and beyond—largely due to his extraordinary ability to articulate, like few others, its ideals and philosophy. In the period beginning with his 1854 anti-Nebraska speech in Peoria and ending with his Cooper Union address in February 1860 (both of which are presented in this volume), Lincoln composed the most memorable speeches of his pre-presidential career in a writing style mixing eloquent and plain, homespun language accessible to audiences and readers alike. Lincoln took his writing seriously, devoting much time to the research, drafting, and revision that each composition required. His eldest son, Robert, provided a description of Lincoln's meticulous approach to writing, whether an important speech or an informal letter:

> He was a very deliberate writer, anything but rapid. I cannot remember any peculiarity about his posture; he wrote sitting at a table and, as I remember, in an ordinary posture. As to dictation, I never saw him dictate to anyone, and it certainly was not his practice to do so. He seemed to think nothing of the labor of writing personally and was accustomed to make many scraps notes and memoranda. In writing a careful letter, he first wrote it himself, then corrected it, and then rewrote the corrected version himself.[14]

Lincoln's laborious writing process was not a completely solitary exercise, for he often read his speeches aloud to advisers and friends, or shared his drafts with them, asking for their opinion.

By 1858, Illinois Republicans nominated Lincoln to challenge Douglas's reelection to the

Rally in front of Lincoln's Springfield residence. Photograph by William Shaw (Springfield, IL, August 8, 1860). Republicans march past the presidential candidate's home, with Lincoln standing by the front door.

U.S. Senate. The issue of slavery in the territories dominated the campaign, which included Lincoln's legendary debates with the "Little Giant." Douglas's impressive debating skills were matched by those of the lanky Springfield lawyer, who was little known at the beginning of the race, outside of Illinois. Although Douglas regained his Senate seat, Lincoln's performance in the debates helped build his national reputation as an emerging leader of the Republican Party, especially when his addresses, rejoinders, and replies appeared in newspaper reprints and, ultimately, a book-length collection that made Lincoln a "bestselling" writer.

In the wake of his strong showing against Douglas in 1858, Lincoln, now a popular speaker throughout the Midwest against the extension of slavery, was put forward by Illinois Republicans as a presidential candidate. His February 1860 speech at New York City's Cooper Union promoting the philosophical underpinnings of the Republican Party both introduced him to Eastern party members and also enhanced his stature as a contender for the party's nomination. Despite his growing reputation among party leaders, Lincoln was considered one of the lesser known candidates and was given little chance of winning the nomination when the Republicans' national convention opened in Chicago in May 1860. He soon emerged as a serious candidate, however, as his managers outmaneuvered the teams of the preconvention favorite, Senator William Henry Seward of New York, and other, better known politicians, among them Salmon Chase of Ohio, Edward Bates of Missouri, and

Currier & Ives, *The Republican Banner for 1860*. Lithograph (New York, 1860). This broadside was issued to promote the Republican Party ticket.

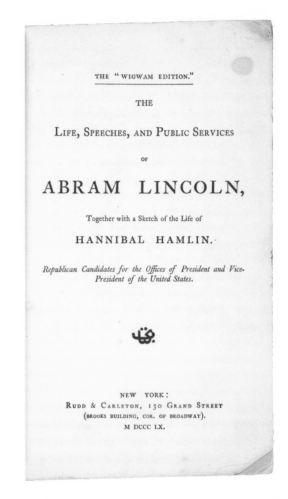

*The Life, Speeches, and Public Services of Abram Lincoln* (New York: Rudd & Carleton, 1860). The title page of the first of several campaign biographies. This one, with an image of Lincoln on the cover based on Mathew Brady's Cooper Union photograph, was written by an anonymous author who was unaware of Lincoln's correct first name.

Simon Cameron of Pennsylvania. To the surprise of many pundits, Lincoln won the nomination on the third ballot.

Lincoln entered the presidential election in a strong position, against a fractured Democratic Party and a third-party candidate. Having failed to find a candidate suitable to both Northern and Southern members, the Democrats fielded two nominees: Stephen A. Douglas, representing the Northern wing of the party and its platform supporting popular sovereignty in the territories, and Vice President John C. Breckinridge of Kentucky, representing

"For President, Abraham Lincoln—Vice President, Hannibal Hamlin." Campaign flag (1860). Flags, such as the ones shown here, were popular campaign ornaments in the nineteenth century.

"Lincoln and Hamlin." Campaign flag (1860).

the Southern wing and its platform espousing a federal slave code. A fourth candidate, John Bell of Tennessee, was nominated by the Constitutional Union Party, a fusion of conservative Whigs and Know-Nothings that rejected the sectional policies of the two major parties in favor of Unionism.

Following tradition, Lincoln did no personal campaigning of his own. He was represented by surrogates, including his former rivals Seward and Chase; a vibrant Republican press and a campaign team that skillfully melded images of Lincoln as a "rail splitter," a man of the people espousing free labor, and as "Honest Abe," a man of integrity; and the intrepid groups of enthusiastic young men who formed the Wide Awake clubs, which held military-style parades throughout the North. Lincoln's public writings achieved wide distribution during the race, even though his private strategy letters remained confidential. The election, held on November 6, exposed the country's deep sectional divisions, with Lincoln winning the presidency despite receiving no Southern support. He carried all of the free states except New Jersey, which he split with Douglas, and garnered 54 percent of the popular vote in the North, though less than 40 percent nationwide.

Fearing that Republican attempts to limit slavery's spread constituted the first steps toward total abolition, many Southern leaders, especially those from the Deep South, refused to accept the election results and threatened secession. While Lincoln had no intention of interfering with slavery where it already existed (privately assuring several Southerners on this point before his inauguration), he refused to retreat on the issue of slavery's extension, working behind the scenes to prevent Republican congressmen from participating in any

D. Wentworth, "Honest Old Abe." Sheet music (Buffalo: Blodgett and Bradford, 1860). One of many pro-Lincoln campaign songs issued during the 1860 election.

effort at compromise, sought by both conservative Northern and moderate Southern politicians, that would negate this key Republican principle. On December 20, 1860, South Carolina became the first of seven Southern states to secede from the Union prior to Lincoln's inauguration. Eventually, eleven states seceded, forming the Confederate States of America, with Jefferson Davis of Mississippi as president.

Facing a crisis that no other U.S. president, before or after, has ever had to address, Lincoln saw his leadership abilities severely tested. Many Americans had no idea what to expect from the man known as Honest Abe and the Rail Splitter, and few Democrats, not to mention the nation's intelligentsia, expected a response equal to the emergency. Despite Lincoln's well-crafted, eloquent prewar speeches and writings, he was still considered an intel-

Louis Maurer, *The Rail Candidate.* Lithograph (New York: Currier & Ives, 1860). Cartoon emphasizing Lincoln's image as the Rail Splitter from the frontier.

lectual lightweight. As one of his White House secretaries, John G. Nicolay, recalled, many people were surprised by the president's "remarkable power of literary expression." But Nicolay and others in Lincoln's circle of friends and advisers knew better; they were familiar with his enormous capacity to lead through the written and spoken word. "The remarkable thing," Nicolay explained, was that Lincoln "learned to write—learned to appreciate the value of the pen as an instrument to formulate and record his thought, and the more clearly, forcibly, and elegantly to express it."[15] Even Lincoln himself, despite his inner confidence in his own intellectual capacity, did not think of himself as a great writer. "Nothing would have more amazed him while he lived than to hear himself called a man of letters," wrote Nicolay and John Hay years after Lincoln's death.[16]

The major events of Lincoln's presidency have been chronicled by many fine historians and thus require no retelling here. Suffice it to say, Lincoln's presidency was historic and transformative; he led the country through a long and bloody civil war and addressed criti-

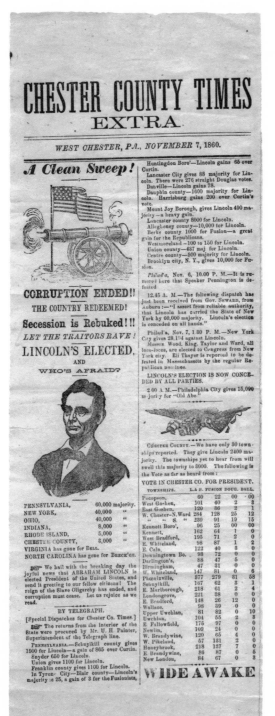

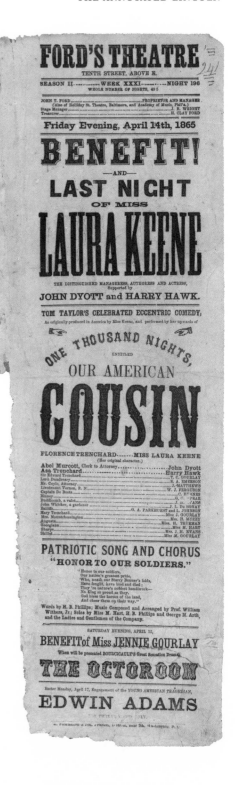

*A Clean Sweep . . . Lincoln's Elected, and Who's Afraid? Chester County Times Extra.* Broadside (West Chester, PA, November 7, 1860). This extra edition published by a Republican newspaper in Pennsylvania celebrates Lincoln's election as president with glowing headlines, such as "Corruption Ended!!," "The Country Redeemed!" and "Secession Is Rebuked!!!"

*Ford's Theatre . . . Friday Evening, April 14th, 1865 . . . Our American Cousin.* Broadside (Washington, DC: H. Polkinhorn and Son, 1865). Playbill announcing the program at Ford's Theatre the night Lincoln was assassinated.

cal issues, such as race and equality and individual freedoms in time of war, that continue to resound in our nation a century and a half later. Lincoln's remarkable achievements as president have tended to overshadow his talents as a writer. Today, in the age of professional speechwriters, it is hard for us to imagine a president of the United States writing his or her own speeches without the assistance of White House staff. Lincoln was his own speechwriter. His artistry with words and his extraordinary ability to inform and inspire the American people and to shape public opinion proved indispensable to his greatness as a leader. Lincoln, according to one historian, achieved "a capacity to express himself and the national concerns more effectively than any president ever had," with the possible exception of Thomas Jefferson.[17] Lincoln's contemporaries Ralph Waldo Emerson and Harriet Beecher Stowe, who knew a thing or two about writing, praised his ability to reach the people through the written word. Emerson credited the self-taught rail splitter with the ability to communicate sincerity and conviction through his writing: "What pregnant definitions; what unerring common sense; what foresight; and, on great occasion, what lofty, and more than national, what human tone! His brief speech at Gettysburg will not easily be surpassed by words on any recorded occasion." To Stowe, the celebrated author of *Uncle Tom's Cabin,* there were passages in Lincoln's writings "that could not be better put," for they were "absolutely perfect." They were, she said, "worthy to be inscribed in letters of gold."[18] Days after Lincoln delivered his second inaugural address, Charles Francis Adams Jr., the son of Lincoln's minister to Great Britain, wrote to his father of his surprise at the ability of the uneducated Lincoln to communicate to the American people:

> What do you think of the inaugural? That rail-splitting lawyer is one of the wonders of the day. Once at Gettysburg and now again on a greater occasion he has shown a capacity for rising to the demands of the hour which should not be expected from orators of men of the schools. The inaugural strikes me in its grand simplicity and directness as being for all time the historical keynote of this war; in it a people seemed to speak in the sublimely simple utterances of ruder times.[19]

Today, Lincoln is almost universally considered this country's greatest president and the author of some of the greatest speeches in the English language, and his words continue to inspire and uplift people from all walks of life and all parts of the globe.

This volume is designed for a wide audience that includes the general reader, scholars, teachers, students, and Lincoln enthusiasts. Considering all of the attention Abraham Lincoln has received from innumerable scholars and popular writers, not to mention his iconic status in American culture, it is surprising that no extensive annotated volume of his writings has been published until now. Lincoln continues to attract scholarly attention and to stir the imagination of the general public 150 years after his tragic death by an assassin's bullet. There are more books written about Lincoln than about any other American.

Over the past century and a half Lincoln has been interpreted and reinterpreted by scholars, popular historians, journalists, novelists, playwrights, and screenwriters, and invoked to justify various causes and movements. Yet one cannot derive meaning from and fully appreciate Lincoln's life and career without understanding what he wrote. In *The Annotated Lincoln,* we guide readers through a selection of Lincoln's essential writings, examining the extraordinary man who produced them and explaining the context in which they were composed. In doing so, we attempt to bring Lincoln's correspondence, memoranda, and speeches more generally into the scope of contemporary scholarship, quoting selectively in the book's margins from leading works of biography, history, and criticism to offer a larger appreciation of Lincoln's writing, thought, and political career.[20]

Comprising almost one hundred letters, speeches, and presidential messages drawn primarily from *The Collected Works of Abraham Lincoln,* complemented by some one hundred illustrations, *The Annotated Lincoln* documents three decades of Lincoln's life and career, from his initial political campaign for state assemblyman through his historic presidency.[21] Through our commentary, we examine Lincoln the popular country lawyer, awkward suitor and loving father, engaging jokester and humorist, ambitious politician and shrewd party leader, resilient and resolute commander in chief and president, whose enormous capacity for growth enabled him to overcome the prejudices of his time to restore the founding principles of American republicanism and freedom. Our annotations explore Lincoln's positions on the critical issues of his time, including slavery, racial equality, secession, and civil liberties in time of war. *The Annotated Lincoln* locates Lincoln's essential writings in contexts necessary for understanding, appreciating, and teaching the life and times of this remarkable man.

# NOTES

1 See "Lecture on Discoveries and Inventions, February 11, 1859," in this volume.

2 Lincoln's reference to his "defective" education can be found in *The Collected Works of Abraham Lincoln,* ed. Roy P. Basler, 9 vols. (New Brunswick, NJ: Rutgers University Press, 1953–1955), 2:459 (hereafter cited as *CW*). The lack of educational opportunities available to Lincoln and others raised in similar circumstances in early nineteenth-century America is covered by Myron Marty, "Schooling in Lincoln's America and Lincoln's Extraordinary Self-Schooling," in *Lincoln's America 1809–1865,* ed. Joseph R. Fornieri and Sara Vaughn Gabbard (Carbondale: Southern Illinois University Press, 2008), 55–71. On Lincoln's self-education, see Frank J. Williams, "The Educated Mr. Lincoln," in *The Living Lincoln,* ed. Thomas A. Horrocks, Harold Holzer, and Frank J. Williams (Carbondale: Southern Illinois University Press, 2011), 9–19. For Lincoln's study of grammar, see *CW,* 4:62.

3 Regarding Lincoln's reading of the Bible, see Ferenc Morton Szasz and Margaret Connell Szasz, *Lincoln and Religion* (Carbondale: Southern Illinois University Press, 2014), 4; Wayne C. Temple, *Abraham Lincoln: From Skeptic to Prophet* (Mahomet, IL: Mayhaven Publishing, 1995), 9; and David C. Mearns, "Mr. Lincoln and the Books He Read," in *Three Presidents and Their Books* (Urbana: University of Illinois Press, 1955), 72–73.

4 Sarah Bush Johnston brought several books with her when she accompanied Lincoln's father from Kentucky to Indiana. David Herbert Donald, *Lincoln* (New York: Simon & Schuster, 1995), 31. On books read by Lincoln in his youth, see Robert Bray, *Reading with Lincoln* (Carbondale: Southern Illinois University Press, 2010), 4.

5 James Engel, *The Committed Word: Literature and Public Values* (University Park: Pennsylvania State University Press, 1999), 143–146; Bray, *Reading with Lincoln,* 4–9, 41–42; Fred Kaplan, *Lincoln: A Biography of a Writer* (New York: Harper, 2008), 10–11, 32; Marty, "Schooling in Lincoln's America," 61–63; and Donald, *Lincoln,* 29, 48. Lincoln's assertion concerning Murray's work and his study of Kirkham's *English Grammar* are cited in William H. Herndon and Jesse W. Weik, *Herndon's Lincoln,* ed. Douglas L. Wilson and Rodney O. Davis (Urbana: Knox College Lincoln Studies Center and the University of Illinois Press, 2006), 36, 64–65. The dates in parentheses refer to the original editions of the works of Dilworth, Scott, and Murray. The editions used by the editors are: Thomas Dilworth, *A New Guide to the English Tongue* (Philadelphia: John Bioren, 1819); William Scott, *Lessons in Elocution, or a Selection of Pieces in Prose and Verse, for the Improvement of Youth in Reading and Speaking* (Montpelier, VT: E. P. Walton, 1820); Lindley Murray, *The English Reader, or Pieces in Prose and Poetry, Selected from the Best Writers* (Haverhill, NH: White and Rand, 1824); and Samuel Kirkham, *English Grammar in Familiar Lessons* (Rochester, NY: Marshall and Dean, 1833).

6 Lincoln's stepmother is cited in Douglas L. Wilson and Rodney O. Davis, ed., *Herndon's Informants: Letters, Interviews, and Statements about Abraham Lincoln* (Urbana: University of Illinois Press, 1998), 107.

7    Kaplan, *Lincoln,* 21–22. Lincoln was quoted as saying, "I never read an entire novel in my life. . . . I once commenced 'Ivanhoe' but never finished it." Francis B. Carpenter, *The Inner Life of Abraham Lincoln: Six Months in the White House* (Boston: Houghton, Osgood and Company, 1880), 115; and Donald, *Lincoln,* 47.

8    William E. Barton, *Abraham Lincoln and His Books* (Chicago: Marshall Field and Co., 1920), 18; Bray, *Reading with Lincoln,* 200–208.

9    For "Abraham Lincoln is my name," see *CW,* 1:1.

10   Ninian Wirt Edwards is cited in Wilson and Davis, *Herndon's Informants,* 446. Herndon is cited in Herndon and Weik, *Herndon's Lincoln,* 199. On Lincoln's admiration of Shakespeare, see Robert Berkelman, "Lincoln's Interest in Shakespeare," *Shakespeare Quarterly* 2 (1951): 303–312.

11   Douglas L. Wilson, "The Frigate and the Frugal Chariot: Jefferson and Lincoln as Readers," in *Lincoln before Washington: New Perspectives on the Illinois Years* (Urbana: University of Illinois Press, 1997), 8.

12   For an account of Lincoln's understanding of and relationship with the press, see Harold Holzer, *Lincoln and the Power of the Press: The War for Public Opinion* (New York: Simon & Schuster, 2014). See also Richard Carwardine, "Abraham Lincoln and the Fourth Estate: The White House and the Press during the American Civil War," *American Nineteenth Century History* 7 (March 2006): 1–27; and Michael Burlingame, "Lincoln Spins the Press," in *Lincoln Reshapes the Presidency,* ed. Charles M. Hubbard (Macon, GA: Mercer University Press, 2003), 65–78.

13   The "skinning" of Thomas is related in Herndon and Weik, *Herndon's Lincoln,* 130.

14   Robert Todd Lincoln is cited in Douglas L. Wilson, *Lincoln's Sword: The Presidency and the Power of Words* (New York: Alfred A. Knopf, 2006), 5.

15   John G. Nicolay cited in ibid., 4.

16   John G. Nicolay and John Hay, *Abraham Lincoln: A History,* 10 vols. (New York: Century Co., 1890), 10:351.

17   Kaplan, *Lincoln,* 320.

18   Stowe and Emerson are cited in Wilson, *Lincoln's Sword,* 196, 279.

19   Cited in ibid., 281.

20   We have provided a Selected Bibliography in the back of this volume so the reader can easily locate full citations of works appearing in an abbreviated format in the annotations.

21   We used the *Collected Works* (*CW*) as the source for all but two of the documents presented in this volume. For the "House Divided" speech we referred to *Abraham Lincoln: Speeches and Writings, 1832–1858: Speeches, Letters, and Miscellaneous Writings: The Lincoln-Douglas Debates,* edited by Don E. Fehrenbacher (Library of America, 1989), and for the Cooper Union address, we turned to the original 1860 published version.

# Message to the People of Sangamo County

## March 9, 1832

*In the 1830s many Americans still adhered to the tradition that political candidates were sought by the people to serve, and it was considered unseemly for candidates to seek political office. Less than seven months after settling in New Salem, Illinois, the twenty-three-year-old Lincoln flouted this tradition when he attempted his first run for public office, for a seat in the Illinois House of Representatives. Not only did the young Lincoln publicly ask for votes, he also openly admitted to possessing a burning ambition to succeed and to win the admiration of his friends, neighbors, and peers.*

FELLOW-CITIZENS: HAVING BECOME A CANDIDATE FOR THE HONorable office of one of your representatives in the next General Assembly of this state, in accordance with an established custom, and the principles of true republicanism, it becomes my duty to make known to you—the people whom I propose to represent—my sentiments with regard to local affairs.[1]

Time and experience have verified to a demonstration, the public utility of internal improvements. That the poorest and most thinly populated countries would be greatly benefitted [*sic*] by the opening of good roads, and in the clearing of navigable streams within their limits, is what no person will deny. But yet it is folly to undertake works of this or any other kind, without first knowing that we are able to finish them—as half finished work generally proves to be labor lost. There cannot justly be any objection to having rail roads and canals, any more than to other good things, provided they cost nothing. The only objection is paying for them; and the objection to paying arises from the want of ability to pay.

With respect to the county of Sangamo, some more easy means of communication than we now possess, for the purpose of facilitating the task of exporting the surplus products of its fertile soil, and importing necessary articles from abroad, are indispensably necessary. A meeting has been held of the citizens of Jacksonville, and the adjacent country, for the purpose of deliberating and enquiring into the expediency of constructing a rail road from some eligible point on the Illinois river, through the town of Jacksonville, in Morgan county, to the town of Springfield, in Sangamo county. This is, indeed, a very desirable object. No other improvement that reason will justify us in hoping for, can equal in utility the rail road. It is a never failing source of communication, between places of business remotely situated from each other. Upon the rail road the regular progress of commer-

1   *Sangamo Journal,* March 15, 1832. John G. Nicolay and John Hay, in their biography of Lincoln, claim that Lincoln announced his candidacy via a handbill dated March 9, 1832. Roy P. Basler, in *CW,* noted that no copies of the handbill have been found. Nicolay and Hay, *Abraham Lincoln,* 1:101; *CW,* 1:9n1. This announcement, written with the assistance of New Salem merchant John McNamar and, possibly, local schoolteacher William Mentor Graham (1800–1886), adheres to principles of the emerging Whig Party, that government should create opportunities and economic independence for American citizens willing to work for it through internal improvements, protective tariffs, and a centralized banking system. Lincoln joined a political party that was strong in the central part of a solidly Democratic state. Economic issues, particularly internal improvements, dominated Lincoln's attention early in his political career. Although a proponent of railroads, the young candidate argued against a costly proposed railroad project in favor of a more affordable alternative, that of improving navigation on the Sangamon River, which would provide a significant economic boost to New Salem. In addition explaining his stance on this issue, Lincoln, regretting his own deficient schooling, expressed his strong support for public education. He ended his announcement by reminding voters

Samuel Whiteside, Muster roll of Capt. Abraham Lincoln's Company of the 4th Regiment of Mounted Volunteers commanded by Brig. Genl. Samuel Whiteside mustered out of service at the mouth of the Fox River. Manuscript (May 27, 1832). Lincoln signed this document as captain.

of his humble origins, an aspect of his life that caused him some embarrassment and yet one he was not averse to using for political advantage at appropriate times. Within weeks of his announcement, Lincoln's campaign was interrupted by his service in the Black Hawk War, which was fought between the United States and Native American tribes in 1832, after several tribes led by Black Hawk, a Sauk chief, crossed the Mississippi into Illinois. Returning to New Salem with less than two weeks to campaign before the August 6 election, Lincoln faced the daunting task of introducing himself to voters in the vast central Illinois district. On election day the top four candidates out of the thirteen running won seats in the state assembly. Lincoln finished eighth in voting, but he did extremely well in New Salem, winning 277 votes out of the 300 cast, a testament to his personal popularity. Michael Burlingame,

cial intercourse is not interrupted by either high or low water, or freezing weather, which are the principal difficulties that render our future hopes of water communication precarious and uncertain. Yet, however desirable an object the construction of a rail road through our country may be; however high our imaginations may be heated at thoughts of it—there is always a heart appalling shock accompanying the account of its cost, which forces us to shrink from our pleasing anticipations. The probable cost of this contemplated rail road is estimated at $290,000;—the bare statement of which, in my opinion, is sufficient to justify the belief, that the improvement of Sangamo river is an object much better suited to our infant resources.

Respecting this view, I think I may say, without fear of being contradicted, that its navigation may be rendered completely practicable, as high as the mouth of the South Fork, or probably higher, to vessels of from 25 to 30 tons burthen, for at least one half of all common years, and to vessels of much greater burthen a part of that time. From my peculiar circumstances, it is probable that for the last twelve months I have given as particular attention to the stage of the water in this river, as any other person in the country. In the month of March, 1831, in company with others, I commenced

Restored Lincoln-Berry store, New Salem, Illinois. Photograph (n.d.) After losing his first run for public office, Lincoln became a storekeeper here in 1833, in partnership with William F. Berry. Although Lincoln sold his interest in the store to Berry after a few months, he assumed Berry's debts after the latter died in 1835.

the building of a flat boat on the Sangamo, and finished and took her out in the course of the spring.[2] Since that time, I have been concerned in the mill at New Salem.[3] These circumstances are sufficient evidence, that I have not been very inattentive to the stages of the water. The time at which we crossed the mill dam, being in the last days of April, the water was lower than it had been since the breaking of winter in February, or than it was for several weeks after. The principal difficulties we encountered in descending the river, were from the drifted timber, which obstructions all know is not difficult to be removed. Knowing almost precisely the height of water at that time, I believe I am safe in saying that it has as often been higher as lower since.

From this view of the subject, it appears that my calculations with regard to the navigation of the Sangamo, cannot be unfounded in reason; but whatever may be its natural advantages, certain it is, that it never can be practically useful to any great extent, without being greatly improved by art. The drifted timber, as I have before mentioned, is the most formidable barrier to this object. Of all parts of this river, none will require so much labor in proportion, to make it navigable, as the last thirty or thirty-five miles; and going with the meanderings of the channel, when we are this distance above its mouth, we are only between twelve and eighteen miles above Beardstown, in something near a straight direction; and this route is upon

*Abraham Lincoln: A Life,* 2 vols. (Baltimore: Johns Hopkins University Press, 2008), 1:71–74; Donald, *Lincoln,* 41–43; Douglas L. Wilson, *Honor's Voice: The Transformation of Abraham Lincoln* (New York: Knopf, 1998), 146–147. For Lincoln's economic philosophy, see Gabor S. Boritt, *Lincoln and the Economics of the American Dream* (1978; Urbana: University of Illinois Press, 1994).

2    In March 1831, soon after leaving the family farm for good, Lincoln was hired, along with his cousin John Hanks (1802–?) and his stepbrother John D. Johnston (1811–1854), by Denton Offutt (ca. 1803–186?), a local—and unscrupulous—businessman, to take a flatboat of farm products to New Orleans. As a result of Offutt's failure to obtain a flatboat in time for the trip, Lincoln and the others constructed one at Sangamo Town before they departed for New Orleans in late April. After the boat ran aground on a milldam at the tiny village of New Salem and began to take on water, Lincoln devised the ingenious solution of boring a hole in the bow of the vessel to drain out the water, and unloading barrels in the rear in order to lift the boat over the dam—an idea that led to a mechanism he later patented. This trip was Lincoln's second flatboat excursion to New Orleans; the first took place in 1828. Burlingame, *Abraham Lincoln,* 1:52–53, 56; Richard Campanella, *Lincoln in New Orleans: The 1828–1831 Flatboat Voyages and Their Place in History* (Lafayette: University of Louisiana at Lafayette Press, 2010). For more on Lincoln's solution for freeing vessels that have run aground, see his "Lecture on Discoveries and Inventions, February 11, 1859," note 9, in this volume.

3    After settling in New Salem, Lincoln worked as a clerk in a store owned by Offutt. He also worked in a flour mill and a saw mill that Offutt acquired. Donald, *Lincoln,* 40–41.

such low ground as to retain water in many places during the season, and in all parts such as to draw two-thirds or three-fourths of the river at all high stages.

This route is upon prairie land the whole distance;—so that it appears to me, by removing the turf, a sufficient width and damming up the old channel, the whole river in a short time would wash its way through, thereby curtailing the distance; and increasing the velocity of the current very considerably, while there would be no timber upon the banks to obstruct its navigation in future; and being nearly straight, the timber which might float in at the head, would be apt to go clear through. There are so many places above this where the river, in its zig zag course, forms such complete peninsulas, as to be easier cut through at the necks than to remove the obstructions from the bends—which if done, would also lesson [*sic*] the distance.

What the cost of this work would be, I am unable to say. It is probable, however, it would not be greater than is common to streams of the same length. Finally, I believe the improvement of the Sangamo river, to be vastly important and highly desirable to the people of this county; and if elected, any measures in the legislature having this for its object, which may appear judicious, will meet my approbation, and shall receive my support.

It appears that the practice of loaning money at exorbitant rates of interest, has already been opened as a field for discussion; so I suppose I may enter upon it without claiming the honor, or risking the danger, which may await its first explorer. It seems as though we are never to have an end to this baneful and corroding system, acting almost as prejudicial to the general interests of the community as a direct tax of several thousand dollars annually laid on each county, for the benefit of a few individuals only, unless there be a law made setting a limit to the rates of usury. A law for this purpose, I am of opinion, may be made, without materially injuring any class of people. In cases of extreme necessity there could always be means found to cheat the law, while in all other cases it would have its intended effect. I would not favor the passage of a law upon this subject, which might be very easily evaded. Let it be such that the labor and difficulty of evading it, could only be justified in cases of the greatest necessity.

Upon the subject of education, not presuming to dictate any plan or system respecting it, I can only say that I view it as the most important subject which we as a people can be engaged in. That every man may receive at least, a moderate education, and thereby be enabled to read the histories of his own and other countries, by which he may duly appreciate the value of our free institutions, appears to be an object of vital importance, even on this account alone, to say nothing of the advantages and satisfaction to be derived from all being able to read the scriptures and other works, both of a religious and moral nature, for themselves. For my part, I desire to see the time when education, and by its means, morality, sobriety, enterprise and industry, shall become much more general than at present, and should be gratified to have it in my power to contribute something to the advancement of any measure which might have a tendency to accelerate the happy period.

With regard to existing laws, some alterations are thought to be necessary. Many respectable men have suggested that our estray laws—the law respecting the issuing of executions, the road law, and some others, are deficient in their present form, and require alterations. But considering the great probability that the framers of those laws were wiser than myself, I should prefer [not?] meddling with them, unless they were first attacked by others, in which case I should feel it both a privilege and a duty to take that stand, which in my view, might tend most to the advancement of justice.

But, Fellow-Citizens, I shall conclude. Considering the great degree of modesty which should always attend youth, it is probable I have already been more presuming than becomes me. However, upon the subjects of which I have treated, I have spoken as I thought. I may be wrong in regard to any or all of them; but holding it a sound maxim, that it is better to be only sometimes right, than at all times wrong, so soon as I discover my opinions to be erroneous, I shall be ready to renounce them.

Every man is said to have his peculiar ambition. Whether it be true or not, I can say for one that I have no other so great as that of being truly esteemed by my fellow men, by rendering myself worthy of their esteem. How far I shall succeed in gratifying this ambition, is yet to be developed. I am young and unknown to many of you. I was born and have ever remained in the most humble walks of life. I have no wealthy or popular relations to recommend me. My case is thrown exclusively upon the independent voters of this county, and if elected they will have conferred a favor upon me, for which I shall be unremitting in my labors to compensate. But if the good people in their wisdom shall see fit to keep me in the background, I have been too familiar with disappointments to be very much chagrined. Your friend and fellow-citizen,

New Salem, March 9, 1832.
A. Lincoln

# Letter to the Editor of the *Sangamo Journal,* New Salem

## June 13, 1836

Simeon Francis, editor of the *Sangamo Journal.* Photograph (ca. 1861). Lincoln and Francis became good friends and political allies. Lincoln promoted Francis's paper and the editor promoted Lincoln's political career.

To the Editor of the Journal:[1]

In your paper of last Saturday, I see a communication over the signature of "Many Voters," [in] which the candidates who are announced in the Journal, are called upon to "show their hands." Agreed. Here's mine!

I go for all sharing the privileges of the government, who assist in bearing its burthens. Consequently I go for admitting all whites to the right of suffrage, who pay taxes or bear arms, (by no means excluding females.)[2]

If elected, I shall consider the whole people of Sangamon my constituents, as well as those that oppose, as those that support me.

While acting as their representative, I shall be governed by their will, on all subjects upon which I have the means of knowing what their will is; and upon all others, I shall do what my own judgment teaches me will best advance their interests. Whether elected or not, I go for distributing the proceeds of the sales of the public lands to the several states, to enable our state, in common with others, to dig canals and construct rail roads, without borrowing money and paying interest on it.

If alive on the first Monday in November, I shall vote for Hugh L. White for President.[3]

Very respectfully,
A. LINCOLN.

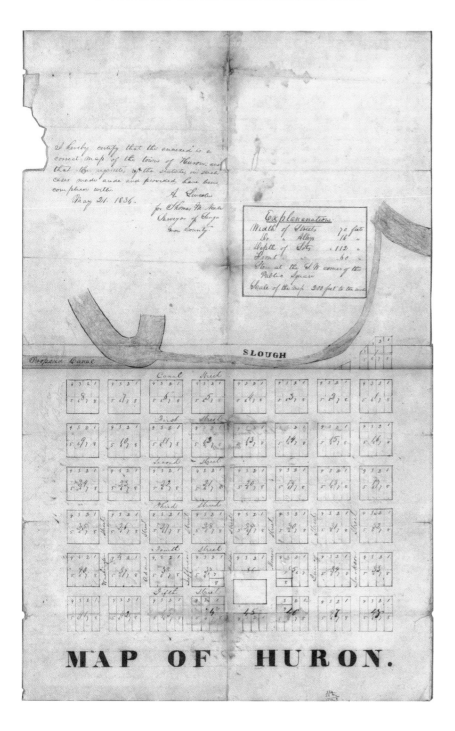

MAP OF HURON.

*Lincoln again ran for a seat in the Illinois House of Representatives in 1834 and won with the second highest number of votes among the declared candidates. His 1836 announcement for reelection, more concise and far less specific on issues than four years earlier, reflected Lincoln's support for the national trend toward expanding suffrage to all white male citizens.*

1  Lincoln's letter appeared in the *Sangamo Journal*, June 18, 1836. See *CW*, 1:48.

2  His remarks about women's suffrage may have been an attempt at humor, since women in Illinois did not pay taxes or serve in the militia. On August 1, 1836, Lincoln received more votes than the other sixteen candidates in the race. Donald, *Lincoln*, 59–60; Burlingame, *Abraham Lincoln*, 1:103–104, 112.

3  Hugh Lawson White (1773–1840), a United States senator from Tennessee, was one of three Whigs running against Democrat Martin Van Buren, Andrew Jackson's vice president, in the 1836 presidential election. Biographical Directory of the United States Congress, http://bioguide.congress.gov/scripts/biodisplay.pl?index=W000376 (accessed October 30, 2014).

Abraham Lincoln, Town plat, survey of Huron. Manuscript (May 21, 1836). Lincoln worked for a while as a surveyor, and in 1836 he plotted out the proposed town of Huron, Illinois.

*Lincoln's protest, aimed against resolutions passed with overwhelming support in both houses of the legislature that condemned abolitionist societies and declared that slavery was protected by the U.S. Constitution, marked his first public statement on slavery.*

1   House Journal, Tenth General Assembly, First Session, 817–818. Cited in *CW,* 1:76. Lincoln drafted a statement that reflected his moderate stance on the issue: opposing slavery but objecting to abolitionist activities as counterproductive, as well as acknowledging slavery's protection under the Constitution in states where it already existed. Burlingame, *Abraham Lincoln,* 1:122; Donald, *Lincoln,* 63–64.

2   Daniel Stone (1800–?) was elected to the Illinois legislature from Sangamon County in 1838. Norman F. Boas, *Abraham Lincoln: Illustrated Biographical Dictionary: Family and Associates, 1809–1861* (Mystic, CT: Seaport Autograph Press, 2009), 426.

# Protest on Slavery in Illinois Legislature

## March 3, 1837

The following protest was presented to the House, which was read and ordered to be spread on the journals, to wit:[1]

"Resolutions upon the subject of domestic slavery having passed both branches of the General Assembly at its present session, the undersigned hereby protest against the passage of the same.

They believe that the institution of slavery is founded on both injustice and bad policy; but that the promulgation of abolition doctrines tends rather to increase than to abate its evils.

They believe that the Congress of the United States has no power, under the constitution, to interfere with the institution of slavery in the different States.

They believe that the Congress of the United States has the power, under the constitution, to abolish slavery in the District of Columbia; but that that power ought not be exercised unless at the request of the people of said District.

The difference between these opinions and those contained in the said resolutions, is their reason for entering this protest."

DAN STONE[2]
A. LINCOLN,
Representatives from the county of Sangamon.

# Public Sale of Negroes,

## By RICHARD CLAGETT.

*On Tuesday, March 5th, 1833 at 1:00 P. M. the following Slaves will be sold at Potters Mart, in Charleston, S. C.*

*Miscellaneous Lots of Negroes, mostly house servants, some for field work.*

*Conditions:* ½ cash, balance by bond, bearing interest from date of sale. Payable in one to two yea s to be secured by a mortgage of the Negroes, and appraised personal security. *Auctioneer will pay for the papers.*

---

A valuable Negro woman, accustomed to all kinds of house work. Is a good plain cook, and excellent dairy maid, washes and irons. She has four children, one a girl about 13 years of age, another 7, a boy about 5, and an infant 11 months old. 2 of the children will be sold with mother, the others separately, if it best suits the purchaser.

A very valuable Blacksmith, wife and daughters; the Smith is in the prime of life, and a perfect master at his trade. His wife about 27 years old, and his daughters 12 and 10 years old have been brought up as house servants, and as such are very valuable. Also for sale 2 likely young negro wenches, one of whom is 16 the other 13, both of whom have been taught and accustomed to the duties of house servants. The 16 year old wench has one eye.

A likely yellow girl about 17 or 18 years old, has been accustomed to all kinds of house and garden work. She is sold for no fault. Sound as a dollar.

House servants: The owner of a family described herein, would sell them for a good price only, they are offered for no fault whatever, but because they can be done without, and money is needed. He has been offered $1250. They consist of a man 30 to 33 years old, who has been raised in a genteel Virginia family as house servant, Carriage driver etc., in all which he excels. His wife a likely wench of 25 to 30 raised in like manner, as chamber maid, seamstress, nurse etc., the r two children, girls of 12 and 4 or 5. They are bright mulattoes, of mild tractable dispositions, unassuming manners, and of genteel appearance and well worthy the no ice of a gentleman of fortune needing such.

Also 14 Negro Wenches ranging from 16 to 25 years of age, all sound and capable of doing a good days work in the house or field.

*Public Sale of Negroes, by Richard Claget.* Broadside (Charleston, SC, 1833).

Mary Owens. Photograph (n.d). She rejected Lincoln's half-hearted marriage proposal.

*Inexperienced in romantic relationships with women, Lincoln apparently reached an understanding concerning marriage with twenty-six-year-old Mary Owens of Kentucky. In August 1837 Mary appears to have demanded a commitment on Lincoln's part. Not sure of his own feelings toward her, an agonized Lincoln in this letter sought a resolution concerning marriage—either a response from Mary releasing him from a pledge he felt honor bound to keep, or a statement from her indicating a wish to pursue a more committed relationship.*

1 Lincoln began courting Mary S. Owens (1808–1877) in the fall of 1836. The well-educated daughter of a wealthy Kentucky planter, Mary was the sister of Mrs. Bennett Abell of New Salem, with whom Lincoln boarded for a time. She and Lincoln first met in the fall of 1833 when she visited her sister, and Lincoln apparently was impressed by

# Letter to Mary Owens

## August 16, 1837

Friend Mary, Springfield Aug. 16th 1837

You will, no doubt, think it strange, that I should write you a letter on the same day on which we parted; and I can only account for it by supposing, that seeing you lately makes me think of you more than usual, while at our late meeting we had but few expressions of thoughts.[1] You must know that I can not see you, or think of you, with entire indifference; and yet it may be, that you, are mistaken in regard to what my real feelings towards you are. If I knew you were not, I should not trouble you with this letter. Perhaps any other man would know enough without further information; but I consider it *my* peculiar right to plead ignorance, and your bounden duty to allow the plea. I want in all cases to do right, and most particularly so, in all cases with women. I want, at this particular time, more than any thing else, to do right with you, and if I *knew* it would be doing right, as I rather suspect it would, to let you alone, I would do it. And for the purpose of making the matter as plain as possible, I now say, that you can now drop the subject, dismiss your thoughts (if you ever had any) from me forever, and leave this letter unanswered, without calling forth one accusing murmer [*sic*] from me. And I will even go further, and say, that if it will add any thing to your comfort, or peace of mind, to do so, it is my sincere wish that you should. Do not understand by this, that I wish to cut your acquaintance. I mean no such thing. What I do wish is, that our further acquaintance shall depend upon yourself. If such further acquaintance would contribute nothing to your happiness, I am sure it would not to mine. If you feel yourself in any degree bound to me, I am now willing to release you, provided you wish it; while, on the other hand, I am willing, and even anxious to bind you faster, if I can be convinced that it will, in any considerable degree, add to your happiness. This, indeed, is the whole question with me.

Nothing would make me more miserable than to believe you miserable—nothing more happy, than to know you were so.

In what I have now said, I think I can not be misunderstood; and to make myself understood, is the only object of this letter.

If it suits you best to not answer this—farewell—a long life and a merry one attend you. But if you conclude to write back, speak plainly as I do. There can be neither harm nor danger, in saying, to me, any thing you think, just in the manner you think it.

My respects to your sister.
Your friend LINCOLN.

his landlady's attractive, sophisticated, intellectual, fun-loving guest. Three years later Mrs. Abell offered to invite Mary back to New Salem if Lincoln would agree to marry her, a proposal that he—seriously or in jest—accepted. As a result, Mary returned and resided in New Salem from the spring of 1836 through 1838, during which time Lincoln moved to Springfield, Illinois. The courtship was troubled from the start, with Lincoln, awkward and uncomfortable around women, unsure of both his own feelings toward Mary and her intentions toward him. It is not known if Mary Owens ever wrote a reply to Lincoln's August 16 letter, as none has been found. Lincoln later reported on the relationship's demise in a letter to a woman friend. See "Letter to Mrs. Orville H. Browning, April 1, 1838," in this volume. See also Wilson, *Honor's Voice,* 129–141.

*In one of his first public speeches, delivered two months after the murder of abolitionist newspaper editor Elijah P. Lovejoy by a proslavery mob in Alton, Illinois, Lincoln urged his audience to reject mob rule and revere the rule of law. Although Lincoln did not mention Lovejoy by name, he alluded to the incident when citing several other examples of mob violence, which he considered a serious threat to the free American government created by the Founding Fathers. Respect for the nation's Constitution and its laws, Lincoln declared, must become the "political religion" of the nation.*

1   Lincoln's address was printed in the *Sangamo Journal* on February 3, 1838. *CW,* 1:108. Springfield's Young Men's Lyceum was founded around 1835, two years after the founding of the Sangamon County Lyceum. While the latter's programs addressed culture, health and medicine, history, politics, and science, the Young Men's Lyceum focused more on civic responsibility, with lectures concentrating on the leading political issues of the time, including slavery, foreign policy, and immigration. This emphasis on such topics was not surprising, since the purpose of the Lyceum was to prepare young men to be future leaders. Thomas F. Schwartz, "The Springfield Lyceums and Lincoln's 1838 Speech," *Illinois Historical Journal* 83 (Spring 1990): 45, 48.

2   Bracketed sections in the text were supplied by John George Nicolay and John Hay, who compiled the *Complete Works of Abraham Lincoln,* 12 vols. (New York: Francis D. Tandy Company, 1905). Cited in *CW,* 1:115.

3   Napoleon Bonaparte (1769–1821).

# Address to the Young Men's Lyceum of Springfield, Illinois

## January 27, 1838

### The Perpetuation of Our Political Institutions

As a subject for the remarks of the evening, *the perpetuation of our political institutions,* is selected.[1]

In the great journal of things happening under the sun, we, the American People, find our account running, under date of the nineteenth century of the Christian era. We find ourselves in the peaceful possession, of the fairest portion of the earth, as regards extent of territory, fertility of soil, and salubrity of climate. We find ourselves under the government of a system of political institutions, conducting more essentially to the ends of civil and religious liberty, than any of which the history of former times tells us. We, when mounting the stage of existence, found ourselves the legal inheritors of these fundamental blessings. We toiled not in the acquirement or establishment of them—they are a legacy bequeathed us, by a *once* hardy, brave, and patriotic, but *now* lamented and departed race of ancestors. Their's [*sic*] was the task (and nobly they performed it) to possess themselves, and through themselves, us, of this goodly land; and to uprear upon its hills and its valleys, a political edifice of liberty and equal rights; 'tis ours only, to transmit these, the former, unprofaned by the foot of an invader; the latter, undecayed by the lapse of time, and untorn by [usurpation—to the latest generation that fate shall permit the world to know. This task of gratitude to our fathers, justice to][2] ourselves, duty to posterity, and love for our species in general, all imperatively require us faithfully to perform.

How, then, shall we perform it? At what point shall we expect the approach of danger? By what means shall we fortify against it? Shall we expect some transatlantic military giant, to step the Ocean, and crush us at a blow? Never! All the armies of Europe, Asia and Africa combined, with all the treasure of the earth (our own excepted) in their military chest; with a

*Attack on the office of the Alton* Observer (1837). Engraved illustration in Henry Tanner, *Martyrdom of Lovejoy: An Account of the Life, Trials, and Perils of the Rev. Elijah P. Lovejoy* (Chicago, 1881).

Buonaparte[3] for a commander, could not by force, take a drink from the Ohio, or make a track on the Blue Ridge, in a trial of a thousand years.

At what point then is the approach of danger to be expected? I answer, if it ever reach us, it must spring up amongst us. It cannot come from abroad. If destruction be our lot, we must ourselves be its author and finisher. As a nation of freemen, we must live through all time, or die by suicide.

I hope I am over wary; but if I am not, there is, even now, something of ill-omen amongst us. I mean the increasing disregard for law which pervades the country; the growing disposition to substitute the wild and furious passions, in lieu of the sober judgment of Courts; and the worse than savage mobs, for the executive ministers of justice. This disposition is awfully fearful in any community; and that it now exists in ours, though grating to our feelings to admit, it would be a violation of truth, and an insult

4 The 1820s and, especially, the 1830s, witnessed an upsurge in rioting in many American towns and cities. Ethnic animosities, religious bigotry, and racial prejudice, heightened by the rise of a market economy, economic downturns, the increase in immigration, and the spread of urbanization, fueled most of this unrest. Abolitionists and free blacks became targets of many violent acts perpetrated by mobs in response to the growing antislavery movement. Concerns about lawlessness and mob violence were shared by many in the Whig Party, including Lincoln; a year before, in a speech in the Illinois legislature on the state bank, Lincoln had declared his opposition to "that lawless and mobocratic spirit, whether in relation to the bank or any thing else, which is already abroad in the land" and spreading "with rapid and fearful impetuosity, to the ultimate overthrow of every institution, or even moral principle, in which persons and property have hitherto found security." *CW,* 1:69. Whigs tended to blame former president Andrew Jackson (1767–1845) and his followers within the Democratic Party for inciting uncontrolled lawlessness among the people. While Lincoln shared this opinion, he did not view Jackson as negatively as many of his fellow Whigs did. In fact, parts of his address echo concerns of mob violence raised by Jackson in his farewell address. "You have no longer any cause to fear danger from abroad," declared Jackson. "It is from within," he warned, "from cupidity, from corruption, from disappointed ambition, and inordinate thirst for power, that factions will be formed and liberty endangered." John Channing Briggs asserts that Lincoln used Jackson's farewell address and the inaugural address of Martin Van Buren (1782– 1862), who also warned against the dangers posed by mob rule and sectional strife over slavery, in preparing these remarks. But Lincoln offered a remedy far broader in scope than Jackson's resort to force or Van Buren's call for strengthening fraternal

N[athaniel]. Currier, *Andrew Jackson.* Lithograph (New York, ca. 1835–1837).

to our intelligence, to deny. Accounts of outrages committed by mobs, form the every-day news of the times. They have pervaded the country, from New England to Louisiana;—they are neither peculiar to the eternal snows of the former, nor the burning suns of the latter;—they are not the creature of climate—neither are they confined to the slaveholding, or the non-slaveholding States. Alike, they spring up among the pleasure hunting masters of Southern slaves, and the order loving citizens of the land of steady habits. Whatever, then, their cause may be, it is common to the whole country.[4]

*King Andrew the First.* Lithograph (1833). Anti-Jackson cartoon by an unknown printmaker portraying its subject as a despot.

feelings among the citizenry: that of "reverence for the laws" and the principles of self-government becoming the "*political religion* of the nation." John Channing Briggs, *Lincoln's Speeches Reconsidered* (Baltimore: Johns Hopkins University Press, 2005), 32–36, 47; Jackson's quote from his farewell address and Van Buren's inaugural address are found in *The Addresses and Messages of the Presidents of the United States, from 1789 to 1839* (New York: McLean and Taylor, 1839), 570, 571–577. See also Major L. Wilson, "Lincoln and Van Buren in the Steps of the Fathers: Another Look at the Lyceum Address," in *On Lincoln,* ed. John T. Hubbell (Kent: Kent State University Press, 2014), 14–15; and Daniel Walker Howe, *The Political Culture of the American Whigs* (Chicago: University of Chicago Press, 1979). On urban rioting in the 1830s, see Daniel Walker Howe, *What Hath God Wrought: The Transformation of America, 1815–1848* (New York: Oxford University Press, 2007), 430–439, and Michel Feldberg, *The Turbulent Era: Riot and Disorder in Jacksonian America* (New York: Oxford University Press, 1980). Antiabolition mob violence in America during the Jacksonian period is covered by Leonard L. Richards, *"Gentlemen of Property and Standing": Anti-Abolition Mobs in Jacksonian America* (New York: Oxford University Press, 1970).

5   Lincoln refers to an event that took place in Vicksburg, Mississippi, in the summer of 1835, in which vigilantes captured and hung five men for gambling. Cited in *Lincoln's Selected Writings,* ed. David S. Reynolds (New York: W. W. Norton, 2014), 9n2.

6   In Mississippi, the same summer that the gamblers were hung by the mob, a rumor of a slave rebellion resulted in the rounding up of a group of enslaved blacks and two white men alleged to be associated with the revolt. Not only were the enslaved blacks and the two white men hanged,

It would be tedious, as well as useless, to recount the horrors of all of them. Those happening in the State of Mississippi, and at St. Louis, are, perhaps, the most dangerous in example, and revolting to humanity. In the Mississippi case, they first commenced by hanging the regular gamblers: a set of men, certainly not following for the livelihood, a very useful, or very honest occupation; but one which, so far from being forbidden by the laws, was actually licensed by an act of the Legislature, passed but a single year before.[5] Next, negroes, suspected of conspiring to raise an insurrection, were caught up and hanged in all parts of the State: then, white men, supposed to be leagued with the negroes; and finally, strangers, from neighboring States, going thither on business, were, in many instances, subjected to the same fate.[6] Thus went on this process of hanging, from gamblers to negroes, from negroes to white citizens, and from these to strangers; till, dead men were seen literally dangling from the boughs of trees upon every road side; and in numbers almost sufficient, to rival the native Spanish moss of the country, as a drapery of the forest.

but the associated hysteria led to additional lynchings. Cited in ibid.

7   Francis L. McIntosh, a free black Saint Louis boat worker, was tied to a tree and burned alive by a mob on April 28, 1836. McIntosh had attempted to prevent the arrest of one or two of his friends. When his friend or friends escaped, McIntosh was apprehended and informed he would be whipped and imprisoned for five years for interfering with police activity. McIntosh resisted arrest and, in doing so, killed a police officer. He was then lynched. Ibid.; see also Richard Lawrence Miller, *Lincoln and His World: Prairie Politician 1834–1842* (Mechanicsburg, PA: Stackpole Books, 2008), 210.

Turn, then, to that horror-striking scene at St. Louis.[7] A single victim was only sacrificed there. His story is very short; and is, perhaps, the most highly tragic, of any thing of its length, that has ever been witnessed in real life. A mulatto man, by the name of McIntosh, was seized in the street, dragged to the suburbs of the city, chained to a tree, and actually burned to death; and all within a single hour from the time he had been a freeman, attending to his own business, and at peace with the world.

Such are the effects of mob law; and such are the scenes, becoming more and more frequent in this land so lately famed for love of law and order; and the stories of which, have even now grown too familiar, to attract any thing more, than an idle remark.

But you are, perhaps, ready to ask, "What has this to do with the perpetuation of our political institutions?" I answer, it has much to do with it. Its direct consequences are, comparatively speaking, but a small evil; and much of its danger consists, in the proneness of our minds, to regard its direct, as its only consequences. Abstractly considered, the hanging of the gamblers at Vicksburg, was of but little consequence. They constitute a portion of the population in a[ny community; and their death, if no perni]cious example be set by it, is never [a] matter of reasonable regret with any one. If they were annually swept, from the stage of existence, by the plague or small pox, honest men would, perhaps, be much profited, by the operation. Similar too, is the correct reasoning, in regard to the burning of the negro at St. Louis. He had forfeited his life, by the perpetration of an outrageous murder, upon one of the most worthy and respectable citizens of the city; and had he not died as he did, he must have died by the sentence of the law, in a very short time afterwards. As to him alone, it was as well the way it was, as it could otherwise have been. But the example in either case, was fearful. When men take it into their heads to day, to hang gamblers, or burn murderers, they should recollect, that, in the confusion usually attending such transactions, they will [be] as likely to hang or burn some one, who is neither a gambler nor a murderer [as] one who is; and that, acting upon the [exam]ple they set, the mob of to-morrow, may an[d] probably will, hang and burn some of them, [by th]e very same mistake. And not only so; the innocent, those who have ever set their faces against violations of law in every shape, alike with the guilty, fall victims to the ravages of mob law; and thus it goes on, step by step, till all the walls erected for the defence of the persons and property of individuals, are trodden down, and disregarded. But all this even, is not the full extent of the evil. By such examples, by instances of the perpetrators of such acts going unpunished, the lawless in spirit, are encouraged to become lawless in practice; and having been used to no restraint, but dread of punishment, they thus become, absolutely un-restrained.[8] Having ever regarded Government as their deadliest bane, they make a jubilee of the suspension of its operations; and pray for nothing so much, as its total annihilation. While, on the other hand, good men, men who love tranquility, who desire to abide by the laws, and enjoy their bene-fits, who would gladly spill their blood in the defence of their country; see-ing their property destroyed; their families insulted, and their lives endan-gered; their persons injured; and seeing nothing in prospect that forebodes a change for the better; become tired of, and disgusted with, a Government that offers them no protection; and are not much averse to a change in which they imagine they have nothing to lose. Thus, then, by the operation of this mobocratic spirit, which all must admit, is now abroad in the land, the strongest bulwark of any Government, and particularly of those consti-tuted like ours, may effectively be broken down and destroyed—I mean the *attachment* of the People. Whenever this effect shall be produced among us; whenever the vicious portion of population shall be permitted to gather in bands of hundreds and thousands, and burn churches, ravage and rob pro-vision stores, throw printing presses into rivers, shoot editors,[9] and hang and burn obnoxious persons at pleasure, and with impunity; depend on it, this Government cannot last. By such things, the feelings of the best citizens will become more or less alienated from it; and thus it will be left with-out friends, or with too few, and those few too weak, to make their friend-ship effectual. At such time and under such circumstances, men of sufficient tal[ent and ambition will not be want]ing to seize [the opportunity, strike the blow, and over-turn that fair fabric], which for the last half century, has been the fondest hope, of the lovers of freedom, throughout the world.

I know the American People are *much* attached to their Government;—I know they would suffer *much* for its sake;—I know they would endure evils long and patiently, before they would ever think of exchanging it for an-other. Yet, notwithstanding all this, if the laws be continually despised and disregarded, if their rights to be secure in their persons and property, are held by no better tenure than the caprice of a mob, the alienation of their affections from the Government is the natural consequence; and to that, sooner or later, it must come.

Here, then, is one point at which danger may be expected.

The question recurs "how shall we fortify against it?" The answer is sim-ple. Let every American, every lover of liberty, every well wisher to his pos-terity, swear by the blood of the Revolution, never to violate in the least

8   Lincoln made it clear that he did not condone the actions of the gamblers in Mississippi or the free black boatman in Saint Louis. However, their fates should have been decided by courts of law, not by mob rule. Mob rule, warned Lincoln, diminishes citizens' respect for laws and their government, resulting in either anarchy or tyranny and the destruction of the institutions established by the Founding Fathers.

9   Lincoln alluded to the recent murder of the journalist Lovejoy (1802–1837). The editor, who had published an abolitionist newspaper in Saint Louis, moved to Alton after a mob destroyed his printing presses in response to his condemnation of the lynching of Francis McIntosh in April 1836. In November 1837 an Alton mob threw Lovejoy's presses into the river after shooting him to death when he tried to defend his property.

particular, the laws of the country; and never to tolerate their violation by others. As the patriots of seventy-six did to support the Declaration of Independence, so to the support of the Constitution and Laws, let every American pledge his life, his property, and his sacred honor;—let every man remember that to violate the law, is to trample on the blood of his father, and to tear the character [charter?] of his own, and his children's liberty. Let reverence for the laws, be breathed by every American mother, to the lisping babe, that prattles on her lap—let it be taught in schools, in seminaries, and in colleges;—let it be written in Primmers [*sic*], spelling books, and in Almanacs;—let it be preached from the pulpit, proclaimed in legislative halls, and enforced in courts of justice. And, in short, let it become the *political religion* of the nation; and let the old and the young, the rich and the poor, the grave and the gay, of all sexes and tongues, and colors and conditions, sacrifice unceasingly upon its altars.

While ever a state of feeling, such as this, shall universally, or even, very generally prevail throughout the nation, vain will be every effort, and fruitless every attempt, to subvert our national freedom.

When I so pressingly urge a strict observance of the laws, let me not be understood as saying there are no bad laws, nor that grievances may not arise, for the redress of which, no legal provisions have been made. I mean to say no such thing. But I do mean to say, that, although bad laws, if they exist, should be repealed as soon as possible, still while they continue in force, for the sake of example, they should be religiously observed. So also in unprovided cases. If such arise, let proper legal provisions be made for them with the least possible delay; but till then, let them if not too intolerable, be borne with.

There is no grievance that is a fit object of redress by mob law. In any case that arises, as for instance, the promulgation of abolitionism, one of two positions is necessarily true; that is, the thing is right within itself, and therefore deserves the protection of all law and all good citizens; or, it is wrong, and therefore proper to be prohibited by legal enactments; and in neither case, is the interposition of mob law, either necessary, justifiable, or excusable.

But it may be asked, why suppose danger to our political institutions? Have we not preserved them for more than fifty years? And why may we not for fifty times as long?

We hope there is no *sufficient* reason. We hope all dangers may be overcome; but to conclude that no danger may ever arise, would itself be extremely dangerous. There are now, and will hereafter be, many causes, dangerous in their tendency, which have not existed heretofore; and which are not too insignificant to merit attention. That our government should have been maintained in its original form from its establishment until now, is not much to be wondered at. It had many props to support it through that period, which are now decayed, and crumbled away. Through that period, it was felt by all, to be an undecided experiment; now, it is understood to be a successful one. Then, all that sought celebrity and fame, and distinction, expected to find them in the success of that experiment. Their *all* was staked upon it:—their destiny was *inseparably* linked with it. Their ambition aspired to display before an admiring world, a practical demonstration of the truth of a proposition, which had hitherto been considered, at best no better, than problematical; namely, *the capacity of a people to govern themselves.* If they succeeded, they were to be immortalized; their names were to be transferred to counties and cities, and rivers and mountains; and to be revered and sung, and toasted through all time. If they failed, they were to be called knaves and fools, and fanatics for a fleeting hour; then to sink and be forgotten. They succeeded. The experiment is successful; and thousands have won their deathless names in making it so. But the game is caught; and I believe it is true, that with the catching, end the pleasures of the chase. The field of glory is harvested, and the crop is already appropriated. But new reapers will arise, and *they,* too, will seek a field. It is to deny, what the history of the world tells us is true, to suppose that men of ambition and talents will not continue to spring up amongst us. And, when they do, they will as naturally seek the gratification of their ruling passion, as others have *so* done before them. The question then, is, can that gratification be found in supporting and maintaining an edifice that has been erected by others? Most certainly it cannot. Many great and good men sufficiently qualified for any task they should undertake, may ever be found, whose ambition would aspire to nothing beyond a seat in Congress, a gubernatorial or a presidential chair; *but such belong not to the family of the lion, or the tribe of the eagle.* What! think you these places would satisfy an Alexander,[10] a Ceasar,[11] or a Napoleon? Never! Towering genius disdains a beaten path. It seeks regions hitherto unexplored. It sees *no distinction* in adding story to story, upon the monuments of fame, erected to the memory of others. It *denies* that it is glory enough to serve under any chief. It *scorns* to tread in the footsteps of *any* predecessor, however illustrious. It thirsts and burns for distinction; and, if possible, it will have it, whether at the expense of emancipating slaves, or enslaving freemen. Is it unreasonable then to expect, that some man possessed of the loftiest genius, coupled with ambition sufficient

10 Alexander the Great (356–323 BCE).

11 Julius Caesar (100–44 BCE)

Philip Haas, after Henry Inman, *Martin Van Buren.*
Lithograph (Washington, DC, ca. 1837).

12  Lincoln's remarks concerning the possible rise
of an ambitious "towering genius" have received
much scholarly attention. Was Lincoln, aware of
his own burning ambition, unconsciously or
subconsciously referring to himself or to someone
else, such as Martin Van Buren or Stephen A.
Douglas? Using psychoanalytical interpretations,
Edmund Wilson, in *Patriotic Gore: Studies in the
Literature of the American Civil War* (New York:
Oxford University Press, 1962), 106–108, asserted
that Lincoln consciously projected himself into the
very role of the ambitious genius that he warns
against, while George B. Forgie, in *Patricide in the
House Divided: A Psychological Interpretation of
Lincoln and His Age* (New York: W. W. Norton,
1979), 84–85, and Charles B. Strozier, in *Lincoln's
Quest for Union: Public and Private Meanings* (New
York: Basic Books, 1982), 59–61, argued that
Lincoln was projecting himself unconsciously.
Dwight G. Anderson, on the other hand, in

to push it to its utmost stretch, will at some time, spring up among us? And
when such one does, it will require the people to be united with each other,
attached to the government and laws, and generally intelligent, to successfully frustrate his designs.[12]

Distinction will be his paramount object; and although he would as willingly, perhaps more so, acquire it by doing good as harm; yet, that opportunity being past, and nothing left to be done in the way of building up, he
would set boldly to the task of pulling down.

Here then, is a probable case, highly dangerous, and such a one as could
not have well existed heretofore.

Another reason which *once was,* but which, to the same extent, is *now no
more,* has done much in maintaining our institutions thus far. I mean that
powerful influence which the interesting scenes of the revolution had upon
the *passions* of the people as distinguished from their judgment. By this influence, the jealousy, envy, and avarice, incident to our nature, and so common to a state of peace, prosperity, and conscious strength, were, for the
time, in a great measure smothered and rendered inactive; while the deep
rooted principles of *hate,* and the powerful motive of *revenge,* instead of being turned against each other, were directed exclusively against the British
nation. And, thus, from the force of circumstances, the basest principles of
our nature, were either made to lie dormant, or to become active agents in
the advancement of the noblest of cause[s?]—that of establishing and maintaining civil and religious liberty.

But this state of feeling *must fade, is fading, has faded,* with the circumstances that produced it.

I do not mean to say, that the scenes of the revolution *are now* or *ever will
be* entirely forgotten; but that like every thing else, they must fade upon the
memory of the world, and grow more and more dim by the lapse of time. In
history, we hope, they will be read of, and recounted, so long as the bible
shall be read;—but even granting that they will, their influence *cannot be*
what it heretofore has been. Even then, they *cannot be* so universally known,
nor so vividly felt, as they were by the generation just gone to rest. At the
close of that struggle, nearly every adult male had been a participator in
some of its scenes. The consequence was, that of those scenes, in the form
of a husband, a father, a son or a brother, a *living history was* to be found in
every family—a history bearing the indubitable testimonies of its own authenticity, in the limbs mangled, in the scars of wounds received, in the
midst of the very scenes related—a history, too, that could be read and understood alike by all, the wise and the ignorant, the learned and the un-

learned. But *those* histories are gone. They *can* be read no more forever. They *were* a fortress of strength; but, what invading foeman could *never do*, the silent artillery of time *has done;* the leveling of its walls. They are gone. They *were* a forest of giant oaks; but the all-resistless hurricane has swept over them, and left only, here and there, a lonely trunk, despoiled of its verdure, shorn of its foliage; unshading and unshaded, to murmur in a few more gentle breezes, and to combat with its mutilated limbs, a few more ruder storms, then to sink, and be no more.

They *were* pillars of the temple of liberty; and now, that they have crumbled away, that temple must fall, unless we, their descendants, supply their places with other pillars, hewn from the solid quarry of sober reason. Passion has helped us; but can do so no more. It will in future be our enemy. Reason, cold, calculating, unimpassioned reason, must furnish all the materials for our future support and defence. Let those [materials] be moulded into *general intelligence,* [*sound*] *morality* and, in particular, *a reverence for the constitution and laws;* and, that we improve to the last; that we remained free to the last; that we revered his name to the last; [tha]t, during his long sleep, we permitted no hostile foot to pass over or desecrate [his] resting place; shall be that which to le[arn the last] trump shall awaken our WASH[INGTON.

Upon these] let the proud fabric of freedom r[est, as the] rock of its basis; and as truly as has been said of the only greater institution, "*the gates of hell shall not prevail against it.*"[13]

*Abraham Lincoln: The Quest for Immortality* (New York: Alfred A. Knopf, 1982), 68–78, not only agreed with Wilson that Lincoln consciously identified with those who might become a tyrant, but also contended that Lincoln wanted to become a godlike figure who sought immortality by destroying what the Founding Fathers had created. In contrast, Harry V. Jaffa, in *Crises of the House Divided* (New York: Doubleday, 1959), 183–232, viewed Lincoln and his speech in a positive light. More recently, Burlingame, in *Abraham Lincoln,* 1:140–142, argued that Lincoln was referring to Stephen A. Douglas. Others, such as Major L. Wilson, in "Lincoln and Van Buren"; David Donald, in *Lincoln;* and Douglas Wilson, in *Honor's Voice,* 195–198, posited that Lincoln's remarks were conventional for the time. For a review of the Lyceum speech and its interpretations, see Mark E. Neely Jr., "Lincoln's Lyceum Speech and the Origins of a Modern Myth," *Lincoln Lore,* nos. 1776–1777 (February and March 1987): 1–3, 1; Richard O. Curry, "Lincoln after 175 Years: Conscious or Subconscious Caesarism? A Critique of Recent Scholarly Attempts to Put Lincoln on the Analyst's Couch," *Journal of the Illinois State Historical Society* 77 (1984): 67–71; Richard N. Current, "Lincoln after 175 Years: The Myth of the Jealous Son," *Journal of the Abraham Lincoln Association* 6 (1984): 15–24; and Major L. Wilson, "Lincoln on the Perpetuation of Republican Institutions: Whig and Republican Strategies," *Journal of the Abraham Lincoln Association* 16 (1995): 15–25. See also Gabor S. Boritt, ed., *The Historian's Lincoln: Pseudohistory, Psychohistory, and History* (Urbana: University of Illinois Press, 1988), 211–312.

13 Matthew 16:18: "And I say also unto thee, That thou art Peter, and upon this rock I will build my church; and the gates of hell shall not prevail against it."

*In this letter to one of his few women friends—and the wife of a fellow legislator—Lincoln wrote of his mortification resulting from Mary Owens's rejection of his marriage proposal. Lincoln related the history of the awkward affair in a jocular, sometimes cruel vein, making fun of Mary as well as himself. While his exaggerated descriptions of Mary were intended to be humorous, they also served another purpose, that of rationalizing a humiliating experience. Admitting he was "really a little in love" with Mary Owens, Lincoln realized he had not only misunderstood his own feelings toward her but also failed completely to comprehend her feelings toward him.*

1 Eliza Caldwell of Kentucky married Orville Hickman Browning, also a Kentuckian, in 1836. Browning (1806–1881) had moved in 1831 from Kentucky to Quincy, Illinois, where he practiced law. In the same year that he was married, Browning was elected state senator and met Lincoln in Vandalia, then the capital of Illinois. Both Browning and his wife, Eliza, became Lincoln's close friends, with the latter serving as a valued confidant. Mark E. Neely Jr., *The Abraham Lincoln Encyclopedia* (New York: Da Capo Press, 1984), 38–39; Boas, *Biographical Dictionary,* 76–78.

2 Elizabeth Abell (ca. 1804–?). She and her husband, Bennett Abell, resided in New Salem, Illinois, and Lincoln lived for a time with the couple. She, along with Eliza, was a confidant of Lincoln's. Elizabeth Abell was the sister of Mary Owens, and she promoted the courtship between her sister and Lincoln. Wilson and Davis, *Herndon's Informants,* 738; Boas, *Biographical Dictionary,* 2–3.

3 Mary S. Owens.

4 Disturbed. Cited in *Lincoln's Selected Writings,* 15n3.

# Letter to Mrs. Orville H. Browning

## April 1, 1838

Dear Madam: Springfield, April 1. 1838[1]

Without appologising [*sic*] for being egotistical, I shall make the history of so much of my own life, as has elapsed since I saw you, the subject of this letter. And by the way I now discover, that, in order to give a full and inteligible [*sic*] account of things I have done and suffered *since* I saw you, I shall necessarily have to relate some that happened *before*.

It was, then, in the autumn of 1836, that a married lady of my acquaintance,[2] and who was a great friend of mine, being about to pay a visit to her father and other relatives residing in Kentucky, proposed to me, that on her return she would bring a sister of hers[3] with her, upon condition that I would engage to become her brother-in-law with all convenient dispatch. I, of course, accepted the proposal; for you know I could not have done otherwise, had I really been averse to it; but privately between you and me, I was most confoundedly well pleased with the project. I had seen the said sister some three years before, thought her inteligent [*sic*] and agreeable, and saw no good objection to plodding life through hand in hand with her. Time passed on, the lady took her journey and in due time returned, sister in company sure enough. This stomached[4] me a little; for it appeared to me, that her coming so readily showed that she was a trifle too willing; but on reflection it occured [*sic*] to me, that she might have been prevailed on by her married sister to come, without any thing concerning me ever having been mentioned to her; and so I concluded that if no other objection presented itself, I would consent to wave [*sic*] this. All this occured [*sic*] upon my *hearing* of her arrival in the neighbourhood; for, be it remembered, I had not yet *seen* her, except three years previous, as before mentioned.

In a few days we had an interview, and although I had seen her before, she did not look as my immagination [*sic*] had pictured her. I knew she was

5   Sir John Falstaff, the rotund comic character in Shakespeare's *Henry IV* and *The Merry Wives of Windsor.*

*Orville Hickman Browning.* Photograph (n.d.).

over-size, but she now appeared a fair match for Falstaff;[5] I knew she was called an "old maid", and I felt no doubt of the truth of at least half the appelation [*sic*]; but now, when I beheld her, I could not for my life avoid thinking of my mother; and this, not from withered features, for her skin was too full of fat, to permit its contracting in to wrinkles; but from her want of teeth, weather-beaten appearance in general, and from a kind of notion that ran in my head, that *nothing* could have commenced at the size of infancy, and reached her present bulk in less than thirty five or forty years;

6   Perhaps a reference to *Firm as the Surge Repelling Rock,* the title of the frontispiece to the fourth edition of David Ramsay's *Life of George Washington* (Baltimore: Joseph Cushing, 1815), which depicted a large rock bearing Washington's name, holding firm against a violent surge of waves during a storm.

and, in short, I was not all pleased with her. But what could I do? I had told her sister that I would take her for better or for worse; and I made a point of honor and conscience in all things, to stick to my word, especially if others had been induced to act on it, which in this case, I doubted not they had, for I was now fairly convinced, that no other man on earth would have her, and hence the conclusion that they were bent on holding me to my bargain. Well, thought I, I have said it, and, be consequences what they may, it shall not be my fault if I fail to do it. At once I determined to consider her my wife; and this done, all my powers of discovery were put to the rack, in search of perfections in her, which might be fairly set-off against her defects. I tried to imagine she was handsome, which, but for her unfortunate corpulency, was actually true. Exclusive of this, no woman that I have seen, has a finer face. I also tried to convince myself, that the mind was much more to be valued than the person; and in this, she was not inferior, as I could discover, to any with whom I had been acquainted.

Shortly after this, without attempting to come to any positive understanding with her, I set out for Vandalia, where and when you first saw me. During my stay there, I had letters from her, which did not change my opinion of either her intelect [*sic*] or intention; but on the contrary, confirmed it in both.

All this while, although I was fixed "firm as the surge repelling the rock"[6] in my resolution, I found I was continually repenting the rashness, which had led me to make it. Through life I have been in no bondage, either real or immaginary [*sic*] from the thralldom of which I so much desired to be free.

After my return home, I saw nothing to change my opinion of her in any particular. She was the same and so was I. I now spent my time between planning how I might get along through life after my contemplated change of circumstances should have taken place; and how I might procrastinate the evil day for a time, which I really dreaded as much—perhaps more, than the Irishman does the halter.

After all my suffering upon this deeply interesting subject, here I am, wholly unexpectedly, completely out of the "scrape"; and I now want to know, if you can guess how I got out of it. Out clear in every sense of the term; no violation of word, honor or conscience. I dont [*sic*] believe you can guess, and so I may as well tell you at once. As the lawyers say, it was done in the manner following, towit [*sic*]. After I had delayed the matter as long as I thought I could in honor do, which by the way had brought me round into the last fall, I concluded I might as well bring it to a consumation [*sic*] without further delay; and so I mustered my resolution, and made the proposal to her direct; but, shocking to relate, she answered, No. At first I supposed she did it through an affectation of modesty, which I thought but ill-become her, under the peculiar circumstances of her case; but on my renewal of the charge, I found she repeled [*sic*] it with greater firmness than before. I tried it again and again, but with the same success, or rather with the same want of success.[7] I finally was forced to give it up, at which I verry [*sic*] unexpectedly found myself mortified almost beyond endurance. I was mortified, it seemed to me, in a hundred different ways. My vanity was deeply wounded by the reflection, that I had so long been too stupid to discover her intentions, and at the same time never doubting that I understood them perfectly; and also, that she whom I had taught myself to believe no body else would have, had actually rejected me with all my fancied greatness; and to cap the whole, I then, for the first time, began to suspect that I was really a little in love with her. But let it all go. I'll try and out live it. Others have been made fools of by the girls; but this can never be with truth said of me. I most emphatically, in this instance, made a fool of myself. I have now come to the conclusion never again to think of marrying; and for this reason; I can never be satisfied with any one who would be block-head enough to have me.

When you receive this, write me a long yarn about something to amuse me. Give my respects to Mr. Browning. Your sincere friend

Mrs. O. H. Browning.   A. LINCOLN

7   It is not known if Mary Owens offered Lincoln specific reasons for rejecting his marriage proposal. A year after Lincoln's death, she informed Lincoln's former law partner William Henry Herndon (1818–1891), who was conducting interviews for a biography of Lincoln, that Lincoln "was deficient in those little links which make up the chain of woman's happiness. . . . Not that I believed it proceeded from a lack of goodness of heart; but that his training had been different from mine; hence there was not that congeniality which would otherwise have existed." She provided Herndon with at least two examples of Lincoln's deficiencies, including his seeming lack of concern or sensitivity concerning her safety when they were riding their horses across a creek with several other couples. Lincoln supposedly belittled the incident when Mary brought it to his attention. She came to the conclusion that while Lincoln was a good man, he would not make a good husband. Herndon and Weik, *Herndon's Lincoln,* 100–101. Soon after ending her relationship with Lincoln, Owens married Jessie Vineyard, and together they had five children. She became a widow in 1862 and was living in Weston, Missouri, when she corresponded with Herndon regarding Lincoln. Neely, *Lincoln Encyclopedia,* 230.

*In September 1841, following a six-week visit to the Speed family plantation in Farmington, Kentucky, Lincoln and his close friend Joshua Speed took a boat trip to Saint Louis. Lincoln wrote to his friend's older half sister to report on his encounter aboard the vessel with a group of chained slaves. While he would recall years later how this experience continued to torment him, his description in this letter is muted, lacking the emotion one would expect from an ardent opponent of slavery. In this instance Lincoln may have toned down his response to the episode out of friendship for Joshua and his stepsister and out of respect for the slave-holding Speed family, whose warm hospitality, including the services of a slave, had been extended to him.*

1   Mary Speed (1800–?) was the daughter of John Speed (1772–1840) by his first wife and thus the half sister to Lincoln's friend Joshua F. Speed (1814–1882). *CW,* 1:261n1. During his visit to Farmington, Lincoln had developed a friendship with Mary.

2   Farmington was located in Jefferson County, Kentucky, near Louisville.

3   Speed returned to Springfield with Lincoln, staying for several weeks in order to finalize several business affairs before traveling back to Farmington the following January. *CW,* 1:261n3.

4   From Laurence Sterne's *Sentimental Journal through France and Italy by Mr. Yorick* (London, 1768), in which Sterne quotes a French proverb first recorded by Henri Estienne in the sixteenth century.

5   Lincoln paraphrased Cervantes in *Don Quixote:* "Don Quixote would not break his fast; for, as it is said, he resolved to subsist upon savoury remembrances." Cited in *The Life and Exploits of the Ingenious Gentleman Don Quixote de la Mancha* (Boston: L .C. Page and Company, 1910), 28.

# Letter to Mary Speed

## September 27, 1841

Miss Mary Speed, Bloomington, Illinois
Louisville, Ky. Sept. 27th. 1841[1]

My Friend: Having resolved to write to some of your mother's family, and not having the express permission of any one of them [to] do so, I have had some little difficulty in determining on which to inflict the task of reading what I now feel must be a most dull and silly letter; but when I remembered that you and I were something of cronies while I was at Farmington,[2] and that, while there, I once was under the necessity of shutting you up in a room to prevent your committing an assault and battery upon me, I instantly decided that you should be the devoted one.

I assume that you have not heard from Joshua & myself since we left, because I think it doubtful whether he has written.

You remember there was some uneasiness about Joshua's health when we left. That little indisposition of his turned out to be nothing serious; and it was pretty nearly forgotten when we reached Springfield.[3] We got on board the Steam Boat Lebanon, in the locks of the Canal about 12. o'clock. M. of the day we left, and reached St. Louis the next monday at 8 P.M. Nothing of interest happened during the passage, except the vexatious delays occasioned by the sand bars be thought interesting. By the way, a fine example was presented on board the boat for contemplating the effect of *condition* upon human happiness. A gentleman had purchased twelve negroes in different parts of Kentucky and was taking them to a farm in the South. They were chained six and six together. A small iron clevis was around the left wrist of each, and this fastened to the main chain by a shorter one at a convenient distance from, the others; so that the negroes were strung together precisely like so many fish upon a trot-line. In this condition they were being separated forever from the scenes of their childhood, their friends, their

Artist unknown, *Joshua Fry Speed*. Oil on canvas? (ca. 1830s). Speed was Lincoln's closest and most intimate friend.

fathers and mothers, and brothers and sisters, and many of them, from their wives and children, and going into perpetual slavery where the lash of the master is proverbially more ruthless and unrelenting than any other where; and yet amid all these distressing circumstances, as we would think them, they were the most cheerful and apparently happy creatures on board. One, whose offense for which he had been sold was an over-fondness for his wife, played the fiddle almost continually; and the others danced, sung, cracked jokes, and played various games with cards from day to day. How true it is that "God tempers the wind to the shorn lamb,"[4] or in other words, that He renders the worst of human conditions tolerable, while He permits the best, to be nothing better than tolerable.

To return to the narrative. When we reached Springfield, I staid [*sic*] but one day when I started on this tedious circuit where I now am. Do you remember my going to the city while I was in Kentucky, to have a tooth extracted, and making a failure of it? Well, that same old tooth got to paining me so much, that about a week since I had it torn out, bringing with it a bit of the jawbone; the consequences of which is that my mouth is now so sore that I can neither talk nor eat. I am litterally [*sic*] "subsisting on savoury remembrances"[5]—that is, being unable to eat, I am living upon the remembrance of the delicious dishes of peaches and cream we used to have at your house.

6    At the time Lincoln wrote this letter, Joshua was engaged to Fanny Henning (1820–1902), whom he had courted during Lincoln's visit to Farmington. He married her on February 14, 1842. Burlingame, *Abraham Lincoln,* 1:188; Wilson, *Honor's Voice,* 249–250.

7    Lincoln referred either to Lucy Gilmer Davis (1840–1924), the two-year-old daughter of Joshua Speed's sister Susan Fry Speed Davis (1817–1888), or to Mary Speed's younger sister Eliza Davis Speed (1805–?), another stepsister of Joshua's. *CW,* 1:261n6.

8    Lincoln visited Farmington months after he broke his engagement with Mary Todd, an event that brought on a period of deep depression. To help ease Lincoln's "blues," Speed's mother gave her guest an "Oxford" Bible before he returned to Springfield. Wilson, *Honor's Voice,* 249.

9    Lincoln probably referred to Emma Keats, who married Joshua Speed's younger brother Philip. *CW,* 1:261n8.

10    Joshua Speed's elder sister, Peachy Walker Speed Peay (1813–1891), who was married to Austin Peay (1803–1849). *CW,* 1:261n9.

When we left, Miss Fanny Henning[6] was owing you a visit, as I understood. Has she paid it yet? If she has, are you not convinced that she is one of the sweetest girls in the world? There is but one thing about her, so far as I could perceive, that I would have otherwise than as it is. That is something of a tendency to melancholly [*sic*]. This, let it be observed, is a misfortune not a fault. Give her an assurance of my verry [*sic*] highest regard, when *you* see her.

Is little Siss Eliza Davis[7] at your house yet? If she is kiss her "o'er and o'er again" for me.

Tell your mother that I have not got her "present" with me; but I intend to read it regularly when I return home.[8] I doubt not that it is really, as she says, the best cure for the "Blues" could one but take it according to the truth.

Give my respects to all your sisters (including "Aunt Emma")[9] and brothers. Tell Mrs. Peay,[10] of whose happy face I shall long retain a pleasant remembrance, that I have been trying to think of a name for her homestead, but as yet, can not satisfy myself with one. I shall be verry [*sic*] happy to receive a line from you, soon after you receive this; and, in case you choose to favour me with one, address it to Charleston, Coles Co. Ills as I shall be there about the time to receive it. Your sincere friend A. LINCOLN

# Address to the Springfield Washington Temperance Society

## February 22, 1842

*Although he was a partner in a New Salem store that sold liquor, Lincoln seldom drank alcoholic beverages, and he was a supporter of the antebellum temperance movement. In this address, he criticized the early Calvinistic, church-centered, fire-and-brimstone approach, which condemned both drinkers and sellers of alcoholic beverages but offered no assistance to reform them. Instead, Lincoln favored the reform methods of moral suasion and redemption practiced by the Washingtonian temperance organizations. Lincoln compared the bondage of intemperance with that of slavery; over the next decade the latter would emerge as a signature issue for Lincoln while the former was deemphasized for political reasons.*

ALTHOUGH THE TEMPERANCE cause[1] HAS BEEN IN PROGRESS FOR nearly twenty years, it is apparent to all, that it is, *just now,* being crowned with a degree of success, hitherto unparalleled.[2]

The list of friends is daily swelled by the additions of fifties, of hundreds, and of thousands. The cause itself seems suddenly transformed from a cold abstract theory, to a living, breathing, active, and powerful chieftain, going forth "conquering, and to conquer."[3] The citadels of his great adversary are daily being stormed and dismantled; his temples and his altars, where the rites of his idolatrous worship have long been performed, and where human sacrifices have long been wont to be made, are daily desecrated and deserted. The trump of the conqueror's fame is sounding from hill to hill, from sea to sea, and from land to land, and calling millions to his standard at a blast.

For this new and splendid success, we heartily rejoice. That the success is so much greater *now* than *heretofore,* is doubtless owing to rational causes; and if we would have it to continue, we shall do well to enquire what those causes are. The warfare heretofore waged against the demon of Intemperance, has, some how or other, been erroneous. Either the champions engaged, or the tactics they adopted, have not been the most proper. These champions for the most part, have been Preachers, Lawyers, and hired agents. Between these and the mass of mankind, there is a want of *approachability,* if the term be admissible, partially at least, fatal to their success. They are supposed to have no sympathy or feeling of interest, with those very persons whom it is their object to convince and persuade.[4]

And again, it is so easy and so common to ascribe motives to men of these classes, other than those they profess to act upon. The *preacher,* it is said, advocates temperance because he is a fanatic, and desires a union of Church and State; the *lawyer,* from his pride and vanity of hearing himself speak; and the *hired agent,* for his salary. But when one, who has long been

1    The Springfield Washington Temperance Society was organized in mid-December 1841. Within six months it attracted 700 members in the town and some 2,000 in Sangamon County. Part of a movement of local groups named in honor of George Washington, the Springfield society held its first meeting, appropriately enough, on the former president's birthday. Lincoln was the principal speaker at this meeting, held in Springfield's Presbyterian Church. Paul M. Angle, *"Here I Have Lived": A History of Lincoln's Springfield 1821–1865* (Springfield, IL: The Abraham Lincoln Association, 1935), 193–194. Though Lincoln supported the temperance movement, there is no evidence that he was a member of this or any other temperance organization. In 1854, when asked by Illinois senator Stephen A. Douglas if he belonged to a temperance society, Lincoln replied that he did not, but that he was "temperate in that I don't drink anything." Cited in Burlingame, *Abraham Lincoln,* 1:377.

2    By the end of the eighteenth century many Americans were drinking alcohol as part of their daily routine. It was believed by many that alcoholic drinks, when consumed in moderation, were conducive to good health. With the increasing availability of cheap whiskey in the early

decades of the nineteenth century, drinking in the United States increased significantly, with a typical adult American consuming more than seven gallons a year (average consumption in the late 1990s was less than three gallons). Responding to the rise of drinking and its perceived deleterious effects on Americans' physical and moral health as well as on society in general, a temperance movement emerged in which all alcoholic beverages were denounced and proscribed. At first championed by physicians, clergymen, merchants, and other elites, the temperance movement, influenced by the evangelical revivals of the 1820s and 1830s, gathered momentum and a broader base of support, including many middle-class women. During the 1830s and 1840s, alcohol consumption by Americans was reduced significantly. For a concise review of the antebellum temperance movement, see Steven Mintz, *Moralists & Modernizers: America's Pre–Civil War Reformers* (Baltimore: Johns Hopkins University Press, 1995), 72–76. See also Bruce Dorsey, *Reforming Men and Women: Gender in the Antebellum City* (Ithaca: Cornell University Press, 2002), 90–135; Stephen Nissenbaum, *Sex, Diet, and Debility in Jacksonian America: Sylvester Graham and Health Reform* (Westport, CT: Greenwood Press, 1980), 69–85; W. J. Rorabaugh, *The Alcoholic Republic: An American Tradition* (New York: Oxford University Press, 1979), 187; Ian R. Tyrrell, *Sobering Up: From Temperance to Prohibition in Antebellum America* (Westport, CT: Greenwood Press, 1979); and Joseph R. Gusfield, *Symbolic Crusade: Status Politics and the American Temperance Movement* (Urbana: University of Illinois Press, 1963).

3    Revelation 6:2.

4    In this passage and several that follow, Lincoln repudiated as counterproductive the self-righteous approach taken by early leaders of the temperance movement, "Preachers, Lawyers, and hired agents" who condemned and sought to coerce "dram

known as a victim of intemperance, bursts the fetters that have bound him, and appears before his neighbors "clothed, and in his right mind,"[5] a redeemed specimen of long lost humanity, and stands up with tears of joy trembling in eyes, to tell of the miseries *once* endured, *now* to be endured no more forever; of his once naked and starving children, now clad and fed comfortably; of a wife long weighed down with woe, weeping, and a broken heart, now restored to health, happiness, and renewed affection; and how easily it all is done, once it is resolved to be done; however simple his language, there is a logic, and an eloquence in it, that few, with human feelings can resist. They cannot say that *he* desires a union of church and state, for he is not a church member; they can not say *he* is vain of hearing himself speak, for his whole demeanor shows, he would gladly avoid speaking at all; they cannot say *he* speaks for pay for he receives none, and asks for none. Nor can his sincerity in any way be doubted; or his sympathy for those he would persuade to imitate his example, be denied.

In my judgment, it is to the battles of this new class of champions that our late success is greatly, perhaps chiefly, owing. But, had the old school of champions themselves, been of the most wise selecting, was their *system* of tactics, the most judicious? It seems to me, it was not. Too much denunciation against dram sellers and dram-drinkers was indulged in. This, I think, was both impolitic and unjust. It was *impolitic,* because, it is not much in the nature of man to be driven to any thing; still less to be driven about that which is exclusively his own business; and least of all, where such driving is to be submitted to, at the expense of pecuniary interest, or burning appetite. When the dram-seller and drinker, were incessantly told, not in the accents of entreaty and persuasion, diffidently addressed by erring man to an erring brother; but in the thundering tones of anathema and denunciation, with which the lordly Judge often groups together all the crimes of the felon's life, and thrusts them in his face just ere he passes sentence of death upon him, that *they* were the authors of all the vice and misery and crime in the land; that *they* were the manufacturers and material of all the thieves and robbers and murderers that infested the earth; that *their* houses were the workshops of the devil; and that *their persons* should be shunned by all the good and virtuous, as moral pestilences—I say, when they were told all this, and in this way, it is not wonderful that they were slow, *very slow,* to acknowledge the truth of such denunciations, and to join the ranks of their denouncers, in a hue and cry against themselves.

To have expected them to do otherwise than as they did—to have expected them not to meet denunciation with denunciation, crimination with

N. Currier, *The Drunkard's Progress. From the First Glass to the Grave.* Lithograph (New York, 1846). A gentleman's progress on the archway of nine steps depicts the rise and fall of a drunkard.

crimination, and anathema with anathema, was to expect a reversal of human nature, which is God's decree, and never can be reversed. When the conduct of men is designed to be influenced, *persuasion,* kind, unassuming persuasion, should ever be adopted. It is an old and a true maxim, that a "drop of honey catches more flies than a gallon of gall."[6] So with men. If you would win a man to your cause, *first* convince him that you are his sincere friend. Therein is a drop of honey that catches his heart, which, say what he will, is the great high road to his reason, and which, when once gained, you will find but little trouble in convincing his judgment of the justice of your cause, if indeed that cause really be a just one. On the contrary, assume to dictate to his judgment, or to command his action, or to mark him as one to be shunned and despised, and he will retreat within himself, close all the avenues to his head and heart; and tho' your cause be naked truth itself, transformed to the heaviest lance, harder than steel, and sharper than steel can be made, and tho' you throw it with more than Her-

sellers and dram drinkers" to change their ways. Lincoln endorsed voluntary abstinence when it came to drinking, favoring "*persuasion,* kind, unassuming persuasion," over denunciation or prohibition, as the most effective and prudent course toward reforming the alcoholic. As one historian asserted, Lincoln's attitude toward alcoholics and saloon keepers foreshadowed "that compassion and absence of self-righteousness for which he was to become famous." Howe, *Political Culture of American Whigs,* 272.

5   Luke 8:35.

6   An English proverb. Other variations include: "A drop of honey catches more flies than a hogshead of vinegar," "flies are easier caught with

honey than vinegar," "more wasps are caught by
honey than by vinegar," and "you will catch more
flies with a spoonful of honey than with a gallon of
vinegar." Emanuel Strauss, comp., *Concise
Dictionary of European Proverbs* (New York:
Routledge, 1998), 112.

7    Lincoln is paraphrasing the hymn "Let Dogs
Delight to Bark and Bite" (1715) by the English
hymn writer Isaac Watts (1674–1784). Cited in
*Lincoln's Selected Writings,* 32n4.

8    The Washingtonian movement Lincoln praised
began in 1840 with the establishment of the
Washington Temperance Society in Baltimore.
This organization was founded by a group of
reformed drinkers who chose a life of total
abstinence after they attended a temperance lecture
at a local church. Other Washingtonian societies
emerged throughout the North over the next few
years, attracting middle-class and working-class
men and women. The Washingtonians spurned the
Calvinistic view of the drinker as a sinner beyond
redemption and instead offered assistance and
support. Unlike the old-guard evangelical temperance advocates who viewed reform as strictly
church-based, Washingtonians engaged in parades,
picnics, and other public events. They claimed to
have millions of followers by the mid-1840s. Mintz,
*Moralists & Modernizers,* 74; Dorsey, *Reforming
Men and Women,* 120–121.

culean force and precision, you shall no more be able to pierce him, than to
penetrate the hard shell of a tortoise with a rye straw.

Such is man, and so *must* he be understood by those who would lead
him, even to his own best interest.

On this point, the Washingtonians greatly excel the temperance advocates of former times. Those whom *they* desire to convince and persuade,
are their old friends and companions. They know they are not demons, nor
even the worst of men. *They* know that generally, they are kind, generous
and charitable, even beyond the example of their more staid and sober
neighbors. *They* are practical philanthropists; and *they* glow with a generous
and brotherly zeal, that mere theorizers are incapable of feeling. Benevo-
lence and charity possess *their* hearts entirely; and out of the abundance of
their hearts, their tongues give utterance, "Love through all their actions
runs, and all their words are mild."[7] In this spirit they speak and act, and in
the same, they are heard and regarded. And when such is the temper of the
advocate, and such of the audience, no good cause can be unsuccessful.[8]

But I have said that denunciations against dram-sellers and dram-
drinkers, are *unjust* as well as impolitic. Let us see.

I have not enquired at what period of time the use of intoxicating drinks
commenced; nor is it important to know. It is sufficient that to all of us who
now inhabit the world, the practice of drinking them, is just as old as the
world itself,—that is, we have seen the one, just as long as we have seen the
other. When all such of us, as have now reached the years of maturity, first
opened our eyes upon the stage of existence, we found intoxicating liquor,
recognized by every body, used by every body, and repudiated by nobody. It
commonly entered into the first draught of the infant, and the last draught
of the dying man. From the sideboard of the parson, down to the ragged
pocket of the houseless loafer, it was constantly found. Physicians prescribed
it in this, that, and the other disease. Government provided it for its soldiers
and sailors; and to have a rolling or raising, a husking or hoe-down, any
where without it, was *positively insufferable.*

So too, it was every where a respectable article of manufacture and of
merchandize. The making of it was regarded as an honorable livelihood;
and he who could make most, was the most enterprising and respectable.
Large and small manufactories of it were every where erected, in which all
the earthly good of their owners were invested. Wagons drew it from town
to town—boats bore it from clime to clime, and the winds wafted it from
nation to nation; and merchants bought and sold it, by wholesale and by
retail, with precisely the same feelings, on the part of the seller, buyer, and

bystander, as are felt at the selling and buying of flour, beef, bacon, or any other of the real necessaries of life. Universal public opinion not only tolerated, but recognized and adopted its use.

It is true, that even *then,* it was known and acknowledged, that many were greatly injured by it; but none seemed to think the injury arose from the *use* of a *bad thing,* but from the *abuse* of a *very good thing.* The victims to it were pitied and compassionated, just as now are, the heirs of consumptions, and other hereditary diseases.

Their failing was treated as a *misfortune,* and not as a *crime,* or even as a *disgrace.*

If, then, what I have been saying be true, is it wonderful, that *some* should think and act *now,* as *all* thought and acted *twenty years ago?* And is it *just* to assail, *contemn,* or despise them, for doing so? The universal *sense* of mankind, on any subject, is an argument, or at least an *influence* not easily overcome. The success of the argument in favor of the existence of an overruling Providence, mainly depends upon that sense; and men ought not, in justice, to be denounced for yielding to it, in any case, or for giving it up slowly, *especially,* where they are backed by interest, fixed habits, or burning appetites.

Another error, as it seems to me, into which the old reformers fell, was, the position that all habitual drunkards were utterly incorrigible, and therefore, must be turned adrift, and damned without remedy, in order that the grace of temperance might abound to the temperate *then,* and to all mankind some hundred years *thereafter.* There is in this something so repugnant to humanity, so uncharitable, so cold-blooded and feelingless, that it never did, nor ever can enlist the enthusiasm of a popular cause. We could not love the man who taught it—we could not hear him with patience. The heart could not throw open its portals to it. The generous man could not adopt it. It could not mix with his blood. It looked so fiendishly selfish, so like throwing fathers and brothers overboard, to lighten the boat for our security—that the noble minded shrank from the manifest meanness of the thing.

And besides this, the benefits of a reformation to be effected by such a system, were too remote in point of time, to warmly engage many in its behalf. Few can be induced to labor exclusively for posterity; and none will do it enthusiastically. Posterity has done nothing for us; and theorise on it as we may, practically we shall do very little for it, unless we are made to think, we are, at the same time, doing something for ourselves. What an ignorance of human nature does it exhibit, to ask or expect a whole community to rise

N. Currier, *The Tree of Intemperance.* Lithograph (New York, 1849). This print depicts a dying tree, the life being squeezed out of it by the snake of "alcohol."

up and labor for the *temporal* happiness of *others* after *themselves* shall be consigned to the dust, a majority of which community take no pains whatever to secure their own eternal welfare, at a no greater distant day? Great distance, in either time or space, has wonderful power to lull and render quiescent the human mind. Pleasures to be enjoyed, or pains to be endured, *after* we shall be dead and gone, are but little regarded, even in our *own* cases, and much less in the cases of others.

Still, in addition to this, there is something so ludicrous in *promises* of good, or *threats* of evil, a great way off, as to render the whole subject with which they are connected, easily turned into ridicule. "Better lay down that spade you're stealing, Paddy,—if you don't you'll pay for it at the day of judgment." "By the powers, if ye'll credit me so long, I'll take another, jist."

By the Washingtonians, this system of consigning the habitual drunkard to hopeless ruin, is repudiated. *They* adopt a more enlarged philanthropy. *They* go for present as well as future good. *They* labor for all *now* living, as well as all *hereafter* to live. *They* teach *hope* to all—*despair* to none. As applying to *their* cause, *they* deny the doctrine of unpardonable sin. As in Christianity it is taught, so in this *they* teach, that "While the lamp holds out to burn, the vilest sinner may return."9

And, what is matter of the most profound gratulation, they, by experiment upon experiment, and example upon example, prove the maxim to be no less true in the one case than in the other. On every hand we behold those, who but yesterday, were the chief of sinners, now the chief apostles of the cause. Drunken devils are cast out by ones, by sevens, and by legions; and their unfortunate victims, like the poor possessed, who was redeemed from his long and lonely wanderings in the tombs, are publishing to the ends of the earth, how great things have been done for them.

To these *new champions,* and this *new* system of tactics, our late success is mainly owing; and to *them* we must chiefly look for final consummation. The ball is now rolling gloriously on, and none are so able as *they* to increase its speed, and its bulk—to add to its momentum, and its magnitude. Even though unlearned in letters, for this task, none others are so well educated. To fit them for this work, they have been taught in the true school. *They* have been in *that* gulf, from which they would teach others the means of escape. *They* have passed that prison wall, which others have long declared impassable; and who that has not, shall dare to weigh opinions with *them,* as to the mode of passing.

But if it be true, as I have insisted, that those who have suffered by intemperance *personally,* and have reformed, are the most powerful and efficient instruments to push the reformation to ultimate success, it does not follow, that those who have not suffered, have no part left them to perform. Whether or not the world would be vastly benefitted by a total and final banishment from it of all intoxicating drinks, seems to me not *now* to be an open question. Three-fourths of mankind confess the affirmative with their *tongues,* and, I believe, all the rest acknowledge it in their *hearts.*

Ought *any,* then, to refuse their aid in doing what the good of the *whole* demands? Shall he, who cannot do *much,* be, for that reason, excused if he do *nothing?* "But," says one, "what good can I do by signing the pledge? I never drink even without signing." This question has already been asked and answered more than millions of times. Let it be answered once more. For the man to suddenly, or in any other way, to break off from the use of drams, who has indulged in them for a long course of years, and until his appetite for them has become ten or a hundred fold stronger, and more craving, than any natural appetite can be, requires a most powerful moral effort. In such an undertaking, he needs every moral support and influence, that can possibly be brought to his aid, and thrown around him. And not only so; but every moral prop, should be taken *from* whatever argument might rise in his mind to lure him to his backsliding. When he casts his eyes around him, he should be able to see, all that he respects, all that he admires, and all that [he] loves, kindly and anxiously pointing him onward; and none beckoning him back, to his former miserable "wallowing in the mire."

But it is said by some, that men will *think* and *act* for themselves; that none will disuse spirits or any thing else, merely because his neighbors do; and that *moral influence* is not that powerful engine contended for. Let us examine this. Let me ask the man who would maintain this position most stiffly, what compensation he will accept to go to church some Sunday and sit during the sermon with his wife's bonnet upon his head? Not a trifle, I'll venture. And why not? There would be nothing irreligious in it: nothing immoral, nothing uncomfortable. Then why not? Is it not because there would be something egregiously unfashionable in it? Then it is the influence of *fashion;* and what is the influence of fashion, but the influence that *other* people's actions have [on our own] actions, the strong inclination each of us feels to do as we see our neighbors do? Nor is the influence of fashion confined to any particular thing or class of things. It is just as strong on one subject as another. Let us make it as unfashionable to withhold our names from the temperance pledge as for husbands to wear their wives [*sic*] bonnets to church, and instances will be just as rare in the one case as the other.

Arthur I. Keller, *Abraham Lincoln Pledges Cleopas Breckenridge to Total Abstinence.* Drawing, used as frontispiece in Louis Albert Banks, *The Lincoln Legion: The Story of Its Founder and Forerunners* (New York: The Mershon Company, 1903). Lincoln delivered several temperance speeches during the summers of 1846 and 1847. Cleopas Breckenridge claimed that he attended one of these events as a boy and signed a temperance pledge after the speech. He alleged that Lincoln told him, "Now, sonny, you keep that pledge, and it will be the best act of your life!"

10   William H. Herndon, Lincoln's law partner, a temperance advocate, and sometimes a heavy drinker, claimed this passage of the address offended many of the church members who were present. The assertion, wrote Herndon, that "certain Christians" objected to associating with drunkards, "even with the chance of reforming them[,] . . . proved to be an unfortunate thing for Lincoln. The professing Christians regarded the suspicion suggested in the first sentence as a reflection on the sincerity of their belief, and the last one had no better effect in reconciling them to his views. I was at the door of the church as the people passed out, and heard them discussing the speech. Many of them were open in the expression of their displeasure." Herndon and Weik, *Herndon's Lincoln,* 166.

11   From Ezekiel 37:9–10.

12   As was the case in his 1838 address to the Young Men's Lyceum, Lincoln advocated reason and self-control over unrestrained passion as essential components for preserving individual as well as political freedom. According to historian Daniel Walker Howe, Lincoln's glorification of mind over matter and reason over passion was "typical of American moral philosophy and Whig modernization." Lincoln also equated the bondage of intemperance with that of slavery, a link many temperance and antislavery advocates would have understood, owing to the overlap of participants in the two reform movements. Lincoln's views on the two reform movements were similar: just as he saw the self-righteousness approach as detrimental to the success of the temperance movement, Lincoln also viewed radical abolitionists and their strident tactics as counterproductive to the antislavery cause. Like his approach to temperance, Lincoln favored a moderate course concerning the fight against slavery. In the 1850s Lincoln and the Republican Party minimized the temperance issue for political reasons, not wishing to alienate

"But," say some, "we are no drunkards; and we shall not acknowledge ourselves such by joining a reformed drunkard's society, whatever our influence might be." Surely no Christian will adhere to this objection. If they believe, as they profess, that Omnipotence condescended to take on himself the form of sinful man, and, as such, to die an ignominious death for their sakes, surely they will not refuse submission to the infinitely lesser condescension, for the temporal, and perhaps eternal salvation, of a large, erring, and unfortunate class of their own fellow creatures. Nor is the condescension very great.[10]

In my judgment, such of us as have never fallen victims, have been spared more from the absence of appetite, than from any mental or moral superiority over those who have. Indeed, I believe, if we take habitual drunkards as a class, their heads and their hearts will bear an advantageous comparison with those of any other class. There seems ever to have been a proneness in the brilliant, and the warm-blooded, to fall into this vice. The demon of intemperance ever seems to have delighted in sucking the blood of genius and of generosity. What one of us but can call to mind some dear relative, more promising in youth than all his fellows, who has fallen a sacrifice to his rapacity? He ever seems to have gone forth, like the Egyptian angel of death, commissioned to slay if not the first, the fairest born of every family. Shall he now be arrested in his desolating career? In that arrest, all can give aid that will; and who shall be excused that *can,* and will not? Far around as human breath has ever blown, he keeps our fathers, our brothers, our sons, and our friends, prostrate in the chains of moral death. To all the living every where, we cry, "come sound the moral resurrection trump, that these may rise and stand up, an exceeding great army"—"Come from the four winds, O breath! and breathe upon these slain, that they may live."[11]

If the relative grandeur of revolutions shall be estimated by the great amount of human misery they alleviate, and the small amount they inflict, then, indeed, will this be the grandest the world shall ever have seen. Of our political revolution of '76, we all are justly proud. It has given us a degree of political freedom, far exceeding that of any other of the nations of the earth. In it the world has found a solution of that long mooted problem, as to the capability of man to govern himself. In it was the germ which has vegetated, and still is to grow and expand into the universal liberty of mankind. But with all these glorious results, past, present, and to come, it had its evils too. It breathed forth famine, swam in blood and rode on fire; and long, long after, the orphan's cry, and the widow's wail, continued to break the sad silence that ensued. These were the price, the inevitable price, paid for the blessings it bought.

Turn now, to the temperance revolution. In *it,* we shall find a stronger bondage broken; a viler slavery, manumitted; a greater tyrant deposed. In *it,* more of want supplied, more disease healed, more sorrow assuaged. By *it* no orphans starving, no widows weeping. By *it,* none wounded in feeling, none injured in interest. Even the dram-maker, and dram seller, will have glided into other occupations *so* gradually, as never to have felt the shock of change; and will stand ready to join all others in the universal song of gladness.

And what a noble ally this, to the cause of political freedom. With such an aid, its march cannot fail to be on and on, till every son of earth shall drink in rich fruition, the sorrow quenching draughts of perfect liberty. Happy day, when, all appetites controlled, all passions subdued, all matters subjected, *mind,* all conquering *mind,* shall live and move the monarch of the world. Glorious consummation! Hail fall of Fury! Reign of Reason, all hail![12]

And when the victory shall be complete—when there shall be neither a slave nor a drunkard on earth—how proud the title of that *Land,* which may truly claim to be the birth-place and the cradle of both those revolutions, that shall have ended in that victory. How nobly distinguished that People, who shall have planted, and nurtured to maturity, both the political and moral freedom of their species.

This is the one hundred and tenth anniversary of the birth-day of Washington. We are met to celebrate this day. Washington is the mightiest name of earth—*long since* mightiest in the cause of civil liberty; *still* mightiest in moral reformation. On that name, an [*sic*] eulogy is expected. It cannot be. To add brightness to the sun, or glory to the name of Washington, is alike impossible. Let none attempt it. In solemn awe pronounce the name, and in its naked deathless splendor, leave it shining on.[13]

immigrant Irish and, especially, German Protestant voters, who viewed the movement as an overzealous attempt to impose morality. Howe, *Political Culture of American Whigs,* 272.

13  George Washington, whose success as a general, president, and statesman was attributed to his temperate behavior and self-control, inspired the temperance movement that used his name. The nation's first president was greatly admired by Lincoln, who as a youth was captivated by Mason Locke Weems's romanticized *Life of George Washington.*

*Lincoln offered consolation and support to his closest friend, who was undergoing a crisis of confidence concerning his upcoming marriage. Lincoln had recently undergone a similar emotional crisis that resulted in the temporary breaking of his engagement to Mary Todd. Lincoln and Speed's relationship was such that each shared with the other his innermost thoughts concerning women, courtships, and marriage, subjects Lincoln rarely discussed with other friends and acquaintances.*

1   Joshua Fry Speed was born near Louisville, Kentucky, moved to Springfield, Illinois, in 1835 and became a partner in a general store. Speed and Lincoln met when the latter arrived in Springfield from New Salem in 1837. Lincoln entered Speed's store and inquired about lodging in town, whereupon Speed offered to share his room above the store. Lincoln accepted and the two lived together, sharing the same bed, for the next four years, with Speed becoming Lincoln's most intimate friend. After Speed moved to Kentucky and both he and Lincoln married, they drifted apart. Speed's conservative views on slavery clashed with Lincoln's, though Speed remained loyal to the Union during the Civil War and continued to offer counsel to a president determined to keep his native state out of the Confederacy. Neely, *Lincoln Encyclopedia*, 284–285. Debates concerning Lincoln's sexuality emerged in the 1990s and reached their peak in 2005 with the long-awaited publication of C. A. Tripp's *The Intimate World of Abraham Lincoln* (New York: Free Press), which contended that Lincoln had sexual relationships with several men, including Speed. As evidence of Lincoln and Speed's intense relationship, Tripp pointed to Lincoln's sentence in the first paragraph of this letter, which Tripp characterized as "perhaps the clearest smoking gun" in their correspondence supporting claims of their sexual relationship. According to Tripp, Lincoln's trauma was caused by his realization that his relationship with Speed

# Letter to Joshua F. Speed

## February 25, 1842

Dear Speed:[1] Springfield, Feb: 25- 1842-

I received yours of the 12th. written the day you went down to William's place, some days since; but delayed answering it, till I should receive the promised one, of the 16th., which came last night. I opened the latter, with intense anxiety and trepidation—so much, that although it turned out better than I expected, I have hardly yet, at the distance of ten hours, become calm.[2]

I tell you, Speed, our *forebodings,* for which you and I are rather peculiar, are all the worst sort of nonsense. I fancied, from the time I received your letter of *saturday,* that the one of *wednesday* was never to come; and yet it *did* come, and what is more, it is perfectly clear, both from it's [*sic*] tone and *handwriting,* that you were much *happier,* or, if you think the term preferable, *less miserable,* when you wrote *it,* than when you wrote the last one before. You had so obviously improved, at the verry [*sic*] time I so much feared, you would have grown worse. You say that "something indescribably horrible and alarming still haunts you." You will not say *that* three months from now, I will venture. When your nerves once get steady now, the whole trouble will be over forever. Nor should you become impatient at their being even verry [*sic*] slow, in becoming steady. Again; you say you much fear that that Elysium of which you have dreamed so much, is never to be realized. Well, if it shall not, I dare swear, it will not be the fault of her who is now your wife. I now have no doubt that it is the peculiar misfortune of both you and me, to dream dreams of Elysium far exceeding all that any thing earthly can realize. Far short of your dreams as you may be, no woman could do more to realize them, than that same black eyed Fanny. If you could but contemplate her through my imagination, it would appear ridiculous to you, that any one should for a moment think of being unhappy

George P. A. Healy, *Joshua Fry Speed and Fanny Henning Speed.* Oil on canvas (ca. 1840s).

had changed forever. Tripp's evidence to support his views of Lincoln's sexual relationship with Speed and other men is questionable, however, and based on misinterpretations of anecdotal material. Speed's letters to Lincoln are lost. Tripp, *Intimate World,* 38.

2　When Lincoln was in the midst of the serious and debilitating emotional crisis that led to the breaking of his engagement with Mary Todd, in the winter of 1840–41, Speed served as his friend's main source of solace and support, culminating in an invitation to Lincoln to spend time at the Speed plantation in Kentucky. A year later, their roles were reversed when Lincoln wrote a series of letters to Speed in the early weeks of 1842, including this one, in which he offered advice and support to Speed, who, after a whirlwind courtship, had proposed marriage to Fanny Henning and was experiencing his own crisis of confidence. Wilson, *Honor's Voice,* 245–52; Burlingame, *Abraham Lincoln,* 1:188–189. For Lincoln's letters to Speed during this period, in addition to this one, see *CW,* 1:265–266, 267–268, 269–270, 281.

with her. My old Father used to have a saying that "If you make a bad bargain, *hug* it the tighter"; and it occurs to me, that if the bargain you have just closed can possibly be called a bad one, it is certainly the most *pleasant* one for applying that maxim to, which my fancy can, by any effort, picture.

I write another letter enclosing this, which you can show her, if she desires it. I do this, because, she would think strangely perhaps should you tell her that you receive no letters from me; or, telling her you do, should refuse to let her see them.

I close this, entertaining the confident hope, that every successive letter I shall have from you, (which I here pray may not be few, nor far between) may show you possessing a more steady hand, and cheerful heart, than the last preceding it. As ever, your friend LINCOLN

*That Lincoln was afforded unlimited access to the columns of Springfield's Whig newspaper is not surprising; he was a leader of the city's Whig Party and a close friend of the newspaper's editor. Over the years, the paper published numerous anonymous contributions penned by Lincoln, among which the most ludicrous was the "Rebecca" letter, which appeared in the September 2, 1842, issue. The letter, a satirical attack on Democrat James Shields, Illinois state auditor, caused an immediate sensation in and around Springfield and extreme embarrassment to its intended victim. Writing as a semiliterate widow living on a farm in the fictional location of the "Lost Townships," Lincoln used vernacular dialect for comic effect as he skewered Shields unmercifully. When Shields discovered Lincoln was the author, he challenged him to a duel. Lincoln reluctantly accepted the challenge, though the duel was avoided as a result of negotiations on the day the encounter was scheduled. Lincoln was ashamed of his participation in the dueling episode and regretted it for the rest of his life.*

1 Appearing in the *Sangamo Journal* on September 2, 1842, this was actually the second of four "Rebecca" letters published by the newspaper. The first, dated August 10, appeared in the August 19 issue, and the third (dated August 29) and fourth (dated September 8) in the September 9 issue. The September 16 issue carried several verses of doggerel that announced the wedding of Shields and Rebecca. Roy Basler, chief editor of Lincoln's *Collected Works* and an authority on the "Rebecca" letters, asserted that Simeon Francis (1796–1872), editor of the *Sangamo Journal,* was the author of an earlier series of "Lost Township" letters published in his paper in 1838 as well as of the first and third "Rebecca" letters, owing to the similarity of the writing style. *CW,* 1:297n2; see also Basler, "The Authorship of the 'Rebecca' Letters," *Abraham Lincoln Quarterly* (June 1942): 88. Julia Jayne and Mary Todd may have authored the fourth letter.

# The "Rebecca" Letter

## August 27, 1842

LETTER FROM THE LOST TOWNSHIPS.
Dear Mr. Printer: Lost Townships, Aug. 27, 1842.

I see you printed that long letter I sent you a spell ago—I'm quite encouraged by it, and can't keep from writing again.[1] I think the printing of my letters will be a good thing all round,—it will give me the benefit of being known by the world, and give the world the advantage of knowing what's going on in the Lost Townships, and give your paper respectability besides. So here come another. Yesterday afternoon I hurried through cleaning up the dinner dishes, and stepped over to neighbor S—— to see if his wife Peggy was as well as mought be expected, and hear what they called the baby. Well, when I got there, and just turned round the corner of his log cabin, there he was setting on the door-step reading a newspaper.

"How are you Jeff," says I,—he sorter started when he heard me, for he hadn't seen me before. "Why," says he, "I'm mad as the devil, aunt Becca."

"What about," says I, "aint its hair the right color? None of that nonsense, Jeff—there aint an honester woman in the Lost Township than—"

"Than who?" says he, "what the mischief are you about?"

I began to see I was running the wrong trail, and so says I, "O nothing, I guess I was mistaken a little, that's all. But what is it you're mad about?"

"Why," says he, "I've been tugging ever since harvest getting out wheat and hauling it to the river, to raise State Bank paper enough to pay my tax this year, and a little school debt I owe; and now just as I've got it, here I open this infernal Extra Register, expecting to find it full of 'glorious democratic victories,' and 'High Comb'd Cocks,' when, lo and behold, I find a set of fellows calling themselves *officers of State,* have forbidden the tax collectors and school commissioners to receive State paper at all; and so here it is, dead on my hands. I don't now believe all the plunder I've got will fetch ready cash enough to pay my taxes and that school debt."[2]

I was a good deal thunderstruck myself; for that was the first I had heard of the proclamation, and my old man was pretty much in the same fix with Jeff. We both stood a moment, staring at one another without knowing what to say. At last says I, "Mr. S—— let me look at that paper." He handed it to me, when I read the proclamation over.

"There now," says he, "did you ever see such a piece of impudence and imposition as that?" I saw Jeff was in a good tune for saying some ill-natured things, and so I tho't I would just argue a little on the contrary side, and make him rant a spell if I could.

"Why," says I, looking as dignified and thoughtful as I could, "it seems pretty tough to be sure, to have to raise silver where there's none to be raised; but then you see *there will be danger of loss*' if it aint done."

"Loss, damnation!" says he, "I defy Daniel Webster, I defy King Solomon, I defy the world,—I defy—I defy—yes, I defy even you, aunt Becca, to show how people can lose any thing by paying their taxes in State paper." "Well," says I, "you will see what the *officers of State* say about it, and they are a desarnin set of men." "But," says I, "I guess you're mistaken about what the proclamation says; it don't say *the people* will lose any thing by the paper money being taken for taxes. It only says '*there will be danger of loss*,' and though it is tolerable plain that the people can't lose by paying their taxes in something they can get easier than silver, instead of having to pay silver; and though it is just as plain, that the State can't lose by taking State Bank paper, however low it may be, while she owes the Bank more than the whole revenue, and can pay that paper over her debt, dollar for dollar; still *there is danger of loss* to the '*officers of State*,' and you know Jeff, we can't get along without *officers of State*."

"Damn officers of State," says he, "that's what you whigs are always hurraing for." "Now don't swear so Jeff," says I, "you know I belong to the meetin, and swearin hurts my feelins." "Beg pardon, aunt Becca," says he, "but I do say its enough to make Dr. Goddard[3] swear, to have tax to pay in silver, for nothing only that Ford[4] may get his two thousand a year, and Sheilds[5] his twenty four hundred a year, and Carpenter[6] his sixteen hundred a year, and all without 'danger of loss' by taking it in State paper. Yes, yes, it's plain enough now what these *officers of State* mean by 'danger of loss.' Wash,[7] I spose, actually lost fifteen hundred dollars out of three thousand that two of these 'officers of State' let him steal from the Treasury, by be-

Jayne, daughter of a Springfield physician and politician who served with Lincoln in the Illinois legislature, was a close friend of Mary Todd's and served as her bridesmaid when Todd married Lincoln. Jayne later married Lyman Trumbull (1813–1896), who served Illinois as a U.S. senator, was a supporter of Lincoln, and authored the Thirteenth Amendment to the Constitution. Mary Todd, who broke with Julia after her husband defeated Lincoln for a seat in the U.S. Senate in 1855, later claimed to have written only the verses that appeared in the September 16 issue of the *Sangamo Journal*. Wilson, *Honor's Voice*, 270. Information on Julia Jayne is from Boas, *Biographical Dictionary*, 246.

2    The Illinois economy was hit hard by the 1837 panic and, by 1842 the state was mired in debt owing to commitments made for internal improvement projects passed in the state legislature by Lincoln and his fellow Whigs. With the state bank collapsing because of the depreciation of its currency, Democratic state officers were forced to make harsh decisions to deal with a bleak economic situation for which they were not solely to blame. State auditor James Shields (1806–1879) issued a proclamation ordering state officials to refuse state bank notes as payment of taxes. With residents forced to pay state taxes with other legal tender, which was scarce, the proclamation was extremely unpopular. Illinois Whigs, including Lincoln, sought to take advantage of the situation.

3    According to *CW*, 1:297n5, this is probably Methodist minister Dr. Addison S. Goddard.

4    Thomas Ford (1800–1850), a Democrat, served as governor of Illinois from 1842 to 1846. National Governors Association http://www.nga.org/cms/home/past-governors-bios/page_illinois/col2-content/main-content-list/title_ford_thomas.html (accessed January 19, 2015).

5    James Shields served as auditor of the State of Illinois from 1839 to 1843. Born in Ireland, he settled in Illinois in 1829 and was serving in the state legislature by 1836. Appointed to the Illinois Supreme Court in 1843 by Governor Ford, Shields served and was wounded in the Mexican-American War and was elected U.S. senator in 1849. Shields later moved to Minnesota and served that state in the U.S. Senate (1858–1859) before he moved to California. Though he supported Southern Democrat John C. Breckinridge (1821–1875) for president in 1860 and believed the South acted in self-defense when rebelling against the North, he supported the Union in the Civil War. Despite their past differences and Shields's pro-Southern sentiments, Lincoln appointed him brigadier general of U.S volunteers in 1861. Shields resigned his post in 1863. He later served as senator from Missouri in 1879. Neely, *Lincoln Encyclopedia,* 277; Lawrence Frederick Kohl, "Shields, James," in *The Political Lincoln: An Encyclopedia,* ed. Paul Finkelman and Martin J. Hershock (Washington, DC: CQ Press, 2009), 599–600.

6    Milton Carpenter (1807–1848) was a Democrat who served as state treasurer. Cited in *CW,* 1:297n7; obituary in *Illinois State Register,* August 15, 1848.

7    Milton H. Wash (1819–?) served as a clerk in James Shields's office and embezzled $1,161 of state funds. Cited in *CW,* 1:297n8.

8    Thomas Carlin (1789–1852), a Democrat, served Illinois as governor from 1838 to 1842. National Governors Association, http://www.nga.org/cms/home/governors/past-bios/page_illinois/col2-content/main-content-list/title_carlin_thomas.html (accessed January 19, 2015).

9    John Tyler (1790–1862) was president of the United States from 1841 to 1845. In 1840 he was elected vice president on the Whig Party ticket headed by William Henry Harrison, and he

ing compelled to take it in State paper. Wonder if we don't have a proclamation before long, commanding us to make up this loss to Wash in silver."

And so he went on, till his breath run out, and he had to stop. I couldn't think of any thing to say just then: and so I begun to look over the paper again. "Aye! Here's another proclamation, or something like it." "Another!" says Jeff, "and whose egg is it, pray?" I looked at the bottom of it, and read aloud, "Your obedient servant, JAS SHEILDS, Auditor."

"Aha!", says Jeff, "one of them same three fellows again. Well read it, and let's hear what of it." I read on till I came to where it says "*The object of this measure is to suspend the collection of revenue for the current year.*" "Now stop, now stop," says he, "that's a lie aready, and I don't want to hear of it." "O may be not," says I.

"I say *it—is—a—lie.*—Suspend the collection, indeed! Will the collectors that have taken their oaths to make the collection DARE to suspend it? Is there any thing in the law requiring them to perjure themselves at the bidding of Jas. Shields? Will the greedy gullet of the penitentiary be satisfied with swallowing *him* instead of all *them* if they should venture to obey him? And would he not discover some 'danger of loss' and be off, about the time it came to taking their places?"

"And suppose the people attempt to suspend by refusing to pay, what then? The collectors would just jerk up their horses, and cows, and the like, and sell them to the highest bidder for silver in hand, without valuation or redemption. Why, Shields didn't believe that story himself—it was never meant for the truth. If it was true, why was it not writ till five days after the proclamation? Why didn't Carlin[8] and Carpenter sign it as well as Shields? Answer me that, aunt Becca. I say it's a lie, and not a well told one at that. It grins out like a copper dollar. Shields is a fool as well as a liar. With him truth is out of the question, and as for getting a good bright passable lie out of him, you might as well try to strike fire from a cake of tallow. I stick to it, its all an infernal whig lie."

"A *whig* lie,—Highty! Tighty!!"

"Yes, a *whig* lie; and its just like every thing the cursed British whigs do. First they'll do some devilment, and then they'll tell a lie to hide it. And they don't care how plain a lie it is; they think they can cram any sort of a one down the throats of the ignorant loco focus, as they call the democrats."

"Why, Jeff, you're crazy—you don't mean to say Shields is a whig."

"*Yes I do.*"

"Why, look here, the proclamation is in your own democratic paper as you call it."

"I know it, and what of that? They only printed it to let us democrats see the deviltry the whigs are at."

"Well, but Shields is the Auditor of this loco—I mean this democratic State."

"So he is, and Tyler[9] appointed him to office."

"Tyler appointed him?"

"Yes (if you must chaw it over) Tyler appointed him, or if it wasn't him it was old granny Harrison,[10] and that's all one. I tell you, aunt Becca, there's no mistake about his being a whig—why his very looks show it—every thing about him shows it—if I was deaf and blind I could tell him by the smell. I seed him when I was down in Springfield last winter. They had a sort of a gatherin there one night, among the grandees, they called a fair. All the galls about town was there, and all the handsome widows, and married women, finickin about, trying to look like galls, tied as tight in the middle, and puffed out at both ends like bundles of fodder that hadn't been stacked yet, but wanted stackin pretty bad. And then they had tables all round the house kivered over with baby caps, and pin-cushions, and ten thousand such little knik-nacks, tryin to sell 'em to the fellows that were bowin and scrapin, and kungeerin about 'em. They wouldn't let no democrats in, for fear they'd disgust the ladies, or scare the little galls, or dirty the floor. I looked in at the window, and there was this same fellow Shields floatin about on the air, without heft or earthly substance, just like a lock of cat-fur where cats had been fightin."

"He was paying his money to this one and that one, and tother one, and sufferin great loss because it wasn't silver instead of State paper; and the sweet distress he seemed to be in,—his very features, in the exstatic agony of his soul, spoke audibly and distinctly—'Dear girls, *it is distressing,* but I cannot marry you all. Too well I know how much you suffer; but do, *do* remember, it is not my fault that I am *so* handsome and *so* interesting.'"

"As this last was expressed by a most exquisite contortion of his face, he seized hold of one of their hands and squeezed, and held on to it about a quarter of an hour. O, my good fellow, says I to myself, if that was one of our democratic galls in the Lost Township, the way you'd get a brass pin let into you, would be about up to the head. He's a democrat! Fiddle-sticks! I tell you, aunt Becca, he's a whig, and no mistake: nobody but a whig could make such a conceity dunce of himself."[11]

"Well," says I, "may be he is, but if he is, I'm mistaken the worst sort."

"May be so; may be so; but if I am I'll suffer by it; I'll be a democrat if it

James T. Shields. Photograph (n.d.).

became president on April 6, 1841, upon the death of Harrison.

10  William Henry Harrison (1773–1841), president of the United States in 1841, was the first Whig to be elected to that office. Sixty-eight years old when inaugurated, Harrison died in office after serving only thirty-two days.

11  Shields reacted angrily to the Rebecca letters, assuming that they were all written by the same person. Lincoln's letter undoubtedly garnered the most attention, referring to Shields as a liar, a

Globe Tavern, Springfield, Illinois. Photograph by Samuel M. Fassett (Springfield, May 3, 1865). Abraham and Mary Lincoln lived here after they were married. Their first son, Robert, was born at the Globe.

crook, and a fool. In addition to besmirching Shields's character, Lincoln lampooned his vanity concerning his looks and his attractiveness to women. After the appearance of the second (Lincoln's) Rebecca letter, Shields sent a friend to Simeon Francis demanding the name of the author. Having been informed by Francis (with Lincoln's permission) that Lincoln wrote the letter published in the September 2 issue, Shields wrote to Lincoln on September 17 demanding a "full, positive and absolute retraction of all offensive allusions . . . in relation to my private character and standing as a man," and "an apology for the insults conveyed in them." Acting on the advice of a friend, Springfield physician Elias H. Merryman (1802–1855), a man experienced in the art of

turns out that Shields is a whig; considerin you shall be a whig if he turns out a democrat."

"A bargain, by jingoes," says he, "but how will we find out."

"Why," says I, "we'll just write and ax the printer." "Agreed again," says he, "and by thunder if it does turn out that Shields is a democrat, I never will—"

"Jefferson,—Jefferson—"

"What do you want, Peggy."

"Do get through your everlasting clatter some time, and bring me a gourd of water; the child's been crying for a drink this live-long hour."

"Let it die, then, it may as well die for water as to be taxed to death to fatten *officers of State*."

Jeff run off to get the water though, just like he hadn't been sayin any thing spiteful; for he's a rall good hearted fellow, after all, once you get at the foundation of him.

I walked into the house, and "why Peggy," says I, "I declare, we like to forgot you altogether." "O yes," says she, "when a body can't help themselves, every body soon forgets 'em; but thank God by day after to-morrow I shall be well enough to milk the cows and pen the calves, and wring the contrary one's tails for 'em, and no thanks to nobody." "Good evening, Peggy," says I, and so I sloped, for I seed she was mad at me, for making Jeff neglect her so long.

And now Mr. Printer, will you be sure to let us know in your next paper whether this Shields is a whig or a democrat? I don't care about it for myself, for I know well enough how it is already, but I want to convince Jeff. It may do some good to let him, and others like him, know *who* and *what* these *officers of State* are. It may help to send the present hypocritical set to where they belong, and to fill the places they now disgrace with men who will do more work, for less pay, and take fewer airs while they are doing it. It aint sensible to think that the same men who get us into trouble will change their course; and yet its pretty plain, if some change for the better is not made, its not long that neither Peggy, or I, or any of us, will have a cow left to milk, or a calf's tail to wring. Yours, truly, REBECCA.

dueling, Lincoln refused to acknowledge writing the letter and rejected Shields's complaints. When Shields renewed his demands, Lincoln refused to consider them until Shields retracted his first letter. It was then that Shields demanded satisfaction, a challenge which Lincoln, although opposed to the practice, reluctantly accepted. Since he had the choice of weapons, Lincoln, on the advice of a friend, chose broadswords with the view that they would be an advantage to a man of Lincoln's size (six feet four) versus Shields (five feet eight). Since dueling was illegal in Illinois, the duel was scheduled for September 22 on Bloody Island in Missouri. The letters between Lincoln and Shields are cited in *CW*, 1:299–300. The instructions concerning the duel are found in ibid., 1:300–303. As the participants gathered on Bloody Island, the seconds agreed to a compromise whereby Shields retracted his letters and Lincoln admitted to writing only the September 2 letter and claimed that he had "had no intention of injuring" Shields's "personal or private character, or standing as a man or a gentleman." Lincoln's acknowledgment is cited in Burlingame, *Abraham Lincoln,* 1:193. Some historians have claimed that by the time of the Rebecca letters, Lincoln and Mary Todd had not only resumed their relationship but also collaborated in writing several of the letters, with Lincoln honorably protecting Mary from involvement by claiming to have written ones that she wrote. While Lincoln had resumed his relationship with Mary and married her a few weeks after the letters controversy, there is no concrete evidence that he and Mary collaborated on writing the letters. In addition, Lincoln admitted to writing only the September 2 letter. See Donald, *Lincoln,* 90–93; Harold Holzer, *Lincoln and the Power of the Press: The War for Public Opinion* (New York: Simon & Schuster, 2014), 48–49. Wilson, in *Honor's Voice,* 265–276, argues against the Lincoln-Todd collaboration and examines the lack of evidence.

*In May 1846 Lincoln was nominated by the Illinois Whig Party to represent the state's Seventh District in the United States House of Representatives. These two letters, written to the editor of a Whig newspaper six months before he won the nomination, show that he had developed into a shrewd infighter and political operator who was comfortable using persuasion and arm-twisting to achieve his objectives.*

1  Besides serving as editor of the *Tazewell Whig* (published in Tremont, near Pekin, Illinois), Benjamin F. James was an attorney, chairman of the Whig District Central Committee, and a friend and supporter of Lincoln. Guy C. Fraker, *Lincoln's Ladder to the Presidency: The Eighth Judicial Circuit* (Carbondale: Southern Illinois University Press, 2012), 144.

2  In his letter to James of November 17, Lincoln conveyed incorrect information he had heard, that a paper in Pekin was nominating John J. Hardin (1810–1847) for governor and an Alton newspaper was "indirectly" nominating Hardin for Congress. He told James these events would "give Hardin a great start, and perhaps use me up, if the Whig papers of the District should nominate him for *Congress*." He then urged James to "let nothing appear in your paper which may operate against me. You understand." Lincoln said that "Baker is certainly off the track, and I fear Hardin intends to be on it." *CW,* 1:349. After deciding not to seek reelection to the Illinois state legislature in 1841, Lincoln wanted to run for Congress as early as 1842, when the Illinois Seventh Congressional District was created. He was one of three Whigs interested in the seat, along with Hardin of Morgan County and Edward Dickinson Baker (1811–1861) of Sangamon County. The district convention, held in Pekin, nominated Hardin and agreed to an informal plan, proposed by Lincoln, that Baker would get the nod in 1844 and Lincoln in 1846. Hardin stepped down in 1844 so Baker could run. Baker won election and agreed to step

# Letters to Benjamin F. James

## November 24, 1845
## December 6, 1845

Friend James:[1] Springfield, Novr. 24th. 1845

Yours of the 19th. was not received till this morning. The error I fell into in relation to the *Pekin* paper, I discovered myself the day after I wrote you.[2] The way I fell into it was, that Stuart (John T)[3] met me in the court & told me about a nomination having been made in the Pekin paper, and about the comments upon it in the Alton paper; and without seeing either paper myself, I wrote you. In writing to you, I only meant to call your attention to the matter; and that done, I knew all would be right with you. Of course I should not have thought this necessary, if, at the time, I had known that the nomination had been made in your paper. And let me assure you, that if there is any thing in my letter indicating an opinion that the nomination for *Governor,* which I suppose to have been made in the Pekin paper, was opperating [*sic*], or could opperate [*sic*] against me, such was not my meaning.[4] Now, that I know that nomination was made by you, I say that it *may* do me good while I do not see that it *can* do me harm. But, while the subject is in agitation, should any of the papers in the District nominate the same man for *Congress* that would do me harm; and it was that which I wished to guard against. Let me assure that I do not, for a moment, suppose, that what you *have* done is ill-judged; or that any thing you shall do, will be. It was not to object to the course of the *Pekin* paper (as I then thought it) but to guard against any falling into the wake of the *Alton* paper, that I wrote.

You, perhaps, have noticed the Journal's article of last week, upon the same subject. It was written without any consultation with me, but I was told by Francis[5] of it's [*sic*] purport before it was published. I chose to let it go as it was, lest it should be suspected that I was attempting to juggle Hardin out of a nomination for congress by juggling him into one for Governor. If you, and the other papers, a little more distant from me, choose, to take the same course you have, of course I have no objection. After you shall have received this, I think we shall fully understand each other, and that our views as to the effects of these things are not dissimilar. Confidential of course Yours as ever

A. LINCOLN

---

Friend James: Springfield, Decr. 6, 1845.[6]

Yours of the 4th., informing me of Hardin's communication and letter, is received. I had ascertained that such documents had been sent you, even before I received your letter. Nor is the conclusion they lead to—the certainty that he intends to run for congress—matter of surprise to me. I was almost confident of it before. Now as to the probable result of a contest with him. To succeed, I must have 17 votes in convention. To secure these, I think I may safely claim—Sangamon 8—Menard 2—Logan 1, making 11, so that, if you and other friends can secure Dr. Boal's entire senatorial district—that is Tazewell 4—Woodford 1, and Marshall 1, it just covers the case.[7] Besides this, I am not without some chance in Putnam and Mason, the latter which I verily believe I can secure by close attention. The other counties—that is to say—Morgan, Scott and Cass, he will undoubtedly get. Some of Baker's particular friends in Cass, and who are now my friends, I think I could carry that county; but I do not think there is any chance for it. Upon the whole, it is my intention to give him the trial, unless clouds should rise, which are not yet discernable. This determination you need not, however, as yet, announce in your paper—at least not as coming from me.[8]

If Tazewell, Woodford & Marshall, can be made safe, all will be safe. Of the first, Tazewell, I suppose there is little or no doubt—and while I believe there is good ground of hope in Woodford & Marshall, still I am not quite so easy about them. It is desirable that a sharp look-out should be kept, and every whig met with from those counties, talked to, and initiated. If you and John H. Morrison and Niel Johnson, Dr. Shaw, and others, will see to this; together with what I have done, and will do, those counties can be saved. In doing this, let nothing be said against Hardin . . . nothing deserves to be said against him. Let the pith of the whole argument be "*Turn about is fair play.*"

aside in 1846. Hardin, however, decided to run again that year and geared up for a fight against Lincoln, who, in return, sought enough pledges from party leaders and Whig newspaper editors to dissuade Hardin from entering the race. Burlingame, *Abraham Lincoln,* 1:231; Donald, *Lincoln,* 111–115; Donald W. Riddle, *Congressman Abraham Lincoln* (Urbana: University of Illinois Press, 1957), 5.

3  John Todd Stuart (1807–1885) met Lincoln in the Black Hawk War and became his political mentor and his first law partner. Neely, *Lincoln Encyclopedia,* 292.

4  To keep faith with the Pekin agreement and clear the way for Lincoln's nomination, many Whigs supporting Lincoln urged Hardin to run for governor. Conversely, Whigs supporting Hardin urged Lincoln to run for governor. Donald, *Lincoln,* 113; Riddle, *Congressman Abraham Lincoln,* 5.

5  Simeon Francis, ardent Whig and a friend of Lincoln's, was editor of the *Sangamo Journal,* Springfield's Whig newspaper. Holzer, *Lincoln and the Power of the Press,* 11–14, 46–47.

6  Lincoln's December 6, 1845, letter to James that appears in *CW* is incomplete, thus the editors have used the full version of the letter that appears in *Abraham Lincoln: Speeches and Writings 1832–1858,* 115–116.

7  Illinois's Seventh Congressional District included the counties of Putnam, Marshall, Woodford, Tazewell, Mason, Logan, Cass, Menard, Sangamon, and Jacksonville. Dr. Robert Boal (1806–1903) served in the Illinois state senate and represented Tazewell, Woodford, and Marshall counties. Lincoln wrote to Boal on January 7, 1846, seeking his help. *CW,* 1:353. Boal subsequently turned down Hardin's request for support based on the fair-play argument. Burlingame, *Abraham Lincoln,* 1:231–232.

8   James's paper supported Lincoln's nomination. Burlingame, *Abraham Lincoln,* 1:232.

9   David Dickinson, who served for a time as deputy sheriff of Sangamon County, first met Lincoln in New Salem. Boas, *Biographical Dictionary,* 136.

10  For a cogent discussion of Lincoln as crafty politician and party leader, see Matthew Pinsker, "Boss Lincoln: A Reappraisal of Abraham Lincoln's Party Leadership," in *The Living Lincoln,* ed. Thomas A. Horrocks, Harold Holzer, and Frank J. Williams (Carbondale: Southern Illinois University Press, 2011), 20–37.

More than this, I want you to watch, and whenever you see a "moccasin track" as indian fighters say, notify me of it. You understand.

I fear I shall be of a great trouble to you in this matter; but rest assured, that I *will* be grateful when I can. The Lacon paper you sent me I never got, but I learned it's [sic] contents from David Dickinson,[9] formerly of our town, but now residing in Lacon. After I left Tremont last fall, I went up to Lacon and saw Dr. Boal, who said to me that it had always been his understanding since the Pekin convention, that the race of 1846 was to be mine. I have reason to believe, tho, I did not know, that he induced the articles in the Lacon paper. I am sure also that he or Dickinson did, as I have never spoken to the editor on the subject. This letter is, of course, confidential; tho I should have no objection to it's [sic] being seen by a few friends, in your discretion, being *sure* first that they are friends.[10]

Write me frequently if you can spare time. Yours as ever

A. LINCOLN

P.S. Will you not visit Springfield this winter? I should be glad of a personal interview with you.

# "My Childhood-Home I See Again"

## [February 25?] 1846

*Lincoln's Indiana Home.* Engraving (n.d.).

My childhood-home I see again,[1]
And gladden with the view;
And still as mem'ries crowd my brain,
There's sadness in it too.

O memory! Thou mid-way world
'Twixt Earth and Paradise,
Where things decayed, and loved ones lost
In dreamy shadows rise.

And freed from all that's gross or vile,
Seem hallowed, pure, and bright,
Like scenes in some enchanted isle,
All bathed in liquid light.

As distant mountains please the eye,
When twilight chases day—
As bugle-tones, that, passing by,
In distance die away—

As leaving some grand water-fall
We ling'ring, list it's roar,
So memory will hallow all
We've known, but know no more.

Now twenty years have passed away,
Since here I bid farewell
To woods, and fields, and scenes of play
And school-mates loved so well.

*In 1844, while campaigning in southwestern Indiana on behalf of Whig presidential candidate Henry Clay, Lincoln returned to the neighborhood of his Indiana boyhood home for the first time in fifteen years. Revisiting the area where his mother and sister were buried and reconnecting with old friends and neighbors inspired Lincoln to compose a poem to express emotions and memories he rarely if ever discussed with friends and associates.*

1    The editors of *CW* dated this document February 25, 1846, the day following Lincoln's February 24 letter to Andrew Johnston (1811–?), a Quincy, Illinois, attorney, in which he enclosed a copy of one of his favorite poems, William Knox's "Mortality," and referred to a poem "of my own" making, "a piece that is almost done." *CW,* 1: 366–367. Johnston published anonymously (at Lincoln's request) some of Lincoln's poems, including the first two cantos of this poem, in the *Quincy Whig.* Burlingame, *Abraham Lincoln,* 1:241. Lincoln developed an interest in poetry as a young man that lasted throughout his life. His favorite poets included Robert Burns, Lord Byron,

Alexander Pope, and Shakespeare. For Lincoln's interest in poetry, see David J. Harkness and R. Gerald McMurtry, *Lincoln's Favorite Poets* (Knoxville: University of Tennessee Press, 1959); Donald, *Lincoln,* 47–48; Douglas L. Wilson, "Abraham Lincoln and the 'Spirit of Mortal,'" in *Lincoln before Washington: New Perspectives on the Illinois Years* (Urbana: University of Illinois Press, 1997), 133–148; Kaplan, *Lincoln,* 10–12, 29, 62–63, 155; and Bray, *Reading with Lincoln* , 82–139.

2   In an April 18, 1846, letter to Johnston, Lincoln enclosed the first ten stanzas of the poem he referred to in his February 24 letter, informing Johnston that in the fall of 1844, he "went into the neighborhood . . . in which I was raised, where my mother and only sister were buried, and from which I had been absent about fifteen years." Southern Indiana, according to Lincoln, was "as unpoetical as any spot of the earth; but still seeing it and its objects and inhabitants aroused feelings in me which were certainly poetry; though whether my expression of those feelings is poetry is quite another question." Lincoln indicated that the part of the poem he enclosed was the first of "four little divisions or cantos." *CW,* 1:378–379.

Where many were, how few remain
Of old familiar things!
But seeing these to mind again
The lost and absent brings.

The friends I left that parting day—
How changed, as time has sped!
Young childhood grown, strong manhood grey,
And half of all are dead.

I hear the lone survivors tell
How nought from death could save,
Till every sound appears a knell,
And every spot a grave.

I range the fields with pensive tread,
And pace the hollow rooms;
And feel (companions of the dead)
I'm living in the tombs.[2]

A[nd] here's an object more of dread,
Than ought the grave contains—
A human-form, with reason fled,
While wretched life remains.

Poor Matthew! Once of genius bright,—
A fortune-favored child—
Now locked for aye, in mental night,
A haggard mad-man wild.

Poor Matthew! I have ne'er forgot
When first with maddened will,
Yourself you maimed, your father fought,
And mother strove to kill;

And terror spread, and neighbours ran,
Your dang'rous strength to bind;
And soon a howling crazy man,
Your limbs were fast confined.

How then you writhed and shrieked aloud,
Your bones and sinews bared;
And fiendish on the gaping crowd,
With burning eye-balls glared.

And begged, and swore, and wept, and prayed,
With maniac laughter joined—
How fearful are the signs displayed,
By pangs that kill the mind!

And when at length, tho' drear and long,
Time soothed your fiercer woes—
How plaintively your mournful song,
Upon the still night rose.

I've heard it oft, as if I dreamed,
Far-distant, sweet, and lone;
The funeral dirge it ever seemed
Of reason dead and gone.

To drink it's [sic] strains, I've stole away,
All silently and still,
Ere yet the rising god of day
Had streaked the Eastern hill.

Air held his breath; the trees all still
Seemed sorr'wing angels round.
Their swelling tears in dew-drops fell
Upon the list'ning ground.

But this is past, and nought remains
That raised you o'er the brute.
Your mad'ning shrieks and soothing strains
Are like forever mute.

Now fare thee well: more thou the cause
Than subject now of woe.
All mental pangs, but time's kind laws,
Hast lost the power to know.[3]

3　This ends the second canto, in which Lincoln recounts the emotional trauma he experienced when his childhood friend Matthew Gentry, at age nineteen, attempted to murder his parents during a mental breakdown. Gentry was diagnosed as insane and locked up in an institution. He was still alive in 1844 when Lincoln visited. In a September 6, 1846, letter to Johnston, in which he included a slightly revised version of this canto devoted to Gentry, Lincoln wrote that Gentry "was still lingering in this wretched condition." *CW*, 1:384–386. This section of the poem may reflect Lincoln's preoccupation with his own mental well-being. Those close to Lincoln believed he had experienced serious episodes of melancholy in the wake of the death of Ann Rutledge, with whom Lincoln was alleged to be engaged, in 1835 and again after he broke his engagement with Mary Todd in 1841. Joshua Wolf Shenk, *Lincoln's Melancholy: How Depression Challenged a President and Fueled His Greatness* (Boston: Houghton Mifflin, 2005), 19–22, 57–62; and Kaplan, *Lincoln*, 159.

4    This and the next stanza are all that survive of a
third canto. Apparently Lincoln never completed
the poem as planned.

And now away to seek some scene[4]
Less painful than the last—
With less of horror mingled in
The present and the past.

The very spot where grew the bread
That formed my bones, I see.
How strange, old field, on thee to tread,
And feel I'm part of thee!

Nancy Hanks Lincoln's gravesite. Photograph (n.d.).

# Handbill Replying to Charges of Infidelity

## July 31, 1846

*A few weeks before the congressional election, Lincoln's opponent, a Methodist minister, accused Lincoln of being an infidel in his religious beliefs. Ever sensitive to such perceptions concerning his unorthodox religious views, and acutely aware of the damage such a charge might inflict on his campaign, Lincoln published a handbill defending himself against these claims.*

*To the Voters of the Seventh Congressional District.*
FELLOW CITIZENS:

A charge having got into circulation in some of the neighborhoods of this District, in substance that I am an open scoffer at Christianity, I have by advice of some friends concluded to notice the subject in this form.[1] That I am not a member of any Christian Church, is true; but I have never denied the truth of the Scriptures; and I have never spoken with intentional disrespect of religion in general, or of any denomination of Christians in particular. It is true that in early life I was inclined to believe in what I understand is called the "Doctrine of Necessity"—that is, that the human mind is impelled to action, or held in rest by some power, over which the mind itself has no control; and I have sometimes (with one, two or three, but never publicly) tried to maintain this opinion in argument. The habit of arguing thus however, I have, entirely left off for more than five years. And I add here, I have always understood this same opinion to be held by several of the Christian denominations. The foregoing, is the whole truth, briefly stated, in relation to myself, upon this subject.[2]

I do not think I could myself, be brought to support a man for office, whom I knew to be an open enemy of, and scoffer at, religion. Leaving the higher matter of eternal consequences, between him and his Maker, I still do not think any man has the right thus to insult the feelings, and injure the morals, of the community in which he may live. If, then, I was guilty of such conduct, I should blame no man who should condemn me for it; but I do blame those, whoever they may be, who falsely put such a charge in circulation against me.[3]

July 31, 1846. A. LINCOLN.

1   Democrat Peter Cartwright (1785–1872), Lincoln's opponent for Congress, was a Methodist circuit-riding preacher. Neely, *Lincoln Encyclopedia*, 49. With the Seventh Congressional District solidly Whig, thus favoring Lincoln, Cartwright's last-minute accusations may have been driven by desperation rather than conviction. It was not the first time Lincoln's religious views were scrutinized; in 1843, when seeking the Whig nomination for Congress, he faced similar criticism. Lincoln's response to Cartwright's charge was originally issued as a handbill and was later published in the *Illinois Gazette* (August 15, 1846) and the *Tazewell Whig* (August 22, 1846) after the August 3 election, the purpose of which, the editors of *CW* suggest, was to "set the record straight, perhaps with an eye on his future political career." *CW,* 1:384.

2   Lincoln, raised in a hard-shell Calvinistic Baptist tradition, grew into a skeptic as he developed a familiarity with the King James Bible, noting contradictions therein. Lincoln's unorthodox religious views were well known among his friends and associates from his New Salem years and early days in Springfield. Several claimed that Lincoln openly rejected certain tenets of Christianity and dismissed as false several passages in the Bible. Some referred to Lincoln as an atheist. Others recalled seeing a manuscript written by Lincoln in which he criticized the Bible and advocated Deism. After Lincoln married and developed a legal and political career, he became more discreet in sharing his religious views. In this handbill Lincoln admitted that he was not a

member of a Christian church. Yet his other statements were carefully constructed in lawyer-like fashion to evade the charge of infidelity concerning Christian doctrine. His claim that he "never denied the truth of the Scriptures" may not have been true, since it contradicts observations made by several of his friends. And while he denied ever speaking with *intentional* disrespect of religion in *general,* he may have intentionally criticized particular aspects of Christianity. Regarding the "Doctrine of Necessity," that all human conduct was compelled by natural laws, Lincoln avoided denying it by claiming he had not argued for a belief in fatalism in several years. He also reminded voters that several Christian denominations adhered to the Doctrine of Necessity. Szasz and Szasz, *Lincoln and Religion,* 22–24, 27–28; Wilson, *Honor's Voice,* 310–312; Burlingame, *Abraham Lincoln,* 1:238–240; Donald, *Lincoln,* 15; Allen C. Guelzo, "Abraham Lincoln and the Doctrine of Necessity," *Journal of the Abraham Lincoln Association* 18 (Winter 1997): 57–81.

3    It is not clear what, if any, influence Cartwright's allegations of Lincoln's infidelity had on the outcome of the election, since Lincoln won handily over his opponent, winning 56 percent of the vote. Burlingame, *Abraham Lincoln,* 1:240.

Victor David Brenner, after Anthony Berger, bas-relief medallion commemorating centennial of Lincoln's birth. Bronze (ca. 1909). The image on this medallion was adopted for the Lincoln penny profile.

# "Spot" Resolutions in the U.S. House of Representatives

## December 22, 1847

Abraham Lincoln. Daguerreotype by Nicholas H. Shepherd (Springfield, ca. 1846). Earliest known photograph of Lincoln, thought to have been taken soon after his election to Congress in August 1846.

WHEREAS THE PRESIDENT OF THE UNITED STATES, IN HIS MESSAGE of May 11th.1846, has declared that "The Mexican Government not only refused to receive him" (the envoy of the U.S.) "or to listen to his propositions, but, after a long continued series of menaces, have at last invaded *our teritory* [*sic*], and shed the blood of our fellow *citizens* on *our own soil*"

And again, in his message of December 8, 1846 that "We had ample cause of war against Mexico, long before the breaking out of hostilities. But even then we forbore to take redress into our own hands, until Mexico herself became the aggressor by invading *our soil* in hostile array, and shedding the blood of our *citizens*"

And yet again, in his message of December 7- 1847 that "The Mexican Government refused even to hear the terms of adjustment which he" (our minister of peace) "was authorized to propose; and finally, under wholly unjustifiable pretexts, involved the two countries in war, by invading the teritory [*sic*] of the State of Texas, striking the first blow, and shedding the blood of our *citizens* on *our own soil*"[1]

And whereas this House desires to obtain full knowledge of all the facts which go to establish whether the particular spot of soil on which the blood of our *citizens* was so shed, was, or was not, *our own soil,* at that time; there-fore

Resolved by the House of Representatives, that the President of the United States be respectfully requested to inform this House—[2]

First: Whether the spot of soil on which the blood of our *citizens* was shed, as in his messages declared, was, or was not, within the teritories [*sic*] of Spain, at least from the treaty of 1819 until the Mexican revolution

Second: Whether that spot is, or is not, within the teritory [*sic*] which was wrested from Spain, by the Mexican revolution.

*Three weeks after his arrival in Congress, the thirty-eight-year-old Lincoln offered eight resolutions challenging President James Knox Polk's rationale for waging war on Mexico in May 1846. Arguing that the war was unnecessary and unconstitutional, Lincoln demanded that the president prove that the exact spot on which Mexican troops had shed American blood was in fact U.S. soil.*

1   When Texas declared independence from Mexico in 1836, it claimed the Rio Grande as its boundary with Mexico, while the latter asserted that Texas's boundary was 150 miles north at the

Laurent Deroy, after Augustus Köllner, *Washington, Chamber of Representatives.* Lithograph (New York and Paris: Goupil, Vibert & Co., 1848). The interior of the old House of Representatives as Lincoln knew it as a congressman.

Nueces River, as it was during Mexican rule. After the annexation of Texas, President Polk, ignoring Mexico's claims, sent American soldiers into the disputed area. On April 25, 1846, those troops were attacked by Mexican soldiers, resulting in sixteen U.S. troops killed or injured and more than fifty captured. On May 11 Polk requested and received from Congress a declaration of war against Mexico, contending that Mexico "has passed the boundary of the United States, has invaded our territory and shed American blood upon American soil." Polk cited in Amy S. Greenberg, *A Wicked War: Polk, Clay, Lincoln, and the 1846 U.S. Invasion of Mexico* (New York: Alfred A. Knopf, 2012), 104. Useful histories of the war with Mexico are Jack K. Bauer, *The Mexican War: 1846–1848* (New York: Macmillan, 1974); John D. Eisenhower, *So Far from God: The U.S. War with Mexico, 1846–1848* (Norman: University of Oklahoma Press, 2000); and David A. Clary, *Eagles and Empire: The United States,*

Third: Whether that spot is, or is not, within a settlement of people, which settlement had existed ever since long before the Texas revolution, until it's [*sic*] inhabitants fled from the approach of the U.S. Army.

Fourth: Whether the settlement is, or is not, isolated from any and all other settlements, by the Gulf of Mexico, and the Rio Grande, on the South and West, and by wide uninhabited regions of the North and East.

Fifth: Whether the *People* of that settlement, or a *majority* of them, or *any* of them, had ever, previous to the bloodshed, mentioned in his messages, submitted themselves to the government or laws of Texas, or of the United States, by *consent,* or by *compulsion,* either by accepting office, or voting at elections, or paying taxes, or serving on juries, or having process served upon them, or in *any other way.*

Sixth: Whether the People of that settlement, did, or did not, flee from the approach of the United States Army, leaving unprotected their homes and their growing crops, *before* the blood was shed, as in his messages stated; and whether the first blood so shed, was, or was not shed, within the *inclosure* of the People, or some of them, who had thus fled from it.

Seventh: Whether our *citizens,* whose blood was shed, as in his messages declared, were, or were not, at that time, *armed* officers, and *soldiers,* sent into that settlement, by the military order of the President through the Secretary of War—and

Eighth: Whether the military force of the United States, including those *citizens,* was, or was not, so sent into that settlement, after Genl. Taylor[3] had, more than once, intimated to the War Department that, in his opinion, no such movement was necessary to the defence or protection of Texas.

*Mexico, and the Struggle for a Continent* (New York: Bantam, 2009).

2   Many Whigs, including Lincoln, condemned the Mexican War, questioning Polk's claims that the provocative Mexican attack had occurred on American soil. In what became known as his "spot" resolutions, Lincoln demanded that Polk identify the exact spot on which American blood was shed, convinced that the president had misled Congress and the American people concerning the rationale for waging war, that it was American troops who had provoked the attack by Mexican soldiers on what might have been Mexican soil. Congress tabled Lincoln's resolutions and Polk never responded to them. Lincoln's inaugural speech in Congress was praised by Whig newspapers in Illinois and repudiated by Democrats, who sarcastically nicknamed him "spotty" Lincoln, a sobriquet they used against him throughout the next decade. For example, Stephen A. Douglas (1813–1861) raised the issue in 1858 in his debate with Lincoln in Charleston, Illinois. See "Fourth Debate with Stephen A. Douglas at Charleston, Illinois, September 18, 1853," in this volume; Burlingame, *Abraham Lincoln,* 1:264–265; Donald, *Lincoln,* 124–125.

3   Zachary Taylor (1784–1850).

82

# Speech in Congress against the War with Mexico

## January 12, 1848

*During his 1846 campaign for Congress Lincoln said little publicly concerning the war with Mexico, though there is no evidence that he ever supported the conflict. Once in Congress, however, he emerged as a leading Whig critic of the war. After introducing a series of resolutions on December 22, 1847, questioning President Polk's argument for war, Lincoln voted for an amendment condemning the conflict and delivered this hard-hitting speech, in which he castigated the president for deceiving the American people concerning the cause of the conflict.*

1   Lincoln referred to a resolution proposed by Congressman George Ashmun (1804–1870) of Massachusetts that ordered President Polk to provide evidence that Mexico had invaded American soil and asserted that the war with Mexico was "unnecessarily and unconstitutionally commenced by the president." The amendment was adopted on January 3, 1848, with Lincoln casting one of the eighty-five votes in favor, against eighty-one opposed. Ashmun was in his second term in Congress when he met Lincoln; like the Illinois freshman, he lived at Mrs. Ann Sprigg's boardinghouse located across the street from the U.S. Capitol (on the location where the Library of Congress's Jefferson Building now stands). Ashmun served in Congress from 1845 to 1851 and chaired the Republican National Convention in 1860 that nominated Lincoln for president. Lincoln was not the first Whig in Congress to question Polk's claim that American blood had been shed on American soil; several Whig congressmen had sought proof from Polk before war was declared. Ashmun was one of the "Immortal Fourteen" congressmen who voted against President Polk's declaration of war on May 14, 1846. Greenberg, *A Wicked War,* 243–244, 250; Neely, *Lincoln Encyclopedia,* 10–11; "Ashmun, George," Biographical Directory of the United States Congress, http://bioguide.congress.gov/

Mr. Chairman: January 12, 1848

Some, if not all the gentlemen on, the other side of the House, who have addressed the committee within the last two days, have spoken rather complainingly, if I have rightly understood them, of the vote given a week or ten days ago, declaring that the war with Mexico was unnecessarily commenced by the President. I admit that such a vote should not be given, in mere party wantonness, and that the one given, is justly censurable, if it have no other, or better foundation. I am one of those who joined in that vote; and I did so under my best impression of the *truth* of the case.[1] How I got this impression, and how it may possibly be removed, I will now try to show. When the war began, it way [was] my opinion that all those who, because of knowing too *little,* or because of knowing too *much,* could not conscientiously approve the conduct of the President, in the beginning of it, should, nevertheless, as good citizens and patriots, remain silent on that point, at least till the war should be ended. Some leading democrats, including Ex President Van Buren,[2] have taken this same view, as I understand them; and I adhered to it, and acted upon it, until since I took my seat here; and I think I should still adhere to it, were it not that the President and his friends will not allow it to be so.[3] Besides the continual effort of the President to argue every silent vote given for supplies, into an endorsement of the justice and wisdom of his conduct—besides that singularly candid paragraph, in his late message[4] in which he tells us that Congress, with great unanimity, only two in the Senate and fourteen in the House dissenting, had declared that "by the act of the Republic of Mexico, a state of war exists between that Government and the United States," when the same journals that informed him of this, also informed him, that when that declaration stood disconnected from the question of supplies, sixtyseven in the House, and not fourteen merely,

James Knox Polk. Photograph by Mathew Brady (Washington, DC, February 14, 1849).

scripts/biodisplay.pl?index=A000318 (accessed November 4, 2014).

2    Martin Van Buren (1782–1862), eighth president of the United States, served one term in office, from 1837 to 1841. Before assuming the presidency, the New York Democrat served in the U.S. Senate from 1821 to 1828; as governor of New York from January 1, 1829, to March 12, 1829, when he resigned; as President Andrew Jackson's secretary of state from March 28, 1829, to May 23, 1831; and as Jackson's vice president from March 4, 1833, to March 3, 1837. After his defeat for reelection to the presidency in 1840, Van Buren unsuccessfully sought the Democratic nomination for president in 1844. Four years later he was nominated for president by the Free Soil Party, but he received no electoral votes in the election. Van Buren opposed the annexation of Texas and supported the Wilmot Proviso, a proposal that would have banned slavery in any territory acquired from Mexico. See John Niven, *Martin Van Buren: The Romantic Age of American Politics* (New York: Oxford University Press, 1983).

voted against it—besides this open attempt to prove, by telling the *truth,* what he could not prove by telling the *whole truth*—demanding of all who will not submit to be misrepresented, in justice to themselves, to speak out—besides all this, one of my colleagues (Mr. Richardson)[5] at a very early day in the session brought in a set of resolutions, expressly endorsing the original justice of the war on the part of the President. Upon these resolutions, when they shall be put on their passage I shall be *compelled* to vote; so that I can not be silent, if I would. Seeing this, I went about preparing myself to give the vote understandingly when it should come. I carefully

3   Acutely aware that his patriotism was and would be questioned as a result of his opposition to the war, Lincoln presented himself as a loyal American who was and remained willing to change his views of the war if only the president would cooperate with opponents of the conflict by providing answers concerning his rationale for requesting a declaration of war.

4   President Polk's annual message to Congress, December 7, 1847, in which he stated, "This act declaring 'the war to exist by the act of the Republic of Mexico,' and making provision for its prosecution 'to a speedy and successful termination,' was passed with great unanimity by Congress, there being but two negative votes in the Senate and but fourteen in the House of Representatives." For Polk's 1847 annual address, see http:// www.presidency.ucsb.edu/ws/?pid=29488 (accessed January 20, 2015).

5   William Alexander Richardson (1811–1875), a Democratic congressman from Rushville, Illinois, who was elected to fill the vacancy caused by the resignation of Stephen A. Douglas when the latter moved up from the House of Representatives to the Senate. Richardson introduced resolutions in the House on December 20, 1847—two days before Lincoln introduced his own resolutions— supporting President Polk's rationale for declaring war. Richardson's resolutions were defeated. *CW,* 1: 442n3, 448n3; Bauer, *The Mexican War,* 369–370; "Richardson, William Alexander," Biographical Directory of the United States Congress, http:// bioguide.congress.gov/scripts/biodisplay. pl?index=R000228 (accessed November 4, 2014).

6   Unlike some other Whigs, who condemned the war as one of conquest to gain territory to expand slavery, Lincoln chose to avoid the slavery issue in order to concentrate on the border question at the heart of President Polk's rationale for war. He saw Polk's war primarily as a war of conquest "to catch

examined the President's messages, to ascertain what he himself had said and proved upon the point. The result of this examination was to make the impression, that taking for true, all the President states as facts, he falls far short of proving his justification; and that the President would have gone farther with his proof, if it had not been for the small matter, that the *truth* would not permit him. Under the impression thus made, I gave the vote before mentioned. I propose now to give, concisely, the process of the examination I made, and how I reached the conclusion I did. The President, in his first war message of May 1846, declares that the soil was *ours* on which hostilities were commenced by Mexico; and he repeats that declaration, almost in the same language, in each successive annual message, thus showing that he esteems that point, a highly essential one. In the importance of that point, I entirely agree with the President. To my judgment, it is the *very point,* upon which he should be justified, or condemned.[6] In his message of Decr. 1846, it seems to have occurred to him, as is certainly true, that title— ownership—to soil, or any thing else, is not a simple fact; but is a conclusion following one or more simple facts; and that it was incumbent upon him, to present the facts, from which he concluded, the soil was ours, on which the first blood of the war was shed.

Accordingly a little below the middle of page twelve in the message last referred to, he enters upon that task; forming an issue, and introducing testimony, extending the whole, to a little below the middle of page fourteen. Now I propose to try to show, that the whole of this,—issue and evidence— is, from beginning to end, the sheerest deception. The issue, as he presents it, is in these words "But there are those who, conceding all this to be true, assume the ground that the true western boundary of Texas is the Nueces, instead of the Rio Grande; and that, therefore, in marching our army to the east bank of the latter river, we passed the Texan line, and invaded the teritory [*sic*] of Mexico." Now this issue, is made up of two affirmatives and no negative. The main deception of it is, that it assumes as true, that *one* river or the *other* is necessarily the boundary; and cheats the superficial thinker entirely out of the idea, that *possibly* the boundary is somewhere *between* the two, and not actually at either. A further deception is, that it will let in *evidence,* which a true issue would exclude. A true issue, made by the President, would be about as follows "I say, the soil *was ours,* on which the first blood was shed; there are those who say it was not."

I now proceed to examine the Presidents [*sic*] evidence, as applicable to such an issue. When that evidence is analized [*sic*], it is all included in the following propositions:

1. That the Rio Grande was the Western boundary of Louisiana as we purchased it of France in 1803.

2. That the Republic of Texas always *claimed* the Rio Grande, as her Western boundary.

3. That by various acts, she had claimed it *on paper.*

4. That Santa Anna, in his treaty with Texas, recognised the Rio Grande, as her boundary.

5. That Texas *before,* and the U. S. *after,* annexation had *exercised* jurisdiction *beyond* the Nueces—*between* the two rivers.

6. That our Congress, *understood* the boundary of Texas to extend beyond the Nueces.

Now for each of these in it's [*sic*] turn.

His first item is, that the Rio Grande was the Western boundary of Louisiana, as we purchased it of France in 1803; and seeming to expect this to be disputed, he argues over the amount of nearly a page, to prove it true; at the end of which he lets us know, that by the treaty of 1819, we sold to Spain the whole country from the Rio Grande eastward, to the Sabine. Now, admitting for the present, that the Rio Grande, was the boundary of Louisiana, what, under heaven, had that to do with the *present* boundary between us and Mexico? How, Mr. Chairman, the line, that once divided your land and mine, can *still* be the boundary between us, *after* I have sold my land to you, is, to me beyond all comprehension. And how any man, with an honest purpose only, of proving the truth, could ever have *thought* of introducing such a fact to prove such an issue, is equally incomprehensible.[7] His next piece of evidence is that "The Republic of Texas always *claimed* this river (Rio Grande) as her western boundary[.]" That is not true, in fact. Texas *has* claimed it, but she has not *always* claimed it. There is, at least, one distinguished exception. Her state constitution,—the republic's most solemn, and well considered act—that which may, without impropriety, be called her last will and testament revoking all others—makes no such claim. But suppose she had always claimed it. Has not Mexico always claimed the contrary? so that there is but *claim* against *claim,* leaving nothing proved, until we get back of the claims, and find which has the better *foundation.* Though not in order in which the President presents his evidence, I now consider that class of his statements, which are, in substance, nothing more than that Texas has, by various acts of her convention and congress, claimed the Rio Grande, as her boundary, *on paper.* I mean here what he says about the fix-

votes." Although antislavery like many Northern Whigs, Lincoln joined several Southern Whigs in supporting General Zachary Taylor, a slaveholder, for president, believing it was in the Whigs' best interests politically to deemphasize slavery as an issue in the 1848 election. Many Northern or "Conscience" Whigs were angry at Lincoln for supporting Taylor and downplaying the slavery issue for political purposes. Greenberg, *A Wicked War,* 251; Eric Foner, *The Fiery Trial: Abraham Lincoln and American Slavery* (New York: W. W. Norton, 2010), 54–55. Lincoln quote "to catch votes" is from Neely, *Lincoln Encyclopedia,* 210.

7  As cited in *CW,* 1:442n4, Lincoln inserted in the *Congressional Globe* version of his speech this clarification: "The outrage upon common *right,* of seizing as our own what we have once sold, merely because its *was* ours *before* we sold it, is only equalled by the outrage on common *sense* of any attempt to justify it." John Channing Briggs noted this clarification was not included in the printed version of the speech that Lincoln circulated to his constituents. He suggested that Lincoln may have used his original draft of the speech for the printed version or he may have purposely omitted this clarification because he realized that his analogy gave "unintended support to slavery advocates and their argument that persons 'sold' by those who brought slaves to America could not be liberated, even for compensation, on the basis of an inalienable right that revoked the sale." Briggs, *Lincoln's Speeches Reconsidered,* 96. Lincoln wished to "distinguish" himself in Congress and hoped this speech would make a significant impression on his constituents and raise his standing among his fellow congressmen. *CW,* 1:420. He sent the text of his speech off to Simeon Francis to be published in the *Illinois State Journal* and it appeared in that paper about a month later. Francis reissued it as a pamphlet that Lincoln could send to constituents by using his congressional franking privileges.

Alfred Jones, after Richard Caton Woodville, *Mexican News.* Engraving (n.p., ca. 1853). Print depicting Americans' deep interest in news of the Mexican War.

According to historian Gabor Boritt, Lincoln outspent most of his fellow representatives in printing and circulating his speeches, publishing thousands of copies of this one. Gabor S. Boritt, "A Question of Political Suicide: Lincoln's Opposition to the Mexican War," *Journal of the Illinois State Historical Society* 67 (1974): 89. See also Holzer, *Lincoln and the Power of the Press*, 82.

ing of the Rio Grande as her boundary in her old constitution (not her state constitution) about forming congressional districts, counties, &c &c. Now all of this is but naked *claim;* and what I have already said about claims is strictly applicable to this. If I should claim your land, by word of mouth, that certainly would not make it mine; and if I were to claim it by deed which I had made myself, and with which, you had nothing to do, the claim would be quite the same, in substance—or rather, in utter nothingness. I next consider the President's statement that Santa Anna in his *treaty* with Texas, recognised the Rio Grande, as the western boundary of Texas.

Besides the position, so often taken that Santa Anna, while a prisoner of war—a captive—*could* not bind Mexico by a treaty,[8] which I deem conclusive—besides this, I wish to say something in relation to this treaty, so called by the President, with Santa Anna. If any man would like to be amused by a sight of that *little* thing, which the President calls by that *big* name, he can have it, by turning to Niles' Register volume 50, page 336. And if any one should suppose that Niles' Register is a curious repository of so mighty a document, as a solemn treaty between nations, I can only say that I learned, to a tolerable degree [of] certainty, by enquiry at the State Department, that the President himself, never saw it any where else. By the way, I believe I should not err, if I were to declare, that during the first ten years of the existence of that document, it was never, by any body, *called* a treaty—that it was never so called, till the President, in his extremity, attempted, by so calling it, to wring something from it in justification of himself in connection with the Mexican war. It has none of the distinguishing features of a treaty. It does not call itself a treaty. Santa Anna does not therein, assume to bind Mexico; he assumes only to act as the President-Commander-in-chief of the Mexican Army and Navy; stipulates that the then present hostilities should cease, and that he would not *himself* take up arms, nor *influence* the Mexican people to take up arms, against Texas during the existence of the war of independence. He did not recognise the independence of Texas; he did not assume to put an end to the war; but clearly indicated his expectation of it's [*sic*] continuance; he did not say one word about boundary, and, most probably, never thought of it. It *is* stipulated therein that the Mexican forces should evacuate the teritory [*sic*] of Texas, *passing to the other side of the Rio Grande;* and in another article, it is stipulated that, to prevent collisions between the armies, the Texas army should not approach nearer than within five leagues—of *what* is not said—but clearly, from the object stated it is— of the Rio Grande. Now, if this is a treaty, recognising the Rio Grande, as the boundary of Texas, it contains the singular feature, of stipulating, that Texas shall not go within five leagues of *her own* boundary.

Next comes the evidence of Texas before annexation, and the United States, afterwards, *exercising* jurisdiction *beyond* the Nueces, and *between* the two rivers. This actual *exercise* of jurisdiction, is the very class or quality of evidence we want. It is excellent so far as it goes; but does it go far enough? He tells us it went *beyond* the Nueces; but he does not tell us it went *to* the Rio Grande. He tells us, jurisdiction was exercised *between* the two rivers, but he does not tell us it was exercised over *all* the teritory [*sic*] between them. Some simple minded people, think it is *possible,* to cross one river and

8   Treaty is cited in full in *CW,* 1:435n5.

9  *CW,* 1:442n6, cites the *Congressional Globe* version of the speech, in which Lincoln emended this sentence as follows: "In this strange omission chiefly consists the deception of the President's evidence—an omission which, it does seem to me, could scarcely have occurred but by design."

10  As cited in *CW,* 1:442n7, Lincoln emended "point arising in the case" to "position pressed upon him by the prosecution."

go *beyond* it without going *all the way* to the next—that jurisdiction may be exercised *between* two rivers without covering *all* the country between them. I know a man, not very unlike myself, who exercises jurisdiction over a piece of land between the Wabash and the Mississippi; and yet so far is this from being *all* there is between those rivers, that it is just one hundred and fiftytwo feet long by fifty wide, and no part of it much within a hundred miles of either. He has a neighbour between him and the Mississippi,—that is, just across the street, in that direction—whom, I am sure, he could neither *persuade* nor *force* to give up his habitation; but which nevertheless, he could certainly annex, if it were to be done, by merely standing on his own side of the street and *claiming* it, or even, sitting down, and writing a *deed* for it.

But next the President tells us, the Congress of the United States *understood* the state of Texas they admitted into the union, to extend *beyond* the Nueces. Well, I suppose they did. *I* certainly so understood it. But how *far* beyond? That Congress did *not* understand it to extend clear to the Rio Grande, is quite certain by the fact of their joint resolutions, for admission, expressly leaving all questions of boundary to future adjustment. And it may be added, that Texas herself, is proved to have had the same understanding of it, that our Congress had, by the fact of the exact conformity of her new constitution, to those resolutions.

I am now through the whole of the President's evidence; and it is a singular fact, that if any one should declare the President sent the army into the midst of a settlement of Mexican people, who had never submitted, by consent or by force, to the authority of Texas or of the United States, and that *there,* and *thereby,* the first blood of the war was shed, there is not one word in all the President has said, which would either admit or deny the declaration. This strange omission, it does seem to me, could not have occurred but by design.[9] My way of living leads me to be about the courts of justice; and there, I have sometimes seen a good lawyer, struggling for his client's neck, in a desparate [*sic*] case, employing every artifice to work round, befog, and cover up, with many words, some point arising in the case,[10] which he *dared* not admit, and yet *could* not deny. Party bias may help to make it appear so; but with all the allowance I can make for such bias, it still does appear, to me, that just such, and from just such necessity, is the President's struggle in this case.

Some time after my colleague (Mr. Richardson) introduced the resolutions I have mentioned, I introduced a preamble, resolution, and interrogatories, intended to draw the President out, if possible, on this hitherto untrodden ground.[11] To show their relevancy, I propose to state my understanding of the true rule for ascertaining the boundary between Texas and Mexico. It is, that *wherever* Texas was *exercising* jurisdiction, was hers; and *wherever Mexico* was exercising jurisdiction, was hers; and that *whatever* separated the actual exercise of jurisdiction of the one, from that of the other, was the true boundary between them. If, as is probably true, Texas was exercising jurisdiction along the western bank of the Nueces, and Mexico was exercising it along the eastern bank of the Rio Grande, then *neither* river was the boundary; but the uninhabited country between the two, was. The extent of our teritory [*sic*] in that region depended, not on any *treaty-fixed* boundary (for no treaty had attempted it) but on revolution. Any people anywhere, being inclined and having the power, have the right to *rise* up, and shake off the existing government, and form a new one that suits them better. This is a most valuable,—a most sacred right—a right, which we hope and believe, is to liberate the world. Nor is this right confined to cases in which the whole people of an existing government, may choose to exercise it. Any portion of such people that *can, may* revolutionize, and make their *own,* of so much of the teritory [*sic*] as they inhabit. More than this, a majority of any portion of such people may revolutionize, putting down a *minority,* intermingled with, or near about them, who may oppose their movement.[12] Such minority, was precisely the case, of the tories of our own revolution. It is the quality of revolutions not to go by *old* lines, or *old* laws; but to break up both, and make new ones. As to the country now in question, we bought it of France in 1803, and sold it to Spain in 1819, according to the President's statements. After this, all Mexico, including Texas, revolutionized against Spain; and still later, Texas revolutionized against Mexico. In my view, just so far as she carried her revolution, by obtaining the *actual,* willing or unwilling, submission of the people, *so far,* the country was hers, and no farther. Now sir, for the purpose of obtaining the very best evidence, as to whether Texas had actually carried her revolution, to the place where the hostilities of the present war commenced, let the President answer the interrogatories, I proposed, as before mentioned, or some other similar ones. Let him answer, fully, fairly, and candidly. Let him answer with *facts,* and not with arguments. Let him remember he sits where Washington sat, and so remembering, let him answer, as Washington would answer. As a nation *should* not, and the Almighty *will* not, be evaded, so let him attempt no evasion—no equivocation. And if, so answering, he can show that the soil was ours, where the first blood of the war was shed—that it was not within an inhabited country, or, if within such, that the inhabitants had submitted

11  Lincoln referred to his resolutions on the Mexican War, read and submitted to the House of Representatives. See "'Spot' Resolutions in the U.S. House of Representatives, December 22, 1847," in this volume.

12  Lincoln appeared to be using the same argument Confederate states used years later when justifying their rebellion against the United States. Burlingame suggests that Lincoln's purpose may have been to "curry favor with Southern Whigs resentful of Northern congressmen . . . who had denied the legitimacy of the Texas revolution of 1836." After all, he was working with "several Southern Whig congressmen in an attempt to help General Zachary Taylor of Louisiana win their party's presidential nomination." Burlingame, *Abraham Lincoln,* 1:267. Briggs argues that although Lincoln is defending "the right of revolution even for minority causes, he distinguishes . . . between legitimate and illegitimate revolutionary claims to territory." Briggs, *Lincoln's Speeches Reconsidered,* 101. See also Thomas J. Pressly, "Bullets and Ballots: Lincoln and the 'Right of Revolution,'" *American Historical Review* 67 (1962): 647–662.

**13** As cited in *CW,* 1:442n9, Lincoln emended his speech to read "; that he ordered General Taylor into the midst of a peaceful Mexican settlement, purposely to bring on a war; that originally having some strong motive—," etc. Lincoln's remarks invoking heavenly forces against Polk, according to Harold Holzer, were similar to those of Horace Greeley's in an article that appeared a year earlier in the *New York Tribune,* a newspaper undoubtedly read by Lincoln. Greeley declared that the nation was embarked on a war "in which Heaven must take part against us." Cited in Holzer, *Lincoln and the Power of the Press,* 80–81.

themselves to the civil authority of Texas, or of the United States, and that the same is true of the site of Fort Brown, then I am with him for his justification. In that case I, shall be most happy to reverse the vote I gave the other day. I have a selfish motive for desiring that the President may do this. I expect to give some votes, in connection with the war, which, without his so doing, will be of doubtful propriety in my own judgment, but which will be free from the doubt if he does so. But if he *can* not, or *will* not do this— if on any pretence, or no pretence, he shall refuse to omit it, then I shall be fully convinced, of what I more than suspect already, that he is deeply conscious of being in the wrong—that he feels the blood of this war, like the blood of Abel, is crying to Heaven against him.[13] That originally having some strong motive—what, I will not stop to give my opinion concerning—to involve the two countries in a war, and trusting to escape scrutiny, by fixing the public gaze upon the exceeding brightness of military glory— that attractive rainbow, that rises in showers of blood—that serpent's eye, that charms to destroy—he plunged into it, and has swept, *on and on,* till, disappointed in his calculation of the ease with which Mexico might be subdued, he now finds himself, he knows not where. How like the half insane mumbling of a fever-dream, is the whole war part of his late message! At one time telling us that Mexico has nothing whatever, that we can get, but teritory [*sic*]; at another, showing us how we can support the war, by levying contributions on Mexico. At one time, urging the national honor, the security of the future, the prevention of foreign interference, and even, the good of Mexico herself, as among the objects of the war; at another, telling us, that "to reject indemnity, by refusing to accept a cession of teritory [*sic*], would be to abandon all our just demands, and to wage the war, bearing all it's [*sic*] expenses, *without a purpose or definite object.*" So then, the national honor, security of the future, and every thing but teritorial [*sic*] indemnity, may be considered the *no-purposes,* and *indefinite,* objects of the war! But, having it now settled that teritorial [*sic*] indemnity is the only object, we are urged to seize, by legislation here, all that he was content to take, a few months ago, and the whole province of lower California to boot, and to still carry on the war—to take *all* we are fighting for, and *still* fight on. Again, the President is resolved, under all circumstances, to have full teritorial [*sic*] indemnity for the expenses of the war; but he forgets to tell us how we are to get the *excess,* after all those expenses shall have surpassed the value of the *whole* of the Mexican teritory [*sic*]. So again, he insists that the separate national existence of Mexico, shall be maintained; but he does not tell us *how* this can be done, after we shall have taken *all* her territory [*sic*].

Lest the questions, I here suggest, be considered speculative merely, let me be indulged a moment in trying [to] show they are not. The war has gone on some twenty months; for the expenses of which, together with an inconsiderable old score, the President now claims about one half of the Mexican teritory [sic]; and that, by far the better half, so far as concerns our ability to make any thing out of it. *It* is comparatively uninhabited; so that we could establish land offices in it, and raise some money in that way. But the other half is already inhabited, as I understand it, tolerably densely for the nature of the country; and all it's [sic] lands, or all that are valuable, already appropriated as private property. How then are we to make any thing out of these lands with this incumbrance on them? or how, remove the incumbrance? I suppose no one will say we should kill the people, or drive them out, or make slaves of them, or even confiscate their property. How then can we make much out of this part of the teritory [sic]? If the prosecution of the war has, in expenses, already equalled the *better* half of the country, how long it's [sic] future prosecution, will be in equalling, the less valuable half, is not a speculative, but a *practical* question, pressing closely upon us. And yet it is a question which the President seems to never have thought of. As to the mode of terminating the war, and securing peace, the President is equally wandering and indefinite. First, it is to be done by a more vigorous prossecution [sic] of the war in the vital parts of the enemies [sic] country; and, after apparently, talking himself tired, on this point, the President drops down into a half despairing tone, and tells us that "with a people distracted and divided by contending factions, and a government subject to constant changes, by successive revolutions, *the continued success of our arms may fail to secure a satisfactory peace.*" Then he suggests the propriety of wheedling the Mexican people to desert the counsels of their own leaders, and trusting in our protection, to set up a government from which we can secure a satisfactory peace; telling us, that "*this may become the only mode of obtaining such as peace.*" But soon he falls into doubt of this too; and then drops back on to the already half abandoned ground of "more vigorous prossecution [sic]." All this shows that the President is, in no wise, satisfied with his own positions. First he takes up one, and in attempting to argue us *into* it, he argues himself *out* of it; then seizes another, and goes through the same process; and then, confused at being able to think of nothing new, he snatches up the old one again, which he has some time before cast off. His mind, tasked beyond it's [sic] power, is running hither and thither, like some tortured creature, on a burning surface, finding no position, on which it can settle down, and be at ease.

14  Winfield Scott (1786–1866), along with Zachary Taylor, was a successful general in the war with Mexico and, as a result, was considered a war hero. Scott was a confirmed Whig and thus was distrusted within the Polk administration. He was recalled from Mexico on January 2, 1848. Lincoln voted on January 31 and April 17, 1848, for resolutions requesting that President Polk explain Scott's recall. Cited in *CW,* 1:442n10.

Again, it is a singular omission in this message, that it, no where intimates *when* the President expects the war to terminate. At it's [*sic*] beginning, Genl. Scott[14] was, by this same President, driven into disfavor, if not disgrace, for intimating that peace could not be conquered in less than three or four months. But now, at the end of about twenty months, during which time our arms have given us the most splendid successes—every department, and every part, land and water, officers and privates, regulars and volunteers, doing all that men *could* do, and hundreds of things which it had ever before been thought men could *not* do,—after all this, this same President gives us a long message, without showing us, that, *as to the end,* he himself, has, even an immaginary [*sic*] conception. As I have before said, he knows not where he is. He is a bewildered, confounded, and miserably perplexed man. God grant he may be able to show, there is not something about his conscience, more painful than all his mental perplexity!

N. Currier, *The Landing of American Forces under Genl. Scott, at Vera Cruz, March 9th, 1847.* Lithograph (New York, 1847).

# Letter to William H. Herndon

## February 15, 1848

*Weeks after delivering his speech condemning President Polk's rationale for war with Mexico, Lincoln defended his criticism of the war in a letter to his Springfield law partner, William Herndon, a fellow antislavery Whig who supported both the conflict and a president's prerogative to invade a country to protect the United States from a potential attack.*

Dear William:[1] Washington, Feb. 15. 1848

Your letter of the 29th. Jany. was received last night. Being exclusively a constitutional argument, I wish to submit some reflections upon it in the same spirit of kindness that I know actuates you. Let me first state what I understand to be your question. It is, that if it shall become *necessary, to repel invasion,* the President may, without violation of the Constitution, cross the line, and *invade* the teritory [*sic*] of another country; and that whether such *necessity* exists in any given case, the President is to be the *sole* judge.[2]

Before going further, consider well whether this is, or is not your position. If it is, it is a position that neither the President himself, nor any friend of his, so far as I know, has ever taken. Their only positions are first, that the soil was *ours* where hostilities commenced, and second, that whether it was rightfully *ours* or not, *Congress had annexed it,* and the President, for that reason was bound to defend it, both of which are as clearly proved to be false in fact, as you can prove that your house is not mine. That soil was not ours; and Congress did not annex or attempt to annex it. But to return to your position: Allow the President to invade a neighboring nation, whenever *he* shall deem it necessary to repel an invasion, and you allow him to do so, *whenever he may choose to say* he deems it necessary for such purpose— and you allow him to make war at pleasure. Study to see if you can fix *any limit* to his power in this respect, after you have given him so much as you propose. If, to-day, he should choose to say he thinks it necessary to invade Canada, to prevent the British from invading us, how could you stop him? You may say to him, "I see no probability of the British invading us" but he will say to you "be silent; I see it, if you dont."[3]

The provision of the Constitution giving war-making power to Congress, was dictated, as I understand it, by the following reasons. Kings had

1 Herndon commenced his legal studies in 1841 and became Lincoln's law partner in 1844. Their partnership continued until Lincoln departed Springfield to assume the presidency. Neely, *Lincoln Encyclopedia,* 145–147; David Donald, *Lincoln's Herndon* (New York: Alfred A. Knopf, 1948).

2 In a letter to Herndon dated January 19, 1848, Lincoln wrote that he would send "by next mail" a pamphlet of his January 12 speech against the war. In the meantime, hearing of Lincoln's vote for the Ashmun resolution, Herndon wrote a letter conveying his displeasure, concerned that Lincoln would not support supplying American soldiers in Mexico, an action that would cause trouble with local Whigs who served in the war. After Lincoln responded on February 1, 1848, defending his vote for the resolutions and assuring Herndon of his intentions to vote for supplies for the troops, he received Herndon's letter of January 29, in which his law partner argued that it is not unconstitutional for a president to invade another country in order to repel an invasion. *CW,* 1:445, 446–448; Donald, *Lincoln,* 125–126.

3 Historians have long debated whether Lincoln's opposition to the war with Mexico was unpopular with his constituents in particular and in Illinois in general. A majority of Whigs in Illinois and throughout the country were, like Lincoln, opposed to the conflict. Negative reaction to Lincoln's opposition to the war came primarily from Democratic newspapers and politicians.

William Henry Herndon. Photograph (n.d.). Lincoln and Herndon practiced law together from 1844 until Lincoln left Springfield to assume the presidency in 1861.

Lincoln's decision not to run for reelection to the Congress was based more on his loyalty to the Pekin agreement to step aside after one term than on negative reaction to his antiwar stance. That Whig Stephen T. Logan (1800–1880) lost a close election for Lincoln's seat was attributed by Democrats, and by Logan himself, to Lincoln's opposition to the war. Lincoln's antiwar stance was only one factor in the Whigs' losing a traditionally safe seat. Boritt, "A Question of Political Suicide," 79–100; Mark E. Neely Jr., "Lincoln and the Mexican War: An Argument by Analogy," *Civil War History* 25 (1978): 5–24. See also Donald, *Lincoln*, 125–126, and Burlingame, *Abraham Lincoln*, 1:268–272.

always been involving and impoverishing their people in wars, pretending generally, if not always, that the good of the people was the object. This, our Convention understood to be the most oppressive of all Kingly oppressions; and they resolved to so frame the Constitution that *no one man* should hold the power of bringing this oppression upon us. But your view destroys the whole matter, and places our President where kings have always stood. Write soon again. Yours truly, A. LINCOLN

# Letter to Mary Todd Lincoln

〜〜〜〜〜〜〜〜〜〜〜〜〜〜〜

## June 12, 1848

My dear wife: Washington, June 12. 1848—

On my return from Philadelphia, yesterday, where, in my anxiety I had been led to attend the whig convention[,] I found your last letter.[1] I was so tired and sleepy, having ridden all night, that I could not answer it till to-day; and now I have to do so in the H. R. The leading matter in your letter, is your wish to return to this side of the Mountains. Will you be a *good girl* in all things, if I consent?[2] Then come along, and that as *soon* as possible. Having got the idea in my head, I shall be impatient till I see you. You will not have money enough to bring you; but I presume your uncle will supply you, and I will refund him here. By the way you do not mention whether you have received the fifty dollars I sent you. I do not much fear but that you got it; because the want of it would have induced you [to?] say something in relation to it. If your uncle is already at Lexington, you might induce him to start on earlier than the first of July; he could stay in Kentucky longer on his return, and so make up for lost time. Since I began this letter, the H. R. has passed a resolution for adjourning on the 17th. July, which probably will pass the Senate. I hope this letter will not be disagreeable to you; which, together with the circumstances under which I write, I hope will excuse me for not writing a longer one. Come on just as soon as you can. I want to see you, and our dear—*dear* boys very much. Every body here wants to see our dear Bobby.[3] Affectionately A. LINCOLN

Mary Lincoln. Daguerreotype by Nicholas H. Shepherd (Springfield, ca. 1846). Earliest known photograph of Lincoln's wife, thought to have been taken in August 1846.

*Lincoln, along with his wife and two sons, moved to the nation's capital in December of 1847 to take his seat in Congress. For reasons unknown, Mary and the two children left early in 1848 for her father's home in Lexington, Kentucky. In this letter, written after months of separation, Lincoln grants Mary's wish to return with the children.*

1   Lincoln attended the Whig Party's national convention in Philadelphia, held June 7–9, 1848. Earl Schenck Miers, ed., *Lincoln Day by Day: A Chronology 1809–1865*, 3 vols. (Washington, DC: Lincoln Sesquicentennial Commission, 1960), 1:312.

2   Lincoln, his wife, Mary, and their two boys, Robert, age five and a half, and Eddy, not quite two, had resided at a boardinghouse located near

Carroll Row (at left), including Mrs. Sprigg's Boarding House, Congressman Abraham Lincoln's residence in Washington, DC. Photograph (ca. 1860–1880).

the Capitol since their arrival in Washington. It is not clear exactly why Mary Lincoln left Washington. Lincoln's request that she be a "*good girl* in all things" suggests that he was either unhappy with her behavior or that she demanded too much of his time while she was in Washington. With her husband immersed in congressional duties, and having limited financial means to host social events of her own, Mary spent most of her time in their rented rooms, managing two young boys who had no other children to play with. In an April 16, 1848, letter to his wife, Lincoln wrote, "When you were here, I thought you hindered me some in attending to business." He soon qualified this statement by stating he was lonely without her, having to "stay in this old room by myself." *CW,* 1:465; Catherine Clinton, *Mrs. Lincoln: A Life* (New York: Harper, 2009), 82–83.

3   Robert Todd Lincoln (1843–1926) was the eldest and only son of Abraham and Mary Lincoln to reach adulthood and survive both his parents. Neely, *Lincoln Encyclopedia,* 184–187.

# Letters to Thomas Lincoln and John D. Johnston

## December 24, 1848

*Having achieved success through hard work and a regimen of self-improvement, Lincoln wrote a few months before his fortieth birthday to two people with whom he had little in common when it came to ambition and success. While he complied with his father's request for money, he expressed doubts concerning its real purpose. His stepbrother's request for financial assistance is repaid with a harsh lecture on the value of work.*

1   Lincoln's father, Thomas (1776 or 1778–1851), moved with his family from Virginia to Kentucky in the 1780s. Little is known of his early life except that his father, Abraham, was killed by Indians when Thomas was a child, and he received little if any education during his youth. He settled in Hardin County, Kentucky, in 1802, purchased a

My dear father:[1] Washington, Decr. 24th. 1848—

Your letter of the 7th. was received night before last. I very cheerfully send you the twenty dollars, which sum you say is necessary to save your land from sale. It is singular that you should have forgotten a judgment against you; and it is more singular that the plaintiff should have let you forget it so long, particularly as I suppose you have always had property enough to satisfy a judgment of that amount. Before you pay it, it would be well to be sure you have not paid it; or, at least, that you can not prove you have paid it.[2] Give my love to Mother,[3] and all the connections. Affectionately your son

A. LINCOLN

Dear Johnston:

Your request for eighty dollars, I do not think it best, to comply with now. At the various times when I have helped you a little, you have said to me "We can get along very well now" but in a very short time I find you in the same difficulty again. Now this can only happen by some defect in your *conduct*. What that defect is I think I know. You are not *lazy,* and still you *are* an *idler.* I doubt whether since I saw you, you have done a good whole day's work, in any one day.[4] You do not very much dislike to work; and still you do not work much, merely because it does not seem to you that you could get much for it. This habit of uselessly wasting time, is the whole difficulty; and it is vastly important to you, and still more so to your children that you should break this habit. It is more important to them, because they

Thomas Lincoln. Photograph (n.d.). This is traditionally believed to be a photograph of Lincoln's father.

Lincoln home in Coles County, Illinois. Photograph (ca. 1890s). Built in 1831 by Thomas and Abraham Lincoln near Farmington, Coles County, Illinois, this was the last home of Lincoln's father and stepmother. Both died here, Thomas Lincoln in 1851 and Sarah in 1869.

238-acre farm, and in 1806 married Nancy Hanks. An industrious farmer and skilled carpenter, Thomas owned three farms in Kentucky but, owing to the state's confusing land laws, the titles to those properties were defective, and the Lincoln family was forced to move within Kentucky and subsequently to Indiana in 1816. A year after Nancy Lincoln's death in 1818, Thomas married Sarah Bush Johnston (1788–1869), a widow from Elizabethtown, Kentucky. Thomas later moved his family to Illinois, first to Macon County in 1830, and then to Coles County in 1831, where he lived for the remainder of his life. Neely, *Lincoln Encyclopedia*, 187–188.

2    Thomas Lincoln had requested twenty dollars

have longer to live, and can keep out of an idle habit before they are in it; easier than they can get out after they are in.

You are in need of some ready money; and what I propose is, that you shall go to work, "tooth and nails" for some body who will give you money [for] it. Let father and your boys take charge of things at home—prepare for a crop, and make the crop; and you go to work for the best money wages, or in discharge of any debt you owe, that you can get. And to secure you a fair reward for your labor, I now promise you, that for every dollar you will, between this and the first of next May, get for your own labor, either in money, or in your own indebtedness, I will then give you one other dollar. By this, if you hire yourself at ten dolla[rs] a month, from me you will get ten more, making twenty dollars a month for your work. In this, I do not mean you shall go off to St. Louis, or the lead mines, or the gold mines, in Calif[ornia,] but I [mean for you to go at it for the best wages you] can get close to home [in] Coles county. Now if you will do this, you will soon be out of debt, and what is better, you will have a habit that will keep you from getting in debt again. But if I should now clear you out, next year you will be just as deep in as ever. You say you would almost give your place in Heaven for $70 or $80. Then you value your place in Heaven very cheaply for I am sure you can with the offer I make you get the seventy or eighty dollars for four or five months work. You say if I furnish you with the money you will deed me the land, and, if you dont [*sic*] pay the money back, you will deliver possession. Nonsense! If you cant [*sic*] now live *with* the land, how will you then live without it? You have always been [kind] to me, and I do not now mean to be unkind to you. On the contrary, if you will but follow my advice, you will find it worth more than eight times eighty dollars to you. Affectionately Your brother

A. LINCOLN

to pay an old debt and thus prevent the family farm from being sold. Lincoln, as he had done with previous requests of this kind, readily complied, in spite of his doubts concerning the details. David Donald surmised that Lincoln may have suspected John D. Johnston, who wrote letters for his stepfather, of using the debt story to get money from Lincoln. Donald, *Lincoln,* 152. Lincoln did not have a close relationship with his father. He not only believed his father lacked ambition to better himself but also resented his father's lack of support for or understanding of his own efforts at self-improvement. When his father was dying, Lincoln declined a request to visit him, citing several other commitments and claiming that it would be "doubtful" whether a visit "would not be more painful than pleasant." He did not attend his father's funeral. Lincoln rarely visited his father and stepmother after he left the family farm and never introduced them to his wife and children. *CW,* 2:97; Burlingame, *Abraham Lincoln,* 1:42.

3  Lincoln developed a loving relationship with his stepmother, who, unlike his father, encouraged Lincoln's desire for learning and self-improvement. Donald, *Lincoln,* 152.

4  Johnston, the youngest son of Lincoln's stepmother, grew up with Lincoln from the time his father remarried until Lincoln left for New Salem in 1831. He continued to live with Lincoln's father until the latter's death in 1851. Despite having a wife and eight children, Johnston attempted to earn money through schemes rather than steady work, a trait that ran afoul of Lincoln's strong work ethic. Chronically in debt, Johnston turned frequently to Lincoln for financial assistance. Neely, *Lincoln Encyclopedia,* 165–166; Burlingame, *Abraham Lincoln,* 1:29.

1   John Wentworth (1815–1888) was editor, manager, and later publisher of the *Chicago Democrat* until 1864. A Democrat who later joined the Republican Party and became a political ally of Lincoln's, Wentworth served in Congress from 1843 to 1851 and from 1853 to 1855. "Wentworth, John," Biographical Directory of the United States Congress, http://bioguide.congress.gov/scripts/biodisplay.pl?index=W000295 (accessed January 21, 2015).

2   With the Mexican-American War ended and Zachary Taylor elected president, many Northern Whigs were determined to keep slavery out of territory acquired from Mexico and to end slavery in the District of Columbia, the latter having been an objective of abolitionists from the time of the establishment of the city of Washington in 1800. William Lee Miller, *Arguing about Slavery: The Great Battle in the United States Congress* (New York: Alfred A. Knopf, 1996), 28; Foner, *The Fiery Trial*, 55.

3   During Lincoln's tenure in Congress, the black population of the District of Columbia numbered 52,000, including 10,000 free blacks and some 3,700 slaves. Washington was home to a thriving slave trade, with slave pens operating throughout the city, some close to the Capitol building, which appalled many in the North. Despite his long-standing opposition to slavery, Lincoln for most of his term in Congress was not a leader in the fight to abolish slavery in the nation's capital. It was

# Remarks and Resolution concerning the Abolition of Slavery in the District of Columbia, U.S. House of Representatives

## January 10, 1849

Mr. LINCOLN appealed to his colleague [Mr. WENTWORTH][1] to withdraw his motion, to enable him to read a proposition which he intended to submit, if the vote should be reconsidered.[2]

Mr. WENTWORTH again withdrew his motion for that purpose.

Mr. LINCOLN said, that by the courtesy of his colleague, he would say, that if the vote on the resolution was reconsidered, he should make an effort to introduce the amendment, which he should now read.[3]

And Mr. L read as follows:

Strike out all before and after the word "Resolved" and insert the following, towit: That the Committee on the District of Columbia be instructed to report a bill in substance as follows, towit:

Section 1. Be it enacted by the Senate and House of Representatives of the United States of America, in Congress assembled: That no person not now within the District of Columbia, nor now owned by any person or persons now resident within it, nor hereafter born within it, shall ever be held in slavery within said District.

Section 2. That no person now within said District, or now owned by any person, or persons now resident within the same, or hereafter born within it, shall ever be held in slavery without the limits of said District: *Provided,* that officers of the government of the United States, being citizens of the slave-holding states, coming into said District on public business, and remaining only so long as may be reasonably necessary for that object, may be attended into, and out of, said District, and while there, by the necessary servants of themselves and their families, without their right to hold such servants in service, being thereby impaired.

Section 3. That all children born of slave mothers within said District on, or after the first day of January in the year of our Lord one thousand, eight hundred and fifty shall be free; but shall be reasonably supported and edu-

*Slave Market of America* (New York: American Anti-Slavery Society, 1836). Broadside condemning the sale and keeping of slaves in the District of Columbia.

Lincoln's boardinghouse colleague, Ohio congressman Joshua Giddings (1795–1864), along with others, such as John Gorham Palfrey (1796–1881) of Massachusetts and Daniel Gott (1794–1864) of New York, who worked tirelessly on the issue. In December 1848 Palfrey sought permission to introduce legislation abolishing slavery and the slave trade in Washington, D.C., which the House denied. Lincoln was one of six Northern Whigs who opposed Palfrey's request because it did not include compensation for slave owners. When Giddings introduced a bill on December 18 allowing District of Columbia residents over the age of twenty-one, including both free and enslaved African Americans, to vote for either slavery or its abolition, it was tabled by a 106–80 vote, with Lincoln joining nine other Northern Whigs in opposition. Several days later, Gott introduced a resolution instructing the House Committee for the District of Columbia to draft legislation abolishing the slave trade in the nation's capital. The resolution passed, but Lincoln voted to table it because he believed its preamble, which declared the slave trade "contrary to natural justice," anti-Christian, and antithetical to "republican liberty," would alienate Southern Whigs. On January 10 the House voted to reconsider Gott's resolution, with Lincoln voting with the majority. By this time Lincoln was working on his own legislation. Upon reconsideration of Gott's resolution, Lincoln announced he would submit his own bill as a substitute, legislation that would take effect only if approved by a majority of "free white male citizens." Foner, *The Fiery Trial,* 55–58; Burlingame, *Abraham Lincoln,* 1:286–289.

4   Lincoln did not respond to requests by several congressmen to share the names of citizens of the district who supported his measure. He never formally submitted his legislation, later admitting that he abandoned the measure when its original

cated, by the respective owners of their mothers or by their heirs or representatives, and shall owe reasonable service, as apprentices, to such owners, heirs and representatives until they respectively arrive at the age of ___ years when they shall be entirely free; and the municipal authorities of Washington and Georgetown, within their respective jurisdictional limits, are hereby empowered and required to make all suitable and necessary provisions for forcing obedience to this section, on the part of both masters and apprentices.

Section 4. That all persons now within said District lawfully held as slaves, or now owned by any person or persons now resident within said District, shall remain such, at the will of their respective owners, their heirs and legal representatives: *Provided* that any such owner, or his legal representative, may at any time receive from the treasury of the United States the full value of his or her slave, of the class in this section mentioned, upon which such slave shall be forthwith and forever free: and *provided further* that the President of the United States, the Secretary of State, and the Secretary of the Treasury shall be a board for determining the value of such slaves as their owners may desire to emancipate under this section; and whose duty it shall be to hold a session for the purpose, on the first monday of each calendar month; to receive all applications; and, on satisfactory evidence in each case, that the person presented for valuation, is a slave, and of the class in this section mentioned, and is owned by the applicant, shall value such slave at his or her full cash value, and give to the applicant an order on the treasury for the amount; and also to such slave a certificate of freedom.

Section 5. That the municipal authorities of Washington and Georgetown, within their respective jurisdictional limits, are hereby empowered and required to provide active and efficient means to arrest, and deliver up to their owners, all fugitive slaves escaping into said District.

Section 6. That the election officers within said District of Columbia, are hereby empowered and required to open polls at all the usual places of holding elections, on the first monday of April next, and receive the vote of every free white male citizen above the age of twentyone years, having resided within said District for the period of one year or more next preceding the time of such voting, for, or against this act; to proceed, in taking said votes, in all respects not herein specified, as at elections under the municipal laws; and, with as little delay as possible, to transmit correct statements of the votes so cast to the President of the United States. And it shall be the duty of

backers withdrew their support. His proposal received no Southern support and offended several antislavery congressmen. Burlingame, *Abraham Lincoln,* 1:289.

U.S. Capitol Building. Daguerreotype by John Plumbe (Washington, DC, 1846). The earliest photograph of the Capitol, with its original dome.

the President to canvass said votes immediately, and, if a majority of them be found to be for this act, to forthwith issue his proclamation giving notice of the fact; and this act shall only be in full force and effect on, and after the day of such proclamation.

Section 7. That involuntary servitude for the punishment of crime, whereof the party shall have been duly convicted shall in no wise be prohibited by this act.

Section 8. That for all the purposes of this act the jurisdictional limits of Washington are extended to all parts of the District of Columbia not now included within the present limits of Georgetown.

Mr. LINCOLN then said, that he was authorized to say, that of about fifteen of the leading citizens of the District of Columbia to whom this proposition had been submitted, there was not one but who approved of the adoption of such a proposition.[4] He did not wish to be misunderstood. He did not know whether or not they would vote for this bill on the first Monday of April; but he repeated, that out of fifteen persons to whom it had been submitted, he had the authority to say that every one of them desired that some proposition like this should pass.

*It is not known exactly when and for what purpose Lincoln recorded these thoughts. Whenever they were written, these fragments highlight what Lincoln considered the fundamental qualities of a successful lawyer, such as diligence and honesty.*

1 Nicolay and Hay (*Complete Works*, 2:140–143) date this document July 1, 1850, but offer no evidence in support of their claim. Basler, in *CW*, 2:82n1, assigns this date with extreme caution, suggesting that Lincoln probably wrote these notes "several years later." The editors of the Lincoln Legal Papers project (http://papersofabrahamlin-coln.org/the-documents/series-i) posit that Lincoln may have drafted these notes as a result of an invitation to speak at Ohio State and Union Law College in 1858. Cited in Brian Dirck, *Lincoln the Lawyer* (Urbana: University of Illinois Press, 2007), 1n2.

2 Lincoln may be referring to his informal legal training and what he saw as his inadequate knowledge of the law. By the 1850s, however, he had achieved success as a lawyer, especially in comparison to his political career. Lincoln began his study of law by reading standard legal text-books that he borrowed. Obtaining his Illinois law license in 1836, Lincoln established himself in the profession through partnerships with John Todd Stuart, Stephen T. Logan, and William H. Herndon, the latter lasting from 1841 to 1861. Over his career he handled more than 5,000 cases and provided his family with a comfortable middle-class living. Although Lincoln participated in almost 200 criminal cases, including murder, the bulk of his practice involved debt collection, contract disputes, divorce, and slander. His success as a lawyer benefited greatly his political career, as he became well known on the Illinois Eighth Judicial Circuit, which he rode for more than twenty years. See Dirck, *Lincoln the Lawyer;* Mark E. Steiner, *An Honest Calling: The Law Practice of Abraham Lincoln* (De Kalb: Northern Illinois

# Notes for a Law Lecture

## [July 1, 1850?]

I AM NOT AN ACCOMPLISHED LAWYER.[1] I FIND QUITE AS MUCH MATE-rial for a lecture, in those points wherein I have failed, as in those wherein I have been moderately successful.[2] The leading role for the lawyer, as for the man, of every other calling, is *diligence.* Leave nothing for to-morrow, which can be done today. Never let your correspondence fall behind. Whatever piece of business you have in hand, before stopping, do all the labor per-taining to it which can *then* be done. When you bring a common-law suit, if you have the facts for doing so, write the declaration at once. If a law point be involved, examine the books, and note the authority you rely on upon the declaration itself, where you are sure to find it when wanted. The same of defences and pleas. In business not likely to be litigated,—ordinary collection cases, foreclosures, partitions, and the like,—make all examina-tions of titles, and note them, and even draft orders and decrees in advance. This course has a tripple [*sic*] advantage; it avoids omissions and neglect, *saves* your labor when once done, performs the labor out of court when you *have* leisure, rather than in court, when you have not. Extemporaneous speaking should be practised and cultivated. It is the lawyer's avenue to the public. However able and faithful he may be in other respects, people are slow to bring him business, if he cannot make a speech. And yet there is not a more fatal error to young lawyers, than relying too much on speech-making. If any one, upon his rare powers of speaking, shall claim an exemp-tion from the drudgery of the law, his case is a failure in advance.[3]

Discourage litigation. Persuade your neighbors to compromise whenever you can. Point out to them how the *nominal* winner is often the *real* loser—in fees, and expenses, and waste of time. As a peace-maker the lawyer has a superior opportunity of being a good man. There will still be business enough.[4]

Abraham Lincoln, legal brief, *Illinois Central Railroad v. McLean County.* Manuscript (February 1854).

University Press, 2006); and Fraker, *Lincoln's Ladder to the Presidency.*

3    Lincoln was well known for his oratorical skills in the courtroom. A folksy speaker armed with humorous anecdotes and stories, he was particularly accomplished at persuading juries. His success was due in large part to his ability to relate to the ordinary citizens who sat on juries and served as witnesses. Dirck, *Lincoln the Lawyer,* 102; Frank J. Williams, "Lincoln's Lessons for Lawyers," in Roger Billings and Frank J. Williams, eds., *Abraham Lincoln, Esq.: The Legal Career of America's Greatest President* (Lexington: University Press of Kentucky, 210), 26–28.

4    When it came to avoiding litigation, Lincoln practiced what he preached, often seeking a peaceful settlement outside the courtroom rather than going to trial. Examples of this can be found in Williams, "Lincoln's Lessons," 33; and Steiner, *An Honest Calling,* 58, 85, 99–100, 102, 143.

Never stir up litigation. A worse man can scarcely be found than one who does this. Who can be more nearly a fiend than he who habitually overhauls the Register of deeds, in search of defects in titles, whereon to stir up strife, and put money in his pocket? A moral tone ought to be infused into the profession, which should drive such men out of it.

5   On average Lincoln charged his clients modest fees and made a living by handling a large number of cases. The popular image of Lincoln as a folksy, ill-trained, backwoods attorney who represented only the innocent and the poor for little compensation is grossly inaccurate; he represented both rich and poor, plaintiffs and defendants, ordinary citizens and business interests, and the guilty as well as the innocent. Steiner, *An Honest Calling,* 70–72; Dirck, *Lincoln the Lawyer,* 159–161.

The matter of fees is important far beyond the mere question of bread and butter involved. Properly attended to fuller justice is done to both lawyer and client. An exorbitant fee should never be claimed. As a general rule, never take your whole fee in advance, nor any more than a small retainer. When fully paid before hand, you are more than a common mortal if you can feel the same interest in the case, as if something was still in prospect for you, as well as for your client. And when you lack interest in the case, the job will very likely lack skill and diligence in the performance. Settle the *amount* of fee, and take a note in advance. Then you will feel that you are working for something, and you are sure to do your work faithfully and well. Never sell a fee note—at least, not before the consideration service is performed. It leads to negligence and dishonesty—negligence, by losing interest in the case, and dishonesty in refusing to refund, when you have allowed the consideration to fail.[5]

There is a vague popular belief that lawyers are necessarily dishonest. I say *vague,* because when we consider to what extent *confidence,* and *honors* are reposed in, and conferred upon lawyers by the people, it appears improbable that their *impression* of dishonesty is very distinct and vivid. Yet the impression is common—almost universal. Let no young man choosing the law for a calling, for a moment yield to the popular belief.—Resolve to be honest at all events; and if, in your own judgment, you cannot be an honest lawyer, resolve to be honest without being a lawyer. Choose some other occupation, rather than one in the choosing of which you do, in advance, consent to be a knave.

Louis Bonhajo, *Lincoln the Circuit Rider.* Oil on canvas (ca. 1939–1940). A romanticized rendering of Lincoln riding the vast Eighth Judicial Circuit in Illinois.

# Eulogy for Zachary Taylor

## July 25, 1850

*Researched and written in less than two days, Lincoln's eulogy of Zachary Taylor is one of his least-known major compositions. In praising the man he had actively campaigned for in the 1848 presidential election, Lincoln focused on Taylor's military career and his virtues of wisdom and patriotism, virtues that Lincoln himself not only sought to emulate but also believed were essential to political leadership.*

GENERAL ZACHARY TAYLOR, THE ELEVENTH PRESIDENT OF THE United States, is dead.[1] He was born Nov. 2nd,[2] 1784, in Orange county, Virginia; and died July the 9th 1850, in the sixty-sixth year of his age, at the White House in Washington City. He was the second son[3] of Richard Taylor, a Colonel in the army of the revolution. His youth was passed among the pioneers of Kentucky, whither his parents emigrated soon after his birth; and where his taste for military life, probably inherited, was greatly stimulated. Near the commencement of our last war with Great Britain, he was appointed by President Jefferson,[4] a lieutenant in the 7th regiment of Infantry. During the war, he served under Gen. Harrison[5] in his North Western campaign against the Indians; and, having been promoted to a captaincy, was intrusted with the defence of Fort Harrison,[6] with fifty men, half of them unfit for duty. A strong party of Indians, under the Prophet,[7] brother of Tecumseh, made a midnight attack on the Fort; but Taylor, though weak in his force, and without preparation, was resolute, and on the alert; and, after a battle, which lasted till after daylight, completely repulsed them. Soon after, he took a prominent part in the expedition under Major Gen. Hopkins[8] against the Prophet's town; and, on his return, found a letter from President Madison,[9] who had succeeded Mr. Jefferson, conferring on him a major's brevet for his gallant defense of Fort Harrison.

After the close of the British war, he remained in the frontier service of the West, till 1818. He was then transferred to the Southern frontier, where he remained, most of the time in active service till 1826. In 1819, and during his service in the South, he was promoted to the rank of lieutenant colonel. In 1826 he was again sent to the North West, where he continued until 1836. In 1832, he promoted to the rank of a colonel. In 1836 he was ordered South to engage in what is well known as the Florida War.[10] In the autumn of 1837, he fought and conquered in the memorable battle of Okeechobee,[11]

1 Lincoln was in Chicago on July 9, 1850, representing the defendant in *Parker v. Hoyt*, a patent infringement case concerning a waterwheel, when President Taylor died in Washington, D.C., after a short illness (acute gastroenteritis). On July 22, Lincoln was asked by a group of Chicago Whigs to deliver a eulogy of the late president on the afternoon of July 25. Although concerned that the "want of time for preparation" would "make the task, for me, very difficult," Lincoln accepted the invitation on July 24, obviously not wishing to pass up the opportunity to deliver a widely reported speech before a large crowd in Chicago. *CW*, 2:82. The speech appeared in the *Chicago Daily Journal* on July 27 and the *Chicago Weekly Journal* on August 5, 1850. *CW*, 2:82; Kaplan, *Lincoln*, 206–207.

2 Taylor was born on November 24, 1784, not November 2. With less than forty-eight hours to compose Taylor's eulogy, Lincoln probably relied on one or more Taylor obituaries and on biographies produced for the 1848 election. Presidential campaign biographies were produced in haste, usually in the first several weeks after a candidate was nominated, and factual errors are often encountered in these publications. In this instance, Lincoln may have left out the "4" by mistake when quickly writing the eulogy. See W. Burlie Brown, *The People's Choice: The Presidential Image in the Campaign Biography* (Baton Rouge: Louisiana State University Press, 1960).

3   Taylor was the third child and son, not the second, among the nine children of Richard Taylor and Sarah Dabney Stroher Taylor. This mistake appears in John Frost's *Life of Major General Zachary Taylor* (New York: D. Appleton; Philadelphia: G. S. Appleton, 1847), one of numerous Taylor campaign biographies issued in 1847 and 1848 and one that Lincoln may have consulted. Of the sixteen Taylor campaign biographies consulted by the editors, Frost's is the only one that includes this mistake. For biographical information on Taylor, see K. Jack Bauer, *Zachary Taylor: Soldier, Planter, and Statesman of the Old Southwest* (Baton Rouge: Louisiana State University Press, 1985).

4   Thomas Jefferson (1743–1826), third president of the United States.

5   William Henry Harrison was born in Virginia and began his military career during the American Revolution, serving as an aide-de-camp to General Anthony Wayne. In 1799 he was elected as the Northwest Territory's delegate to the U.S. Congress, and a year later President John Adams appointed him territorial governor of Indiana. Harrison's defeat of the Shawnees led by Tecumseh (1768–1813) at the Battle of Tippecanoe in 1811 earned him the popular sobriquet "Old Tippecanoe." In 1839 the Whig Party nominated Harrison for president, and he was elected the next year. Freeman Cleaves, *Old Tippecanoe: William Henry Harrison and His Times* (Port Washington, NY: Kennikat Press, 1939).

6   Fort Harrison, a small stockade post, was built by General William Henry Harrison on a bluff overlooking the Wabash River near what is now Terre Haute, Indiana. Robert M. Owens, *Mr. Jefferson's Hammer: William Henry Harrison and the Origins of American Indian Policy* (Norman: University of Oklahoma Press, 2007), 216; Bauer, *Zachary Taylor*, 11–12.

7   Tenskwatawa (1768–1836), known as the

one of the most desperate struggles known to the annals of Indian warfare. For this, he was honored with the rank of Brigadier General; and, in 1838 was appointed to succeed Gen. Jessup[12] in command of the forces in Florida. In 1841 he was ordered to Fort Gibson[13] to take command of the Second Military department of the United States; and in September, 1844, was directed to hold the troops between the Red River and the Sabine in readiness to march as might be indicated by the Charge of the United States, near Texas. In 1845 his forces were concentrated at Corpus Christi.

In obedience to orders, in March 1846, he planted his troops on the Rio Grande opposite Mattamoras. Soon after this, and near this place, a small detachment of Gen. Taylor's forces, under Captain Thornton,[14] was cut to pieces by a party of Mexicans. Open hostilities being thus commenced, and Gen. Taylor being constantly menaced by Mexican forces vastly superior to his own, in numbers, his position became exceedingly critical. Having erected a fort, he might defend himself against great odds while he could remain within it; but his provisions had failed, and there was no supply nearer than Point Isabel, between which and the new fort, the country was open to, and full of, armed Mexicans. His resolution was at once taken. He garrisoned Fort Brown, (the new fort) with a force of about four hundred; and, putting himself at the head of the main body of his troops, marched forthwith for Point Isabel. He met no resistance on his march. Having obtained his supplies, he began his return march, to the relief of Fort Brown, which he at first knew, would be, and then knew had been besieged by the enemy, immediately upon his leaving it. On the first or second day of this return march, the Mexican General, Arista,[15] met General Taylor in front, and offered battle. The Mexicans numbered six or eight thousand, opposed to whom were about two thousand Americans. The moment was a trying one. Comparatively, Taylor's forces were but a handful; and few, of either officers or men, had ever been under fire. A brief council was held; and the result was, the battle commenced. The issue of that contest all remember— remember with mingled sensations of pride and sorrow, that then, American valor and powers triumphed, and then the gallant and accomplished, and noble Ringgold[16] fell.

The Americans passed the night on the field. The General knew the enemy was still in his fort; and the question rose upon him, whether to advance or retreat. A council was again held; and, it is said, the General overruled the majority, and resolved to advance. Accordingly in the morning, he moved rapidly forward. At about four or five miles from Fort Brown he again met the enemy in force, who had selected his position, and made some hasty fortification. Again the battle commenced, and raged till toward nightfall, when the Mexicans were entirely routed, and the General with his fatigued and bleeding, and reduced battalions marched into Fort Brown. There was a joyous meeting. A brief hour before, whether all *within* the fort had perished, all *without* feared, but none could tell—while the incessant roar of artillery, wrought those *within* to the highest pitch of apprehension, that their brethren *without* were being massacred to the last man. And now the din of battle nears the fort and sweeps obliquely by; a gleam of hope flies through the half imprisoned few; they fly to the wall; every eye is strained—it is—it is—the stars and stripes are still aloft! Anon the anxious brethren meet; and while hand strikes hand, the heavens are rent with a loud, long, glorious, gushing cry of victory! victory!! victory!!!

Soon after these two battles, Gen. Taylor was breveted a Major General in the U. S. Army.

In the mean time, war having been declared to exist between the United States and Mexico, provisions were made to reinforce Gen. Taylor; and he was ordered to march into the interior of Mexico.[17] He next marched upon Monterey [*sic*], arriving there on the 19th of September. He commenced an assault upon the city, on the 21st, and on the 23d was about carrying it at the point of the bayonet, when Gen. Ampudia[18] capitulated. Taylor's forces consisted of 425 officers, and 9,220 men. His artillery consisted of one 10 inch mortar, two 24 pound Howitzers, and four light field batteries of four guns—the mortar being the only piece serviceable for the siege. The Mexican works were armed with forty-two pieces of canon, and manned with a force of at least 7000 troops of the line, and from 2000 to 3000 irregulars.

Next we find him advancing further into the interior of Mexico, and at the head of 5,400 men, not more than 600 being regular troops.

At Agua Nueva he received intelligence that Santa Anna,[19] the greatest military chieftain of Mexico, was advancing after him; and he fell back to Buena Vista, a strong position a few miles in advance of Saltillo. On the 22nd of Feb., 1847, the battle, now called the battle of Buena Vista, was commenced by Santa Anna at the head of 20,000 well appointed soldiers. This was Gen. Taylor's great battle. The particulars of it are familiar to all. It continued through the 23rd; and although Gen. Taylor's defeat seemed to be inevitable, yet he succeeded by skill, and by the courage and devotion of his officers and men, in repulsing the overwhelming forces of the enemy, and throwing them back into the desert. This was the battle of the chiefest interest fought during the Mexican war. At the time it was fought, and for some weeks after, Gen. Taylor's communication with the United States was

Shawnee Prophet, led the Native American resistance against President Jefferson's program to wrest from them cheap cessions of Indian lands. Owens, *Mr. Jefferson's Hammer,* 107.

8   Samuel Hopkins (1753–1819) was a veteran of the Revolutionary War, a congressman, and a major general in the Kentucky militia. Bauer, *Zachary Taylor,* 17–18.

9   James Madison (1751–1836), fourth president of the United States.

10   The Second Seminole War (1835–1842).

11   The Battle of Lake Okeechobee, fought in December 1837, was, according to one historian, "one of the bloodiest in all the history of nineteenth-century Indian warfare." Bauer, *Zachary Taylor,* 82.

12   Major General Thomas Sidney Jesup (1788–1860) was Taylor's mentor and supporter in his early military career. Ibid., 32, 37.

13   Fort Gibson, located near the Arkansas River, was erected in 1824 and was known at the time as the unhealthiest post in the army. Ibid., 99.

14   Seth B. Thornton (1815–1847). On April 25, 1846, Thornton's troops were ambushed twenty miles from camp, and he was captured, along with most of his men. This incident was used by President Polk to ask Congress for a declaration of war against Mexico. He and his surviving officers were later exchanged for Mexican prisoners. Thornton was killed in May 1847 while investigating the defenses of San Antonio. Bauer, *The Mexican War,* 48, 81, 291.

15   Mariano Arista (1802–1855) commanded Mexican troops along the Rio Grande. Ibid., 21.

16   Major Samuel Ringgold (1796–1846), a commander of a light artillery unit, was mortally wounded at the Battle of Palo Alto. James Wynne,

*Memoir of Major Samuel Ringgold* (Baltimore: John Murphy, 1847).

17  Lincoln does not mention his or his party's fierce opposition to the war and his harsh criticisms of President Polk. See "Speech in Congress against the War with Mexico, January 12, 1848," in this volume.

18  The Cuban-born major general Pedro de Ampudia (1803–1868) served the Mexican army as commander of the Division of the North. Clary, *Eagles and Empire,* 81.

19  Antonia Lopez de Santa Anna (1794–1876) was a major figure in the history of early national Mexico. He was known to Americans as the leader of Mexican forces at the attack of the Alamo. Santa Anna retired in disgrace after signing the treaty giving Texas its independence but returned to power in 1838, after defeating French forces that landed in Veracruz to enforce repayment of Mexico's debt. He was later imprisoned and banished to Cuba in 1845. He returned to Mexico in August 1846 with the aid of President Polk, who believed that Santa Anna, as leader of Mexico, would agree to any terms the United States might dictate. Once back in power, however, Santa Anna not only refused to negotiate with the United States but also led Mexican troops against Taylor's army. Greenberg, *A Wicked War,* 147–149.

20  Lieutenant Colonel Henry Clay (1811–1847), the son of the famous statesman Henry Clay and a graduate of West Point, was killed at the Battle of Buena Vista. Robert V. Remini, *Henry Clay: Statesman for the Union* (New York: W. W. Norton, 1991), 31, 339, 684.

21  Colonel William R. McKee (1808–1847) of the Second Kentucky Infantry. Bauer, *The Mexican War,* 210.

22  Colonel Archibald Yell (1797?–1847) was commander of the Arkansas Mounted Volunteers.

cut off; and the road was in possession of parties of the enemy. For many days after full intelligence of it, should have been in all parts of this country, nothing certain, concerning it, was known, while vague and painful rumors were afloat, that a great battle had been fought, and that Gen. Taylor, and his whole force had been annihilated.

At length the truth came, with its thrilling details of victory and blood—of glory and grief. A bright and glowing page was added to our Nation's history; but then too, in eternal silence, lay Clay,[20] and Mc'Kee,[21] and Yell,[22] and Lincoln,[23] and our own beloved Hardin.[24]

This also was Gen. Taylor's *last* battle. He remained in active service in Mexico, till the autumn of the same year, when he returned to the United States.

Passing in review, Gen. Taylor's military history, some striking peculiarities will appear. No one of the six battles which he fought, excepting perhaps, that of Monterey [*sic*], presented a field, which would have been selected by an ambitious captain upon which to gather laurels. So far as fame was concerned, the prospect—the promise in advance, was "you may lose, but you can not win." Yet Taylor, in his blunt business-like view of things, seems never to have thought of this.

It did happen to Gen. Taylor once in his life, to fight a battle on equal terms, or on terms advantageous to himself—and yet he was never beaten, and never retreated. In *all,* the odds was [*sic*] greatly against him; in each, defeat seemed inevitable; and yet *in all,* he triumphed. Wherever he has led, while the battle still raged, the issue was painfully doubtful; yet in *each* and *all,* when the din had ceased, and the smoke had blown away, our country's flag was still seen, fluttering in the breeze.

Gen. Taylor's battles were not distinguished for brilliant military manoeuvers; but in all, he seems rather to have conquered by the exercise of a sober and steady judgment, coupled with a dogged incapacity to understand that defeat was possible. His rarest military trait, was a combination of negatives—absence of *excitement* and absence of *fear.* He could not be *flurried,* and he could not be *scared.*

In connection with Gen. Taylor's military character, may be mentioned his relations with his brother officers, and his soldiers. Terrible as he was to his country's enemies, no man was so little disposed to have difficulty with his friends. During the period of his life, *duelling* was a practice not quite uncommon among gentlemen in the peaceful avocations of life, and still more common, among the officers of the Army and Navy. Yet, so far as I can learn, a *duel* with Gen. Taylor, has never been talked of.

He was alike averse to *sudden,* and to *startling* quarrels; and he pursued no man with *revenge.* A notable, and a noble instance of this, is found in his conduct to the gallant and now lamented Gen. Worth.[25] A short while before the battles of the 8th and 9th of May, some questions of precedence arose between Worth, (then a colonel) and some other officer, which question it seems Gen. Taylor's duty to decide. He decided against Worth. Worth was greatly offended, left the Army, came to the United States, and tendered his resignation to the authorities at Washington. It is said, that in his passionate feeling, he hesitated not to speak harshly and disparagingly of Gen. Taylor. He was an officer of the highest character; and his word, on military subjects, and about military men, could not, with the country, pass for nothing. In this absence from the army of Col. Worth, the unexpected turn of things brought on the battles of the 8th and 9th. He was deeply mortified—in almost absolute desperation—at having lost the opportunity of being present, and taking part in those battles. The laurels won by his previous service, in his own eyes, seemed withering away. The Government, both *wisely* and *generously,* I think, declined accepting his resignation; and he returned to Gen. Taylor. Then came Gen. Taylor's *opportunity* for revenge. The battle of Monterey [*sic*] was approaching, and even at hand. Taylor *could* if he *would,* so place Worth in that battle, that his name would scarcely be noticed in the report. But no. He felt it was due to the service, to assign the real post of honor to some one of the best officers; he knew Worth was one of the best, and he felt that it was *generous* to allow him, then and there, to retrieve his secret loss. Accordingly he assigned Col. Worth in that assault, what was *par excellence,* the post of honor; and, the duties of which, he executed so well, and so brilliantly, as to eclipse, in that battle, even Gen. Taylor himself.

As to Gen[.] Taylor's relations with his soldiers, details would be endless. It is perhaps enough to say—and it is far from the *least* of his honors that we can *truly* say—that of the many who served with him through the long course of forty years, all testify to the uniform kindness, and his constant care for, and hearty sympathy with, their every want and every suffering; while none can be found to declare, that he was ever a tyrant anywhere, in anything.

Going back a little point of time, it is proper to say that so soon as the news of the battles of the 8th and 9th of May 1846, had fairly reached the United States, Gen. Taylor began to be named for next Presidency, by letter writers, newspapers, public meetings and conventions in various parts of the country.

He served his state as governor and in Congress. "Yell, Archibald," *Biographical Directory of the United States Congress,* http://bioguide.congress. gov/scripts/biodisplay.pl?index=Y000017 (accessed January 21, 2015).

23  Captain George Lincoln (1816–1847) of Massachusetts was a son of Levi Lincoln and a distant relative of Abraham Lincoln. William Lincoln, *History of Worcester, Massachusetts: From Its Earliest Settlement to September 1836* (Worcester, MA: Charles Hersey, 1862), 385.

24  John J. Hardin of Illinois was a cousin of Mary Todd Lincoln; a stepnephew of Henry Clay; and the son of Martin Hardin, U.S. senator, member of the Kentucky Supreme Court, and decorated veteran of the War of 1812. Hardin County, Kentucky, where Lincoln was born, was named in honor of John Hardin's grandfather. Hardin served in Lincoln's militia company in the Black Hawk War, and the two of them became good friends as well as fellow Whigs in the Illinois state legislature. It was Hardin who helped avert a duel between Lincoln and James Shields; see "The 'Rebecca' Letter, August 27, 1842," in this volume. Along with Edward D. Baker, Hardin and Lincoln emerged as leaders of Illinois's Whig Party in the 1840s. All three coveted the state's Seventh Congressional District seat in the House of Representatives and agreed to a party resolution that each would serve only one term so that all three would have a chance to represent the district in Congress. After the war with Mexico was declared, Hardin was elected colonel of the First Illinois Regiment of Volunteers, on June 30, 1846. Neeley, *Lincoln Encyclopedia,* 139–140.

25  William J. Worth (1794–1849). The issue of rank arose between Colonel Worth and Colonel David E. Twiggs (1790–1862) while they were stationed in Corpus Christi. Although Twiggs was senior to Worth as a colonel, the latter had a brevet

commission as a brigadier general. The issue was a critical one, since the senior of the two would serve as second-in-command of the army. Since the issue was not covered by army regulations, a ruling was warranted. General Winfield Scott ruled in favor of Worth, but Taylor reversed Scott's ruling. President Polk also sided with Twiggs, as a result of which Worth refused to serve under Twiggs and resigned his position. He soon withdrew his resignation, but later had a falling out with General Scott. Bauer, *The Mexican War,* 35–36; Bauer, *Zachary Taylor,* 123n39; Clary, *Eagles and Empire,* 406.

**26** Lewis Cass (1782–1866), senator from Michigan, was nominated for president of the United States by the Democratic Party. He lost the 1848 election to Zachary Taylor. Cass later served as secretary of state in the Buchanan administration. "Cass, Lewis," Biographical Directory of the United States Congress, http://bioguide.congress.gov/scripts/biodisplay.pl?index=c000233 (accessed January 22, 2015).

**27** Despite his profound admiration for Henry Clay, Lincoln early in 1848 supported Taylor for the Whig nomination for president, joining a group of pro-Taylor congressional Whigs known as the "Young Indians." Although the group was dominated by Southerners who believed that Taylor, a slaveholder, would protect the interests of their region, Northern Young Indians like Lincoln were attracted to the popular general because he appeared to be the only Whig nominee with a chance to win the presidency. "I am in favor of Gen. Taylor," Lincoln told a fellow Whig, "because I am satisfied we can elect him, that he would give us a whig administration, and that we can not elect any other whig." *CW,* 2:452. Lincoln asserted to William Herndon that having a Mexican War hero as their standard-bearer would not only defuse attacks against the Whigs' patriotism for having opposed the conflict but also turn the "war thunder" against the Democrats: "The war is now

These nominations were generally put forth as being of a no[-]party character. Up to this time I think it highly probable—nay, almost certain, that Gen. Taylor had never thought of the Presidency in connection with himself. And there is reason for believing that the first intelligence of these nominations rather *amused* than *seriously* interested him. Yet I should be insincere, were I not to confess, that in my opinion, the repeated, and steady manifestations in his favor, *did* beget in his mind a laudable ambition to reach the high distinction of the Presidential chair.

As the time for the Presidential canvas approached, it was seen that general nominations, combining anything near the number of votes necessary to an election, could not be made without some pretty strong and decided reference to party politics. Accordingly, in the month of May, 1848, the great Democratic party nominated as their candidate, an able and distinguished member of their own party, on strictly party grounds.[26] Almost immediately following this, the Whig party, in general convention, nominated Gen. Taylor as their candidate.[27] The election came off in the November following; and though there was also a third candidate, the two former only, received any vote in the electoral college.[28] Gen. Taylor, having the majority of them was duly elected; and he entered on the duties of that high and responsible office, March 5th, 1849. The incidents of his administration up to the time of his death, are too familiar and too fresh to require any direct repetition.

The Presidency, even to the most experienced politicians, is no bed of roses; and Gen. Taylor like others, found thorns within it. No human being can fill that station and escape censure. Still I hope and believe when Gen. Taylor's official conduct shall come to be viewed in the calm light of history, he will be found to have *deserved* as little as any who have succeeded him.

Upon the death of Gen. Taylor, as it would in the case of the death of any President, we are naturally led to consider what will be its effect, politically, upon the country. I will not pretend to believe that all of the wisdom, or all the patriotism of the country, died with Gen. Taylor. But we know that *wisdom* and *patriotism,* in a public office, under institutions like ours, are wholly inefficient and worthless, unless they are sustained by the confidence and devotion of the people. And I confess my apprehensions, that in the death of the late President, we have lost a degree of that confidence and devotion, which will not soon again pertain to any successor. Between public measures regarded as antagonistic, there is often less real difference in its bearing on the public weal, than there is between the dispute being *kept up,* or being *settled* either way. I fear the one *great* question of the day,[29] is not now so likely to be partially acquiesced in by the different sections of the

N. Currier, *Zachary Taylor, People's Candidate for President.*
Lithograph (New York, ca. 1848).

Union, as it would have been, could Gen. Taylor have been spared to us. Yet, under all circumstances, trusting our Maker, and through his wisdom and beneficence, to the great body of our people, we will not despair, nor despond.

In Gen. Taylor's general public relation to his country, what will strongly impress a close observer, was his unostentatious, self-sacrificing, long enduring devotion to his *duty.* He indulged in no recreations, he visited no public places, seeking applause; but quietly, as the earth in its orbit, he was always at his post. Along our whole Indian frontier, thro' summer and winter, in sunshine and storm, like a sleepless sentinel, *he* has *watched,* while *we* have *slept* for forty long years. How well might the dying hero say at last, "I have done my duty, I am ready to go."

Nor can I help thinking that the American people, in electing Gen. Taylor to the presidency, thereby showing their high appreciation, of his ster-

on them, the gallows of Haman, which they built for us, and on which they are doomed to be hanged themselves." *CW,* 2:477. Lincoln's active campaigning on Taylor's behalf included a September speaking tour of New England, where he attempted to dissuade many Whigs, angered by the party's nomination of a slaveholder, from abandoning the party and joining the newly formed Free Soil Party. For Lincoln's tour of Massachusetts, see William F. Hanna, *Abraham among the Yankees* (Taunton, MA: Old Colony Historical Society, 1983). After Taylor's election to the presidency, Lincoln sought to influence patronage appointments, including the post of commissioner of the General Land Office in

Zachary Taylor. Daguerreotype by Mathew Brady (ca. 1844–1849). Lincoln worked hard for Taylor's election as president but was disappointed in not receiving a top patronage appointment as a reward.

Washington, D.C., which he ended up applying for himself. He did not receive the appointment but was offered the positions of secretary and governor of Oregon Territory, both of which he declined. Burlingame, *Abraham Lincoln*, 1:296–307. One historian has suggested that Lincoln's proposed legislation to abolish slavery in the District of Columbia did not help his quest for a patronage appointment in the Taylor administration. William Lee Miller, *Lincoln's Virtues: An Ethical Biography* (New York: Alfred A. Knopf, 2002), 214–215.

**28** The Free Soil Party, founded by antislavery Northern Whigs, abolitionists, and disaffected Democrats, advocated the prohibition of slavery in western territories and the outlawing of the slave trade in Washington, D.C. The party nominated

ling, but unobtrusive qualities, did their *country* a service, and *themselves* an imperishable honor. It is *much* for the young to know, that treading the hard path of duty, as he trod it, *will* be noticed, and *will* lead to high places.

But he is gone. The conqueror at last is conquered. The fruits of his labor, his name, his memory and example, are all that is left us—his example, verifying the great truth, that "he that humbleth himself, shall be exalted"[30] teaching, that to serve one's country with a singleness of purpose, gives assurance of that country's gratitude, secures its best honors, and makes "a dying bed, soft as downy pillows are."[31]

The death of the late President may not be without its use, in reminding us, that *we,* too, must die. Death, abstractly considered, is the same with the high as with the low; but practically, we are not so much aroused to the contemplation of our own mortal natures, by the fall of *many* undistinguished, as that of *one* great, and well known, name. By the latter, we are forced to muse, and ponder, sadly.[32]

"Oh, why should the spirit of mortal be proud"

So the multitude goes, like the flower or the weed,
That withers away to let others succeed;
So the multitude comes, even those we behold,
To repeat every tale that has often been told.

For we are the same, our fathers have been,
We see the same sights our fathers have seen;
We drink the same streams and see the same sun
And run the same course our fathers have run.

*They* loved; but the story *we* cannot unfold;
They scorned, but the heart of the haughty is cold;
They grieved, but no wail from their slumbers will come,
They joyed, but the tongue of their gladness is dumb.

They died! Aye, they died; we things that are now;
That work on the turf that lies on their brow,
And make in their dwellings a transient abode,
Meet the things that they met on their pilgrimage road.

Yea! Hope and despondency, pleasure and pain,
Are mingled together in sun-shine and rain;

And the smile and the tear, and the song and the dirge,
Still follow each other, like surge upon surge.

'Tis the wink of an eye, 'tis the draught of a breath,
From the blossoms of health, to the paleness of death.
From the gilded saloon, to the bier and the shroud.
Oh, why should the spirit of mortal be proud!

former president Martin Van Buren as its candidate. See Frederick J. Blue, *The Free Soilers: Third Party Politics 1848–54* (Urbana: University of Illinois Press, 1973).

29  Lincoln referred to the issue of slavery in the territories, which was then being debated in Congress. The result of these debates was the Compromise of 1850.

30  Luke 14:11: "For whosoever exalteth himself shall be abased; and he that humbleth himself shall be exalted."

31  "Jesus can make a dying bed / Feel soft as downy pillows are": from Isaac Watts's Hymn 31. Thomas Hastings and William Patton, *The Christian Psalmist; or, Watts' Psalms and Hymns* (New York: Ezra Collier, 1836), 574.

32  Lincoln ends the eulogy by reciting one of his favorite poems, William Knox's "Mortality." Years before, Lincoln claimed, "I would give all I am worth, and go in debt, to be able to write so fine a piece as I think that is." *CW*, 1:378. Years later, encouraged by published versions listing Lincoln as its author, many Americans came to believe he had composed it. "There is no truth in it," Lincoln told the artist Francis B. Carpenter (1830–1900) in 1864. "The poem was first shown to me by a young man named 'Jason Duncan' many years ago." F. B. Carpenter, *The Inner Life of Abraham Lincoln: Six Months at the White House* (Boston: Houghton, Osgood and Company, 1880), 59. For Lincoln's interest in poetry, see "My Childhood-Home I See Again, [February 25?] 1846," in this volume.

*In his eulogy of Henry Clay, whom he considered his "beau ideal of a statesman," Lincoln concentrated not on Clay's well-known reputation as a master of the art of compromise but on his life-long devotion to human liberty and his opposition to slavery. Lincoln applauded Clay's moderate approach to the gradual eradication of slavery through a combination of emancipation and colonization of American blacks, an approach he himself pursued until 1862. This represents Lincoln's first public endorsement of colonization.*

1    There was no American political figure more admired by Lincoln than Henry Clay, senator and congressman from Lincoln's native Kentucky, secretary of state under President John Quincy Adams (1767–1848), and three-time presidential candidate. In the first of his famous Illinois senatorial debates with Stephen A. Douglas in 1858, Lincoln referred to Clay as "my beau ideal of a statesman, the man for whom I fought all my humble life." See "First Debate with Stephen A. Douglas at Ottawa, Illinois, August 21, 1858," in this volume. Considered the founder of the Whig Party, Clay proposed an "American System" consisting of a national bank, protective tariffs, and federal support for internal improvements, such as roads and canals. Clay's system became the foundation of the Whig Party's domestic agenda as well as that of the Republican Party during the Civil War and Reconstruction eras. Lincoln adhered to the economic principles of Clay's and later the Whigs' American System from the beginning of his political career to the end of his life, in the belief that government can and should create opportunities for economic independence for Americans willing to work for it. In fact, before the 1850s Lincoln's political career was devoted primarily to economic issues. See Remini, *Henry Clay,* and Boritt, *Lincoln and the Economics of the American Dream.*

# Eulogy for Henry Clay

## July 6, 1852

### Honors to Henry Clay

On the fourth day of July, 1776, the people of a few feeble and oppressed colonies of Great Britain, inhabiting a portion of the Atlantic coast of North America, publicly declared their national independence, and made their appeal to the justice of their cause, and to the God of battles, for the maintenance of that declaration. That people were few in numbers, and without resources, save only their own wise heads and stout hearts. Within the first year of that declared independence, and while its maintenance was yet problematical—while the bloody struggle between those resolute rebels, and their haughty would-be-masters, was still waging, of undistinguished parents, and in an obscure district of one of those colonies, Henry Clay was born. The infant nation, and the infant child began the race of life together. For three quarters of a century they have travelled hand in hand. They have been companions ever. The nation has passed its perils, and is free, prosperous, and powerful. The child has reached his manhood, his middle age, his old age, and is dead. In all that has concerned the nation the man ever sympathised; and now the nation mourns for the man.[1]

The day after his death,[2] one of the public Journals, opposed to him politically, held the following pathetic and beautiful language, which I adopt, partly because such high and exclusive eulogy, originating with a political friend, might offend good taste, but chiefly, because I could not, in any language of my own, so well express my thoughts—

"Alas! who can realize that Henry Clay is dead! Who can realize that never again that majestic form shall rise in the council-chambers of his country to beat back the storms of anarchy which may threaten, or pour the oil of peace upon the troubled billows as they rage and menace around? Who can realize, that the workings of that mighty mind have ceased—that the throbbings of that gallant heart are stilled—that the mighty sweep of that graceful arm will be felt no more, and the magic of that eloquent tongue, which spake as spake no other tongue besides, is hushed—hushed forever! Who can realize that freedom's champion—the champion of a civilized world, and of all tongues and kindreds and people, has indeed fallen! Alas, in those dark hours, which, as they come in the history of all nations, must come in ours—those hours of peril and dread which our land has experienced, and which she may be called to experience again—to whom now may her people look up for that council [*sic*] and advice, which only wisdom and experience and patriotism can give, and which only the undoubting confidence of a nation will receive? Perchance, in the whole circle of the great and gifted of our land, there remains but one on whose shoulders the mighty mantle of the departed statesman may fall—one, while we now write, is doubtless pouring his tears over the bier of his brother and friend—brother, friend ever, yet in political sentiment, as far apart as party could make them. Ah, it is times like these, that the petty distinctions of mere party disappear. We see only the great, the grand, the noble features of the departed statesman; and we do not even beg permission to bow at his feet and mingle our tears with those who have ever been his political adherents—we do [not] beg this permission—we claim it as a right, though we feel it as a privilege. Henry Clay belonged to his country—to the world, mere party cannot claim men like him. His career has been national—his fame has filled the earth—his memory will endure to 'the last syllable of recorded time.'

Henry Clay is dead!—He breathed his last on yesterday at twenty minutes after eleven, in his chamber at Washington. To those who followed his lead in public affairs, it more appropriately belongs to pronounce his eulogy, and pay specific honors to the memory of the illustrious dead—but all Americans may show the grief which his death inspires, for, his character and fame are national property. As on a question of liberty, he knew no North, no South, no East, no West, but only the Union, which held them all in its sacred circle, so now his countrymen will know no grief, that is not as wide-spread as the bounds of the confederacy. The career of Henry Clay was a public career. From his youth he has been devoted to the public service, at a period too, in the world's history justly regarded as a remarkable era in

Henry Clay. Daguerreotype by Mathew Brady (ca. 1850–1852). Clay was Lincoln's "beau ideal of a statesman."

2   Henry Clay died in Washington, D.C., on June 29, 1852, at the age of seventy-five. The cause of death was tuberculosis. Within hours of Clay's passing, President Millard Fillmore (1800–1874) ordered the closings of all federal offices. On July 6 Springfield, Illinois, suspended city business while its citizens held two memorial ceremonies, one of which took place in the state capitol, where Lincoln delivered his eulogy in the Hall of Representatives. Lincoln's address was published in the *Illinois Weekly Journal* on July 21, 1852. See *CW*, 2:132n1, and Ronald C. White, *A. Lincoln: A Biography* (New York: Random House, 2009), 184–185.

3   Simón Bolívar (1783–1830) was a Venezuelan soldier and statesman who led several South American countries to independence from Spain.

4   From the popular poem "Marco Bozzaris" by the American poet Fitz-Greene Halleck (1790–1867), first published in the *New York Review* in June 1825, http://digital.lib.lehigh.edu/pfaffs/p111/ (accessed January 22, 2015).

5   The intense sectional division that resulted in the Compromise of 1850. See note 10.

human affairs. He witnessed in the beginning the throes of the French Revolution. He saw the rise and fall of Napoleon. He was called upon to legislate for America, and direct her policy when all Europe was the battle-field of contending dynasties, and when the struggle for supremacy imperiled the rights of all natural nations. His voice, spoke war and peace in the contest with Great Britain.

When Greece rose against the Turks and struck for liberty, his name was mingled with the battle-cry of freedom. When South America threw off the thralldom of Spain, his speeches were read at the head of her armies by Bolivar.[3] His name has been, and will continue to be, hallowed in two hemispheres, for it is—

'One of the few the immortal names
That were not born to die'[4]

To the ardent patriot and profound statesman, he added a quality possessed by few of the gifted on earth. His eloquence has not been surpassed. In the effective power to move the heart of man, Clay was without an equal, and the heaven born endowment, in the spirit of its origin, has been most conspicuously exhibited against intestine feud. On at least three important occasions, he has quelled our civil commotions, by a power and influence, which belonged to no other statesman of his age and times. And in our last internal discord,[5] when this Union trembled to its center—in old age, he left the shades of private life and gave the death blow to fraternal strife, with the vigor of his earlier years in a series of Senatorial efforts, which in themselves would bring immortality, by challenging comparison with the efforts of any statesman in any age. He exorcised the demon which possessed the body politic, and gave peace to a distracted land. Alas! the achievement cost him his life! He sank day by day to the tomb—his pale, but noble brow, bound with a triple wreath, put there by a grateful country. May his ashes rest in peace, while his spirit goes to take its station among the great and good men who preceded him!"

While it is customary, and proper, upon occasions like the present, to give a brief sketch of the life of the deceased; in the case of Mr. Clay, it is less necessary than most others; for his biography has been written and re-written, and read, and re-read for the last twenty-five years; so that, with the exception of a few of the latest incidents of his life, all is as well known, as it can be. The short sketch which I give is, therefore merely to maintain the connection of this discourse.

Henry Clay was born on the 12th of April 1777, in Hanover county, Virginia. Of his father, who died in the fourth or fifth year of Henry's age, little seems to be known, except that he was a respectable man, and a preacher of the baptist persuasion. Mr. Clay's education, to the end of his life, was comparatively limited. I say *"to the end of his life,"* because I have understood that, from time to time, he added something to his education during the greater part of his whole life. Mr. Clay's lack of a more perfect early education, however it may be regretted generally, teaches at least one profitable lesson; it teaches that in this country, one can scarcely be so poor, but that, if he *will,* he *can* acquire sufficient education to get through the world respectably.[6] In his twenty-third year Mr. Clay was licenced to practice law, and emigrated to Lexington, Kentucky. Here he commenced and continued to practice till the year 1803, when he was first elected to the Kentucky Legislature. By successive elections he was continued in the Legislature till the latter part of 1806, when he was elected to fill a vacancy, of a single session, in the United States Senate. In 1807 he was again elected to the Kentucky House of Representatives, and by that body, chosen its speaker. In 1808 he was re-elected to the same body. In 1809 he was again chosen to fill a vacancy of two years in the United States Senate. In 1811 he was elected to the United States House of Representatives, and on the first day of taking his seat in that body, he was chosen its speaker. In 1813 he was again elected Speaker. Early in 1814, being the period of our last British war, Mr. Clay was sent as commissioner, with others, to negotiate a treaty of peace, which treaty was concluded in the latter part of the same year.[7] On his return from Europe he was again elected to the lower branch of Congress, and on taking his seat in December 1815 was called to his old post—the speaker's chair, a position in which he was retained, by successive elections, with one brief intermission, till the inauguration of John Q. Adams in March 1825. He was then appointed Secretary of State, and occupied that important station till the inauguration of Gen. Jackson in March 1829. After this he returned to Kentucky, resumed the practice of the law, and continued it till the Autumn of 1831, when he was by the Legislature of Kentucky, again placed in the United States Senate. By a re-election he was continued in the Senate till he resigned his seat, and retired, in March 1842. In December 1849 he again took his seat in the Senate, which he again resigned only a few months before his death.

By the foregoing it is perceived that the period from the beginning of

6   Lincoln related to Clay's loss of a parent during childhood and his limited education. Concerning the latter, Lincoln's formal education was limited to less than a year. He embarked on a vigorous regimen of self-improvement, enhancing his reading and writing skills, and finally mastering the fundamentals of grammar in his early twenties.

7   The Treaty of Ghent, which ended the War of 1812 between Great Britain and the United States, was signed on December 24, 1814. The U.S. delegation consisted of John Quincy Adams, James Bayard (1767–1815), Albert Gallatin (1761–1849), Jonathan Russell (1771–1832), and Clay.

8  In 1819, Missouri Territory applied for admission as a slave state and thus threatened the balance between free and slave states. New York congressman James Tallmadge Jr. (1778–1853) responded by introducing an amendment to ban the importation of slaves into the territory and emancipate Missouri's slaves when they reached the age of twenty-five. A fierce debate ensued in Congress between free- and slave-state representatives, with both sides fearing the consequences on their section if the other gained control of the Senate. Amid the stalemate, some Southern congressmen threatened secession. When Maine Territory petitioned Congress for admission as a free state, Clay, serving as speaker of the House of Representatives, saw an opportunity for a solution and devised a compromise. What became known as the Missouri Compromise permitted the admission of Missouri as a slave state and Maine as a free state, and banned slavery north and west of Missouri. The compromise maintained the balance of free and slave states in the Senate and reaffirmed congressional authority to prohibit slavery in the territories. President James Monroe (1758–1831) signed the legislation on March 6, 1820. Remini, *Henry Clay,* 178–184.

9  Henry Clay's American System included imposing tariffs on imported products in order to protect American manufacturing from foreign competition. Northern shippers and, especially, Southern planters objected to the high tariffs because they relied on foreign trade for their business. The Tariff of 1828, which included duties averaging 45 percent, was condemned by its opponents as the "Tariff of Abominations." John C. Calhoun (1782–1850) of South Carolina, vice president of the United States, asserted that a state had the right to nullify an act of Congress if it deemed the measure's impact harmful to citizens of that state. A tariff passed by Congress in 1832, which lowered some rates, did not stem the crisis.

Mr. Clay's official life, in 1803, to the end of it in 1852, is but one year short of half a century; and that the sum of all the intervals in it, will not amount to ten years. But mere duration of time in office, constitutes the smallest part of Mr. Clay's history. Throughout that long period, he has constantly been the most loved, and most implicitly followed by friends, and the most dreaded by opponents, of all living American politicians. In all the great questions which have agitated the country, and particularly in those great and fearful crises, the Missouri question[8]—the Nullification question,[9] and the late slavery question, as connected with the newly acquired territory, involving and endangering the stability of the Union,[10] his has been the leading and most conspicuous part. In 1824 he was first a candidate for the Presidency, and was defeated; and, although he was successively defeated for the same office in 1832, and in 1844, there has never been a moment since 1824 till after 1848 when a very large portion of the American people did not cling to him with an enthusiastic hope and purpose of still elevating him to the Presidency. With other men, to be defeated, was to be forgotten; but to him, defeat was but a trifling incident, neither changing him, or the world's estimate of him. Even those of both political parties, who have been preferred to him for the highest office, have run far briefer courses than he, and left him, still shining, high in the heavens of the political world. Jackson, Van Buren, Harrison, Polk, and Taylor, all rose *after,* and set long before him. The spell—the long enduring spell—with which the souls of men were bound to him, is a miracle. Who can compass it? It is probably true he owed his pre-eminence to no one quality, but to a fortunate combination of several. He was surpassingly eloquent; but many eloquent men fail utterly; and they are not, as a class, generally successful. His judgment was excellent; but many men of good judgment, live and die unnoticed. His will was indomitable; but this quality often secures to its owner nothing better than a character for useless obstinacy. These then were Mr. Clay's leading qualities. No one of them is very uncommon; but all taken together are rarely combined in a single individual; and this is probably the reason why such men as Henry Clay are so rare in the world.

Mr. Clay's eloquence did not consist, as many fine specimens of eloquence does [*sic*], of types and figures—of antithesis, and elegant arrangement of words and sentences; but rather of that deeply earnest and impassioned tone, and manner, which can proceed only from great sincerity and a thorough conviction, in the speaker of the justice and importance of his cause. This it is, that truly touches the chords of human sympathy; and those who heard Mr. Clay, never failed to be moved by it, or ever after-

Robert Whitechurch, after a drawing by P. F. Rothermel, *The United States Senate, A.D. 1850.* Engraving (Philadelphia: John M. Butler and Alfred Long, ca. 1855). Print showing Henry Clay advocating the Compromise of 1850 in the Old Senate Chamber.

wards, forgot the impression. All his efforts were made for practical effect. He never spoke merely to be heard. He never delivered a Fourth of July Oration, or an eulogy on an occasion like this. As a politician or statesman, no one was so habitually careful to avoid all sectional ground. Whatever he did, he did for the whole country. In the construction of his measures he ever carefully surveyed every part of the field, and duly weighed every conflicting interest. Feeling, as he did, and as the truth surely is, that the world's best hope depended on the continued Union of these States, he was ever jealous of, and watchful for, whatever might have the slightest tendency to separate them.

Mr. Clay's predominant sentiment, from first to last, was a deep devotion to the cause of human liberty—a strong sympathy with the oppressed every where, and an ardent wish for their elevation. With him, this was a primary and all controlling passion. Subsidiary to this was the conduct of his whole life. He loved his country partly because it was his own country, but mostly

Calhoun resigned as vice president and returned to South Carolina to lead the fight for nullification of the two tariffs. When South Carolina declared the tariffs null and void and threatened secession if the federal government attempted to force their collection, President Andrew Jackson responded by asking Congress to approve legislation giving him authority to call out the state militia and to use federal ships and troops to enforce the laws and collect federal revenue. Congress passed the Force Bill on February 20, 1833, thus setting the stage for a potential confrontation between the federal government and South Carolina. A crisis was averted when Clay and Calhoun fashioned a compromise tariff bill that reduced tariff rates to 20 percent by 1842. Ibid., 412–431.

10 Lincoln referred to the Compromise of 1850, the congressional measure that averted another sectional crisis over the expansion of slavery. When the United States acquired California, New Mexico, and Utah from Mexico in 1848 as part of the treaty ending the Mexican War, Congress became embroiled in an acrimonious debate over the question of whether slavery should be permitted or prohibited in these areas. Southerners, fearing that the potential emergence of several free states from new territories would upset the balance of political power in Congress, asserted their right to take their slaves into the newly acquired land. Northerners, on the other hand, responding to the growing antislavery movement in their region, attempted to prohibit slavery in the territories. As was the case during the Missouri crisis decades before, sectional tensions caused deadlock in Congress, with some Southerners again threatening secession. Clay, then serving in the Senate, introduced what he called a "comprehensive scheme" that addressed all the major issues in one bill: admit California as a free state; organize the New Mexico and Utah territories, allowing their residents to decide whether they would be free or

slave states; relinquish Texas's claim to New Mexico territory, with the federal government assuming the state's preannexation debts as compensation; block the abolition of slavery in Washington, D.C., without the consent of residents, compensation to slave owners, and the consent of Maryland; abolish the slave trade in the District of Columbia; strengthen the Fugitive Slave Law; and deny Congress the power to interfere with interstate slave trade. Clay failed to garner enough support to pass his omnibus package and left the capital a sick and depressed man. It was left to Senator Stephen A. Douglas of Illinois, chair of the Committee on Territories, to advance individual measures in Clay's package through Congress. Nevertheless, Clay received much acclaim for his role in saving the Union and strengthened his reputation as a leading statesman. Ibid., 730–761. For a concise history of the Compromise of 1850, see Robert V. Remini, *At the Edge of the Precipice: Henry Clay and the Compromise That Saved the Union* (New York: Basic Books, 2010).

11  James Otis (1725–1783) of Massachusetts was a leader in the American colonies' cause against Great Britain. He is best known for his phrase, "Taxation without representation is tyranny."

12  Patrick Henry (1736–1799) was a lawyer, planter, and politician who served as the first and sixth governor of Virginia. Remembered for his "Give me liberty, or give me death" speech, he was an early proponent of American independence from Great Britain; http://www.redhill.org/biography.html (accessed January 22, 2015).

13  Lincoln referred to the Northwest Ordinance, enacted by the Continental Congress on July 13, 1787, to ensure an orderly settlement of the territory to the north and west of the Ohio River. The ordinance included fourteen sections and six articles, the latter addressing religious liberty, due process of law, creation of public schools, relations

because it was a free country; and he burned with a zeal for its advancement, prosperity and glory, because he saw in such, the advancement, prosperity and glory, of human liberty, human right and human nature. He desired the prosperity of his countrymen partly because they were his countrymen, but chiefly to show to the world that freemen could be prosperous.

That his views and measures were always the wisest, needs not to be affirmed; nor should it be, on this occasion, where so many, thinking differently, join in doing honor to his memory. A free people, in times of peace and quiet—when pressed by no common danger—naturally divide into parties. At such times, the man who is of neither party, is not—cannot be, of any consequence. Mr. Clay, therefore, was of a party. Taking a prominent part, as he did, in all the great political questions of his country for the last half century, the wisdom of his course on many, is doubted and denied by a large portion of his countrymen; and of such it is not now proper to speak particularly. But there are many others, about his course upon which, there is little or no disagreement, amongst intelligent and patriotic Americans. Of these last are the War of 1812, the Missouri question, Nullification, and the now recent compromise measures. In 1812 Mr. Clay, though not unknown, was still a young man. Whether we should go to war with Great Britain, being the question of the day, a minority opposed the declaration of war by Congress, while the majority, though apparently inclining to war, had, for years, wavered, and hesitated to act decisively. Meanwhile British aggressions multiplied, and grew more daring and aggravated. By Mr. Clay, more than any other man, the struggle was brought to a decision in Congress. The question, being now fully before congress, came up, in a variety of ways, in rapid succession, on most of which occasions Mr. Clay spoke. Adding to all the logic, of which the subject was susceptible, that noble inspiration, which came to him as it came to no other, he aroused, and nerved, and inspired his friends, and confounded and bore-down all opposition. Several of his speeches, on these occasions, were reported, and are still extant; but the best of these all never was. During its delivery the reporters forgot their vocations, dropped their pens, and sat enchanted from near the beginning to quite the close. The speech now lives only in the memory of a few old men; and the enthusiasm with which they cherish their recollection of it is absolutely astonishing. The precise language of this speech we shall never know; but we do know—we cannot help knowing, that, with deep pathos, it pleaded the cause of the injured sailor—that it invoked the genius of the revolution—that it apostrophised the names of Otis,[11] of Henry[12] and of

Washington—that it appealed to the interest, the pride, the honor and the glory of the nation—that it shamed and taunted the timidity of friends—that it scorned, and scouted, and withered the temerity of domestic foes—that it bearded and defied the British Lion—and rising, and swelling, and maddening in its course, it sounded the onset, till the charge, the shock, the steady struggle, and the glorious victory, all passed in vivid review before the entranced hearers.

Important and exciting as was the War question, of 1812, it never so alarmed the sagacious statesmen of the country for the safety of the republic, as afterwards did the Missouri question. This sprang from that unfortunate source of discord—negro slavery. When our Federal Constitution was adopted, we owned no territory beyond the limits of ownership of the states, except the territory North-West of the River Ohio, and East of the Mississippi. What has since formed into the States of Maine, Kentucky, and Tennessee, was, I believe, within the limits of or owned by Massachusetts, Virginia, and North Carolina. As to the North Western Territory, provision had been made, even before the adoption of the Constitution, that slavery should never go there.[13] On the admission of the States into the Union carved from the territory we owned before the constitution, no question—or at most, no considerable question—arose about slavery—those which were within the limits of or owned by the old states, following, respectively, the condition of the parent state, and those within the North West territory, following the previously made provision. But in 1803 we purchased Louisiana of the French; and it included with much more, what has since been formed into the State of Missouri. With regard to it, nothing had been done to forestall the question of slavery. When, therefore, in 1819, Missouri, having formed a State constitution, without excluding slavery, and with slavery already actually existing within its limits, knocked at the door of the Union for admission, almost the entire representation of the non-slave-holding states, objected. A fearful and angry struggle instantly followed. This alarmed thinking men, more than any previous question, because, unlike all the former, it divided the country by geographical lines. Other questions had their opposing partizans in all localities of the country and in almost every family; so that no division of the Union could follow such, without a separation of friends, to quite as great an extent, as that of opponents. Not so with the Missouri question. On this a geographical line could be traced which, in the main, would separate opponents only. This was the danger, Mr. Jefferson, then in retirement wrote:

with native peoples, how territories become states, and slavery. Article VI was devoted to slavery and stated that "there shall be neither slavery nor involuntary servitude in the said territory." In the many debates over the expansion of slavery in the western territories prior to the Civil War, antislavery Northerners, including Lincoln, referred often to the Northwest Ordinance as evidence that Congress possessed the constitutional power to prohibit slavery in the territories and proof that the Founding Fathers were against slavery's expansion and expected and hoped that the institution would eventually die out. Lincoln often cited the Northwest Ordinance when speaking out against the Kansas-Nebraska Act. See "Speech on the Kansas-Nebraska Act at Peoria, Illinois, October 16, 1854," in this volume. Paul Finkelman argued that the Northwest Ordinance's Article VI on slavery was "ambivalent and far from clear," pointing out that bondage continued in the Northwest "for more than half a century." Paul Finkelman, *Slavery and the Founders: Race and Liberty in the Age of Jefferson* (New York: M. E. Sharpe, 1996), 34–37.

14  Lincoln inserted this passage from Thomas Jefferson, a man he admired almost as he did Clay, in order to place Clay's efforts on behalf of the Missouri Compromise and, later, the Compromise of 1850 in the context of the extreme danger slavery posed to the future of the Union. Moreover, Lincoln agreed with Jefferson's—and Clay's—proposed solution to slavery, a gradual process combining emancipation with "expatriation," or colonization. This passage is from a letter Thomas Jefferson wrote to John Holmes on April 22, 1820, in which he discussed slavery against the background of the Missouri crisis. Jefferson used the phrase "wolf by the ear," not "wolf by the ears" as cited by Lincoln. Thomas Jefferson, *The Writings of Thomas Jefferson,* ed. Paul Leicester Ford, 10 vols. (New York: G. P. Putnam's Sons, 1892–1899), 10:159. The phrase "wolf by the ear" is attributed to the Roman emperor Tiberius. Carl J. Richard, *The Founders and the Classics: Greece, Rome, and the American Enlightenment* (Cambridge, MA: Harvard University Press, 1994), 264n6. On Lincoln's use of and agreement with the Jefferson passage cited in this eulogy, see Kevin R. C. Gutzman, "Abraham Lincoln, Jeffersonian: The Colonization Chimera," in *Lincoln Emancipated: The President and the Politics of Race,* ed. Brian R. Dirck (De Kalb: Northern Illinois University Press, 2007), 65–67.

15  As speaker of the U.S. House of Representatives, Clay was one of this nation's strongest advocates for Latin American independence from Spanish rule, consistently urging the administrations of presidents Madison and Monroe to formally support the independence movement. Finally, on March 8, 1822, in the wake of the military successes of Simón Bolívar's forces in South America, and seven years after Clay first called for recognition, President Monroe agreed to formally recognize the independence of four Latin American countries (Mexico, Peru, Colombia, and

"I had for a long time ceased to read newspapers, or to pay any attention to public affairs, confident they were in good hands, and content to be a passenger in our bark to the shore from which I am not distant. But this momentous question, like a fire bell in the night, awakened, and filled me with terror. I considered it at once as the knell of the Union. It is hushed, indeed, for the moment. But this is a reprieve only, not a final sentence. A geographical line, co-inciding with a marked principle, moral and political, once conceived, and held up to the angry passions of men, will never be obliterated; and every irritation will mark it deeper and deeper. I can say, with conscious truth, that there is not a man on earth who would sacrifice more than I would to relieve us from this heavy reproach, in any *practicable* way. The cession of that kind of property, for so it is misnamed, is a bagatelle which would not cost me a second thought, if, in that way, a general emancipation, and *expatriation* could be effected; and, gradually, and with due sacrifices I think it might be. But as it is, we have the wolf by the ears and we can neither hold him, nor safely let him go. Justice is in one scale, and self-preservation in the other."[14]

Mr. Clay was in congress, and perceiving the danger, at once engaged his whole energies to avert it. It began, as I have said, in 1819; and it did not terminate till 1821. Missouri would not yield the point; and congress—that is, a majority in congress—by repeated votes, showed a determination to not admit the state unless it should yield. After several failures, and great labor on the part of Mr. Clay to so present the question that a majority could consent to admission, it was, by a vote, rejected, and as all seemed to think, finally. A sullen gloom hung over the nation. All felt that the rejection of Missouri, was equivalent to a dissolution of the Union; because those states which already had, what Missouri was rejected for refusing to relinquish, would go with Missouri. All deprecated and deplored this, but none saw how to avert it. For the judgment of Members to be convinced of the necessity of yielding, was not the whole difficulty; each had a constituency to meet, and to answer to. Mr. Clay, though worn down, and exhausted, was appealed to by members, to renew his efforts at compromise. He did so, and by some judicious modifications of his plan, coupled with laborious efforts with individual members, and his own over-mastering eloquence upon the floor, he finally secured the admission of the State. Brightly, and captivating as it had previously shown, it was now perceived that his great eloquence, was a mere embellishment, or, at most, but a helping hand to his inventive genius, and his devotion to his country in the day of her extreme peril.

After the settlement of the Missouri question, although a portion of the American people have differed with Mr. Clay, and a majority even, appear generally to have been opposed to him on questions of ordinary administration, he seems constantly to have been regarded by all, as *the* man for a crisis. Accordingly, in the days of Nullification, and more recently in the reappearance of the slavery question, connected with our territory newly acquired of Mexico, the task of devising a mode of adjustment, seems to have been cast upon Mr. Clay, by common consent—and his performance of the task, in each case, was little else than a literal fulfilment of the public expectation.

Mr. Clay's efforts in behalf of the South Americans,[15] and afterwards, in behalf of the Greeks,[16] in the times of their respective struggles for civil liberty are among the finest on record, upon the noblest of all themes; and bear ample corroboration of what I have said was his ruling passion—a love of liberty and right, unselfishly, and for their own sakes.

Having been led to allude to domestic slavery, so frequently already, I am unwilling to close without referring more particularly to Mr. Clay's views and conduct in regard to it. He ever was, on principle and in feeling, opposed to slavery. The very earliest, and one of the latest public efforts of his life, separated by a period of more than fifty years, were both made in favor of gradual emancipation of the slaves in Kentucky. He did not perceive, that on a question of human right, the negroes were to be excepted from the human race. And yet Mr. Clay was the owner of slaves. Cast into life where slavery was already widely spread and deeply seated, he did not perceive, as I think no wise man has perceived, how it could be at *once* eradicated, without producing a greater evil, even to the cause of human liberty itself. His feeling and his judgment, therefore, ever led him to oppose both extremes of opinion on the subject. Those who would shiver into fragments the Union of these States; tear to tatters its now venerated constitution; and even burn the last copy of the Bible, rather than slavery should continue a single hour, together with all their more halting sympathizers, have received, and are receiving their just execution; and the name, and opinions, and influence of Mr. Clay, are fully, and, as I trust, effectually and enduringly, arrayed against them. But I would also, if I could, array his name, opinions, and influence against the opposite extreme—against a few, but increasing number of men, who, for the sake of perpetuating slavery, are beginning to assail and to ridicule the white-man's charter of freedom—the declaration

Argentina). Latin Americans acknowledged Clay's efforts on their behalf, translating his speeches and erecting statues in his honor. In 1927, on the 150th anniversary of his birth, representatives from twenty Latin American countries gathered in Washington, D.C., to acknowledge his tireless support for their independence. Remini, *Henry Clay,* 154–155, 170, 173, 175–176.

16  In keeping with his support for freedom throughout the world, Clay supported Greek independence from Turkey. The revolt began in 1821, and by January of the next year Greece had declared independence. Clay spoke passionately in Congress for Greek independence, stating that "the Turk with all his power, and in all the elevation of his despotic throne . . . has felt the uncalculating valor of American freemen in some of his dominions; and when he is made to understand, that not only the Executive of this government, but that this nation; that our entire political fabric, base, column and entablature, rulers and people, with heart, soul, mind, and strength, are all on the side of the nation he is crushing, he will be more likely to restrain, than to increase his atrocities upon suffering and bleeding Greece." Ibid., 222–223.

17  Unlike many of the eulogies of Clay, Lincoln's addressed his subject's opposition to slavery. At this time in his career, Lincoln agreed with Clay's gradual, middle-ground approach to eradicating the institution. Like Clay, Lincoln opposed slavery but believed that the immediate emancipation sought by abolitionists was unconstitutional and would lead to disunion. On the other hand, he asserted that all men, including blacks, were created equal, as stated in the Declaration of Independence. Lincoln's views on slavery are discussed in Foner, *The Fiery Trial*. Lincoln's eulogy as it compared with others is addressed in Mark E. Neely Jr., "American Nationalism in the Image of Henry Clay: Abraham Lincoln's Eulogy on Henry Clay in Context," *Register of the Kentucky Historical Society* 73 (January 1975): 57.

18  John C. Calhoun was a zealous advocate of states' rights and slavery. In a June 17, 1848, speech in Congress that Lincoln may have heard and undoubtedly had read, Calhoun denounced the proposition "all men are born free and equal" as the "most false and dangerous of all political errors." According to the South Carolinian, there was no reason to insert the proposition into the Declaration of Independence, since it "made no necessary part of our justification in separating from the parent country, and declaring ourselves independent." John C. Calhoun, *The Collected Works of John C. Calhoun*, ed. Richard K. Crallé, 6 vols. (New York: Appleton, 1851–1854), 4:507–508.

19  The pen name of François-Marie Arouet (1649–1778), an eighteenth-century French philosopher and writer. Cited in *Lincoln's Selected Writings*, 77n6.

20  Henry Clay, *Speech of the Hon. Henry Clay, before the American Colonization Society, in the Hall of the House of Representatives, January 20, 1827* (Washington, 1827), 12–13.

that "all men are created free and equal."[17] So far as I have learned, the first American, of any note, to do or attempt this, was the late John C. Calhoun;[18] and if I mistake not, it soon after found its way into some of the messages of the Governors of South Carolina. We, however, look for, and are not much shocked by, political eccentricities and heresies in South Carolina. But, only last year, I saw with astonishment, what purported to be a letter of a very distinguished and influential clergyman of Virginia, copied with apparent approbation, into a St. Louis newspaper, containing the following, to me, very extraordinary language—

> "I am fully aware that there is a text in some Bibles that is not in mine. Professional abolitionists have made more use of it, than of any passage in the Bible. It came, however, as I trace it, from Saint Voltaire,[19] and was baptized by Thomas Jefferson, and since almost universally regarded as canonical authority '*All men are born free and equal.*' This is a genuine coin in the political currency of our generation. I am sorry to say that I have never seen two men of whom it is true. But I must admit I never saw the Siamese twins, and therefore will not dogmatically say that no man ever saw a proof of this sage aphorism."

This sounds strange in republican America. The like was not heard in the fresher days of the Republic. Let us contrast with it the language of that truly national man, whose life and death we now commemorate and lament. I quote from a speech of Mr. Clay delivered before the American Colonization Society in 1827.

> "We are reproached with doing mischief by the agitation of this question. The society goes into no household to disturb its domestic tranquility; it addresses itself to no slaves to weaken their obligations of obedience. It seeks to affect no man's property. It neither has the power nor the will to affect the property of any one contrary to his consent. The execution of its scheme would augment instead of diminishing the value of the property left behind. The society, composed of free men, concerns itself only with the free. Collateral consequences we are not responsible for. It is not this society which has produced the great moral revolution which the age exhibits. What would they, who thus reproach us, have done? If they would repress all tendencies toward liberty, and ultimate emancipation, they must do more than to put down the benevolent efforts of this society. They must go back to the era of our liberty and independence, and muzzle the cannon

which thunders its annual joyous return. They must renew the slave trade with all its train of atrocities. They must suppress the workings of British philanthropy, seeking to meliorate the condition of the unfortunate West Indian slave. They must arrest the career of South American deliverance from thraldom. They must blow out the moral lights around us, and extinguish that greatest torch of all which America presents to a benighted world—pointing the way to their rights, their liberties, and their happiness. And when they have achieved all those purposes their work will be yet incomplete. They must penetrate the human soul, and eradicate the light of reason, and the love of liberty. Then, and not till then, when universal darkness and despair prevail, can you perpetuate slavery, and repress all sympathy, and all humane, and benevolent efforts among free men, in behalf of the unhappy portion of our race doomed to bondage."[20]

The American Colonization Society was organized in 1816. Mr. Clay, though not its projector, was one of its earliest members; and he died, as for the many preceding years he had been, its President.[21] It was one of the most cherished objects of his direct care and consideration; and the association of his name with it has probably been its very greatest collateral support. He considered it no demerit in the society, that it tended to relieve slave-holders from the troublesome presence of the free negroes; but this was far from being its whole merit in his estimation. In the same speech from which I have quoted he says: "There is a moral fitness in the idea of returning to Africa her children, whose ancestors have been torn from her by the ruthless hand of fraud and violence. Transplanted in a foreign land, they will carry back to their native soil the rich fruits of religion, civilization, law, and liberty. May it not be one of the great designs of the Ruler of the universe, (whose ways are often inscrutable by short-sighted mortals,) thus to transform an original crime, into a signal blessing to that most unfortunate portion of the globe?"[22] This suggestion of the possible ultimate redemption of the African race and African continent, was made twenty-five years ago. Every succeeding year he added strength to the hope of its realization. May it indeed be realized! Pharaoh's country was cursed with plagues, and his hosts were drowned in the Red Sea for striving to retain a captive people who had already served them more than four hundred years. May like disasters never befall us! If as the friends of colonization hope, the present and coming generations of our countrymen shall by any means, succeed in freeing our land from the dangerous presence of slavery; and, at the same time, in re-

21 The American Colonization Society (ACS) was founded in 1816 with the purpose of transporting free American blacks to Africa. Although slavery had been abolished in the North, many whites in the region resented the presence of free blacks. The rapid growth of the free black population in the years after the Revolution gave rise to the idea of colonization as a way to remove free black Americans from the country. As the society grew in popularity in the 1820s, local auxiliaries were established in both the North and the South, with a number of prominent white Americans, including Henry Clay, providing support. In 1819 Congress passed the Slave Trade Act, which included funding for returning slaves rescued from the illegal slave trade. The ACS used the funds to establish a colony of free blacks in Africa. Between its founding and 1860, the ACS transported fewer than 12,000 blacks, most of whom were slaves emancipated by their owners with the intention of deporting them to Liberia. Colonization, however, was resisted by most free blacks and condemned by leading abolitionists, who favored immediate emancipation and the creation of a biracial society in America. Over time, many antislavery leaders turned away from the ACS. Clay and Lincoln, however, remained active promoters of colonization. Clay, a slaveholder, was active in the ACS since its founding, serving as president from 1836 until his death. Gradual emancipation, linked with colonization, was part of his economic plan to transform Kentucky into a vibrant, diversified economy equal to any found in the North. After Clay's death, Lincoln became one of the leading political voices for colonization as part of his gradual, middle-ground approach to ending slavery. He would support colonization until 1862. It must be noted that Lincoln's views on colonization were more moderate compared with those of some of its proponents. He favored voluntary as opposed to forced colonization, and he neither

feared a racial war if free blacks remained in the country, as Jefferson did, nor viewed free blacks as a degraded group who would undermine the stability of American society. The history of the ACS is surveyed in Allan Yarema, *The American Colonization Society: An Avenue to Freedom?* (Lanham, MD: University Press of America, 2006). For a concise analysis of Lincoln's support of colonization, see Eric Foner, "Lincoln and Colonization," in *Our Lincoln: New Perspectives on Lincoln and His World,* ed. Eric Foner (New York: W. W. Norton, 2008), 135–166.

22  Clay, *Speech of the Hon. Henry Clay,* 11–12.

23  In August 1862, President Lincoln, in a letter to John M. Clay acknowledging the gift of a snuffbox owned by his "great and patriotic" father, mentioned that he could still "recognize" Clay's voice, "speaking as it ever spoke, for the Union, the Constitution, and the freedom of mankind." *CW,* 5:364.

storing a captive people to their long-lost father-land, with bright prospects for the future; and this too, so gradually, that neither races nor individuals shall have suffered the change, it will indeed be a glorious consummation. And if, to such a consummation, the efforts of Mr. Clay shall have contributed, it will be what he most ardently wished, and none of his labors will have been more valuable to his country and his kind.

But Henry Clay is dead.[23] His long and eventful life is closed. Our country is prosperous and powerful; but could it have been quite all it has been, and is, and is to be, without Henry Clay? Such a man the times have demanded, and such, in the providence of God was given us. But he is gone. Let us strive to deserve, as far as mortals may, the continued care of Divine Providence, trusting that, in future emergencies, He will not fail to provide us the instruments of safety and security.

# Fragments on Government

## [July 1, 1854?]

*In these two fragments Lincoln expresses his view on the role of government, particularly its encouragement and support of economic opportunity and individual enterprise through education and internal improvements.*

THE LEGITIMATE OBJECT OF GOVERNMENT,[1] IS TO DO FOR A COMMUNITY of people, whatever they need to have done, but can not do, *at all,* or can not, *so well do,* for themselves—in their separate, and individual capacities.

In all that the people can individually do as well for themselves, government ought not to interfere.[2]

The desirable things which the individuals of a people can not do, or can not well do, for themselves, fall into two classes: those which have relation to *wrongs,* and those which have not. Each of these branch off into an infinite variety of subdivisions.

The first—that in relation to wrongs—embraces all crimes, misdemeanors, and non-performance of contracts. The other embraces all which, in its nature, and without wrong, requires combined action, as public roads and highways, public schools, charities, pauperism, orphanage, estates of the deceased, and the machinery of government itself.

From this it appears that if all men were just, there still would be *some,* though not *so much,* need of government.

. . .

Government is a combination of the people of a country to effect certain objects by joint effort. The best framed and best administered governments are necessarily expensive; while by errors in frame and maladministration most of them are more onerous than they need to be, and some of them very oppressive. Why, then, should we have government? Why not each individual take to himself the whole fruit of his labor, without having any of it taxed away, in services, corn, or money? Why not take just so much land as he can cultivate with his own hands, without buying it of any one?

The legitimate object of government is "to do for the people what needs to be done, but which they can not, by individual effort, do at all, or do so

1 Nicolay and Hay, in *Complete Works,* assigned the date to these fragmentary writings on government and it is used in *CW,* although the editor of the latter readily admits that the date was retained "for want of satisfactory evidence to the contrary." *CW,* 2:221n1. It appears that the second piece was written after the first, and was intended as a revision. It is not known if Lincoln ever incorporated these thoughts into a lecture or speech. If he did, the existence of such a lecture or speech is unknown.

2 From his first political campaign Lincoln espoused the Whig economic philosophy that government should aid individual initiative and the right to rise economically, through federal government policies that help individuals to support themselves and become economically independent, such as education, internal improvements, protective tariffs, and defense. Lincoln's philosophy—and that of Whigs in general—differed from that advocated by the Democratic Party, which, based on a strict interpretation of the Constitution, favored a limited role for the federal government in the affairs of the American people, especially in the economic sphere. Lincoln's economic philosophy is covered by Boritt, *Economics of the American Dream.* For Whig and Democratic Party philosophies of government, see Howe, *Political Culture of the American Whigs,* and Joel H. Silbey, *A Respectable Minority: The Democratic Party in the Civil War Era, 1860–1868* (New York: W. W. Norton, 1977).

REVERE HOUSE

WORCESTER & CO

*Daniel Webster Addressing the Citizens of Boston in Front of the Revere House, ca. 1850s.* Engraving (Worcester & Co., ca. 1851). Lincoln admired Webster as an orator, and historians have noted that Lincoln opened his House Divided speech in a vein similar to Webster's famous second reply to Senator Robert Y. Hayne in 1830.

well, for themselves." There are many such things—some of them exist independently of the injustice in the world. Making and maintaining roads, bridges, and the like; providing for the helpless young and afflicted; common schools; and disposing of deceased men's property, are instances.

But a far larger class of objects springs from the injustice of men. If one people will make war upon another, it is a necessity with that other to unite and cooperate for defense. Hence the military department. If some men will kill, or beat, or constrain others, or despoil them of property, by force, or noncompliance with contracts, it is a common object with peaceful and just men to prevent it. Hence the criminal and civil departments.

# Fragments on Slavery

## [April 1, 1854?]

*In these two fragments relating to slavery, Lincoln appeared to be forming an argument against the emerging Southern contention that slave labor was not only beneficial to the slave but was also more productive than free labor.*

. . . DENT TRUTH.[1] MADE SO PLAIN BY OUR GOOD FATHER IN HEAVEN, that all *feel* and *understand* it, even down to brutes and creeping insects. The ant, who has toiled and dragged a crumb to his nest, will furiously defend the fruit of his labor, against whatever robber assails him. So plain, that the most dumb and stupid slave that ever toiled for a master, does constantly *know* that he is wronged. So plain that no one, high or low, ever does mistake it, except in a plainly *selfish* way; for although volume upon volume is written to prove slavery is a very good thing, we never hear of the man who wishes to take the good of it, *by being a slave himself.*[2]

*Most governments* have been based, practically, on the denial of equal rights of men, as I have, in part, stated them; *ours* began, by *affirming* those rights. *They* said, some men are too *ignorant,* and *vicious,* to share in government. Possibly so, said we; and, by your system, you would always keep them ignorant, and vicious. We proposed to give *all* a chance; and we expected the weak to grow stronger, the ignorant, wiser; and all better, and happier together.

We made the experiment; and the fruit is before us. Look at it—think of it. Look at it, in it's [*sic*] aggregate grandeur, of extent of country, and numbers of population—of ship, and steamboat, and rail—

. . .

If A. can prove, however conclusively, that he may, of right, enslave B.—why not B. snatch the same argument, and prove equally, that he may enslave A.?

You say A. is white, and B. is black. It is *color,* then; the lighter, having the right to enslave the darker? Take care. By this rule, you are to be slave to the first man you meet, with a fairer skin than your own.

You do not mean *color* exactly?—You mean the whites are *intellectually*

1 *CW* retains the arbitrary date assigned to these fragments by Nicolay and Hay in *Complete Works,* "for want of conclusive evidence to the contrary." The editor of *CW* believes the fragments may have been part of a speech Lincoln composed in 1858 or 1859. *CW,* 2:222n1.

2 Two recent Lincoln biographers have speculated that Lincoln was responding to proslavery arguments advanced by Southern writers, including George Fitzhugh (1806–1881), the Virginia lawyer and planter who wrote *Sociology for the South, or the Failure of Free Society,* published in Richmond, Virginia, in 1854, a work that not only claimed that slavery was beneficial to enslaved blacks, who could not survive on their own, but also criticized the free-labor society as one in which exploited workers are forced to work for low wages and live in impoverished conditions. Lincoln's law partner, William Herndon, owned a copy of Fitzhugh's book, which Lincoln may have read. Lincoln's message was a clear and simple one: if slavery is such a positive good, why do we not see advocates of slavery choosing it for themselves. Donald, *Lincoln,* 187; White, *A. Lincoln,* 194–195.

Taylor (first name unknown), *The American Slave Market*. Oil on canvas (1852). One of the greatest fears of the enslaved was to be sold and separated from loved ones.

the superiors of the blacks, and, therefore have the right to enslave them? Take care again. By this rule, you are to be slave to the first man you meet, with an intellect superior to your own.

But, say you, it is a question of *interest;* and, if you can make it your *interest,* you have the right to enslave another. Very well. And if he can make it his interest, he has the right to enslave you.

# Speech on the Kansas-Nebraska Act at Peoria, Illinois

## October 16, 1854

THE REPEAL OF THE MISSOURI COMPROMISE, AND THE PROPRIETY OF its restoration, constitute the subject of what I am about to say.[1]

As I desire to present my own connected view of this subject, my remarks will not be, specifically, an answer to Judge Douglas;[2] yet, as I proceed, the main points he has presented will arise, and will receive such respectful attention as I may be able to give them.[3]

I wish further to say, that I do not propose to question the patriotism, or assail the motives of any man, or class of men; but rather to strictly confine myself to the naked merits of the question.[4]

I also wish to be no less than National in all the positions I may take; and whenever I take ground which others have thought, or may think, narrow, sectional and dangerous to the Union, I hope to give a reason, which will appear sufficient, at least to some, why I think differently.[5]

And, as this subject is no other, than part and parcel of the larger general question of domestic-slavery, I wish to MAKE and to KEEP the distinction between the EXISTING institution, and the EXTENSION of it, so broad, and so clear, that no honest man can misunderstand me, and no dishonest one, successfully misinterpret me.[6]

In order to [get?] a clear understanding of what the Missouri Compromise is, a short history of the preceding kindred subjects will perhaps be proper. When we established our independence, we did not own, or claim, the country to which this compromise applies. Indeed, strictly speaking, the confederacy then owned no country at all; the States respectively owned the country within their limits; and some of them owned territory beyond their strict State limits. Virginia thus owned the North-Western territory—the country out of which the principal part of Ohio, all Indiana, all Illinois, all Michigan, and all Wisconsin, have since been formed. She also owned (perhaps within her then limits) what has since been formed into the State of

*The passage of the Kansas-Nebraska Act in 1854 profoundly transformed Lincoln's political career. The purpose of the new law, authored by Illinois senator Stephen A. Douglas, was to give white settlers the power to determine whether their territories would be admitted to the Union as free or slave states. Removing this responsibility from Congress and circumventing the Missouri Compromise of 1820 in the name of "popular sovereignty," the act unleashed indignation in the North, violence and bloodshed in Kansas, and political turmoil that resulted in the death of the Whig Party and the birth of the Republican Party. Aroused "as he had never been before," Lincoln responded by returning to the political arena as a leader of an anti-Nebraska coalition in Illinois, speaking out passionately against what he perceived as a covert attempt to extend slavery into the territories. Of the several speeches he delivered in the fall of 1854, his Peoria speech presented the most complete summary of Lincoln's views at that time on slavery and on African Americans.*

1 The Missouri Compromise of 1820 permitted the admission of Missouri as a slave state and Maine as a free state, and prohibited slavery in territories north and west of Missouri. The measure also reaffirmed Congress's authority to prohibit slavery in the territories. The Missouri Compromise, along with the Compromise of 1850, defused rancorous debates and threats of disunion in Congress over the slavery issue. The relative calm resulting from the 1850 compromise was shattered by the debates over and passage of the Kansas-Nebraska Act in May 1854. Stephen A. Douglas, U.S. senator from Illinois and chair of the Committee on Territories, was a committed expansionist who promoted western settlement along with the construction of a transcontinental railroad, via a northern route, linking the East and West coasts. A route passing through Chicago, the senator believed, would reap enormous economic benefits not only for the city and his constituents

but also for himself as an owner of Chicago real
estate. The area west of Missouri, however, was
unorganized territory in 1854, home to several
Native American tribes and white settlers. With
Southern congressmen refusing to support
legislation to organize the region because slavery
was prohibited in territories north of 36°30′
latitude in accordance with the Missouri Compromise, Douglas devised a solution based on the
concept of "popular sovereignty." Espoused in 1848
by Lewis Cass, Democratic candidate for president
that year, the concept was based on local self-
determination: residents of territories, acting
through their legislatures, make their own
decisions regarding slavery. Despite the outrage
generated in the North in response to Douglas's
legislation, perceived by many as a veiled attempt
to extend slavery into the territories, the Kansas-
Nebraska Act was passed by the Senate on March
3, 1854, and the House on May 22, and signed into
law by President Franklin Pierce (1804–1869).
Southerners supported the bill, believing they
could now take their slaves into western territories
and, hopefully, establish slave states in the region
to maintain the balance of power in the U.S.
Senate. Northerners, including anti-Nebraska
Democrats, rejected the bill for similar reasons,
insisting that it broke faith with the North-South
compromise of 1820 to preserve the territories
north of 36°30′ latitude for free labor. Prominent
antislavery advocates and political leaders harshly
criticized the act and Douglas personally. An
"Appeal of the Independent Democrats," condemning the legislation and castigating Douglas
for plotting to make free Nebraska a "dreary region
of despotism, inhabited by masters and slaves" in
order to aid Douglas in his quest for the presidency
in 1856, appeared in several newspapers. Senators
Salmon P. Chase (1808–1873) of Ohio, Edward
Everett (1794–1865) of Massachusetts, William H.
Seward (1801–1872) of New York, and Charles

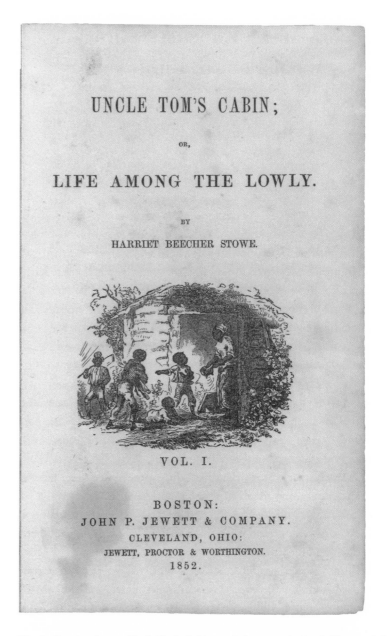

Harriet Beecher Stowe, *Uncle Tom's Cabin; or, Life among the Lowly* (Boston: John P.
Jewett & Company, 1852). Title page of Stowe's runaway best-selling novel, which
changed forever how Americans viewed slavery.

Kentucky. North Carolina thus owned what is now the State of Tennessee; and South Carolina and Georgia, in separate parts, owned what are now Mississippi and Alabama. Connecticut, I think, owned the little remaining part of Ohio—being the same where they now send Giddings[7] to Congress, and beat all creation at making cheese. These territories, together with the States themselves, constituted all the country over which the confederacy then claimed any sort of jurisdiction. We were then living under the Articles of Confederation, which were superceded by the Constitution several years afterwards. The question of ceding these territories to the general government was set on foot. Mr. Jefferson, the author of the Declaration of Independence, and otherwise a chief actor in the revolution; then a delegate in Congress; afterwards twice President; who was, is, and perhaps will continue to be, the most distinguished politician of our history;[8] a Virginian by birth and continued residence, and withal, a slave-holder; conceived the idea of taking that occasion, to prevent slavery ever going into the northwestern territory. He prevailed on the Virginia Legislature to adopt his views, and to cede the territory, making the prohibition of slavery therein, a condition of the deed.[9] Congress accepted the cession, with the condition; and in the first Ordinance (which the acts of Congress were then called) for the government of the territory, provided that slavery should never be permitted therein. This is the famed ordinance of '87 so often spoken of.[10] Thenceforward, for sixty-one years, and until in 1848, the last scrap of this territory came into the Union as the State of Wisconsin, all parties acted in quiet obedience to this ordinance. It is now what Jefferson foresaw and intended—the happy home of teeming millions of free, white, prosperous people, and no slave amongst them.

Thus, with the author of the declaration of Independence, the policy of prohibiting slavery in new territory originated. Thus, away back of the constitution, in the pure fresh, free breath of the revolution, the State of Virginia, and the National congress put that policy in practice. Thus through sixty odd of the best years of the republic did that policy steadily work its great and beneficent end. And thus, in those five states, and five millions of free enterprising people, we have before us the rich fruits of this policy. But *now* new light breaks upon us.[11] Now congress declares this ought never to have been; and the like of it, must never be again. The sacred right of self government is grossly violated by it! We even find some men, who drew their first breath, and every other breath of their lives, under this very restriction, now live in dread of absolute suffocation, if they should be restricted in the "sacred right" of taking slaves to Nebraska. That *perfect* lib-

Sumner (1811–1874) of Massachusetts fiercely opposed the bill. Although Douglas expected the Kansas-Nebraska bill to engender a storm of controversy, he was surprised by the intensity of the criticism. He later remarked that "I could then travel from Boston to Chicago by the light of my own effigies" and that he found "my effigy upon every tree" along the Western Reserve of Ohio. Douglas also failed to anticipate the dramatic impact the Kansas-Nebraska Act would have on the American political system; the bill destroyed the Whig Party, divided the Democratic Party, and led to the birth of the Republican Party. It also inflamed sectional tensions and incited a violent and bloody border war in Kansas. The passage from an "Appeal of the Independent Democrats" is cited in David M. Potter, *The Impending Crisis 1848–1861* (New York: Harper & Row, 1976), 163. Douglas's quotes are cited in his July 17, 1858, speech in Springfield, Illinois, in *Political Speeches and Debates of Abraham Lincoln and Stephen A. Douglas 1854–1861* (Chicago: Scott, Foresman & Company, 1896), 124. For Douglas's role in the drafting and passage of the Kansas-Nebraska Act and the critical responses, see Robert W. Johannsen, *Stephen A. Douglas* (Urbana: University of Illinois Press, 1997), 402–405, 409–410, 432–434, 451; and James Rawley, "Stephen A. Douglas and the Kansas-Nebraska Act," in *The Nebraska-Kansas Act of 1854*, ed. John R. Wunder and Joann M. Ross (Lincoln: University of Nebraska Press, 2008), 70–71, 74–75.

2    In his speeches Lincoln often referred to Douglas as "Judge" because Douglas had once served a brief term on the Illinois Supreme Court. Douglas at this time was considered one of the most prominent Democrats serving in the U.S. Senate. Born in Brandon, Vermont, he resided in upstate New York for several years before settling in Illinois in 1833. Admitted to the Illinois bar in 1834, Douglas, a follower of President Andrew

Jackson, soon became active in the state's Democratic Party. Two years later he was elected to the Illinois House of Representatives, and in 1842 he was named to the Illinois State Supreme Court. Elected to Congress in 1843, the diminutive Douglas, standing five feet four inches tall, earned the nickname "Little Giant" for his aggressive debating skills. In Congress, Douglas emerged as an ardent expansionist and a strong advocate for settling and organizing the western territories. The Whig Lincoln and Democrat Douglas met early in their political careers and developed a rivalry as their careers progressed. By 1854, however, Lincoln's political career appeared at an end while the rising Douglas was perceived by many observers as a future candidate for the presidency. The passage of the Kansas-Nebraska Act revived their rivalry, which would continue through the 1858 Illinois U.S. Senate and 1860 presidential campaigns. The definitive biographical account of Douglas's life and political career is Johannsen, *Stephen A. Douglas.* The Lincoln-Douglas rivalry is reviewed in Roy Morris Jr., *The Long Pursuit: Abraham Lincoln's Thirty-Year Struggle with Stephen Douglas for the Heart and Soul of America* (New York: HarperCollins/Smithsonian Books, 2008). See also, Martin H. Quitt, "In the Shadow of the Little Giant: Lincoln before the Great Debates," *Journal of the Abraham Lincoln Association* 36 (Winter 2015): 18–46.

3    After his one term in Congress ended in 1849 and he failed in his quest for the patronage appointment he desired from President Zachary Taylor, Lincoln entered into a period of political hibernation, emerging only occasionally, to deliver eulogies for Taylor and Henry Clay and to campaign on behalf of Winfield Scott, the Whig candidate for president in 1852. From the time he left Congress until he reentered the political arena in the wake of the Kansas-Nebraska Act, Lincoln concentrated on his law practice. As Lincoln stated years later in two autobiographical sketches (see "Letter to Jesse W. Fell, Enclosing an Autobiographical Sketch, December 20, 1859" and "Autobiography Written for John L. Scripps, [ca. June 1860]," in this volume) he "practiced law more assiduously than ever before" while "losing interest in politics." It was the "repeal of the Missouri compromise," he wrote, that "aroused him as he had never been before," compelling him to continue his political career with renewed passion. Before 1854 Lincoln's political interests were primarily economic. Except for his 1837 protest in the Illinois legislature and his aborted congressional legislation concerning slavery in Washington, D.C., in 1849, Lincoln said little publicly

about slavery. This changed with the Kansas-Nebraska Act: fighting against slavery's expansion became Lincoln's primary political objective for the remainder of the decade. He did not commence his public campaign against the Kansas-Nebraska bill until the late summer of 1854, stumping across Illinois for the anti-Nebraska congressional candidacy of fellow Whig Richard Yates (see note 56), running for the Illinois state legislature himself, and speaking out against the repeal of the Missouri Compromise and the extension of slavery into the territories. His arguments against the legislation were based on thorough preparation, consisting of hours of research in the library of the Illinois Statehouse to familiarize himself with details of the Northwest Ordinance of 1787, the Louisiana Purchase of 1803, the Missouri Compromise of 1820, and their relationship to the slavery question. He spoke against Kansas-Nebraska in Winchester on August 26, Carrollton on August 28, Bloomington on September 12 and 26, and in Springfield on October 4, before he spoke at Peoria, sometimes following Douglas, who had embarked on a speaking tour of the state to defend the act, to the stage. Lincoln's Peoria speech was the fullest version of his previous anti-Nebraska arguments. *CW,* 2:226–227, 229–233, 234–247; Miers, *Lincoln Day by Day,* 2:126–129; and Lewis E. Lehrman, *Lincoln at Peoria: The Turning Point* (Mechanicsburg, PA: Stackpole Books, 2008), 33, 111. Lincoln probably was the author of several anti-Nebraska editorials that appeared in the *Illinois State Journal* during 1854, certainly the one published on September 11, in which he demonstrated in a folksy manner the absurdity of Section 14 of the act: "It repeals the Missouri Compromise; and then puts in a declaration that it is not intended by this repeal to legislate slavery in or exclude it therefrom, the territory. . . . The state of the case in a few words, is this: The Missouri Compromise excluded slavery from the Kansas-Nebraska territory. The repeal opened the territories to slavery. If there is any meaning to the declaration in the 14th section, that it does not mean to legislate slavery into the territories, [it] is this: that it does not require slaves to be sent there. The Kansas and Nebraska territories are now open to slavery as Mississippi or Arkansas were when they were territories. To illustrate the case—Abraham Lincoln has a fine meadow, containing beautiful springs of water, and well fenced, which John Calhoun had agreed with Abraham (originally owning the land in common) should be his, and the agreement had been consummated in the most solemn manner, regarded by both as sacred. John Calhoun, however, in the course of time, had become owner of an extensive herd of cattle—the prairie grass had become dried up and there was no convenient water to be had. John Calhoun then looks with a longing eye on Lincoln's meadow, and goes to it and throws down the fences, and exposes it to the ravages of his starving and famishing cattle. 'You rascal,' says Lincoln, 'what have you done? what do you do this for?' 'Oh,' replies Calhoun, 'everything is right. I have taken down your fence; but nothing more. It is my true intent and meaning not to drive my cattle into your meadow, nor to exclude them therefrom, but to leave them perfectly free to form their own notions of the feed, and to direct their movements in their own way!' Now would not the man who committed this outrage be deemed both a knave and a fool,—a knave in removing the restrictive fence, which he had solemnly pledged himself to sustain;—and a fool in supposing that there could be one man found in the country to believe that he had not pulled down the fence for the purpose of opening the meadow for his cattle?" *CW,* 2:229–230. John Calhoun (1808–1859), referred to in Lincoln's analogy, once served as Sangamon County surveyor in New Salem, Illinois, and in 1833 employed Lincoln as a deputy surveyor. An ardent Jacksonian Democrat, Calhoun was a lawyer and served as mayor of Springfield, Illinois, from 1849 to 1851. He supported the Kansas-Nebraska Act and debated Lincoln on the issue in Springfield on September 9, 1854. Neely, *Lincoln Encyclopedia,* 44; and Lehrman, *Lincoln at Peoria,* 24.

4   Lincoln made similar remarks at the beginning of his October 4 speech in Springfield, stating that it was not his intention to "assail the motives" nor to "impeach the honesty of any man who voted for the Nebraska Bill, much less, his distinguished friend, Judge Douglas." Moreover, he credited Douglas for "honesty of intention and true patriotism—referring whatever of wrong he might happen to find among his actions, entirely to a mistaken sense of duty." Cited in Burlingame, *Abraham Lincoln,* 1:378.

5   In the early afternoon on the day of Lincoln's Peoria speech, Douglas spoke to a large crowd in front of the town's courthouse. Lincoln was in attendance and, as part of an agreement with Douglas, was called to the stage to respond to the senator's remarks. Sensing the crowd was tired and hungry after listening to his rival's three-hour speech, and hoping to attract a larger crowd in the evening, Lincoln asked the crowd to come back later, after dinner: "I do not arise to speak to you now, if I can stipulate with the audience to meet me here at half past 6 or 7 o'clock. It is now

several minutes past five, and Judge Douglas has spoken over three hours. If you hear me at all, I wish you to hear me thro'. It will take me as long as it has taken him. That will carry us beyond eight o'clock at night. Now every one of you who can remain that long, can just as well get his supper, meet me at seven, and remain one hour or two later. The Judge has already informed you that he is to have an hour to reply to me. I doubt not but you have been a little surprised to learn that I have consented to give one of his high reputation and known ability, this advantage of me. Indeed my consenting to it, though reluctant, was not wholly unselfish; for I suspected if it were understood, that the Judge was entirely done, you democrats would leave, and not hear me; but by giving him the close, I felt confident you would stay for the fun of hearing him skin me." Lincoln reportedly asked for the crowd's consent, which he received with a roar of approval. Lincoln spoke for three hours, with Douglas's response lasting approximately an hour. Lincoln's remarks were published in the *Illinois State Journal* in seven installments, on October 21, 23, 24, 25, 26, 27, and 28. *CW,* 2:247–248, 283. Lehrman, *Lincoln at Peoria,* 55–56, 58.

6   Despite his abhorrence of slavery, Lincoln made it clear that he was not an abolitionist. What he espoused was restricting slavery's expansion, not immediate emancipation or interfering with the institution where it already existed. He revered the Constitution, which he acknowledged protected slavery where it was established. This principle became the core philosophy of the future Republican Party.

7   Joshua Reed Giddings was born in Pennsylvania and moved to Ohio in 1806, where he was admitted to the bar in 1821. A committed abolitionist Whig, Giddings served in Congress, off and on, between 1838 and 1859. Douglas referred to him as "Father Giddings, the high priest of Abolition." He was one of Lincoln's fellow lodgers in Mrs. Spriggs's boardinghouse when the latter served in Congress. After his election as president, Lincoln appointed Giddings consul general to British North American Provinces. "Giddings, Joshua Reed," Biographical Directory of the United States Congress, http://bioguide.congress.gov/scripts/biodisplay.pl?index=G000167 (accessed January 23, 2015).

8   Lincoln, who rarely mentioned Jefferson before 1854, honored Jefferson primarily for the Declaration of Independence, but he was not an advocate for Jefferson's agrarian states' rights and antimanu-

facturing philosophy, which contrasted starkly with Whig and, later, Republican Party beliefs. See Sean Wilentz, "Abraham Lincoln and Jacksonian Democracy," in *Our Lincoln: New Perspectives on Lincoln and His World,* ed. Eric Foner (New York: W. W. Norton, 2008), 71–72.

9   Lincoln later admitted this statement was a mistake. In a June 16, 1860, letter to John Locke Scripps (1818–1866), Lincoln wrote that in his Peoria speech, "I have said the prohibition of slavery in the N.W. Territory was made a condition in the Virginia deed of cession. That is an error. Such prohibition is not a condition of the deed." He also referenced his mistake in a letter written on September 13 of that year. *CW,* 4:77, 115.

10   Known as the Northwest Ordinance. See "Eulogy for Henry Clay, July 6, 1852," note 13, in this volume.

11   Having demonstrated the benefits of the Northwest Ordinance of 1787 to the nation by prohibiting slavery in the region, Lincoln used biting sarcasm when referring to Douglas's doctrine of popular sovereignty. He employed similar language in his September 4 Springfield speech: "Were not the people who were to settle that territory and form those States, capable of managing their own affairs—of deciding all questions of domestic concern—slavery included—for themselves? Why, then, did the founders of liberty and republicanism on this continent tie their hands—rob them of popular sovereignty— deny them the right of self government in all things?" The ordinance was accepted and obeyed, with the result that no states in the world "have ever advanced as rapidly in population, wealth, the arts and appliances of life, and now have such promise of prospective greatness, as the very States that were born under the ordinance of '87, and were deprived of the blessings of 'popular sovereignty,' as contained in the Nebraska Bill, and

erty they sigh for—the liberty of making slaves of other people—Jefferson never thought of; their own father never thought of; they never thought of themselves, a year ago. How fortunate for them, they did not sooner become sensible of their great misery! Oh, how difficult it is to treat with respect, such assaults upon all we have ever really held sacred.

But to return to history. In 1803, we purchased what was then called Louisiana, of France. It included the now states of Louisiana, Arkansas, Missouri, and Iowa; also the territory of Minnesota, and the present bone of contention, Kansas and Nebraska. Slavery already existed among the French at New Orleans; and, to some extent, at St. Louis. In 1812 Louisiana came into the Union as a slave state, without controversy. In 1818 or '19, Missouri showed signs of a wish to come in with slavery. This was resisted by northern members of Congress; and thus began the first great slavery agitation in the nation. This controversy lasted several months, and became very angry and exciting; the House of Representatives voting steadily for the prohibition of slavery in Missouri, and the Senate voting as steadily against it. Threats of breaking up the Union were freely made; and the ablest public men of the day became seriously alarmed. At length a compromise was made, in which, like all compromises, both sides yielded something. It was a law passed on the 6th day of March, 1820, providing that Missouri might come into the Union *with* slavery, but that in all the remaining part of the territory purchased of France, which lies north of 36 degrees and 30 minutes north latitude, slavery should never be permitted. This provision of law, *is the Missouri Compromise.* In excluding slavery North of the line, the same language is employed as in the Ordinance of '87. It directly applied to Iowa, Minnesota, and to the present bone of contention, Kansas and Nebraska. Whether there should or should not, be slavery south of that line, nothing was said in the law; but Arkansas constituted the principal remaining part, south of the line; and it has since been admitted as a slave state without serious controversy. More recently, Iowa, north of the line, came in as a free state without controversy. Still later, Minnesota, north of the line, had a territorial organization without controversy. Texas principally south of the line, West of Arkansas; though originally within the purchase from France, had, in 1819, been traded off to Spain, in our treaty for the acquisition of Florida.[12] It had thus become part of Mexico. Mexico revolutionized and became independent of Spain. American citizens began settling rapidly, with their slaves in the southern part of Texas. Soon they revolutionized against Mexico, and established an independent government of their own, adopting a constitution, with slavery, strongly resembling the constitutions

Eyre Crowe, *After the Sale: Slaves Going South from Richmond*. Oil on canvas (1853). Enslaved people being sold in Richmond to owners of large cotton plantations in the Deep South.

of our slave states. By still another rapid move, Texas, claiming a boundary much further West, than when we parted with her in 1819, was brought back to the United States, and admitted into the Union as a slave state. There then was little or no settlement in the northern part of Texas, a considerable portion of which lay north of the Missouri line; and in the resolutions admitting her into the Union, the Missouri restriction was expressly extended westward across her territory. This was 1845, only nine years ago.

Thus originated the Missouri Compromise; and thus has it been respected down to 1845. And even four years later, in 1849, our distinguished Senator, in a public address, held the following language in relation to it:[13]

"The Missouri Compromise had been in practical operation for about a quarter of a century, and had received the sanction and approbation of men of all parties in every section of the Union. It had allayed all

without it the people of Kansas and Nebraska cannot get along at all! I fear . . . that we of the north western States, never knew the depth of our political misfortunes imposed by the ordinance of '87—we never knew how miserable we were!" *CW*, 2:241–242.

12  Lincoln referred to the 1819 Transcontinental Treaty with Spain.

13  In his attempt to demonstrate Douglas's inconsistency concerning the Missouri Compromise, Lincoln quoted from a speech made by the senator in Springfield, Illinois, on October 1849 in which he presented his views on the territories, including his strong support for the Missouri Compromise. In his own remarks on October 4 in Springfield, Lincoln, reported an observer, called Douglas's speech "powerful and eloquent" with

language "choice and rich." "I wish," Lincoln claimed, "I was such a master of language as my friend, the Judge." These remarks are cited in Burlingame, *Abraham Lincoln*, 1:379. In light of Douglas's "extravagant" praise of the Missouri Compromise, Lincoln continued, "it illy became him or others to apply unseemly names and epitaphs to himself [Lincoln] and other American citizens, who still retained a reverence and respect for the honored measure." *CW*, 2:242. Douglas's October speech was published in the *Illinois State Register* on November 1, 2, and 6, 1849, and is cited in Johannsen, *Stephen A. Douglas*, 253.

14  David Wilmot (1814–1868) served as a congressman from Pennsylvania from 1845 to 1851, his second term coinciding with Lincoln's. Entering Congress as a Democrat, Wilmot later joined the Republican Party and was elected to the United States Senate in 1861 to fill the vacancy created by the resignation of fellow Republican Simon Cameron (1799–1889) when the latter assumed the position of secretary of war in President Lincoln's cabinet. In 1863 President Lincoln appointed him a judge of the U.S. Court of Claims, a post he held until his death. "Wilmot, David," Biographical Directory of the United States Congress, http://bioguide.congress.gov/scripts/biodisplay.pl?index=W000566 (accessed January 23, 2015).

15  On August 8, 1846, Wilmot proposed an amendment to an appropriations bill that prohibited slavery in any territory acquired from Mexico as a result of the war with that country. The Wilmot Proviso passed the House of Representatives but failed in the Senate. During Lincoln's term in Congress, the proviso came before the House on numerous occasions but was never adopted. The proviso caused sectional divisions within the ranks of the Whigs and Democrats: Southern Whigs and Democrats united against the amendment, while virtually every Northern Whig supported it. Northern Democrats, on the other

sectional jealousies and irritations growing out of this vexed question, and harmonized and tranquilized the whole country. It had given to Henry Clay, as its prominent champion, the proud sobriquet of the '*Great Pacificator*' and by that title and for that service, his political friends had repeatedly appealed to the people to rally under his standard, as a presidential candidate, as the man who had exhibited the patriotism and the power to suppress, an unholy and treasonable agitation, and preserve the Union. He was not aware that any man or any party from any section of the Union, had ever urged as an objection to Mr. Clay, that he was the great champion of the Missouri Compromise. On the contrary, the effort was made by the opponents of Mr. Clay, to prove that he was not entitled to the exclusive merit of that great patriotic measure, and that the honor was equally due to others as well as to him, for securing its adoption—that it had its origins in the hearts of all patriotic men, who desired to preserve and perpetuate the blessings of our glorious Union—an origin akin that of the constitution of the United States, conceived in the same spirit of fraternal affection, and calculated to remove forever, the only danger, which seemed to threaten, at some distant day, to sever the social bond of union. All the evidences of public opinion at that day, seemed to indicate that this Compromise had been canonized in the hearts of the American people, as a sacred thing which no ruthless hand would ever be reckless enough to disturb."

I do not read this extract to involve Judge Douglas in an inconsistency. If he afterwards thought he had been wrong, it was right of him to change. I bring this forward merely to show the high estimate placed on the Missouri Compromise by all parties up to so late as the year 1849.

But, going back a little, in point of time, our war with Mexico broke out in 1846. When Congress was about adjourning that session, President Polk asked them to place two millions of dollars under his control, to be used by him in the recess, if found practicable and expedient, in negotiating a treaty of peace with Mexico, and acquiring some part of her territory. A bill was duly got up, for the purpose, and was progressing swimmingly, in the House of Representatives, when a member by the name of David Wilmot,[14] a democrat from Pennsylvania, moved as an amendment "Provided that in any territory thus acquired, there shall never be slavery."

This is the origin of the far-famed "Wilmot Proviso."[15] It created a great flutter; but it stuck like wax, was voted into the bill, and the bill passed with it through the House. The Senate, however, adjourned without final action on it and so both appropriation and proviso were lost, for the time. The war continued, and at the next session, the president renewed his request for the appropriation, enlarging the amount, I think, to three million. Again, came the proviso; and defeated the measure. Congress adjourned again, and the war went on. In Dec., 1847, the new congress assembled. I was in the lower House that term. The "Wilmot Proviso" or the principle of it, was constantly coming up in some shape or other, and I think I may venture to say I voted for it at least forty times; during the short term I was there. The Senate, however, held it in check, and it never became law. In the spring of 1848 a treaty of peace was made with Mexico; by which we obtained that portion of her country which now constitutes the territories of New Mexico and Utah, and the now state of California. By this treaty the Wilmot Proviso was defeated, as so far as it was intended to be, a condition of the acquisition of territory. Its friends however, were still determined to find some way to restrain slavery from getting into the new country. This new acquisition lay directly West of our old purchase from France, and extended west to the Pacific ocean—and was so situated that if the Missouri line should be extended straight West, the new country would be divided by such extended line, leaving some North and some South of it. On Judge Douglas' motion a bill, or provision of a bill, passed the Senate to extend the Missouri line. The Proviso men in the House, including myself, voted it down, because by implication, it gave up the Southern part to slavery, while we were bent on having it *all* free.[16]

In the fall of 1848 the gold mines were discovered in California. This attracted people to it with unprecedented rapidity, so that on, or soon after, the meeting of the new congress in Dec., 1849, she already had a population of nearly a hundred thousand, had called a convention, formed a state constitution, excluding slavery, and was knocking for admission into the Union. The Proviso men, of course, were for letting her in, but the Senate, always true to the other side would not consent to her admission. And there California stood, kept *out* of the Union, because she would not let slavery *into* her borders. Under all the circumstances perhaps this was not wrong. There were other points of dispute, connected with the general question of slavery, which equally needed adjustment. The South clamored for a more efficient fugitive slave law.[17] The North clamored for the abolition of a peculiar species of slave trade in the District of Columbia, in connection with which, in view from the windows in the capitol, a sort of negro-livery stable, where droves of negroes were collected, temporarily kept, and finally

hand, were split, with some unwilling to offend Southern members of their party. Foner, *The Fiery Trial,* 51–52.

16 An observer reported that during Lincoln's Springfield speech, Douglas, who was in the audience, pointed out that Lincoln "voted against extending that line." Lincoln responded: "Yes, sir, because I was in favor of running that line much further south." Cited in Burlingame, *Abraham Lincoln,* 1:379.

17 During the Constitutional Convention of 1787, delegates added a fugitive slave clause to the U.S. Constitution, Article IV, Section 2, which stated, "No person held to Service or Labour in one State, under the Laws thereof, escaping into another, shall, in Consequence of any Law or Regulation therein, be discharged from such Service or Labour, but shall be delivered up on Claim of the Party to whom such Service or Labour may be due." This clause did not provide Congress with enforcement powers concerning fugitive slaves, however. Enforcement powers were granted several years later with the passage of the Fugitive Slave Law of 1793. The act stipulated that once a slave owner or his agent captured a runaway slave, the owner or agent must bring the alleged slave before a federal, state, or local judge or magistrate and provide proof of ownership. The judge or magistrate either permitted or denied the captive's return based on the documentation provided by the slave owner or agent. Any individual interfering in this process could be sued for $500 or more by the owner of the alleged slave. Southern slaveholders claimed the right to take their slaves to and enforce their own state's slave codes in Northern states where slavery was prohibited, based on the fugitive slave clause in the Constitution and the 1793 law. In the early decades of the nineteenth century, Northern states passed "personal liberty laws" that provided alleged runaways due-process rights and restricted the right of slaveholders to bring slaves

into their state. Southerners claimed these laws were unconstitutional and called on Congress to strengthen the Fugitive Slave Law of 1793 or enact a new, tougher measure. A new fugitive slave law was enacted as part of the Compromise of 1850. The new act prevented states from recognizing due-process rights for alleged runaway slaves and empowered federal commissioners to adjudicate fugitive-slave cases. Finkelman, *Slavery and the Founders,* 81, 99; James Oakes, *The Scorpion's Sting: Antislavery and the Coming of the Civil War* (New York: W. W. Norton & Company, 2014), 96.

18  See "Remarks and Resolution concerning the Abolition of Slavery in the District of Columbia, U.S. House of Representatives, January 10, 1849," in this volume.

19  See "Eulogy for Henry Clay, July 6, 1852," in which Lincoln referred to the Compromise of 1850.

20  In one of his most passionate statements against slavery, Lincoln condemned Douglas's declared indifference, as well as Congress's abdication, concerning the leading moral issue of the day. Popular sovereignty not only ignored the intentions of the founders of the nation but also rejected a course that had been approved and endorsed by statesmen both North and South, including Douglas, since 1820. By giving slavery new life in the territories, Kansas-Nebraska made a mockery of the Declaration of Independence's principle that all men are created equal; it besmirched the nation's image around the world. As Lincoln asserted in his Springfield speech, to allow slavery in the territories amounted to "a descending from the high republican faith of our ancestors" and a declaration to the world "that we have no longer a choice between freedom and slavery— that both are equal with us—that we yield our territories as readily for one as the other!" We are, Lincoln admonished, "proclaiming ourselves political hypocrites before the world, by thus

taken to Southern markets, precisely like droves of horses, had been openly maintained for fifty years.[18] Utah and New Mexico needed territorial governments; and whether slavery should or should not be prohibited within them, was another question. The indefinite Western boundary of Texas was to be settled. She was received as a slave state; and consequently the farther West the slavery men could push her boundary, the more slave country they secured. And the further East the slavery opponents could thrust the boundary back, the less slave ground was secured. Thus this was just as clearly a slavery question as any of the others.

These points all needed adjustment; and they were all held up, perhaps wisely to make them to adjust one another. The Union, now, as in 1820, was thought to be in danger; and devotion to the Union rightfully inclined men to yield somewhat, in points where nothing else could have so inclined them. A compromise was finally effected. The south got their new fugitive-slave law; and the North got California, (the far best part of our acquisition from Mexico,) as a free State. The south got a provision that New Mexico and Utah, *when admitted as States,* may come in *with* or *without* slavery as they may then choose; and the north got the slave-trade abolished in the District of Columbia. The north got the western boundary of Texas, thence further back eastward than the south desired; but, in turn, they gave Texas ten millions of dollars, with which to pay her old debts. This is the Compromise of 1850.[19]

Preceding the Presidential election of 1852, each of the great political parties, democrats and whigs, met in convention, and adopted resolutions endorsing the compromise of '50; as a "finality," a final settlement, so far as these parties could make it so, of all slavery agitation. Previous to this, in 1851, the Illinois Legislature had indorsed it.

During this long period of time Nebraska had remained, substantially an uninhabited country, but now emigration to, and settlement within it began to take place. It is about one third as large as the present United States, and its importance so long overlooked, begins to come into view. The restriction of slavery by the Missouri Compromise directly applies to it; in fact, was first made, and has since been maintained, expressly for it. In 1853, a bill to give it a territorial government passed the House of Representatives, and, in the hands of Judge Douglas, failed of passing the Senate only for want of time. This bill contained no repeal of the Missouri Compromise. Indeed, when it was assailed because it did not contain such repeal, Judge Douglas defended it in its existing form. On January 4th, 1854, Judge Douglas introduces a new bill to give Nebraska territorial government. He ac-

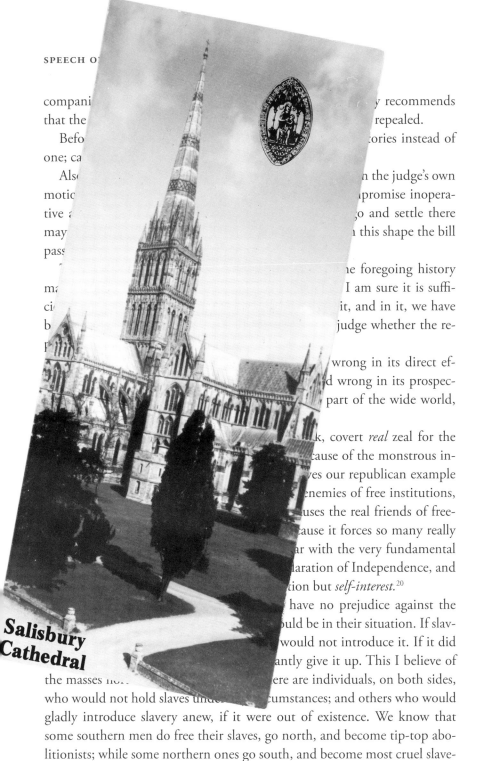

Salisbury Cathedral

compani[...] y recommends that the [...] repealed.

Befo[...] [...]ories instead of one; ca[...]

Als[...] [...] the judge's own motio[...] [...]promise inopera-tive a[...] [...]o and settle there may [...] [...] this shape the bill pass[...]

[...] [...]e foregoing history ma[...] [...] I am sure it is suffi-ci[...] [...] it, and in it, we have b[...] [...] judge whether the re-

[...] wrong in its direct ef-[...]d wrong in its prospec-[...] part of the wide world,

[...]k, covert *real* zeal for the [...]cause of the monstrous in-[...]es our republican example [...]enemies of free institutions, [...]uses the real friends of free-[...]cause it forces so many really [...]r with the very fundamental [...]aration of Independence, and [...]tion but *self-interest*.[20]

[...] have no prejudice against the [...]uld be in their situation. If slav-[...] would not introduce it. If it did [...]antly give it up. This I believe of the masses no[...] [...]ere are individuals, on both sides, who would not hold slaves unde[...] [...]cumstances; and others who would gladly introduce slavery anew, if it were out of existence. We know that some southern men do free their slaves, go north, and become tip-top abo-litionists; while some northern ones go south, and become most cruel slave-masters.

When southern people tell us they are no more responsible for the origin of slavery, than we; I acknowledge the fact. When it is said that the institu-

fostering Human Slavery and proclaiming ourselves, at the same time, the sole friends of Human Freedom." *CW,* 2:244.

21 Despite his abhorrence of slavery and his fight against its expansion into the territories, Lincoln, unlike some abolitionists, resisted demonizing Southerners in general and slaveholders in particular, a position he maintained throughout his presidency. He insisted that Southerners were no more responsible for slavery than Northerners. In his September 12 Bloomington speech, Lincoln avowed that "Southern slaveholders were neither better, nor worse than we of the North, and that we of the North were no better than they. . . . With slavery as existing in the slave States at the time of the formation of the Union, he had nothing to do." Living and working in Illinois, a free state notorious for its antiblack attitudes, especially in the southern part of the state, Lincoln was acutely aware of the prejudices of his audiences and thus concentrated on the shared responsibility of Northerners and Southerners for stopping the spread of slavery. Lincoln's Bloomington speech is cited in *CW,* 2:230. See also Kenneth M. Stampp, "Lincoln's History," in James M. McPherson, ed., *"We Cannot Escape History": Lincoln and the Last Best Hope of Earth* (Urbana: University of Illinois Press, 1995), 28.

**22** Lincoln favored voluntary colonization of American blacks outside of the country as part of his gradual, moderate approach to ending slavery in the United States. His first public statements in support of colonization appeared in his 1852 eulogy of Henry Clay. He continued to advocate colonization until 1862, the second year of his presidency.

**23** In this paragraph, Lincoln revealed that he shared many of the racial prejudices of his time and held a limited view concerning black rights. While he opposed slavery and sought to restrict its extension, he was not ready to acknowledge the political and social equality of blacks. In his 1858 senatorial debates with Douglas, Lincoln argued for the right of blacks to reap the fruits of their labors. He made it clear, however, that he was not willing to go further than that. See, for example, "Fourth Debate with Stephen A. Douglas at Charleston, Illinois, September 18, 1858," in this volume.

**24** Lincoln publicly supported the Fugitive Slave Act of 1850 once it became law. Privately, however, Lincoln condemned the measure as "very obnoxious" and "ungodly." Cited in Burlingame, *Abraham Lincoln*, 1:380.

tion exists; and that it is very difficult to get rid of it, in any satisfactory way, I can understand and appreciate the saying. I surely will not blame them for not doing what I should not know how to do myself. If all earthly power were given me, I should not know what to do, as to the existing institution. My first impulse would be to free all the slaves, and send them back to Liberia,—to their own native land. But a moment's reflection would convince me, that whatever of high hope, (as I think there is) there may be in this, in the long run, its sudden execution is impossible.[22] If they were all landed there in a day, they would all perish in the next ten days; and there are not surplus shipping and surplus money enough in the world to carry them there in many times ten days. What then? Free them all, and keep them among us as underlings? Is it quite certain that this betters their condition? I think I would not hold one in slavery, at any rate; yet the point is not clear enough for me to denounce people upon. What next? Free them, and make them politically and socially, our equals? My own feelings will not admit of this; and if mine would, we well know that those of the great mass of white people will not. Whether this feeling accords with justice and sound judgment, is not the sole question, if indeed, it is any part of it. A universal feeling, whether well or ill-founded, can not be safely disregarded. We can not, then, make them equals. It does seem to me that systems of gradual emancipation might be adopted; but for their tardiness in this, I will not undertake to judge our brethren of the south.[23]

When they remind us of their constitutional rights, I acknowledge them, not grudgingly, but fully, and fairly; and I would give them any legislation for reclaiming of their fugitives, which should not, in its stringency, be more likely to carry a free man into slavery, than our ordinary criminal laws are to hang an innocent one.[24]

But all this; to my judgment, furnishes no more excuse for permitting slavery to go into our own free territory, than it would for reviving the African slave trade by law. The law which forbids the bringing of slaves *from* Africa; and that which has so long forbid the taking them *to* Nebraska, can hardly be distinguished on any moral principle; and the repeal of the former could find quite as plausible excuses as that of the latter.

The arguments by which the repeal of the Missouri Compromise is sought to be justified, are these:

First, that the Nebraska country needed a territorial government.

Second, that in various ways, the public had repudiated it, and demanded the repeal; and therefore should not now complain of it.

And lastly, that the repeal establishes a principle, which is intrinsically right.

I will attempt an answer to each of them in its turn.

First, then, if that country was in need of a territorial organization, could it not have had it as well without as with the repeal? Iowa and Minnesota, to both of which the Missouri restriction applied, had, without its repeal, each in succession, territorial organizations. And even, the year before, a bill for Nebraska itself, was within an ace of passing, without the repealing clause; and this in the hands of the same men who are now the champions of repeal. Why no necessity then for the repeal? But still later, when this very bill was first brought in, it contained no repeal. But, say they, because the public had demanded, or rather commanded the repeal, the repeal was to accompany the organization, whenever that should occur.

Now I deny that the public ever demanded any such thing—ever repudiated the Missouri Compromise—ever commanded its repeal. I deny it, and call for the proof. It is not contended, I believe, that any such command has ever been given in express terms. It is only said that it was done *in principle.* The support of the Wilmot Proviso, is the first fact mentioned, to prove that the Missouri restriction was repudiated in *principle,* and the second is, the refusal to extend the Missouri line over the country acquired from Mexico. These are near enough alike to be treated together. The one was to exclude the chances of slavery from the *whole* new acquisition by the lump; and the other was to reject a division of it, by which one *half* was to be given up to those chances. Now whether this was a repudiation of the Missouri line, in *principle,* depends upon whether the Missouri law contained any *principle* requiring the line to be extended over the country acquired from Mexico. I contend it did not. I insist that it contained no general principle, but that it was, in every sense, specific. That its terms limit it to the country purchased from France, is undenied and undeniable. It could have no principle beyond the intention of those who made it. They did not intend to extend the line to country which they did not own. If they intended to extend it, in the event of acquiring additional territory, why did they not say so? It was just as easy to say, that "in all the country west of the Mississippi, which we now own, *or may hereafter acquire* there shall never be slavery," as to say, what they did say; and they would have said it if they had meant it. An intention to extend the law is not only not mentioned in the law, but is not mentioned in any contemporaneous history. Both the law itself, and the history of the times are a blank as to any *principle* of extension; and by neither the known rules for construing statutes and contracts, nor by common sense, can any such *principle* be inferred.

Another fact showing the *specific* character of the Missouri law—showing that it intended no more than it expressed—showing that the line was not intended as a universal dividing line between free and slave territory, present and prospective—north of which slavery could never go—is the fact that by that very law, Missouri came in as a slave state, *north* of the line. If that law contained any prospective *principle,* the whole law must be looked to in order to ascertain what the *principle* was. And by this rule, the south could fairly contend that inasmuch as they got one slave state north of the line at the inception of the law, they have the right to have another given them *north* of it occasionally—now and then in the indefinite westward extension of the line. This demonstrates the absurdity of attempting to deduce a prospective *principle* from the Missouri Compromise line.

When we voted for the Wilmot Proviso, we were voting to keep slavery *out* of the whole Missouri [Mexican] acquisition; and little did we think we were thereby voting, to let it *into* Nebraska, laying [*sic*] several hundred miles distant. When we voted against extending the Missouri line, little did we think we were voting to destroy the old line, then of nearly thirty years standing. To argue that we thus repudiated the Missouri Compromise is no less absurd than it would be to argue that because we have, so far, forborne to acquire Cuba, we have thereby, *in principle,* repudiated our former acquisitions, and determined to throw them out of the Union! No less absurd than it would be to say that because I may have refused to build an addition to my house, I thereby have decided to destroy the existing house! And if I catch you setting fire to my house, you will turn upon me and say I INSTRUCTED you to do it! The most conclusive argument, however, that, while voting for the Wilmot Proviso, and while voting against the EXTENSION of the Missouri line, we never thought of disturbing the original Missouri Compromise, is found in the facts, that there was then, and still is, an unorganized tract of fine country, nearly as large as the state of Missouri, lying immediately west of Arkansas, and south of the Missouri Compromise line; and that we never attempted to prohibit slavery as to it. I wish particular attention to this. It adjoins the original Missouri Compromise line, by its northern boundary; and consequently is part of the country, into which, by implication, slavery was permitted to go, by that compromise. There it has lain open ever since, and there it still lies. And yet no effort has been made at any time to wrest it from the south. In all our struggles to prohibit slavery within our Mexican acquisitions, we never so much as lifted

Abraham Lincoln. Copy of daguerreotype by Polycarpus Von Schneidau (Chicago, October 27, 1854). Lincoln holds an antislavery newspaper in a photograph taken just weeks after this speech.

a finger to prohibit it, as to this tract. Is not this entirely conclusive that at all times, we have held the Missouri Compromise as a sacred thing; even when against ourselves, as well as when for us?

Senator Douglas sometimes says the Missouri line itself was, *in principle,* only an extension of the line of the ordinance of '87—that is to say, an ex-

25  In his October 4 Springfield speech, Lincoln denied that the Compromise of 1850 sanctioned principles that required repeal of the Missouri Compromise. Lincoln claimed that "not one of the Compromises of 1850 alluded to, or could, by indirection even, be understood to apply to Kansas and Nebraska. Those territories had already been legislated for—that legislation had become 'canonized in the hearts of the people'—it was supposed that 'no ruthless hand' would ever be reckless enough to disturb it—and it could not therefore, in a reasonable mind, be understood that the Compromises of 1850 were meant and intended to disturb it. Those Compromises were good for what they covered—no more." *CW,* 2:243.

tension of the Ohio river. I think this is weak enough on its face. I will remark, however that, as a glance at the map will show, the Missouri line is a long way farther South than the Ohio; and that if our Senator, in proposing his extension, had stuck to the *principle* of jogging southward, perhaps it might not have been voted down so readily.

But next it is said that the compromises of '50 and the ratification of them by both political parties, in '52, established a *new principle,* which required the repeal of the Missouri Compromise.[25] This again I deny. I deny it, and demand the proof. I have already stated fully what the compromises of '50 are. The particular part of those measures, for which the virtual repeal of the Missouri compromise is sought to be inferred (for it is admitted they contain nothing about it, in express terms) is the provision in the Utah and New Mexico laws, which permits them when they seek admission into the Union as States, to come in with or without slavery as they shall then see fit. Now I insist this provision was made for Utah and New Mexico, and for no other place whatever. It had no more direct reference to Nebraska than it had to the territories of the moon. But, say they, it had reference to Nebraska, *in principle.* Let us see. The North consented to this provision, not because they considered it right in itself; but because they were compensated—paid for it. They, at the same time, got California into the Union as a free State. This was far the best part of all they had struggled for by the Wilmot Proviso. They also got the area of slavery somewhat narrowed in the settlement of the boundary of Texas. Also, they got the slave trade abolished in the District of Columbia. For all these desirable objects the North could afford to yield something; and they did yield to the South the Utah and New Mexico provision. I do not mean that the whole North, or even a majority yielded, when the law passed; but enough yielded, when added to the vote of the South, to carry the measure. Now can it be pretended that the *principle* of this arrangement requires us to permit the same provision to be applied to Nebraska, *without any equivalent at all?* Give us another free State; press the boundary of Texas still further back, give us another step toward the destruction of slavery in the District, and you present us a similar case. But ask us not to repeat, for nothing, what you paid for in the first instance. If you wish the thing again, pay again. That is the *principle* of the compromises of '50, if indeed they had any principles beyond their specific terms—it was the system of equivalents.

Again, if Congress, at that time, intended that all future territories should, when admitted as States, come in with or without slavery, at their own option, why did it not say so? With such an universal provision, all know the bills could not have passed. Did they, then—could they—establish *principle* contrary to their own intention? Still further, if they intended to establish the principle that wherever Congress had control, it should be left to the people to do as they thought fit with slavery[,] why did they not authorize the people of the District of Columbia at their adoption to abolish slavery within these limits? I personally know that this has not been left undone, because it was unthought of. It was frequently spoken of by members of Congress and by citizens of Washington six years ago; and I heard no one express a doubt that a system of gradual emancipation, with compensation to owners, would meet the approbation of a large majority of the white people of the District. But without the action of Congress they could say nothing; and Congress said "no." In the measures of 1850 Congress had the subject of slavery in the District expressly in hand. If they were then establishing the *principle* of allowing the people to do as they please with slavery, why did they not apply the *principle* to that people?

Again, it is claimed that by the Resolutions of the Illinois Legislature, passed in 1851, the repeal of the Missouri compromise was demanded. This I deny also.[26] Whatever may be worked out by a criticism of the language of those resolutions, the people have never understood them as being any more than an endorsement of the compromises of 1850; and a release of our Senators from voting for the Wilmot Proviso. The whole people are living witnesses, that this only, was their view. Finally, it is asked "If we did not mean to apply the Utah and New Mexico provision, to all future territories, what did we mean, when we, in 1852, endorsed the compromises of '50?"

For myself, I can answer this question most easily. I meant not to ask a repeal, or modification of the fugitive slave law. I meant not to ask for the abolition of slavery in the District of Columbia. I meant not to resist the admission of Utah and New Mexico, even should they ask to come in as slave States. I meant nothing about additional territories because, as I understood, we then had no territory whose character as to slavery was not already settled. As to Nebraska, I regarded its character as being fixed, by the Missouri compromise, for thirty years—as unalterably fixed as that of my own home in Illinois. As to new acquisitions I said "sufficient unto the day is the evil thereof."[27] When we make new acquaintances [acquisitions], we will, as heretofore, try to manage them some how. That is my answer. That is what I meant and said; and I appeal to the people to say, each for himself, whether that was not also the universal meaning of the free States.

And now, in turn, let me ask a few questions. If by any, or all these matters, the repeal of the Missouri Compromise was commanded, why was not

26  In his October 4 Springfield speech, Lincoln also addressed what he considered Douglas's unjustified claim that the Illinois legislature demanded the repeal of the Missouri Compromise, stating that "he had looked in vain to find those instructions" from the Illinois legislature and could "not find them." At this, Douglas responded by offering a copy of the legislature's resolutions, which Lincoln declined to accept, averring that the resolutions to which Douglas referred "only passed one branch of the legislature." Lincoln asked the senator "to read hereafter, in his public speeches, those resolutions which did pass the legislature, and not those that didn't." Ibid., 2:244.

27  "Sufficient unto the day is the evil thereof" is an aphorism from the Sermon on the Mount in Matthew 6:34: "Take therefore no thought for the morrow: for the morrow shall take thought for the things of itself. Sufficient unto the day is the evil thereof." Lincoln was not a member of any church—his Christianity had been questioned by some of his contemporaries early in his career—but he knew well and often quoted from the King James Bible. On Lincoln's religion, see "Handbill Replying to Charges of Infidelity, July 31, 1846," in this volume.

28 Lincoln's rejection of the argument in favor of repealing the Missouri Compromise on the grounds that it was "intrinsically right" echoed his remarks in Springfield on October 4. In that speech, he demanded to know "what kind of 'right' was meant." There was no "constitutional" right to repeal, he claimed, since the Missouri Compromise "received every sanction that any law could have to establish its constitutionality. It has been originated in principle, in the ordinance of '87, concurrently almost with our Constitution, and by the founders of it, who certainly understood its principles. It has been sustained by all courts and almost every great Statesman down to this day." Lincoln then asked "what *legal* right?" There was no law, Lincoln asserted, that created that right. "The Compromises of 1850 are the only measures relied on, and it is already shown that they re-affirm instead an annual right of Freedom under the Compromise." He continued this line of argument: "What *natural* right requires Kansas and Nebraska to be opened to slavery? Is not slavery universally granted to be, in the abstract, a gross outrage on the law of nature? Have not all civilized nations, our own among them, made the Slave trade capital, and classed it with piracy and murder? Is it not held to be the great wrong of the world? Do not the Southern people, the Slaveholders themselves, spurn the domestic slave dealer, refuse to associate with him, or let their families associate with his family, as long as the taint of his infamous calling is known? What *social* or *political* right, had slavery to demand the repeal of the Missouri Compromise, and claim entrance into States where it has never before existed? The theory of our government is Universal Freedom. 'All men are created free and equal,' says the Declaration of Independence. The word 'Slavery' is not found in the Constitution. . . . All legislation that has recognized or tolerated its extension, has been associated with a compensation—a Compromise—showing that it was something that moved forward, not by

the command sooner obeyed? Why was the repeal omitted in the Nebraska bill of 1853? Why was it omitted in the original bill of 1854? Why, in the accompanying report, was such a repeal characterized as a *departure* from the course pursued in 1850? and its continued omission recommended?

I am aware Judge Douglas now argues that the subsequent express repeal is no substantial alteration of the bill. This argument seems wonderful to me. It is as if one should argue that white and black are not different. He admits, however, that there is a literal change in the bill; and that he made the change in deference to other Senators, who would not support the bill without. This proves that those other Senators thought the change a substantial one; and that the Judge thought their opinions worth deferring to. His own opinions, therefore, seem not to rest on a very firm basis even in his own mind—and I suppose the world believes, and will continue to believe, that precisely on the substance of that change this whole agitation has arisen.

I conclude then, that the public never demanded the repeal of the Missouri compromise.

I now come to consider whether the repeal, with its avowed principle, is intrinsically right. I insist that it is not.[28] Take the particular case. A controversy had arisen between the advocates and opponents of slavery, in relation to its establishment within the country we had purchased of France. The southern, and then the best part of the purchase, was already in as a slave State. The controversy was settled by also letting Missouri in as a slave State; but with the agreement that within all the remaining part of the purchase, North of a certain line, there should never be slavery. As to what was to be done with the remaining part south of the line, nothing was said; but perhaps the fair implication was, that it should come in with slavery if it should so choose. The southern part, except a portion heretofore mentioned, afterwards did come in with slavery, as the State of Arkansas. All these many years since 1820, the Northern part had remained a wilderness. At length settlements began in it also. In due course, Iowa, came in as a free State, and Minnesota was given a territorial government, without removing the slavery restriction. Finally the sole remaining part, North of the line, Kansas and Nebraska, was to be organized; and it is proposed, and carried, to blot out the old dividing line of thirty-four years standing, and to open the whole of that country to the introduction of slavery. Now, this, to my mind, is manifestly unjust. After an angry and dangerous controversy, the parties made friends by dividing the bone of contention. The one party first appropriates her own share, beyond all power to be disturbed in the possession of it;

and then seizes the share of the other party. It is as if two starving men had divided their only loaf; the one had hastily swallowed his half, and then grabbed the other half just as he was putting it to his mouth!

Let me here drop the main argument, to notice what I consider rather an inferior matter. It is argued that slavery will not go to Kansas and Nebraska, *in any event.* This is a *palliation—a lullaby.*[29] I have some hope that it will not; but let us not be too confident. As to climate, a glance at the map shows that there are five slave States—Delaware, Maryland, Virginia, Kentucky, and Missouri—and also the District of Columbia, all north of the Missouri compromise line. The census returns of 1850 show that, within these, there are 867,276 slaves—being more than one-fourth of all slaves in the nation.

It is not climate, then, that will keep slavery out of these territories. Is there any thing in the peculiar nature of the country? Missouri adjoins these territories, by her entire western boundary, and slavery is already within every one of her western counties. I have even heard it said that there are more slaves, in proportion to whites, in the north western county of Missouri, than within any county of the State. Slavery pressed entirely up to the old western boundary of the State, and when, rather recently, a part of that boundary, at the north-west was moved out a little farther west, slavery followed on quite up to the new line. Now, when the restriction is removed, what is to prevent it from going still further? Climate will not. No peculiarity of the country will—nothing in *nature* will. Will the disposition of the people prevent it? Those nearest the scene, are all in favor of the extension. The yankees, who are opposed to it may be more numerous; but in military phrase, the battle-field is too far from *their* base of operations.

But it is said, there now is *no* law in Nebraska on the subject of slavery; and that, in such case, taking a slave there, operates his freedom. That *is* good book-law; but is not the rule of actual practice.[30] Wherever slavery is, it has been first introduced without law. The oldest laws we find concerning it, are not laws introducing it; but *regulating* it, as an already existing thing. A white man takes his slave to Nebraska now; who will inform the negro that he is free? Who will take him before the court to test the question of his freedom? In ignorance of his legal emancipation, he is kept chopping, splitting and plowing. Others are brought, and move on in the same track. At last, if ever the time for voting comes, on the question of slavery, the institution already in fact exists in the country, and cannot well be removed. The facts of its presence, and the difficulty of its removal will carry the vote in its favor. Keep it out until a vote is taken, and a vote in favor of it, can not be

its own right, but by its wrong." Lincoln ended this section of his Springfield speech by demonstrating the fallacy of equating enslaved blacks with property: "It is said that the slaveholder has the same [political] right to take his negroes to Kansas that a freeman has to take his hogs or his horses. This would be true if negroes were property in the same sense that hogs and horses are. But is this the case? It is notoriously not so. Southern men do not treat their negroes as they do their horses. There are 400,000 free negroes in the United States. All the race came into this country as slaves. How came these negroes to be free? At $500 each, their value is $2,000,000. Can you find *two million dollars worth* of any kind of property running around without an owner? These negroes are free, because their owners, in some way and at some time, felt satisfied that the creatures had mind, feeling, souls, family affections, hopes, joys, sorrows—something that made them more than *hogs* or *horses.* Shall the slaveholders require us to be more heartless and mean than they, and treat those beings as property which they themselves have never been able to treat so?" *CW,* 2:245–246.

**29** Lincoln's solution for keeping slavery out of the territories was the continuation of congressional prohibition, such as that imposed by the Missouri Compromise. He rejected the claims by Douglas and others that the climate and soil of Kansas and Nebraska was unsuitable for slavery, providing evidence to back up his claims. In his Springfield address, using a small map he had brought with him, Lincoln demonstrated the implausibility of this argument. Pointing to the northwestern boundary of Missouri, Lincoln claimed that slavery "lost no time going up to the last limits of that boundary." Once the Missouri boundary line was extended over land "adjoining north-west Missouri . . . called the Platte country," claimed Lincoln, slavery "lost no time marching right in and going to the utmost verge of that boundary." Thus, "it is said that there are more slaves in that extreme north-west portion of Missouri, jutting broadside against Kansas and Nebraska than any other equal area in Missouri!" "Will it not go, then," asked Lincoln, "into Kansas and Nebraska, if permitted? Why not? What will hinder? Do cattle nibble a pasture right up to the division fence, crop all close under the fence, and even put their necks through and gather what they can reach, over the line, and still refuse to pass over into that next green pasture, even if the fence shall be thrown down?" *CW,* 2:244.

30  Lincoln demolished the argument that slavery will not be extended into the territories because there "is no law" supporting it by providing evidence disproving the claim. He showed that only a restriction such as imposed by the Missouri Compromise would prevent slavery from being established in a territory, using as an example his own state of Illinois and the Northwest Ordinance of 1787, which banned slavery there. Missouri, on the other hand, lacking such a restriction, became a slave state.

31  Lincoln argued that opening the Kansas and Nebraska territories to slavery would result in the resumption of the African slave trade, outlawed since 1808, due to the increased demand for slaves, leading to the capture of free men and women and selling them in the slave market.

got in any population of forty thousand, on earth, who have been drawn together by the ordinary motives of emigration and settlement. To get slaves into the country simultaneously with the whites, in the incipient stages of settlement, is the precise stake played for, and won in this Nebraska measure.

The question is asked us, "If slaves will go in, notwithstanding the general principle of law liberates them, why would they not equally go in against positive statute law?—go in, even if the Missouri restriction were maintained?" I answer, because it takes a much bolder man to venture in, with his property, in the latter case, than in the former—because the positive congressional enactment is known to, and respected by all, or nearly all; whereas the negative principle that *no* law is free law, is not much known except among lawyers. We have some experience of this practical difference. In spite of the Ordinance of '87, a few negroes were brought into Illinois, and held in a state of quasi slavery; not enough, however, to carry a vote of the people in favor of the institution when they came to form a constitution. But in the adjoining Missouri country, where there was no ordinance of '87—was no restriction—they were carried ten times, nay a hundred times, as fast, and actually made a slave State. This is fact—naked fact.

Another LULLABY argument is, that taking slaves to new countries does not increase their number—does not make any one slave who otherwise would be free. There is some truth to this, and I am glad of it, but it [is] not WHOLLY true. The African slave trade is not yet effectually suppressed; and if we make a reasonable deduction for the white people amongst us, who are foreigners, and the descendants of foreigners, arriving here since 1808, we shall find the increase of the black population out-running that of the white, to an extent unaccountable, except by supposing that some of them too, have been coming from Africa.[31] If this be so, the opening of new countries to the institution, increases the demand for, and augments the price of slaves, and so does, in fact, make slaves of freemen by causing them to be brought from Africa, and sold into bondage.

But, however this may be, we know the opening of new countries to slavery, tends to the perpetuation of the institution, and so does KEEP men in slavery who otherwise would be free. The result we do not FEEL like favoring, and we are under no legal obligation to suppress our feelings in this respect.

Equal justice to the south, it is said, requires us to consent to the extending of slavery to new countries. That is to say, inasmuch as you do not object to my taking my hog to Nebraska, therefore I must not object to you taking your slave.[32] Now, I admit this is perfectly logical, if there is no difference between hogs and negroes. But while you thus require me to deny the humanity of the negro, I wish to ask whether you of the south yourselves, have ever been willing to do as much? It is kindly provided that of all those who come into the world, only a small percentage are natural tyrants. That percentage is no larger in the slave States than in the free. The great majority, south as well as north, have human sympathies, of which they can no more divest themselves than they can of their sensibility to physical pain. These sympathies in the bosoms of the southern people, manifest in many ways, their sense of the wrong of slavery, and their consciousness that, after all, there is humanity in the negro. If they deny this, let me address them a few plain questions. In 1820 you joined the north, almost unanimously, in declaring the African slave trade piracy, and in annexing to it the punishment of death. Why did you do this? If you did not feel that it was wrong, why did you join in providing that men should be hung for it? The practice was no more than bringing wild negroes from Africa, to sell to such as would buy them. But you never thought of hanging men for catching and selling wild horses, wild buffaloes or wild bears.

Again, you have amongst you, a sneaking individual, of the class of native tyrants, known as the "SLAVE-DEALER." He watches your necessities, and crawls up to buy your slave, at a speculating price. If you cannot help it, you sell to him; but if you can help it, you drive him from your door. You despise him utterly. You do not recognize him as a friend, or even as an honest man. Your children must not play with his; they may rollick freely with little negroes, but not with the "slave-dealers" children. If you are obliged to deal with him, you try to get through the job without so much as touching him. It is common with you to join hands with the men you meet; but with the slave dealer you avoid the ceremony—instinctively shrinking from the snaky contact. If he grows rich and retires from business, you still remember him, and still keep up the ban of non-intercourse upon him and his family. Now why is this? You do not so treat the man who deals in corn, cattle or tobacco.

And yet again; there are in the United States and territories, including the District of Columbia, 433,643 free blacks. At $500 per head they are worth over two hundred millions of dollars. How comes this vast amount of property to be running about without owners? We do not see free horses or free cattle running at large. How is this? All these free blacks are the descendants of slaves, or have been slaves themselves, and they would be slaves now, but for SOMETHING which has operated on their white owners,

32 In this section of his speech, Lincoln advanced his core argument against Douglas and supporters of the Kansas-Nebraska Act: their denial of the humanity of the black people. The concept of popular sovereignty espoused by its supporters, according to Lincoln, equated slaves with hogs, property that settlers have a right to take with them into a territory, thereby stripping the slaves of basic rights embodied in the Declaration of Independence. As he did in his October 4 Springfield speech (see note 28), Lincoln offered evidence that even white Southerners have acknowledged the humanity of blacks by treating them differently than they would mere property.

33   Lincoln quoted from one of his favorite poets, Alexander Pope, from "An Essay on Criticism," which was first published in 1711. It is interesting to note that Lincoln referred to these lines as those of "some poet," given that he cited Pope often in conversations, letters, and speeches. Lincoln owned a copy of an 1839 edition of *The Poetical Works of Alexander Pope* (Philadelphia: J. J. Woodward, 1839), presented to him by his friend and the brother-in-law of Mary Todd Lincoln, Ninian Wirt Edwards (1809–1889). In 1861 Lincoln gave several of his books, including this one, to his law partner William Herndon, when he left Springfield for Washington to assume the presidency. It is not known if Lincoln used his own volume of Pope's works when citing the passage in his Peoria speech. Thomas A. Horrocks, "The Travels of Abraham Lincoln's Copy of the Poetical Works of Alexander Pope," in *Other People's Books: Association Copies and the Stories They Tell* (Chicago: Caxton Club, 2011), 90–91. See also F. Lauriston Bullard, "Lincoln's Copy of Pope's Poems," *Abraham Lincoln Quarterly* 4 (1946): 30–35.

34   Lincoln indeed took the "bull by the horns," arguing forcefully that the Kansas-Nebraska Act violated the "sacred right of self-government" by denying the humanity of blacks. This right of self-government, contended Lincoln, was a central principle of the Declaration of Independence, and thus blacks, just as whites, were "endowed by their Creator with certain inalienable rights . . . life, liberty, and the pursuit of happiness." In his Peoria speech, Douglas had defended popular sovereignty by arguing that Northerners who settled in the territories "were as capable of managing their domestic affairs as those who remained behind. They allowed legislation upon every question affecting their welfare as a people, but they were not deemed capable of deciding the question of slavery for themselves [because of the Missouri Compromise]. They were permitted to legislate

inducing them, at vast pecuniary sacrifices, to liberate them. What is that SOMETHING? Is there any mistaking it? In all these cases it is your sense of justice, and human sympathy, continually telling you, that the poor negro has some natural right to himself—that those who deny it, and make mere merchandise of him, deserve kickings, contempt and death.

And now, why will you ask us to deny the humanity of the slave? and estimate him only as an equal of the hog? Why ask us to do what you will not do yourselves? Why ask us to do for *nothing,* what two hundred million of dollars could not induce you to do?

But one great argument in the support of the repeal of the Missouri Compromise, is still to come. That argument is "the sacred right of self government." It seems our distinguished Senator has found great difficulty in getting his antagonists, even in the Senate to meet him fairly on this argument—some poet has said "Fools rush in where angels fear to tread."[33]

At the hazard of being thought one of the fools of this quotation, I meet that argument—I rush in, I take that bull by the horns.[34]

I trust I understand, and truly estimate the right of self-government. My faith in the proposition that each man should do precisely as he pleases with all which is exclusively his own, lies at the foundation of the sense of justice there is in me. I extend the principles to communities of men, as well as to individuals. I so extend it, because it is politically wise, as well as naturally just; politically wise, in saving us from broils about matters which do not concern us. Here, or at Washington, I would not trouble myself with the oyster laws of Virginia, or the cranberry laws of Indiana.

The doctrine of self-government is right—absolutely and eternally right —but it has no just application, as here attempted. Or perhaps I should rather say that whether it has just application depends upon whether a negro is *not* or *is* a man. If he is *not* a man, why in that case, he who is a man may, as a matter of self-government, do just as he pleases with him. But if the negro *is* a man, is it not to that extent, a total destruction of self-government, to say that he too shall not govern *himself?* When the white man governs himself that is self-government; but when he governs himself, and also governs *another* man, that is *more* than self-government—that is despotism. If the negro is a *man,* why then my ancient faith teaches me that "all men are created equal"; and that there can be no moral right in connection with one man's making a slave of another.

Judge Douglas frequently, with bitter irony and sarcasm, paraphrases our argument by saying[,] "The white people of Nebraska are good enough to govern themselves, *but they are not good enough to govern a few miserable negroes!!*"

Well I doubt not that the people of Nebraska are, and will continue to be as good as the average of people elsewhere. I do not say the contrary. What I do say is, that no man is good enough to govern another man, *without that other's consent.* I say this is the leading principle—the sheet anchor of American republicanism. Our Declaration of Independence says: "We hold these truths to be self-evident: that all men are created equal; that they are endowed by their Creator with certain inalienable rights; that among these are life, liberty, and the pursuit of happiness. That to secure these rights, governments are instituted among men, DERIVING THEIR JUST POWERS FROM THE CONSENT OF THE GOVERNED."

I have quoted so much at this time merely to show that according to our ancient faith, the just powers of governments are derived from the consent of the governed. Now the relation of masters and slaves is, PRO TANTO, a total violation of this principle. The master not only governs the slave without his consent; but he governs him by a set of rules altogether different from those which he prescribes for himself. Allow ALL the governed an equal voice in the government, and that, and that only is self government.

Let it not be said I am contending for the establishment of political and social equality between the whites and blacks. I have already said the contrary. I am not now combating the argument of NECESSITY, arising from the fact that the blacks are already amongst us; but I am combating what is set up as MORAL argument for allowing them to be taken where they have never yet been—arguing against the EXTENSION of a bad thing, which where it already exists, we must of necessity, manage as we best can.

In support of his application of the doctrine of self-government, Senator Douglas has sought to bring to his aid the opinions and examples of our revolutionary fathers. I am glad he has done this. I love the sentiments of those old-time men; and shall be most happy to abide by their opinions. He shows us that when it was in contemplation for the colonies to break off from Great Britain, and set up a new government for themselves, several of the states instructed their delegates to go for the measures PROVIDED EACH STATE SHOULD BE ALLOWED TO REGULATE ITS DOMESTIC CONCERNS IN ITS OWN WAY. I do not quote; but this in substance. This was right. I see nothing objectionable in it. I also think it probable that it had some reference to the existence of slavery amongst them. I will not deny that it had. But had it, in any reference to the carrying

upon every subject affecting the white, but were told that they had not sufficient intelligence to legislate for the black man—or to decide the question of slavery for themselves." Popular sovereignty, Lincoln countered, worked only if all men possessed the equal right to make laws. In his September 26 Bloomington speech, Lincoln declared that "if the negro, upon the soil where slavery is not legalized by law and sanctioned by custom, *is* a man, then there is not even the shadow of popular sovereignty in allowing the first settlers upon such soil to decide whether it shall be right in all future time to hold men in bondage." *CW,* 2:239. Douglas is cited in Lehrman, *Lincoln at Peoria,* 127.

35   The doctrine of popular sovereignty as embodied in the Kansas-Nebraska Act, according to Lincoln, allowed settlers of a territory to decide issues of national importance, such as slavery. But because the question of slavery in the territories was a national issue, not a local one, he argued it should be determined by the many across the nation, not by the few in a territory. This, Lincoln insisted, was how democracy worked. "The whole nation is interested that the best use shall be made of these territories," he contended. "We want them for the homes of free white people," but they cannot be of any use "if slavery shall be planted within them." Lincoln may have had his father in mind when he spoke those words, since slavery was one of the reasons his father had moved the family away from Kentucky to Indiana.

of slavery into NEW COUNTRIES? That is the question; and we will let the fathers themselves answer it.

This same generation of men, and mostly the same individuals of the generation, who declared this principle—who declared independence—who fought the war of the revolution through—who afterwards made the constitution under which we still live—these same men passed the ordinance of '87, declaring that slavery should never go to the north-west territory. I have no doubt Judge Douglas thinks they were very inconsistent in this. It is a question of discrimination between them and him. But there is not an inch of ground left for his claiming that their opinions—their example—their authority—are on his side of this controversy.

Again, is not Nebraska, while a territory, a part of us? Do we not own the country? And if we surrender the control of it, do we not surrender the right of self-government? It is part of ourselves. If you say we shall not control it because it is ONLY part, the same is true of every other part; and when all the parts are gone, what has become of the whole? What is then left of us? What use for the general government, when there is nothing left for it [to] govern?

But you say this question should be left to the people of Nebraska, because they are more particularly interested. If this be the rule, you must leave it to each individual to say for himself whether he will have slaves. What better moral right have thirty-one citizens of Nebraska to say, that the thirty-second shall not hold slaves, than the people of thirty-one States have to say that slavery shall not go into the thirty-second State at all?

But if it is a sacred right for the people of Nebraska to take and hold slaves there, it is equally their sacred right to buy them where they can buy them cheapest; and that undoubtedly will be on the coast of Africa; provided you will consent to not hang them for going there to buy them. You must remove this restriction too, from the sacred right of self-government. I am aware you say that taking slaves from the State of Nebraska, does not make slaves of freemen; but the African slave-trader can say just as much. He does not catch free negroes and bring them here. He finds them already slaves in the hands of their black captors, and he honestly buys them at the rate of about a red cotton handkerchief a head. This is very cheap, and it is a great abridgement of the sacred right of self-government to hang men for engaging in this profitable trade!

Another important objection to this application of the right of self-government, is that it enables the first FEW, to deprive the succeeding MANY, a free exercise of the right of self-government.[35] The first few may get slavery IN, and the subsequent many cannot easily get it OUT. How common is the remark now in the slave States—"If we were only clear of our slaves, how much better it would be for us." They are actually deprived of the privilege of governing themselves as they would, by action of a very few, in the beginning. The same thing was true of the whole nation at the time our constitution was formed.

Whether slavery shall go into Nebraska, or other new territories, is not a matter of exclusive concern to the people who may go there. The whole nation is interested that the best use shall be made of these territories. We wanted them for the homes of free white people. This they cannot be, to any considerable extent, if slavery shall be planted within them. Slave States are places for poor white people to remove FROM; not to remove TO. New free States are the places for poor people to go to and better their condition. For this use, the nation needs these territories.

Still further; there are constitutional relations between the slave and free States, which are degrading to the latter. We are under legal obligations to catch and return their runaway slaves to them—a sort of dirty disagreeable job, which I believe, as a general rule the slave-holders will not perform for one another. Then again, in the control of the government—the management of the partnership affairs—they have greatly the advantage of us. By the constitution, each State has two Senators—each has a number of Representatives; in proportion to the number of its people—and each has a number of presidential electors, equal to the whole number of its Senators and Representatives together. But in ascertaining the number of people, for this purpose, five slaves are counted as being equal to three whites.[36] The slaves do not vote; they are only counted and so used, as to swell the influence of the white people's votes. The practical effect of this is more aptly shown by a comparison of the States of South Carolina and Maine. South Carolina has six representatives, and so has Maine; South Carolina has eight presidential electors, and so has Maine. This is precise equality so far; and, of course they are equal in Senators, each having two. Thus in the control of government, the two States are equals precisely. But how are they in the number of their white people? Maine has 581,813—while South Carolina has 274,567. Maine has twice as many as South Carolina, and 32,679 over. Thus each white man in South Carolina is more than the double of any man in Maine. This is all because South Carolina, besides her free people, has 384,984 slaves. The South Carolinian has precisely the same advantage over the white man in every other free State, as well as in Maine.

He is more than the double of any one of us in this crowd. The same ad-

36  Lincoln referred to the so called three-fifths clause of the U.S. Constitution (Article 1, Section 2) which stipulated that each slave held in the United States would equal three-fifths of a person for establishing the representation of a state in the U.S. House of Representatives. The clause was one of the compromises in the Constitutional Convention to secure support in the South. The impact of the three-fifths clause in establishing a slave power in the early republic is addressed in Garry Wills, *"Negro President": Thomas Jefferson and the Slave Power* (Boston: Houghton Mifflin, 2003).

37  While Lincoln disagreed with the three-fifths clause, he accepted it as settled with the adoption of the Constitution. He took issue with admitting new states into the Union under the same terms, however. As Lincoln declared in his October 4 Springfield speech, "He was unwilling that his neighbor, living on an equality by his side in Illinois, should by moving to Kansas be elevated into a state of superiority over himself and become a man and a tenth, whereas before he was formerly only one man, like himself." If this was "equal rights" for the Kansas settler, Lincoln continued, "he would be glad to know what became of his own rights, and the rights of the people of the Free States; while they were thus made into only *fractions of men,* by the creation of *new* Slave States." *CW,* 2:246.

vantage, but not to the same extent, is held by all citizens of the slave States, over those of the free; and it is an absolute truth, without an exception, that there is no voter in any slave State, but who has more legal power in the government, than any voter in any free State. There is no instance of exact equality; and the disadvantage is against us the whole chapter through. This principle, in the aggregate, gives the slave States, in the present Congress, twenty additional representatives—being seven more than the whole majority by which they passed the Nebraska bill.

Now all this is manifestly unfair; yet I do not mention it to complain of it, in so far as it is already settled. It is in the constitution; and I do not, for that cause, or any other cause, propose to destroy, or alter, or disregard the constitution. I stand to it, fairly, fully, and firmly.[37]

But when I am told I must leave it altogether to OTHER PEOPLE to say whether new partners are to be bred up and brought into the firm, on the same degrading terms against me, I respectfully demur. I insist, that whether I shall be a whole man, or only, the half of one, in comparison with others, is a question in which I am somewhat concerned; and one which no other man can have a sacred right of deciding for me. If I am wrong in this—if it really be a sacred right of self-government, in the man who shall go to Nebraska, to decide whether he will be the EQUAL of me or the DOUBLE of me, then after he shall have exercised that right, and thereby shall have reduced me to a still smaller fraction of a man than I already am, I should like for some gentleman deeply skilled in the mysteries of sacred rights, to provide himself with a microscope, and peep about, and find out, if he can, what has become of my sacred rights! They will surely be too small for detection with the naked eye.

Finally, I insist, that if there is ANY THING which it is the duty of the WHOLE PEOPLE to never entrust to any hands but their own, that thing is the preservation and perpetuity, of their own liberties, and institutions. And if they shall think, as I do, that the extension of slavery endangers them, more than any, or all other causes, how recreant to themselves, if they submit the question, and with it, the fate of their country, to a mere handfull of men, bent only on temporary self-interest. If this question of slavery extension were an insignificant one—one having no power to do harm—it might be shuffled aside in this way. But being, as it is, the great Behemoth of danger, shall the strong gripe of the nation be loosened upon him, to entrust him to the hands of such feeble keepers?

I have done with this mighty argument, of self-government. Go, sacred thing! Go in peace.

But Nebraska is urged as a great Union-saving measure.[38] Well I too, go for saving the Union. Much as I hate slavery, I would consent to the extension of it rather than see the Union dissolved, just as I would consent to any GREAT evil, to avoid a GREATER one. But when I go to Union saving, I must believe, at least, that the means I employ has some adaptation to the end. To my mind, Nebraska has no such adaptation.

"It hath no relish of salvation in it."[39]

It is an aggravation, rather, of the only one thing which ever endangers the Union. When it came upon us, all was peace and quiet. The nation was looking to forming of new bonds of Union; and a long course of peace and prosperity seemed to lie before us. In the whole range of possibility, there scarcely appears to me to have been any thing, out of which the slavery agitation could have been revived, except the very project of repealing the Missouri compromise. Every inch of territory we owned, already had a definite settlement of the slavery question, and by which, all parties were pledged to abide. Indeed, there was no uninhabited country on the continent, which we could acquire; if we except some extreme northern regions, which are wholly out of the question. In this state of case, the genius of Discord himself, could scarcely have invented a way of again getting us by the ears, but by turning back and destroying the peace measures of the past. The councils of that genius seem to have prevailed, the Missouri compromise was repealed; and here we are, in the midst of a new slavery agitation, such, I think, as we have never seen before.

Who is responsible for this? Is it those who resist the measure; or those who, causelessly, brought it forward, and pressed it through, having reason to know, and, in fact, knowing it must and would be so resisted? It could not but be expected by its author, that it would be looked upon as a measure for the extension of slavery, aggravated by a gross breach of faith. Argue as you will, and long as you will, this is the naked FRONT and ASPECT, of the measure. And in this aspect, it could not but produce agitation. Slavery is founded in the selfishness of man's nature—opposition to it, is his love of justice. These principles are an eternal antagonism; and when brought into collision so fiercely, as slavery extension brings them, shocks, and throes, and convulsions must ceaselessly follow. Repeal the Missouri compromise—repeal all compromises—repeal the declaration of independence—repeal all past history, you still can not repeal human nature. It still will be the abundance of man's heart, that slavery extension is wrong; and out of the abundance of his heart, his mouth will continue to speak.

The structure, too, of the Nebraska bill is very peculiar. The people are to

38 Owing to his devotion to the Union, Lincoln avowed he would allow slavery's extension into the territories rather than see the Union torn apart. But he did not agree with proponents of the Kansas-Nebraska Act that the measure was a Union-saving measure. Rather, Lincoln saw the act in the opposite light, as posing a threat to the Union by shredding the "new bonds of Union" created by the Missouri Compromise and the Compromise of 1850.

39 Lincoln cites a line from Shakespeare's *Hamlet*, act 3, scene 3, line 92. Shakespeare was one of Lincoln's favorite playwrights and poets. According to William Herndon, Lincoln carried a "well-worn copy" of Shakespeare, "in which he read no little in his leisure moments." Herndon and Weik, *Herndon's Lincoln*, 199. For Lincoln's interest in Shakespeare, see Robert Bray, *Reading with Lincoln*, 189–190, 215–216; and Berkelman, "Lincoln's Interest in Shakespeare."

40 One of Lincoln's criticisms of popular sovereignty concerned when and how settlers decided whether slavery was to be banned in a territory. He saw this issue leading to violent controversy, possibly ending in bloodshed. Lincoln's fear was prescient. With the fate of slavery in the hands of Kansas Territory residents, free-state and slave-state advocates migrated to the territory to vote and even fight for their cause. Fraudulent elections resulted in two territorial governments, one representing free-state residents and the other representing slave-state supporters. By 1856 guerrilla warfare between the two factions broke out, resulting in several violent and bloody skirmishes in the territory that became popularly known as "Bleeding Kansas." Bleeding Kansas was a major influence in the political realignment of the 1850s that included the founding of the Republican Party. For background on Bleeding Kansas, see James A. Rawley, *Race and Politics: "Bleeding Kansas" and the Coming of the Civil War* (Lincoln: University of Nebraska Press, 1979); and Nicole Etcheson, *Bleeding Kansas: Contested Liberty in the Civil War Era* (Lawrence: University Press of Kansas, 2004).

41 Lincoln again countered the assertions of Douglas and his supporters that opposition to the Kansas-Nebraska Act would endanger the Union. He advanced the opposite view, that of restoring the Missouri Compromise for "the sake of the Union." He warned that rejecting the "spirit of mutual concession" which "gave us the constitution" and "thrice saved the nation" would lead to a level of distrust and resentment between North and South that would threaten sectional harmony and, ultimately, the Union.

decide the question of slavery for themselves; but WHEN they are to decide; or HOW they are to decide; or whether, when the question is once decided, it is to remain so, or is it to be subject to an indefinite succession of new trials, the law does not say, Is it to be decided by the first dozen settlers who arrive there? or is it to await the arrival of a hundred? Is it to be decided by a vote of the people? or a vote of the legislature? or, indeed a vote of any sort? To these questions, the law gives no answer. There is mystery about this; for when a member proposed to give the legislature express authority to exclude slavery, it was hooted down by the friends of the bill. This fact is worth remembering. Some yankees, in the east, are sending emigrants to Nebraska, to exclude slavery from it; and, so far as I can judge, they expect the question to be decided by voting, in some way or other. But the Missourians are awake too. They are within a stone's throw of the contested ground. They hold meetings, and pass resolutions, in which not the slightest allusion to voting is made. They resolve that slavery already exists in the territory; that more shall go there; that they, remaining in Missouri will protect it; and that abolitionists shall be hung, or driven away. Through all this, bowie-knives and six-shooters are seen plainly enough; but never a glimpse of the ballot-box. And, really, what is to be the result of this? Each party WITHIN, having numerous and determined backers WITHOUT, is it not probable that the contest will come to blows, and bloodshed? Could there be a more apt invention to bring about collision and violence, on the slavery question, than this Nebraska project is? I do not charge, or believe, that such was intended by Congress; but if they had literally formed a ring, and placed champions within it to fight out the controversy, the fight could be no more likely to come off, than it is. And if this fight should begin, is it likely to take a very peaceful, Union-saving turn? Will not the first drop of blood so shed, be the real knell of the Union?[40]

The Missouri Compromise ought to be restored. For the sake of the Union, it ought to be restored.[41] We ought to elect a House of Representatives which will vote its restoration. If by any means, we omit to do this, what follows? Slavery may or may not be established in Nebraska. But whether it be or not, we shall have repudiated—discarded from the councils of the Nation—the SPIRIT of COMPROMISE; for who after this will ever trust in a national compromise? The spirit of mutual concession—that spirit which gave us the constitution, and which has thrice saved the Union—we shall have strangled and cast from us forever. And what shall we have in lieu of it? The South flushed with triumph and tempted to excesses;

the North, betrayed, as they believe, brooding on wrong and burning for revenge. One side will provoke; the other resent. The one will taunt, the other defy; one agrees [aggresses], the other retaliates. Already a few in the North, defy all constitutional restraints, resist the execution of the fugitive slave law, and even menace the institution of slavery in the states where it exists.

Already a few in the South, claim the constitutional right to take to and hold slaves in the free states—demand the revival of the slave trade; and demand a treaty with Great Britain by which fugitive slaves may be reclaimed from Canada. As yet there are but few on either side. It is a grave question for the lovers of the Union, whether the final destruction of the Missouri Compromise, and with it the spirit of all compromise will or will not embolden and embitter each of these, and fatally increase the numbers of both.

But restore the compromise, and what then? We thereby restore the national faith, the national confidence, the national feeling of brotherhood. We thereby reinstate the spirit of concession and compromise—that spirit which has never failed us in past perils, and which may be safely trusted for all the future. The south ought to join in doing this. The peace of the nation is as dear to them as to us. In memories of the past and hopes of the future, they share as largely as we. It would be on their part, a great act—great its spirit, and great in its effect. It would be worth to the nation a hundred years' purchase of peace and prosperity. And what sacrifice would they make? They only surrender to us, what they gave us for a consideration long, long ago; what they have not now, asked for, struggled or cared for; what has been thrust upon them, not less to their own astonishment than to ours.

But it is said we cannot restore it; that though we elect every member of the lower house, the Senate is still against us. It is quite true, that of the Senators who passed the Nebraska bill, a majority of the whole Senate will retain their seats in spite of the elections of this and the next year. But if at these elections, their several constituencies shall clearly express their will against Nebraska, will these senators disregard their will? Will they neither obey, nor make room for those who will?[42]

But even if we fail to technically restore the compromise, it is still a great point to carry a popular vote in favor of the restoration. The moral weight of such a vote can not be estimated too highly. The authors of Nebraska are not at all satisfied with the destruction of the compromise—an endorsement of this PRINCIPLE, they proclaim to be the great object. With them,

42 Lincoln urged opponents of the Kansas-Nebraska Act to use the ballot box to make their views known to their representatives in Congress. In his September 12 Bloomington speech, Lincoln argued that the repeal of the Missouri Compromise was "done without the consent of the people, and against their wishes, for if the matter had been put to a vote before the people directly . . . they would have indignantly voted it down." *CW,* 2:232–233. Lincoln believed strongly in the power of public opinion in influencing public policy. He once claimed, "Our government rests on public opinion. Whoever can change public opinion, can change the government, practically just so much." *Abraham Lincoln: Speeches and Writings, 1832–1858,* 385.

43 Anti-Nebraska political coalitions established in the wake of passage of the Kansas-Nebraska Act significantly weakened the Whig Party in the North, yet Lincoln for a time remained loyal to the party and wedded to his moderate approach to the ending of slavery. He exhorted fellow Whigs to stand up and oppose Kansas-Nebraska because it was right, and not to worry how they would be perceived by the public. In short, he said, good Whigs stand with anyone, whether a Northern abolitionist or a Southern slave owner, in support of the Constitution and law.

44 What Lincoln meant by "argument of 'Necessity,'" was that the founders had no choice but to include protections for slavery in the Constitution because it already existed in the Southern states; it was an action necessary to obtain Southern support for the Constitution. Lincoln made it clear, however, that the founders' omission of the word "slave" from the Constitution was deliberate, proving their distaste for the institution. He then offered examples of the founders'—as well as the early Congresses'—attempts to restrict slavery's expansion with the intention of ensuring its gradual decline and death.

45 U.S. Constitution, Article IV, Section 2. See note 17.

Nebraska alone is a small matter—to establish a principle, for FUTURE USE, is what they particularly desire.

That future use is to be the planting of slavery wherever in the wide world, local and unorganized opposition can not prevent it. Now if you wish to give them this endorsement—if you wish to establish this principle—do so. I shall regret it; but it is your right. On the contrary if you are opposed to the principle—intend to give it no such endorsement—let no wheedling, no sophistry, divert you from throwing a direct vote against it.

Some men, mostly whigs, who condemn the repeal of the Missouri Compromise, nevertheless hesitate to go for its restoration, lest they be thrown in company with the abolitionist. Will they allow me as an old whig to tell them good humoredly, that I think this is very silly? Stand with anybody that stands RIGHT.[43] Stand with him while he is right and PART with him when he goes wrong. Stand WITH the abolitionist in restoring the Missouri Compromise; and stand AGAINST him when he attempts to repeal the fugitive slave law. In the latter case you stand with the southern disunionist. What of that? you are still right. In both cases you are right. In both cases you oppose the dangerous extremes. In both you stand on middle ground and hold the ship level and steady. In both you are national and nothing less than national. This is good old whig ground. To desert such ground, because of any company, is to be less than a whig—less than a man—less than an American.

I particularly object to the NEW position which the avowed principle of this Nebraska law gives to slavery in the body politic. I object to it because it assumes that there CAN be MORAL RIGHT in the enslaving of one man by another. I object to it as a dangerous dalliance for a few [free] people—a sad evidence that, feeling prosperity[,] we forget right—that liberty, as a principle, we have ceased to revere. I object to it because the fathers of the republic eschewed, and rejected it. The argument of "Necessity" was the only argument they ever admitted in favor of slavery; and so far, and so far only as it carried them, did they ever go.[44] They found the institution existing among us, which they could not help; and they cast blame upon the British King for having permitted its introduction. BEFORE the constitution, they prohibited its introduction into the north-western Territory—the only country we owned, then free from it. At the framing and adoption of the constitution, they forbore to so much as mention the word "slave" or "slavery" in the whole instrument. In the provision for the recovery of fugitives, the slave is spoken of as a "PERSON HELD TO SERVICE OR LABOR."[45] In that prohibiting the abolition of the African slave trade for twenty years, that the trade is spoken of as "The migration or importation of such persons as any of the States NOW EXISTING, shall think proper to admit," &c.[46] These are the only provisions alluding to slavery. Thus, the thing is hid away, in the constitution, just as an afflicted man hides away a wen or a cancer, which he dares not cut out at once, lest he bleed to death; with the promise, nevertheless, that the cutting may begin at the end of a given time. Less than this our fathers COULD not do; and NOW [MORE] they WOULD not do. Necessity drove them so far, and farther, they would not go. But this is not all. The earliest Congress, under the constitution, took the same view of slavery. They hedged and hemmed it in to the narrowest limits of necessity.

In 1794, they prohibited an out-going slave-trade—that is, the taking of slaves FROM the United States to sell.

In 1798, they prohibited the bringing of slaves from Africa, INTO the Mississippi Territory—this territory then comprising what are now the States of Mississippi and Alabama. This was TEN YEARS before they had the authority to do the same thing as to the States existing at the adoption of the constitution.

In 1800 they prohibited AMERICAN CITIZENS from trading in slaves between foreign countries—as, for instance, from Africa to Brazil.

In 1803 they passed a law in aid of one or two State laws, in restraint of the internal slave trade.

In 1807, in apparent hot haste, they passed the law, nearly a year in advance, to take effect the first day of 1808—the very first day the constitution would permit—prohibiting the African slave trade by heavy pecuniary and corporal penalties.

In 1820, finding these provisions ineffectual, they declared the trade piracy, and annexed to it, the extreme penalty of death. While all this was passing in the general government, five or six of the original slave States had adopted systems of gradual emancipation; and by which the institution was rapidly becoming extinct within these limits.

Thus we see, the plain unmistakable spirit of that age, towards slavery, was hostility to the PRINCIPLE, and toleration, ONLY BY NECESSITY.

But NOW it is to be transformed into a "sacred right." Nebraska brings it forth, places it on the high road to extension and perpetuity; and, with a pat on its back, says to it, "Go, and God speed you." Henceforth it is to be the chief jewel of the nation—the very figure-head of the ship of State. Little by little, but steadily as man's march to the grave, we have been giving up the OLD for the NEW faith. Near eighty years ago we began by declaring

46  Ibid., Article I, Section 9.

**47** John Pettit (1808–1877) was a Democrat who represented Indiana in the U.S. House of Representatives (1843–1849) and the Senate (1853–1855). "Pettit, John," Biographical Directory of the United States Congress, http://bioguide.congress.gov/scripts/biodisplay.pl?index=p000277 (accessed October 4, 2014).

**48** Francis Marion (ca. 1732–1795) was born in South Carolina and served as a military officer during the Revolutionary War. Known as the "Swamp Fox," owing to his irregular methods of warfare, Marion led a band of guerrilla fighters against the British during their occupation of South Carolina in 1780 and 1781. See http://www.nps.gov/nisi/historyculture/general-francis-marion.htm (accessed January 24, 2015).

**49** John André (1750–1780) was a British army officer hanged as a spy by American troops during the Revolutionary War; http://www.mountvernon.org/research-collections/digital-encyclopedia/article/john-andre (accessed January 24, 2015).

**50** Lincoln also referred to the Declaration of Independence as the "white-man's charter of freedom" in his eulogy of Clay; see "Eulogy for Henry Clay, July 6, 1852," in this volume.

that all men are created equal; but now from that beginning we have run down to the other declaration, that for SOME men to enslave OTHERS is a "sacred right of self-government." These principles can not stand together. They are opposite as God and mammon; and whoever holds to the one, must despise the other. When Pettit,[47] in connection with his support of the Nebraska bill, called the Declaration of Independence "a self-evident lie" he only did what consistency and candor require all other Nebraska men to do. Of the forty odd Nebraska Senators who sat present and heard him, no one rebuked him. Nor am I apprized that any Nebraska newspaper, or any Nebraska orator, in the whole nation, has ever rebuked him. If this had been said among Marion's men,[48] Southerners though they were, what would have become of the man who said it? If this had been said to the men who captured Andre,[49] the man who said it, would probably have been hung sooner than Andre was. If it had been said in old Independence Hall, seventy-eight years ago, the very door-keeper would have throttled the man, and thrust him into the street.

Let no one be deceived. The spirit of seventy-six and the spirit of Nebraska, are utter antagonisms; and the former is being rapidly displaced by the latter.

Fellow countrymen—Americans south, as well as north, shall we make no effort to arrest this? Already the liberal party throughout the world, express the apprehension "that the one retrograde institution in America, is undermining the principles of progress, and fatally violating the noblest political system the world ever saw." That is not the taunt of enemies, but the warning of friends. Is it quite safe to disregard it—to despise it? Is there no danger to liberty itself, in discarding the earliest practice, and first precept of our ancient faith? In our greedy chase to make profit of the negro, let us beware, lest we "cancel and tear to pieces" even the white man's charter of freedom.[50]

Our republican robe is soiled, and trailed in the dust. Let us repurify it. Let us turn and wash it white, in the spirit, if not the blood, of the Revolution. Let us turn slavery from its claims of "moral right," back upon its existing legal rights, and its arguments of "necessity." Let us return it to the position our fathers gave it; and there let it rest in peace. Let us re-adopt the Declaration of Independence, and with it, the practices, and policy, which harmonize with it. Let north and south—let all Americans—let all lovers of liberty everywhere—join in the great and good work. If we do this, we shall not only have saved the Union; but we shall have so saved it, as to make it, forever worthy of saving. We shall have so saved it, that the succeeding millions of free happy people, the world over, shall rise up, and call us blessed, to the latest generations.

At Springfield, twelve days ago,[51] where I had spoken substantially as I have here, Judge Douglas replied to me—and as he is to reply to me here, I shall attempt to anticipate him, by noticing some of the points he made there.

He commenced by stating that I had assumed all the way through, that the principle of the Nebraska bill, would have the effect of extending slavery. He denied that this was INTENDED, or that this EFFECT would follow.

I will not re-open the argument upon this point. That such was the intention, the world believed at the start, and will continue to believe. This was the COUNTENANCE of the thing; and, both friends and enemies, instantly recognized it as such. That countenance can not now be changed by argument. You can as easily argue the color out of the negroes' skin. Like the "bloody hand" you may wash it, and wash it, the red witness of guilt still sticks, and stares horribly at you.

Next he says, congressional intervention never prevented slavery, any where—that it did not prevent it in the north west territory, now [nor] in Illinois—that in fact, Illinois came into the Union as a slave State—that the principle of the Nebraska bill expelled it from Illinois, from several old States, from every where.[52]

Now this is mere quibbling all the way through. If the ordinance of '87 did not keep slavery out of the north west territory, how happens it that the north west shore of the Ohio river is entirely free from it; while the south east shore, less than a mile distant, along nearly the whole length of the river, is entirely covered with it?

If that ordinance did not keep it out of Illinois, what was it that made the difference between Illinois and Missouri? They lie side by side, the Mississippi river only dividing them; while their early settlements were within the same latitude. Between 1810 and 1820 the number of slaves in Missouri INCREASED 7,211; while in Illinois, in the same ten years, they DECREASED 51. This appears by the census returns. During nearly all of that ten years, both were territories—not States. During this time, the ordinance forbid slavery to go into Illinois; and NOTHING forbid it to go into Missouri. It DID go into Missouri, and did NOT go into Illinois. That is the fact. Can any one doubt as to the reason of it?

But, he says, Illinois came into the Union as a slave State. Silence, perhaps, would be the best answer to this flat contradiction of the known his-

51  Lincoln's October 4, 1854, speech at Spring-field, Illinois. See *CW,* 2:240–247.

52  Douglas, as Lincoln pointed out, erroneously stated that Illinois had been admitted as a slave state; the Northwest Ordinance had defined Illinois as a free territory.

53 According to *CW,* 2:283n3, Lincoln, by omitting "the" before "Nebraska bill," referred to the measure as a person: "Editorials in Illinois newspapers prior to his speech refer to the villain 'Nebraska Bill' as a person, indicating a common usage during the campaign."

tory of the country. What are the facts upon which this bold assertion is based? When we first acquired the country, as far back as 1787, there were some slaves within it, held by the French inhabitants at Kaskaskia. The territorial legislation, admitted a few negroes, from the slave States, as indentured servants. One year after the adoption of the first State constitution the whole number of them was—what do you think? just 117—while the aggregate free population was 55,094—about 470 to one. Upon this state of facts, the people framed their constitution prohibiting the further introduction of slavery, with a sort of guaranty to the owners of the few indentured servants, giving freedom to their children to be born thereafter, and making no mention whatever, of any supposed slave for life. Out of this small number, the Judge manufactures his argument that Illinois came into the Union as a slave State. Let the facts be the answer to the argument.

The principles of the Nebraska bill, he says, expelled slavery from Illinois? The principle of that bill first planted it here—that is, it first came, because there was no law to prevent it—first came before we owned the country; and finding it here, and having the ordinance of '87 to prevent its increasing, our people struggled along, and finally got rid of it as best they could.

But the principle of the Nebraska bill abolished slavery in several of the old States. Well, it is true that several of the old States, in the last quarter of the last century, did adopt systems of gradual emancipation, by which the institution has finally become extinct within their limits; but it MAY or MAY NOT be true that the principle of the Nebraska bill was the cause that led to the adoption of these measures. It is now more than fifty years, since the last of these States adopted its system of emancipation. If Nebraska bill[53] is the real author of these benevolent works, it is rather deplorable, that he has, for so long a time, ceased working all together. Is there not some reason to suspect that it was the principle of the REVOLUTION, and not the principle of Nebraska bill, that led to emancipation in these old States? Leave it to the people of those old emancipating States, and I am quite sure they will decide, that neither that, nor any other good thing, ever did, or ever will come of Nebraska bill.

In the course of my main argument, Judge Douglas interrupted me to say, that the principle [of] the Nebraska bill was very old; that it originated when God made man and placed good and evil before him, allowing him to choose for himself, being responsible for the choice he should make. At the time I thought this was merely playful; and I answered it accordingly. But in his reply to me he renewed it, as a serious argument. In seriousness then, the facts of this proposition are not true as stated. God did not place good and evil before man, telling him to make his choice. On the contrary, he did tell him there was one tree, of the fruit of which, he should not eat, upon pain of certain death. I should scarcely wish so strong a prohibition against slavery in Nebraska.

But this argument strikes me as not a little remarkable in another particular—in its strong resemblance to the old argument for the "Divine right of Kings." By the latter, the King is to do just as he pleases with his white subjects, being responsible to God alone. By the former the white man is to do just as he pleases with his black slaves, being responsible to God alone. The two things are precisely alike; and it is but natural that they should find similar arguments to sustain them.

I had argued, that the application of the principle of self-government, as contended for, would require the revival of the African slave trade—that no argument could be made in favor of a man's right to take slaves to Nebraska, which could not be equally well made in favor of his right to bring them from the coast of Africa. The Judge replied, that the constitution requires the suppression of the foreign slave trade; but does not require the prohibition of slavery in the territories. That is a mistake, in point of fact. The constitution does NOT require action of Congress in either case; and it does AUTHORIZE it in both. And so, there is still no difference between the cases.

In regard to what I had said, the advantage the slave States have over the free, in the matter of representation, the Judge replied that we, in the free States, count five negroes as five white people, while in the slave States, they count five slaves as three whites only; and that the advantage, at last, was on the side of the free States.

Now, in the slave States, they count free negroes just as we do; and it so happens that besides their slaves, they have as many free negroes as we have, and thirty-three thousand over. Thus, their free negroes more than balance ours; and their advantage over us, in consequence of their slaves, still remains as I stated it.

In reply to my argument, that the compromise measures of 1850, were a system of equivalents; and that the provisions of no one of them could fairly be carried to other subjects, without its corresponding equivalent being carried with it, the Judge denied out-right, that these measures had any connection with, or dependence upon, each other. This is mere desperation. If they have no connection, why are they always spoken of in connection? Why has he so spoken of them, a thousand times? Why has he constantly

54 Because of population growth in the northern section of Oregon Territory and the distance between northern settlements and those in the southern parts, there was a push to establish a new territory. Congress created Washington Territory for Oregon's northern settlers. Douglas submitted the bill to the Senate and it was passed without debate. The laws of Oregon were enforced in the new territory, including a ban on slavery. Johannsen, *Stephen A. Douglas,* 396.

called them a SERIES of measures? Why does everybody call them a compromise? Why was California kept out of the Union, six or seven months, if it was not because of its connection with the other measures? Webster's leading definition of the verb "to compromise" is "to adjust and settle a difference, by mutual agreement with concessions of claims by the parties." This conveys precisely the popular understanding of the word compromise. We knew, before the Judge told us, that these measures passed separately, and in distinct bills; and that no two of them were passed by the votes of precisely the same members. But we also know, and so does he know, that no one of them could have passed both branches of Congress but for the understanding that the others were to pass also. Upon this understanding each got votes, which it could have got in no other way. It is this fact, that gives the measures their true character; and it is the universal knowledge of this fact, that has given them the name of compromise so expressive of that true character.

I had asked[,] "If in carrying the provisions of the Utah and New Mexico laws to Nebraska, you could clear away other objection, how can you leave Nebraska 'perfectly free' to introduce slavery BEFORE she forms a constitution—during her territorial government?—while the Utah and New Mexico laws only authorize it WHEN they form constitutions, and are admitted into the Union?" To this Judge Douglas answered that the Utah and New Mexico laws, also authorized it BEFORE; and to prove this, he read from one of their laws, as follows: "That the legislative power of said territory shall extend to all rightful subjects of legislation consistent with the constitution of the United States and the provisions of this act."

Now it is perceived from the reading of this, that there is nothing express upon the subject; but that the authority is sought to be implied merely, for the general provision of "all rightful subjects of legislation." In reply to this, I insist, as a legal rule of construction, as well as the plain popular view of the matter, that the EXPRESS provision for Utah and New Mexico coming in with slavery if they choose, when they shall form constitutions, is an EXCLUSION of all implied authority on the same subject—that Congress, having the subject distinctly in their minds, when they made the express provision, they therein expressed their WHOLE meaning on that subject.

The Judge rather insinuated that I had found it convenient to forget the Washington territorial law passed in 1853.[54] This was a division of Oregon, organizing the northern part, as the territory of Washington. He asserted that, by this act, the ordinance of '87 theretofore existing in Oregon, was repealed; that nearly all the members of Congress voted for it, beginning in the H.R., with Charles Allen of Massachusetts,[55] and ending with Richard Yates, of Illinois;[56] and that he could not understand how those who now oppose the Nebraska bill, so voted then, unless it was because it was then too soon after both the great political parties had ratified the compromises of 1850, and the ratification therefore too fresh, to be then repudiated.

Now I had seen the Washington act before; and have carefully examined it since; and I aver that there is no repeal of the ordinance of '87, or of any prohibition of slavery, in it. In express terms, there is absolutely nothing in the whole law upon the subject—in fact, nothing to lead a reader to THINK of the subject. To my judgment, it is equally free from every thing from which such repeal can be legally implied; but however this may be, are men now to be entrapped by a legal implication, extracted from covert language, introduced perhaps, for the very purpose of entrapping them? I sincerely wish every man could read this law quite through, carefully watching every sentence, and every line, for a repeal of the ordinance of '87 or any thing equivalent to it.

Another point on the Washington act. If it was intended to be modified after the Utah and New Mexico acts, as Judge Douglas, insists, why was it not inserted in it, as in them, that Washington was to come in with or without slavery as she may choose at the adoption of her constitution? It has no such provision in it; and I defy the ingenuity of man to give a reason for the omission, other than that it was not intended to follow the Utah and New Mexico laws in regard to the question of slavery.

The Washington act not only differs vitally from the Utah and New Mexico acts; but the Nebraska act differs vitally from both. By the latter act the people are left "perfectly free" to regulate their own domestic concerns, &; but in all the former, all their laws are to be submitted to Congress, and if disapproved are to be null. The Washington act goes even further; it absolutely prohibits the territorial legislation, by very strong and guarded language, from establishing banks, or borrowing money on the faith of the territory. Is this the sacred right of self-government we hear vaunted so much? No sir, the Nebraska bill finds no model in the acts of '50 or the Washington act. It finds no model in any law from Adam till today. As Phillips[57] says of Napoleon, the Nebraska act is grand, gloomy, and peculiar; wrapped in the solitude of its own originality; without a model, and without a shadow upon the earth.

In the course of his reply, Senator Douglas remarked, in substance, that he had always considered this government was made for the white people and not for the negroes. Why, in point of mere fact, I think so too. But in

55  Charles Allen (1797–1869), a member of the Free Soil Party, served Massachusetts as a U.S. congressman from 1849 to 1853. "Allen, Charles," Biographical Directory of the United States Congress, http://bioguide.congress.gov/scripts/biodisplay.pl?index=A000115 (accessed October 5, 2014).

56  Richard Yates (1815–1873) was a Whig who served Illinois as a U.S. congressman from 1850 to 1854. Like Lincoln, Yates strongly opposed the Kansas-Nebraska Act and spoke out against it in Congress. Yates served as governor of Illinois from 1861 to 1865, followed by one term in the U.S. Senate. Neely, *Lincoln Encyclopedia,* 340–341.

57  Charles Phillips (1787?–1859) was a British lawyer and writer. Lincoln referred to his *Historical Character of Napoleon Bonaparte* (London: Printed for George Herbert, 1817). David James O'Donoghie, "Phillips, Charles (1787?–1859)," *Dictionary of National Biography,* 63 vols. (London: Smith, Elder & Co., 1885–1900), 45:196–197.

58  What Lincoln referred to was Douglas's claim that when various opponents used different arguments against him, it made it difficult for him to respond. When it was proposed to Douglas to engage Lincoln in a debate in Bloomington, Illinois, he rejected the idea, saying, "I come to Chicago, and there I am met by an old line abolitionist; I come down to the center of the State, and I am met by an old line Whig; I go to the south end of the State, and I am met by an anti-administration Democrat." "I can't hold the abolitionist responsible," he continued, "for what the Whig says; I can't hold the Whig responsible for what the abolitionist says; and I can't hold either responsible for what the Democrat says." Cited in Burlingame, *Abraham Lincoln*, 1:376–377.

59  Daniel Webster (1782–1852), along with fellow Whig Henry Clay, was considered one of the leading American orators of his time. Webster served as a U.S. congressman from New Hampshire (1813–1817) and as a U.S. congressman (1823–1827) and senator from Massachusetts (1827–1841, 1845–1850). He was an unsuccessful Whig candidate for president in 1836. He served as secretary of state under presidents William Henry Harrison, John Tyler, and Millard Fillmore. "Webster, Daniel," Biographical Directory of the United States Congress, http://bioguide.congress.gov/scripts/biodisplay.pl?index=w000238 (accessed October 5, 2014).

this remark of the Judge, there is a significance, which I think is the key to the great mistake (if there is any such mistake) which he has made in this Nebraska measure. It shows that the Judge has no very vivid impression that the negro is a human; and consequently has no idea that there can be any moral question in legislating about him. In his view, the question of whether a new country shall be slave or free, is a matter of as utter indifference, as it is whether his neighbor shall plant his farm with tobacco, or stock it with horned cattle. Now, whether this view is right or wrong, it is very certain that the great mass of mankind take a totally different view. They consider slavery a great moral wrong; and their feeling against it, is not evanescent, but eternal. It lies at the very foundation of their sense of justice; and it cannot be trifled with. It is a great and durable element of popular action, and, I think, no statesman can safely disregard it.

Our Senator also objects that those who oppose him in this measure do not entirely agree with one another. He reminds me that in my firm adherence to the constitutional rights of the slave States, I differ widely from others who are co-operating with me in opposing the Nebraska bill; and he says it is not quite fair to oppose him in this variety of ways.[58] He should remember that he took us by surprise—astounded us—by this measure. We were thunderstruck and stunned; and we reeled and fell in utter confusion. But we rose each fighting, grasping whatever he could first reach—a scythe—a pitchfork—a chopping axe, or a butcher's cleaver. We struck in the direction of the sound; and we are rapidly closing in upon him. He must not think to divert us from our purpose, by showing us that our drill, our dress, and our weapons, are not entirely perfect and uniform. When the storm shall be past, he shall find us still Americans; no less devoted to the continued Union and prosperity of the country than heretofore.

Finally, the Judge invokes against me, the memory of Clay and Webster.[59] They were great men; and men of great deeds. But where have I assailed them? For what is it, that their life-long enemy, shall now make profit, by assuming to defend them against me, their life-long friend? I go against the repeal of the Missouri compromise; did they ever go for it? They went for the Compromise of 1850; did I ever go against them? They were greatly devoted to the Union; to the small measure of my ability, was I ever less so? Clay and Webster were dead before this question arose; by what authority shall our Senator say they would espouse his side of it, if alive? Mr. Clay was the leading spirit in making the Missouri compromise; is it very credible that if now alive, he would take the lead in the breaking of it? The truth is that some support from whigs is now a necessity with the Judge, and for thus it is, that the names of Clay and Webster are now invoked. His old friends have deserted him in such numbers as to leave too few to live by. He came to his own, and his own received him not,[60] and Lo! He turns unto the Gentiles.

A word now as to the Judge's desperate assumption that the compromises of '50 had no connection with one another; that Illinois came into the Union as a slave state, and some other similar ones. This is no other than a bold denial of the history of the country. If we do not know that the Com-promises of '50 were dependent on each other; if we do not know that Illi-nois came into the Union as a free state—we do not know any thing. If we do not know these things, we do not know that we ever had a revolutionary war, or such a chief as Washington. To deny these things is to deny our na-tional axioms, or dogmas, at least; and it puts an end to all argument. If a man will stand up and assert, and repeat, and re-assert, that two and two do not make four, I know nothing in the power of argument that can stop him. I think I can answer the Judge so long as he sticks to the premises; but when he flies from them, I can not work an argument into the consistency of a maternal gag, and actually close his mouth with it. In such case I can only commend him to the seventy thousand answers just in from Pennsylvania, Ohio and Indiana.[61]

60 John 1:11.

61 After his Peoria appearance, Lincoln presented similar speeches in Chicago, Quincy, and Urbana. His Peoria speech was condemned by some Democrats for promoting miscegenation, while Republicans viewed it favorably. Antislavery journalist Horace White (1834–1916) claimed Lincoln's October 4 Springfield address was the "greatest" speech ever delivered in Illinois. Lincoln was undoubtedly pleased by the positive response to his series of speeches, noting that they received "more marked attention than they had ever done before." White and Lincoln cited in Foner, *The Fiery Trial*, 69–70; Burlingame, *Abraham Lincoln*, 1:389.

1    George Robertson (1790–1874) was a lawyer and politician. He served in the U.S. House of Representatives from 1817 to 1821, the Kentucky House of Representatives from 1822 to 1827, and as Kentucky's secretary of state in 1828. He later joined the Whig Party, and was elected to represent that party in the Kentucky House of Representatives in 1848, 1851, and 1852. Robertson visited Springfield on July 9, 1855, when Lincoln was in Chicago and left for Lincoln an inscribed copy of his book *Scrapbook on Law and Politics, Men and Times* (Lexington, KY: A. W. Elder, 1855), a collection of his speeches and papers. "Robertson, George," Biographical Directory of the United States Congress, http://bioguide.congress.gov/scripts/biodisplay.pl?index=R000322 (accessed October 11, 2014); *CW,* 2:318n1; Miers, *Lincoln Day by Day,* 2:148–149.

2    Lincoln referred to a speech Robertson delivered in Congress on the Arkansas Territory in which he argued against permitting slavery in the new territory, an issue that generated a sectional crisis that resulted in the Missouri Compromise of 1820. Robertson, *Scrapbook,* 25–27.

3    Lincoln did not foresee the "peaceful extinction" of slavery predicted by Robertson in 1819. In light of the recent fight against the Kansas-Nebraska Act, Lincoln had grown pessimistic. In his view the nation had lost its way on this moral issue, as political leaders rejected the spirit of the American Revolution and of the founders to the point that the once-revered "fourth of July" had become a day merely for firecrackers.

# Letter to George Robertson

## August 15, 1855

Hon: Geo. Robertson Springfield, Ills.
Lexington, Ky. Aug. 15. 1855

My dear Sir: The volume you left for me has been received. I am really grateful for the honor of your kind remembrance, as well as for the book.[1] The partial reading I have already given it, has afforded me much of both pleasure and instruction. It was new to me that the exact question which led to the Missouri compromise, had arisen before it arose in regard to Missouri; and that you had taken so prominent a part in it. Your short, but able and patriotic speech upon that occasion, has not been improved upon since, by those holding the same views; and, with all the lights you then had, the views you took appear to me as very reasonable.[2]

You are not a friend of slavery in the abstract. In that speech you spoke of *"the peaceful extinction of slavery"* and used other expressions indicating your belief that the thing was, at some time, to have an end[.] Since then we have had thirty six years of experience; and this experience has demonstrated, I think, that there is no peaceful extinction of slavery in prospect for us.[3] The signal failure of Henry Clay, and other good and great men, in 1849, to effect any thing in favor of gradual emancipation in Kentucky, together with a thousand other signs, extinguishes that hope utterly. On the question of liberty, as a principle, we are not what we have been. When we were the political slaves of King George, and wanted to be free, we called the maxim that "all men are created equal" a self evident truth; but now when we have grown fat, and have lost all dread of being slaves ourselves, we have become so greedy to be *masters* that we call the same maxim "a self-evident lie." The fourth of July has not quite dwindled away; it is still a great day—*for burning fire-crackers!!!*

That spirit which desired the peaceful extinction of slavery, has itself become extinct, with the *occasion,* and the *men* of the Revolution. Under the impulse of that occasion, nearly half the states adopted systems of emancipation at once; and it is a significant fact, that not a single state has done the like since. So far as peaceful, voluntary emancipation is concerned, the condition of the negro slave in America, scarcely less terrible to the contemplation of a free mind, is now as fixed, and hopeless of change for the better, as that of the lost souls of the finally impenitent. The Autocrat of all the Russias will resign his crown, and proclaim his subjects free republicans sooner than will our American masters voluntarily give up their slaves.

Our political problem now is[,] "Can we, as a nation, continue together *permanently—forever*—half slave, and half free?"[4] The problem is too mighty for me. May God, in his mercy, superintend the solution. Your much obliged friend, and humble servant

A. LINCOLN—

4   Lincoln posed a question that would form the basis of his famous speech three years later: see "'House Divided' Address, Springfield, Illinois, June 16, 1858," in this volume.

*Lincoln wrote to his old friend Speed, a supporter of popular sovereignty, in the midst of the violent and bloody war in Kansas Territory over the slavery issue and rising Northern resistance to the Fugitive Slave Law. Responding to Speed's inquiry concerning his association with the nascent Republican Party, Lincoln reiterated his strong opposition to slavery and its extension, yet assured Speed that he was neither an abolitionist nor an advocate of disunion. Lincoln still considered himself a Whig rather than a Republican—and certainly not a Know-Nothing.*

1   In an 1846 letter to Speed, Lincoln had referred to their strained relationship, citing the "suspension of our correspondence" and his dismay at the prospect that their friendship would "die by degrees." As the slavery issue became the dominant political issue of the 1850s, the gulf between Lincoln and Speed only widened. Despite their political differences, especially concerning slavery, Speed remained loyal to the Union during the Civil War. *CW,* 1:390–391; Neely, *Lincoln Encyclopedia,* 285.

2   As he stated in his Peoria speech and other public addresses, Lincoln, despite his abhorrence of slavery, acknowledged the constitutional rights of slaveholding Southerners and insisted he did not wish to interfere with that right for the sake of protecting the Union.

3   Lincoln described this incident with the shackled slaves in a letter to Mary Speed, Joshua Speed's half-sister (see "Letter to Mary Speed, September 27, 1841," in this volume) but did not mention the torment that the experience had caused him.

4   In light of Speed's willingness to see the Union dissolved in order to protect states' rights, Lincoln contrasted Southerners' tendency to threaten disunion when debating issues concerning slavery with Northerners' willingness to compromise to save the Union.

# Letter to Joshua F. Speed

## August 24, 1855

Dear Speed: Springfield, Aug: 24, 1855

You know what a poor correspondent I am. Ever since I received your very agreeable letter of the 22nd. of May I have been intending to write you in answer to it. You suggest that in political action now, you and I would differ.[1] I suppose we would; not quite as much, however, as you may think. You know I dislike slavery; and you fully admit the abstract wrong of it. So far there is no cause of difference. But you say that sooner than yield your legal right to the slave—especially at the bidding of those who are not themselves interested, you would see the Union dissolved. I am not aware that *any one* is bidding you to yield that right; very certainly *I* am not. I leave that matter entirely to yourself. I also acknowledge *your* rights and *my* obligations, under the constitution, in regard to your slaves. I confess I hate to see the poor creatures hunted down, and caught, and carried back to their stripes, and unrewarded toils; but I bite my lip and keep quiet.[2] In 1841 you and I had together a tedious low-water trip, on a Steam Boat from Louisville to St. Louis. You may remember, as I well do, that from Louisville to the mouth of the Ohio there were, on board, ten or a dozen slaves, shackled together with irons. That sight was a continual torment to me; and I see something like it every time I touch the Ohio, or any other slave-border.[3] It is hardly fair for you to assume, that I have no interest in a thing which has, and continually exercises, the power of making me miserable. You ought rather to appreciate how much the great body of the Northern people do crucify their feelings, in order to maintain their loyalty to the constitution and the Union.[4]

I do oppose the extension of slavery, because my judgment and feelings so prompt me; and I am under no obligation to the contrary. If for this you and I must differ, differ we must. You say if you were President, you would

LETTER TO JOSHUA F. SPEED

send an army and hang the leaders of the Missouri outrages upon the Kansas elections; still, if Kansas fairly votes herself a slave state, she must be admitted, or the Union must be dissolved. But how if she votes herself a slave state *unfairly*—that is, by the very means for which you say you would hang men? Must she still be admitted, or the Union be dissolved? That will be the phase of the question when it first becomes a practical one. In your assumption that there may be a *fair* decision of the slavery question in Kansas, I plainly see you and I would differ about the Nebraska-law. I look upon that enactment not as a *law,* but as *violence* from the beginning. It was conceived in violence, passed in violence, is maintained in violence, and is being executed in violence. I say it was *conceived* in violence, because the destruction of the Missouri Compromise, under the circumstances, was nothing less than violence. It was *passed* in violence, because it could not have passed at all but for the votes of many members, in violent disregard of the known will of their constituents. It is *maintained* in violence because the elections since, clearly demand it's [*sic*] repeal, and this demand is openly disregarded.[5] *You* say men ought to be hung for the way they are executing that law; and *I* say the way it is being executed is quite as good as any of its antecedents. It is being executed in the precise way which was intended from the first; else why does no Nebraska man express astonishment or condemnation? Poor Reeder[6] is the only public man who has been silly enough to believe that anything like fairness was ever intended; and he has been bravely undeceived.

That Kansas will form a Slave constitution, and, with it, will ask to be admitted into the Union, I take to be an already settled question; and so settled by the very means you so pointedly condemn. By every principle of law, ever held by any court, North or South, every negro taken to Kansas is free; yet in utter disregard of this—in the spirit of violence merely—that beautiful Legislature gravely passes a law to hang men who shall venture to inform a negro of his legal rights. This is the substance, and real object of the law. If, like Haman,[7] they should hang upon the gallows of their own building, I shall not be among the mourners for their fate.

In my humble sphere, I shall advocate the restoration of the Missouri Compromise, so long as Kansas remains a territory; and when, by all these foul means, it seeks to come into the Union as a Slave-state, I shall oppose it. I am very loth, in any case, to withhold my assent to the enjoyment of property *acquired,* or *located,* in good faith; but I do not admit that *good faith,* in taking a negro to Kansas, to be held in slavery, is a *possibility* with any man. Any man who has sense enough to be the controller of his own

5   The violence and bloodshed that Lincoln and others feared for Kansas became a reality as free-state and slave-state advocates engaged in a fierce and sometimes bloody battle for control of the future state. Anti-Nebraska coalitions and the nascent Republican Party used "Bleeding Kansas" as an effective weapon against the Democratic Party. In March 1855, with thousands of proslave Missourians crossing the border and voting, a proslavery legislature was fraudulently elected. Despite the governor's veto, the legislature instituted proslavery statutes and expelled the few free-state representatives who were elected. Eventually, two territorial governments were established in Kansas, with the proslavery government located at Lecompton, led by a governor and other officials appointed by the president of the United States, and a free-state government at Topeka, representing a majority of Kansas residents outraged by the fraudulent election. Between November 1855 and May 1856, armed groups representing both factions engaged in violent acts, including murder. In 1857 the Kansas issue would divide the Democratic Party, pitting the forces of President James Buchanan (1791–1868) against those of Stephen A. Douglas. See Potter, *The Impending Crisis,* 209–212. See also Etcheson, *Bleeding Kansas,* and Rawley, *Race and Politics.*

6   Andrew H. Reeder (1807–1864), a popular-sovereignty Democrat from Pennsylvania, was appointed the first territorial governor of Kansas by President Franklin Pierce in June 1854. While Reeder was not antislavery, he took a neutral stance on the issue in Kansas, in keeping with popular sovereignty. He remained in office until he was fired by Pierce in August 1855 for his stance against the fraudulent election held the previous March. Reeder returned to Pennsylvania and joined the Republican Party. In 1861 he declined an appointment as brigadier general from President Lincoln. "Andrew Horatio Reeder," Kansapedia, http://

www.kshs.org/kansapedia/andrew-horatio-reeder/12181 (accessed October 13, 2014).

7   Haman, according to the Old Testament, was a vizier in the Persian empire who, along with his wife, plotted to kill all the Jews in ancient Persia. The plot was discovered and Haman was hanged on his own gallows. Esther 7:6–10.

8   Benjamin F. Stringfellow (1816–1891) was a Virginia-born proslavery lawyer and businessman who became active in Missouri politics. Dedicated to making Kansas a slave state, Stringfellow actively supported the proslavery movement through the Missouri Platte County Self-Defensive Association, which he helped found. Infuriated by Governor Andrew Reeder's vetoes of proslavery legislation and his assertion that he was a "border ruffian," Stringfellow challenged Reeder to a duel. When the governor declined, Stringfellow physically assaulted him. Although both men drew pistols, the encounter was stopped by territorial officials. The proslavery cause was supported by the *Atchison Squatter Sovereign,* a newspaper owned by John H. Stringfellow (1819–1905), the physician brother of Benjamin. "Benjamin F. Stringfellow, 1816–1891," Territorial Kansas Online 1854–1861, http://www.territorialkansasonline.org/~imlskto/cgi-bin/index.php?SCREEN=bio_sketches/stringfellow_benjamin (accessed October 14, 2014); Etcheson, *Bleeding Kansas,* 67.

property, has too much sense to misunderstand the outrageous character of this whole Nebraska business. But I digress. In my opposition to the admission of Kansas I shall have some company; but we may be beaten. If we are, I shall not, on that account, attempt to dissolve the Union. On the contrary, if we succeed, there will be enough of us to take care of the Union. I think it probable, however, we shall be beaten. Standing as a unit among yourselves, you can, directly, and indirectly, bribe enough of our men to carry the day—as you could on an open proposition to establish monarchy. Get hold of some man in the North, whose position and ability is such, that he can make the support of your measure—whatever it may be—a *democratic party necessity,* and the thing is done. *Appropos* [*sic*] of this, let me tell you an anecdote. Douglas introduced the Nebraska bill in January. In February afterwards, there was a call session of the Illinois Legislature. Of the one hundred members composing the two branches of that body, about seventy were democrats. These latter held a caucus, in which the Nebraska bill was talked of, if not formally discussed. It was thereby discovered that just three, and no more, were in favor of the measure. In a day or two Douglas' orders came on to have resolutions passed approving the bill; and they were passed by large majorities!!! The truth of this is vouched for by a bolting democratic member. The masses too, democratic as well as whig, were even, nearer unanamous [*sic*] against it; but as soon as the party necessity of supporting it, became apparent, the way the democracy began to see the *wisdom* and *justice* of it, was perfectly astonishing.

You say if Kansas fairly votes herself a free state, as a christian you will rather rejoice at it. All decent slave-holders *talk* that way; and I do not doubt their candor. But they never *vote* that way. Although in a private letter, or conversation, you will express your preference that Kansas shall be free, you would vote for no man for Congress who would say the same thing publicly. No such man could be elected from any district in any slave-state. You think Stringfellow & Co[8] ought to be hung; and yet, at the next presidential election you will vote for the exact type and representative of Stringfellow. The slave-breeders and slave-traders, are a small, odious and detested class, among you; and yet in politics, they dictate the course of all of you, and are as completely your masters, as you are the masters of your own negroes.

You enquire where I now stand. That is a disputed point. I think I am a whig; but others say there are no whigs, and that I am an abolitionist. When I was at Washington I voted for the Wilmot Proviso as good as forty times, and I never heard of any one attempting to unwhig me for that. I now do no more than oppose the *extension* of slavery.

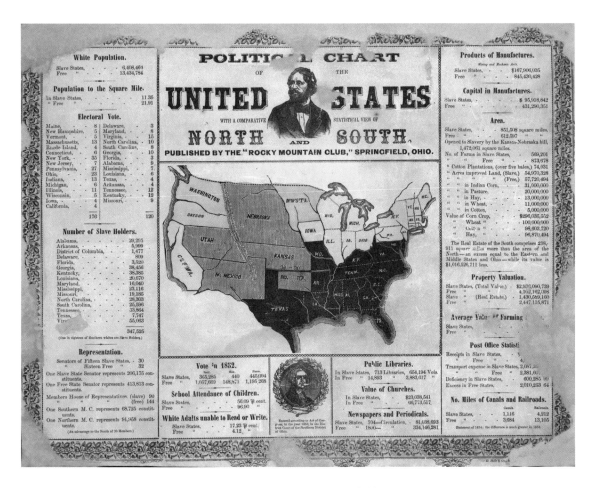

C. F. Bradley, *Political Chart of the United States, 1856.* Broadside (Springfield, OH: Rocky Mountain Club of Springfield, 1856). Republican presidential campaign chart illustrating differences between free and slave states.

I am not a Know-Nothing.[9] That is certain. How could I be? How can any one who abhors the oppression of negroes, be in favor of degrading classes of white people? Our progress in degeneracy appears to me to be pretty rapid. As a nation, we began by declaring that "*all men are created equal.*" We now practically read it "all men are created equal, *except negroes.*" When the Know-Nothings get control, it will read "all men are created equal, except negroes, *and foreigners, and catholics.*" When it comes to this I should prefer emigrating to some country where they make no pretence of loving liberty—to Russia, for instance, where despotism can be taken pure, and without the base alloy of hypocrisy [*sic*].

9 The Know-Nothing Party, or American Party, rose to prominence in the 1850s as part of the realignment of the political system in the midst of the collapse of the Whig Party, the sectional split among Democrats as a result of the Kansas-Nebraska Act, and the high immigration rates during the previous decade. Originally founded as a secret organization, the anti-immigrant and anti-Catholic Know-Nothing movement achieved a modicum of success in the 1850s as disaffected

Whigs and Democrats sought political refuge. Know-Nothings claimed that the influx of immigrants, most of whom were Catholics, posed a threat to the nation. By 1856, the Know-Nothing Party was strong enough to run a presidential candidate, former president and Whig Millard Fillmore, and had replaced the Whigs as the major opposition party to the Democrats. Despite Lincoln's distaste for the Know-Nothings, he was a shrewd politician who understood, as did many in the new Republican Party, that an alliance with Know-Nothings who opposed the expansion of slavery was sound, practical politics. By 1860 the Know-Nothing movement was dead, with many of its former Northern members having joined the Republican Party. Tyler Anbinder, *Nativism and Slavery: The Northern Know-Nothings and the Politics of the 1850s* (New York: Oxford University Press, 1992); and Michael F. Holt, *The Political Crisis of the 1850s* (New York: John Wiley, 1978).

10   Lincoln's wife, Mary Lincoln.

Mary[10] will probably pass a day or two in Louisville in October. My kindest regards to Mrs. Speed. On the leading subject of this letter, I have more of her sympathy than I have of yours.

And yet let say I am Your friend forever

A. LINCOLN—

# Speech at Kalamazoo, Michigan

## August 27, 1856

*By the 1856 presidential election, Lincoln had joined the new Republican Party and was campaigning actively on behalf of its first presidential nominee, John C. Frémont. In this speech, one of more than fifty he delivered throughout Illinois during that campaign, Lincoln spoke ardently against the expansion of slavery. His main objective was to convince conservative Whigs and nativists in Illinois to support the Republican Party rather than the Know-Nothings.*

Fellow countrymen:—Under the Constitution of the U.S. another Presidential contest approaches us.[1] All over this land—that portion at least, of which I know much—the people are assembling to consider the proper course to be adopted by them. One of the first considerations is to learn what the people differ about. If we ascertain what we differ about, we shall be better able to decide. The question of slavery, at the present day, should be not only the greatest question, but very nearly the sole question. Our opponents, however, prefer that this should not be the case. To get at this question, I will occupy your attention but a single moment. The question is simply this:—Shall slavery be spread into the new Territories, or not? This is the naked question. If we should support Fremont successfully in this, it may be charged that we will not be content with restricting slavery in the new territories. If we should charge that James Buchanan,[2] by his platform, is bound to extend slavery into the territories, and that he is in favor of its being thus spread, we should be puzzled to prove it. We believe it, nevertheless. By taking the issue as I present it, whether it shall be permitted as an issue, is made up between the parties. Each takes his own stand. This is the question: Shall the Government of the United States prohibit slavery in the United States.

We have been in the habit of deploring the fact that slavery exists amongst us. We have ever deplored it. Our forefathers did, and they declared, as we have done in later years, the blame rested on the mother Government of Great Britain. We constantly condemn Great Britain for not preventing slavery from coming amongst us. She would not interfere to prevent it, and so individuals were enabled to introduce the institution without opposition. I have alluded to this, to ask you if this is not exactly the policy of Buchanan and his friends, to place this government in the attitude then occupied by the government of Great Britain—placing the nation in the

[1] Created out of political turmoil generated by passage of the Kansas-Nebraska Act, in which the Whig Party disintegrated and the Democratic Party divided, Republicans attracted former Whigs, anti-Nebraska Democrats, abolitionists, Protestant German immigrants, and nativists. Having won several local and state elections in 1855, the Republican Party was poised to challenge the Democratic Party at the national level. Attempts at establishing a Republican organization in Illinois in 1854 failed when many Whigs, including Lincoln, remained loyal to their party and the Know-Nothing movement gained strength. In 1856, however, Lincoln, realizing that an organized anti-Nebraska coalition was essential to restricting slavery's expansion, participated in establishing the Illinois Republican Party. The party held its national convention in Philadelphia, June 17–19, 1856, and adopted a platform calling for the prohibition of slavery's expansion into the territories; the admission of Kansas as a free state; and federal aid for internal improvements, including construction of a railroad to the Pacific. The party nominated the charismatic explorer of the West and former U.S. senator from California John C. Frémont (1813–1890) for president and William L. Dayton (1807–1851), a former Whig from New Jersey, for vice president. To Lincoln's pleasant surprise, he received 110 votes for vice president. Although he campaigned vigorously for Frémont, Lincoln, along with the Illinois delegation, had supported the seventy-one-year-old

former Supreme Court justice John McLean (1785–1861) of Ohio, because he would appeal to the conservative and moderate voters who were critical to the Republican Party's success in a presidential contest. The Democratic Party nominated James Buchanan and the American, or Know-Nothing, Party chose former Whig and former president Millard Fillmore. On the origins of the Republican Party and Lincoln's role in founding the party in Illinois, see William E. Gienapp, *The Origins of the Republican Party, 1852–1856* (New York: Oxford University Press, 1987); and Burlingame, *Abraham Lincoln,* 1:411–423.

2 James Buchanan of Pennsylvania was the Democratic Party's candidate for president in 1856. Prior to his nomination, Buchanan had served in the Pennsylvania House of Representatives (1814–1816), the U.S. House of Representatives (1821–1831), as minister to Russia under President Andrew Jackson (1832–1833), in the U.S. Senate (1834–1845), as secretary of state under President James Knox Polk (1845–1849), and as minister to Great Britain (the Court of St. James's) under President Franklin Pierce (1853–1856). Buchanan had sought and failed to gain the Democratic Party's presidential nomination in 1844, 1848, and 1852. Acknowledging Northern outrage against the Kansas-Nebraska Act, Democrats saw the elderly Buchanan as a safe choice, in contrast to rivals Stephen Douglas and former president Franklin Pierce, who were both tarnished by their association with the controversial legislation; Buchanan was out of the country during the contentious debates. However, the Democratic Party platform in 1856 endorsed popular sovereignty in the territories as embodied in the Kansas-Nebraska Act; the Compromise of 1850, including the Fugitive Slave Act; federal noninterference with slavery; and an aggressive foreign policy in the Gulf of Mexico. The best biographical account of

position to authorize the territories to reproach it, for refusing to allow them to hold slaves. I would like to ask your attention, any gentleman to tell me when the people of Kansas are going to decide. When are they to do it? How are they to do it? I asked that question two years ago—when, and how are [they] to do it?[3] Not many weeks ago, our new Senator from Illinois, (Mr. Trumbull)[4] asked Douglas how it could be done. Douglas is a great man—at keeping from answering questions he don't want to answer. He would not answer. He said it was a question for the Supreme Court to decide. In the North, his friends argue that the people can decide it at any time. The Southerners say there is no power in the people, whatever. We know that from the time that white people have been allowed in the territory, they have brought slaves with them. Suppose the people come up to vote as freely, and with as perfect protection as we could do it here. Will they be at liberty to vote their sentiments? If they can, then all that has ever been said about our provincial ancestors is untrue, and they could have done so, also. We know our Southern friends say that the General Government cannot interfere. The people, say they, have no right to interfere. They could as truly say,—"It is amongst us—we cannot get rid of it."

But I am afraid I waste too much time on this point. I take it as an illustration of the principle, that slaves are admitted into the territories. And, while I am speaking of Kansas, how will that operate? Can men vote truly? We will suppose that there are ten men who go into Kansas to settle. Nine of these are opposed to slavery. One has ten slaves. The slaveholder is a good man in other respects; he is a good neighbor, and being a wealthy man, he is enabled to do the others many neighborly kindnesses. They like the man, though they don't like the system by which he holds his fellow-men in bondage. And here let me say, that in intellectual and physical structure, our Southern brethren do not differ from us. They are, like us, subject to passions, and it is only their odious institution of slavery, that makes the breach between us. These ten men of whom I was speaking, live together three or four years; they intermarry; their family ties are strengthened. And who wonders that in time, the people learn to look upon slavery with complacency? This is the way in which slavery is planted, and gains so firm a foothold. I think this is a strong card that the Nebraska party have played, and won upon, in this game.

I suppose that this crowd are [*sic*] opposed to the admission of slavery into Kansas, yet it is true that in all crowds there are some who differ from the majority. I want to ask the Buchanan men, who are against the spread of slavery, if there be any present, why not vote for the man who is against it? I understand that Mr. Fillmore's position is precisely like Buchanan's.[5] I understand that, by the Nebraska bill, a door has been opened for the spread of slavery in the Territories. Examine, if you please, and see if they have ever done any such thing as try to shut the door. It is true that Fillmore tickles a few of his friends with the notion that he is not the cause of the door being opened. Well; it brings him into this position: he tries to get both sides, one by denouncing those who opened the door, and the other by hinting that he doesn't care a fig for its being open. If he were President, he would have one side or the other—he would either restrict slavery or not. Of course it would be so. There could be no middle way. You who hate slavery and love freedom, why not, as Fillmore and Buchanan are on the same ground, vote for Fremont? Why not vote for the man who takes your side of the question? "Well," says Buchanier, "it is none of our business." But is it not *our* business? There are several reasons why I think it is our business. But let us see how it is. Others have urged these reasons before, but they are still of use. By our Constitution we are represented in Congress in proportion to numbers, and in counting the numbers that give us our representatives, three slaves are counted as two people.[6] The State of Maine has six representatives in the lower house of Congress. In strength South Carolina is equal to her. But stop! Maine has *twice as many* white people, and 32,000 to boot! And is that fair? I don't complain of it. This regulation was put in force when the exigencies of the times demanded it, and could not have been avoided. Now, one man in South Carolina is the same as two men here. Maine should have twice as many men in Congress as South Carolina. It is a fact that any man in South Carolina has more influence and power in Congress today than any two now before me. The same thing is true of all slave States, though it may not be in the same proportion. It is a truth that cannot be denied, that in all the free States no white man is the equal of the white man of the slave States. But this is in the Constitution, and we must stand up to it. The question, then, is, "Have we no interest as to whether the white man of the North shall be the equal of the white man of the South?" Once when I used this argument in the presence of Douglas, he answered that in the North the black man was counted as a full man, and had an equal vote with the white, while at the South they were counted at but three-fifths. And Douglas, when he had made this reply, doubtless thought he had forever silenced the objection.

Have we no interest in the free Territories of the United States—that they should be kept open for the homes of free white people?[7] As our Northern States are growing more and more in wealth and population, we are

Buchanan is Philip Shriver Klein, *President James Buchanan: A Biography* (University Park: Pennsylvania State University Press, 1962). On the election of 1856, see Roy F. Nichols and Philip S. Klein, "Election of 1856," in *The Coming to Power: Critical Presidential Elections in American History,* ed. Arthur M. Schlesinger Jr., Fred L. Israel, and William P. Hansen (New York: Chelsea House, 1972), 91–117.

3 See "Speech on the Kansas-Nebraska Act at Peoria, Illinois, October 16, 1854," in this volume.

4 In the fall 1854 elections, opponents of the Kansas-Nebraska Act performed strongly throughout the North. Lincoln reluctantly ran for a seat in the Illinois legislature and won. He wanted to serve in the U.S. Senate, however, and since a member of the legislature was ineligible for election to the Senate, Lincoln declined to accept his seat in the state legislature so that he could run in 1855 for the Senate seat held by James Shields. Running as an anti-Nebraska Whig, Lincoln faced Democratic governor Joel Matteson (1808–1873) and Lyman Trumbull, the anti-Nebraska candidate of a group of independent Democrats. The decision was in the hands of the Illinois legislature and Lincoln, considered the favorite, led after the first ballot with forty-five votes, five short of what he needed to win. Over the next eight ballots, Lincoln's numbers decreased while Trumbull's and Matteson's increased. Realizing he could not win and fearing the election of a pro-Nebraska Democrat, Lincoln directed his supporters to vote for the anti-Nebraska Trumbull as a compromise choice. Lincoln was bitterly disappointed, although he wrote a colleague soon after the election that he regretted his defeat "moderately" and was "not nervous about it." "On the whole," Lincoln continued, "it is perhaps as well for our general cause that Trumbull is elected. The Neb. Men confess they hate it worse than anything that could have happened. It is a great consolation to see them

worse whipped than I am." Trumbull was a Connecticut-born lawyer who had moved to Illinois in 1837, where he became active in politics as a Democrat. Prior to his election to the U.S. Senate in 1855, he served in the Illinois state senate, as Illinois secretary of state, on the Illinois Supreme Court, and in the U.S. House of Representatives. Trumbull subsequently became a Republican and supported Lincoln in the 1860 presidential election. Trumbull's relationship with President Lincoln, however, was often strained, and he opposed Lincoln's reelection in 1864. Biographical information on Trumbull can be found in Neely, *Lincoln Encyclopedia,* 313–315. For Lincoln's 1855 senate bid, see Donald, *Lincoln,* 177–185. Lincoln's response to his defeat is cited in *CW,* 2:306.

5    Millard Fillmore served as vice president of the United States under Zachary Taylor and assumed the presidency on Taylor's death in July 1850, holding the office until 1853. A Whig from upstate New York, the self-educated Fillmore served for three terms in Congress (1837–1843). A conservative Whig who had no sympathy for the antislavery cause, Fillmore was rejected by his party for the presidency in 1852. Unlike many Northern Whigs, Fillmore did not join the Republican Party. He accepted the Know-Nothing, or American Party, nomination for president in 1856 on a platform that called on Northerners and Southerners to unite against the influx of foreigners into the United States. During the campaign, Fillmore declared that Southerners would have the right to secede if the Republican Frémont was elected. In 1861 he denounced secession but opposed war against the South. For Fillmore's career, see Robert J. Rayback, *Millard Fillmore: Biography of a President* (East Aurora, NY: Henry Stewart, 1959); Paul Finkelman, *Millard Fillmore* (New York: Henry Holt, 2011).

6    As he had done in his anti-Nebraska speeches two years before, Lincoln points to the "three-

continually in want of an outlet, through which it may pass out to enrich our country. In this we have an interest—a deep and abiding interest. There is another thing, and that is the mature knowledge we have—the greatest interest of all. It is the doctrine, that the people are to be driven from the maxims of our free Government, that despises the spirit which for eighty years has celebrated the anniversary of our national independence.

We are a great empire. We are eighty years old. We stand at once the wonder and admiration of the whole world, and we must enquire what it is that has given us so much prosperity, and we shall understand that to give up that one thing, would be to give up all future prosperity. This cause is that every man can make himself. It has been said that such a race of prosperity has been run nowhere else. We find a people on the North-east, who have a different government from ours, being ruled by a Queen. Turning to the South, we see a people who, while they boast of being free, keep their fellow beings in bondage. Compare our Free States with either, shall we say here that we have no interest in keeping that principle alive? Shall we say—"Let it be." No—we have an interest in the maintenance of the principles of the Government, and without this interest, it is worth nothing. I have noticed in Southern newspapers, particularly the Richmond *Enquirer,* the Southern view of the Free States. They insist that slavery has a right to spread. They defend it upon principle. They insist that their slaves are far better off than Northern freemen.[8] What a mistaken view do these men have of Northern laborers! They think that men are always to remain laborers here—but there is no such class. The man who labored for another last year, this year labors for himself, and next year he will hire others to labor for him. These men don't understand when they think in this manner of Northern free labor. When these reasons can be introduced, tell me not that we have no interest in keeping the Territories free for the settlement of free laborers.

I pass, then, from this question. I think we have an ever growing interest in maintaining the free institutions of our country.

It is said that our party is a sectional party.[9] It has been said in high quarters that if Fremont and Dayton were elected the Union would be dissolved. The South do not think so. I believe it! I believe it! It is a shameful thing that the subject is talked of so much. Did we not have a Southern President and Vice-President at one time? And yet the Union has not yet been dissolved. Why, at this very moment, there is a Northern President and Vice-President. Pierce and King were elected, and King died without ever taking his seat.[10] The Senate elected a Northern man from their own numbers, to perform the duties of the Vice-President. He resigned his seat, however, as soon as he got the job of making a slave State out of Kansas. Was not that a great mistake?

Then why didn't he speak what he did mean? Why did not he speak what he ought to have spoken? That was the very thing. He should have spoken manly, and we should then have known where to have found him. It is said we expect to elect Fremont by Northern votes. Certainly we do not think the South will elect him. But let us ask the question differently. Does not Buchanan expect to be elected by Southern votes? Fillmore, however, will go out of this contest the most national man we have. He has no prospect of having a single vote on either side of Mason and Dixon's line, to trouble his poor soul about.

We believe that it is right that slavery should not be tolerated in the new territories, yet we cannot get support for this doctrine, except in one part of the country. Slavery is looked upon by men in the light of dollars and cents. The estimated worth of the slaves at the South is $1,000,000,000, and in a very few years, if the institution shall be admitted into the territories, they will have increased fifty per cent in value.

Our adversaries charge Fremont with being an abolitionist. When pressed to show proof, they frankly confess that they can show no such thing. They then run off upon the assertion that his supporters are abolitionists. But this they have never attempted to prove. I know of no word in the language that has been used so much as that one "abolitionist," having no definition. It has no meaning unless taken as designating a person who is abolishing something. If that be its signification, the supporters of Fremont are not abolitionists.[11] In Kansas all who come there are perfectly free to regulate their own social relations. There has never been a man there who was an abolitionist—for what was there to be abolished? People there had perfect freedom to express what they wished on the subject, when the Nebraska bill was first passed. Our friends in the South, who support Buchanan, have five disunion men to one at the North. This disunion is a sectional question. Who is to blame for it? Are we? I don't care how you express it. This government is sought to be put on a new track. Slavery is to be made a ruling element in our government. The question can be avoided in but two ways. By the one, we must submit, and allow slavery to triumph, or, by the other, we must triumph over the black demon. We have chosen the latter manner. If you of the North wish to get rid of this question, you must decide between these two ways—submit and vote for Buchanan, submit and vote that slavery is a just and good thing and immediately get rid of

fifths" clause in the Constitution, providing one example of why slavery is a national issue which impacts all Americans. See "Speech on the Kansas-Nebraska Act at Peoria, Illinois, October 16, 1854."

7  Lincoln adhered to the Republican Party's philosophy of "Free Soil, Free Labor, and Free Men," and believed it was incompatible with slavery. This ideology was based on the dignity and mobility of free labor, and the idea that one can better one's economic status through hard work. With the accessibility of land in the territories, white citizens had the choice of either working as a wage laborer in a crowded urban center or seeking economic independence by working for themselves as a farmer. In other words, geographical mobility and social mobility were linked. Slavery, in the view of Lincoln and his fellow Republicans, devalued work by robbing it of its nobility and economic incentive. Thus the Southern slave system, which rejected the moral value of hard work while creating a dependence on servile labor, had to be prohibited from the territories or it would pose a threat to bedrock Republican values, including free labor. The best study of this ideology remains Eric Foner, *Free Soil, Free Labor, Free Men: The Ideology of the Republican Party before the Civil War* (New York: Oxford University Press, 1970).

8  Lincoln referred to the *Richmond Enquirer,* a semiweekly newspaper that ran several articles by proslavery advocate George Fitzhugh, who argued that slavery was beneficial to the enslaved, pointing out that they lived better lives than working-class whites in the North. Henry Louis Gates Jr., ed., *Lincoln on Race and Slavery* (Princeton, NJ: Princeton University Press, 2009), 84.

9  Democrats, especially those from the South, charged the Republican Party with being anti-Southern and opposed to the Southern way of life and, as such, a threat to the Union. Lincoln subtly

reminded Southerners of their constant threats of
disunion.

**10**  Franklin Pierce of New Hampshire was elected
president of the United States and William R. King
(1786–1853) of Alabama was elected vice president
in 1852. King died on April 18, 1853, a few weeks
after taking office. Thus David R. Atchison
(1807–1886) of Missouri, an ardent supporter of
Southern rights, was, as president pro tempore of
the Senate, next in the line of succession to the
presidency. Atchison resigned from his office the
following December to sponsor legislation for
organizing Kansas and Nebraska territories for the
proslavery faction in Congress. Larry Gara, *The
Presidency of Franklin Pierce* (Lawrence: University
Press of Kansas, 1991), 76; *CW,* 2:366n2.

**11**  Lincoln reiterated that neither he nor the
Republicans supported the abolition of slavery. He
was clearly concerned that the charge of abolitionism would result in the party's losing the votes of
anti-Nebraska conservatives, former Whigs, and
nativists to the Democratic or Know-Nothing
Parties. His remarks were directed primarily to
these groups of potential voters.

the question; or unite with us, and help us to triumph. We would all like to
have the question done away with, but we cannot submit.

They tell us that we are in company with men who have long been
known as abolitionists. What care we how many may feel disposed to labor
for our cause? Why do not you, Buchanan men, come in and use your influence to make our party respectable? How is the dissolution of the Union
to be consummated? They tell us that the Union is in danger. Who will divide it? Is it those who make the charge? Are they themselves the persons
who wish to see this result? A majority will never dissolve the Union. Can a
minority do it? When this Nebraska bill was first introduced into Congress,
the sense of the Democratic party was outraged. That party has ever prided
itself, that it was the friend of individual, universal freedom. It was that
principle upon which they carried their measures. When the Kansas scheme
was conceived, it was natural that this respect and sense should have been
outraged. Now I make this appeal to the Democratic citizens here. Don't
you find yourself making arguments in support of these measures, which
you never would have made before? Did you ever do it before this Nebraska
bill compelled you to do it? If you answer this in the affirmative, see how a
whole party have been turned away from their love of liberty! And now, my
Democratic friends, come forward. Throw off these things, and come to the
rescue of this great principle of equality. Don't interfere with anything in
the Constitution. That must be maintained, for it is the only safeguard of
our liberties. And not to Democrats alone do I make this appeal, but to all
who love these great and true principles. Come, and keep coming! Strike,
and strike again! So sure as God lives, the victory shall be yours.

# Form Letter to Millard Fillmore Supporters

## September 8, 1856

*Concerned that former Whigs, especially in the central and southern regions of Illinois, would vote for third-party presidential candidate Millard Fillmore, thus taking away votes from Republican nominee, John C. Frémont, Lincoln composed this form letter for use by his old Whig friends, claiming that a vote for Fillmore was really a vote for Buchanan, because the ex-president had no chance of carrying the state.*

Dear Sir, Springfield, Sept. 8, 1856

I understand you are a Fillmore man. Let me prove to you that every vote withheld from Fremont, and given to Fillmore, *in this state,* actually lessens Fillmore's chance of being President.[1]

Suppose Buchanan gets *all* the slave states, and Pennsylvania, and *any other* one state besides; *then he is elected,* no matter who gets all the rest.

But suppose Fillmore gets the two slave states of Maryland and Kentucky; *then* Buchanan *is not* elected; Fillmore goes into the House of Representatives, and may be made President by a compromise.

But suppose again Fillmore's friends throw away a few thousand votes on him, in *Indiana* and *Illinois,* it will inevitably give these states to Buchanan, which will more than compensate him for the loss of Maryland and Kentucky; will elect him, and leave Fillmore no chance in the H.R. or out of it.

This is as plain as the adding up of the weights of three small hogs. As Mr. Fillmore has no possible chance to carry Illinois *for himself,* it is plainly his interest to let Fremont take it, and thus keep it out of the hands of Buchanan. Be not deceived. *Buchanan* is the hard horse to beat in this race. Let him have Illinois, and nothing can beat him; *and he will get Illinois,* if men persist in throwing away votes upon Mr. Fillmore.[2]

Does some one persuade you that Mr. Fillmore can carry Illinois? Nonsense! There are over seventy newspapers in Illinois opposing Buchanan, only three or four of which support Mr. Fillmore, *all* the rest going for Fremont. Are not these newspapers a fair index of the proportion of the voters. If not, tell me why.

Again, of these three or four Fillmore newspapers, *two* at least, are supported, in part, by the Buchanan men, as I understand. Do not they know

[1] Lincoln was convinced Fillmore could not win Illinois and that the only way to prevent a Buchanan victory there was for Republicans and anti-Nebraska Fillmore supporters to unite behind the Republican candidate. Convincing Fillmore supporters to vote for Frémont proved to be a difficult task, as many former Whigs admired Fillmore and were wary of the Republican Party's association with abolitionists. Lincoln had his letter to Fillmore men lithographed in order to reach as many of them as possible and quickly. A Democratic politician got hold of a copy and published it in the Logan County *Democrat,* the first of several opposition newspapers to carry it. Donald, *Lincoln,* 194.

[2] Just as Lincoln feared, Buchanan won Illinois with 105,528 votes to Frémont's 96,528 and Fillmore's 37,531. Nationwide, Democrats carried every Southern state except Maryland and several key Northern states. Although Buchanan was elected with 174 electoral votes to Frémont's 114 and Fillmore's 8, there were positive signs for the new Republican Party in the election returns. Frémont and Fillmore won 55 percent of the popular vote, compared with Buchanan's 45 percent, and the Republicans performed strongly in the North. Lincoln blamed Frémont's loss in Illinois to the lack of cooperation with Fillmore supporters and the Democrats' success in associating the Republican candidate with abolitionists. Burlingame, *Abraham Lincoln,* 1:433.

*Millard Fillmore, American candidate for president of the United States.* Engraving (New York: Baker & Godwin, 1856). Proof for a campaign portrait featuring the Native American Party's 1856 presidential candidate.

where the shoe pinches? They know the Fillmore movement helps *them,* and therefore they help *it.*

Do think these things over, and then act according to your judgment. Yours very truly, A. LINCOLN

(Confidential)

# Speech on the *Dred Scott* Decision at Springfield, Illinois

## June 26, 1857

FELLOW CITIZENS:—I AM HERE TO-NIGHT, PARTLY BY THE INVITA-tion of some of you, and partly by my own inclination.[1] Two weeks ago Judge Douglas spoke here on the several subjects of Kansas, the Dred Scott decision, and Utah.[2] I listened to the speech at the time, and have read the report of it since. It was intended to controvert opinions which I think just, and to assail (politically, not personally,) those men who, in common with me, entertain those opinions. For this reason I wished then, and still wish, to make some answer to it, which I now take the opportunity of doing.

I begin with Utah.[3] If it prove to be true, as is probable, that the people of Utah are in open rebellion to the United States, then Judge Douglas is in favor of repealing their territorial organization, and attaching them to the adjoining States for judicial purposes. I say, too, if they are in rebellion, they ought to be somehow coerced to obedience; and I am not now prepared to admit or deny that the Judge's mode of coercing them is not as good as any. The Republicans can fall in with it without taking back anything they have ever said. To be sure, it would be a considerable backing down by Judge Douglas from his much vaunted doctrine of self-government for the territo-ries; but this is only additional proof of what was very plain from the begin-ning, that that doctrine was a mere deceitful pretense for the benefit of slav-ery.[4] Those who could not see that much in the Nebraska act itself, which forced Governors, and Secretaries, and Judges on the people of the territo-ries, without their choice or consent, could not be made to see, though one should rise from the dead to testify.

But in all this, it is very plain the Judge evades the only question the Re-publicans have ever pressed upon the Democracy in regard to Utah. That question the Judge well knows to be this: "If the people of Utah shall peace-fully form a State Constitution tolerating polygamy, will the Democracy

*On March 6, 1857, two days after James Buchanan's inauguration as the nation's fifteenth president, the United States Supreme Court announced its ruling on the* Dred Scott v. Sandford *case. By a seven to two vote, the court's decision held that blacks could not bring suit in federal court because they could never be citizens, and that the Missouri Compromise was unconstitutional. In this speech, Lincoln responded to the court's decision as well as to Stephen Douglas's speech defending it in Springfield two weeks before.*

1   Lincoln's speech was published in the *Illinois State Journal,* a Republican newspaper, on June 29, 1857. The paper announced that copies of Lincoln's remarks were available for sale. At least two other Illinois newspapers, the *Illinois State Chronicle* in Decatur, on July 2, and the *Central Transcript* in Clinton, on July 9, also published the speech. Cited in *CW,* 2:410n1.

2   Douglas's speech, on June 12, 1857, was published as a pamphlet entitled *Remarks of the Hon. Stephen A. Douglas, on Kansas, Utah, and the Dred Scott Decision* (Chicago: Daily Times Book and Job Office, 1857).

3   Founded in 1830 in upstate New York by Joseph Smith (1805–1844), the Church of Latter Day Saints endured years of hardship and persecu-tion as its members migrated westward to settle-ments in Ohio, Illinois, and Missouri. Everywhere they settled, Mormons attracted suspicion and condemnation for their religious practices, especially polygamy. In 1846, Smith's successor, the charismatic Brigham Young (1801–1877), led his flock to the Salt Lake region of what later became Utah territory. Young was appointed governor of Utah by President Millard Fillmore in September of 1850, soon after Congress established the territory. Seeing himself as accountable to no one but God and the territory as a religious kingdom independent of federal control, Young challenged federal officials and laws by raising a militia that

fought with federal agents and judges and harassed non-Mormon emigrants passing through Utah. In May 1857, about a month before Lincoln's speech, Buchanan decided to act. With reports of violence and even murder at the hands of Young's militia, the president, concerned about the safety of federal agents and officials in Utah, moved to replace Young as governor with the non-Mormon Alfred Cumming (1802–1873) of Georgia and also appointed two associate justices, a secretary, a marshal, and a new secretary of Indian Affairs for the territory. In addition, Buchanan, without informing Congress, ordered 2,500 troops to accompany and provide protection for Cumming. Douglas enthusiastically endorsed Buchanan's actions in his Springfield speech, and proposed, if the reports of violence and lawlessness were validated, that Congress disband the Utah territory. In December of 1857 Buchanan stated that the situation in Utah was "the first rebellion which has existed in our Territories" and should be put down "in such a manner that it shall be the last." The threat of military action convinced Young, with the aid of a mediator, that resistance would be futile. A settlement was achieved, with Young turning over the governorship to Cumming and guaranteeing that federal laws would be observed, and Washington agreeing not to interfere with the Mormons' religion or practices. In June 1858, Buchanan announced that peace had been restored in the territory. Thomas A. Horrocks, *President James Buchanan and the Crisis of National Leadership* (New York: Nova Publishers, 2012), 53–54. Buchanan is cited in *The Works of James Buchanan Comprising His Speeches, State Papers, and Private Correspondence,* ed. John Bassett Moore, 12 vols. (New York: Antiquarian Press, 1960), 10:153–154. See also William P. MacKinnon, "Prelude to Armageddon: James Buchanan, Brigham Young, and a President's Initiation to Bloodshed," in John W. Quist and Michael J. Birkner, eds., *James Buchanan and the Coming of*

Abraham Lincoln. Ambrotype by Anton T. Joslin (Danville, IL, May 27, 1857). Portrait taken of Lincoln a month before this speech.

admit them into the Union?" There is nothing in the United States Constitution or law against polygamy; and why is it not a part of the Judge's "sacred right of self-government" for that people to have it, or rather to *keep* it, if they choose? These questions, so far as I know, the Judge never answers. It might involve the Democracy to answer them either way, and they go unanswered.

As to Kansas.[5] The substance of the Judge's speech on Kansas is an effort to put the free State men in the wrong for not voting at the election of delegates to the Constitutional Convention. He says: "*There is every reason to hope and believe that the law will be fairly interpreted and impartially executed, so as to insure to every bona fide inhabitant the free and quiet exercise of the elective franchise.*"[6]

It appears extraordinary that Judge Douglas should make such a statement. He knows that, by the law, no one can vote who has not been registered; and he knows that the free State men place their refusal to vote on the ground that but few of them have been registered.[7] It is *possible* this is not true, but Judge Douglas knows it is asserted to be true in letters, newspapers and public speeches, and borne by every mail, and blown by every breeze to the eyes and ears of the world. He knows it is boldly declared that the people of many whole counties, and many whole neighborhoods in others, are left unregistered; yet, he does not venture to contradict the declaration, nor to point out how they *can* vote without being registered; but he just slips along, not seeming to know there is any such question of fact, and complacently declares: "There is every reason to hope and believe that the law will be fairly and impartially executed, so as to insure to every *bona fide* inhabitant the free and quiet exercise of the elective franchise."

I readily agree that if all had a chance to vote, they ought to have voted. If, on the contrary, as they allege, and Judge Douglas ventures not to particularly contradict, few only of the free State men had a chance to vote, they were perfectly right in staying from the polls in a body.

By the way[,] since the Judge spoke, the Kansas election has come off. The Judge expressed his confidence that all the Democrats in Kansas would do their duty—including "free state Democrats" of course. The returns received here as yet are very incomplete; but so far as they go, they indicate that only about one sixth of the registered voters, have really voted; and this too, when not more, perhaps, than one half of the rightful voters have been registered, thus showing the thing to have been altogether the most exquisite farce ever enacted. I am watching with considerable interest, to ascertain what figure "the free state Democrats" cut in the concern. Of course they voted—all democrats do their duty—and of course they did not vote for slave-state candidates. We soon shall know how many delegates *they* elected, how many candidates they had, pledged for a free state; and how many votes were cast for them.

Allow me to barely whisper my suspicion that there were no such things in Kansas "as free state Democrats"—that they were altogether mythical, good only to figure in newspapers and speeches in the free states. If there should prove to be one real living free state Democrat in Kansas, I suggest that it might be well to catch him, and stuff and preserve his skin, as an interesting specimen of that soon to be extinct variety of the genus, Democrat.

And now as to the Dred Scott decision.[8] That decision declares two propositions—first, that a negro cannot sue in the U.S. Courts; and secondly, that Congress cannot prohibit slavery in the Territories. It was made by a divided court—dividing differently on the different points. Judge Douglas does not discuss the merits of the decision; and, in that respect, I

*the Civil War* (Gainesville: University Press of Florida, 2013), 46–85; Elbert B. Smith, *The Presidency of James Buchanan* (Lawrence: University Press of Kansas, 1975), 68; and Johannsen, *Stephen A. Douglas,* 568.

4   Lincoln pointed out Douglas's inconsistency concerning the doctrine of popular sovereignty: the senator's approval of federal intervention in Utah compared with his advocacy of federal nonintervention in the Kansas and Nebraska territories.

5   Lincoln responded to Douglas's optimistic remarks, made weeks earlier at Springfield, concerning the situation in Kansas, recently the scene of violent and bloody conflicts between slave-state and free-state proponents. The senator believed the territory's troubles had passed and looked forward to the admission of Kansas to statehood, with slavery to be decided peacefully by Kansas inhabitants, in keeping with popular sovereignty. Douglas claimed that Kansas would choose to be a free state, unless a majority of free-state residents declined to participate in the election of delegates to a constitutional convention, thus "leaving the Free State Democrats in a minority, and securing a pro-slavery constitution in opposition to the wishes of the majority of the people." If this occurred, he asserted, Republicans would be to blame—that is, "those who, for partisan purposes, will sacrifice the principles they profess to cherish and promote." Douglas, *Remarks on Kansas, Utah, and the Dred Scott Decision,* 4; Johannsen, *Stephen A. Douglas,* 567.

6   This statement appears in Douglas, *Remarks on Kansas, Utah, and the Dred Scott Decision,* 3–4.

7   Lincoln challenged Douglas's claims regarding voting by free-state proponents by pointing out that many were not registered to vote. The proslave government in Kansas had conducted a census that left many free-state residents unaccounted for on the voting rolls while counting hundreds of

Missouri residents who crossed over the border. As a result, less than half the adult males in the territory were on the voting lists. When the election of delegates to the Kansas constitutional convention took place in mid-June, registered free-state residents boycotted, fearing that they would be bound by a fraudulent election. Etcheson, *Bleeding Kansas,* 142; Kenneth M. Stamp, *America in 1857: A Nation on the Brink* (New York: Oxford University Press, 1990), 162–163, 167; Potter, *The Impending Crisis,* 300.

8   Dred Scott (ca. 1799–1858), born into slavery in Virginia around 1800, was sold in 1830 to an army surgeon, Dr. John Emerson (?–1843), who lived in Missouri. Scott lived with Emerson when the latter moved to Illinois, which prohibited slavery, and to the Wisconsin territory, where slavery was banned by the Missouri Compromise. In 1846, after Emerson's death, Scott sued to gain freedom for himself and his family, which consisted of his wife and two daughters, claiming that living for a time in a free state and a free territory made them free. Although a Saint Louis court sided with Scott, his case was overturned by the Missouri Supreme Court. When Emerson's widow moved to Massachusetts, she transferred ownership of Scott to her brother, John F. A. Sanford (1806–1857), who lived in New York City. Scott again sued for freedom and his case made its way to the U.S. Supreme Court. The court heard arguments on the case in early 1856 but decided to postpone its decision until after the 1856 presidential election. In his inaugural address, James Buchanan dismissed the debate over slavery in the territories, indicating it would soon be resolved by the Supreme Court's impending *Dred Scott* decision. The new president declared that he, "in common with all good citizens," would "cheerfully submit" to the court's verdict. Two days later, Chief Justice Roger B. Taney (1777–1864), supported by six of the other eight justices, delivered the court's majority

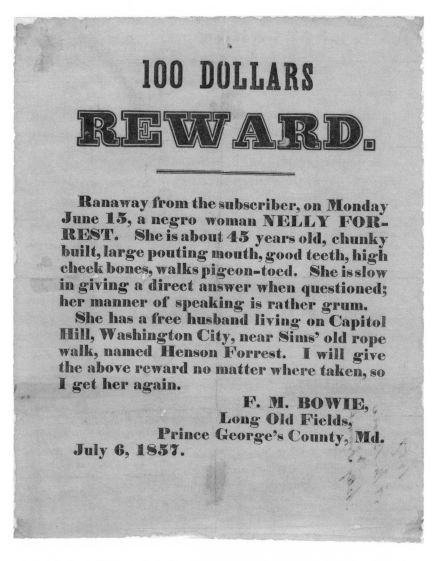

*100 Dollars Reward.* Broadside (July 6, 1857). Poster offering a reward for the return of Nelly Forrest, a runaway slave, to her owner, F. M. Bowie of Prince George's County, Maryland.

shall follow his example, believing I could no more improve on McLean and Curtis, than he could on Taney.[9]

He denounces all who question the correctness of that decision, as offering violent resistance to it.[10] But who resists it? Who has, in spite of the decision, declared Dred Scott free, and resisted the authority of his master over him?

Judicial decisions have two uses—first, to absolutely determine the case decided, and secondly, to indicate to the public how other similar cases will be decided when they arise. For the latter use, they are called "precedents" and "authorities."

We believe, as much as Judge Douglas, (perhaps more) in obedience to, and respect for the judicial department of government. We think its decisions on Constitutional questions, when fully settled, should control, not only the particular cases decided, but the general policy of the country, subject to be disturbed only by amendments of the Constitution as provided in that instrument itself. More than this would be revolution. But we think the Dred Scott decision is erroneous. We know the court that made it, has often over-ruled its own decisions, and we shall do what we can to have it to over-rule this. We offer no *resistance* to it.

Judicial decisions are of greater or less authority as precedents, according to circumstances. That this should be so, accords both with common sense, and the customary understanding of the legal profession.

If this important decision had been made by the unanimous concurrence of the judges, and without any apparent partisan bias, and in accordance with legal public expectation, and with the steady practice of the departments throughout our history, and had been in no part, based on assumed historical facts which are not really true; or, if wanting in some of these, it had been before the court more than once, and had there been affirmed and re-affirmed through a course of years, it then might be, perhaps would be, factious, nay, even revolutionary, to not acquiesce in it as a precedent.

But when, as it is true we find it wanting in all these claims to the public confidence, it is not resistance, it is not factious, it is not even disrespectful, to treat it as not having yet quite established a settled doctrine for the country—But Judge Douglas considers this view awful. Hear him:

"The courts are the tribunals prescribed by the Constitution and created by the authority of the people to determine, expound and enforce the law. Hence, whoever resists the final decision of the highest judicial tribunal, aims a deadly blow to our whole Republican system of government—a blow, which if successful would place all our rights and liberties at the mercy of passion, anarchy and violence. I repeat, therefore, that if resistance to the decisions of the Supreme Court of the United States, in a matter like the points decided in the Dred Scott case, clearly within their jurisdiction as defined by the Constitution, shall be forced upon the country as a political issue, it will be-

decision, which was, in the words of one historian, "one of the most infamous" in its history. Taney ruled that blacks could never be citizens of the United States and thus Scott could not sue in a federal court of law; that Congress was prevented by the Constitution from passing laws regulating the territories; and, because the Constitution protected the right to property in slaves, slave owners could bring them into federal territories, thereby rendering the Missouri Compromise unconstitutional and undermining the main objective of the Republican Party. Southerners and many Northern Democrats welcomed the court's ruling, but Republicans and free-soil Democrats were outraged. Recalling the court's decision to postpone its ruling until after the presidential election, Republicans, including Lincoln, asserted it had been politically motivated. Moreover, some in the North believed there was a conspiracy between Buchanan and the court to open up all territories to slavery. These critics pointed to Buchanan's brief conversation with Taney during the inaugural ceremonies and the president's remarks concerning his support of the forthcoming decision. Buchanan and Taney never divulged the content of their short chat, though existing evidence proves that the president not only knew how the court would rule but also played a direct and inappropriate role in influencing the decision. Buchanan was less concerned about Scott's status than he was about the issue of slavery in the territories, which he knew could derail the objectives he set for his administration. He longed to eliminate the main plank of the Republican Party, ease sectional tensions caused by antislavery agitation, and solidify the Democrats' standing as the only national party. Wishing to say something about the issue of slavery in the territories in his inaugural address, president-elect Buchanan wrote in early February 1857 to his old friend Justice James Catron (1786–1865) of Tennessee, wanting to know if a decision on *Dred Scott* would be handed down before the inauguration. In subsequent communications, Catron informed Buchanan that it was likely the court's decision against Scott would be along sectional lines and that the Supreme Court was divided on whether to address the larger issue of slavery in the territories. Catron suggested that if Buchanan desired a definitive verdict on the issue, he should make his wishes known to his friend and fellow Pennsylvanian, Justice Robert Grier (1794–1870). Buchanan immediately contacted Grier and, although no letter from Buchanan to Grier has been found, it is clear from Grier's response that the president-elect informed him of his wish for a comprehensive ruling with at least one Northern judge joining the majority. When the court's decision was handed down, Grier's name was listed on Taney's majority report. Don E. Fehrenbacher, *The Dred Scott Case: Its Significance in American Law and Politics* (New York: Oxford University Press, 1978); and Paul Finkelman, *Dred Scott v. Sandford: A Brief History with Documents* (Boston: Bedford Books, 1997). Buchanan's inaugural address is cited in *Works of James Buchanan,* 10:105–109. The quote about the Supreme Court's "infamous" decision comes from Foner, *The Fiery Trial,* 92. Buchanan's intervention in the Supreme Court's deliberations is discussed in Paul Finkelman, "James Buchanan, Dred Scott, and the Whisper of Conspiracy," in John W. Quist and Michael J. Birkner, eds., *James Buchanan and the Coming of the Civil War* (Gainesville: University Press of Florida, 2013), 20–45.

9   Lincoln subsequently referred to the *Dred Scott* case as "that burlesque upon judicial decisions." *CW,* 2:454.

10   Though the decision negated the principle of popular sovereignty central to his Kansas-Nebraska Act, Douglas publicly supported the Supreme Court's verdict. In his Springfield speech, Douglas criticized Republicans for unloading "torrents of abuse and misrepresentations not only upon the

come a distinct and naked issue between the friends and the enemies of the Constitution—the friends and the enemies of the supremacy of the laws."[11]

Why this same Supreme court once decided a national bank to be constitutional; but Gen. Jackson, as President of the United States, disregarded the decision, and vetoed a bill for a re-charter, partly on constitutional ground, declaring that each public functionary must support the Constitution, "*as he understands it.*" But hear the General's own words. Here they are, taken from his veto message:

"It is maintained by the advocates of the bank, that its constitutionality, in all its features, ought to be considered as settled by precedent, and by the decision of the Supreme Court. To this conclusion I cannot assent. Mere precedent is a dangerous source of authority, and should not be regarded as deciding questions of constitutional power, except where the acquiescence of the people and the States can be considered as well settled. So far from this being the case on this subject, an argument against the bank might be based on precedent. One Congress in 1791, decided in favor of a bank; another in 1811, decided against it. One Congress in 1815 decided against a bank; another in 1816 decided in its favor. Prior to the present Congress, therefore the precedents drawn from that source were equal. If we resort to the States, the expressions of legislative, judicial and executive opinions against the bank have been probably to those in its favor as four to one. There is nothing in precedent, therefore, which if its authority were admitted, ought to weigh in favor of the act before me."[12]

I drop the quotations merely to remark that all there ever was, in the way of precedent up to the Dred Scott decision, on the points therein decided, had been against that decision. But hear Gen. Jackson further—

"If the opinion of the Supreme court covered the whole ground of this act, it ought not to control the co-ordinate authorities of this Government. The Congress, the executive and the court, must each for itself be guided by its own opinion of the Constitution. Each public officer, who takes an oath to support the Constitution, swears that he will support it as he understands it, and not as it is understood by others."[13]

Again and again have I heard Judge Douglas denounce that bank decision, and applaud Gen. Jackson for disregarding it. It would be interesting for him to look over his recent speech, and see how exactly his fierce philippics against us for resisting Supreme Court decisions, fall upon his own head. It will call to his mind a long and fierce political war in this country, upon an issue which, in his own language, and, of course, in his own changeless estimation, was "a distinct and naked issue between the friends and the enemies of the Constitution," and in which war he fought in the ranks of the enemies of the Constitution.

I have said, in substance, that the Dred Scott decision was, in part, based on assumed historical facts which were not really true; and I ought not to leave the subject without giving some reasons for saying this; I therefore give an instance or two, which I think fully sustain me. Chief Justice Taney, in delivering the opinion of the majority of the Court, insists at great length that negroes were no part of the people who made, or for whom was made, the Declaration of Independence, or the Constitution of the United States.[14]

On the contrary, Judge Curtis, in his dissenting opinion, shows that in five of the then thirteen states, to wit, New Hampshire, Massachusetts, New York, New Jersey and North Carolina, free negroes were voters, and, in proportion to their numbers, had the same part in making the Constitution that the white people had. He shows this with so much particularity as to leave no doubt of its truth; and, as a sort of conclusion on that point, holds the following language:

> "The Constitution was ordained and established by the people of the United States, through the action, in each State, of those persons who were qualified by its laws to act thereon in behalf of themselves and all other citizens of the State. In some of the States, as we have seen, colored persons were among those qualified by law to act on the subject. These colored persons were not only included in the body of 'the people of the United States,' by whom the Constitution was ordained and established; but in at least five of the States they had the power to act, and, doubtless, did act, by their suffrages, upon the question of its adoption."[15]

Again, Chief Justice Taney says: "It is difficult, at this day to realize the state of public opinion in relation to that unfortunate race, which prevailed in the civilized and enlightened portions of the world at the time of the Declaration of Independence, and when the Constitution of the United States was framed and adopted."[16] And again, after quoting from the Declaration, he says: "The general words above quoted would seem to include the

decision, but upon the character and motives of the venerable chief justice and his illustrious associates on the bench," and for forgetting their obligations to society by calling for "violent resistance to the final decision of the highest tribunal on earth." While the "Republicans or Abolition party" pronounced the court's decision "cruel, inhumane and infamous" and called on Americans "to disregard and refuse to obey it," Douglas urged citizens to fight them. Douglas, *Remarks on Kansas, Utah, and the Dred Scott Decision,* 5, 11.

11 Ibid., 5.

12 *Addresses and Messages of the Presidents of the United States, from 1789 to 1839,* 403.

13 Ibid.

14 In his majority opinion Chief Justice Taney wrote that "the words 'people of the United States' and 'citizens' are synonymous terms, and mean the same thing. They both describe the political body who, according to our republican institutions, form the sovereignty, and who hold the power and conduct the Government through their representatives. They are what we familiarly call the 'sovereign people,' and every citizen is one of this people, and a constituent member of this sovereignty. The question before us is, whether the class of persons described in the plea in abatement compose a portion of this people, and are constituent members of this sovereignty? We think they are not, and that they are not included, and were not intended to be included, under the word 'citizens' in the Constitution, and can therefore claim none of the rights and privileges which that instrument provides for and secures to citizens of the United States. On the contrary, they were at that time considered as a subordinate and inferior class of beings, who had been subjugated by the dominant race, and, whether emancipated or not, yet remained subject to their authority, and had no

rights or privileges but such as those who held power and the Government might choose to grant them." Benjamin Howard, *Report of the Decision of the Supreme Court of the United States . . . in the Case of Dred Scott versus John F. A. Sandford* (Washington, DC, 1857), 10–11.

15  Ibid., 182. Justice Benjamin R. Curtis (1809–1857) was a Massachusetts lawyer and politician. A Whig in politics, Curtis was appointed to the Supreme Court by President Millard Fillmore in 1851. In his dissenting opinion, he claimed that at the time of ratification of the Articles of Confederation, "all free native-born inhabitants of the States of New Hampshire, Massachusetts, New York, New Jersey, and North Carolina, though descended from African slaves, were not only citizens of those States, but such of them as had the other necessary qualifications possessed the franchise of electors, on equal terms with other citizens." Ibid., 178–179. "Benjamin R. Curtis, 1851–1857," http://supremecourthistory.org/timeline_curtis.html (accessed November 6, 2014).

16  Howard, *Report of the Decision of the Supreme Court*, 13.

17  Ibid., 16. After this sentence, Taney continued by declaring that "the enslaved African race were not intended to be included, and formed no part of the people who framed and adopted this declaration; for if the language, as understood in that day, would embrace them, the conduct of the distinguished men who framed the Declaration of Independence would have been utterly and flagrantly inconsistent with the principles they asserted."

18  Here Lincoln expanded on views he expressed in an earlier letter in which he bemoaned the lack of improvement for blacks, especially the enslaved, in the United States. See "Letter to George Robertson, August 15, 1855," in this volume. In his Springfield remarks, Lincoln conveyed a passion

whole human family, and if they were used in a similar instrument at this day, would be so understood."[17]

In these the Chief Justice does not directly assert, but plainly assumes, as a fact, that the public estimate of the black man is more favorable *now* than it was in the days of the Revolution. This assumption is a mistake. In some trifling particulars, the condition of that race has been ameliorated; but, as a whole, in this country, the change between then and now is decidedly the other way; and their ultimate destiny has never appeared so hopeless as in the last three or four years.[18] In two of the five States—New Jersey and North Carolina—that then gave the free negro the right of voting, the right has since been taken away; and in a third—New York—it has been greatly abridged; while it has not been extended, so far as I know, to a single additional State, though the number of the States has more than doubled. In those days, as I understand, masters could, at their own pleasure, emancipate their slaves; but since then, such legal restraints have been made upon emancipation, as to amount almost to prohibition. In those days, Legislatures held the unquestioned power to abolish slavery in their respective States; but now it is becoming quite fashionable for State Constitutions to withhold that power from the Legislatures. In those days, by common consent, the spread of the black man's bondage to new countries was prohibited; but now, Congress decides that it *will* not continue the prohibition, and the Supreme Court decides that it *could* not if it would. In those days, our Declaration of Independence was held sacred by all, and thought to include all; but now, to aid in making the bondage of the negro universal and eternal, it is assailed, and sneered at, and construed, and hawked at, and torn, till, if its framers could rise from their graves, they could not at all recognize it. All the powers of earth seem rapidly combining against him. Mammon is after him; ambition follows, and philosophy follows, and the Theology of the day is fast joining the cry. They have him in his prison house; they have searched his person, and left no prying instrument with him. One after another they have closed the heavy iron doors upon him, and now they have him, as it were, bolted in with a lock of a hundred keys, which can never be unlocked without the concurrence of every key; the keys in the hands of a hundred different men, and they scattered to a hundred different and distant places; and they stand musing as to what invention, in all the dominions of mind and matter, can be produced to make the impossibility of his escape more complete than it is.

It is grossly incorrect to say or assume, that the public estimate of the negro is more favorable now than it was at the origin of the government.

Three years and a half ago, Judge Douglas brought forward his famous Nebraska bill. The country was at once in a blaze. He scorned all opposition, and carried it through Congress. Since then he has seen himself superseded in a Presidential nomination, by one indorsing the general doctrine of his measure, but at the same time standing clear of the odium of its untimely agitation, and its gross breach of national faith; and he has seen that successful rival Constitutionally elected, not by the strength of friends, but by the division of adversaries, being in a popular minority of nearly four hundred thousand votes.[19] He has seen his chief aids in his own State, Shields and Richardson, politically speaking, successively tried, convicted, and executed, for an offense not their own, but his. And now he sees his own case, standing next on the docket for trial.[20]

There is a natural disgust in the minds of nearly all white people, to the idea of an indiscriminate amalgamation of the white and black races; and Judge Douglas evidently is basing his chief hope, upon the chances of being able to appropriate the benefit of this disgust to himself.[21] If he can, by much drumming and repeating, fasten the odium of that idea upon his adversaries, he thinks he can struggle through the storm. He therefore clings to this hope, as a drowning man to the last plank. He makes an occasion for lugging it in from the opposition to the Dred Scott decision. He finds the Republicans insisting that the Declaration of Independence includes ALL men, black as well as white; and forthwith he boldly denies that it includes negroes at all, and proceeds to argue gravely that all who contend it does, do so only because they want to vote, and eat, and sleep, and marry with negroes! He will have it that they cannot be consistent else. Now I protest against that counterfeit logic which concludes that, because I do not want a black woman for a *slave* I must necessarily want her for a *wife*. I need not have her for either, I can just leave her alone. In some respects she certainly is not my equal; but in her natural right to eat the bread she earns with her own hands without asking leave of any one else, she is my equal, and the equal of all others.

Chief Justice Taney, in his opinion in the Dred Scott case, admits that the language of the Declaration is broad enough to include the whole human family, but he and Judge Douglas argue that the authors of that instrument did not intend to include negroes, by the fact that they did not at once, actually place them on an equality with the whites. Now this grave argument comes to just nothing at all, by the other fact, that they did not at once, *or ever afterwards,* actually place all white people on an equality with one or another. And this is the staple argument of both the Chief Justice

that was seldom present in previous statements on the condition of African Americans.

19  Douglas lost the 1856 Democratic Party presidential nomination to James Buchanan, who had returned to the country on completing his tenure as U.S. minister to Great Britain in 1855. Buchanan was elected president, receiving 1,838,169 popular votes against a combined total of 2,215,798 for Republican John C. Frémont (1,341,264) and Know-Nothing Millard Fillmore (874,534), or 45 percent of the total popular vote cast.

20  Lincoln referred to Douglas's fellow Illinois Democrats William Alexander Richardson, who ran for governor of Illinois in 1856 and was defeated by William Bissell (1811–1860), the first Republican governor of the state, and James Shields, Douglas's candidate in 1855 for the open U.S. senate seat for Illinois, who lost to anti-Nebraska candidate Lyman Trumbull. Richardson and Shields were both victims of the strong anti-Nebraska movement in Illinois. Lincoln's remarks about Douglas "standing next on the docket" referred to the upcoming election in Illinois, in which the senator would be judged by Illinois voters.

21  Lincoln criticized Douglas for resorting to antiblack rhetoric while acknowledging his own racial prejudice, using language similar to that he would later use in his fourth debate with Douglas. See "Fourth Debate with Stephen A. Douglas at Charleston, Illinois, September 18, 1858," in this volume.

and the Senator, for doing this obvious violence to the plain unmistakable language of the Declaration. I think the authors of that notable instrument intended to include *all* men, but they did not intend to declare all men equal *in all respects.* They did not mean to say all were equal in color, size, intellect, moral developments, or social capacity. They defined with tolerable distinctness, in what respects they did consider all men created equal—equal in "certain inalienable rights, among which are life, liberty, and the pursuit of happiness." This they said, and this meant. They did not mean to assert the obvious untruth, that all were then actually enjoying that equality, nor yet, that they were about to confer it immediately upon them. In fact they had no power to confer such a boon. They meant simply to declare the *right,* so that the *enforcement* of it might follow as fast as circumstances should permit. They meant to set up a standard maxim for free society, which should be familiar to all, and revered by all; constantly looked to, constantly labored for, and even though never perfectly attained, constantly approximated, and thereby constantly spreading and deepening its influence, and augmenting the happiness and value of life to all people of all colors everywhere. The assertion that "all men are created equal" was of no practical use in effecting our separation from Great Britain; and it was placed in the Declaration, not for that, but for future use. Its authors meant it to be, thank God, it is now proving itself, a stumbling block to those who in after times might seek to turn a free people back into the hateful paths of despotism. They knew the proneness of prosperity to breed tyrants, and they meant when such should re-appear in this fair land and commence their vocation they should find left for them at least one hard nut to crack.

I have now briefly expressed my view of the *meaning* and *objects* of that part of the Declaration of Independence which declares that "all men are created equal."

Now let us hear Judge Douglas' view of the same subject, as I find it in the printed report of his late speech. Here it is:

"No man can vindicate the character, motives and conduct of the signers of the Declaration of Independence, except upon the hypothesis that they referred to the white race alone, and not to the African, when they declared all men to have been created equal—that they were speaking of British subjects on this continent being equal to British subjects born and residing in Great Britain—that they were entitled to the same inalienable rights, and among them were enumerated life, liberty and the pursuit of happiness. The Declaration was adopted for the purpose of justifying the colonists in the eyes of the civilized world in withdrawing their allegiance from the British crown, and dissolving their connection with the mother country."[22]

My good friends, read that carefully over some leisure hour, and ponder well upon it—see what a mere wreck—mangled ruin—it makes of our once glorious Declaration.

"They were speaking of British subjects on this continent being equal to British subjects born and residing in Great Britain!" Why, according to this, not only negroes but white people outside of Great Britain and America are not spoken of in that instrument. The English, Irish and Scotch, along with white Americans, were included to be sure, but the French, Germans and other white people of the world are all gone to pot along with the Judge's inferior races.

I had thought the Declaration promised something better than the condition of British subjects; but no, it only meant that we should be *equal* to them in their own oppressed and *unequal* condition. According to that, it gave no promise that having kicked off the King and Lords of Great Britain, we should not at once be saddled with a King and Lords of our own.

I had thought the Declaration contemplated the progressive improvement in the condition of all men everywhere; but no, it merely "was adopted for the purpose of justifying the colonists in the eyes of the civilized world in withdrawing their allegiance from the British crown, and dissolving their connection with the mother country." Why, that object having been effected some eighty years ago, the Declaration is of no practical use now— mere rubbish—old wadding left to rot on the battle-field after the victory is won.

I understand you are preparing to celebrate the "Fourth," to-morrow week. What for? The doings of that day had no reference to the present; and quite half of you are not even descendants of those who were referred to at that day. But I suppose you will celebrate; and will even go so far as to read the Declaration. Suppose after you read it once in the old fashioned way, you read it once more with Judge Douglas' version. It will then run thus: "We hold these truths to be self-evident that all British subjects who were on this continent eighty-one years ago, were created equal to all British subjects born and *then* residing in Great Britain."[23]

And now I appeal to all—to Democrats as well as others,—are you really willing that the Declaration shall be thus frittered away?—thus left no more at most, than an interesting memorial of the dead past? thus shorn of its

22 Douglas, *Remarks on Kansas, Utah, and the Dred Scott Decision,* 9–10.

23 See "Letter to George Robertson, August 15, 1855," in which Lincoln decried proslavery attacks on the "all men are created equal" passage in the Declaration of Independence as "a self-evident lie." As a result, Lincoln claimed, the fourth of July "has not quite dwindled away; it is still a great day—*for burning fire-crackers!!!*"

24 Lincoln assured his listeners that he did not favor amalgamation of the races. He used Douglas's racial argument against him by arguing that race mixing occurred mostly between black slaves and white masters, and that prohibiting slavery in the territories would do more to prevent amalgamation than would popular sovereignty, which would open up the possibility of bringing blacks into the territories in large numbers.

vitality, and practical value; and left without the *germ* or even the *suggestion* of the individual rights of man in it?

But Judge Douglas is especially horrified at the thought of the mixing of blood by the white and black races: agreed for once—a thousand times agreed. There are white men enough to marry all the white women, and black men enough to marry all the black women; and so let them be married. On this point we fully agree with the Judge; and when he shall show that his policy is better adapted to prevent amalgamation than ours we shall drop ours, and adopt his.[24] Let us see. In 1850 there were in the United States, 405,751, mulattoes. Very few of these are the offspring of whites and *free* blacks; nearly all have sprung from black *slaves* and white masters. A separation of the races is the only perfect preventive of amalgamation but as an immediate separation is impossible the next best thing is to *keep* them apart *where* they are not already together. If white and black people never get together in Kansas, they will never mix blood in Kansas. That is at least one self-evident truth. A few free colored persons may get into the free States, in any event; but their number is too insignificant to amount to much in the way of mixing blood. In 1850 there were in the free states, 56,649 mulattoes; but for the most part they were not born there—they came from the slave States, ready made up. In the same year the slave States had 348,874 mulattoes all of home production. The proportion of free mulattoes to free blacks—the only colored classes in the free states—is much greater in the slave than in the free states. It is worthy of note too, that among the free states those which make the colored man the nearest to equal the white, have, proportionably the fewest mulattoes [and] the least of amalgamation. In New Hampshire, the State which goes farthest towards equality between the races, there are just 184 Mulattoes while there are in Virginia—how many do you think? 79,775, being 23,126 more than in all the free States together.

These statistics show that slavery is the greatest source of amalgamation; and next to it, not the elevation, but the degeneration of the free blacks. Yet Judge Douglas dreads the slightest restraints on the spread of slavery, and the slightest human recognition of the negro, as tending horribly to amalgamation.

This very Dred Scott case affords a strong test as to which party most favors amalgamation, the Republicans or the dear Union-saving Democracy. Dred Scott, his wife and two daughters were all involved in the suit. We desired the court to have held that they were citizens so far at least as to entitle them to a hearing as to whether they were free or not; and then, also, that they were in fact and in law really free. Could we have had our way, the chances of these black girls, ever mixing their blood with that of white people, would have been diminished at least to the extent that it could not have been without their consent. But Judge Douglas is delighted to have them decided to be slaves, and not human enough to have a hearing, even if they were free, and thus left subject to the forced concubinage of their masters, and liable to become the mothers of mulattoes in spite of themselves—the very state of case that produces nine tenths of all the mulattoes—all the mixing of blood in the nation.

Of course, I state this case as an illustration only, not meaning to say or intimate that the master of Dred Scott and his family, or any more than a per centage of masters generally, are inclined to exercise this particular power which they hold over their female slaves.

I have said that the separation of the races is the only perfect preventive of amalgamation. I have no right to say all the members of the Republican party are in favor of this, nor to say that as a party they are in favor of it. There is nothing in their platform directly on the subject. But I can say a very large proportion of its members are for it, and that the chief plank in their platform—opposition to the spread of slavery—is most favorable to that separation.

Such separation, if ever effected at all, must be effected by colonization; and no political party, as such, is now doing anything directly for colonization.[25] Party operations at present only favor or retard colonization incidentally. The enterprise is a difficult one; but "when there is a will there is a way"; and what colonization needs most is a hearty will. Will springs from the two elements of moral sense and self-interest. Let us be brought to believe it is morally right, and, at the same time, favorable to, or, at least, not against, our interest, to transfer the African to his native clime, and we shall find a way to do it, however great the task may be. The children of Israel, to such numbers as to include four hundred thousand fighting men, went out of Egyptian bondage in a body.

How differently the respective courses of the Democratic and Republican parties incidentally bear on the question of forming a will—a public sentiment—for colonization, is easy to see. The Republicans inculcate, with whatever of ability they can, that the negro is a man; that his bondage is cruelly wrong, and that the field of his oppression ought not to be enlarged. The Democrats deny his manhood; deny, or dwarf to insignificance, the wrong of his bondage; so far as possible, crush all sympathy for him, and cultivate and excite hatred and disgust against him; compliment themselves

25  Lincoln reiterated his support for colonization of African Americans outside the United States.

as Union-savers for doing so; and call the indefinite outspreading of his bondage "a sacred right of self-government."

The plainest print cannot be read through a gold eagle; and it will be ever hard to find many men who will send a slave to Liberia, and pay his passage while they can send him to a new country, Kansas for instance, and sell him for fifteen hundred dollars, and the rise.

# Speech to the Jury in the Rock Island Bridge Case, Chicago

## September 22 and 23, 1857

*In one of the most celebrated cases of his legal career, Lincoln served as a member of the defense team retained by the Rock Island Bridge Company and its parent company, the Chicago and Rock Island Railroad, to fight a suit filed by the owner of the* Effie Afton, *a steamboat that had crashed into a bridge owned by the company. In recognition of his skill in persuading juries, Lincoln was chosen as lead defense counsel in a case that pitted steamboat interests against railroad companies; he took two days to present his closing argument. With the jury unable to reach a decision, the judge dismissed the case, preventing the plaintiffs from recovering damages.*

THIRTEENTH DAY
Tuesday, September 23[1]

Mr. A. Lincoln addressed the jury:[2] He said he did not purpose to assail anybody, that he expected to grow earnest as he proceeded, but not ill-natured. There is some conflict of testimony in the case, but one quarter of such a number of witnesses, seldom agree, and even if all had been on one side some discrepancy might have been expected. We are to try and reconcile them, and to believe that they are not intentionally erroneous, as long as we can. He had no prejudice against steamboats or steamboatmen, nor any against St. Louis, for he supposed they went about as other people would do in their situation.[3] St. Louis as a commercial place, may desire that this bridge should not stand, as it is adverse to her commerce, diverting a portion of it from the river; and it might be that she supposed that the additional cost of railroad transportation upon the productions of Iowa, would force them to go to St. Louis if this bridge was removed. The meetings in St. Louis[4] were connected with this case, only as some witnesses were in it and thus had some prejudice [to] add color to their testimony.

The last thing that would be pleasing to him would be, to have one of these great channels, extending almost from where it never freezes to where it never thaws, blocked up. But there is a travel from East to West, whose demands are not less important than that of the river. It is growing larger and larger, building up new countries with a rapidity never before seen in the history of the world. He alluded to the astonishing growth of Illinois, having grown within his memory to a population of a million and a half, to Iowa and the other young and rising communities of the Northwest.

This current of travel has its rights, as well as that north and south. If the

1   Because it involved interstate traffic, the trial was held in the U.S. Circuit Court in Chicago, located on the top floor of the city's historic Saloon Building; it ran from September 8 through September 23, 1857. Newspapers, such as the *Chicago Daily Democratic Press* and the *Saint Louis Missouri Republican,* aware of the reading public's interest in a trial that pitted steamboat interests against the emerging railroad industry, provided daily reports on the trial, including Lincoln's closing arguments on September 22 and 23. *Chicago Daily Democratic Press* version of Lincoln's closing remarks cited in *CW,* 2:415–422. Henry Binmore (1833–1907), strongly pro-steamboat and anti-bridge, covered the trial for the *Missouri Republican,* and Robert R. Hitt (1830–1906) performed the same task for the *Chicago Daily Democratic Press,* which favored the railroad interests. Both Binmore and Hitt worked as reporters in covering the Lincoln-Douglas debates the following year. Brian McGinty, *Lincoln's Greatest Case: The River, the Bridge, and the Making of America* (New York: Liveright, 2015), 94, 101–102; and Jenry Morsman, "Collision of Interests: The Effie Afton, the Rock Island Bridge, and the Making of America," *Common-Place* 6, no. 4 (July 2006), http://www.common-place.org/vol-06/

no-04/morsman/ (accessed November 21, 2014); *CW,* 2:422n1.

2    The Rock Island Bridge, completed on April 21, 1856, was the first railroad bridge to span the Mississippi River; it connected Rock Island, Illinois, and Davenport, Iowa. Fifteen days after it opened, on May 6, 1856, the bridge was struck by the steamship *Effie Afton,* which collided with several piers supporting the structure and caught fire. Although its 200 passengers and crew escaped, the vessel sank, losing all of its cargo, some 350 tons, including livestock, machinery, and groceries. The fire from the steamship burned some of the bridge's wooden trusses, causing sections of the bridge to collapse. Jacob S. Hurd (1816–1866), captain and co-owner of the *Effie Afton,* filed a suit in the U.S. Circuit Court in Chicago against the Rock Island Bridge Company, claiming that the bridge was illegal because it obstructed free navigation on the Mississippi River and caused the accident with his vessel. He sought damages from the company for the loss of the ship and its cargo, a sum of $50,000. The Rock Island Bridge Company responded by charging that the accident was intentional and premeditated by the ship's owners, who were against the bridge's construction. Supreme Court justice John McLean presided over the trial, in which Lincoln, along with Norman B. Judd (1815–1878), Lincoln's friend, fellow lawyer, and a director of the Rock Island Railroad, and Joseph Knox (1805–1891), also a railroad company lawyer, represented the bridge owners. Judd reportedly urged the bridge company to hire Lincoln because he was "one of the best men to state a case forcibly and convincingly that I ever heard, and his personality will appeal to any judge or jury hereabouts." Judd is cited in Burlingame, *Abraham Lincoln,* 1:337. See also McGinty, *Lincoln's Greatest Case,* 68, 72–73, 109–112; Morsman, "Collision of Interests"; David A. Pfeiffer, "Bridging the Mississippi: The Railroads and Steamboats

Abraham Lincoln. Ambrotype by Abraham Byers (May 7, 1858). Photograph taken in Beardstown, Illinois, after Lincoln successfully defended William "Duff" Armstrong against a murder charge in the famous "almanac trial."

river had not the advantage in priority and legislation, we could enter into free competition with it and we would surpass it. This particular line has a great importance, and the statement of its business during little less than a year shows this importance. It is in evidence that from September 8, 1856, to August 8, 1857, 12,586 freight cars and 74,179 passengers passed over this bridge. Navigation was closed four days short of four months last year, and during this time, while the river was of no use, this road and bridge were equally valuable. There is, too, a considerable portion of time, when floating or thin ice makes the river useless, while the bridge is as useful as ever. This shows that this bridge must be treated with respect in this court and is not to be kicked about with contempt.[5]

The other day Judge Wead alluded to the strife of the contending interests, and even a dissolution of the Union. Mr. Lincoln thought the proper mood for all parties in this affair, is to "live and let live," and then we will find a cessation of this trouble about the bridge.[6] What mood were the steamboat men in when this bridge was burned? Why there was a shouting, a ringing of bells and whistling on all the boats as it fell. It was a jubilee, a greater celebration than follows an excited election.[7]

The first thing I will proceed to is the record of Mr. Gurney[8] and the complaint of Judge Wead, that it did not extend back over all the time from the completion of the bridge. The principal part of the navigation after the bridge was burned passed through the span. When the bridge was repaired and the boats were a second time confined to the draw, it was provided that this record should be kept. That is the simple history of that book.

From April 19, 1856, to May 6—17 days—there were 20 accidents, and all the time since then, there has been but 20 hits, including 7 accidents; so that the dangers of this place are tapering off, and, as the boatmen get cool, the accidents get less. We may soon expect, if this ratio is kept up, that there will be no accidents at all.

Judge Wead said, while admitting that the floats went straight through, there was a difference between a float and a boat, but I do not remember that he indulged us with an argument in support of this statement. Is it because there is a difference in size? Will not a small body and a large one, float the same way, under the same influence? True, a flat boat would float faster than an egg-shell, and the egg-shell might be blown away by the wind, but if under the *same influence* they would go the same way. Logs, floats, boards, various things, the witnesses say all show the same current. Then is not this test reliable? At all depths too, the direction of the current is the same. A series of these floats would make a line as long as a boat, and would show any influence upon any part, and all parts of the boat.

I will now speak of the angular position of the piers. What is the amount of the angle? The course of the river is a curve and the pier is straight. If a line is produced from the upper end of the long pier straight with the pier to a distance of 350 feet, and a line is drawn from a point in the channel opposite this point to the head of the pier, Col. Mason[9] says they will form an

Clash at the Rock Island Bridge," *Prologue* 36 (Summer 2004); http://www.archives.gov/ publications/prologue/2004/summer/bridge.html (accessed November 21, 2014).

3   Having piloted two flatboats to Louisiana, Lincoln understood river commerce and travel and sympathized with those employed in business connected to the waterways. Moreover, in 1851 he served as legal counsel for insurers of a canal boat that had sunk as a result of a crash into a railroad bridge spanning the Illinois River. The Columbus Insurance Company sued the bridge builders for damages, with Lincoln challenging that the defendants' claim that construction of the bridge was legal because it was authorized by the state legislature. The trial ended in a hung jury and was settled out of court. Donald, *Lincoln,* 156–157; Steiner, *An Honest Calling,* 69.

4   Lincoln referred to meetings of the Chamber of Commerce of Saint Louis at which steamboat owners and pilots were apprised of the economic importance of river commerce and navigation to the city. *CW,* 2:422n2. Hezekiah M. Wead (1810–1877) of Peoria, Illinois, one of the lawyers representing Hurd, sought to make the trial a symbol of the fight for free navigation of the Mississippi River, which was central to St. Louis' economy. The press publicized the trial as a battle between Saint Louis, a river town dependent on steamboats for its livelihood, and Chicago, whose economic future was tied to the railroad. Railroad men and their supporters believed that the outcome of the case would determine the future of bridge construction over waterways. Morsman, "Collision of Interests."

5   Lincoln, by the time of the trial, was an experienced railroad lawyer, having handled several cases for the Illinois Central Railroad and the Alton & Sangamon Railroad. He argued for the importance of railroads to the nation's commerce

and the development of the West. Railroad transportation was especially critical in areas of the country where rivers tend to freeze and in locations where there are no waterways; he made use of statistics to bolster his claim. Steiner, *An Honest Calling*, 69.

6   In his closing statement, Wead contended that the Rock Island Bridge was improperly designed and thus posed an extreme danger to river traffic. He placed the case within the long tradition of the right of U.S. citizens to free navigation of the Mississippi River; Americans had come to believe free access to waterways was a right of citizenship and even a requirement of Union. McGinty, *Lincoln's Greatest Case*, 145–146.

7   As parts of the bridge caught fire and collapsed, steamboat pilots on the river celebrated by blowing their whistles and ringing their bells. This cheering in the wake of the accident led bridge owners and advocates to suspect the steamboat crash was planned by bridge opponents. When one river captain, Joseph Boyd, was asked if he and other steamboat captains had blown their whistles when they observed the bridge on fire, Boyd responded that he did not ring his bell or blow a whistle, "but when the bridge fell I blew one—a long and loud one. . . . So many were blowing and the bells were ringing so on the boats and in the town that I could not hear." Questions were raised by local newspapers as to why the *Effie Afton* was far north of her usual route at night. Also there was no record of her destination or information on her cargo, which convinced railroad supporters that the vessel was carrying flammable material with the intent to crash. Boyd is cited in ibid., 125. See also Pfeiffer, "Bridging the Mississippi."

8   Seth Gurney, superintendent of the Rock Island Bridge from the time that it had opened in April 1856, testified that the bridge had been repaired less than three months after the collision

angle of 20 degrees; but the angle if measured at the pier, is 7 degrees—that is, we would have to move the pier 7 degrees, and then it would be exactly straight with the current. Would that make the navigation better or worse? The witnesses of the plaintiffs seemed to think it was only necessary to say that the pier was angling to the current, and that settled the matter. Our more careful and accurate witnesses say, that though they have been accustomed to seeing the piers placed straight with the current, yet, they could see that here the current has been made straight by us, in having made this slight angle—that the water now runs just right now—that it is straight and cannot be improved. They think that if the pier was changed the eddy would be divided, and the navigation improved; and that as it is, the bridge is placed in the best manner possible.

I am not now going to discuss the question what is a material obstruction? We do not very greatly differ about the law. The cases produced here, are, I suppose, proper to be taken into consideration by the Court in instructing the jury. Some of them I think are not exactly in point, but still I am willing to trust his honor, Judge McLean,[10] and take his instructions as law.

What is *reasonable* skill and care? This is a thing of which the jury are to judge. I differ from them in saying that they are bound to exercise no more care than they took before the building of the bridge. If we are allowed by the Legislature to build a bridge, which will require them to do more than before, when a pilot comes along, it is unreasonable for him to dash on, heedless of this structure, which has been *legally put there*. The Afton came there on the 5th, and lay at Rock Island until next morning. When the boat lies up, the pilot has a holiday, and would not any of these jurors have then gone around there, and got acquainted with the place? Parker[11] has shown here that he does not understand the draw. I heard him say that the fall from the head to the foot of that pier was four feet! He needs information. He could have gone there that day and have seen there was no such fall. He should have discarded passion, and the chances are that he would have had no disaster at all. He was bound to make himself acquainted with it.

McCammon[12] says that "the current and the swell coming from the long pier, drove her against the long pier." Drove her towards the very pier from which the current came! It is an absurdity, an impossibility. The only reconciliation I can find for this contradiction, is in a current which White[13] says strikes out from the long pier, and then, like a ram's horn, turns back, and this might have acted somehow in this manner.

It is agreed by all that the plaintiffs' boat was destroyed; that it was destroyed upon the head of the short pier; that she moved from the channel, where she was, with her bow above the head of the long pier, till she struck the short one, swung around under the bridge, and there was crowded under the bridge and destroyed.

I shall try to prove that the average velocity of the current through the draw with the boat in it, should be five and a half miles an hour; that it is slowest at the head of the pier,—swiftest at the foot of the pier. Their lowest estimate, in evidence, is six miles an hour, their highest twelve miles. This was the testimony of men who had made no experiment—only conjecture. We have adopted the most exact means. The water runs swiftest in high water, and we have taken the point of nine feet above low water. The water, when the Afton was lost, was seven feet above low water, or at least a foot lower than our time. Brayton[14] and his assistants timed the instruments— the best known instruments for measuring currents. They timed them under various circumstances, and they found the current five miles an hour, and no more. They found that the water, at the upper end, ran slower than five miles; that below it was swifter than five miles, but that the average was five miles. Shall men, who have taken no care, who conjecture, some of whom speak of twenty miles an hour be believed, against those who have had such a favorable and well-improved opportunity? They should not even *qualify* the result. Several men have given their opinions as to the distance of the Carson,[15] and I suppose if *one* should go and *measure* that distance, you would believe him in preference to all of them.

These measurements were made when the boat was not in the draw. It has been ascertained what is the area of the cross-section of the stream, and the area of the face of the piers, and the engineers say, that the piers being put there will increase the current proportionably as the space is decreased. So with the boat in the draw. The depth of the channel was 22 feet, the width 116 feet—multiply these and you have the square feet across the water of the draw, viz.: 2,552 feet. The Afton was 35 feet wide and drew five feet, making a fourteenth of the sum. Now one-fourteenth of five miles is five-fourteenths of one mile—about one-third of a mile—the increase of the current. We will call the current 5 1/2 miles per hour.

The next thing I will try to prove is that the plaintiffs' boat had power to run six miles an hour in that current. It has been testified that she was a strong, swift boat, able to run eight miles an hour up stream in a current of four miles an hour, and fifteen miles down stream. Strike the average and you will find what is her average—about 11 1/2 miles. Take the 5 1/2 miles which is the speed of the current in the draw, and it leaves the power of the

and that he had recorded in a log book 958 passages of boats under the bridge in the thirteen months since its reopening, with only 7 boats suffering any kind of damage. Lincoln and the defense team pointed to this statistic to counter the testimony of more than fifty boat captains and river pilots that the bridge posed a danger to river traffic. Their main argument was that the crash was the fault of the pilot and crew of the *Effie Afton,* thus Lincoln devoted much of his closing statement to the length and speed of the current under the bridge, the positions of the piers, and testimony concerning the actions of the *Effie Afton* and its crew. McGinty, *Lincoln's Greatest Case,* 132–133. See also Morsman, "Collision of Interests"; Dirck, *Lincoln the Lawyer,* 97.

9  Roswell B. Mason (1805–1892), from Dubuque, Iowa, was one of six civil engineers called as witnesses for the defense concerning the bridge and its effect upon the river current. He served as mayor of Chicago from 1869 to 1871. McGinty, *Lincoln's Greatest Case,* 137–138.

10  John McLean of Ohio was appointed associate justice of the U.S. Supreme Court in 1829 by President Andrew Jackson. He was a contender for the Whig nomination for president in 1848 and the Republican nomination for president in 1856. Timothy L. Hall, *Supreme Court Justices: A Biographical Dictionary* (New York: Facts on File, 2001), 78–81.

11  Nathaniel W. Parker was the pilot of the *Effie Afton.* Although Lincoln and the defense team asserted that carelessness and incompetence caused the accident, they also suspected the fire on the vessel may have been set intentionally because it was only insured against fire. McGinty, *Lincoln's Greatest Case,* 72–73; 122–123.

12  Joseph McCammant, hired to pilot the *Effie Afton,* was replaced by Nathaniel Parker at Saint Louis. McCammant remained on the crew and, at

the time of the crash, was in the wheelhouse of the vessel. Ibid., 71–72, 154–155.

13  William White, a Galena (Illinois)-based river pilot for more than twenty years, testified on behalf of the plaintiffs that there was "a risk of life and property in going through the bridge." White cited in Morsman, "Collision of Interests."

14  Benjamin B. Brayton was the engineer in charge of building the Rock Island Bridge. In early September, in preparation for the trial, Lincoln inspected the rebuilt bridge with Brayton, measured the river's currents, and interviewed several boatmen. McGinty, *Lincoln's Greatest Case,* 66, 104–105; Donald, *Lincoln,* 157; Allen D. Spiegel, *A. Lincoln, Esquire: A Shrewd, Sophisticated Lawyer in His Time* (Macon, GA: Mercer University Press, 2002), 98.

15  The steamer *J. B. Carson,* which the defense contended the *Effie Afton* engaged in a race to the bridge, which would have affected the angle at which the latter vessel approached the draw. Morsman, "Collision of Interests."

16  John A. Baker was a member of the crew of the *Effie Afton. CW,* 2:422n10.

boat in that draw at six miles an hour, 528 feet per minute, and 8 4/5 feet to the second.

Next I propose to show that there are no cross currents. I know their witnesses say that there are cross currents—that, as one witness says, there are three cross currents and two eddies. So far as mere statement without experiment, and mingled with mistakes can go, they have proved. But can these men's testimony be compared with the nice, exact, thorough experiments of our witnesses. Can you believe that these floats go across the currents? It is inconceiveable [*sic*] that they could not have discovered every possible current. How do boats find currents that floats cannot discover? We assume the position then that those cross currents are not there. My next proposition is that the Afton passed between the S. B. Carson and Iowa shore. That is undisputed.

Next I shall show that she struck first the short pier, then the long pier, then the short one again and there she stopped. Mr. Lincoln cited the testimony of eighteen witnesses on this point. How did the boat strike Baker[16] when she went in! Here is an endless variety of opinion. But ten of them say what pier she struck; three of them testify that she struck first the short, then the long, then the short pier for the last time. None of the rest substantially contradict this. I assume that these men have got the truth, because I believe it an established fact.

My next proposition is that after she struck the short and long pier and before she got back to the short pier the boat got right with her bow out. So says the Pilot Parker—that he "got her through until her starboard wheel passed the short pier." This would make her head about even with the head of the long pier. He says her head was as high or higher than the head of the long pier. Other witnesses confirm this one. The final stroke was in the splash door, aft the wheel. Witnesses differ but the majority say that she struck thus.

Court adjourned.

FOURTEENTH DAY
Wednesday, September 23

Mr. A. Lincoln resumed. He said he should conclude as soon as possible. He said the colored map of the plaintiffs, which was brought in during the advanced stages of the trial, showed itself that the cross currents alleged did not exist; that the current as represented would drive an ascending boat to the long pier, but not to the short pier as they urged. He explained from a model of a boat where the splash door is, just behind the wheel.[17] The boat struck on the lower shoulder of the short pier, as she swung round, in the splash door, then as she went on round she struck the point or end of the pier, where she rested. Her engineers say the starboard wheel then was rushing round rapidly. Then the boat must have struck the upper point of the pier so far back as not to disturb the wheel. It is forty feet from the stern of the Afton to the splash door, and thus it appears that she had but forty feet to go to clear the pier.

How was it that the Afton, with all her power, flanked over from the channel to the short pier without moving one inch ahead? Suppose she was in the middle of the draw, her wheel would have been 31 feet from the short pier. The reason she went over thus is, her starboard wheel was not working. I shall try to establish the fact that that wheel was not running, and, that after she struck, she went ahead strong on this same wheel. Upon the last point the witnesses agree—that the starboard wheel was running after she struck—and no witnesses say that it was running while she was out in the draw flanking over. Mr. Lincoln read from the testimony of various witnesses to prove that the starboard wheel was not working while she was out in the stream. Other witnesses show that the captain said something of the machinery of the wheel, and the inference is that he knew the wheel was not working. The fact is undisputed, that she did not move one inch ahead, while she was moving this 31 feet sideways. There is evidence proving that the current there is only five miles an hour, and the only explanation is that her power was not all used—that only one wheel was working. The pilot says he ordered the engineers to back her out. The engineers differ from him and say that they kept one going ahead. The bow was so swung that the current pressed it over; the pilot pressed the stern over with the rudder, though not so fast but that the bow gained on it, and, only one wheel being in motion, the boat merely stood still so far as motion up and down is concerned, and thus she was thrown upon this pier.

The Afton came into the draw after she had just passed the Carson, and, as the Carson no doubt kept the true course, the Afton going around her, got out of the proper way, got across the current, into the eddy which is west of a straight line drawn down from the long pier, was compelled to resort to these changes of wheels, which she did not do with sufficient adroitness to save her. Was it not her own fault that she entered wrong? so far, wrong that she never got right. Is the defence to blame for that?

For several days we were entertained with depositions about boats "smell-

17 Using a model of the *Effie Afton*, which he brought to the court on the second day of his closing statement, Lincoln demonstrated that the failure of the starboard wheel to run properly played a significant role in the crash. McGinty, *Lincoln's Greatest Case*, 158; Albert A. Woldman, *Lawyer Lincoln* (1936; repr. New York: Carroll & Graff, 2001), 184.

18  Lincoln, along with the defense team, was able to convince nine members of the jury of twelve. With the panel unable to reach a unanimous verdict, Judge McLean dismissed the case and Jacob Hurd and his associates did not recover damages. The legal battle against the bridge dragged on until 1862, when the U.S. Supreme Court overturned a lower court order to remove a part of the bridge. McGinty, *Lincoln's Greatest Case,* 160–162, 185–190. According to one attorney, Lincoln's performance was one of his "ablest efforts." "His illustrations," the lawyer continued, "were apt and forcible, his statements clear and logical, and his reasons in favor of policy (and necessarily right) to bridge the river . . . were broad and statesmanlike." According to one historian, "As a practical matter, Lincoln's side won," since "the case was not retried." Steiner, *An Honest Calling,* 69. Quote about Lincoln is cited in Burlingame, *Abraham Lincoln,* 1:338.

ing a bar." Why did the Afton then, after she had come up smelling so close to the long pier sheer off so strangely? When she got to the centre of the very nose she was smelling, she seems suddenly to have lost her sense of smell and flanks over to the short pier.

Mr. Lincoln said there was no practicability in the project of building a tunnel under the river, for there is not a tunnel that is a successful project, in the world. A suspension bridge cannot be built so high, but that the chimneys of the boats will grow up till they cannot pass. The steamboatmen will take pains to make them grow. The cars of a railroad, cannot, without immense expense, rise high enough to get even with a suspension bridge, or go low enough to get down through a tunnel. Such expense is unreasonable.

The plaintiffs have to establish that the bridge is a material obstruction, and that they managed their boat with reasonable care and skill. As to the last point, high winds have nothing to do with it, for it was not a windy day. They must show "due skill and care." Difficulties going down stream, will not do, for they were going up stream. Difficulties with barges in tow, have nothing to do with it, for they had no barge. He said he had much more to say, many things he could suggest to the jury, but he would close to save time.[18]

# "House Divided" Address, Springfield, Illinois

## June 16, 1858

*Accepting the Illinois Republican Party's nomination to challenge incumbent, two-term Democratic senator Stephen A. Douglas, Lincoln delivered one of his most eloquent and forceful speeches against the extension of slavery. Focusing on Douglas's Kansas-Nebraska Act and the Supreme Court's Dred Scott decision, Lincoln pointed to what he saw as a conspiracy by Douglas and Northern Democrats to open the territories to slavery and ultimately nationalize the institution. He urged his fellow Republicans to firmly resist the movement to expand slavery by defeating Douglas, one of its chief proponents, famously asserting that a "house divided against itself cannot stand."*

Mr. PRESIDENT and Gentlemen of the Convention.[1]

If we could first know *where* we are, and *whither* we are tending, we could then better judge *what* to do, and *how* to do it.[2]

We are now far into the *fifth* year, since a policy was initiated,[3] with the *avowed* object, and *confident* promise, of putting an end to slavery agitation.

Under the operation of that policy, that agitation has not only, *not ceased,* but has *constantly augmented.*

In *my* opinion, it *will* not cease, until a *crisis* shall have been reached, and passed.

"A house divided against itself cannot stand."[4]

I believe this government cannot endure, permanently half *slave* and half *free.*

I do not expect the Union to be *dissolved*—I do not expect the house to *fall*—but I *do* expect it will cease to be divided.

It will become *all* one thing, or *all* the other.

Either the *opponents* of slavery, will arrest the further spread of it, and place it where the public mind shall rest in the belief that it is in course of ultimate extinction; or its *advocates* will push it forward, till it shall become alike lawful in *all* the States, *old* as well as *new*—*North* as well as *South.*

Have we no *tendency* to the latter condition?

Let any one who doubts, carefully contemplate that now almost complete legal combination—piece of *machinery* so to speak—compounded of the Nebraska doctrine, and the Dred Scott decision.[5] Let him consider not only *what work* the machinery is adapted to do, and *how well* adapted; but also, let him study the *history* of its construction, and trace, if he can, or

[1]   The Illinois Republican convention was held in the statehouse in Springfield, where Lincoln was unanimously nominated for the U.S. Senate. After weeks of assiduous preparation, Lincoln delivered his address that evening in the Hall of Representatives. Lincoln had a lock on the nomination before the convention began, with ninety-five Republican county conventions declaring support for his candidacy prior to the Springfield meeting. Early in 1858 some Illinois Republicans and prominent Eastern party members considered an alliance with Douglas against slavery's extension owing to his break with President Buchanan over the Kansas constitution. Desiring the admission of Kansas as a Democrat-controlled state, with or without slavery, Buchanan attempted to quell the violence and division in the territory by appointing Robert J. Walker (1801–1869) of Mississippi, a former treasury secretary and a prominent Democrat, territorial governor. Walker accepted the post after Buchanan pledged to support only a constitution that was submitted to residents of the territory for approval. The governor soon turned to Buchanan for support when free-state men refused to participate in the 1857 election to send delegates to a constitutional convention, held in the town of Lecompton, that resulted in a proslavery minority producing a constitution permitting slavery and

prohibiting any changes to the document until 1865. The constitution would be submitted to Congress after a popular vote only on the question of whether new slaves could be brought into the territory. The Lecompton constitution was adopted by a limited vote, as free-state residents again refused to participate in what they considered a fraudulent election. Aware that a majority of Kansans opposed slavery, Walker expected Buchanan to fulfill his pledge to reject a constitution not approved in its entirety by a popular referendum. But the president, under severe pressure from Southern congressmen and governors, accepted the constitution and submitted it to Congress with his full support. Outraged over the president's willingness to accept a constitution that repudiated popular sovereignty enshrined in the Democratic Party platform of 1856, Douglas broke with Buchanan and led the fight in Congress against the Lecompton constitution. To the chagrin of Lincoln and other Illinois Republicans, several prominent Eastern Republicans, led by Horace Greeley, editor of the influential *New York Tribune,* which had a wide circulation in the state, toyed with the idea of joining forces with Douglas. Lincoln worked actively behind the scenes to keep his fellow Republicans in line, constantly reminding them that while Douglas disagreed with Buchanan on Lecompton, he supported the president on every other issue that Republicans opposed and, more important, he was indifferent to the cause of the eventual eradication of slavery. Burlingame, *Abraham Lincoln,* 1:445–458; Don E. Fehrenbacher, *Prelude to Greatness: Lincoln in the 1850s* (Stanford: Stanford University Press, 1962), 70; Horrocks, *President James Buchanan,* 56–59.

2    Historians have noted that Lincoln opened his speech in a vein similar to Daniel Webster's famous second reply to Robert Y. Hayne (1791–1839) delivered in the U.S. Senate on March 7, 1830, which Lincoln considered "the very best speech

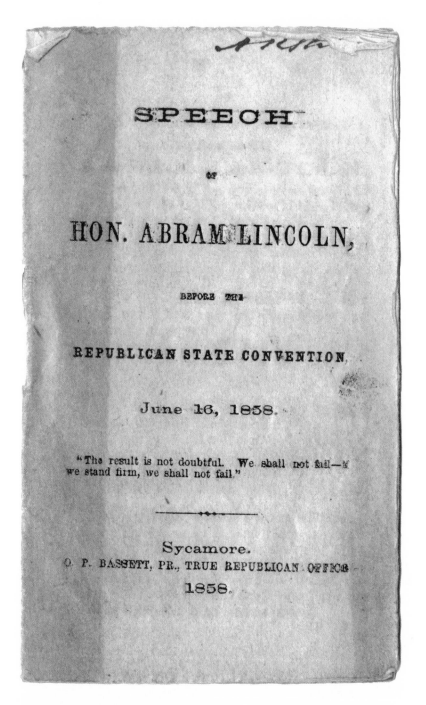

SPEECH

OF

HON. ABRAM LINCOLN,

BEFORE THE

REPUBLICAN STATE CONVENTION,

June 16, 1858.

"The result is not doubtful. We shall not fail—if we stand firm, we shall not fail."

Sycamore.
O. P. BASSETT, PR., TRUE REPUBLICAN OFFICE.
1858.

Abraham Lincoln, *Speech of Hon. Abram Lincoln, before the Republican State Convention, June 16, 1858* (Sycamore, IL, 1858). Title page of the printed version of Lincoln's House Divided speech.

rather *fail,* if he can, to trace the evidences of design, and concert of action, among its chief bosses, from the beginning.

The new year of 1854 found slavery excluded from more than half the States by State Constitutions, and from most of the national territory by Congressional prohibition.[6]

Four days later, commenced the struggle, which ended in repealing that Congressional prohibition.

This opened all the national territory to slavery; and was the first point gained.

But, so far, *Congress* only, had acted; and an *indorsement* by the people, *real* or apparent, was indispensable, to *save* the point already gained, and give chance for more.

This necessity had not been overlooked; but had been provided for, as well as might be, in the notable argument of "*squatter sovereignty,*"[7] otherwise called "*sacred right of self government,*" which latter phrase, though expressive of the only rightful basis of any government, was so perverted in this attempted use of it as to amount to just this: That if any *one* man, choose to enslave *another,* no *third* man shall be allowed to object.

That argument was incorporated into the Nebraska bill itself, in the language which follows: "*It being the true intent and meaning of this act not to legislate slavery into any Territory or state, nor to exclude it therefrom; but to leave the people thereof perfectly free to form and regulate their domestic institutions in their own way, subject only to the Constitution of the United States.*"

Then opened the roar of loose declamation in favor of "Squatter Sovereignty," and "Sacred right of self government."

"But," said opposition members, "let us be more *specific*—let us *amend* the bill so as to expressly declare that the people of the territory *may* exclude slavery." "Not we," said the friends of the measure; and down they voted the amendment.

While the Nebraska bill was passing through congress, a *law case,* involving the question of a negroe's [*sic*] freedom, by reason of his owner having voluntarily taken him first into a free state and then a territory covered by the congressional prohibition, and held him as a slave, for a long time in each, was passing through the U.S. Circuit Court for the District of Missouri; and both Nebraska bill and law suit were brought to a decision in the same month of May, 1854. The negroe's [*sic*] name was "Dred Scott," which name now designates the decision finally made in the case.

*Before* the *then* next Presidential election, the law case came *to,* and was argued *in* the Supreme Court of the United States; but the *decision* of it was

that was ever delivered." See, for example, Donald, *Lincoln,* 206. Webster began his address with this passage: "When the mariner has been tossed for many days in thick weather and on an unknown sea, he naturally avails himself of the first pause in the storm, the earliest glance at the sun, to take his latitude and ascertain how far the elements have driven him from his course. Let us imitate this prudence, and, before we float further on the waves of this debate, refer to the point from which we departed, that we may at least be able to conjecture where we now are." Daniel Webster, *Papers of Daniel Webster, 1800–1833,* ed. Charles M. Wiltse, 2 vols. (Hanover, NH: University Press of New England, 1986), 1:287.

3    Popular sovereignty, as enshrined in the Kansas-Nebraska Act of 1854.

4    The "house divided" quotation used by Lincoln would have been familiar to virtually everyone who heard or read his speech, since it appeared in three of the Gospels: Matthew 12:25, "Every kingdom divided against itself is brought to desolation; and every city or house divided against itself shall not stand"; Mark 3:25, "And if a house be divided against itself, that house cannot stand"; and Luke 11:17, "Every kingdom divided against itself is brought to desolation; and a house divided against a house falleth." While Lincoln's speech is well known because of this phrase, it was not the first time the metaphor was used to describe the incompatibility of slavery and freedom. Both Northerners and Southerners and antislavery and proslavery advocates had expressed similar ideas. With great interest Lincoln had read a few years before an editorial by proslavery zealot George Fizhugh in the *Richmond Enquirer* that discussed the war between slavery and freedom. Lincoln himself had previously used the "house divided" phrase—in private—in a letter and a draft of a speech. "Letter to George Robertson, August 15, 1855," in this volume; *CW,* 2:452. Lincoln's law

partner Herndon claimed that he used the same argument in an 1856 speech in Bloomington (the famous "Lost Speech"). Herndon and Weik, *Herndon's Lincoln*, 244. See also Burlingame, *Abraham Lincoln*, 1:461–463; Donald, *Lincoln*, 206–207.

5   The U.S. Supreme Court case, *Dred Scott v. Sandford*, 1857. See "Speech on the *Dred Scott* Decision at Springfield, Illinois, June 26, 1857," in this volume.

6   The Missouri Compromise of 1820, which prohibited slavery in territory acquired by the Louisiana Purchase (1803) that lay above parallel 36°30' north.

7   Term used by Lincoln to belittle "popular sovereignty."

8   Senator Lyman Trumbull of Illinois.

9   Lincoln pointed out that Democratic candidate, James Buchanan, was elected president with only 45 percent of the popular vote, garnering fewer than the approximately 378,000 votes that Republican Charles C. Frémont and Know-Nothing Millard Fillmore received, combined.

10   Democrat Franklin Pierce, the fourteenth president of the United States (1853–1857).

11   In his inaugural address, James Buchanan, referring to the pending decision of the Supreme Court on the *Dred Scott* case, declared that he would, "in common with all good citizens . . . cheerfully submit." See "Speech on the *Dred Scott* Decision at Springfield, Illinois, June 26, 1857," note 8.

12   The *Dred Scott* decision was announced on March 6, 1857.

13   Douglas's speech was delivered in Springfield on June 12, 1857, and was quickly published in pamphlet form. See Douglas, *Remarks on Kansas, Utah, and the Dred Scott Decision.*

deferred until *after* the election. Still, *before* the election, Senator Trumbull,[8] on the floor of the Senate, requests the leading advocate of the Nebraska bill to state *his opinion* whether the people of a territory can constitutionally exclude slavery from their limits; and the latter answers, "That is a question for the Supreme Court."

The election came. Mr. Buchanan was elected, and the *indorsement,* such as it was, secured. That was the *second* point gained. The indorsement, however, fell short of a clear popular majority by nearly four hundred thousand votes, and so, perhaps, was not overwhelmingly reliable and satisfactory.[9]

The *outgoing* President,[10] in his last annual message, as impressively as possible *echoed back* upon the people the *weight* and *authority* of the indorsement.

The Supreme Court met again; *did not* announce their decision, but ordered a re-argument.

The Presidential inauguration came, and still no decision of the court; but the *incoming* President, in his inaugural address, fervently exhorted the people to abide by the forthcoming decision, *whatever it might be.*[11]

Then, in a few days, came the decision.[12]

The reputed author of the Nebraska bill finds an early occasion to make a speech at this capitol indorsing the Dred Scott Decision, and vehemently denouncing all opposition to it.[13]

The new President, too, seizes the early occasion of the Silliman letter to *indorse* and strongly *construe* that decision, and to express his *astonishment* that any different view had ever been entertained.[14]

At length a squabble springs up between the President and the author of the Nebraska bill, on the *mere* question of *fact,* whether the Lecompton constitution was or was not, in any just sense, made by the people of Kansas; and in that squabble the latter declares that all he wants is a fair vote for the people, and that he *cares* not whether slavery be voted *down* or voted *up.*[15] I do not understand his declaration that he cares not whether slavery be voted down or voted up, to be intended by him other than as an *apt definition* of the *policy* he would impress upon the public mind—the *principle* for which he declares he has suffered much, and is ready to suffer to the end.

And well may he cling to that principle. If he has any parental feeling, well may he cling to it. That principle, is the only *shred* left of his original Nebraska doctrine. Under the Dred Scott decision, "squatter sovereignty" squatted out of existence, tumbled down like temporary scaffolding—like the mould at the foundry served through one blast and fell back into loose sand—helped to carry an election, and then was kicked to the winds. His

Old State House, Springfield, Illinois. Photograph (Springfield, ca. 1898).

late *joint* struggle with the Republicans, against the Lecompton Constitution, involves nothing of the original Nebraska doctrine. That struggle was made on a point, the right of a people to make their own constitution, upon which he and the Republicans have never differed.

The several points of the Dred Scott decision, in connection with Senator Douglas' "care not" policy, constitute the piece of machinery, in its *present* state of advancement. This was the third point gained.

The *working* points of that machinery are:

First, that no negro slave, imported as such from Africa, and no descendant of such slave can ever be a *citizen* of any State, in the sense of that term as used in the Constitution of the United States.

This point is made in order to deprive the negro, in every possible event, of the benefit of this provision of the United States Constitution, which declares that—

"The citizens of each State shall be entitled to all privileges and immunities of citizens in the several States."[16]

Secondly, that "subject to the Constitution of the United States," neither

14  On August 15, 1857, President Buchanan replied to a letter signed by forty-three antislavery advocates from Connecticut, including the eminent scientist Benjamin Silliman (1779–1864), complaining of Kansas governor Robert Walker's use of the military to aid proslavery forces in the territory. They requested that the president intervene against Walker's use of military force. Buchanan defended the use of the military as necessary to protect residents "from the violence of lawless men," whom he identified as free-state partisans determined to establish a "revolutionary government" in Kansas. Stamp, *America in 1857,* 179–180; *Works of James Buchanan,* 10:117–122.

15  When Buchanan proclaimed his support for the proslavery Lecompton constitution, which was not supported by a majority of Kansas residents, Douglas broke with the administration because he

believed the constitution violated the principle of popular sovereignty. Lincoln downplayed the intensity of the Douglas-Buchanan feud, referring to it as a "squabble," in order to strengthen his case against the senator. See note 1.

16   Article IV, Section 2.

*Congress* nor a *Territorial Legislature* can exclude slavery from any United States territory.

This point is made in order that individual men may *fill up* the territories with slaves, without danger of losing them as property, and thus to enhance the chances of *permanency* to the institution through all the future.

Thirdly, that whether the holding a negro in actual slavery in a free State, makes him free, as against the holder, the United States courts will not decide, but will leave to be decided by the courts of any slave State the negro may be forced into by the master.

This point is made, not to be pressed *immediately;* but, if acquiesced in for a while, and apparently *indorsed* by the people at an election, *then* to sustain the logical conclusion that what Dred Scott's master might lawfully do with Dred Scott, in the free State of Illinois, every other master may lawfully do with any other *one,* or one *thousand* slaves, in Illinois, or in any other free State.

Auxiliary to all this, and working hand in hand with it, the Nebraska doctrine, or what is left of it, is to *educate* and *mould* public opinion, at least *Northern* public opinion, to not *care* whether slavery is voted *down* or voted *up.*

This shows exactly where we now *are;* and *partially* also, whither we are tending.

It will throw additional light on the latter, to go back, and run the mind over the string of historical facts already stated. Several things will *now* appear less *dark* and *mysterious* than they did *when* they were transpiring. The people were to be left "perfectly free" "subject only to the Constitution." What the *Constitution* had to do with it, outsiders could not *then* see. Plainly enough *now,* it was an exactly fitted *niche,* for the Dred Scott decision to afterwards come in, and declare the *perfect freedom* of the people, to be just no freedom at all.

Why was the amendment, expressly declaring the right of the people to exclude slavery, voted down? Plainly enough *now,* the adoption of it, would have spoiled the niche for the Dred Scott decision.

Why was the court decision held up? Why, even a Senator's individual opinion withheld, till *after* the Presidential election? Plainly enough *now,* the speaking out *then* would have damaged the "*perfectly free*" argument upon which the election was to be carried.

Why the *outgoing* President's felicitation on the indorsement? Why the delay of a reargument? Why the incoming President's *advance* exhortation in favor of the decision?

These things *look* like the cautious *patting* and *petting* of a spirited horse, preparatory to mounting him, when it is dreaded that he may give the rider a fall.

And why the hasty after indorsements of the decision by the President and others?

We can not absolutely *know* that all these exact adaptations are the result of preconcert. But when we see a lot of framed timbers, different portions of which we know have been gotten out at different times and places and by different workmen—Stephen, Franklin, Roger and James,[17] for instance—and when we see these timbers joined together, and see they exactly make the frame of a house or a mill, all the tenons and mortices exactly fitting, and all the lengths and proportions of the different pieces exactly adapted to their respective places, and not a piece too many or too few—not omitting even scaffolding—or, if a single piece be lacking, we can see the place in the frame exactly fitted and prepared to yet bring such piece in—in *such* a case, we find it impossible to not *believe* that Stephen and Franklin and Roger and James all understood one another from the beginning, and all worked upon a common *plan* or *draft* drawn up before the first lick was struck.

It should not be overlooked that, by the Nebraska bill, the people of a *State* as well as *Territory,* were to be left *"perfectly free"* *"subject only to the Constitution."*

Why mention a *State*? They were legislating for *territories,* and not *for* or *about* States. Certainly the people of a State *are* and *ought to be* subject to the Constitution of the United States; but why is mention of this *lugged* into this merely *territorial* law? Why are the people of a *territory* and the people of a *state* therein *lumped* together, and their relation to the Constitution therein treated as being *precisely* the same?

While the opinion of *the Court,* by Chief Justice Taney, in the Dred Scott case, and the separate opinions of all the concurring Judges, expressly declare that the Constitution of the United States neither permits Congress nor a Territorial legislature to exclude slavery from any United States territory, they all *omit* to declare whether or not the same Constitution permits a *state,* or the people of a State, to exclude it.

*Possibly,* this was a mere *omission;* but who can be *quite* sure, if McLean[18] or Curtis[19] had sought to get into the opinion a declaration of unlimited power in the people of a *state* to exclude slavery from their limits, just as Chase[20] and Macy[21] sought to get such declaration, in behalf of the people of a territory, into the Nebraska bill—I ask, who can be quite *sure* that it

17 Douglas, Franklin Pierce, Chief Justice Roger B. Taney, and James Buchanan. Lincoln used the analogy of several workmen constructing a house to support his allegation of a conspiracy among Douglas and his Democratic and proslavery associates to expand slavery throughout the nation. Lincoln's charge was an exaggeration in view of Douglas's break with Buchanan Democrats who were undermining, with the assistance of Illinois Republicans, his reelection bid. Fehrenbacher, *Prelude to Greatness,* 113.

18 Justice John McLean was one of the two dissenting Supreme Court justices in the *Dred Scott* case, arguing that Scott should be recognized as a free man. Howard, *Report of the Decision of the Supreme Court,* 135–170.

19 Justice Benjamin R. Curtis was the other dissenting justice in the *Dred Scott* case.

20 Salmon B. Chase of Ohio was a U.S. senator who, along with several other leading antislavery congressmen, condemned the Kansas-Nebraska Act as violating a sacred compact between North and South to prohibit slavery in the territories. An aspirant for the Republican nomination for president in 1860, Chase was appointed secretary of the treasury by Lincoln in 1861. Potter, *The Impending Crisis,* 162–163.

21 John B. Macy (1799–1856), Democratic representative from Wisconsin. "Macy, John," Biographical Directory of the United States Congress, http://bioguide.congress.gov/scripts. biodisplay.pl?index=M000036 (accessed January 26, 2015).

**22** Samuel Nelson (1792–1872), Supreme Court justice and a Democrat from New York, agreed with the court's majority opinion that Scott and his family remained slaves, but in his concurring opinion he ignored the question of Congress's power to ban slavery in the territories and focused entirely on the ability of Missouri's Supreme Court to determine the status of blacks in its jurisdiction. Fehrenbacher, *The Dred Scott Case,* 390–394.

**23** Lincoln warned of the possibility of another Supreme Court decision similar to *Dred Scott,* one that would protect slavery not just in the territories but in all states. Lincoln was aware that the case *Lemmon v. The People,* concerning the right of a Virginia slaveholder to bring his slaves into the state of New York for shipment to Texas, was possibly headed to the Supreme Court. In October 1857 the New York Supreme Court upheld a New York state law that stipulated that "no person imported, introduced or brought into this State" could be held in bondage. In light of the *Dred Scott* decision, antislavery opponents feared the Supreme Court would overturn the New York court's decision. The case had not reached the U.S. Supreme Court by the time Virginia seceded. Burlingame, *Abraham Lincoln,* 1:463; Foner, *The Fiery Trial,* 101–102.

**24** Lincoln closed his address with a call for party unity along with a harsh indictment of Douglas's role in aiding and abetting the movement to nationalize slavery, urging Republicans leaning toward supporting the senator, owing to his break with the Buchanan administration, to reject him because he was and always had been strongly opposed to Republican principles.

**25** Previously comparing himself with Douglas, Lincoln sarcastically wrote that "with *me,* the race of ambition has been a failure—a flat failure; with *him* it has been one of splendid success. His name fills the nation; and is not unknown, even in foreign lands." *CW,* 2:383.

would not have been voted down, in the one case, as it had been in the other.

The nearest approach to the point of declaring the power of a State over slavery, is made by Judge Nelson.[22] He approaches it more than once, using the precise idea, and *almost* the language too, of the Nebraska act. On one occasion his exact language is, "except in cases where the power is restrained by the Constitution of the United States, the law of the State is supreme over the subject of slavery within its jurisdiction."

In what *cases* the power of the *states is* so restrained by the U.S. Constitution, is left an *open* question, precisely as the same question, as to the restraint on the power of the *territories* was left open in the Nebraska act. Put *that* and *that* together, and we have another nice little niche, which we may, ere long, see filled with another Supreme Court decision, declaring that the Constitution of the United States does not permit a *state* to exclude slavery from its limits.[23]

And this may especially be expected if the doctrine of "care not whether slavery be voted *down* or voted *up,*" shall gain upon the public mind sufficiently to give promise that such a decision can be maintained when made.

Such a decision is all that slavery now lacks of being alike lawful in all the States.

Welcome or unwelcome, such decision *is* probably coming, and will soon be upon us, unless the power of the present political dynasty shall be met and overthrown.

We shall *lie down* pleasantly dreaming that the people of *Missouri* are on the verge of making their State *free;* and we shall *awake* to the *reality,* instead, that the *Supreme* Court has made *Illinois* a *slave* State.

To meet and overthrow the power of that dynasty, is the work now before all those who would prevent that consummation.

That is *what* we have to do.

But *how* can we best do it?

There are those who denounce us *openly* to their *own* friends, and yet whisper to *us softly,* that *Senator Douglas* is the *aptest* instrument there is, with which to effect that object. *They* do *not* tell us, nor has *he* told us, that he *wishes* any such object to be effected. They wish us to *infer* all, from the facts, that he now has a little quarrel with the present head of the dynasty; and that he has regularly voted with us, on a single point, upon which, he and we, have never differed.[24]

They remind us that *he* is a very *great man,* and that the largest of *us* are very small ones.[25] Let this be granted. But "a *living dog* is better than a *dead*

Hall of Representatives, Old State House, Springfield, Illinois. Photograph (ca. 1898). The Hall of Representatives as it looked forty years after Lincoln delivered the House Divided address.

lion."[26] Judge Douglas, if not a *dead* lion *for this work,* is at least a *caged* and *toothless* one. How can he oppose the advances of slavery? He *don't* care anything about it. His avowed *mission is impressing* the "public heart" to *care* nothing about it.

A leading Douglas Democratic newspaper thinks Douglas' superior talent will be needed to resist the revival of the African slave trade.

Does Douglas believe an effort to revive that trade is approaching? He has not said so. Does he *really* think so? But if it is, how can he resist it? For years he has labored to prove it a *sacred right* of white men to take negro slaves into the new territories. Can he possibly show that it is *less* a sacred right to *buy* them where they can be bought cheapest? And, unquestionably they can be bought *cheaper in Africa* than in *Virginia.*

26 Ecclesiastes 9:4, "For to him that is joined to all the living there is hope: for a living dog is better than a dead lion."

**27** A reference to the 1,341,264 popular votes received by Republican candidate Frémont in the 1856 presidential election.

**28** Lincoln's speech inaugurated the 1858 senate campaign, which featured the famous series of debates between the two candidates. The Republican press in Illinois and around the country praised the speech, but some of Lincoln's associates feared the house-divided reference would be interpreted as a full-scale attack on the institution of slavery that would lead to civil war, alienating moderate swing voters in the middle of the state. Aware that the speech might be perceived by some as too radical, Lincoln shared a draft with Herndon and other close advisers in advance of the convention, and only his law partner approved. In response to a colleague who admired the speech but claimed that the house-divided reference was too "ultra" for many who would normally vote Republican, Lincoln said he was mortified that "any part of it should be construed so differently from anything intended by me," claiming that he had "declared a thousand times, and now repeat that, in my opinion, neither the General Government, nor any other power outside of the slave states, can constitutionally or rightfully interfere with slaves or slavery where it already exists." In Douglas's opinion, Lincoln's speech called for "a war of sections, a war of the North against the South, of the free states against the slave states," and equality and amalgamation of the races, charges he would direct at Lincoln during their subsequent debates. Burlingame, *Abraham Lincoln,* 1:465–466; Donald, *Lincoln,* 209; Herndon and Weik, *Herndon's Lincoln,* 244. For Lincoln's response see *CW,* 1:471; Douglas is quoted in Johannsen, *Stephen A. Douglas,* 642.

He has done all in his power to reduce the whole question of slavery to one of a mere *right of property;* and as such, how can *he* oppose the foreign slave trade—how can he refuse that trade in that "property" shall be "perfectly free"—unless he does it as a *protection* to the home production? And as the home *producers* will probably not *ask* the protection, he will be wholly without a ground of opposition.

Senator Douglas holds, we know, that a man may rightfully be *wiser to-day* than he was *yesterday*—that he may rightfully *change* when he finds himself wrong.

But, can we for that reason, run ahead, and *infer* that he *will* make any particular change, of which he, himself, has given no intimation? Can we *safely* base *our* action upon any such *vague* inference?

Now, as ever, I wish to not *misrepresent* Judge Douglas' *position,* question his motives, or do ought that can be personally offensive to him.

Whenever, *if ever,* he and we can come together on *principle* so that *our great cause* may have assistance from *his great ability,* I hope to have interposed no adventitious obstacle.

But clearly, he is not *now* with us—he does not *pretend* to be—he does not *promise* to *ever* be.

Our cause, then, must be intrusted to, and conducted by its own undoubted friends—those whose hands are free, whose hearts are in the work—who *do care* for the result.

Two years ago the Republicans of the nation mustered over thirteen hundred thousand strong.[27]

We did this under the single impulse of resistance to a common danger, with every external circumstance against us.

Of *strange, discordant,* and even, *hostile* elements, we gathered from the four winds, and *formed* and fought the battle through, under the constant hot fire of a disciplined, proud, and pampered enemy.

Did we brave all *then,* to *falter* now?—*now*—when that same enemy is *wavering,* dissevered and belligerent?

The result is not doubtful. We shall not fail—if we stand firm, we shall not fail.

*Wise councils* may *accelerate* or *mistakes delay* it, but, sooner or later the victory is *sure* to come.[28]

# First Debate with Stephen A. Douglas at Ottawa, Illinois

≈≈≈≈≈≈≈≈≈≈≈≈≈≈≈≈≈≈≈≈≈≈≈≈

## August 21, 1858

### Mr. Douglas' Speech.

Ladies and gentlemen:[1] I appear before you to-day for the purpose of discussing the leading political topics which now agitate the public mind. By an arrangement[2] between Mr. Lincoln and myself, we are present here to-day for the purpose of having a joint discussion as the representatives of the two great political parties of the State and Union, upon the principles in issue between these parties and this vast concourse of people, shows the deep feeling which pervades the public mind in regard to the questions dividing us.[3]

. . .

During the session of Congress of 1853–'54, I introduced into the Senate of the United States a bill to organize the Territories of Kansas and Nebraska on that principle which had been adopted in the compromise measures of 1850, approved by the Whig party and the Democratic party in Illinois in 1851, and endorsed by the Whig party and the Democratic party in national convention in 1852. In order that there might be no misunderstanding in relation to the principle involved in the Kansas and Nebraska bill, I put forth the true intent and meaning of the act in these words: "It is the true intent and meaning of this act not to legislate slavery into any State or Territory, or to exclude it therefrom, but to leave the people thereof perfectly free to form and regulate their domestic institutions in their own way, subject only to the federal constitution." Thus, you see, that up to 1854, when the Kansas and Nebraska bill was brought into Congress for the purpose of carrying out the principles which both parties had up to that time endorsed

*In the first of his seven historic debates with Stephen A. Douglas, Lincoln repeated the criticisms of the Kansas-Nebraska Act and the* Dred Scott *ruling expressed in his Peoria and recent "House Divided" speeches, reiterating that they were contrary to the Founding Fathers' intention of placing slavery on a course of eventual extinction. He also affirmed his belief that Douglas was part of a proslavery conspiracy to extend slavery nationally, possibly ending with a Supreme Court decision allowing slavery in all states. For his part, Douglas accused Lincoln of being an abolitionist who promoted black equality and sectional conflict, a charge Lincoln sought to refute. While Lincoln agreed with Douglas that blacks would never be equal with whites in some aspects, he passionately disagreed with his opponent over the question whether African Americans were included in the definition of equality—having an equal right to life, liberty, and the pursuit of happiness—enshrined in the Declaration of Independence. Unlike Douglas, Lincoln firmly believed that the "all men are created equal" phrase in the Declaration meant all men, black and white.*

1    As is the case with all of the documents presented in this book, the versions of the Ottawa, Freeport, and Charleston, Illinois, debates are from *CW,* which used transcriptions from the scrapbook assembled and lightly edited by Lincoln after the 1858 campaign and later published as *Political Debates between Hon. Abraham Lincoln and Hon. Stephen A. Douglas* in 1860. The scrapbook contained transcriptions from newspapers friendly to both candidates, the Republican *Chicago Press and Tribune* and the Democratic *Chicago Times.* Lincoln's remarks are from the *Chicago Press and Tribune* and Douglas's from the *Chicago Times.* The *Press and Tribune* hired Robert R. Hitt, a future congressman from Illinois, and the *Times* used the English-born journalist Henry Binmore and James B. Sheridan (?–ca. 1905), sent by the pro-Douglas *Philadelphia Press,* to report the debates verbatim,

using shorthand. The reporters and editors of each paper made every effort to present their candidate in the best light, and as a result, the clippings gathered by Lincoln represent edited and sanitized versions of each candidate's remarks. Harold Holzer, ed., *The Lincoln-Douglas Debates: The First Complete and Unexpurgated Text* (New York: Fordham University Press, 2004), 10–11; Allen C. Guelzo, *Lincoln and Douglas: The Debates that Defined America* (New York: Simon & Schuster, 2008), 116–117. The publishing history of the *Political Debates* is covered by David H. Leroy, *Mr. Lincoln's Book: Publishing the Lincoln-Douglas Debates* (New Castle, DE: Oak Knoll Books; Chicago: Abraham Lincoln Book Shop, 2009).

2   In the wake of Lincoln's "House Divided" speech, Douglas opened his campaign for reelection with a July 9, 1858, speech in Chicago, responding to the various points raised by his Republican opponent. Both candidates delivered speeches across the state, with Lincoln appearing in Chicago (July 10), Springfield (July 17), Clinton (July 27), Monticello (July 29), Beardstown (August 12), Havana (August 14), Bath (August 16), Lewistown (August 17), and Peoria (August 19), offering rejoinders to Douglas's speeches in those towns while also reiterating points made in his "House Divided" oration. *CW,* 2:484–502, 504–521, 525–527, 538–547; Miers, *Lincoln Day by Day,* 2:221–222, 224–225. While Lincoln thought his tactic of following Douglas from town to town was "the very thing—it is, in fact, a concluding speech on him," other Republicans considered it seriously flawed because it favored Douglas, who drew "the crowd" while Lincoln got "the leavings," and opened up Lincoln to admonishment and ridicule by Democrats and the Democratic press. The *Chicago Times,* for example, wrote that Lincoln was nothing more than a "desperate creature," using Douglas to attract crowds he could not get on his own, which was a "mean, sneaking, and disreputable" practice. Republican leaders, both in Illinois and elsewhere, suggested debates between the two men. "Let Mr. Douglas and Mr. Lincoln agree to canvas the State together," urged the Republican-supporting *Chicago Press and Tribune.* Fully aware of Douglas's aggressive debating skills and his ability to draw large crowds of loyal supporters, Lincoln was at first wary of the idea. Despite his reluctance, Lincoln wrote to Douglas on July 24 proposing that "you and myself to divide time, and address the same audiences during the present canvas." The incumbent had no wish to share a stage with a little-known

challenger; there was little to be gained by providing visibility to Lincoln. Considering Lincoln a worthy foe, Douglas admitted to a Democratic newspaperman that "I will have my hands full. He is a strong man . . . full of wit, facts, dates . . . and the best stump speaker, with his droll ways and dry jokes, in the West. He is honest as he is shrewd, and if I beat him my victory will be hardly won." And Lincoln was not Douglas's only problem; he feared the Buchanan faction of the Democratic Party would enter its own candidate who would seek to join the debates, resulting in the senator's having to face two opponents. The pugnacious Douglas, however, could not pass up a fight: he accepted Lincoln's challenge the same day he received it. However, having scheduled many appearances across the state he was unwilling to debate Lincoln at most of them. The senator instead proposed joint meetings at one location in each of the nine congressional districts in the state except the two where they had already given speeches (Chicago and Springfield), suggesting Freeport, Ottawa, Galesburg, Quincy, Alton, Jonesboro, and Charleston. On July 29, Lincoln agreed to debate in the seven towns proposed by Douglas and asked for equal time and for "conclusions" to be assigned on a rotating basis. Douglas replied a day later with the following schedule of debates: Ottawa (LaSalle County) on August 21, Freeport (Stevenson County) on August 27, Jonesboro (Union County) on September 15, Charleston (Coles County) on September 18, Galesburg (Knox County) on October 7, Quincy (Adams County) on October 13, and Alton (Madison County) on October 15. He agreed with Lincoln's suggestion that the order of opening and closing arguments should alternate at each location, proposing that he (Douglas) would speak first in Ottawa for one hour, then Lincoln for one hour and a half, followed with his own half-hour concluding response. The candidates would then switch speaking slots at each subsequent debate. Lincoln accepted Douglas's proposed dates and format on July 31. Burlingame, *Abraham Lincoln,* 1:483; Guelzo, *Lincoln and Douglas,* 90–91. Lincoln's correspondence with Douglas concerning debates is found in *CW,* 2: 522, 530–531. For Douglas's view of Lincoln as an opponent and his response to Lincoln concerning debates, see Johannsen, *Stephen A. Douglas,* 640–641, 663–665. The best presentations of the Lincoln-Douglas debates are Rodney O. Davis and Douglas L. Wilson, ed., *The Lincoln-Douglas Debates: The Lincoln Studies Center Edition* (Urbana: Knox College Lincoln Studies Center and University of Illinois Press, 2008); and Holzer, *The Lincoln-Douglas Debates.*

3    Ottawa, the location of the first debate, is eighty miles southwest of Chicago and the seat of LaSalle County. Although LaSalle County was a hotbed of anti-Nebraska fervor in 1854 and supported the 1856 Republican presidential candidate, John C. Frémont, it remained Democratic throughout the 1850s. Based on the county's recent political history, the huge crowd attending the debate was probably evenly split between Democrats and Republicans. The debate drew an estimated crowd of more than 12,000, almost double the town's population. The crush of people assembling in Washington Square in the steamy midday heat caused the start of the debate to be delayed a half hour from the scheduled two o'clock start time. Davis and Wilson, *The Lincoln-Douglas Debates,* 1–2; Guelzo, *Lincoln and Douglas,* 113–115.

Abraham Lincoln. Photograph (Springfield, IL, 1860). This full-length portrait of Lincoln was made soon after he received the Republican nomination for president. Contrast this image with the full-length photograph of Douglas.

4   The resolution, introduced by Lincoln's associate and brother-in-law, Ninian Wirt Edwards, was adopted by the Illinois legislature on January 22, 1851: "Resolved, That our liberty and independence are based upon the right of people to form themselves such a government as they may choose; that this great principle, the birthright of freemen, the gift of Heaven, secured to us by the blood of our ancestors, ought to be extended to future generations, and no limitation ought to be extended to this power in the organization of any territory of the U.S. of either territorial government or state constitution, provided the government so established shall be Republican, and in conformity with the Constitution of the United States." *Illinois House Journal* (1851): 128, cited in Davis and Wilson, *The Lincoln-Douglas Debates,* 7n3.

5   Lyman Trumbull was elected U.S. senator from Illinois in 1855 as an anti-Nebraska Democrat after defeating Lincoln in a contest decided by the state legislature. He had joined the Republican Party by 1858. A fierce opponent of Douglas, Trumbull worked closely with Lincoln to prevent Illinois Republicans from supporting the senator for reelection because of his break with the Buchanan administration.

6   James H. Matheny (1818–1890), best man at Lincoln's wedding in 1842, was for many years a close political and legal associate of Lincoln's. During the Civil War Matheny would serve as an officer in the Union army. From 1873 until his death, he served as judge of Sangamon County. Douglas referred to a speech that Matheny delivered prior to the presidential election of 1856. At the time, he was a member of the Know-Nothing Party and was politically estranged from Lincoln. Cited in Davis and Wilson, *The Lincoln-Douglas Debates,* 8n4. For biographical information, see Neely, *Lincoln Encyclopedia,* 207.

and approved, there had been no division in this country in regard to that principle except the opposition of the abolitionists. In the House of Representatives of the Illinois Legislature, upon a resolution asserting that principle,[4] every Whig and every Democrat in the House voted in the affirmative, and only four men voted against it, and those four were old line Abolitionists. (*Cheers*)

In 1854, Mr. Abraham Lincoln and Mr. Trumbull[5] entered into an arrangement, one with the other, and each with his respective friends, to dissolve the old Whig party on the one hand, and to dissolve the old Democratic party on the other, and to connect the members of both into an Abolition party under the name and disguise of a Republican party. (*Laughter and cheers, "hurrah for Douglas"*) The terms of that arrangement between Mr. Lincoln and Mr. Trumbull have been published to the world by Mr. Lincoln's special friend, James H. Matheny, Esq.,[6] and they were that Lincoln should have Shields'[7] place in the U.S. Senate, which was then about to become vacant, and that Trumbull should have my seat when my term expired. (*Great laughter*) Lincoln went to work to abolitionize the Old Whig party all over the State, pretending that he was then as good a Whig as ever; (*laughter*) and Trumbull went to work in his part of the State preaching Abolitionism in its milder and lighter form, and trying to abolitionize the Democratic party, and bring old Democrats handcuffed and bound hand and foot into the Abolition camp. (*"Good," "hurrah for Douglas," and cheers*) In pursuance of the arrangement, the parties met at Springfield in October, 1854, and proclaimed their new platform[.]

Lincoln was to bring into the Abolition camp the old line Whigs, and transfer them over to Giddings,[8] Chase,[9] Ford,[10] Douglass[11] and Parson Lovejoy,[12] who were ready to receive them and christen them in their new faith. (*Laughter and cheers*) They laid down on that occasion a platform for their new Republican party, which was to be thus constructed. I have the resolutions of their State convention then held, which was the first mass State Convention ever held in Illinois by the Black Republican party, and I now hold them in my hands and will read a part of them, and cause the others to be printed. Here is the most important and material resolution of this Abolition platform.[13]

1.  *Resolved,* That we believe this truth to be self-evident, that when parties become subversive of the ends for which they are established, or incapable of restoring the government to the true principles of the constitution, it is the right and duty of the people to dissolve the political bands by which they may have been connected therewith, and to organize new parties upon

such principles and with such views as the circumstances and exigencies of the nation may demand.

2. *Resolved,* That the times imperatively demand the reorganization of parties, and repudiating all previous party attachments, names and predilections, we unite ourselves together in defence of the liberty and constitution of the country, and will hereafter co-operate as the Republican party, pledged to the accomplishment of the following purposes: to bring the administration of the government back to the control of first principles; to restore Nebraska and Kansas to the position of free territories; that, as the constitution of the United States, vests in the States, and not in Congress, the power to legislate for the extradition of fugitives from labor, to repeal and entirely abrogate the fugitive slave law; to restrict slavery to those States in which it exists; to prohibit the admission of any more slave States into the Union; to abolish slavery in the District of Columbia; to exclude slavery from all the territories over which the general government has exclusive jurisdiction; and to resist the acquirements of any more territories unless the practice of slavery therein forever shall have been prohibited.

3. *Resolved,* That in furtherance of these principles we will use such constitutional and lawful means as shall seem best adapted to their accomplishment, and that we will support no man for office, under the general or State government, who is not positively and fully committed to the support of these principles, and whose personal character and conduct is not a guaranty that he is reliable, and who shall not have abjured old party allegiance and ties.

(*The resolutions, as they were read, were cheered throughout*)

Now, gentlemen, your Black Republicans have cheered every one of those propositions, (*"good" and cheers*) and yet I venture to say that you cannot get Mr. Lincoln to come out and say that he is now in favor of each one of them. (*Laughter and applause. "Hit him again"*) That these propositions, one and all, constitute the platform of the Black Republican party of this day, I have no doubt, (*"good"*) and when you were not aware for what purpose I was reading them, your Black Republicans cheered them as good Black Republican doctrines. (*"That's it,"* etc.) My object in reading these resolutions, was to put the question to Abraham Lincoln this day, whether he now stands and will stand by each article in that creed and carry it out. (*"Good" "Hit him again"*) I desire to know whether Mr. Lincoln to-day stands as he did in 1854, in favor of the unconditional repeal of the fugitive slave law. I desire him to answer whether he stands pledged to-day, as he did in 1854, against the admission of any more slave States into the Union, even

7 James Shields was elected to the U.S. Senate in 1849. Lincoln coveted his senate seat and sought support for it in 1855, but in a deadlock withdrew in favor of anti-Nebraska Democrat Lyman Trumbull. On Lincoln's relationship with Shields, see "The 'Rebecca' Letter, August 27, 1842," notes 5 and 11, in this volume. Lincoln's 1855 campaign for Shields's U.S. Senate seat is mentioned in "Speech at Kalamazoo, Michigan, August 27, 1856," note 4, in this volume.

8 Joshua R. Giddings of Ohio.

9 Salmon B. Chase. See "'House Divided' Address, Springfield, Illinois, June 16, 1858," note 20.

10 Thomas H. Ford (1814–1868) was an antislavery politician from Ohio. He served as lieutenant governor of Ohio under Salmon Chase from 1856 to 1858. He was appointed government printer by the U.S. House of Representatives in 1860 and served in the Ohio militia during the Civil War. Joseph P. Smith, ed., *History of the Republican Party in Ohio,* 2 vols. (Chicago: Lewis Publishing Co., 1898), 1:44.

11 Frederick Douglass (1818–1895), born Frederick Washington Augustus Bailey to Harriet Bailey, an enslaved field hand, and a white man, possibly Aaron Anthony, Douglass's first master. After escaping from slavery in 1838 Douglass became the North's leading African American abolitionist. While Douglass admired Lincoln and supported him for president in 1860 and 1864, he sometimes criticized Lincoln for his slow approach to achieving emancipation and equal rights for blacks. James Oaks, *The Radical and the Republican: Frederick Douglass, Abraham Lincoln, and the Triumph of Antislavery Politics* (New York: W. W. Norton, 2007); and John Stauffer, *Giants: The Political Lives of Frederick Douglass and Abraham Lincoln* (New York: Twelve, 2008).

12   Owen Lovejoy (1811–1864) of Illinois was a minister and politician, serving in the U.S. House of Representatives from 1857 to 1864. An ardent abolitionist, he was the brother of Elijah Lovejoy (1802–1837), a Presbyterian minister, journalist, newspaper editor, and abolitionist who was killed by a proslavery mob in Alton, Illinois, on November 7, 1837. "Lovejoy, Owen," Biographical Directory of the United States Congress, http://bioguide.congress.gov/scripts/biodisplay.pl?index=L000462 (accessed December 14, 2014).

13   Douglas was mistaken here in his assertions concerning the 1854 Springfield resolutions. First of all, the Springfield resolutions were drawn up by a committee that did not include Lincoln. Second, the resolutions to which he refers were not those adopted at Springfield. In transcribing Douglas's remarks, *Chicago Press and Tribune* reporter Hitt discovered that Douglas was reading resolutions not from the platform of the Illinois Republican Party but those passed at a meeting of abolitionists at Aurora, Illinois, in October of the same year. Douglas was citing an 1856 speech given by a fellow Democrat, claiming that the radical Aurora resolutions were adopted by the 1854 Republican state convention. In fact, the Republican state convention adopted a moderate platform compared with that referred to by Douglas in the debate. Republicans and the Republican press lambasted Douglas for deliberate misrepresentation. The *Chicago Press and Tribune,* for example, blasted the senator as a liar: "What a man, who, indebted to the people of Illinois for everything that he has been and is, attempts to delude and mislead them by a cheat?" Douglas defended himself by first claiming he was misled and then pugnaciously asserting that he and everyone else had "abundant reason" to believe the Aurora resolutions represented the views of Illinois Republicans. Guelzo, *Lincoln and Douglas,* 131–133; Burlingame, *Abraham Lincoln,* 1:489–491.

if the people want them. I want to know whether he stands pledged against the admission of a new State into the Union with such a constitution as the people of that State may see fit to make. (*"That's it," "put it at him"*) I want to know whether he stands to-day pledged to the abolition of slavery in the District of Columbia. I desire him to answer whether he stands pledged to the prohibition of the slave trade between the different States. (*"He does"*) I desire to know whether he stands pledged to prohibit slavery in all the territories of the United States, North as well as South of the Missouri Compromise line, (*"Kansas too"*) I desire him to answer whether he is opposed to the acquisition of any more territory unless slavery is first prohibited therein. I want his answer to these questions. Your affirmative cheers in favor of this Abolition platform is [*sic*] not satisfactory. I ask Abraham Lincoln to answer these questions, in order that when I trot him down to lower Egypt[14] I may put the same questions to him. (*Enthusiastic applause*) My principles are the same everywhere. (*Cheers, and "hark"*) I can proclaim them alike in the North, the South, the East, and the West. My principles will apply wherever the Constitution prevails and the American flag waves. (*"Good," and applause*) I desire to know whether Mr. Lincoln's principles will bear transplanting from Ottawa to Jonesboro?[15] I put these questions to him to-day distinctly, and ask an answer. I have a right to an answer (*"that's so," "he can't dodge you," etc.*), for I quote from the platform of the Republican party, made by himself and others at the time that party was formed, and the bargain made by Lincoln to dissolve and kill the old Whig party, and transfer its members, bound hand and foot, to the Abolition party, under the direction of Giddings and Fred Douglass. (*Cheers*) In the remarks I have made on this platform, and the position of Mr. Lincoln upon it, I mean nothing personally disrespectful or unkind to that gentleman. I have known him for nearly twenty-five years. There were many points of sympathy between us when we first got acquainted. We were both comparatively boys, and both struggling with poverty in a strange land. I was a school-teacher in the town of Winchester, and he a flourishing grocery-keeper in the town of Salem.[16] (*Applause and laughter*) He was more successful in his occupation than I was in mine, and hence more fortunate in this world's goods. Lincoln is one of those peculiar men who perform with admirable skill everything which they undertake. I made as good a school-teacher as I could and when a cabinet maker I made a good bedstead and tables, although my old boss said I succeeded better with bureaus and secretaries than anything else; (*cheers*) but I believe that Lincoln was always more successful in business than I, for his business enabled him to get into the Legislature.[17] I met him there, however, and had a sympathy with him, because of the up hill struggle we both had in life. He was then just as good at telling an anecdote as now. (*"No doubt"*) He could beat any of the boys wrestling, or running a foot race, in pitching quoits or tossing a copper, could ruin more liquor than all the boys of the town together, (*uproarious laughter*) and the dignity and impartiality with which he presided at a horse race or fist fight, excited the admiration and won the praise of everybody that was present and participated. (*Renewed laughter*) I sympathised with him, because he was struggling with difficulties and so was I. Mr. Lincoln served with me in the Legislature in 1836, when we both retired, and he subsided, or became submerged, and he was lost sight of as a public man for some years. In 1846, when Wilmot introduced his celebrated proviso,[18] and the Abolition tornado swept over the country, Lincoln again turned up as a member of Congress from the Sangamon district. I was then in the Senate of the United States, and was glad to welcome my old friend and companion. Whilst in Congress, he distinguished himself by his opposition to the Mexican war, taking the side of the common enemy against his own country;[19] (*"that's true"*) and when he returned home he found that the indignation of the people followed him everywhere, and he was again submerged or obliged to retire into private life, forgotten by his former friends. (*"And will be again"*) He came up again in 1854, just in time to make this Abolition or Black Republican platform, in company with Giddings, Lovejoy, Chase, and Fred Douglass for the Republican party to stand upon. (*Laughter, "Hit him again," &c.*) Trumbull, too, was one of our own contemporaries. He was born and raised in old Connecticut, was bred a federalist, but removing to Georgia, turned nullifier when nullification was popular, and as soon as he disposed of his clocks and wound up his business, migrated to Illinois, (*laughter*) turned politician and lawyer here, and made his appearance in 1841, as a member of the Legislature. He became noted as the author of the scheme to repudiate a large portion of the State debt of Illinois, which, if successful, would have brought infamy and disgrace upon the fair escutcheon of our glorious State.[20] The odium attached to that measure consigned him to oblivion for a time. I helped to do it. I walked into a public meeting in the hall of the House of Representatives and replied to his repudiating speeches, and resolutions were carried over his head denouncing repudiation, and asserting the moral and legal obligation of Illinois to pay every dollar of the debt she owed and every bond that bore her seal. (*"Good," and cheers*) Trumbull's malignity has followed me since I thus defeated his infamous scheme.

14  "Egypt" was the name given to southern Illinois, a part of the state that was culturally, economically, and politically more aligned with the South than the North. Why this region was referred to as "Egypt" is unclear. Two possible explanations are that the confluence of the Ohio and Mississippi Rivers looked much like the Nile Delta, and that one of the region's towns is named Cairo. Holzer, *The Lincoln-Douglas Debates,* 136. Douglas asserted that Lincoln changed his views according to the region of the state in which he appeared. Although Douglas was guilty of exaggeration, his charge was not completely erroneous, for Lincoln tended to deemphasize his association with the Republican Party in the central part of the state, home to former Whigs and anti-Nebraska Democrats. There, he was advised to hold meetings of "friends of Lincoln" rather than "Republican" gatherings because "we can gain something from the old Whigs, who may be wavering, and soften down the prejudice of others." T. J. Pickett to Lincoln, August 3, 1858, cited in David Zarefsky, *Lincoln, Douglas, and Slavery: In the Crucible of Public Debate* (Chicago: University of Chicago Press, 1990), 46.

15  Jonesboro, located in Union County in southern Illinois, or "Egypt," was the site of the third Lincoln-Douglas debate, on September 15, 1858.

16  By referencing Lincoln's ownership of a grocery—or, its nineteenth-century usage, a saloon—in New Salem and claiming that he (Lincoln) could "ruin more liquor," Douglas sought to create the false impression that his opponent was a drinker. See "Address to the Springfield Washington Temperance Society, February 22, 1842," in this volume, for Lincoln's views on drinking as well as his own relationship with alcohol.

17  Born in Brandon, Vermont, in 1813, Douglas at

fifteen years of age worked several months for a cabinetmaker in Middlebury, Vermont. After settling in Illinois in 1833 at the age of twenty, before he became active in Illinois politics and while studying the law, Douglas opened and taught in a school in Winchester until March 1834. He later served in the U.S. House of Representatives, from 1843 to 1847, and in the U.S. Senate from 1847 to 1861. Johannsen, *Stephen A. Douglas,* 9, 20–21.

18   The Wilmot Proviso. See "Speech on the Kansas-Nebraska Act at Peoria, Illinois, October 16, 1854," notes 14 and 15, in this volume.

19   Douglas used Lincoln's opposition to the Mexican War to falsely accuse him of not supporting American soldiers. Despite his stance against the conflict, Lincoln had voted for supplies for soldiers and veterans' benefits.

20   Douglas wrongly accused Trumbull of voting for legislation repudiating Illinois's internal improvement liability when he was a member of the Illinois House of Representatives from 1840 to 1841. While Trumbull supported an early version of the bill, he voted against the final version. *Illinois House Journal* (1841): 118–119, 511, cited in Davis and Wilson, *The Lincoln-Douglas Debates,* 11n12.

21   Archibald Williams (1801–1863) was a Quincy, Illinois, attorney, politician, and associate of Lincoln's, and served in the Illinois legislature for a number of years. From 1849 to 1853 Williams served as U.S. attorney for Illinois. A Whig in politics, he was active in Illinois's anti-Nebraska movement and later joined the Republican Party. He campaigned for Lincoln against Douglas's reelection in 1858. In 1861, President Lincoln appointed Williams U.S. district judge for Kansas. Boas, *Biographical Dictionary,* 476.

22   Orville Hickman Browning was a Quincy, Illinois, lawyer and politician who served in the

These two men having formed this combination to abolitionize the old Whig party and the old Democratic party, and put themselves into the Senate of the United States, in pursuance of their bargain, are now carrying out that arrangement. Matheny states that Trumbull broke faith; that the bargain was that Lincoln should be the Senator in Shields' place, and Trumbull was to wait for mine; (*laughter and cheers*) and the story goes, that Trumbull cheated Lincoln, having control of four or five abolitionized Democrats who were holding over in the Senate; he would not let them vote for Lincoln, and which obliged the rest of the Abolitionists to support him in order to secure an Abolition Senator. There are a number of authorities for the truth of this besides Matheny, and I suppose that even Mr. Lincoln will not deny it. (*Applause and laughter*)

Mr. Lincoln demands that he shall have the place intended for Trumbull, as Trumbull cheated him and got his, and Trumbull is stumping the State traducing me for the purpose of securing that position for Lincoln, in order to quiet him. (*"Lincoln can never get it," &c.*) It was in consequence of this arrangement that the Republican Convention was empanelled to instruct for Lincoln and nobody else, and it was on this account that they passed resolutions that he was their first, their last, and their only choice. Archy Williams[21] was nowhere, Browning[22] was nobody, Wentworth[23] was not to be considered, they had no man in the Republican party for the place except Lincoln, for the reason that he demanded that they should carry out the arrangement. (*"Hit him again"*)

Having formed this new party for the benefit of deserters from Whiggery, and deserters from Democracy, and having laid down the Abolition platform which I have read, Lincoln now takes his stand and proclaims his Abolition doctrines. Let me read a part of them. In his speech at Springfield[24] to the convention which nominated him for the Senate, he said:

"In my opinion it will not cease until a crisis shall have been reached and passed. 'A house divided against itself cannot stand.' I believe this Government *cannot endure permanently half Slave and half Free.* I do not expect the Union to be dissolved—I do not expect the house to fall—*but I do expect it will cease to be divided.* It will become all one thing, or all the other. Either the opponents of Slavery *will arrest the further spread of it,* and place it where the public mind shall rest in the belief *that it is in the course of ultimate extinction;* or its advocates *will push it forward till it shall become alike lawful in all the States*—old as well as new, North as well as South."

(*"Good," "good," and cheers*)

I am delighted to hear you Black Republicans say "good." (*Laughter and cheers*) I have no doubt that doctrine expresses your sentiments (*"hit them again," "that's it"*) and I will prove to you now, if you will listen to me, that it is revolutionary and destructive of the existence of this Government. (*"Hurrah for Douglas," "good" and cheers*) Mr. Lincoln, in the extract from which I have read, says that this Government cannot endure permanently in the same condition in which it was made by its framers—divided into free and slave States. He says that it has existed for about seventy years thus divided, and yet he tells you that it cannot endure permanently on the same principles and in the same relative condition in which our fathers made it. (*"Neither can it"*) Why can it not exist divided into free and slave States? Washington, Jefferson, Franklin, Madison, Hamilton, Jay, and the great men of that day, made this Government divided into free States and slave States, and left each State perfectly free to do as it pleased on the subject of slavery. (*"Right, right"*) Why can it not exist on the same principles on which our fathers made it? (*"It can"*) They knew when they framed the Constitution that in a country as wide and broad as this, with such a variety of climate, production and interest, the people necessarily required different laws and institutions in different localities. They knew that the laws and regulations which would suit the granite hills of New Hampshire would be unsuited to the rice plantations of South Carolina, (*"right, right"*) and they, therefore, provided that each State should retain its own Legislature, and its own sovereignty with the full and complete power to do as it pleased within its own limits, in all that was local and not national. (*Applause*) One of the reserved rights of the States, was the right to regulate the relations between Master and Servant, on the slavery question. At the time the Constitution was formed, there were thirteen States in the Union, twelve of which were slaveholding States and one a free State.[25] Suppose this doctrine of uniformity preached by Mr. Lincoln, that the States should all be free or all be slave had prevailed and what would have been the result? Of course, the twelve slaveholding States would have overruled the one free State, and slavery would have been fastened by a Constitutional provision on every inch of the American Republic, instead of being left as our fathers wisely left it, to each State to decide for itself. (*"Good, good," and three cheers for Douglas*) Here I assert that uniformity in the local laws and institutions of the different States is neither possible or desirable. If uniformity had been adopted when the government was established, it must inevitably have been the uniformity of slavery ev-

Illinois House of Representatives from 1836 to 1843 as a Whig and later joined the anti-Nebraska coalition, attending the May 1856 convention in Bloomington, Illinois, which led to the founding of the Republican Party. He was appointed U.S. senator to fill the vacancy resulting from the death of Senator Douglas in 1861. He served in that capacity until 1863. Browning was President Andrew Johnson's secretary of the interior from 1866 to 1869. "Browning, Orville Hickman," *Biographical Directory of the United States Congress,* http://bioguide.congress.gov/scripts/biodisplay.pl?index=b000960 (accessed December 16, 2014).

23  John Wentworth. Boas, *Biographical Dictionary,* 472; "Wentworth, John," Biographical Directory of the United States Congress, http://bioguide.congress.gov/scripts/biodisplay.pl?index=W000295 (accessed December 16, 2014).

24  Douglas quoted from Lincoln's "House Divided" speech. See "'House Divided' Address, Springfield, Illinois, June 16, 1858."

25  When the Constitutional Convention met in Philadelphia in 1787, the states of Vermont, Massachusetts, and New Hampshire had abolished slavery. The states of Pennsylvania, Rhode Island, and Connecticut had made provisions for its gradual extinction. Cited in Davis and Wilson, *The Lincoln-Douglas Debates,* 13n14.

Stephen A. Douglas. Photograph (1860). This full-length image of the "Little Giant" offers a stark contrast to that of Lincoln.

erywhere, or else the uniformity of negro citizenship and negro equality everywhere.

We are told by Lincoln that he is utterly opposed to the Dred Scott decision, and will not submit to it, for the reason that he says it deprives the negro of the rights and privileges of citizenship. (*Laughter and applause*) That is the first and main reason which he assigns for his warfare on the Supreme Court of the United States and its decision. I ask you, are you in favor of conferring upon the negro the rights and privileges of citizenship? (*"No, no"*) Do you desire to strike out of our State Constitution that clause which keeps slaves and free negroes out of the State, and allow the free negroes to flow in, (*"never"*) and cover your prairies with black settlements? Do you desire to turn this beautiful State into a free negro colony, (*"no, no"*) in order that when Missouri abolishes slavery she can send one hundred thousand emancipated slaves into Illinois, to become citizens and voters, on an equality with yourselves? (*"Never," "no"*) If you desire negro citizenship, if you desire to allow them to come into the State and settle with the white man, if you desire them to vote on an equality with yourselves, and to make them eligible to office, to serve on juries, and to adjudge your rights, then support Mr. Lincoln and the Black Republican party, who are in favor of the citizenship of the negro. (*"Never, never"*) For one, I am opposed to negro citizenship in any and every form. (*Cheers*) I believe this government was made on the white basis. (*"Good"*) I believe it was made by white men, for the benefit of white men and their posterity for ever, and I am in favour of confining citizenship to white men, men of European birth and descent, instead of conferring it upon negroes, Indians and other inferior races. (*"Good for you." "Douglas forever"*)

Mr. Lincoln, following the example and lead of all the little Abolition orators, who go around and lecture in the basements of schools and churches, reads from the Declaration of Independence, that all men were created equal, and then asks how can you deprive a negro of that equality which God and the Declaration of Independence awards to him. He and they maintain that negro equality is guarantied by the laws of God, and that it is asserted in the Declaration of Independence. If they think so, of course they have a right to say so, and so vote. I do not question Mr. Lincoln's conscientious belief that the negro was made his equal, and hence is his brother, (*laughter*) but for my own part, I do not regard the negro as my equal, and positively deny that he is my brother or any kin to me whatever. (*"Never." "Hit him again" and cheers*) Lincoln has evidently learned by heart Parson Lovejoy's catechism. (*Laughter and applause*) He can repeat it as well as

Farnsworth,[26] and he is worthy of a medal from father Giddings and Fred Douglass for his Abolitionism. (*Laughter*) He holds that the negro was born his equal and yours, and that he was endowed with equality by the Almighty, and that no human law can deprive him of these rights which were guarantied to him by the Supreme ruler of the Universe. Now, I do not believe that the Almighty ever intended the negro to be the equal of the white man. (*"Never, never"*) If he did, he has been a long time demonstrating the fact. (*Cheers*) For thousands of years the negro has been a race upon the earth, and during all that time, in all latitudes and climates, wherever he has wandered or been taken, he has been inferior to the race which he has there met. He belongs to an inferior race, and must always occupy an inferior position. (*"Good," "that's so," &c.*) I do not hold that because the negro is our inferior that therefore he ought to be a slave. By no means can such a conclusion be drawn from what I have said. On the contrary, I hold that humanity and christianity both require that the negro shall have and enjoy every right, every privilege, and every immunity consistent with the safety of the society in which he lives. (*"That's so"*) On that point, I presume, there can be no diversity of opinion. You and I are bound to extend to our inferior and dependent being every right, every privilege, every facility and immunity consistent with the public good. The question then arises what rights and privileges are consistent with the public good. This is a question which each State and each Territory must decide for itself—Illinois has decided it for herself. We have provided that the negro shall not be a slave, and we have also provided that he shall not be a citizen, but protect him in his civil rights, in his life, his person and his property, only depriving him of all political rights whatsoever, and refusing to put him on an equality with the white man. (*"Good"*) That policy of Illinois is satisfactory to the Democratic party and to me, and if it were to the Republicans, there would then be no question upon the subject; but the Republicans say that he ought to be made a citizen, and when he becomes a citizen he becomes your equal, with all your rights and privileges. (*"He never shall"*) They assert the Dred Scott decision to be monstrous because it denies that the negro is or can be a citizen under the Constitution. Now, I hold that Illinois had a right to abolish and prohibit slavery as she did, and I hold that Kentucky has the same right to continue and protect slavery that Illinois had to abolish it. I hold that New York had as much right to abolish slavery as Virginia has to continue it, and that each and every State of this Union is a sovereign power, with the right to do as it pleases upon this question of slavery, and upon all its domestic institutions. Slavery is not the only question which comes up

26 John Franklin Farnsworth (1820–1897) was a lawyer and Republican politician from Chicago. He served in Congress from 1857 to 1861. In the Civil War, as a colonel of the Eighth Regiment, Illinois Volunteer Cavalry, Farnsworth attained the rank of brigadier general before he resigned to serve again in Congress from 1863 to 1873. Boas, *Biographical Dictionary*, 165; "Farnsworth, John Franklin," Biographical Directory of the United States Congress, http://bioguide.congress.gov/scripts/biodisplay.pl?index=F000024 (accessed December 16, 2014).

*Lincoln-Douglas Debate.* Lantern slide (Chicago: McIntosh Stereopticon Co., ca. 1915). McIntosh issued a series of glass slides depicting various scenes from Lincoln's life, including this one of the Lincoln-Douglas debates.

in this controversy. There is a far more important one to you, and that is, what shall be done with the free negro? We have settled the slavery question as far as we are concerned; we have prohibited it in Illinois forever, and in doing so, I think we have done wisely, and there is no man in the State who would be more strenuous in his opposition to the introduction of slavery than I would; (*cheers*) but when we settled it for ourselves, we exhausted all our power over that subject. We have done our whole duty, and can do no more. We must leave each and every other State to decide for itself the same question. In relation to the policy to be pursued towards the free negroes, we have said that they shall not vote; whilst Maine, on the other hand, has said that they shall vote. Maine is a sovereign State, and has the power to regulate the qualifications of voters within her limits. I would never consent to confer the right of voting and of citizenship upon a negro, but still I am not going to quarrel with Maine for differing from me in opinion. Let Maine take care of her own negroes and fix the qualifications of her own voters to suit herself, without interfering with Illinois, and Illinois will not interfere with Maine. So with the State of New York. She allows the negro to vote provided he owns two hundred and fifty dollars' worth of property, but not otherwise. While I would not make any distinction whatever between a negro who held property and one who did not; yet if the sovereign State of New York chooses to make that distinction it is her business and not mine, and I will not quarrel with her for it. She can do as she pleases on this question if she minds her own business, and we will do the same thing. Now, my friends, if we will only act conscientiously and rigidly upon this great principle of popular sovereignty which guarantees to each State and Territory the right to do as it pleases on all things local and domestic instead of Congress interfering, we will continue at peace one with another. Why should Illinois be at war with Missouri, or Kentucky with Ohio, or Virginia with New York, merely because their institutions differ? Our fathers intended that our institutions should differ. They knew that the North and the South having different climates, productions and interests, required different institutions. This doctrine of Mr. Lincoln's of uniformity among the institutions of the different States is a new doctrine, never dreamed of by Washington, Madison, or the framers of this Government. Mr. Lincoln and the Republican party set themselves up as wiser than these men who made this government, which has flourished for seventy years under the principle of popular sovereignty, recognizing the right of each State to do as it pleased. Under that principle, we have grown from a nation of three or four millions to a nation of about thirty millions of people; we have crossed the Allegheny mountains and filled up the whole North West, turning the prairie into a garden, and building up churches and schools, thus spreading civilization and christianity where before there was nothing but savage-barbarism. Under that principle we have become from a feeble nation, the most powerful on the face of the earth, and if we only adhere to that principle, we can go forward increasing in territory, in power, in strength and in glory until the Republic of America shall be the North Star that shall guide the friends of freedom throughout the civilized world. (*"Long may you live," and great applause*) And why can we not adhere to the great principle of self-government,

27  Lincoln did not attend the meeting; he left Springfield to attend court in Tazewell County. Miers, *Lincoln Day by Day,* 2:129. See also note 13 above.

upon which our institutions were originally based. (*"We can"*) I believe that this new doctrine preached by Mr. Lincoln and his party will dissolve the Union if it succeeds. They are trying to array all the Northern States in one body against the South, to excite a sectional war between the free States and the slave States, in order that the one or the other may be driven to the wall.

I am told that my time is out. Mr. Lincoln will now address you for an hour and a half, and I will then occupy a half hour in replying to him. (*Three times three cheers were here given for Douglas*)

## Mr. Lincoln's Reply.

MY FELLOW-CITIZENS: When a man hears himself somewhat misrepresented, it provokes him—at least, I find it so with myself; but when the misrepresentation becomes very gross and palpable, it is more apt to amuse him. (*Laughter*) The first thing I see fit to notice, is the fact that Judge Douglas alleges, after running through the history of the old Democratic and the old Whig parties, that Judge Trumbull and myself made an arrangement in 1854, by which I was to have the place of Gen. Shields in the United States Senate, and Judge Trumbull was to have the place of Judge Douglas. Now all I have to say upon that subject is, that I think no man—not even Judge Douglas—can prove it, *because it is not true.* (*Cheers*) I have no doubt he is "*conscientious*" in saying it. (*Laughter*) As to those resolutions that he took such a length of time to read, as being the platform of the Republican party in 1854, I say I never had anything to do with them, and I think Trumbull never had. (*Renewed laughter*) Judge Douglas cannot show that either one of us ever did have any thing to do with them. I believe *this* is true about those resolutions: There was a call for a Convention to form a Republican party at Springfield, and I think that my friend Mr. Lovejoy, who is here upon this stand, had a hand in it. I think this is true, and I think if he will remember accurately, he will be able to recollect that he tried to get me into it, and I would not go in.[27] (*Cheers and laughter*) I believe it is also true, that I went away from Springfield when the Convention was in session, to attend court in Tazewell County. It is true they did place my name, though without authority, upon the Committee, and afterwards wrote me to attend the meeting of the Committee, but I refused to do so, and I never had anything to do with that organization. This is the plain truth about all that matter of the resolutions.

Now, about this story that Judge Douglas tells of Trumbull bargaining to

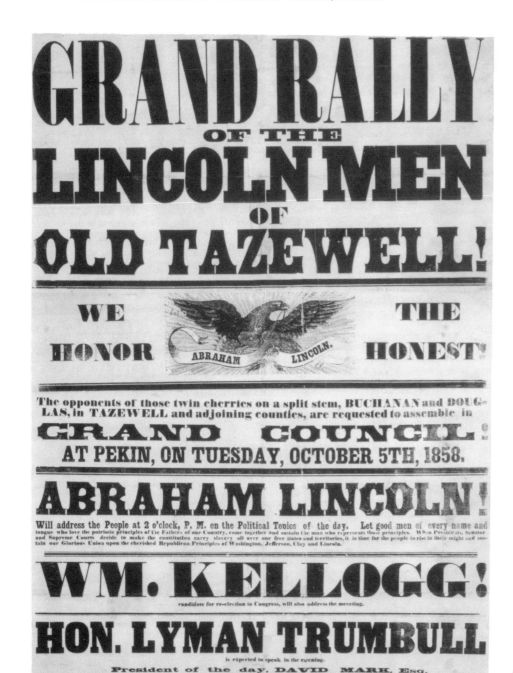

*Grand Rally of the Lincoln Men of Old Tazewell!* Broadside (Pekin, IL, 1858). Republican poster from the 1858 Lincoln-Douglas senatorial campaign.

**28** Lincoln quoted a long passage from his 1854 Peoria speech. For the full speech, see "Speech on the Kansas-Nebraska Act at Peoria, Illinois, October 16, 1854."

sell out the old Democratic party, and Lincoln agreeing to sell out the old Whig party, I have the means of *knowing* about that; (*Laughter*) Judge Douglas cannot have; and I know there is no substance to it whatever. (*Applause*) Yet I have no doubt he is "*conscientious*" about it. (*Laughter*) I know that after Mr. Lovejoy got into the Legislature that winter, he complained of me that I had told all the old Whigs in his district that the old Whig party was good enough for them, and some of them voted against him because I told them so. Now I have no means of totally disproving such charges as this which the Judge makes. A man cannot prove a negative, but he has a right to claim that when a man makes an affirmative charge, he must offer some proof to show the truth of what he says. I certainly cannot introduce testimony to show the negative about things, but I have a right to claim that if a man says he *knows* a thing, then he must show *how* he knows it. I always have a right to claim this, and it is not satisfactory to me that he may be "conscientious" on the subject. (*Cheers and laughter*)

Now gentlemen, I hate to waste my time on such things, but in regard to that general abolition tilt that Judge Douglas makes, when he says that I was engaged at that time in selling out and abolitionizing the old Whig party—I hope you will permit me to read a part of a printed speech that I made then at Peoria,[28] which will show altogether a different view of the position I took in that contest of 1854.

VOICE—Put on your specs.

MR. LINCOLN—Yes, sir, I am obliged to do so. I am no longer a young man. (*Laughter*)

"This is the *repeal* of the Missouri Compromise. The foregoing history may not be precisely accurate in every particular; but I am sure it is sufficiently so, for all the uses I shall attempt to make of it, and in it, we have before us, the chief materials enabling us to correctly judge whether the repeal of the Missouri Compromise is right or wrong.

I think, and shall try to show, that it is wrong; wrong in its direct effect, letting slavery into Kansas and Nebraska—and wrong in its prospective principle, allowing it to spread to every other part of the wide world, where men can be found inclined to take it.

This *declared* indifference, but as I must think, covert *real* zeal for the spread of slavery, I can not but hate. I hate it because of the monstrous injustice of slavery itself. I hate it because it deprives our republican example of its just influence in the world—enables the enemies of free institutions, with plausibility, to taunt us as hypocrites—causes the real friends of freedom to doubt our sincerity, and especially because it forces so many really good men amongst ourselves into an open war with the very fundamental principles of civil liberty—criticising the Declaration of Independence, and insisting that there is no right principle of action but *self-interest.*

Before proceeding, let me say I think I have no prejudice against the Southern people. They are just what we would be in their situation. If slavery did not now exist amongst them, they would not introduce it. If it did now exist amongst us, we should not instantly give it up. This I believe of the masses north and south. Doubtless there are individuals, on both sides, who would not hold slaves under any circumstances; and others who would gladly introduce slavery anew, if it were out of existence. We know that some southern men do free their slaves, go north, and become tip-top abolitionists; while some northern ones go south, and become most cruel slave-masters.

When southern people tell us they are no more responsible for the origin of slavery, than we; I acknowledge the fact. When it is said that the institution exists, and that it is very difficult to get rid of it, in any satisfactory way, I can understand and appreciate the saying. I surely will not blame them for not doing what I should not know how to do myself. If all earthly power were given me, I should not know what to do, as to the existing institution. My first impulse would be to free all the slaves, and send them to Liberia,—to their own native land. But a moment's reflection would convince me, that whatever of high hope, (as I think there is) there may be in this, in the long run, its sudden execution is impossible. If they were all landed there in a day, they would all perish in the next ten days; and there are not surplus shipping and surplus money enough in the world to carry them there in many times ten days. What then? Free them all, and keep them among us as underlings? Is it quite certain that this betters their condition? I think I would not hold one in slavery, at any rate; yet the point is not clear enough to me to denounce people upon. What next? Free them, and make them politically and socially, our equals? My own feelings will not admit of this; and if mine would, we well know that those of the great mass of white people will not. Whether this feeling accords with justice and sound judgment, is not the sole question, if indeed, it is any part of it. A universal feeling, whether well or ill-founded, can not be safely disregarded. We can not, then, make them equals. It does seem to me that systems of gradual emancipation might be adopted; but for their tardiness in this, I will not undertake to judge our brethren of the south.

When they remind us of their constitutional rights, I acknowledge them, not grudgingly, but fully, and fairly; and I would give them any legislation for the reclaiming of their fugitives, which should not, in its stringency, be more likely to carry a free man into slavery, than our ordinary criminal laws are to hang an innocent one.

But all this; to my judgment, furnishes no more excuse for permitting slavery to go into our own free territory, than it would for reviving the African slave trade by law. The law which forbids the bringing of slaves *from* Africa; and that which has so long forbid the taking them *to* Nebraska, can hardly be distinguished on any moral principle; and the repeal of the former could find quite as plausible excuses as that of the latter."

I have reason to know that Judge Douglas *knows* that I said this. I think he has the answer here to one of the questions he put to me. I do not mean to allow him to catechise me unless he pays back for it in kind. I will not answer questions one after another unless he reciprocates, but as he made this inquiry and I have answered it before, he has got it without my getting anything in return. He has got my answer on the Fugitive Slave Law.

Now gentlemen, I don't want to read at any greater length, but this is the true complexion of all I have ever said in regard to the institution of slavery and the black race. This is the whole of it, and anything that argues me into his idea of perfect social and political equality with the negro, is but a specious and fantastic arrangement of words, by which a man can prove a horse chestnut to be a chestnut horse. (*Laughter*) I will say here, while upon this subject, that I have no purpose directly or indirectly to interfere with the institution of slavery in the States where it exists. I believe I have no lawful right to do so, and I have no inclination to do so. I have no purpose to introduce political and social equality between the white and the black races. There is a physical difference between the two, which in my judgment will probably forever forbid their living together upon the footing of perfect equality, and inasmuch as it becomes a necessity that there must be a difference, I, as well as Judge Douglas, am in favor of the race to which I belong, having the superior position. I have never said anything to the contrary, but I hold that notwithstanding all this, there is no reason in the world why the negro is not entitled to all the natural rights enumerated in the Declaration of Independence, the right to life, liberty and the pursuit of happiness.

(*Loud cheers*) I hold that he is as much entitled to these as the white man. I agree with Judge Douglas he is not my equal in many respects—certainly not in color, perhaps not in moral or intellectual endowment. But in the right to eat the bread, without leave of anybody else, which his own hand earns, *he is my equal and the equal of Judge Douglas, and the equal of every living man.* (*Great applause*)

Now I pass on to consider one or two more of these little follies. The Judge is wofully [*sic*] at fault about his early friend Lincoln being a "grocery keeper." (*Laughter*) I don't know as it would be a great sin, if I had been, but he is mistaken. Lincoln never kept a grocery anywhere in the world. (*Laughter*) It is true that Lincoln did work the latter part of one winter in a small still house, up at the head of a hollow. (*Roars of laughter*) And so I think my friend, the Judge, is equally at fault when he charges me at the time when I was in Congress of having opposed our soldiers who were fighting in the Mexican war. The Judge did not make his charge very distinctly but I can tell you what he can prove by referring to the record. You remember I was an old Whig, and whenever the Democratic party tried to get me to vote that the war had been righteously begun by the President, I would not do it. But whenever they asked for any money, or land warrants, or anything to pay the soldiers there, during all that time, I gave the same votes that Judge Douglas did. (*Loud applause*) You can think as you please as to whether that was consistent. Such is the truth; and the Judge has the right to make all he can out of it. But when he, by a general charge, conveys the idea that I withheld supplies from the soldiers who were fighting in the Mexican war, or did anything else to hinder the soldiers, he is, to say the least, grossly and altogether mistaken, as a consultation of the records will prove to him.

As I have not used up so much of my time as I had supposed, I will dwell a little longer upon one or two of these minor topics upon which the Judge has spoken. He has read from my speech in Springfield, in which I say that "a house divided against itself cannot stand." Does the Judge say it *can* stand? (*Laughter*) I don't know whether he does or not. The Judge does not seem to be attending to me just now, but I would like to know if it is his opinion that a house divided against itself *can stand.* If he does, then there is a question of veracity, not between him and me, but between the Judge and an authority of a somewhat higher character.[29] (*Laughter and applause*)

Now, my friends, I ask your attention to this matter for the purpose of saying something seriously. I know that the Judge may readily enough agree with me that the maxim which was put forth by the Saviour is true, but he may allege that I misapply it; and the Judge has a right to urge that, in my

29 Lincoln sarcastically accused Douglas of disagreeing with Jesus Christ, who, according to the Gospel of Matthew, used the phrase to rebuke the Pharisees (Matthew 12:25).

30  Article 1, Section 9 of the Constitution protected the slave trade for twenty years. After 1808 the slave trade was prohibited.

application, I do misapply it, and then I have a right to show that I do *not* misapply it. When he undertakes to say that because I think this nation, so far as the question of Slavery is concerned, will all become one thing or all the other, I am in favor of bringing about a dead uniformity in the various States, in all their institutions, he argues erroneously. The great variety of the local institutions in the States, springing from differences in the soil, differences in the face of the country, and in the climate, are bonds of Union. They do not make "a house divided against itself," but they make a house united. If they produce in one section of the country what is called for by the wants of another section, and this other section can supply the wants of the first, they are not matters of discord but bonds of union, true bonds of union. But can this question of slavery be considered as among *these* varieties in the institutions of the country? I leave it to you to say whether, in the history of our government, this institution of slavery has not always failed to be a bond of union, and, on the contrary, been an apple of discord and an element of division in the house. (*Cries of "Yes, yes," and applause*) I ask you to consider whether, so long as the moral constitution of men's minds shall continue to be the same, after this generation and assemblage shall sink into the grave, and another race shall arise, with the same moral and intellectual development we have—whether, if that institution is standing in the same irritating position in which it now is, it will not continue an element of division? (*Cries of "Yes, yes"*) If so, then I have a right to say that in regard to this question, the Union is a house divided against itself, and when the Judge reminds me that I have often said to him that the institution of slavery has existed for eighty years in some States, and yet it does not exist in some others, I agree to the fact, and I account for it by looking at the position in which our fathers originally placed it—restricting it from the new Territories where it had not gone, and legislating to cut off its source by the abrogation of the slave trade,[30] thus putting the seal of legislation *against its spread.* The public mind *did* rest in the belief that it was in the course of ultimate extinction. (*Cries of "Yes, yes"*) But lately, I think—and in this I charge nothing on the Judge's motives—lately, I think, that he, and those acting with him, have placed that institution on a new basis, which looks to the *perpetuity and nationalization of slavery.* (*Loud cheers*) And while it is placed upon this new basis, I say, and I have said, that I believe we shall not have peace upon the question until the opponents of slavery arrest the further spread of it, and place it where the public mind shall rest in the belief that it is in the course of ultimate extinction; or, on the other hand, that its advocates will push it forward until it shall become alike

31   The "House Divided" speech.

lawful in all the States, old as well as new, North as well as South. Now, I believe if we could arrest the spread, and place it where Washington, and Jefferson, and Madison placed it, it *would be* in the course of ultimate extinction, and the public mind *would,* as for eighty years past, believe that it was in the course of ultimate extinction. The crisis would be past and the institution might be let alone for a hundred years, if it should live so long, in the States where it exists, yet it would be going out of existence in the way best for both the black and the white races. (*Great cheering*)

A VOICE—Then do you repudiate Popular Sovereignty?

MR. LINCOLN—Well, then, let us talk about Popular Sovereignty! (*Laughter*) What is Popular Sovereignty? (*Cries of "A humbug," "a humbug"*) Is it the right of the people to have Slavery or not have it, as they see fit, in the territories? I will state—and I have an able man to watch me—my understanding is that Popular Sovereignty, as now applied to the question of Slavery, does allow the people of a Territory to have Slavery if they want to, but does not allow them *not* to have it if they *do not* want it. (*Applause and laughter*) I do not mean that if this vast concourse of people were in a Territory of the United States, any one of them would be obliged to have a slave if he did not want one; but I do say that, as I understand the Dred Scott decision, if any one man wants slaves, all the rest have no way of keeping that one man from holding them.

When I made my speech at Springfield,[31] of which the Judge complains, and from which he quotes, I really was not thinking of the things which he ascribes to me at all. I had no thought in the world that I was doing anything to bring about a war between the free and slave States. I had no thought in the world that I was doing anything to bring about a political and social equality of the black and white races. It never occurred to me that I was doing anything or favoring anything to reduce to a dead uniformity all the local institutions of the various States. But I must say, in all fairness to him, if he thinks I am doing something which leads to these bad results, it is none the better that I did not mean it. It is just as fatal to the country, if I have any influence in producing it, whether I intend it or not. But can it be true, that placing this institution upon the original basis—the basis upon which our fathers placed it—can have any tendency to set the Northern and the Southern States at war with one another, or that it can have any tendency to make the people of Vermont raise sugar cane, because they raise it in Louisiana, or that it can compel the people of Illinois to cut pine logs on the Grand Prairie, where they will not grow, because they cut pine logs in Maine, where they do grow? (*Laughter*) The Judge says this is a new princi-

32  According to Davis and Wilson, *The Lincoln-Douglas Debates,* 23n20, Lincoln may have referred to Douglas's earliest Senate speech, in January 1854, in which he defended the Kansas-Nebraska Act.

33  Although Lincoln seldom used the term "nigger," he used it twice in this debate. In Douglas's July 9, 1858, speech in Chicago, he charged that Lincoln's statements in his "House Divided" speech would lead to sectional crisis and equality and amalgamation of the races. See "'House Divided' Address, Springfield, Illinois, June 16, 1858," note 28.

34  Lincoln may have meant his July 10, 1858, Chicago speech, which was his response to Douglas's speech of the day before. In his July 17 Springfield speech, to which he referred, Lincoln made similar statements concerning his belief that the federal government had no constitutional right to interfere with slavery in states where it already existed and that he was not calling for such action. *CW,* 2:493, 513.

35  Speech given by Douglas in Bloomington, Illinois, on July 16, 1858, in which he stated, "Well, I never did suppose that he [Lincoln] ever dreamed of entering into Kentucky to make war upon her institutions; nor will any Abolitionist ever enter into Kentucky to wage such war. Their mode of making war is not to enter into those States where slavery exists, and there interfere, and render themselves responsible for the consequences. Oh no! They stand on the other side of the Ohio River and shoot across. They stand in Bloomington, and shake their fists at the people of Lexington; they threaten South Carolina from Chicago. And they call that bravery!" *Political Speeches and Debates of Abraham Lincoln and Stephen A. Douglas 1854–1861* (Chicago: Scott, Foresman & Company, 1896), 102.

36  Speech by Douglas at Springfield, Illinois, on July 17, 1858, in which he claimed Lincoln's

ple started in regard to this question. Does the Judge claim that he is working on the plan of the founders of government? I think he says in some of his speeches—indeed I have one here now—that he saw evidence of a policy to allow slavery to be south of a certain line, while north of it it should be excluded, and he saw an indisposition on the part of the country to stand upon that policy, and therefore he set about studying the subject upon *original principles,* and upon *original principles* he got up the Nebraska bill![32] I am fighting it upon these "original principles"—fighting it in the Jeffersonian, Washingtonian, and Madisonian fashion. (*Laughter and applause*)

Now my friends I wish you to attend for a little while to one or two other things in that Springfield speech. My main object was to show, so far as my humble ability was capable of showing to the people of this country, what I believed was the truth—that there was a *tendency,* if not a conspiracy among those who have engineered this slavery question for the last four or five years, to make slavery perpetual and universal in this nation. Having made that speech principally for that object, after arranging the evidences that I thought tended to prove my proposition, I concluded with this bit of comment:

> "We cannot absolutely know that these exact adaptations are the result of pre-concert, but when we see a lot of framed timbers, different portions of which we know have been gotten out at different times and places, and by different workmen—Stephen, Franklin, Roger and James, for instance—and when we see these timbers joined together, and see they exactly make the frame of a house or a mill, all the tenons and mortices exactly fitting and all the lengths and proportions of the different pieces exactly adapted to their respective places and not a piece too many or too few—not omitting even the scaffolding—or if a single piece be lacking we see the place in the frame exactly fitted and prepared yet to bring such piece in—in such a case we fell [feel] it impossible not to believe that Stephen and Franklin, and Roger and James, all understood one another from the beginning, and all worked upon a common plan or draft drawn before the first blow [lick] was struck." (*Great cheers*)

When my friend, Judge Douglas, came to Chicago, on the 9th of July, this speech having been delivered on the 16th of June, he made an harangue there, in which he took hold of this speech of mine, showing that he had carefully read it; and while he paid no attention to *this* matter at all, but complimented me as being a "kind, amiable, and intelligent gentleman," notwithstanding I had said this; he goes on and eliminates, or draws out, from my speech this tendency of mine to set the States at war with one another, to make all the institutions uniform, and set the niggers and white people to marrying together.[33] (*Laughter*) Then, as the Judge had complimented me with these pleasant titles, (I must confess to my weakness,) I was a little "taken," (*Laughter*) for it came from a great man. I was not very much accustomed to flattery, and it came the sweeter to me. I was rather like the Hoosier, with the gingerbread, when he said he reckoned he loved it better than any other man, and got less of it. (*Roars of laughter*) As the Judge had so flattered me, I could not make up my mind that he meant to deal unfairly with me; so I went to work to show him that he misunderstood the whole scope of my speech, and that I really never intended to set the people at war with one another. As an illustration, the next time I met him, which was at Springfield,[34] I used this expression, that I claimed no right under the Constitution, nor had I any inclination, to enter into the Slave States and interfere with the institutions of slavery. He says upon that: Lincoln will not enter into the Slave States, but will go to the banks of the Ohio, on this side, and shoot over![35] (*Laughter*) He runs on, step by step, in the horse-chestnut style of argument, until in the Springfield speech, he says, "Unless he shall be successful in firing his batteries until he shall have extinguished slavery in all the States, the Union shall be dissolved."[36] Now I don't think that was exactly the way to treat a kind, amiable, intelligent gentleman. (*Roars of laughter*) I know if I had asked the Judge to show when or where it was I had said that, if I didn't succeed in firing into the Slave States until slavery should be extinguished, the Union should be dissolved, he could not have shown it. I understand what he would do. He would say, "I don't mean to quote from you, but this was the *result* of what you say." But I have the right to ask, and I do ask now, Did you not put it in such a form that an ordinary reader or listener would take it as an expression *from me?* (*Laughter*)

In a speech at Springfield, on the night of the 17th, I thought I might as well attend to my own business a little, and I recalled his attention as well as I could to this charge of conspiracy to nationalize Slavery. I called his attention to the fact that he had acknowledged, in my hearing twice, that he had carefully read the speech, and, in the language of the lawyers, as he had twice read the speech, and still had put in no plea or answer, I took a default on him. I insisted that I had a right then to renew that charge of conspiracy.[37] Ten days afterwards, I met the Judge at Clinton[38]—that is to say, I was on the ground, but not in the discussion—and heard him make a speech. Then he comes in with his plea to this charge, for the first time, and his plea

intention was to pit free states against slave states: "Thus, Mr. Lincoln is going to plant his Abolition batteries all along the banks of the Ohio River, and throw his shells into Virginia and Kentucky and into Missouri, and blow up the institution of slavery; and when we arraign him for his unjust interference with the institutions of other States, he says 'Why, I never did enter into Kentucky to interfere with her; I do not propose to do it; I only propose to take care of my own head by keeping on this side of the river, out of harm's way.' But yet he says he is going to persevere in this system of sectional warfare, and I have no doubt he is sincere in what he says. He says that the existence of the Union depends upon his success in firing into these Slave States until he exterminates them. He says that unless he shall play his batteries successfully, so as to abolish slavery in every one of the States, that the Union shall be dissolved; and he says that a dissolution of the Union would be a terrible calamity." Ibid., 129.

37  In his Springfield speech on July 17, 1858, Lincoln reiterated his belief in Douglas's role in a possible conspiracy to perpetuate and nationalize slavery: "One more point on this Springfield speech [the "House Divided" speech] which Judge Douglas says he read so carefully. I expressed my belief in the existence of a conspiracy to perpetuate and nationalize slavery. I did not profess to know it, nor do I now. I showed the part Judge Douglas had played in the string of facts, constituting to my mind, the proof of that conspiracy. I showed the parts played by others. I charged that the people had been deceived into carrying the last Presidential election, by the impression that the people of the Territories might exclude slavery if they chose, when it was known in advance by the conspirators, that the Court was to decide that neither Congress nor the people could so exclude slavery. . . . Judge Douglas has carefully read and re-read that speech. He has not, so far as I know, contradicted those

charges. In the two speeches which I heard he certainly did not. On his own tacit admission I renew that charge. I charge him with having been a party to that conspiracy and to that deception for the sole purpose of nationalizing slavery." *CW,* 2:521.

38  Both Douglas and Lincoln spoke at Clinton, Illinois, on July 27, 1858. The senator spoke in the afternoon and Lincoln was in the audience. Lincoln spoke later that evening. *CW,* 2:525–527.

when put in, as well as I can recollect it, amounted to this: that he never had any talk with Judge Taney or the President of the United States with regard to the Dred Scott decision before it was made. I (Lincoln) ought to know that the man who makes a charge without knowing it to be true, falsifies as much as he who knowingly tells a falsehood; and lastly, that he would pronounce the whole thing a falsehood; but he would make no personal application of the charge of falsehood, not because of any regard for the "kind, amiable, intelligent gentleman," but because of his own personal self-respect! (*Roars of laughter*) I have understood since then, (but [*turning to Judge Douglas*] will not hold the Judge to it if he is not willing) that he has broken through the "self-respect," and has got to saying the thing *out.* The Judge nods to me that it is so. (*Laughter*) It is fortunate for me that I can keep as good-humored as I do, when the Judge acknowledges that he has been trying to make a question of veracity with me. I know the Judge is a great man, while I am only a small man, but *I feel that I have got him.* (*Tremendous cheering*) I demur to that plea. I waive all objections that it was not filed till after default was taken, and demur to it upon the merits. What if Judge Douglas never did talk with Chief Justice Taney and the President, before the Dred Scott decision was made, does it follow that he could not have had as perfect an understanding without talking, as with it? I am not disposed to stand upon my legal advantage. I am disposed to take his denial as being like an answer in chancery, that he neither had any knowledge, information or belief in the existence of such a conspiracy. I am disposed to take his answer as being as broad as though he had put it in these words. And now, I ask, even if he has done so, have not I a right to *prove it on him,* and to offer the evidence of more than two witnesses, by whom to prove it; and if the evidence proves the existence of the conspiracy, does his broad answer denying all knowledge, information, or belief, disturb the fact? It can only show that he was *used* by conspirators, and was not a *leader* of them. (*Vociferous cheering*)

Now in regard to his reminding me of the moral rule that persons who tell what they do not know to be true, falsify as much as those who knowingly tell falsehoods. I remember the rule, and it must be borne in mind that in what I have read to you, I do not say that I *know* such a conspiracy to exist. To that, I reply *I believe it.* If the Judge says that I do *not* believe it, then *he* says what *he* does not know, and falls within his own rule, that he who asserts a thing which he does not know to be true, falsifies as much as he who knowingly tells a falsehood. I want to call your attention to a little discussion on that branch of the case, and the evidence which brought my mind to the conclusion which I expressed as my *belief*. If, in arraying that evidence, I had stated anything which was false or erroneous, it needed but that Judge Douglas should point it out, and I would have taken it back with all the kindness in the world. I do not deal in that way. If I have brought forward anything not a fact, if he will point it out, it will not even ruffle me to take it back. But if he will not point out anything erroneous in the evidence, is it not rather for him to show, by a comparison of the evidence that I have *reasoned* falsely, than to call the "kind, amiable, intelligent gentleman," a liar? (*Cheers and laughter*) If I have reasoned to a false conclusion, it is the vocation of an able debater to show by argument that I have wandered to an erroneous conclusion. I want to ask your attention to a portion of the Nebraska Bill, which Judge Douglas has quoted: "It being the true intent and meaning of this act, not to legislate slavery into any Territory or State, nor to exclude it therefrom, but to leave the people thereof perfectly free to form and regulate their domestic institutions in their own way, subject only to the Constitution of the United States." Thereupon Judge Douglas and others began to argue in favor of "Popular Sovereignty"—the right of the people to have slaves if they wanted them, and to exclude slavery if they did not want them. "But," said, in substance, a Senator from Ohio, (Mr. Chase, I believe,) "we more than suspect that you do not mean to allow the people to exclude slavery if they wish to, and if you do mean it, accept an amendment which I propose expressly authorizing the people to exclude slavery." I believe I have the amendment here before me, which was offered, and under which the people of the Territory, through their proper representatives, might if they saw fit, prohibit the existence of slavery therein. And now I state it as a *fact,* to be taken back if there is any mistake about it, that Judge Douglas and those acting with him, *voted that amendment down. (Tremendous applause)* I now think that those men who voted it down, had a *real reason* for doing so. They know what that reason was. It looks to us, since we have seen the Dred Scott decision pronounced holding that "under the Constitution" the people cannot exclude slavery—I say it looks to outsiders, poor, simple, "amiable, intelligent gentlemen," (*great laughter*) as though the niche was left as a place to put that Dred Scott decision in—(*laughter and cheers*)—a niche which would have been spoiled by adopting the amendment. And now, I say again, if *this* was not the reason, it will avail the Judge much more to calmly and good-humoredly point out to these people what that *other* reason was for voting the amendment down, than, swelling himself up, to vociferate that he may be provoked to call somebody a liar. (*Tremendous applause*)

39 Lincoln feared another *Dred Scott*–like decision from the Supreme Court that would nationalize slavery. See "'House Divided' Address, Springfield, Illinois, June 16, 1858," note 23.

40 Douglas's speech was published in the *Chicago Times,* July 30, 1858.

Again: there is in that same quotation from the Nebraska bill this clause—"It being the true intent and meaning of this bill not to legislate slavery into any Territory or *State.*" I have always been puzzled to know what business the word "State" had in that connection. Judge Douglas knows. *He put it there.* He knows what he put it there for. We outsiders cannot say what he put it there for. The law they were passing was not about States, and was not making provisions for States. What was it placed there for? After seeing the Dred Scott decision, which holds that the people cannot exclude slavery from a *Territory,* if another Dred Scott decision shall come,[39] holding that they cannot exclude it from a *State,* we shall discover that when the word was originally put there, it was in view of something which was to come in due time, we shall see that it was the *other half* of something. (*Applause*) I now say again, if there is any different reason for putting it there, Judge Douglas, in a good-humored way, without calling anybody a liar, *can tell what the reason was.* (*Renewed cheers*)

When the Judge spoke at Clinton, he came very near making a charge of falsehood against me. He used, as I found it printed in a newspaper, which I remember was very nearly like the real speech, the following language:

"I did not answer the charge [of conspiracy] before, for the reason that I did not suppose there was a man in America with a heart so corrupt as to believe such a charge could be true. I have too much respect for Mr. Lincoln to suppose he is serious in making the charge."[40]

I confess this is rather a curious view, that out of respect for me he should consider I was making what I deemed rather a grave charge in fun. (*Laughter*) I confess it strikes me rather strangely. But I let it pass. As the Judge did not for a moment believe that there was a man in America whose heart was so "corrupt" as to make such a charge, and as he places me among the "men in America" who have hearts base enough to make such a charge, I hope he will excuse me if I hunt out another charge very like this; and if it should turn out that in hunting I should find that other, and it should turn out to be Judge Douglas himself who made it, I hope he will reconsider this question of the deep corruption of heart he has thought fit to ascribe to me. (*Great applause and laughter*) In Judge Douglas' speech of March 22d, 1858, which I hold in my hand, he says:

"In this connection there is another topic to which I desire to allude. I seldom refer to the course of newspapers, or notice the articles which they publish in regard to myself; but the course of the Washington

*Union* has been so extraordinary, for the last two or three months, that I think it well enough to make some allusion to it. It has read me out of the Democratic party every other day, at least for two or three months, and keeps reading me out, (*laughter*) and, as if it had not succeeded still continues to read me out, using such terms as "traitor," "renegade," "deserter," and other kind and polite epithets of that nature. Sir, I have no vindication to make of my democracy against the Washington *Union,* or any other newspapers. I am willing to allow my history and action for the last twenty years to speak for themselves as to my political principles, and my fidelity to political obligations. The Washington *Union* has a personal grievance. When its editor was nominated for Public Printer I declined to vote for him, and stated that at some time I might give my reasons for doing so. Since I declined to give that vote, this scurrilous abuse, these vindictive and constant attacks have been repeated almost daily on me. Will my friend from Michigan read the article to which I allude."[41]

This is a part of the speech. You must excuse me from reading the entire article of the Washington *Union,* as Mr. Stuart[42] read it for Mr. Douglas. The Judge goes on and sums up, as I think correctly:

"Mr. President, you here find several distinct propositions advanced boldly by the Washington *Union* editorially and apparently *authoritatively,* and every man who questions any of them is denounced as an Abolitionist, a Free-Soiler, a fanatic. The propositions are, first, that the primary object of all government at its original institution is the protection of person and property; second, that the Constitution of the United States declares that the citizens of each State shall be entitled to all the privileges and immunities of citizens in the several States; and that, therefore, thirdly, all State laws, whether organic or otherwise, which prohibit the citizens of one State from settling in another with their slave property, and especially declaring it forfeited, are direct violations of the original intention of the Government and Constitution of the United States; and fourth, that the emancipation of the slaves of the northern States was a gross outrage on the rights of property, inasmuch as it was involuntarily done on the part of the owner.

Remember that this article was published in the *Union* on the 17th of November, and on the 18th appeared the first article giving the ad-

41  Lincoln quoted from a pamphlet: Stephen A. Douglas, *Speech of Senator Douglas, of Illinois, against the Admission of Kansas under the Lecompton Constitution* (Washington, DC: Lemuel Towers, 1858), 21.

42  Charles E. Stuart (1810–1887), Democrat from Michigan, served in the U.S. House of Representatives from 1847 to 1849 and from 1851 to 1853, and in the U.S. Senate from 1853 to 1859. "Stuart, Charles E.," Biographical Directory of the United States Congress, http://bioguide.congress.gov/scripts/biodisplay.pl?index=S001033 (accessed December 17, 2014).

43 Douglas, *Speech of Senator Douglas against the Admission of Kansas,* 23.

44 Ibid., 24.

hesion of the *Union* to the Lecompton constitution. It was in these words:

'KANSAS AND HER CONSTITUTION.—The vexed question is settled. The problem is solved. The dread point of danger is passed. All serious trouble to Kansas affairs is over and gone.'

And a column, nearly of the same sort. Then, when you come to look into the Lecompton Constitution, you find the same doctrine incorporated in it which was put forth editorially in the *Union.* What is it?

'ARTICLE 7, Section 1. The right of property is before and higher than any constitutional sanction; and the right of the owner of a slave to such slave and its increase is the same and as inviolable as the right of the owner of any property whatever.'

Then in the schedule is a provision that the Constitution may be amended after 1864 by a two-thirds vote.

'But no alteration shall be made to affect the right of property in the ownership of slaves.'

It will be seen by these clauses in the Lecompton Constitution that they are identical in spirit with this *authoritative* article in the Washington *Union* of the day previous to its indorsement of this Constitution."[43]

I pass over some portions of the speech, and I hope that any one who feels interested in this matter will read the entire section of the speech, and see whether I do the Judge injustice. He proceeds:

"When I saw that article in the *Union* of the 17th of November, followed by the glorification of the Lecompton Constitution on the 18th of November, and this clause in the Constitution asserting the doctrine that a State has no right to prohibit slavery within its limits, I saw that there was a *fatal blow* being struck at the sovereignty of the States of this Union."[44]

I stop the quotation there, again requesting that it may all be read. I have read all of the portion I desire to comment upon. What is this charge that the Judge thinks I must have a very corrupt heart to make? It was a purpose on the part of certain high functionaries to make it impossible for the people of one State to prohibit the people of any other State from entering it with their "property," so called, and making it a slave State. In other words, it was a charge implying a design to make the institution of slavery national.

And now I ask your attention to what Judge Douglas has himself done here. I know he made that part of the speech as a reason why he had refused to vote for a certain man for public printer, but when we get at it, the charge itself is the very one I made against him, that he thinks I am so corrupt for uttering. Now whom does he make that charge against? Does he make it against that newspaper editor merely? No; he says it is identical in spirit with the Lecompton Constitution, and so the framers of that Constitution are brought in with the editor of the newspaper in that "fatal blow being struck." He did not call it a "conspiracy." In his language it is a "fatal blow being struck." And if the words carry the meaning better when changed from a "conspiracy" into a "fatal blow being struck," I will change *my* expression and call it "fatal blow being struck." (*Cheers and laughter*) We see the charge made not merely against the editor of the *Union* but all the framers of the Lecompton Constitution; and not only so, but the article was an *authoritative* article. By whose authority? Is there any question but he means it was by the authority of the President, and his Cabinet—the Administration?

Is there any sort of question but he means to make that charge? Then there are the editors of the *Union,* the framers of the Lecompton Constitution, the President of the United States and his Cabinet, and all the supporters of the Lecompton Constitution in Congress and out of Congress, who are all involved in this "fatal blow being struck." I commend to Judge Douglas' consideration the question of *how corrupt a man's heart must be to make such a charge!* (*Vociferous cheering*)

Now my friends, I have but one branch of the subject, in the little time I have left, to which to call your attention, and as I shall come to a close at the end of that branch, it is probable that I shall not occupy quite all the time allotted to me. Although on these questions I would like to talk twice as long as I have, I could not enter upon another head and discuss it properly without running over my time. I ask the attention of the people here assembled and elsewhere, to the course that Judge Douglas is pursuing every day as bearing upon this question of making slavery national. Not going back to the records but taking the speeches he makes, the speeches he made yesterday[45] and day before and makes constantly all over the country—I ask your attention to them. In the first place what is necessary to make the institution national? Not war. There is no danger that the people of Kentucky will shoulder their muskets and with a young nigger stuck on every bayonet march into Illinois and force them upon us. There is no danger of our going over there and making war upon them. Then what is necessary for the

45 It is not clear to which speeches Lincoln referred. Douglas was in Ottawa on August 20, the day before the debate, and in Peoria and Lacon on August 19. Guelzo, *Lincoln and Douglas,* 105–106.

46 President Andrew Jackson in 1832 vetoed legislation rechartering the Bank of the United States. The Supreme Court's *McCulloch v. Maryland* decision in 1819 upheld Congress's authority under the Constitution to charter the bank. Jackson, in his veto message, declared that he did not agree with the claim that the bank's constitutionality "in all its features ought to be considered as settled by the supreme court." According to Jackson, "Congress, the Executive and the Court, must each for itself, be guided by his own opinion of the Constitution." Jackson's veto message is in *Addresses and Messages of the Presidents of the United States, from 1789 to 1839*, 403.

47 The Democratic Party's 1856 platform, adopted at its national convention in Cincinnati, included a clause stating that "Congress has no power to charter a national bank; that we believe such an institution one of deadly hostility to the best interests of the country." See http://www.presidency.ucsb.edu/ws/?pid=29576 (accessed December 17, 2014).

nationalization of slavery? It is simply the next Dred Scott decision. It is merely for the Supreme Court to decide that no *State* under the Constitution can exclude it, just as they have already decided that under the Constitution neither Congress nor the Territorial Legislature can do it. When that is decided and acquiesced in, the whole thing is done. This being true, and this being the way as I think that slavery is to be made national, let us consider what Judge Douglas is doing every day to that end. In the first place, let us see what influence he is exerting on public sentiment. In this and like communities, public sentiment is everything. With public sentiment, nothing can fail; without it nothing can succeed. Consequently he who moulds public sentiment, goes deeper than he who enacts statutes or pronounces decisions. He makes statutes and decisions possible or impossible to be executed. This must be borne in mind, as also the additional fact that Judge Douglas is a man of vast influence, so great that it is enough for many men to profess to believe anything, when they once find out that Judge Douglas professes to believe it. Consider also the attitude he occupies at the head of a large party—a party which he claims has a majority of all the voters in the country. This man sticks to a decision which forbids the people of a Territory from excluding slavery, and he does so not because he says it is right in itself—he does not give any opinion on that—but because it has been *decided by the court*, and being decided by the court, he is, and you are bound to take it in your political action as *law*—not that he judges at all of its merits, but because a decision of the court is to him a "*Thus saith the Lord.*" (*Applause*) He places it on that ground alone, and you will bear in mind that thus committing himself unreservedly to this decision, *commits him to the next one* just as firmly as to this. He did not commit himself on account of the merit or demerit of the decision, but it is a *Thus saith the Lord*. The next decision, as much as this, will be a *thus saith the Lord*. There is nothing that can divert or turn him away from this decision. It is nothing that I point out to him that his great prototype, Gen. Jackson, did not believe in the binding force of decisions. It is nothing to him that Jefferson did not so believe. I have said that I have often heard him approve of Jackson's course in disregarding the decision of the Supreme Court pronouncing a National Bank constitutional.[46] He says, I did not hear him say so. He denies the accuracy of my recollection. I say he ought to know better than I, but I will make no question about this thing, though it still seems to me that I heard him say it twenty times. (*Applause and laughter*) I will tell him though, that he now claims to stand on the Cincinnati platform,[47] which affirms that Congress *cannot* charter a National Bank, in the teeth of that old standing decision that Congress *can* charter a bank. (*Loud applause*) And I remind him of another piece of history on the question of respect for judicial decisions, and it is a piece of Illinois history, belonging to a time when the large party to which Judge Douglas belonged, were displeased with a decision of the Supreme Court of Illinois, because they had decided that a Governor could not remove a Secretary of State. You will find the whole story in Ford's History of Illinois,[48] and I know that Judge Douglas will not deny that he was then in favor of overslaughing that decision by the mode of adding five new Judges, so as to vote down the four old ones. Not only so, but it ended in *the Judge's sitting down on that very bench as one of the five new Judges to break down the four old ones.*[49] (*Cheers and laughter*) It was in this way precisely that he got his title of Judge. Now, when the Judge tells me that men appointed conditionally to sit as members of a court, will have to be catechised beforehand upon some subject, I say[,] "You know Judge; you have tried it." (*Laughter*) When he says a court of this kind will lose the confidence of all men, will be prostituted and disgraced by such a proceeding, I say, "You know best, Judge; you have been through the mill." (*Great laughter*) But I cannot shake Judge Douglas' teeth loose from the Dred Scott decision. Like some obstinate animal (I mean no disrespect) that will hang on when he has once got his teeth fixed, you may cut off a leg, or you may tear away an arm, still he will not relax his hold. And so I may point out to the Judge, and say that he is bespattered all over, from the beginning of his political life to the present time, with attacks upon judicial decisions—I may cut off limb after limb of his public record, and strive to wrench him from a single dictum of the Court—yet I cannot divert him from it. He hangs to the last, to the Dred Scott decision. (*Loud cheers*) These things show there is a purpose *strong as death and eternity* for which he adheres to this decision, and for which he will adhere to *all other decisions* of the same Court. (*Vociferous applause*)

A HIBERNIAN.—Give us something besides Dred Scott.

MR. LINCOLN.—Yes; no doubt you want to hear something that don't hurt. (*Laughter and applause*) Now, having spoken of the Dred Scott decision, one more word and I am done. Henry Clay, my beau ideal of a statesman, the man for whom I fought all my humble life—Henry Clay once said of a class of men who would repress all tendencies to liberty and ultimate emancipation, that they must, if they would do this, go back to the era of our Independence, and muzzle the cannon which thunders its annual joyous return; they must blow out the moral lights around us; they must penetrate the human soul, and eradicate there the love of liberty; and

48 Thomas Ford, *A History of Illinois, from its Commencement as a State in 1818 to 1847* (Chicago: S. C. Griggs, 1854), 214–221.

49 Illinois Democrats favored voting rights for aliens, since most would support the party. Expecting the state supreme court, dominated by Whigs, to deny aliens the right to vote, the Democrat-controlled General Assembly passed legislation in the 1840–1841 session to pack the court with five additional justices, all of them Democrats. Douglas, one of the new judges, was involved in promoting the legislation that resulted in the appointment of new judges. See ibid., 214–221.

50  Lincoln referred to the conclusion of Henry Clay's 1827 speech to the American Colonization Society, when he criticized opponents of the organization's goals: "What would they, who thus reproach us, have done? If they would repress all tendencies towards liberty and ultimate emancipation, they must do more than put down the benevolent efforts of this Society. They must go back to the era of our Liberty and independence, and muzzle the cannon which thunders its annual joyous return. They must revive the slave trade, with all its train of atrocities. They must suppress the workings of British philanthropy, seeking to meliorate the condition of the unfortunate West Indian slaves. They must arrest the career of South American deliverance from thralldom. They must blow out the moral lights around us, and extinguish that greatest torch of all which America presents to a benighted world, pointing the way to their rights, their liberties, and their happiness." Clay, *Speech of the Hon. Henry Clay, before the American Colonization Society,* 13.

51  Douglas used his half-hour closing statement by again raising the questions he posed to Lincoln in his opening remarks, asserting that Lincoln was in Springfield when the Republican convention was held and its resolutions adopted. Lincoln responded angrily to this charge, springing up from his chair and interrupting Douglas several times with denials, before two Republican committeemen led him back to his seat. Douglas reminded the audience that Lincoln failed to answer the questions concerning the Republican resolutions, and ridiculed Lincoln's "charge of conspiracy against me," claiming that his opponent "acknowledges he does not know it to be true." Douglas ended his remarks by renewing his assertion that Lincoln's house-divided doctrine would result in the dissolution of the Union. *CW,* 2:30–37.

then and not till then, could they perpetuate slavery in this country![50] (*Loud cheers*) To my thinking, Judge Douglas is, by his example and vast influence, doing that very thing in this community, (*Cheers*) when he says that the negro has nothing in the Declaration of Independence. Henry Clay plainly understood the contrary. Judge Douglas is going back to the era of our Revolution, and to the extent of his ability, muzzling the cannon which thunders its annual joyous return. When he invites any people willing to have slavery, to establish it, he is blowing out the moral lights around us. (*Cheers*) When he says he "cares not whether slavery is voted down or voted up,"—that it is a sacred right of self government—he is in my judgment penetrating the human soul and eradicating the light of reason and the love of liberty in this American people. (*Enthusiastic and continued applause*) And now I will only say that when, by all these means and appliances, Judge Douglas shall succeed in bringing public sentiment to an exact accordance with his own views—when these vast assemblages shall echo back all these sentiments—when they shall come to repeat his views and to avow his principles, and to say all that he says on these mighty questions—then it needs only the formality of the second Dred Scott decision, which he endorses in advance, to make Slavery alike lawful in all the States—old as well as new, North as well as South.

My friends, that ends the chapter. The Judge can take his half-hour.[51]

# Second Debate with Stephen A. Douglas at Freeport, Illinois

## August 27, 1858

### Mr. Lincoln's Speech[1]

LADIES AND GENTLEMEN—On Saturday last, Judge Douglas and myself first met in public discussion.[2] He spoke one hour, I an hour-and-a-half, and he replied for half an hour. The order is now reversed. I am to speak an hour, he an hour-and-a-half, and then I am to reply for half an hour.[3] I propose to devote myself during the first hour to the scope of what was brought within the range of his half hour speech at Ottawa. Of course there was brought within the scope in that half hour's speech something of his own opening speech. In the course of that opening argument Judge Douglas proposed to me seven distinct interrogatories. In my speech of an hour and a half, I attended to some other parts of his speech, and incidentally, as I thought, answered one of the interrogatories then. I then distinctly intimated to him that I would answer the rest of his interrogatories on condition only that he should agree to answer as many for me. He made no intimation at the time of the proposition, nor did he in his reply allude at all to that suggestion of mine. I do him no injustice in saying that he occupied at least half of his reply in dealing with me as though I had *refused* to answer his interrogatories. I now propose that I will answer any of the interrogatories, upon condition that he will answer questions from me not exceeding the same number. I give him an opportunity to respond. The Judge remains silent. I now say to you that I will answer his interrogatories, whether he answers mine or not; (*Applause*) and that after I have done so, I shall propound mine to him. (*Applause*)[4]

I have supposed myself, since the organization of the Republican party at Bloomington, in May, 1856, bound as a party man by the platforms of the party, then and since. If in any interrogatories which I shall answer I go be-

*In his second debate with Douglas, Lincoln, on the recommendation of close advisers, went on the offense against his opponent by posing several questions intended to force the senator to explain the perceived incompatibility between popular sovereignty and the Dred Scott decision. Douglas's answer to Lincoln's second question, in which he asserted the right of residents of a territory to prohibit slavery before that territory adopted a state constitution, a position violating the Supreme Court's Dred Scott decision, assumed mythical proportions long after the debate. The exaggerated legend has it that Lincoln sacrificed the Senate seat for the presidency two years later, knowing that Douglas's "Freeport Doctrine" might win him reelection but would alienate Southerners and thus destroy his presidential aspirations in 1860.*

1    The second Lincoln-Douglas debate was held in Freeport, Illinois, the county seat of Stephenson County, located in the northwest region of the state bordering Wisconsin. Freeport was solidly Republican in its politics; its residents voted overwhelmingly for the 1856 Republican presidential candidate, John C. Frémont, over Democrat James Buchanan and the Know-Nothing candidate, Millard Fillmore. A crowd of approximately 15,000, double the size of the town's population, attended the debate amid chilly, damp, and cloudy weather conditions. Of all of the debate crowds, this would have been the most supportive of Lincoln. Wearing his ever-present stovepipe hat and a "course looking coat with sleeves far too short, and baggy looking trousers so short they showed his rough boots," Lincoln was driven, along with an escort of farmers, the short distance from his boardinghouse to the debate platform in a Conestoga wagon. Douglas, adorned in finer clothing, including a ruffled shirt, a blue coat with shiny buttons, and polished shoes, stayed at the same boardinghouse as Lincoln, but at the last minute chose to forgo using a carriage and walked to the

debate in the company of supporters. Guelzo, *Lincoln and Douglas,* 145–148; Holzer, *The Lincoln-Douglas Debates,* 87–88, includes description of Lincoln's clothing.

2    Due to the crush of people surrounding the debate platform, Robert Hitt, the reporter for the Republican *Chicago Press and Tribune,* had trouble making his way through the crowd and was not on the stage when Lincoln began his opening statement. Before Lincoln commenced speaking, he was interrupted by William "Deacon" Bross (1813–1890) of the *Press and Tribune,* who requested that Lincoln delay his remarks, since "Hitt ain't here, and there is no use of your speaking unless the *Press and Tribune* has a report." According to one observer, Lincoln, giving the friendly reporter time to get onto the platform, began by speaking very slowly. Quotation cited in Burlingame, *Abraham Lincoln,* 1:502; Guelzo, *Lincoln and Douglas,* 149.

3    Lincoln's speaking style, as his physical appearance, presented a dramatic contrast to Douglas's. Standing six feet four inches tall, Lincoln was slender, stoop shouldered, somewhat awkward, looked older than his forty-nine years, and spoke with a high-pitched voice. One unimpressed witness to a Lincoln speech observed that his "pronunciation is bad, his manners uncouth and his general appearance anything but prepossessing." An attendee at the Ottawa debate described Lincoln's gestures on the stage as "awfully awkward" but nevertheless effective: "He elongated himself to his full height and delivered himself awkwardly, it is true, but with the greatest animation and with one single gesture delivered with his right forefinger . . . in fact that forefinger seemed to be continually scratching away out in front of the speaker. If I recall it rightly, he wore one of those old-fashioned satin stocks or chokers, and it was worn and evidently impeded full use of his organs of speech, for he pulled it off and threw it down. A few moments later, with nervous impatience he pulled off his shirt collar, tearing loose the buttons and throwing it to the winds, and continued his speech minus both necktie and collar; and the old farmers cheered and howled." Douglas, on the other hand, was, in the words of one historian, "a hurricane of passion." A foot shorter than Lincoln, Douglas possessed a stocky body with short legs and a paunch. Whereas Lincoln tended to speak in an earnest and measured manner, the Illinois senator was much more animated in his speech and gestures, pacing around a platform and speaking with verve, passion, precision, and charisma, in a deep, powerful voice. Guelzo, *Lincoln*

*and Douglas,* 99–102; quotation about Lincoln's style of speaking on p. 100. Newspaper reporter Henry Villard (1835–1900), biased in favor of Lincoln, described both candidates in action at the Ottawa debate: "The Democratic spokesman commanded a strong, sonorous voice, a rapid, vigorous utterance, a telling play of countenance, impressive gestures, and all the other arts of the practiced speaker. As far as all external conditions were concerned, there was nothing in favor of Lincoln. He had a lean, lank, indescribably gawky figure, and odd-featured, wrinkled, inexpressive, and altogether uncomely face. He used singularly awkward, almost absurd, up-and-down and sidewise movements of his body to give emphasis to his arguments. His voice was naturally good, but he frequently raised it to an unnatural pitch. Yet the unprejudiced mind felt at once that, while there was on the one side a skillful dialectician and debater arguing a wrong and weak cause, there was on the other a thoroughly earnest and truthful man, inspired by sound convictions in conscience with the true spirit of American institutions. There was nothing in all Douglas' powerful effort that appealed to the higher instincts of human nature, while Lincoln always touched sympathetic chords." Cited in Holzer, *The Lincoln-Douglas Debates,* 19.

4    Douglas's questions posed in the first debate relating to resolutions adopted at an October 1854 abolitionist meeting in Aurora, Illinois, must have taken Lincoln by surprise, since Douglas claimed, incorrectly, that they were adopted by a Republican meeting in Springfield, which Lincoln did not attend, in the same year. See "First Debate with Stephen A. Douglas at Ottawa, Illinois, August 21, 1858," note 13, in this volume. Though he may have been caught off guard by his opponent at the beginning of the earlier debate, Lincoln was praised by Republicans and the party press for his performance in Ottawa. Simply holding his own with a well-known figure noted for his oratorical skills was undoubtedly looked upon as a victory for Lincoln. Yet several members of the Republican state committee thought Lincoln spent too much time defending himself against Douglas's charges when he should have taken the fight to the senator. For the second debate he was urged to dispense with Douglas's questions quickly and then pose "a few ugly questions" of his own relating to slavery in the territories and the incompatibility between popular sovereignty and the *Dred Scott* decision. Guelzo, *Lincoln and Douglas,* 144–145. See also Burlingame, *Abraham Lincoln,* 1:495–496, 501.

Louis O. Lussier, *Stephen A. Douglas.* Oil on canvas (ca. 1855). Portrait of Douglas as he appeared at the peak of his power in the U.S. Senate.

5    The Fugitive Slave Law passed by Congress as part of the Compromise of 1850 penalized officials, North or South, who did not arrest alleged runaway slaves. The law required the arrest of persons suspected of being runaway slaves, without due process. Any person assisting a runaway slave was subject to imprisonment and a fine. Lincoln privately opposed the law, once admitting to a slaveholding friend that he hated "to see the poor creatures hunted down, and caught, and carried back to their stripes, and unrewarded toils; but I bite my lip and keep quiet." Publicly Lincoln would not call for flouting the measure so long as it was law. See "Letter to Joshua F. Speed, August 24, 1855," in this volume. For background on the Fugitive Slave Law, see "Speech on the Kansas-Nebraska Act at Peoria, Illinois, October 16, 1854," note 17.

yond the scope of what is within these platforms it will be perceived that no one is responsible but myself.

Having said thus much, I will take up the Judge's interrogatories as I find them printed in the Chicago *Times,* and answer them *seriatim.* In order that there may be no mistake about it, I have copied the interrogatories in writing, and also my answers to them. The first one of these interrogatories is in these words:

Question 1. "I desire to know whether Lincoln to-day stands, as he did in 1854, in favor of the unconditional repeal of the fugitive slave law?"[5]

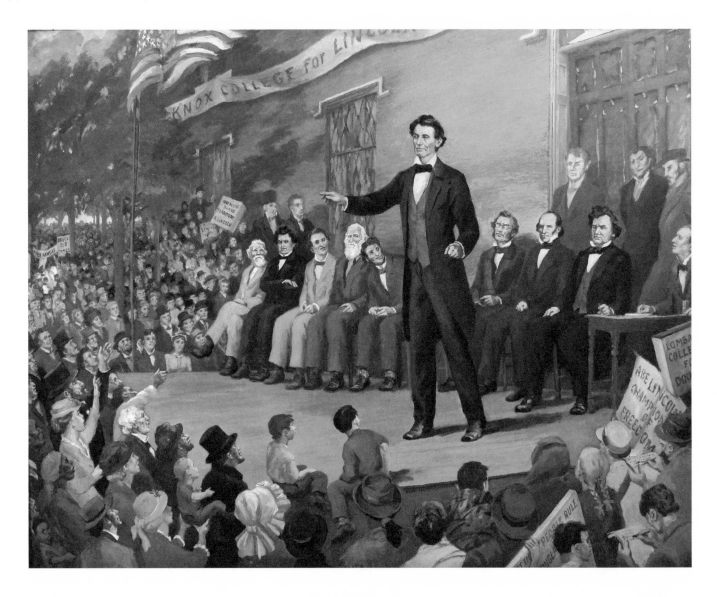

Ralph Seymour, mural (1958) painted at Knox
College to commemorate the Lincoln-Douglas
debate at Galesburg, Illinois.

Answer. I do not now, nor ever did, stand in favor of the unconditional
repeal of the fugitive slave law. (*Cries of "Good," "Good"*)

Q. 2. "I desire him to answer whether he stands pledged to-day, as he did
in 1854, against the admission of any more slave States into the Union, even
if the people want them?"

A. I do not now, nor ever did, stand pledged against the admission of any
more slave States into the Union.

Q. 3. "I want to know whether he stands pledged against the admission of a new State into the Union with such a Constitution as the people of that State may see fit to make."

A. I do not stand pledged against the admission of a new State into the Union, with such a Constitution as the people of that State may see fit to make. (*Cries of "good," "good"*)

Q. 4. "I want to know whether he stands to-day pledged to the abolition of slavery in the District of Columbia?"

A. I do not stand to-day pledged to the abolition of slavery in the District of Columbia.

Q. 5. "I desire him to answer whether he stands pledged to the prohibition of the slave trade between the different States?"

A. I do not stand pledged to the prohibition of the slave trade between the different States.

Q. 6. "I desire to know whether he stands pledged to prohibit slavery in all the Territories of the United States, North as well as South of the Missouri Compromise line."

A. I am impliedly, if not expressly, pledged to a belief in the *right* and *duty* of Congress to prohibit slavery in all the United States Territories. (*Great applause*)

Q. 7. "I desire him to answer whether he is opposed to the acquisition of any new territory unless slavery is first prohibited therein."

A. I am not generally opposed to honest acquisition of territory; and, in any given case, I would or would not oppose such acquisition, accordingly as I might think such acquisition would or would not agravate [*sic*] the slavery question among ourselves. (*Cries of "good," "good"*)

Now, my friends, it will be perceived upon an examination of these questions and answers, that so far I have only answered that I was not *pledged* to this, that or the other. The Judge has not framed his interrogatories to ask me anything more than this, and I have answered in strict accordance with the interrogatories, and have answered truly that I am not *pledged* at all upon any of the points to which I have answered. But I am not disposed to hang upon the exact form of his interrogatory. I am rather disposed to take up at least some of these questions, and state what I really think upon them.

As to the first one, in regard to the Fugitive Slave Law, I have never hesitated to say, and I do not now hesitate to say, that I think, under the Constitution of the United States, the people of the Southern States are entitled to a Congressional Fugitive Slave Law. Having said that, I have had nothing to say in regard to the existing Fugitive Slave Law further than that I think it should have been framed so as to be free from some of the objections that

6   The views Lincoln expressed concerning the abolition of slavery in the District of Columbia were in keeping with legislation he proposed but never formally submitted to Congress in 1849. See "Remarks and Resolution concerning Abolition of Slavery in the District of Columbia, U.S. House of Representatives, January 10, 1849," in this volume. Lincoln misquoted Clay concerning slavery in the nation's capital. In his January 20, 1827, speech to the American Colonization Society, Clay declared, "[If] I could be the instrument in eradicating the deepest stain upon the character of our country, and removing all cause of reproach on account of it, by foreign nations—if I could only be the instrument in ridding of this foul blot that revered State that gave me birth, or that not less beloved State which kindly adopted me as her son, I would not exchange the proud satisfaction which I should enjoy for the honour of all the triumphs ever decreed to the most successful conqueror." In this instance Clay is referring to Virginia, the state of his birth. Clay, *Speech of the Hon. Henry Clay, before the American Colonization Society,* 11.

pertain to it, without lessening its efficiency. And inasmuch as we are not now in an agitation in regard to an alteration or modification of that law, I would not be the man to introduce it as a new subject of agitation upon the general question of slavery.

In regard to the other question of whether I am pledged to the admission of any more slave States into the Union, I state to you very frankly that I would be exceedingly sorry ever to be put in a position of having to pass upon that question. I should be exceedingly glad to know that there would never be another slave State admitted into the Union; (*Applause*) but I must add, that if slavery shall be kept out of the Territories during the territorial existence of any one given Territory, and then the people shall, having a fair chance and a clear field, when they come to adopt the Constitution, do such an extraordinary thing as to adopt a Slave Constitution, uninfluenced by the actual presence of the institution among them, I see no alternative, if we own the country, but to admit them into the Union. (*Applause*)

The third interrogatory is answered by the answer to the second, it being, as I conceive, the same as the second.

The fourth one is in regard to the abolition of slavery in the District of Columbia. In relation to that, I have my mind very distinctly made up. I should be exceedingly glad to see slavery abolished in the District of Columbia. (*Cries of "good," "good"*) I believe that Congress possesses the constitutional power to abolish it. Yet as a member of Congress, I should not with my present views, be in favor of *endeavoring* to abolish slavery in the District of Columbia, unless it would be upon these conditions. *First,* that the abolition should be gradual. *Second,* that it should be on a vote of the majority of qualified voters in the District, and *third,* that compensation should be made to unwilling owners. With these three conditions, I confess I would be exceedingly glad to see Congress abolish slavery in the District of Columbia, and, in the language of Henry Clay, "sweep from our Capital that foul blot upon our nation."[6] (*Loud applause*)

In regard to the fifth interrogatory, I must say here, that as to the question of the abolition of the Slave Trade between the different States, I can truly answer, as I have, that I am *pledged* to nothing about it. It is a subject to which I have not given that mature consideration that would make me feel authorized to state a position so as to hold myself entirely bound by it. In other words, that question has never been prominently enough before me to induce me to investigate whether we really have the Constitutional power to do it. I could investigate it if I had sufficient time, to bring myself to a conclusion upon that subject, but I have not done so, and I say so frankly to you here, and to Judge Douglas. I must say, however, that if I should be of opinion that Congress does possess the Constitutional power to abolish the slave trade among the different States, I should still not be in favor of the exercise of that power unless upon some conservative principle as I conceive it, akin to what I have said in relation to the abolition of slavery in the District of Columbia.

My answer as to whether I desire that slavery should be prohibited in all the Territories of the United States is full and explicit within itself, and cannot be made clearer by any comments of mine. So I suppose in regard to the question whether I am opposed to the acquisition of any more territory unless slavery is first prohibited therein, my answer is such that I could add nothing by way of illustration, or making myself better understood, than the answer which I have placed in writing.

Now in all this, the Judge has me and he has me on the record. I suppose he had flattered himself that I was really entertaining one set of opinions for one place and another set for another place—that I was afraid to say at one place what I uttered at another. What I am saying here I suppose I say to a vast audience as strongly tending to Abolitionism as any audience in the State of Illinois, and I believe I am saying that which, if it would be offensive to any persons and render them enemies to myself, would be offensive to persons in this audience.

I now proceed to propound to the Judge the interrogatories, so far as I have framed them. I will bring forward a new installment when I get them ready. (*Laughter*) I will bring them forward now, only reaching to number four.

The first one is—

Question 1. If the people of Kansas shall, by means entirely unobjectionable in all other respects, adopt a State Constitution, and ask admission into the Union under it, *before* they have the requisite number of inhabitants according to the English Bill—some ninety-three Thousand—will you vote to admit them? (*Applause*)

Q. 2. Can the people of a United States Territory, in any lawful way, against the wish of any citizen of the United States, exclude slavery from its limits prior to the formation of a State Constitution?[7] (*Renewed applause*)

Q. 3. If the Supreme Court of the United States shall decide that States can not exclude slavery from their limits, are you in favor of acquiescing in, adopting and following such decision as a rule of political action? (*Loud applause*)

Q. 4. Are you in favor of acquiring additional territory, in disregard of

7    Lincoln's second question and Douglas's answer assumed mythical proportions in the years following the debates. Several Lincoln associates and biographers claimed Lincoln sought to trap his opponent, forcing him to either disown popular sovereignty and lose support among his supporters in Illinois or reject the *Dred Scott* decision in favor of popular sovereignty and thus exacerbate the divisions with the Buchanan administration and alienate the Southern supporters essential to an 1860 presidential victory. By following the latter course, subsequently known as the "Freeport Doctrine," Douglas may have won the senate race but doomed his chances to be president two years later. According to the legend, Lincoln was advised not to ask the question because it would provide Douglas a chance to solidify his chances of reelection. Supposedly, Lincoln, already thinking beyond the debates to the 1860 presidential election, rejected the advice and posed the question because, he said, "I am killing larger game. The battle of 1860 is worth a hundred of this." Evidence does not support this version of events, especially Lincoln's sacrificing his chance of being elected senator in favor of winning the presidency in 1860. As pointed out in note 4, Lincoln was urged by advisers to ask questions concerning the incompatibility of Douglas's support of popular sovereignty and the *Dred Scott* decision. Moreover, Douglas's answer to Lincoln's second question was nothing new, since he had been making similar statements in previous speeches and appearances across Illinois. Finally, while Southern newspapers condemned Douglas's Freeport Doctrine, his standing with Southerners was already on shaky ground owing to his break with President Buchanan over the Lecompton constitution. The quote from Lincoln regarding "larger game" is from John Locke Scripps, *Life of Abraham Lincoln* (New York: Horace Greeley & Co., 1860), 28, just one of several biographies that promulgated the myth.

Historians have downplayed the importance of Lincoln's Freeport question. According to David Potter, the question was "one of the great non-events of American history." Potter, *Impending Crisis,* 338. See also Fehrenbacher, *Prelude to Greatness,* 121–142; Burlingame, *Abraham Lincoln,* 1:504–505.

8   See "First Debate with Stephen A. Douglas at Ottawa, Illinois," note 13, concerning Douglas's assertions surrounding the 1854 Republicans' resolutions.

9   The radical resolutions to which Douglas referred were adopted at an 1854 meeting of abolitionists in the town of Aurora, which is located in Kane County, Illinois.

how such acquisition may affect the nation on the slavery question? (*Cries of "good," "good"*)

As introductory to these interrogatories which Judge Douglas propounded to me at Ottawa, he read a set of resolutions which he said Judge Trumbull and myself had participated in adopting, in the first Republican State Convention held at Springfield, in October, 1854.[8] He insisted that I and Judge Trumbull, and perhaps, the entire Republican party were responsible for the doctrines contained in the set of resolutions which he read, and I understand that it was from that set of resolutions that he deduced the interrogatories which he propounded to me, using these resolutions as a sort of authority for propounding those questions to me. Now I say here to-day that I do not answer his interrogatories because of their springing at all from that set of resolutions which he read. I answered them because Judge Douglas thought fit to ask them. (*Applause*) I do not now, nor never did recognize any responsibility upon myself in that set of resolutions. When I replied to him on that occasion, I assured him that I never had anything to do with them. I repeat here to-day, that I never in any possible form had anything to do with that set of resolutions. It turns out, I believe, that those resolutions were never passed in any Convention held in Springfield. (*Cheers and laughter*) It turns out that they were never passed at any Convention or any public meeting that I had any part in. I believe it turns out in addition to all this, that there was not, in the fall of 1854, any Convention holding a session in Springfield, calling itself a Republican State Convention; yet it is true there was a Convention, or assemblage of men calling themselves a Convention, at Springfield, that did pass *some* resolutions. But so little did I really know of the proceedings of that Convention, or what set of resolutions they had passed, though having a general knowledge that there had been such an assemblage of men there, that when Judge Douglas read the resolutions, I really did not know but they had been the resolutions passed then and there. I did not question that they were the resolutions adopted. For I could not bring myself to suppose that Judge Douglas could say what he did upon this subject without *knowing* that it was true. (*Cheers and laughter*) I contented myself, on that occasion, with denying, as I truly could, all connection with them, not denying or affirming whether they were passed at Springfield. Now it turns out that he had got hold of some resolutions passed at some Convention or public meeting in Kane County.[9] (*Renewed laughter*) I wish to say here that I don't conceive that in any fair and just mind this discovery relieves me at all. I had just as much to do with the Convention in Kane County as that in Springfield. I am just as much responsible for the resolutions at Kane County as those at Springfield, the amount of the responsibility being exactly nothing in either case; no more than there would be in regard to a set of resolutions passed in the moon. (*Laughter and loud cheers*)

I allude to this extraordinary matter in this canvas for some further purpose than anything yet advanced. Judge Douglas did not make his statement upon that occasion as matters that he believed to be true, but he stated them roundly as *being true,* in such form as to pledge his veracity for their truth. When the whole matter turns out as it does, and when we consider who Judge Douglas is—that he is a distinguished Senator of the United States—that he has served nearly twelve years as such—that his character is not at all limited as an ordinary Senator of the United States, but that his name has become of world-wide renown—it is *most extraordinary* that he should so far forget all the suggestions of justice to an adversary, or of prudence to himself, as to venture upon the assertion of that which the slightest investigation would have shown him to be wholly false. (*Cheers*) I can only account for his having done so upon the supposition that that evil genius which has attended him through his life, giving to him an apparent astonishing prosperity, such as to lead very many good men to doubt there being any advantage in virtue over vice—(*Cheers and laughter*) I say I can only account for it on the supposition that that evil genius has at last made up its mind to forsake him. (*Continued cheers and laughter*)

And I may add that another extraordinary feature of the Judge's conduct in this canvass—made more extraordinary by this incident—is that he is in the habit, in almost all the speeches he makes, of charging falsehood upon his adversaries—myself and others. I now ask whether he is able to find in anything that Judge Trumbull, for instance, has said, or in anything that I have said, a justification at all compared with what we have, in this instance, for that sort of vulgarity. (*Cries of "good," "good," "good"*)

I have been in the habit of charging as a matter of belief on my part, that, in the introduction of the Nebraska bill into Congress, there was a conspiracy to make slavery perpetual and national. I have arranged from time to time the evidence which establishes and proves the truth of this charge. I recurred to this charge at Ottawa. I shall not now have time to dwell upon it at very great length, but inasmuch as Judge Douglas in his reply of half an hour, made some points upon me in relation to it, I propose noticing a few of them.

The Judge insists that, in the first speech I made, in which I very distinctly made that charge,[10] he thought for a good while I was in fun! that I

10  Lincoln referred to his "House Divided" speech. See "'House Divided' Address, Springfield, Illinois, June 16, 1858," note 17.

11  *U.S. Statutes at Large,* 10:283. Cited in David
and Wilson, *The Lincoln-Douglas Debates,* 52n4.

12  The *Dred Scott* decision.

was playful—that I was not sincere about it—and that he only grew angry and somewhat excited when he found that I insisted upon it as a matter of earnestness. He says he characterised it as a falsehood as far as I implicated his *moral character* in that transaction. Well, I did not know, till he presented that view that I had implicated his moral character. He is very much in the habit, when he argues me up into a position I never thought of occupying, of very cosily saying he has no doubt Lincoln is "conscientious" in saying so. He should remember that I did not know but what *he* was ALTOGETHER "CONSCIENTIOUS" in that matter. (*Great laughter*) I can conceive it possible for men to conspire to do a good thing, and I really find nothing in Judge Douglas' course or arguments that is contrary to or inconsistent with his belief of a conspiracy to nationalize and spread slavery as being a good and blessed thing, (*Continued laughter*) and so I hope he will understand that I do not at all question but that in all this matter he is entirely "conscientious." (*More laughter and cheers*)

But to draw your attention to one of the points I made in this case, beginning at the beginning. When the Nebraska bill was introduced, or a short time afterwards, by an amendment I believe, it was provided that it must be considered "the true intent and meaning of this act not to legislate slavery into any State or Territory, or to exclude it therefrom, but to leave the people thereof perfectly free to form and regulate their own domestic institutions in their own way, subject only to the Constitution of the United States."[11] I have called his attention to the fact that when he and some others began arguing that they were giving an increased degree of liberty to the people in the Territories over and above what they formerly had on the question of slavery, a question was raised whether the law was enacted to give such unconditional liberty to the people, and to test the sincerity of this mode of argument, Mr. Chase, of Ohio, introduced an amendment, in which he made the law—if the amendment were adopted—expressly declare that the people of the Territory should have the power to exclude slavery if they saw fit. I have asked attention also to the fact that Judge Douglas and those who acted with him, voted that amendment down, notwithstanding it expressed exactly the thing they said was the true intent and meaning of the law. I have called attention to the fact that in subsequent times, a decision of the Supreme Court has been made in which it has been declared that a Territorial Legislature has no constitutional right to exclude slavery.[12] And I have argued and said that for men who did intend that the people of the territory should have the right to exclude slavery absolutely and unconditionally, the voting down of Chase's amendment is wholly inexplicable. It is a puzzle—a riddle. But I have said that with men who did look forward to such a decision, or who had it in contemplation, that such a decision of the Supreme Court would or might be made, the voting down of that amendment would be perfectly rational and intelligible. It would keep Congress from coming in collision with the decision when it was made. Anybody can conceive that if there was an intention or expectation that such a decision was to follow, it would not be a very desirable party attitude to get into for the Supreme Court—all or nearly all its members belonging to the same party—to decide one way, when the party in Congress had decided the other way. Hence it would be very rational for men expecting such a decision, to keep the niche in that law clear for it. After pointing this out, I tell Judge Douglas that it looks to me as though here was the reason why Chase's amendment was voted down. I tell him that as he did it, and knows why he did it, if it was done for a reason different from this, *he knows what that reason was, and can tell us what it was.* I tell him, also, it will be vastly more satisfactory to the country, for him to give some other plausible, intelligible reason *why* it was voted down than to stand upon his dignity and call people liars. (*Loud cheers*) Well, on Saturday[13] he did make his answer, and what do you think it was? He says if I had only taken upon myself to tell the whole truth about that amendment of Chase's no explanation would have been necessary on his part—or words to that effect. Now, I say here, that I am quite unconscious of having suppressed anything material to the case, and I am very frank to admit if there is any sound reason other than that which appeared to me material, it is quite fair for him to present it. What reason does he propose? That when Chase came forward with his amendment expressly authorizing the people to exclude slavery from the limits of every Territory, Gen. Cass[14] proposed to Chase, if he (Chase) would add to his amendment that the people should have the power to *introduce* or exclude, they would let it go. (This is substantially all of his reply.) And because Chase would not do that, they voted his amendment down. Well, it turns out, I believe, upon examination, that General Cass took some part in the little running debate upon that amendment, and then ran away *and did not vote on it at all.* (*Laughter*) Is not that the fact? So confident, as I think, was Gen. Cass, that there was a snake somewhere about, he chose to run away from the whole thing. This is an inference I draw from the fact that though he took part in the debate, his name does not appear in the ayes and noes [nays]. But does Judge Douglas' reply amount to a satisfactory answer? (*Cries of "yes," "yes," and "no," "no"*) There is some little difference of opinion here. (*Laughter*) But I ask attention to a

13  In the Ottawa debate.

14  Lewis Cass was a Democratic senator from Michigan. See "Eulogy for Zachary Taylor, July 25, 1850," note 26, in this volume.

15   In a July 17, 1858 speech at Springfield, Illinois, Lincoln renewed his charge, made in his "House Divided" speech of June 16, of a conspiracy involving Douglas, former president Pierce, President Buchanan, and Chief Justice Taney to nationalize slavery. See "First Debate with Stephen A. Douglas at Ottawa, Illinois," note 37. Douglas denied the conspiracy charge in a July 27, 1858, speech in Clinton, Illinois, and in his closing remarks at the first debate in Ottawa. At the Ottawa debate Douglas responded strongly to Lincoln's charge: "[Lincoln] then said that when he made it he did not know whether it was true or not, but inasmuch as Judge Douglas had not denied it . . . he repeated it as a charge of conspiracy against me, thus charging me with moral turpitude." Labeling the charge "an infamous lie," Douglas proceeded to attack his opponent's honesty: "Mr. Lincoln has not the character enough for integrity and truth merely on his own *ipse dixit* to arraign President Buchanan, President Pierce, and nine judges of the Supreme Court." "There is an unpardonable presumption in a man," he continued, "putting himself up before thousands of people, and pretending that his *ipse dixit,* without proof, without fact and without truth, is enough to bring down and destroy the purest and best of living men." Douglas again questioned Lincoln's honesty concerning these charges in his response to Lincoln in the Freeport debate. *CW,* 2:521; 3:34–35.

few more views bearing on the question of whether it amounts to a satisfactory answer. The men, who were determined that that amendment should not get into the bill and spoil the place where the Dred Scott decision was to come in, sought an excuse to get rid of it somewhere. One of these ways—one of these excuses—was to ask Chase to add to his proposed amendment a provision that the people might *introduce* slavery if they wanted to. They very well knew Chase would do no such thing—that Mr. Chase was one of the men differing from them on the broad principle of his insisting that freedom was *better* than slavery—a man who would not consent to enact a law, penned with his own hand, by which he was made to recognize slavery on the one hand and liberty on the other as *precisely equal;* and when they insisted on his doing this, they very well knew they insisted on that which he would not for a moment think of doing, and that they were only bluffing him. I believe (I have not, since he made his answer, had a chance to examine the journals or *Congressional Globe,* and therefore speak from memory)—I believe the state of the bill at that time, according to parliamentary rules, was such that no member could propose an additional amendment to Chase's amendment. I rather think this is the truth—the Judge shakes his head. Very well. I would like to know, then, *if they wanted Chase's amendment fixed over, why somebody else could not have offered to do it?* If they wanted it amended, why did they not offer the amendment? Why did they stand there taunting and quibbling at Chase? (*Laughter*) Why did they not *put it in themselves?* But to put it on the other ground; suppose that there was such an amendment offered, and Chase's was an amendment to an amendment; until one is disposed of by parliamentary law, you cannot pile another on. Then all these gentlemen had to do was to vote Chase's on, and then in the amended form in which the whole stood, add their own amendment to it if they wanted it put in that shape. This was all they were obliged to do, and the ayes and noes [nays] show that there were 36 who voted it down, against 10 who voted in favor of it. The 36 held entire sway and control. They could in some form or other have put that bill in the exact shape they wanted. If there was a rule preventing their amending it at the time, they could pass that, and then Chase's amendment being merged, put it in the shape they wanted. They did not choose to do so, but they went into a quibble with Chase to get him to add what they knew he would not add, and because he would not, they stand upon that flimsy pretext for voting down what they argued was the meaning and intent of their own bill. They left room thereby for this Dred Scott decision, which goes very far to make slavery national throughout the United States.

I pass one or two points I have because my time will very soon expire, but I must be allowed to say that Judge Douglas recurs again, as he did upon one or two other occasions,[15] to the enormity of Lincoln—an insignificant individual like Lincoln—upon his *ipse dixit*[16] charging a conspiracy upon a large number of members of Congress, the Supreme Court and two Presidents, to nationalize slavery. I want to say that, in the first place, I have made no charge of this sort upon my *ipse dixit*. I have only arrayed the evidence tending to prove it, and presented it to the understanding of others, saying what I think it proves, but giving you the means of judging whether it proves it or not. This is precisely what I have done. I have not placed it upon my *ipse dixit* at all. On this occasion, I wish to recall his attention to a piece of evidence which I brought forward at Ottawa[17] on Saturday, showing that he had made substantially the *same charge* against substantially the *same persons,* excluding his dear self from the category. I ask him to give some attention to the evidence which I brought forward, that he himself had discovered a "fatal blow being struck" against the right of the people to exclude slavery from their limits, which fatal blow he assumed as in evidence in an article in the Washington *Union,* published "by authority." I ask by whose authority? He discovers a similar or identical provision in the Lecompton Constitution. Made by whom? The framers of that Constitution. Advocated by whom? By all the members of the party in the nation, who advocated the introduction of Kansas into the Union under the Lecompton Constitution.

I have asked his attention to the evidence that he arrayed to prove that such a fatal blow was being struck, and to the facts which he brought forward in support of that charge—being identical with the one which he thinks so villainous in me. He pointed it not at a newspaper editor merely, but at the President and his Cabinet and the members of Congress advocating the Lecompton Constitution and those framing that instrument. I must again be permitted to remind him, that although my *ipse dixit* may not be as great as his, yet it somewhat reduces the force of his calling my attention to the *enormity* of my making a like charge against him. (*Loud applause*)

Go on, Judge Douglas.

## Mr. Douglas' Speech

Ladies and Gentlemen[18]—The silence with which you have listened to Mr. Lincoln during his hour is creditable to this vast audience, composed of

16 An assertion made but not proved.

17 In the Ottawa debate Lincoln quoted passages from a March 22, 1858, Douglas speech in which the senator made a similar conspiracy charge against the *Washington Union* and the Buchanan administration it supported. See "First Debate with Stephen A. Douglas, at Ottawa, Illinois," notes 41 and 43.

18 As Douglas rose to speak he was hit on his shoulder by a melon thrown by someone in the crowd. Burlingame, *Abraham Lincoln,* 1:504.

men of various political parties. Nothing is more honorable to any large mass of people assembled for the purpose of a fair discussion, than that kind and respectful attention that is yielded not only to your political friends, but to those who are opposed to you in politics.

. . .

In a few moments I will proceed to review the answers which he has given to these interrogatories; but in order to relieve his anxiety I will first respond to those which he has presented to me. Mark you, he has not presented interrogatories which have ever received the sanction of the party with which I am acting, and hence he has no other foundation for them than his own curiosity. (*"That's a fact"*)

First, he desires to know if the people of Kansas shall form a constitution by means entirely proper and unobjectionable and ask admission into the Union as a State, before they have the requisite population for a member of Congress, whether I will vote for that admission. Well, now, I regret exceedingly that he did not answer that interrogatory himself before he put it to me, in order that we might understand, and not be left to infer, on which side he is. (*"Good," "good"*) Mr. Trumbull, during the last session of Congress, voted from the beginning to the end against the admission of Oregon, although a free State, because she had not the requisite population for a member of Congress. (*"That's it"*) Mr. Trumbull would not consent, under any circumstances, to let a State, free or slave, come into the Union until it had the requisite population. As Mr. Trumbull is in the field, fighting for Mr. Lincoln, I would like to have Mr. Lincoln answer his own question and tell me whether he is fighting Trumbull on that issue or not. (*"Good, put it to him," and cheers.*) But I will answer his question. In reference to Kansas; it is my opinion, that as she has population enough to constitute a slave State, she has people enough for a free State. (*Cheers*) I will not make Kansas an exceptional case to the other States of the Union. (*"Sound," and "hear, hear"*) I hold it to be a sound rule of universal application to require a territory to contain the requisite population for a member of Congress, before it is admitted as a State into the Union. I made that proposition in the Senate in 1856, and I renewed it during the last session, in a bill providing that no territory of the United States should form a constitution and apply for admission until it had the requisite population. On another occasion I proposed that neither Kansas, or [*sic*] any other territory, should be admitted until it had the requisite population. Congress did not adopt any of my propositions containing this general rule, but did make an exception of Kansas. I will not stand by that exception. (*Cheers*) Either Kansas must come in as a free State, with whatever population she may have, or the rule must be applied to all the other territories alike. (*Cheers*) I therefore answer at once, that it having been decided that Kansas has people enough for a slave State, I hold that she has enough for a free State. (*"Good," and applause*) I hope Mr. Lincoln is satisfied with my answer; (*"He ought to be," and cheers*) and now I would like to get his answer to his own interrogatory—whether or not he will vote to admit Kansas before she has the requisite population. (*"Hit him again"*) I want to know whether he will vote to admit Oregon before that Territory has the requisite population. Mr. Trumbull will not, and the same reason that commits Mr. Trumbull against the admission of Oregon, commits him against Kansas, even if she should apply for admission as a free State. (*"You've got him," and cheers*) If there is any sincerity, any truth in the argument of Mr. Trumbull in the Senate against the admission of Oregon because she had not 93,420 people, although her population was larger than that of Kansas, he stands pledged against the admission of both Oregon and Kansas until they have 93,420 inhabitants. I would like Mr. Lincoln to answer this question. I would like him to take his own medicine. (*Laughter*) If he differs with Mr. Trumbull, let him answer his argument against the admission of Oregon, instead of poking questions at me. (*"Right, good, good," laughter and cheers*)

The next question propounded to me by Mr. Lincoln is, can the people of a territory in any lawful way against the wishes of any citizen of the United States; exclude slavery from their limits prior to the formation of a State Constitution? I answer emphatically, as Mr. Lincoln has heard me answer a hundred times from every stump in Illinois, that in my opinion the people of a territory can, by lawful means, exclude slavery from their limits prior to the formation of a State Constitution. (*Enthusiastic applause*) Mr. Lincoln knew that I had answered that question over and over again. He heard me argue the Nebraska bill on that principle all over the State in 1854, in 1855 and in 1856, and he has no excuse for pretending to be in doubt as to my position on that question. It matters not what way the Supreme Court may hereafter decide as to the abstract question whether slavery may or may not go into a territory under the constitution, the people have the lawful means to introduce it or exclude it as they please, for the reason that slavery cannot exist a day or an hour anywhere, unless it is supported by local police regulations. (*"Right, right"*) Those police regulations can only be established by the local legislature, and if the people are opposed to slavery they will elect representatives to that body who will by unfriendly legislation ef-

19 Douglas's answer to Lincoln's second question is his so-called Freeport Doctrine that, according to legend, destroyed his chances of winning the 1860 presidential election because it alienated Southern Democrats. The senator's answer may have attracted votes in the senate race from moderate Illinois voters who were supporters of popular sovereignty. See Holzer, *The Lincoln-Douglas Debates,* 89.

20 William Henry Seward of New York was a Whig and later a Republican in politics. He served his state as governor from 1838 to 1842 and as a U.S. senator from 1849 to 1861. He was appointed secretary of state by President Lincoln and served in that post from 1861 to 1869. Neely, *Lincoln Encyclopedia,* 272–275; "Seward, William Henry," Biographical Directory of the United States Congress, http://bioguide.congress.gov/scripts/biodisplay.pl?index=s000261 (accessed December 22, 2014).

21 James Parker Hale (1806–1873) of New Hampshire began his political career as a Democrat, but switched to the Free Soil Party and later joined the Republican Party. He served in the U.S. Congress as a Democrat from 1843 to 1845. In 1846 he was elected to the U.S. Senate as a member of the Free Soil Party and served in that chamber from 1847 to 1853. He was a candidate for president of the United States on the Free Soil ticket in 1852. He returned to the U.S. Senate in 1855, serving until 1865. "Hale, James Parker," Biographical Directory of the United States Congress, http://bioguide.congress.gov/biodisplay.pl?index=H000034 (accessed December 22, 2014).

fectually prevent the introduction of it into their midst. If, on the contrary, they are for it, their legislation will favor its extension. Hence, no matter what the decision of the Supreme Court may be on that abstract question, still the right of the people to make a slave territory or a free territory is perfect and complete under the Nebraska bill. I hope Mr. Lincoln deems my answer satisfactory on that point.[19]

. . .

The third question which Mr. Lincoln presented is, if the Supreme Court of the United States shall decide that a State of this Union cannot exclude slavery from its own limits will I submit to it? I am amazed that Lincoln should ask such a question. (*"A school boy knows better"*) Yes, a school boy does know better. Mr. Lincoln's object is to cast an imputation upon the Supreme Court. He knows that there never was but one man in America, claiming any degree of intelligence or decency, who ever for a moment pretended such a thing. It is true that the Washington *Union,* in an article published on the 17th of last December, did put forth that doctrine, and I denounced the article on the floor of the Senate, in a speech which Mr. Lincoln now pretends was against the President. The *Union* had claimed that slavery had a right to go into the free States, and that any provision in the Constitution or laws of the free States to the contrary were null and void. I denounced it in the Senate, as I said before, and I was the first man who did. Lincoln's friends, Trumbull, and Seward,[20] and Hale,[21] and Wilson,[22] and the whole Black Republican side of the Senate were silent. They left it to me to denounce it. (*Cheers*) And what was the reply made to me on that occasion? Mr. Toombs,[23] of Georgia, got up and undertook to lecture me on the ground that I ought not to have deemed the article worthy of notice, and ought not to have replied to it; that there was not one man, woman or child south of the Potomac, in any slave State, who did not repudiate any such pretension. Mr. Lincoln knows that that reply was made on the spot, and yet now he asks this question. He might as well ask me, suppose Mr. Lincoln should steal a horse would I sanction it; (*Laughter*) and it would be as genteel in me to ask him, in the event he stole a horse, what ought to be done with him. He casts an imputation upon the Supreme Court of the United States by supposing that they would violate the Constitution of the United States. I tell him that such a thing is not possible. (*Cheers*) It would be an act of moral treason that no man on the bench could ever descend to. Mr. Lincoln himself would never in his partizan feelings so far forget what was right as to be guilty of such an act. (*"Good, good"*)

The fourth question of Mr. Lincoln is, are you in favor of acquiring additional territory in disregard as to how such acquisition may effect [*sic*] the Union on the slavery questions. This question is very ingeniously and cunningly put.

The Black Republican creed lays it down expressly, that under no circumstances shall we acquire any more territory unless slavery is first prohibited in the country. I ask Mr. Lincoln whether he is in favor of that proposition. Are you (addressing Mr. Lincoln) opposed to the acquisition of any more territory, under any circumstances, unless slavery is prohibited in it? That he does not like to answer. When I ask him whether he stands up to that article in the platform of his party, he turns, yankee-fashion, and without answering it, asks me whether I am in favor of acquiring territory without regard to how it may affect the Union on the slavery question. (*"Good"*) I answer that whenever it becomes necessary, in our growth and progress to acquire more territory, that I am in favor of it, without reference to the question of slavery, and when we have acquired it, I will leave the people free to do as they please, either to make it slave or free territory, as they prefer. It is idle to tell me or you that we have territory enough. Our fathers supposed that we had enough when our territory extended to the Mississippi river, but a few years' growth and expansion satisfied them that we needed more, and the Louisiana territory, from the West branch of the Mississippi, to the British possessions, was acquired. Then we acquired Oregon, then California and New Mexico. We have enough now for the present, but this is a young and a growing nation. It swarms as often as a hive of bees, and as new swarms are turned out each year, there must be hives in which they can gather and make their honey. (*"Good"*) In less than fifteen years, if the same progress that has distinguished this country for the last fifteen years continues, every foot of vacant land between this and the Pacific ocean, owned by the United States, will be occupied. Will you not continue to increase at the end of fifteen years as well as now? I tell you, increase, and multiply, and expand, is the law of this nation's existence. (*"Good"*) You cannot limit this great republic by mere boundary lines, saying, "thus far shalt thou go, and no further." Any one of you gentlemen might as well say to a son twelve years old that he is big enough, and must not grow any larger, and in order to prevent his growth put a hoop around him to keep him to his present size. What would be the result? Either the hoop must burst and be rent asunder, or the child must die. So it would be with this great nation. With our natural increase, growing with a rapidity unknown in any other part of the globe, with the tide of emigration that is fleeing

22 Henry Wilson (1812–1875) was a Republican from Massachusetts. He was elected to the U.S. Senate by a coalition of Free-Soilers, Know-Nothings, antislavery Whigs, and anti-Nebraska Democrats on January 31, 1855, to fill the vacancy caused by the resignation of Edward Everett. Wilson soon joined the Republican Party. He served in the Senate from 1855 to 1873. In 1872 he was elected vice president of the United States on the Republican ticket headed by Ulysses Grant. He served as vice president from March 4, 1873, to his death on November 22, 1875. "Wilson, Henry," ibid., http://bioguide.congress.gov/biodisplay. pl?index=W000585 (accessed December 22, 2014).

23 Robert Augustus Toombs (1810–1885) was a congressman and senator from Georgia. He was elected to the U.S. House of Representatives as a Whig and served in that chamber from 1845 to 1853. He was elected to the U.S. Senate as a Democrat in 1852 and held his seat until he withdrew in 1861. During the Civil War, he served in the Confederate congress and as secretary of state of the Confederate States of America. "Toombs, Robert Augustus," ibid., http:// bioguide.congress.gov/biodisplay. pl?index=T000313 (accessed December 22, 2014).

Frederick Douglass. Photograph (ca. 1840s). Earliest known photograph of Douglass. During the Freeport debate, Stephen Douglas attempted to connect Lincoln to the well-known African American abolitionist.

24 Douglas may have been referring to H. Ford Douglas (1831–1865), a black abolitionist; born into slavery in Virginia, he escaped soon after his fifteenth birthday. Self-educated, this Douglas moved to Cleveland and later Chicago, where he became active in the city's free black community and an ardent supporter of black emigration to Africa, Haiti, Central America, and Canada, and of the abolition of slavery. Douglas was no relation to Frederick Douglass. Robert L. Harris Jr., "H. Ford Douglas Afro-American Antislavery Emigrationist," *Journal of Negro History* 62 (July 1997): 217–234.

from despotism in the old world to seek a refuge in our own, there is a constant torrent pouring into this country that requires more land, more territory upon which to settle, and just as fast as our interests and our destiny require additional territory in the north, in the south, or on the islands of the ocean, I am for it, and when we acquire it will leave the people, according to the Nebraska bill, free to do as they please on the subject of slavery and every other question. (*"Good, good," "hurrah for Douglas"*)

I trust now that Mr. Lincoln will deem himself answered on his four points. He racked his brain so much in devising these four questions that he exhausted himself, and had not strength enough to invent the others. (*Laughter*) As soon as he is able to hold a council with his advisers, Lovejoy, Farnsworth, and Fred. Douglass, he will frame and propound others. (*"Good, good," &c. Renewed laughter, in which Mr. Lincoln feebly joined, saying that he hoped with their aid to get seven questions, the number asked him by Judge Douglas, and so make conclusions even*) You Black Republicans who say good, I have no doubt think that they are all good men. (*"White, white"*) I have reason to recollect that some people in this country think that Fred. Douglass is a very good man. The last time I came here to make a speech, while talking from the stand to you, people of Freeport, as I am doing to-day, I saw a carriage and a magnificent one it was, drive up and take a position on the outside of the crowd; a beautiful young lady was sitting on the box seat, whilst Fred. Douglass and her mother reclined inside, and the owner of the carriage acted as driver. (*Laughter, cheers, cries of "right, what have you to say against it," &c.*) I saw this in your own town. (*"What of it"*) All I have to say of it is this, that if you, Black Republicans, think that the negro ought to be on a social equality with your wives and daughters, and ride in a carriage with your wife, whilst you drive the team, you have a perfect right to do so. (*"Good, good," and cheers, mingled with hooting and cries of "white, white"*) I am told that one of Fred. Douglass' kinsmen, another rich black negro, is now traveling in this part of the State making speeches for his friend Lincoln as the champion of black men.[24] (*"White men, white men," and "what have you got to say against it." "That's right," &c.*) All I have to say on that subject is that those of you who believe that the negro is your equal and ought to be on an equality with you socially, politically, and legally; have a right to entertain those opinions, and of course will vote for Mr. Lincoln. (*"Down with the negro," "no, no," &c.*)

I have a word to say on Mr. Lincoln's answer to the interrogatories contained in my speech at Ottawa, and which he has pretended to reply to here to-day. Mr. Lincoln makes a great parade of the fact that I quoted a platform as having been adopted by the Black Republican party at Springfield in 1854, which, it turns out, was adopted at another place. Mr. Lincoln loses sight of the thing itself in his ecstasies over the mistake I made in stating the place where it was done. He thinks that that platform was not adopted on the right "spot."[25]

When I put the direct questions to Mr. Lincoln to ascertain whether he now stands pledged to that creed—to the unconditional repeal of the fugitive slave law, a refusal to admit any more slave States into the Union even if the people want them, a determination to apply the Wilmot Proviso[26] not only to all the territory, we now have, but all that we may hereafter acquire, he refused to answer, and his followers say, in excuse, that the resolutions upon which I based my interrogatories were not adopted at the "*right spot.*" (*Laughter and applause*) Lincoln and his political friends are great on "*spots.*" (*Renewed laughter*) In Congress, as a representative of this State, he declared the Mexican war to be unjust and infamous, and would not support it, or acknowledge his own country to be right in the contest, because he said that American blood was not shed on American soil in the "*right spot.*" (*"Lay on to him"*) And now he cannot answer the questions I put to him at Ottawa because the resolutions I read were not adopted at the *"right spot."* It may be possible that I was led into an error as to the *spot* on which the resolutions I then read were proclaimed, but I was not, and am not in error as to the fact of their forming the basis of the creed of the Republican party when that party was first organized.

. . .

Mr. Lincoln made a speech when he was nominated for the U.S. Senate[27] which covers all these abolition platforms. He there lays down a proposition so broad in its abolitionism as to cover the whole ground.

> "In my opinion it (the slavery agitation) will not cease until a crisis shall have been reached and passed. 'A house divided against itself cannot stand.' I believe this Government cannot endure permanently half Slave and half Free. I do not expect the house to fall—but I do expect it will cease to be divided. It will become all one thing or all the other. Either the opponents of Slavery will arrest the further spread of it, and place it where the public mind shall rest in the belief that it is in the course of ultimate extinction, or its advocates will push it forward till it shall become alike lawful in all the States—old as well as new, North as well as South."

25 In the paragraph that follows, Douglas ridiculed Lincoln's "Spot" resolutions against the Mexican War, introduced by Lincoln in the U.S. House of Representatives on December 22, 1847. Lincoln was pilloried by Democrats at the time as "Spotty" Lincoln. See "'Spot' Resolutions in the U.S. House of Representatives, December 22, 1847," in this volume.

26 An amendment offered in the U.S. House of Representatives by Pennsylvania congressman David Wilmot that banned slavery in all territory gained as a result of the War with Mexico. See "Speech on the Kansas-Nebraska Act at Peoria, Illinois, October 16, 1854," notes 14 and 15.

27 See "'House Divided' Address, Springfield, Illinois, June 16, 1858."

There you find that Mr. Lincoln lays down the doctrine that this Union cannot endure divided as our Fathers made it, with free and slave States. He says they must all become one thing, or all the other; that they must be all free or all slave, or else the Union cannot continue to exist. It being his opinion that to admit any more slave States, to continue to divide the Union into free and slave States, will dissolve it. I want to know of Mr. Lincoln whether he will vote for the admission of another Slave state. (*Cries of "Bring him out"*)

He tells you the Union cannot exist unless the States are all free or all slave; he tells you that he is opposed to making them all slave, and hence he is for making them all free, in order that the Union may exist; and yet he will not say that he will not vote against the admission of another slave State, knowing that the Union must be dissolved if he votes for it. (*Great laughter*) I ask you if that is fair dealing? The true intent and inevitable conclusion to be drawn from his first Springfield speech is, that he is opposed to the admission of any more slave States under any circumstance. If he is so opposed why not say so? If he believes this Union cannot endure divided into free and slave States, that they must all become free in order to save the Union, he is bound, as an honest man, to vote against any more slave States. If he believes it he is bound to do it. Show me that it is my duty in order to save the Union to do a particular act, and I will do it if the constitution does not prohibit it. (*Applause*) I am not for the dissolution of the Union under any circumstances. (*Renewed applause*) I will pursue no course of conduct that will give just cause for the dissolution of the Union. The hope of the friends of freedom throughout the world rests upon the perpetuity of this Union. The down-trodden and oppressed people who are suffering under European despotism all look with hope and anxiety to the American Union as the only resting place and permanent home of freedom and self-government.

Mr. Lincoln says that he believes that this Union cannot continue to endure with slave States in it, and yet he will not tell you distinctly whether he will vote for or against the admission of any more slave States, but says he would not like to be put to the test. (*Laughter*) I do not think he will be put to the test. (*Renewed laughter*) I do not think that the people of Illinois desire a man to represent them who would not like to be put to the test on the performance of a high constitutional duty. (*Cries of "good"*) I will retire in shame from the Senate of the United States when I am not willing to be put to the test in the performance of my duty. I have been put to severe tests. (*"That is so"*) I have stood by my principles in fair weather and in foul, in the sunshine and in the rain. I have defended the great principles of self-government here among you when Northern sentiment ran in a torrent against me. (*A VOICE,—"that is so"*) and I have defended that same great principle when Southern sentiment came down like an avalanche upon me. I was not afraid of any test they put to me. I knew I was right—I knew my principles were sound—I knew that the people would see in the end that I had done right, and I knew that the God of Heaven would smile upon me if I was faithful in the performance of my duty. (*Cries of "good," cheers and laughter*)

Mr. Lincoln makes a charge of corruption against the Supreme Court of the United States, and two Presidents of the United States, and attempts to bolster it up by saying that I did the same against the Washington *Union*. Suppose I did make that charge of corruption against the Washington *Union,* when it was true, does that justify him in making a false charge against me and others? That is the question I would put. He says that at the time the Nebraska bill was introduced, and before it was passed there was a conspiracy between the Judges of the Supreme Court, President Pierce, President Buchanan and myself by that bill, and the decision of the Court to break down the barrier and establish slavery all over the Union. Does he not know that that charge is historically false as against President Buchanan? He knows that Mr. Buchanan was at that time in England, representing this country with distinguished ability at the Court of St. James, that he was there for a long time before and did not return for a year or more after.[28] He knows that to be true, and that fact proves his charge to be false as against Mr. Buchanan. (*Cheers*) Then again, I wish to call his attention to the fact that at the time the Nebraska bill was passed the Dred Scott case was not before the Supreme Court at all; it was not upon the docket of the Supreme Court; it had not been brought there, and the Judges in all probability, knew nothing of it. Thus the history of the country proves the charge to be false as against them. As to President Pierce, his high character as a man of integrity and honor is enough to vindicate him from such a charge, (*Laughter and applause*) and as to myself, I pronounce the charge an infamous lie, whenever and wherever made, and by whomsoever made.

. . .

28 James Buchanan served as minister to the Court of St. James's (Great Britain) under President Franklin Pierce from 1853 to 1855.

## Mr. Lincoln's Rejoinder

My friends, it will readily occur to you that I cannot in half an hour notice all the things that so able a man as Judge Douglas can say in an hour and a half, and I hope, therefore, if there be anything that he has said upon which you would like to hear something from me, but which I omit to comment upon, you will bear in mind that it would be expecting an impossibility for me to go over his whole ground. I can but take up some of the points that he has dwelt upon, and employ my half-hour specially on them.

The first thing I have to say to you is a word in regard to Judge Douglas' declaration about the "vulgarity and blackguardism" in the audience—that no such thing, as he says, was shown by any Democrat while I was speaking. Now, I only wish, by way of reply on this subject, to say that while *I* was speaking *I* used no "vulgarity or blackguardism" towards any Democrat. (*Great laughter and applause*)

Now, my friends, I come to all this long portion of the Judge's speech—perhaps half of it—which he has devoted to the various resolutions and platforms that have been adopted in the different counties in the different Congressional districts, and in the Illinois Legislature—which he supposes are at variance with the positions I have assumed before you to-day. It is true that many of these resolutions are at variance with the positions I have here assumed. All I have to ask is that we talk reasonably and rationally about it. I happen to know, the Judge's opinion to the contrary notwithstanding, that I have never tried to conceal my opinions, nor tried to deceive any one in reference to them. He may go and examine all the members who voted for me for United States Senator in 1855, after the election of 1854. They were pledged to certain things here at home, and were determined to have pledges from me, and if he will find any of these persons who will tell him anything inconsistent with what I say now, I will resign, or rather retire from the race, and give him no more trouble. (*Applause*) The plain truth is this: At the introduction of the Nebraska policy, we believed there was a new era being introduced in the history of the Republic, which tended to the spread and perpetuation of slavery. But in our opposition to that measure we did not agree with one another in everything. The people in the north end of the State were for stronger measures of opposition than we of the central and southern portions of the State, but we were all opposed to the Nebraska doctrine. We had that one feeling and that one sentiment in common. You at the north end met in your Conventions and passed your resolutions. We in the middle of the State and further south did not hold such Conventions and pass the same resolutions, although we had in general a common view and a common sentiment. So that these meetings which the Judge has alluded to, and the resolutions he has read from were local and did not spread over the whole State. We at last met together in 1856 from all parts of the State, and we agreed upon a common platform. You, who held more extreme notions either yielded those notions, or if not wholly yielding them, agreed to yield them practically, for the sake of embodying the opposition to the measures which the opposite party were pushing forward at that time. We met you then, and if there was anything yielded, it was for practical purposes. We agreed then upon a platform for the party throughout the entire State of Illinois, and now we are all bound as a party, *to that platform.*[29] And I say here to you, if any one expects of me—in the case of my elec[tion]—that I will do anything not signified by our Republican platform and my answers here to-day, I tell you very frankly that person will be deceived. I do not ask for the vote of any one who supposes that I have secret purposes or pledges that I dare not speak out. Cannot the Judge be satisfied? If he fears, in the unfortunate case of my election, (*Laughter*) that my going to Washington will enable me to advocate sentiments contrary to those which I expressed when you voted for and elected me, I assure him that his fears are wholly needless and groundless. Is the Judge really afraid of any such thing? (*Laughter*) I'll tell you what he is afraid of. *He is afraid we'll all pull together.* (*Applause, and cries of "we will, we will"*) This is what alarms him more than anything else. (*Laughter*) For my part, I do hope that all of us, entertaining a common sentiment in opposition to what appears to us a design to nationalize and perpetuate slavery, will waive minor differences on questions which either belong to the dead past or the distant future, and all pull together in this struggle. What are your sentiments? (*"We will, we will," and loud cheers*) If it be true, that on the ground which I occupy—ground which I occupy as frankly and boldly as Judge Douglas does his—my views, though partly coinciding with yours, are not as perfectly in accordance with your feelings as his are, I do say to you in all candor, Go for him and not for me. I hope to deal in all things fairly with Judge Douglas, and with the people of the State, in this contest. And if I should never be elected to any office, I trust I may go down with no stain of falsehood upon my reputation,—notwithstanding the hard opinions Judge Douglas chooses to entertain of me. (*Laughter*)

The Judge has again addressed himself to the abolition tendencies of a speech of mine, made at Springfield in June last. I have so often tried to answer what he is always saying on that melancholy theme, that I almost turn

29 Lincoln referred to a meeting held in Bloomington, Illinois, on May 29, 1856, which is considered the founding convention of the state's Republican Party. Conservatives and moderates controlled the meeting, at which delegates drafted a platform that was anything but radical. The platform called for the prohibition of slavery's extension into territories "heretofore free" and the admission of Kansas as a free state. It was deliberately vague concerning slavery in other territories and the admission of other slave states. Gienapp, *Origins of the Republican Party,* 295.

with disgust from the discussion—from the repetition of an answer to it. I trust that nearly all of this intelligent audience have read that speech. (*"We have; we have"*) If you have, I may venture to leave it to you to inspect it closely, and see whether it contains any of those "bugaboos" which frighten Judge Douglas. (*Laughter*)

The Judge complains that I did not fully answer his questions. If I have the sense to comprehend and answer those questions, I have done so fairly. If it can be pointed out to me how I can more fully and fairly answer him, I aver I have not the sense to see how it is to be done. He says I do not declare I would in any event vote for the admission of a slave State into the Union. If I have been fairly reported he will see that I did give an explicit answer to his interrogatories. I did not merely say that I would dislike to be put to the test; but I said clearly, if I were put to the test, and a Territory from which slavery had been excluded should present herself with a State Constitution sanctioning slavery—a most extraordinary thing and wholly unlikely ever to happen—I did not see how I could avoid voting for her admission. But he refuses to understand that I said so, and he wants this audience to understand that I did not say so. Yet it will be so reported in the printed speech that he cannot help seeing it.

He says if I should vote for the admission of a Slave State I would be voting for a dissolution of the Union, because I hold that the Union can not permanently exist half slave and half free. I repeat that I do not believe this Government *can* endure permanently half slave and half free, yet I do not admit, nor does it at all follow, that the admission of a single Slave State will permanently fix the character and establish this as a universal slave nation. The Judge is very happy indeed at working up these quibbles. (*Laughter and cheers*) Before leaving the subject of answering questions I aver as my confident belief, when you come to see our speeches in print, that you will find every question which he has asked me more fairly and boldly and fully answered than he has answered those which I put to him. Is not that so? (*Cries of "yes, yes"*) The two speeches may be placed side by side; and I will venture to leave it to impartial judges whether his questions have not been more directly and circumstantially answered than mine.

Judge Douglas says he made a charge upon the editor of the Washington *Union, alone,* of entertaining a purpose to rob the States of their power to exclude slavery from their limits. I undertake to say, and I make the direct issue, that he did *not* make his charge against the editor of the *Union* alone. (*Applause*) I will undertake to prove by the record here, that he made that charge against more and higher dignitaries than the editor of the Washington *Union.* I am quite aware that he was shirking and dodging around the form in which he put it, but I can make it manifest that he leveled his "fatal blow" against more persons than this Washington editor. Will he dodge it now by alleging that I am trying to defend Mr. Buchanan against the charge? Not at all. Am I not making the same charge myself? (*Laughter and applause*) I am trying to show that you, Judge Douglas, are a witness on my side. (*Renewed laughter*) I am not defending Buchanan, and I will tell Judge Douglas that in my opinion, when he made that charge, he had an eye farther North than he was to-day. He was then fighting against people who called *him* a Black Republican and an Abolitionist.

It is mixed all through his speech, and it is tolerably manifest that his eye was a great deal farther North than it is to-day. (*Cheers and laughter*) The Judge says that though he made this charge Toombs got up and declared there was not a man in the United States, except the editor of the *Union,* who was in favor of the doctrines put forth in that article. And thereupon, I understand that the Judge withdrew the charge. Although he had taken extracts from the newspaper, and then from the Lecompton Constitution, to show the existence of a conspiracy to bring about a "fatal blow," by which the States were to be deprived of the right of excluding slavery, it all went to pot as soon as Toombs got up and told him it was not true. (*Laughter*) It reminds me of the story that John Phoenix,[30] the California railroad surveyor, tells. He says they started out from the Plaza to the Mission of Dolores. They had two ways of determining distances. One was by a chain and pins taken over the ground. The other was by a "go-it-ometer"—an invention of his own—a three-legged instrument, with which he computed a series of triangles between the points. At night he turned to the chain-man to ascertain what distance they had come, and found that by some mistake he had merely dragged the chain over the ground without keeping any record. By the "go-it-ometer" he found he had made ten miles. Being skeptical about this, he asked a drayman who was passing how far it was to the plaza. The drayman replied it was just half a mile, and the surveyor put it down in his book—just as Judge Douglas says, after he had made his calculations and computations, he took Toombs' statement. (*Great laughter*) I have no doubt that after Judge Douglas had made his charge, he was as easily satisfied about its truth as the surveyor was of the drayman's statement of the distance to the plaza. (*Renewed laughter*) Yet it is a fact that the man who put forth all that matter which Douglas deemed a "fatal blow" at State sovereignty, was elected by the Democrats as public printer.

Now, gentlemen, you may take Judge Douglas' speech of March 22d,

30 John Phoenix, a pseudonym used by the California humorist George Horatio Derby (1823–1861). Lincoln's reference is to the book *Phoenixiana; or, Sketches and Burlesques* (New York: D. Appleton and Company, 1856), 20. See "'Phoenix' Revisited: Another Look at George Horatio Derby," *Journal of San Diego History* 26 (1980), http://www.sandiegohistory.org/journal/80spring/derby.htm (accessed December 23, 2014).

1858, beginning about the middle of page 21, and reading to the bottom of page 24, and you will find the evidence on which I say that he did not make his charge against the editor of the *Union* alone. I cannot stop to read it, but I will give it to the reporters. Judge Douglas said:

> "Mr. President, you here find several distinct propositions advanced boldly by the Washington *Union* editorially and apparently *authoritatively*, and every man who questions any of them is denounced as an abolitionist, a Free-Soiler, a fanatic. The propositions are, first, that the primary object of all government at its original institution is the protection of persons and property; second, that the Constitution of the United States declares that the citizens of each State shall be entitled to all the privileges and immunities of citizens in the several States; and that, therefore, thirdly, all State laws, whether organic or otherwise, which prohibit the citizens of one State from settling in another with their slave property, and especially declaring it forfeited, are direct violations of the original intention of the Government and Constitution of the United States; and fourth, that the emancipation of the slaves of the Northern States was a gross outrage on the rights of property, inasmuch as it was involuntarily done on the part of the owner.

> Remember that this article was published in the *Union* on the 17th of November, and on the 18th appeared the first article giving the adhesion of the *Union* to the Lecompton Constitution. It was in these words:

> > 'KANSAS AND HER CONSTITUTION—The vexed question is settled. The problem is solved. The dread point of danger is passed. All serious trouble to Kansas affairs is over and gone.'

> And a column, nearly, of the same sort. Then, when you come to look into the Lecompton Constitution, you find the same doctrine incorporated in it which was put forth editorially in the *Union*. What is it?

> > 'ARTICLE 7. *Section* 1. The right of property is before and higher than any constitutional sanction; and the right of the owner of a slave to such slave and its increase is the same and as inviolable as the right of the owner of any property whatever.'

> Then in the schedule is a provision that the Constitution may be amended after 1864 by a two-thirds vote.

> > 'But no alteration shall be made to affect the right of property in the ownership of slaves.'

It will be seen by these clauses in the Lecompton Constitution that they are identical in spirit with this *authoritative* article in the Washington *Union* of the day previous to its indorsement of this Constitution. . . .

When I saw that article in the *Union* of the 17th of November, followed by the glorification of the Lecompton Constitution on the 18th of November, and this clause in the Constitution asserting the doctrine that a State has no right to prohibit slavery within its limits, I saw that there was a *fatal blow* being struck at the sovereignty of the States of this Union."[31]

Here he says, "Mr. President, you here find several distinct propositions advanced boldly, and apparently *authoritatively.*" By whose authority, Judge Douglas? (*Great cheers and laughter*) Again, he says in another place, "It will be seen by these clauses in the Lecompton Constitution, that they are identical in spirit with this *authoritative* article." *By whose authority?* (*Renewed cheers*) Who do you mean to say authorized the publication of these articles? He knows that the Washington *Union* is considered the organ of the Administration. *I* demand of Judge Douglas *by whose authority* he meant to say those articles were published, if not by the authority of the President of the United States and his Cabinet? I defy him to show whom he referred to, if not to these high functionaries in the Federal Government. More than this, he says the articles in that paper and the provisions of the Lecompton Constitution are "identical," and being identical, he argues that the authors are co-operating and conspiring together. He does not use the word "conspiring," but what other construction can you put upon it? He winds up with this:

> "When I saw that article in the *Union* of the 17th of November,[32] followed by the glorification of the Lecompton Constitution on the 18th of November, and this clause in the Constitution asserting the doctrine that a State has no right to prohibit slavery within its limits, I saw that there was a *fatal blow* being struck at the sovereignty of the States of this Union."

I ask him if all this fuss was made over the editor of this newspaper. (*Laughter*) It would be a terribly "*fatal* blow" indeed which a single man could strike, when no President, no Cabinet officer, no member of Congress, was giving strength and efficiency to the movement. Out of respect to Judge Douglas' good sense I must believe he didn't manufacture his idea

31 Douglas, *Speech of Senator Douglas against the Admission of Kansas,* 23–24

32 The correct date of the *Washington Union* article referred to by Douglas is December 17, 1857, not November 17.

33   Views of the debate by Democratic and Republican newspapers were predictable: in each case their respective candidate won handily. One pro-Douglas sheet proclaimed, "Lincoln Again Routed! He Can't Find the Spot!"—a snide reference to Lincoln's "Spot" resolutions against the Mexican War. Pro-Lincoln papers equaled Democratic organs in hyperbole, with one running a headline declaring the "Great Caving-In on the Ottawa Forgery," ridiculing Douglas's false claim that Lincoln participated in drafting the radical Aurora platform in 1854. Cited in Zarefsky, *Lincoln, Douglas, and Slavery,* 57.

of the "fatal" character of that blow out of such a miserable scapegrace as he represents that editor to be. But the Judge's eye is farther south now. (*Laughter and cheers*) Then, it was very peculiarly and decidedly North. His hope rested on the idea of visiting the great "Black Republican" party, and making it the tail of his new kite. (*Great laughter*) He knows he was then expecting from day to day to turn Republican and place himself at the head [of] our organization. He has found that these despised "Black Republicans" estimate him by a standard which he has taught them none too well. Hence he is crawling back into his old camp, and you will find him eventually installed in full fellowship among those whom he was then battling, and with whom he now pretends to be at such fearful variance. (*Loud applause and cries of "go on, go on"*) I cannot, gentlemen, my time has expired.[33]

# Fourth Debate with Stephen A. Douglas at Charleston, Illinois

## September 18, 1858

### Mr. Lincoln's Speech[1]

LADIES AND GENTLEMEN: It will be very difficult for an audience so large as this to hear distinctly what a speaker says, and consequently it is important that as profound silence be preserved as possible.[2]

While I was at the hotel to-day an elderly gentleman called upon me to know whether I was really in favor of producing a perfect equality between the negroes and white people. (*Great laughter*) While I had not proposed to myself on this occasion to say much on that subject, yet as the question was asked me I thought I would occupy perhaps five minutes in saying something in regard to it. I will say then that I am not, nor ever have been in favor of bringing about in any way the social and political equality of the white and black races (*Applause*)—that I am not nor ever have been in favor of making voters or jurors of negroes, nor of qualifying them to hold office, nor to intermarry with white people; and I will say in addition to this that there is a physical difference between the white and black races which I believe will for ever forbid the two races living together on terms of social and political equality.[3] And inasmuch as they cannot so live, while they do remain together there must be the position of superior and inferior, and I as much as any other man am in favor of having the superior position assigned to the white race. I say upon this occasion I do not perceive that because the white man is to have the superior position the negro should be denied everything. I do not understand that because I do not want a negro woman for a slave I must necessarily want her for a wife. (*Cheers and laughter*) My understanding is that I can just let her alone. I am now in my fiftieth year, and I certainly never have had a black woman for either a slave or a wife. So it seems to me quite possible for us to get along without making either

1   The Charleston debate was the fourth of seven held between Lincoln and Douglas. After Ottawa and Freeport, a third debate took place in Jonesboro on September 15, 1858. Located in Union County, Jonesboro was a small town located in "Egypt," the southern portion of Illinois, a region known for its hostility to blacks and Republicans. For example, in the 1856 presidential election, Republican John C. Frémont received less than 4 percent in the surrounding Ninth Congressional District. Before the smallest crowd to witness the debates, a pro-Douglas audience estimated at twelve to fifteen hundred (approximately double the town's population), Douglas and Lincoln continued to argue over issues discussed in previous debates. Douglas, speaking first, accused Lincoln of adhering to a dangerous "house divided" philosophy, consorting with abolitionists, favoring equal rights for blacks, and participating in a conspiracy to win a Senate seat in 1855. Lincoln in turn denied Douglas's charges while arguing that popular sovereignty was incompatible with the *Dred Scott* decision, and again asserted that Douglas's policy would lead to the nationalization of slavery, a course opposite to that of ultimate

extinction set by the Founding Fathers. Davis and Wilson, *The Lincoln-Douglas Debates,* 83–84; Holzer, *The Lincoln-Douglas Debates,* 137–138; Guelzo, *Lincoln and Douglas,* 171–180.

2    Unlike in Jonesboro, Lincoln was in familiar territory in Charleston, the seat of Coles County in central Illinois. He had practiced law in the region when he traveled the Eighth Judicial Circuit, and he also had family ties to the surrounding area. When the Lincolns moved to Illinois from Indiana in 1830, they first settled in Macon County, near the town of Decatur. Seven years later the family moved to a farm twelve miles east of Charleston. Lincoln's father died on that farm in 1851 and was buried nearby. Lincoln's seventy-eight-year-old stepmother, Sarah Bush Lincoln, whom Lincoln rarely visited, lived in a log cabin near Charleston, and several relatives also lived in the area. Politically, Charleston and Coles County were traditionally Whig, voting solidly for Whig presidential candidates. In the 1856 election, James Buchanan won the county only because former Whigs split their votes between Republican Frémont and Know-Nothing Millard Fillmore. The large crowd at the debate (estimates range from twelve and twenty thousand) was treated to elaborate processions bearing both candidates to the debate platform, located on fairgrounds on the east side of town. Davis and Wilson, *The Lincoln-Douglas Debates,* 127–128; Guelzo, *Lincoln and Douglas,* 187–190.

3    Lincoln responded to Douglas's remarks at the Jonesboro debate accusing him of favoring the equality of blacks and whites. Commenting on Lincoln's disagreement with the *Dred Scott* decision, Douglas had compared his own views on the relationship between the two races with Lincoln's: "Mr. Lincoln objects to that decision [*Dred Scott*], first and mainly because it deprives the negro the rights of citizenship. I am as much opposed to his reason for that objection as I am to the objection itself. I hold that a negro is not and never ought to be a citizen of the United States. I hold that this government was made on the white basis, by white men, for the benefit of white men and their posterity forever, and should be administered by white men and none others. I do not believe that the Almighty made the negro capable of self-government. I am aware that all the abolition lecturers that you find traveling about through the country are in the habit of reading the Declaration of Independence to prove that all men were created equal and endowed by their Creator with certain inalienable rights, among which are life, liberty, and the pursuit of happiness. Mr. Lincoln is very much in the habit of following in the track of Lovejoy in this particular, by reading that part of the Declaration of Independence to prove that the negro was endowed by the Almighty with the inalienable right of equality with white men." *CW,* 3:112–113. After Jonesboro, Douglas stopped on September 17 at Centralia, Illinois, on his way to Charleston, where he again accused Lincoln of favoring equal rights for blacks. If Lincoln were elected senator, Douglas warned, he would fight to end slavery in the South and would give freed slaves "citizenship, the right to vote, to hold office, to become legislators, jurors and judges, and finally to marry white women." Douglas cited in Guelzo, *Lincoln and Douglas,* 186. Douglas's racial pronouncements reflected the beliefs of many among his audiences. Although Illinois was a free state, it was strongly antiblack in its laws and the attitudes of its residents. While a proslavery bias may have been confined to the southern region of the state, prejudice against blacks was pervasive throughout Illinois. By the time of the debates, Illinois laws prohibited blacks from entering the state, and blacks in the state could not vote, sue in court, serve as witnesses, hold property, or serve in the militia. Moreover, blacks had to show a certificate of freedom to reside in the state. Thus any candidate espousing equal rights for blacks would have been viewed as a dangerous radical by most Illinois residents, especially moderate former Whig voters in the central part of the state who may have hated slavery but abhorred the idea of racial equality. Lincoln and his advisers, acutely aware of the damaging effects of Douglas's charges, sought to address the senator's allegations at Charleston. As one Charleston Republican suggested, Lincoln must convince voters that he had no intention of promoting emancipation or black equality: "That as for Negro equality . . . you neither believe in it nor desire it. You desire to offer no temptations to negroes to come among us or remain with us, and therefore you do not propose to confer upon them any further social or political rights than they are now entitled." Lincoln required little prodding; his comments emphatically denying that he favored full equality for blacks, repugnant as they were to abolitionists then and seem to the modern reader now, reflected not only political calculation but also his personal beliefs at the time. Although he hated slavery and believed in the humanity of blacks and in their natural rights as codified in the Declaration of Independence, he did not favor full equality between the white and black races. He reiterated his Charleston comments throughout the rest of the campaign. In terms of his views on racial equality,

Robert Marshall Root, *Lincoln and Douglas Debate.* Oil on canvas (1918). A twentieth-century rendering of the Charleston "joint meeting."

slaves or wives of negroes. I will add to this that I have never seen to my knowledge a man, woman or child who was in favor of producing a perfect equality, social and political, between negroes and white men. I recollect of but one distinguished instance that I ever heard of so frequently as to be entirely satisfied of its correctness—and that is the case of Judge Douglas' old friend Col. Richard M. Johnson.[4] (*Laughter*) I will also add to the remarks I have made, (for I am not going to enter at large upon this subject,) that I have never had the least apprehension that I or my friends would marry negroes if there was no law to keep them from it, (*Laughter*) but as Judge Douglas and his friends seem to be in great apprehension that they might, if there were no law to keep them from it, (*Roars of laughter*) I give him the most solemn pledge that I will to the very last stand by the law of this State, which forbids the marrying of white people with negroes. (*Continued laughter and applause*) I will add one further word, which is this, that I do not understand there is any place where an alteration of the social and political relations of the negro and the white man can be made except in the

Lincoln was still evolving. Quotation is from Guelzo, *Lincoln and Douglas,* 187. See also Zarefsky, *Lincoln, Douglas, and Slavery,* 18; Foner, *The Fiery Trial,* 107–108.

4   Richard M. Johnson (1780–1850) was a Kentucky Democrat who served in the U.S. Congress from 1807 to 1819 and 1829 to 1837, and in the U.S. Senate from 1819 to 1829. He was vice president of the United States under Martin Van Buren from 1837 to 1841. Lincoln snidely referred to Johnson's sexual relationship with an African American woman who was his slave, with whom he had two mixed-race daughters. "Johnson, Richard M." Biographical Directory of the United States Congress, http://bioguide.congress.gov/

scripts/biodisplay.pl?index=j000170 (accessed December 28, 2014).

5   Lyman Trumbull gave a speech in Chicago on August 7, 1858.

6   Trumbull's speech in Alton, Illinois, occurred on August 27, 1858.

7   Douglas's Jacksonville, Illinois, speech was delivered on September 6, 1858.

8   Lincoln repeated a well-known remark made by President Andrew Jackson when he ordered the removal of federal deposits from the Bank of the United States in 1833. When his Treasury Secretary William Duane (1780–1865) refused to transfer the deposits, he was fired by the president. See Jackson's letter to Duane of June 26, 1833, in John Spencer Bassett, ed., *The Correspondence of Andrew Jackson* (Washington, DC: Carnegie Institute of Washington, 1931), 5:128. Cited in Davis and Wilson, *The Lincoln-Douglas Debates*, 133n4.

9   Trumbull's August 7 and August 27, 1858, speeches were published in the *Chicago Press and Tribune* on August 9 and August 31, 1858. Lincoln quoted from Trumbull's Alton speech using an unidentified newspaper clipping, which he included in his debates scrapbook. David C. Mearns, ed., *The Illinois Political Campaign of 1858: A Facsimile of the Printer's Copy of His Debates with Stephen A. Douglas as Edited and Prepared for the Press by Abraham Lincoln* (Washington, DC: Library of Congress, n.d.), 142 (hereafter cited as Debates Scrapbook). Trumbull's August 27 speech can also be found in *Political Debates between Hon. Abraham Lincoln and Hon. Stephen A. Douglas,* 161–165, and *CW,* 3:186–194.

10   William Bigler (1814–1880) was a Democratic politician from Pennsylvania. He was elected governor of Pennsylvania in 1851 for one term. He served his state in the U.S. Senate from 1856 to 1861. "Bigler, William," Biographical Directory of

State Legislature—not in the Congress of the United States—and as I do not really apprehend the approach of any such thing myself, and as Judge Douglas seems to be in constant horror that some such danger is rapidly approaching, I propose as the best means to prevent it that the Judge be kept at home and placed in the State Legislature to fight the measure. (*Uproarious laughter and applause*) I do not propose dwelling longer at this time on this subject.

When Judge Trumbull, our other Senator in Congress, returned to Illinois in the month of August, he made a speech at Chicago[5] in which he made what may be called a *charge* against Judge Douglas, which I understand proved to be very offensive to him. The Judge was at that time out upon one of his speaking tours through the country, and when the news of it reached him, as I am informed, he denounced Judge Trumbull in rather harsh terms for having said what he did in regard to that matter. I was traveling at that time and speaking at the same places with Judge Douglas on subsequent days, and when I heard of what Judge Trumbull had said of Douglas and what Douglas had said back again, I felt that I was in a position where I could not remain entirely silent in regard to the matter. Consequently upon two or three occasions I alluded to it, and alluded to it in no other wise than to say that in regard to the charge brought by Trumbull against Douglas, I *personally* knew nothing and sought to say nothing about it—that I did personally know Judge Trumbull—that I believed him to be a man of veracity—that I believed him to be a man of capacity sufficient to know very well whether an assertion he was making as a conclusion drawn from a set of facts, was true or false; and as a conclusion of my own from that, I stated it as my belief, if Trumbull should ever be called upon he would prove everything he had said. I said this upon two or three occasions. Upon a subsequent occasion, Judge Trumbull spoke again before an audience at Alton,[6] and upon that occasion not only repeated his charge against Douglas, but arrayed the evidence he relied upon to substantiate it. This speech was published at length; and subsequently at Jacksonville Judge Douglas alluded to the matter. In the course of his speech, and near the close of it, he stated in regard to myself what I will now read:[7] "Judge Douglas proceeded to remark that he should not hereafter occupy his time in refuting such charges made by Trumbull, but that Lincoln having indorsed the character of Trumbull for veracity, he should hold him (Lincoln) responsible for the slanders." I have done simply what I have told you, to subject me to this invitation to notice the charge. I now wish to say that it had not originally been my purpose to discuss that matter at all. But inasmuch as it seems to be the wish of Judge Douglas to hold me responsible for it, then for once in my life I will play General Jackson and to the just extent I take the responsibility.[8] (*Great applause and cries of "good, good," "hurrah for Lincoln," etc.*)

I wish to say at the beginning that I will hand to the reporters that portion of Judge Trumbull's Alton speech which was devoted to this matter, and also that portion of Judge Douglas' speech made at Jacksonville in answer to it. I shall thereby furnish the readers of this debate with the complete discussion between Trumbull and Douglas. I cannot now read them, for the reason that it would take half of my first hour to do so. I can only make some comments upon them. Trumbull's charge is in the following words: "Now, the charge is, that there was a plot entered into to have a constitution formed for Kansas and put in force without giving the people an opportunity to vote upon it, and that Mr. Douglas was in the plot."[9] I will state, without quoting further, for all will have an opportunity of reading it hereafter, that Judge Trumbull brings forward what he regards as sufficient evidence to substantiate this charge.

It will be perceived Judge Trumbull shows that Senator Bigler,[10] upon the floor of the Senate, had declared there had been a conference among the Senators, in which conference it was determined to have an Enabling Act passed for the people of Kansas to form a Constitution under, and in this conference it was agreed among them that it was best not to have a provision for submitting the Constitution to a vote of the people after it should be formed. He then brings forward to show, and showing, as he deemed, that Judge Douglas reported the bill back to the Senate with that clause stricken out. He then shows that there was a new clause inserted into the bill, which would in its nature *prevent* a reference of the Constitution back for a vote of the people—if, indeed, upon a mere silence in the law, it could be assumed that they had the right to vote upon it. These are the general statements that he has made.[11]

I propose to examine the points in Judge Douglas' speech, in which he attempts to answer that speech of Judge Trumbull's. When you come to examine Judge Douglas' speech, you will find that the first point he makes is—"Suppose it were true that there was such a change in the bill, and that I struck it out—is that a proof of a plot to force a Constitution upon them against their will?"[12] His striking out such a provision, if there was such a one in the bill, he argues does not establish the proof that it was stricken out for the purpose of robbing the people of that right. I would say, in the first place, that that would be a *most manifest* reason for it. It is true, as Judge

the United States Congress, http://bioguide.congress.gov/scripts/biodisplay.pl?index=b000459 (accessed December 29, 2014).

11  Bigler cited in Trumbull's August 27 speech. Debates Scrapbook, 143.

12  Lincoln cited Douglas's September 6, 1858, speech in Jacksonville, Illinois, from an unidentified newspaper clipping; Debates Scrapbook, 146. Douglas's speech is also found in *Political Debates between Hon. Abraham Lincoln and Hon. Stephen A. Douglas,* 165–170, and *CW,* 3:194–201.

13  In 1856, against the backdrop of violence in Kansas, Robert Toombs of Georgia introduced a bill in the Senate that would provide for an orderly process for admitting the territory as a state, including a census sponsored by the federal government, the appointment of a federal commission to ensure fair elections, and the election of a constitutional convention to draft a state constitution to be approved by a popular vote by the residents of Kansas. The bill was sent to the Committee on Territories, which was chaired by Douglas. The bill was returned to the floor of the Senate minus the popular referendum on the constitution. A clause was inserted to prevent such a vote. Although this clause was subsequently removed, Douglas was accused by anti-Nebraska senators, including Trumbull and Bigler, of hypocrisy regarding popular sovereignty—of using it as a cloak to hide his real intention of nationalizing slavery in order to curry favor with Southern slaveholders. Zarefsky, *Lincoln, Douglas, and Slavery,* 97; Guelzo, *Lincoln and Douglas,* 142–143.

14  Douglas's September 6 speech. Debates Scrapbook, 146.

Douglas states, that many Territorial bills have passed without having such a provision in them. I believe it is true, though I am not certain, that in some instances, Constitutions framed, under such bills have been submitted to a vote of the people, with the law silent upon the subject, but it does not appear that they once had their Enabling Acts framed with an express provision *for* submitting the Constitution to be framed, to a vote of the people, and then that they were stricken out when Congress did not mean to alter the effect of the law. That there have been bills which never had the provision in, I do not question; but when was that provision taken out of one that it was in? More especially does this evidence tend to prove the proposition that Trumbull advanced, when we remember that the provision was stricken out of the bill almost simultaneously with the time that Bigler says there was a conference among certain Senators, and in which it was agreed that a bill should be passed leaving that out. Judge Douglas, in answering Trumbull, omits to attend to the testimony of Bigler, that there was a meeting in which it was agreed they should so frame the bill that there should be no submission of the Constitution to a vote of the people. The Judge does not notice this part of it. If you take this as one piece of evidence, and then ascertain that simultaneously Judge Douglas struck out a provision that did require it to be submitted, and put the two together, I think it will make a pretty fair show of proof that Judge Douglas did, as Trumbull says, enter into a plot to put in force a Constitution for Kansas without giving the people any opportunity of voting upon it.

But I must hurry on. The next proposition that Judge Douglas puts is this: "But upon examination it turns out that the Toombs bill[13] never did contain a clause requiring the Constitution to be submitted."[14] This is a mere question of fact, and can be determined by evidence. I only want to ask this question—Why did not Judge Douglas say that these words were not stricken out of the Toombs bill, or this bill from which it is alleged the provision was stricken out—a bill which goes by the name of Toombs, because he originally brought it forward? I ask why, if the Judge wanted to make a direct issue with Trumbull, did he not take the exact proposition Trumbull made in his speech, and say it was not stricken out? Trumbull has given the exact words that he says were in the Toombs bill, and he alleges that when the bill came back, they were stricken out. Judge Douglas does not say that the words which Trumbull says were stricken out, were not so stricken out, but he says there was no provision in the Toombs bill to submit the Constitution to a vote of the people. We see at once that he is merely making an issue upon the meaning of the words. He has not under-

Abraham Lincoln. Photograph by Calvin Jackson (Pittsfield, IL, October 1, 1858) taken two weeks before the seventh and final debate with Douglas.

taken to say that Trumbull tells a lie about these words being stricken out; but he is really, when pushed up to it, only taking an issue upon the meaning of the words. Now, then, if there be any issue upon the meaning of the words, or if there be upon the question of fact as to whether these words were stricken out, I have before me what I suppose to be a genuine copy of the Toombs bill, in which it can be shown that the words Trumbull says were in it, were, in fact, originally there. If there be any dispute upon the fact, I have got the documents here to show they were there. If there be any

15  Trumbull's August 27 speech, Debates
Scrapbook, 143.

16  Ibid.

controversy upon the sense of the words—whether these words which were stricken out really constituted a provision for submitting the matter to a vote of the people, as that is a matter of argument, I think I may as well use Trumbull's own argument. He says that the proposition is in these words: "That the following propositions be and the same are hereby offered to the said convention of the people of Kansas when formed, for their free acceptance or rejection; which, if accepted by the convention *and ratified by the people at the election for the adoption of the Constitution,* shall be obligatory upon the United States and the said State of Kansas."[15]

Now, Trumbull alleges that these last words were stricken out of the bill when it came back, and he says this was a provision for submitting the Constitution to a vote of the people, and his argument is this: "Would it have been possible to ratify the land propositions at the election for the adoption of the Constitution, unless such an election was to be held?"[16] (*Applause and laughter*) That is Trumbull's argument. Now Judge Douglas does not meet the charge at all, but he stands up and says there was no such proposition in that bill for submitting the Constitution to be framed to a vote of the people. Trumbull admits that the language is not a direct provision for submitting it, but it is a provision necessarily implied from another provision. He asks you how it is possible to ratify the land proposition at the election for the adoption of the Constitution, if there was no election to be held for the adoption of the Constitution. And he goes on to show that it is not any less a law because the provision is put in that indirect shape than it would be if it was put directly. But I presume I have said enough to draw attention to this point, and I pass it by also.

Another one of the points that Judge Douglas makes upon Trumbull, and at very great length, is, that Trumbull, while the bill was pending, said in a speech in the Senate that he supposed the Constitution to be made would have to be submitted to the people. He asks, if Trumbull thought so then, what ground is there for anybody thinking otherwise now? Fellow citizens, this much may be said in reply: That bill had been in the hands of a party to which Trumbull did not belong. It had been in the hands of the Committee at the head of which Judge Douglas stood. Trumbull perhaps had a printed copy of the original Toombs bill. I have not the evidence on that point, except a sort of inference I draw from the general course of business there. What alterations, or what provisions in the way of altering, were going on in committee, Trumbull had no means of knowing, until the altered bill was reported back. Soon afterwards, when it was reported back, there was a discussion over it, and perhaps Trumbull in reading it hastily in

Coles County Court House, Charleston, Illinois. Photograph (ca. 1860–1898). Lincoln often argued law cases here. On September 18, 1858, hours after his fourth debate with Douglas, he made a short speech on this site.

the altered form did not perceive all the bearings of the alterations. He was hastily borne into the debate, and it does not follow that because there was something in it Trumbull did not perceive, that something did not exist. More than this, is it true that what Trumbull did can have any effect on what Douglas did? (*Applause*) Suppose Trumbull had been in the plot with these other men, would that let Douglas out of it? (*Applause and laughter*) Would it exonerate Douglas that Trumbull didn't then perceive he was in the plot? He also asks the question: Why didn't Trumbull propose to amend the bill if he thought it needed any amendment? Why, I believe that everything Judge Trumbull had proposed, particularly in connection with this question of Kansas and Nebraska, since he had been on the floor of the Senate, had been promptly voted down by Judge Douglas and his friends. He had no promise that an amendment offered by him to anything on this subject would receive the slightest consideration. Judge Trumbull did bring to the notice of the Senate at that time the fact that there was no provision for submitting the Constitution about to be made for the people of Kansas, to a vote of the people. I believe I may venture to say that Judge Douglas made some reply to this speech of Judge Trumbull's, *but he never noticed*

17 From the Toombs bill that was reported to the Senate on June 30, 1856. Both Trumbull and Douglas cite this passage in their August 27 and September 6 speeches. Ibid., 144, 146.

18 Lincoln misquoted Douglas. The senator used similar words in his September 6 speech: "Mr. Trumbull, when at Chicago, rested his charge upon the allegation that the clause requiring submission was originally in the bill and was stricken out by me. When that falsehood was exposed by a publication of the record he went to Alton and made another speech, repeating the charge, and referring to other and different evidence to sustain it. He saw that he was caught in his first falsehood, so he changed the issue." Ibid., 146.

*that part of it at all.* And so the thing passed by. I think, then, the fact that Judge Trumbull offered no amendment, does not throw much blame upon him; and if it did, it does not reach the question of fact *as to what Judge Douglas was doing.* (*Applause*) I repeat that if Trumbull had himself been in the plot, it would not at all relieve the others who were in it from blame. If I should be indicted for murder, and upon the trial it should be discovered that I had been implicated in that murder, but that the prosecuting witness was guilty too, that would not at all touch the question of my crime. It would be no relief to my neck that they discovered this other man who charged the crime upon me to be guilty too.

Another one of the points Judge Douglas makes upon Judge Trumbull is, that when he spoke in Chicago he made his charge to rest upon the fact that the bill had the provision in it for submitting the Constitution to a vote of the people, when it went into his (Judge Douglas') hands, that it was missing when he reported it to the Senate, and that in a public speech he had subsequently said the alteration in the bill was made while it was in committee, and that they were made in consultation between him (Judge Douglas) and Toombs. And Judge Douglas goes on to comment upon the fact of Trumbull's adducing in his Alton speech the proposition that the bill not only came back with that proposition stricken out, but with another clause and another provision in it, saying that "until the complete execution of this act there shall be no election in said Territory,"[17]—which Trumbull argued was not only taking the provision for submitting to a vote of the people out of the bill, but was adding an affirmative one, in that it prevented the people from exercising the right under a bill that was merely silent on the question. Now in regard to what he says, that Trumbull shifts the issue—that he shifts his ground—and I believe he uses the term, that "it being proven false, he has changed ground"[18]—I call upon all of you, when you come to examine that portion of Trumbull's speech, (for it will make a part of mine,) to examine whether Trumbull has shifted his ground or not. I say he did not shift his ground, but that he brought forward his original charge and the evidence to sustain it yet more fully, but precisely as he originally made it. Then, in addition thereto, he brought in a new piece of evidence. He shifted no ground. He brought no new piece of evidence inconsistent with his former testimony, but he brought a new piece, tending, as he thought, and as I think, to prove his proposition. To illustrate: A man brings an accusation against another, and on trial the man making the charge introduces A and B to prove the accusation. At a second trial he introduces the same witnesses, who tell the same story as before, and a third witness, who tells the same thing, and in addition, gives further testimony corroborative of the charge. So with Trumbull. There was no shifting of ground, nor inconsistency of testimony between the new piece of evidence and what he originally introduced.

But Judge Douglas says that he himself moved to strike out that last provision of the bill, and that on his motion it was stricken out and a substitute inserted. That I presume is the truth. I presume it is true that that last proposition was stricken out by Judge Douglas. Trumbull has not said it was not. Trumbull has himself said that it was so stricken out. He says: "I am speaking of the bill as Judge Douglas reported it back. It was amended somewhat in the Senate before it passed, but I am speaking of it as he brought it back."[19] Now when Judge Douglas parades the fact that the provision was stricken out of the bill when it came back, he asserts nothing contrary to what Trumbull alleges. Trumbull has only said that he originally put it in— not that he did not strike it out. Trumbull says it was not in the bill when it went to the committee. When it came back it was in, and Judge Douglas said the alterations were made by him in consultation with Toombs. Trumbull alleges therefore as his conclusion that Judge Douglas put it in. Then if Douglas wants to contradict Trumbull and call him a liar, let him say he did not put it in, and not that he didn't take it out again. It is said that a bear is sometimes hard enough pushed to drop a cub, and so I presume it was in this case. (*Loud applause*) I presume the truth is that Douglas put it in and afterwards took it out. (*Laughter and cheers*) That I take it is the truth about it. Judge Trumbull says one thing; Douglas says another thing, and the two don't contradict one another at all. The question is, what did he put it in for? In the first place what did he take the other provision out of the bill for?—the provision which Trumbull argued was necessary for submitting the Constitution to a vote of the people? What did he take that out for, and having taken it out, what did he put this in for? I say that in the run of things it is not unlikely forces conspire, to render it vastly expedient for Judge Douglas to take that latter clause out again. The question that Trumbull has made is that Judge Douglas put it in, and he don't meet Trumbull at all unless he denies that.

In the clause of Judge Douglas' speech upon this subject he uses this language towards Judge Trumbull. He says: "He forges his evidence from beginning to end, and by falsifying the record he endeavors to bolster up his false charge."[20] Well, that is a pretty serious statement. Trumbull forges his evidence from beginning to end. Now upon my own authority I say that it is not true. (*Great cheers and laughter*) What is a forgery? Consider the

19  This exact quote does not appear in Trumbull's August 27 speech. Either Lincoln referred to Trumbull's August 7 speech or he misquoted the senator. Trumbull used similar words in the August 27 speech: "The Toombs bill did not pass in the exact shape in which Judge Douglas reported it. Several amendments were made to it in the Senate. I am now dealing with the action of Judge Douglas, as connected with that bill, and speak of the bill as he recommended it." Ibid., 144.

20  Douglas's September 6 speech. Ibid., 146.

**21** Trumbull's August 27 speech. Ibid., 143.

**22** Trumbull cited the *Congressional Globe,* 35th Congress, 1st Session, Senate, December 9, 1857. Ibid., 143; Davis and Wilson, *The Lincoln-Douglas Debates,* 140n15.

evidence that Trumbull has brought forward. When you come to read the speech, as you will be able to, examine whether the evidence is a forgery from beginning to end. He had the bill or document in his hand like that (*holding up a paper*). He says that is a copy of the Toombs bill—the amendment offered by Toombs. He says that is a copy of the bill as it was introduced and went into Judge Douglas' hands. Now, does Judge Douglas say that is a forgery? That is one thing Trumbull brought forward. Judge Douglas says he forged it from beginning to end! That is the "beginning," we will say. Does Douglas say that is a forgery? Let him say it to-day and we will have a subsequent examination upon this subject. (*Loud applause*) Trumbull then holds up another document like this and says that is an exact copy of the bill as it came back in the amended form out of Judge Douglas' hands. Does Judge Douglas say that is a forgery? Does he say it in his general sweeping charge? Does he say so now? If he does not, then take this Toombs bill and the bill in the amended form and it only needs to compare them to see that the provision is in the one and not in the other; it leaves the inference inevitable that it was taken out. (*Applause*)

But while I am dealing with this question let us see what Trumbull's other evidence is. One other piece of evidence I will read. Trumbull says there are in this original Toombs bill these words: "That the following propositions be, and the same are hereby offered to the said convention of the people of Kansas, when formed, for their free acceptance or rejection; which, if accepted by the convention and ratified by the people at the election for the adoption of the constitution, shall be obligatory upon the United States and the said State of Kansas."[21] Now, if it is said that this is a forgery, we will open the paper here and see whether it is or not. Again, Trumbull says as he goes along, that Mr. Bigler made the following statement in his place in the Senate, December 9, 1857.

"I was present when that subject was discussed by Senators before the bill was introduced, and the question was raised and discussed, whether the constitution, when formed, should be submitted to a vote of the people. It was held by those most intelligent on the subject, that in view of all the difficulties surrounding that Territory, the danger of any experiment at that time of a popular vote, it would be better there should be no such provision in the Toombs bill; and it was my understanding, in all the intercourse I had, that the Convention would make a constitution, and send it here without submitting it to the popular vote."[22]

Then Trumbull follows on: "In speaking of this meeting again on the 21st December, 1857, (*Congressional Globe,* same vol., page 113,) Senator Bigler said:

"Nothing was further from my mind than to allude to any social or confidential interview. The meeting was not of that character. Indeed, it was semi-official and called to promote the public good. My recollection was clear that I left the conference under the impression that it had been deemed best to adopt measures to admit Kansas as a State through the agency of one popular election, and that for delegates to this Convention. This impression was stronger because I thought the spirit of the bill infringed upon the doctrine of non-intervention, to which I had great aversion; but with the hope of accomplishing a great good, and as no movement had been made in that direction in the Territory, I waived this objection, and concluded to support the measure. I have a few items of testimony as to the correctness of these impressions, and with their submission I shall be content. I have before me the bill reported by the Senator from Illinois on the 7th of March, 1856, providing for the admission of Kansas as a State, the third section of which reads as follows:

> 'That the following propositions be, and the same are hereby offered to the said Convention of the people of Kansas, when formed, for their free acceptance or rejection; which if accepted by the Convention and ratified by the people at the election for the adoption of the Constitution, shall be obligatory upon the United States and the said State of Kansas.'

The bill read in his place by the Senator from Georgia, on the 25th of June, and referred to Committee on Territories, contained the same section, word for word. Both these bills were under consideration at the conference referred to; but, Sir, when the Senator from Illinois reported the Toombs bill to the Senate with amendments, the next morning it did not contain that portion of the third section which indicated to the Convention that the Constitution should be approved by the people. The words 'AND RATIFIED BY THE PEOPLE AT THE ELECTION FOR THE ADOPTION OF THE CONSTITUTION,' had been stricken out."[23]

Now these things Trumbull says were stated by Bigler upon the floor of the Senate on certain days, and that they are recorded in the "Congressional Globe" on certain pages. Does Judge Douglas say this is a forgery? Does

23  Trumbull cited Cong. Globe, 35th Cong., 1st Sess., December 21, 1857. Debates Scrapbook, 143; Davis and Wilson, *The Lincoln-Douglas Debates,* 140n16.

24  Trumbull cited Douglas's speech from Cong. Globe, 35th Cong., 1st Sess., December 9, 1857. Debates Scrapbook, 143–144; Davis and Wilson, *The Lincoln-Douglas Debates,* 141n17.

25  Trumbull cited Douglas from Cong. Globe, 35th Cong., 1st Sess., December 9, 1857. Debates Scrapbook, 144; Davis and Wilson, *The Lincoln-Douglas Debates,* 141n18.

he say there is no such thing in the "Congressional Globe?" What does he mean when he says Judge Trumbull forges his evidence from beginning to end? So again he says in another place, that Judge Douglas, in his speech Dec. 9, 1857, ("Congressional Globe," part 1, page 15) stated:

> "That during the last session of Congress I (Mr. Douglas) reported a bill from the Committee on Territories, to authorize the people of Kansas to assemble and form a Constitution for themselves. Subsequently the Senator from Georgia (Mr. Toombs) brought forward a substitute for my bill, which, *after having been modified by him and myself in consultation*, was passed by the Senate."[24]

Now Trumbull says this is a quotation from a speech of Douglas, and is recorded in the "Congressional Globe." Is *it* a forgery? Is it there or not? It may not be there, but I want the Judge to take these pieces of evidence, and distinctly say they are forgeries if he dare do it. (*Great applause*)

A VOICE—"He will."

MR. LINCOLN—Well, sir, you had better not commit him. (*Cheers and laughter*) He gives other quotations—another from Judge Douglas. He says:

> "I will ask the Senator to show me an intimation, from any one member of the Senate, in the whole debate on the Toombs bill, and in the Union, from any quarter, that the Constitution was not to be submitted to the people. I will venture to say that on all sides of the chamber it was so understood at the time. If the opponents of the bill had understood it was not, they would have made the point on it; and if they had made it, we should certainly have yielded to it; and put in the clause. That is a discovery made since the President found out that it was not safe to take it for granted that that would be done, which ought in fairness to have been done."[25]

Judge Trumbull says Douglas made that speech and it is recorded. Does Judge Douglas say it is a forgery and was not true? Trumbull says somewhere, and I propose to skip it, but it will be found by any one who will read this debate, that he did distinctly bring it to the notice of those who were engineering the bill, that it lacked that provision, and then he goes on to give another quotation from Judge Douglas, where Judge Trumbull uses this language:

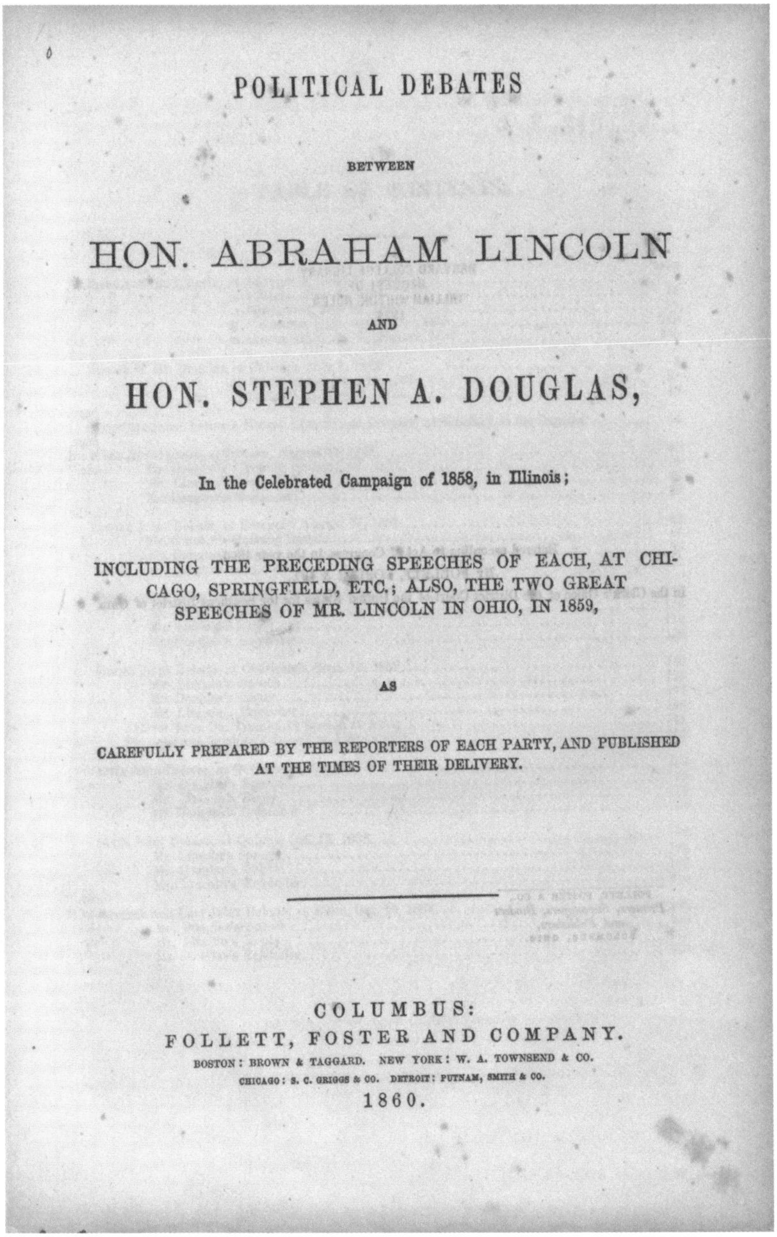

POLITICAL DEBATES

BETWEEN

HON. ABRAHAM LINCOLN

AND

HON. STEPHEN A. DOUGLAS,

In the Celebrated Campaign of 1858, in Illinois;

INCLUDING THE PRECEDING SPEECHES OF EACH, AT CHI-
CAGO, SPRINGFIELD, ETC.; ALSO, THE TWO GREAT
SPEECHES OF MR. LINCOLN IN OHIO, IN 1859,

AS

CAREFULLY PREPARED BY THE REPORTERS OF EACH PARTY, AND PUBLISHED
AT THE TIMES OF THEIR DELIVERY.

———————

COLUMBUS:
FOLLETT, FOSTER AND COMPANY.
BOSTON: BROWN & TAGGARD.   NEW YORK: W. A. TOWNSEND & CO.
CHICAGO: S. C. GRIGGS & CO.   DETROIT: PUTNAM, SMITH & CO.
1860.

*Political Debates between Hon. Abraham Lincoln and Hon. Stephen A. Douglas, in the Celebrated Campaign of 1858, in Illinois* (Columbus, OH: Follett, Foster and Company, 1860). Title page of what became an instant "best seller."

"Judge Douglas, however, on the same day and in the same debate, probably recollecting or being reminded of the fact that I had object-ed to the Toombs bill when pending that it did not provide for a sub-mission of the Constitution to the people, made another statement,

26  Trumbull cited Douglas from Cong. Globe, 35th Cong., 1st Sess., December 9, 1857. Debates Scrapbook, 144; Davis and Wilson, *The Lincoln-Douglas Debates*, 142n19.

which is to be found in the same volume of the *Globe*, page 22, in which he says:

> 'That the bill was silent on this subject was true, and my attention was called to that about the time it was passed; and I took the fair construction to be, that powers not delegated were reserved, and that of course the Constitution would be submitted to the people.'

Whether this statement is consistent with the statement just before made, that had the point been made it would have been yielded to, or that it was a new discovery, you will determine."[26]

So I say, I do not know whether Judge Douglas will dispute this, and yet maintain his position that Trumbull's evidence "was forged from beginning to end." I will remark that I have not got these Congressional Globes with me. They are large books and difficult to carry about, and if Judge Douglas shall say that on these points where Trumbull has quoted from them, there are no such passages there, I shall not be able to prove they are there upon this occasion, but I will have another chance. Whenever he points out the forgery and says, "I declare that this particular thing which Trumbull has uttered is not to be found where he says it is," then my attention will be drawn to that, and I will arm myself for the contest—stating now that I have not the slightest doubt on earth that I will find every quotation just where Trumbull says it is. Then the question is, how can Douglas call that a forgery? How can he make out that it is a forgery? What is a forgery? It is the bringing forward something in writing or in print purporting to be of certain effect when it is altogether untrue. If you come forward with my note for one hundred dollars when I have never given such a note, there is a forgery. If you come forward with a letter purporting to be written by me which I never wrote, there is another forgery. If you produce anything in writing or print saying it is so and so, the document not being genuine, a forgery has been committed. How do you make this a forgery when every piece of the evidence is genuine? If Judge Douglas does say these documents and quotations are false and forged he has a full right to do so, but until he does it specifically we don't know how to get at him. If he does say they are false and forged, I will then look further into it, and I presume I can procure the certificates of the proper officers that they are genuine copies. I have no doubt each of these extracts will be found exactly where Trumbull says it is. Then I leave it to you if Judge Douglas, in making his sweeping charge that Judge Trumbull's evidence is forged from beginning to end, at all meets the case—if that is the way to get at the facts. I repeat again, if he will point out which one is a forgery, I will carefully examine it, and if it proves that any one of them is really a forgery it will not be me who will hold to it any longer. I have always wanted to deal with every one I meet candidly and honestly. If I have made any assertion not warranted by facts, and it is pointed out to me, I will withdraw it cheerfully. But I do not choose to see Judge Trumbull calumniated, and the evidence he has brought forward branded in general terms, "a forgery from beginning to end." This is not the legal way of meeting a charge, and I submit to all intelligent persons, both friends of Judge Douglas and of myself, whether it is.

Now coming back—how much time have I left?

THE MODERATOR—Three minutes.

MR. LINCOLN—The point upon Judge Douglas is this. The bill that went into his hands had the provision in it for a submission of the constitution to the people; and I say its language amounts to an express provision for a submission, and that he took the provision out. He says it was known that the bill was silent in this particular; *but I say, Judge Douglas, it was not silent when you got it.* (*Great applause*) It was vocal with the declaration when you got it, for a submission of the constitution to the people. And now, my direct question to Judge Douglas is, to answer why, if he deemed the bill silent on this point, he found it necessary to strike out those particular harmless words. If he had found the bill silent and without this provision, he might say what he does now. If he supposed it was implied that the constitution would be submitted to a vote of the people, how could these two lines so encumber the statute as to make it necessary to strike them out? How could he infer that a submission was still implied, after its express provision had been stricken from the bill? I find the bill vocal with the provision, while he silenced it. He took it out, and although he took out the other provision preventing a submission to a vote of the people, I ask, *why did you first put it in*? I ask him whether he took the original provision out, which Trumbull alleges was in the bill? If he admits that he did take it, *I ask him what he did it for*? It looks to us as if he had altered the bill. If it looks differently to him—if he has a different reason for his action from the one we assign him—he can tell it. I insist upon knowing why he made the bill silent upon that point when it was vocal before he put his hands upon it.

I was told, before my last paragraph, that my time was within three minutes of being out. I presume it is expired now. I therefore close. (*Three tremendous cheers were given as Mr. Lincoln retired*)

## Senator Douglas' Speech

LADIES AND GENTLEMEN:—I had supposed that we assembled here to-day for the purpose of a joint discussion between Mr. Lincoln and myself upon the political questions that now agitate the whole country. The rule of such discussions is, that the opening speaker shall touch upon all the points he intends to discuss in order that his opponent, in reply, shall have the opportunity of answering them. Let me ask you what questions of public policy relating to the welfare of this State or the Union, has Mr. Lincoln discussed before you? (*"None, none," and great applause*) Gentlemen, allow me to suggest that silence is the best compliment you can pay me. I need my whole time, and your cheering only occupies it. Mr. Lincoln simply contented himself at the outset by saying, that he was not in favor of social and political equality between the white man and the negro, and did not desire the law so changed as to make the latter voters or eligible to office. I am glad that I have at last succeeded in getting an answer out of him upon this question of negro citizenship and eligibility to office, for I have been trying to bring him to the point on it ever since this canvass commenced.

I will now call your attention to the question which Mr. Lincoln has occupied his entire time in discussing. He spent his whole hour in retailing a charge made by Senator Trumbull against me. The circumstances out of which that charge was manufactured, occurred prior to the last Presidential election, over two years ago. If the charge was true, why did not Trumbull make it in 1856, when I was discussing the questions of that day all over this State with Lincoln and him, and when it was pertinent to the then issue. He was then as silent as the grave on the subject. If that charge was true, the time to have brought it forward was the canvass of 1856, the year when the Toombs bill passed the Senate. When the facts were fresh in the public mind, when the Kansas question was the paramount question of the day, and when such a charge would have had a material bearing on the election. Why did he and Lincoln remain silent then, knowing that such a charge could be made and proven if true? Were they not false to you and false to the country in going through that entire campaign, concealing their knowledge of this enormous conspiracy which, Mr. Trumbull says, he then knew and would not tell? (*Laughter*) Mr. Lincoln intimates in his speech, a good reason why Mr. Trumbull would not tell, for, he says, that it might be true, as I proved that it was at Jacksonville, that Trumbull was also in the plot, yet that the fact of Trumbull's being in the plot would not in any way relieve me. He illustrates this argument by supposing himself on trial for murder,

and says that it would be no extenuating circumstance if, on his trial, another man was found to be a party to his crime. Well, if Trumbull was in the
plot, and concealed it in order to escape the odium which would have fallen
upon himself, I ask you whether you can believe him now when he turns
State's evidence, and avows his own infamy in order to implicate me. (*"He is
a liar, and a traitor. We couldn't believe Lyman Trumbull under oath," &c.*) I
am amazed that Mr. Lincoln should now come forward and endorse that
charge, occupying his whole hour in reading Mr. Trumbull's speech in support of it. Why, I ask, does not Mr. Lincoln make a speech of his own instead of taking up his time reading Trumbull's speech at Alton? (*Cheers*) I
supposed that Mr. Lincoln was capable of making a public speech on his
own account, or I should not have accepted the banter from him for a joint
discussion. (*Cheers, and voices: "How about the charges?"*) Do not trouble
yourselves, I am going to make my speech in my own way, and I trust as
the Democrats listened patiently and respectfully to Mr. Lincoln, that his
friends will not interrupt me when I am answering him. When Mr. Trumbull returned from the East, the first thing he did when he landed at Chicago was to make a speech wholly devoted to assaults upon my public character and public action. Up to that time I had never alluded to his course
in Congress, or to him directly or indirectly, and hence his assaults upon
me were entirely without provocation and without excuse. Since then he
has been traveling from one end of the State to the other repeating his vile
charge. I propose now to read it in his own language:

> "Now, fellow citizens, I make the distinct charge, that there was a pre-
> concerted arrangement and plot entered into by the very men who
> now claim credit for opposing a constitution formed and put in force
> without giving the people any opportunity to pass upon it. This, my
> friends, is a serious charge, but I charge it to-night that the very men
> who traverse the country under banners proclaiming popular sover-
> eignty, by design concocted a bill on purpose to force a constitution
> upon that people."

In answer to some one in the crowd, who asked him a question, Trumbull
said:

> "And you want to satisfy yourself that he was in the plot to force a
> constitution upon that people? I will satisfy you. I will cram the truth
> down any honest man's throat until he cannot deny it. And to the
> man who does deny it, I will cram the lie down his throat till he shall

27  Douglas quoted from Trumbull's August 7, 1858, speech in Chicago, published in the *Chicago Press and Tribune*. Cited in Davis and Wilson, *The Lincoln-Douglas Debates*, 146n21.

cry enough. (*"Shameful," "that's decency for you," &c.*) It is preposterous—it is the most damnable effrontery that man ever put on, to conceal a scheme to defraud and cheat the people out of their rights and then claim credit for it."[27]

That is the polite language Senator Trumbull applied to me, his colleague, when I was two hundred miles off. (*"That's like him"*) Why did he not speak out as boldly in the Senate of the United States, and cram the lie down my throat when I denied the charge, first made by Bigler, and made him take it back. You all recollect how Bigler assaulted me when I was engaged in a hand to hand fight, resisting a scheme to force a constitution on the people of Kansas against their will. He then attacked me with this charge; but I proved its utter falsity; nailed the slander to the counter, and made him take the back track. There is not an honest man in America who read that debate who will pretend that the charge is true. (*"Hurrah for Douglas"*) Trumbull was then present in the Senate, face to face with me, and why did he not then rise and repeat the charge, and say he would cram the lie down my throat. (*"He was afraid"*) I tell you that Trumbull then knew it was a lie. He knew that Toombs denied that there ever was a clause in the bill he brought forward calling for and requiring a submission of the Kansas constitution to the people. I will tell you what the facts of the case were. I introduced a bill to authorize the people of Kansas to form a constitution, and come into the Union as a State whenever they should have the requisite population for a member of Congress, and Mr. Toombs proposed a substitute, authorizing the people of Kansas, with their then population of only 25,000, to form a constitution, and come in at once. The question at issue was, whether we would admit Kansas with a population of 25,000, or make her wait until she had the ratio entitling her to a representative in Congress, which was 93,420. That was the point of dispute in the Committee of Territories, to which both my bill and Mr. Toombs' substitute had been referred. I was overruled by a majority of the committee, my proposition rejected, and Mr. Toombs' proposition to admit Kansas then, with her population of 25,000, adopted. Accordingly, a bill to carry out his idea of immediate admission was reported as a substitute for mine—the only points at issue being, as I have already said, the question of population, and the adoption of safeguards against frauds at the election. Trumbull knew this—the whole Senate knew it—and hence he was silent at that time. He waited until I became engaged in this canvass, and finding that I was showing up Lincoln's Abolitionism and negro equality doctrines (*Cheers*), that I was driving Lincoln to the wall, and white men would not support his rank Abolitionism, he came back from the East and trumped up a system of charges against me, hoping that I would be compelled to occupy my entire time in defending myself, so that I would not be able to show up the enormity of the principles of the Abolitionists. Now, the only reason, and the true reason, why Mr. Lincoln has occupied the whole of his first hour in this issue between Trumbull and myself is, to conceal from this vast audience the real questions which divide the two great parties. (*"That's it," and cheers*)

. . .

Now, let me ask how is it, that since that time so many of you Whigs have wandered from the true path marked out by Clay and carried out broad and wide by the great Webster? How is it that so many old line Democrats have abandoned the old faith of their party and joined with Abolitionism and Freesoilism to overturn the platform of the old Democrats, and the platform of the old Whigs? You cannot deny that since 1854, there has been a great revolution on this one question. How has it been brought about? I answer, that no sooner was the sod grown green over the grave of the immortal Clay, no sooner was the rose planted on the tomb of the Godlike Webster, than many of the leaders, of the Whig party, such as Seward, of New York and his followers, led off and attempted to abolitionize the Whig party, and transfer all your old Whigs bound hand and foot into the abolition camp. Seizing hold of the temporary excitement produced in this country by the introduction of the Nebraska bill, the disappointed politicians in the Democratic party, united with the disappointed politicians in the Whig party, and endeavored to form a new party composed of all the abolitionists, of abolitionized Democrats and abolitionized Whigs, banded together in an abolition platform.

And who led that crusade against National principles in this State? I answer, Abraham Lincoln on behalf of the Whigs, and Lyman Trumbull on behalf of the Democrats, formed a scheme by which they would abolitionize the two great parties in this State on condition that Lincoln should be sent to the United States Senate in place of Gen. Shields, and that Trumbull should go to Congress from the Belleville district, until I would be accommodating enough either to die or resign for his benefit, and then he was to go to the Senate in my place.

. . .

28 Ebenezer Peck (1805–1881) was an Illinois lawyer and politician. Originally a Democrat, he broke with the Democratic Party in 1854 over the Kansas-Nebraska bill. After serving in the state legislature for a brief period, Peck was chief clerk for the Illinois Supreme Court from 1841 to 1845 and the court's reporter from 1850 to 1863. He and Norman Judd advised Lincoln after the first debate at Ottawa to take the offensive against Douglas. Guelzo, *Lincoln and Douglas,* 144–145; "Mr. Lincoln & Friends," The Lincoln Institute, http://www.mrlincolnandfriends.org/inside.asp?pageID=45&subjectID=3 (accessed December 30, 2014).

29 John McAuley Palmer (1817–1900) began his career as a Democrat but switched to the Republican Party in 1856. An associate of Lincoln's, Palmer pushed Lincoln's nomination for vice president at the 1856 Republican national convention in Philadelphia. He actively supported Lincoln in his 1858 senate campaign against Douglas. An unsuccessful Republican candidate for Congress in 1859, Palmer endorsed Lincoln for president in 1860 and served as a delegate at the Republican convention in 1860. During the Civil War he was appointed colonel of the Fourteenth Regiment, Illinois Volunteer Infantry. Palmer served as governor of Illinois from 1869 to 1873. He returned to the Democratic Party in the 1880s, representing that party in the U.S. Senate from 1891 to 1897. Neely, *Lincoln Encyclopedia,* 232; "Palmer, John McAuley," Biographical Directory of the United States Congress, http://bioguide.congress.gov/scripts/biodisplay.pl?index=p000042 (accessed December 30, 2014).

And now I will explain to you what has been a mystery all over the State and Union, the reason why Lincoln was nominated for the United States Senate by the Black Republican convention. You know it has never been usual for any party, or any convention to nominate a candidate for United States Senator. Probably this was the first time that such a thing was ever done. The Black Republican convention had not been called for that purpose, but to nominate a State ticket, and every man was surprised and many disgusted when Lincoln was nominated. Archie Williams thought he was entitled to it. Browning knew that he deserved it, Wentworth was certain that he would get it, Peck[28] had hopes, Judd felt sure that he was the man, and Palmer[29] had claims and had made arrangements to secure it; but to their utter amazement, Lincoln was nominated by the convention, (*Laughter*) and not only that, but he received the nomination unanimously, by a resolution declaring that Abraham Lincoln was "the first, last, and only choice" of the Republican party. How did this occur? Why, because they could not get Lincoln's friends to make another bargain with "rogues," (*Laughter*) unless the whole party would come up as one man and pledge their honor that they would stand by Lincoln first, last and all the time, and that he should not be cheated by Lovejoy this time, as he was by Trumbull before. Thus, by passing this resolution, the Abolitionists are all for him, Lovejoy and Farnsworth are canvassing for him, Giddings is ready to come here in his behalf, and the negro speakers are already on the stump for him, and he is sure not to be cheated this time. He would not go into the arrangement until he got their bond for it, and Trumbull is compelled now to take the stump, get up false charges against me, and travel all over the State to try and elect Lincoln, in order to keep Lincoln's friends quiet about the bargain in which Trumbull cheated them four years ago. You see, now, why it is that Lincoln and Trumbull are so mighty fond of each other. (*Tremendous laughter*) They have entered into a conspiracy to break me down by these assaults on my public character, in order to draw my attention from a fair exposure of the mode in which they attempted to abolitionize the old Whig and the old Democratic parties and lead them captive into the Abolition camp. ("*That's so,*" *and* "*hear, hear*") Do you not all remember that Lincoln went around here four years ago making speeches to you, and telling you that you should all go for the Abolition ticket, and swearing that he was as good a Whig as he ever was; (*Laughter*) and that Trumbull went all over the State making pledges to the old Democrats, and trying to coax them into the Abolition camp, swearing by his Maker, with the uplifted hand, that he was still a Democrat, always intended to be, and that never would he desert the Democratic party. (*Laughter*) He got your votes to elect an Abolition legislature, which passed Abolition resolutions, attempted to pass Abolition laws, and sustained Abolitionists for office, State and national. Now, the same game is attempted to be played over again. Then Lincoln and Trumbull made captives of the old Whigs and old Democrats and carried them into the Abolition camp where Father Giddings, the high priest of Abolitionism, received and christened them in the dark cause just as fast as they were brought in.

. . .

I am told that I have but eight minutes more. I would like to talk to you an hour and a half longer, but I will make the best use I can of the remaining eight minutes. Mr. Lincoln said in his first remarks that he was not in favor of the social and political equality of the negro with the white man. Everywhere up north he has declared that he was not in favor of the social and political equality of the negro, but he would not say whether or not he was opposed to negroes voting and negro citizenship. I want to know whether he is for or against negro citizenship? He declared his utter opposition to the Dred Scott decision, and advanced as a reason that the court had decided that it was not possible for a negro to be a citizen under the constitution of the United States. If he is opposed to the Dred Scott decision for that reason he must be in favor of conferring the right and privilege of citizenship upon the negro! I have been trying to get an answer from him on that point, but have never yet obtained one, and I will show you why. In every speech he made in the north he quoted the Declaration of Independence to prove that all men were created equal, and insisted that the phrase "all men," included the negro as well as the white man, and that the equality rested upon Divine law. Here is what he said on that point:

> "I should like to know if, taking this old declaration of independence, which declares that all men are equal upon principle, and making exceptions to it where will it stop. If one man says it does not mean a negro, why may not another say it does not mean some other man? If that declaration is not the truth let us get the statute book in which we find it and tear it out!"[30]

Lincoln maintains there that the Declaration of Independence asserts that the negro is equal to the white man, and that under Divine law, and if he believes so it was rational for him to advocate negro citizenship, which, when allowed, puts the negro on an equality under the law. (*"No negro equality for us," "down with Lincoln"*) I say to you in all frankness, gentle-

30 Douglas quoted from Lincoln's July 10, 1858, speech in Chicago. *CW,* 2:500–501.

31 Douglas referred to Lincoln's "House Divided" speech.

men, that in my opinion a negro is not a citizen, cannot be, and ought not to be, under the constitution of the United States. (*"That's the doctrine"*) I will not even qualify my opinion to meet the declaration of one of the Judges of the Supreme Court in the Dred Scott case, "that a negro descended from African parents, who was imported into this country as a slave, is not a citizen, and cannot be." I say that this government was established on the white basis. It was made by white men, for the benefit of white men and their posterity forever, and never should be administered by any except white men. (*Cheers*) I declare that a negro ought not to be a citizen, whether his parents were imported into this country as slaves or not, or whether or not he was born here. It does not depend upon the place a negro's parents were born, or whether they were slaves or not, but upon the fact that he is a negro, belonging to a race incapable of self government, and for that reason ought not to be on an equality with white men. (*Immense applause*)

My friends, I am sorry that I have not time to pursue this argument further, as I might have done but for the fact that Mr. Lincoln compelled me to occupy a portion of my time in repelling those gross slanders and falsehoods that Trumbull has invented against me and put in circulation. In conclusion, let me ask you why should this government be divided by a geographical line—arraying all men North in one great hostile party against all men South? Mr. Lincoln tells you, in his speech at Springfield, "that a house divided against itself cannot stand; that this government, divided into free and slave States, cannot endure permanently; that they must either be all free or all slave; all one thing or all the other."[31] Why cannot this government endure divided into free and slave States, as our fathers made it? When this government was established by Washington, Jefferson, Madison, Jay, Hamilton, Franklin, and the other sages and patriots of that day, it was composed of free States and slave States, bound together by one common constitution. We have existed and prospered from that day to this thus divided, and have increased with a rapidity never before equalled in wealth, the extension of territory, and all the elements of power and greatness, until we have become the first nation on the face of the globe. Why can we not thus continue to prosper? We can if we will live up to and execute the government upon those principles upon which our fathers established it. During the whole period of our existence Divine Providence has smiled upon us, and showered upon our nation richer and more abundant blessings than have ever been conferred upon any other.

## Mr. Lincoln's Rejoinder

32  "House Divided" speech.

Fellow Citizens—It follows as a matter of course that a half-hour answer to a speech of an hour-and-a-half can be but a very hurried one. I shall only be able to touch upon a few of the points suggested by Judge Douglas, and give them a brief attention, while I shall have to totally omit others for the want of time.

Judge Douglas has said to you that he has not been able to get from me an answer to the question whether I am in favor of negro-citizenship. So far as I know, the Judge never asked me the question before. (*Applause*) He shall have no occasion to ever ask it again, for I tell him very frankly that I am not in favor of negro citizenship. (*Renewed applause*) This furnishes me an occasion for saying a few words upon the subject. I mentioned in a certain speech of mine[32] which has been printed, that the Supreme Court had decided that a negro could not possibly be made a citizen, and without saying what was my ground of complaint in regard to that, or whether I had any ground of complaint, Judge Douglas has from that thing manufactured nearly every thing that he ever says about my disposition to produce an equality between the negroes and the white people. (*Laughter and applause*) If any one will read my speech, he will find I mentioned that as one of the points decided in the course of the Supreme Court opinions, but I did not state what objection I had to it. But Judge Douglas tells the people what my objection was when I did not tell them myself. (*Loud applause and laughter*) Now my opinion is that the different States have the power to make a negro a citizen under the Constitution of the United States if they choose. The Dred Scott decision decides that they have not that power. If the State of Illinois had that power I should be opposed to the exercise of it. (*Cries of "good," "good," and applause*) That is all I have to say about it.

Judge Douglas has told me that he heard my speeches north and my speeches south—that he had heard me at Ottawa and at Freeport in the north, and recently at Jonesboro in the south, and there was a very different cast of sentiment in the speeches made at the different points. I will not charge upon Judge Douglas that he wilfully misrepresents me, but I call upon every fair-minded man to take these speeches and read them, *and I dare him to point out any difference between my printed speeches north and south.* (*Great cheering*) While I am here perhaps I ought to say a word, if I have the time, in regard to the latter portion of the Judge's speech, which was a sort of declamation in reference to my having said I entertained the belief that this government would not endure, half slave and half free. I have said so and I did not say it without what seemed to me to be good reasons. It perhaps would require more time than I have now to set forth these reasons in detail; but let me ask you a few questions. Have we ever had any peace on this slavery question? (*"No, no"*) When are we to have peace upon it if it is kept in the position it now occupies? (*"Never"*) How are we ever to have peace upon it? That is an important question. To be sure if we will all stop and allow Judge Douglas and his friends to march on in their present career until they plant the institution all over the nation, here and wherever else our flag waves, and we acquiesce in it, there will be peace. But let me ask Judge Douglas how he is going to get the people to do that? (*Applause*) They have been wrangling over this question for at least forty years. This was the cause of the agitation resulting in the Missouri Compromise—this produced the troubles at the annexation of Texas, in the acquisition of the territory acquired in the Mexican war. Again, this was the trouble which was quieted by the Compromise of 1850, when it was settled *"forever,"* as both the great political parties declared in their National Conventions. That "forever" turned out to be just four years, (*Laughter*) *when Judge Douglas himself re-opened it.* (*Immense applause, cries of "hit him again," &c.*) When is it likely to come to an end? He introduced the Nebraska bill in 1854 to put *another end* to the slavery agitation. He promised that it would finish it all up immediately, and he has never made a speech since until he got into a quarrel with the President about the Lecompton Constitution, in which he has not declared that we are *just at the end* of the slavery agitation. But in one speech, I think last winter, he did say that he didn't quite see when the end of the slavery agitation would come. (*Laughter and cheers*) Now he tells us again that it is all over, and the people of Kansas have voted down the Lecompton Constitution. How is it over? That was only one of the attempts at putting an end to the slavery agitation—one of these "final settlements." (*Renewed laughter*) Is Kansas in the Union? Has she formed a Constitution that she is likely to come in under? Is not the slavery agitation still an open question in that Territory? Has the voting down of that Constitution put an end to all the trouble? Is that more likely to settle it than every one of these previous attempts to settle the slavery agitation. (*Cries of "No," "No"*) Now, at this day in the history of the world we can no more foretell where the end of this slavery agitation will be than we can see the end of the world itself. The Nebraska-Kansas bill was introduced four years and a half ago, and if the agitation is ever to come to an end, we may say we are four years and a half nearer the end. So, too, we can say we are four years and a half nearer the end of the world; and we can just as clearly see the end of the world as we can see the end of this agitation. (*Applause*) The Kansas settlement did not conclude it. If Kansas should sink to-day, and leave a great vacant space in the earth's surface, this vexed question would still be among us. I say, then, there is no way of putting an end to the slavery agitation amongst us but to put it back upon the basis where our fathers placed it, (*Applause*) no way but to keep it out of our new Territories (*Renewed applause*)—to restrict it forever to the old States where it now exists. (*Tremendous and prolonged cheering; cries of "That's the doctrine," "Good," "Good," &c.*) Then the public mind *will* rest in the belief that it is in the course of ultimate extinction. That is one way of putting an end to the slavery agitation. (*Applause*)

The other way is for us to surrender and let Judge Douglas and his friends have their way and plant slavery over all the States—cease speaking of it as in any way a wrong—regard slavery as one of the common matters of property, and speak of negroes as we do of our horses and cattle. But while it drives on in its state of progress as it is now driving, and as it has driven for the last five years, I have ventured the opinion, and I say to-day, that we will have no end to the slavery agitation until it takes one turn or the other. (*Applause*) I do not mean that when it takes a turn towards ultimate extinction it will be in a day, nor in a year, nor in two years. I do not suppose that in the most peaceful way ultimate extinction would occur in less than a hundred years at the least; but that it will occur in the best way for both races in God's own good time, I have no doubt. (*Applause*) But, my friends, I have used up more of my time than I intended on this point.

Now, in regard to this matter about Trumbull and myself having made a bargain to sell out the entire Whig and Democratic parties in 1854—Judge Douglas brings forward no evidence to sustain his charge, except the speech Matheny is said to have made in 1856,[33] in which he told a cock-and-bull story of that sort, upon the same moral principles that Judge Douglas tells it here to-day. (*Loud applause*) This is the simple truth. I do not care greatly for the story, but this is the truth of it, and I have twice told Judge Douglas to his face, that from beginning to end there is not one word of truth in it. (*Thunders of applause*) I have called upon him for the proof, and he does not at all meet me as Trumbull met him upon that of which we were just talking, by producing the record. He didn't bring the record, because there was no record for him to bring. (*Cheers and laughter*) When he asks if I am ready to indorse Trumbull's veracity after he has broken a bargain with me, I reply that if Trumbull *had* broken a bargain with me, I would not be likely to indorse his veracity (*Laughter and applause*); but I am ready to indorse his veracity because *neither in that thing, nor in any other, in all the years that I*

33  In the preceding debate at Jonesboro on September 15, 1858, Douglas quoted a passage from a speech made by James H. Matheny in 1856. The senator referred to Matheny as "Mr. Lincoln's especial confidential friend for the last twenty years." He then read an extract from Matheny's 1856 speech which, according to Douglas, proved there was a bargain between Lincoln, Trumbull, and abolitionists: "The Whigs, Abolitionists, Know Nothings, and renegade Democrats made a solemn compact for the purpose of carrying this State against the Democracy, on this plan: 1st. That they would all combine and elect Mr. Trumbull to Congress, and thereby carry his district for the legislature, in order to throw all the strength that could be obtained into that body against the Democrats. 2nd. That when the legislature should meet, the officers of that body, such as speaker, clerks, doorkeepers, &c., would be given to the Abolitionists; and 3d, That the Whigs were to have the United States Senator. That, accordingly, in good faith, Trumbull was elected to Congress, and his district carried for the legislature, and, when it convened, the Abolitionists got all the officers of that body, and thus far the 'bond' was fairly executed. The Whigs, on their part, demanded the election of Abraham Lincoln to the United States Senate, that the bond might be fulfilled, the other parties to the contract having already secured to themselves all that was called for. But, in the most perfidious manner, they refused to elect Mr. Lincoln; and the mean, low-lived, sneaking Trumbull succeeded, by pledging all that was required by any party, in thrusting Lincoln aside and foisting himself, an excrescence from the rotten bowels of Democracy, into the United States Senate: and thus it has ever been, that an *honest* man makes a bad bargain when he conspires or contracts with rogues." *CW,* 3:108–109. According to Davis and Wilson, Douglas read this extract from an article in the *Chicago Times* of June 24,

1858, which cited the Petersburg, Illinois, news-paper, the *Menard Index*, which "brings forth from its files" an extract of Matheny's 1856 speech; see *The Lincoln-Douglas Debates*, 92n5.

**34** In his remarks [not included in this text —Eds.], Douglas commented on Lincoln's and Trumbull's charges: "I am not going to allow them to waste much of my time with these personal mat-ters. I have lived in this State twenty-five years, most of that time have been in public life, and my record is open to you all. If that record is not enough to vindicate me from these petty, malicious assaults, I despise ever to be elected to office by slandering my opponents and traducing other men. (*Cheers*) Mr. Lincoln asks you to elect him to the United States Senate to-day solely because he and Trumbull can slander me. Has he given any other reason? (*'No, no'*) Has he avowed what he was desirous to do in Congress on any one question? (*'No, no'*) He desires to ride into office not upon his own merits, not upon the merits and soundness of his principles, but upon his success in fastening a stale old slander upon me. (*'That's the truth,' 'Hear, hear'*)" *CW*, 3:161–162.

**35** Douglas raised the issue of Lincoln's congres-sional record concerning the Mexican War in their first meeting. See "First Debate with Stephen A. Douglas at Ottawa, Illinois, August 21, 1858," note 19.

**36** According to Davis and Wilson, Lincoln cited the June 26, 1858, admission by the Democratic *Illinois State Register* that it was not Lincoln but his immediate predecessor in Congress, the Whig John Henry (1800–1882), who voted against medical supplies for American troops fighting in the Mexican War. The charge against Lincoln was made by the Democratic *Chicago Times* on June 23, 1858. Davis and Wilson, *The Lincoln-Douglas Debates*, 167n42.

**37** Orlando Bell Ficklin (1808–1886) was a lawyer

have known Lyman Trumbull, have I known him to fail of his word or tell a falsehood, large or small. (*Great cheering*) It is for that reason that I indorse Lyman Trumbull.

MR. JAMES BROWN—(Douglas Post Master):—What does Ford's history say about him?

MR. LINCOLN—Some gentleman asks me what Ford's History says about him. My own recollection is, that Ford speaks of Trumbull in very disrespectful terms in several portions of his book, *and that he talks a great deal worse of Judge Douglas.* (*Roars of laughter and applause*) I refer you, sir, to the history for examination. (*Cheers*)

Judge Douglas complains, at considerable length, about a disposition on the part of Trumbull and myself to attack him personally.[34] I want to attend to that suggestion a moment. I don't want to be unjustly accused of dealing illiberally or unfairly with an adversary, either in court, or in a political can-vass, or anywhere else. I would despise myself if I supposed myself ready to deal less liberally with an adversary than I was willing to be treated myself. Judge Douglas, in a general way, without putting it in a direct shape, revives the old charge against me, in reference to the Mexican War.[35] He does not take the responsibility of putting it in a very definite form, but makes a gen-eral reference to it. That charge is more than ten years old. He complains of Trumbull and myself, because he says we bring charges against him one or two years old. He knows, too, that in regard to the Mexican War story, the more respectable papers of his own party throughout the State have been compelled to take it back and acknowledge that it was a lie.[36] (*Continued and vociferous applause*)

(*Here Mr. Lincoln turned to the crowd on the platform, and selecting Hon. Orlando B. Ficklin,[37] led him forward and said*):

I do not mean to do anything with Mr. Ficklin except to present his face and tell you that *he personally knows it to be a lie!* He was a member of Con-gress at the only time I was in Congress, and he (Ficklin) knows that when-ever there was an attempt to procure a vote of mine which would indorse the origin and justice of the war, I refused to give such indorsement, and voted against it; but I never voted against the supplies for the army, and he knows, as well as Judge Douglas, that whenever a dollar was asked by way of compensation or otherwise, for the benefit of the soldiers, *I gave all the votes that Ficklin or Douglas did, and perhaps more.* (*Loud applause*)

MR. FICKLIN—My friends, I wish to say this in reference to the mat-ter. Mr. Lincoln and myself are just as good personal friends as Judge Doug-las and myself. In reference to this Mexican war, my recollection is that when Ashmun's resolution (amendment)[38] was offered by Mr. Ashmun of Massachusetts, in which he declared that the Mexican war was unnecessarily and unconstitutionally commenced by the President—my recollection is that Mr. Lincoln voted for that resolution.

MR. LINCOLN—That is the truth. Now you all remember that was a resolution censuring the President for the manner in which the war was *begun*. You know they have charged that I voted against the supplies, by which I starved the soldiers who were out fighting the battles of their country. I say that Ficklin knows it is false. When that charge was brought forward by the Chicago *Times*, the Springfield *Register* ([a] Douglas organ) reminded the *Times* that the charge really applied to John Henry: and I do know that John Henry *is now making speeches and fiercely battling for Judge Douglas*. (*Loud applause*) If the Judge now says that he offers this as a sort of a set-off to what I said to-day in reference to Trumbull's charge, then I remind him that he made this charge before I said a word about Trumbull's. He brought this forward at Ottawa, the first time we met face to face; and in the opening speech that Judge Douglas made, he attacked me in regard to a matter ten years old. Isn't he a pretty man to be whining about people making charges against him only *two* years old. (*Cheers*)

The Judge thinks it is altogether wrong that I should have dwelt upon this charge of Trumbull's at all. I gave the apology for doing so in my opening speech. Perhaps it didn't fix your attention. I said that when Judge Douglas was speaking at places where I spoke on the succeeding day, he used very harsh language about this charge. Two or three times afterwards I said I had confidence in Judge Trumbull's veracity and intelligence; and my own opinion was, from what I knew of the character of Judge Trumbull, that he would vindicate his position, and prove whatever he had stated to be true. This I repeated two or three times; and then I dropped it, without saying anything more on the subject for weeks—perhaps a month. I passed it by without noticing it at all till I found at Jacksonville, Judge Douglas, in the plenitude of his power, is not willing to answer Trumbull and let me alone; but he comes out there and uses this language: "He should not hereafter occupy his time in refuting such charges made by Trumbull, but that Lincoln, having indorsed the character of Trumbull for veracity, he should hold him (Lincoln) responsible for the slanders."[39] What was Lincoln to do? (*Laughter*) Did he not do right, when he had the fit opportunity of meeting Judge Douglas here, to tell him he was ready for the responsibility? (*Enthusiastic cheering, "good, good," "Hurrah for Lincoln!"*) I ask a candid audience whether in doing thus Judge Douglas was not the assailant rather than I?

and Democratic politician from Charleston, Illinois. He served in the U.S. Congress from 1843 to 1849, covering the tenure of Lincoln's single term in the House of Representatives. Spotting Ficklin seated on the debate platform, Lincoln saw an opportunity to use the former congressman as a witness against Douglas's charge. When the time came, Lincoln allegedly approached Ficklin's chair, grabbed the collar of the Democrat's coat, and walked him to the front of the platform. While Ficklin supported Lincoln's claim that he voted for the Ashmun resolution declaring the war as unnecessary and unconstitutional, he said nothing about the charge that Lincoln voted against supplies for the troops. Surprisingly, Lincoln did not push Ficklin to respond to the charge. "Ficklin, Orlando Bell," Biographical Directory of the United States Congress, http://bioguide.congress. gov/scripts/biodisplay.pl?index=F000101 (accessed December 31, 2014); Guelzo, *Lincoln and Douglas*, 199–200.

38 George Ashmun, a Whig congressman from Massachusetts, submitted a resolution in the House of Representatives on January 3, 1848, claiming that President Polk commenced the war against Mexico "unnecessarily and unconstitutionally," which passed with Lincoln's support. See "Speech in Congress against the War with Mexico, January 12, 1848," note 1.

39 Douglas's September 6, 1858, speech at Jacksonville. Debates Scrapbook, 146.

(*"Yes, yes," "Hit him again!"*) Here I meet him face to face and say I am ready to take the responsibility so far as it rests upon me.

Having done so, I ask the attention of this audience to the question whether I have succeeded in sustaining the charge (*"Yes," "yes"*), and whether Judge Douglas has at all succeeded in rebutting it? (*Loud cries of "no, no"*) You all heard me call upon him to say *which of these pieces of evidence was a forgery?* Does he say that what I present here as a copy of the original Toombs bill is a forgery? (*"No," "no"*) Does he say that what I present as a copy of the bill reported by himself is a forgery? (*"No," "no," "no"*) Or what is presented as a transcript from the *Globe*, of the quotations from Bigler's speech is a forgery? (*"No," "no," "no"*) Does he say the quotations from his own speech are forgeries? (*"No," "no," "no"*) Does he say this transcript from Trumbull's speech is a forgery? (*Loud cries of "no, no." "He didn't deny one of them"*) *I would then like to know how it comes about, that when each piece of a story is true, the whole story turns out false?* (*Great cheers and laughter*) I take it these people have some sense; they see plainly that Judge Douglas is playing cuttlefish, (*Laughter*) a small species of fish that has no mode of defending itself when pursued except by throwing out a black fluid, which makes the water so dark the enemy cannot see it and thus it escapes. (*Roars of laughter*) Ain't the Judge playing the cuttlefish? (*"Yes, yes," and cheers*)

Now I would ask very special attention to the consideration of Judge Douglas' speech at Jacksonville; and when you shall read his speech of to-day, I ask you to watch closely and see which of these pieces of testimony, every one of which he says is a forgery, he has shown to be such. *Not one of them has he shown to be a forgery.* Then I ask the original question, if each of the pieces of testimony is true, *how is it possible that the whole is a falsehood?* (*Loud and continued cheers*)

In regard to Trumbull's charge that he (Douglas) inserted a provision into the bill to prevent the Constitution being submitted to the people, what was his answer? He comes here and reads from the *Congressional Globe* to show that on his motion that provision was struck out of the bill. Why, Trumbull has not said it was not stricken out, but Trumbull says he (Douglas) put it in, and it is no answer to the charge to say he afterwards took it out. Both are perhaps true. It was in regard to that thing precisely that I told him he had dropped the cub. (*Roars of laughter*) Trumbull shows you that by his introducing the bill it was his cub. (*Laughter*) It is no answer to that assertion to call Trumbull a liar merely because he did not specially say Douglas struck it out. Suppose that were the case, does it answer Trumbull? (*"No, no"*) I assert that you (*pointing to an individual*) are here to-day, and you undertake to prove me a liar by showing that you were in Mattoon yesterday. (*Laughter*) I say that you took your hat off your head, and you prove me a liar by putting it on your head. (*Roars of laughter*) That is the whole force of Douglas' argument.

Now, I want to come back to my original question. Trumbull says that Judge Douglas had a bill with a provision in it for submitting a Constitution to be made to a vote of the people of Kansas. Does Judge Douglas deny that fact? (*Cries of "no, no"*) Does he deny that the provision which Trumbull reads was put in that bill? (*"No, no"*) Then Trumbull says he struck it out. Does he dare to deny that? (*"No, no, no"*) He does not, and I have the right to repeat the question—*why, Judge Douglas took it out?* (*Immense applause*) Bigler has said there was a combination of certain Senators, among whom he did not include Judge Douglas, by which it was agreed that the Kansas bill should have a clause in it not to have the Constitution formed under it submitted to a vote of the people. He did not say that Douglas was among them, but we prove by another source that about the same time Douglas comes into the Senate *with that provision stricken out of the bill.* Although Bigler cannot say they were all working in concert, yet it looks very much as if the thing was agreed upon and done with a mutual understanding after the conference; and while we do not know that it was absolutely so, yet it looks so probable that we have a right to call upon the man who knows the true reason why it was done, *to tell what the true reason was.* (*Great cheers*) When he will not tell what the true reason was, he stands in the attitude of an accused thief who has stolen goods in his possession, and when called to account, refuses to tell where he got them. (*Immense applause*) Not only is this the evidence, but when he comes in with the bill having the provision stricken out, he tells us in a speech, not then but since, that these alterations and modifications in the bill *had been made by* HIM, *in consultation with Toombs, the originator of the bill.* He tells us the same today. He says there were certain modifications made in the bill in committee that he did not vote for. I ask you to remember while certain amendments were made which he disapproved of, but which a majority of the committee voted in, he has himself told us that in this particular *the alterations and modifications were made by him upon consultation with Toombs.* (*Enthusiastic cheering*) We have his own word that these alterations were made *by him* and not by the committee. (*"That's so," "good, good"*) Now, I ask what is the reason Judge Douglas is so chary about coming to the exact question? What is the reason he will not tell you anything about HOW it was made, BY WHOM it was made, or that he remembers it being made at all? Why does

40  In an autobiography Lincoln wrote for the 1860 presidential campaign, he claimed to have "studied and nearly mastered the Six-books of Euclid, since he was a member of Congress." According to William H. Herndon, Lincoln, in the years after he served in Congress, carried "his Euclid" along with "a well-worn copy of Shakespeare." See "Autobiography Written for John L. Scripps [ca. June 1860]," in this volume; Herndon and Weik, *Herndon's Lincoln,* 199.

41  After Charleston, Lincoln and Douglas debated three more times, in Galesburg on October 7, Quincy on October 13, and Alton on October 15, where they would reiterate arguments and accusations made in the previous four debates. While the debates have become legendary, they were only seven events in a long campaign in which Lincoln traveled more than 4,000 miles by train, carriage, and riverboat and delivered more than 60 speeches, and Douglas covered more than 5,000 miles and gave more than 70 speeches. Republican candidates won the majority of votes in the election, but with control of the Illinois state legislature (which at the time chose the state's U.S. senators) in the hands of the Democrats, it elected Douglas to a third term by a vote of 54 to 46. Despite his loss, Lincoln, as a result of the media coverage of the debates, was provided with a national platform that raised his visibility not only in Illinois but throughout the West as a leading Republican voice. Zarefsky, *Lincoln, Douglas, and Slavery,* 51; Guelzo, *Lincoln and Douglas,* 281–293.

he stand playing upon the meaning of words, and quibbling around the edges of the evidence? If he can explain all this, but leaves it unexplained, I have a right to infer that Judge Douglas understood it was the purpose of his party, in engineering that bill through, to make a Constitution and have Kansas come into the Union with that Constitution, *without its being submitted to a vote of the people.* (*"That's it"*) If he will explain his action on this question, by giving a *better reason* for the facts that happened, than he has done, it will be satisfactory. But until he does that—until he gives a better or more plausible reason than he has offered against the evidence in the case—*I suggest to him it will not avail him at all that he swells himself up, takes on dignity, and calls people liars.* (*Great applause and laughter*) Why, sir, there is not a word in Trumbull's speech that depends on Trumbull's veracity at all. He has only arrayed the evidence and told you what follows as a matter of reasoning. There is not a statement in the whole speech that depends on Trumbull's word. If you have ever studied geometry, you remember that by a course of reasoning Euclid[40] proves that all the angles in a triangle are equal to two right angles. Euclid has shown you how to work it out. Now, if you undertake to disprove that proposition, and to show that it is erroneous, would you prove it to be false by calling Euclid a liar? (*Roars of laughter and enthusiastic cheers*) They tell me that my time is out, and therefore I close.[41]

# Lecture on Discoveries and Inventions

## February 11, 1859

*Many nineteenth-century politicians yearned to demonstrate their high-mindedness by delivering lectures on philosophical or scientific subjects. Eager to join that pantheon, Lincoln chose as his subject discoveries and inventions. Though he refined the manuscript over time, the lecture never won the praise its author, an inventor himself, yearned for. Lincoln was said to have once refunded the price of admission to an audience that complained about the presentation.*

WE HAVE ALL HEARD OF YOUNG AMERICA.[1] HE IS THE MOST *CURRENT* youth of the age.[2] Some think him conceited, and arrogant; but has he not reason to entertain a rather extensive opinion of himself? Is he not the inventor and owner of the *present,* and sole hope of the *future?* Men, and things, everywhere, are ministering unto him. Look at his apparel, and you shall see cotten [*sic*] fabrics from Manchester and Lowell; flax-linen from Ireland; wool-cloth from [Spain;] silk from France; furs from the Arctic regions, with a buffalo-robe from the Rocky Mountains, as a general outsider. At his table, besides plain bread and meat made at home, are sugar from Louisiana; coffee and fruits from the tropics; salt from Turk's Island; fish from New-foundland; tea from China, and spices from the Indies. The whale of the Pacific furnishes his candle-light; he has a diamond-ring from Brazil; a gold-watch from California, and a spanish cigar from Havanna [*sic*]. He not only has a present supply of all these, and much more; but thousands of hands are engaged in producing fresh supplies, and other thousands, in bringing them to him. The iron horse is panting, and impatient, to carry him everywhere, in no time; and the lightening stands ready harnessed to take and bring his tidings in a trifle less than no time. He owns a large part of the world, by right of possessing it; and all the rest by right of *wanting* it, and *intending* to have it. As Plato[3] had for the immortality of the soul, so Young America has "a pleasing hope—a fond desire—a longing after"[4] teritory [*sic*]. He has a great passion—a perfect rage—for the *"new";* particularly new men for office, and the new earth mentioned in the revelations, in which, being no more sea, there must be about three times as much land as in the present. He is a great friend of humanity; and his desire for land is not selfish, but merely an impulse to extend the area of freedom. He is very anxious to fight for the liberation of enslaved nations and colonies,

1   In Lincoln's time, public lectures by literary figures and politicians were popular with American upper- and middle-class audiences seeking general knowledge as well as practical advice. Organized and funded by thousands of lecture societies and organizations, primarily located in Northern states, public lectures, depending on the speaker and subject, drew large crowds. Lincoln had tried delivering talks on "The Perpetuation of Our Political Institutions" (see "Address to the Young Men's Lyceum of Springfield, Illinois, January 27, 1838," in this volume) and temperance ("Address to the Springfield Washington Temperance Society, February 22, 1842"). It appears he also intended to prepare lectures on Niagara Falls and on the law. His fragment on Niagara Falls, possibly drafted in 1848, is in *CW,* 2:10–11. See also "Notes for a Law Lecture [July 1, 1850?]," in this volume. It is not surprising that Lincoln chose discoveries and inventions as a topic for a lecture, given his inquisitive nature, his constant thirst for knowledge, and his lifelong fascination with mechanical gadgetry and technology. Besides his inventing a mechanism for buoying vessels over shoals (see note 9 below), during his presidency Lincoln was, as historian Robert Bruce has shown, his own bureau of scientific development, welcoming to the White House a parade of inventors and ordnance experts with the hope of enhancing the Union army's tools of war. It was long thought that Lincoln had prepared and delivered two versions of his lecture on discoveries and inventions, with the

first delivered in Bloomington, Illinois, on April 6, 1858 (see *CW,* 2: 437–432), and the second delivered in Jacksonville, Illinois, on February 11, 1859. It has been proven by Lincoln scholar Wayne Temple that the two versions are different parts of one lecture. There is evidence that there was a final draft of the lecture that has been lost. Besides the two lectures mentioned, there were at least two additional presentations, both given in Springfield, on February 21, 1859, and April 26, 1860. It is probable he also delivered a lecture in Decatur, Illinois, sometime in March 1859, and possibly one in Pontiac, Illinois, on January 27, 1860. One scheduled presentation, a repeat performance in Bloomington, was canceled owing to low turnout. It is known that Lincoln turned down several lecture invitations because of other commitments. While it is unclear how audiences reacted to Lincoln's lecture, it was not well received by most contemporaries and has been mostly ignored by historians. John Nicolay, for example, thought it was a "literary experiment" that deserved little attention and that Lincoln drafted it as a way to escape the "monotony of law and politics." In William Herndon's opinion, the lecture was "commonplace" and proved that Lincoln "was no lecturer." It appears that Lincoln took the lecture more seriously than originally supposed, with evidence suggesting that he planned to revise and publish it. According to Noah Brooks, President Lincoln, after a conversation with the Harvard scientist Louis Agassiz (1807–1873), claimed that when he left the White House he intended to "finish it [the discoveries lecture] up, perhaps, and get my friend [Noah Brooks?] to print it somewhere." The best study of Lincoln's interest in inventions and as an inventor is Jason Emerson, *Lincoln the Inventor* (Carbondale: Southern Illinois University Press, 2009), especially 35–53. See Wayne C. Temple, "Lincoln as a Lecturer on 'Discoveries, Inventions, and Improvements,'" *Jacksonville Journal Courier,*

provided, always, they *have* land, and have *not* any liking for his interference. As to those who have no land, and would be glad of help from any quarter, he considers *they* can afford to wait a few hundred years longer. In knowledge he is particularly rich. He knows all that can possibly be known; inclines to believe in spiritual rappings, and is the unquestioned inventor of "*Manifest Destiny.*"[5] His horror is for all that is old, particularly "Old Fogy"; and if there be any thing old which he can endure, it is only old whiskey and old tobacco.

If the said Young America really is, as he claims to be, the owner of all present, it must be admitted that he has considerable advantage of Old Fogy. Take, for instance, the first of all fogies, father Adam. There he stood, a very perfect physical man, as poets and painters inform us; but he must have been very ignorant, and simple in his habits. He had had no sufficient time to learn much by observation; and he had no near neighbors to teach him anything. No part of his breakfast had been brought from the other side of the world; and it is quite probable, he had no conception of the world having any other side. In all of these things, it is very plain, he was no equal of Young America; the most that can be said is, that *according to his chance* he may have been quite as much of a man as his very self-complaisant descendant. Little as was what he knew, let the Youngster discard all he has learned from others, and then show, if he can, any advantage on his side. In the way of *land,* and *live stock,* Adam was quite in the ascendant. He had dominion over all the earth, and all the living things upon, and round about it. The land has been sadly divided out since; but never fret, Young America will *re-annex* it.

The great difference between Young America and Old Fogy, is the result of *Discoveries, Inventions,* and *Improvements.* These, in turn, are the result of *observation, reflection* and *experiment.* For instance, it is quite certain that ever since water has been boiled in covered vessels, men have seen the lids of the vessels rise and fall a little, with a sort of fluttering motion, by force of the steam; but so long as this was not specially observed, and reflected and experimented upon, it came to nothing. At length however, after many thousand years, some man observes this long-known effect of hot water lifting a pot-lid, and begins a train of reflection upon it. He says "Why, to be sure, the force that lifts the pot-lid, will lift any thing else, which is no heavier than the pot-lid." "And, as man has much hard lifting to do, can not this hot-water power be made to help him?" He has become a little excited on the subject, and he fancies he hears a voice answering "Try me[.]" He does try it; and the *observation, reflection,* and *trial* gives to the world the control of that tremendous, and now well known agent, called steam-power. This is not the actual history in detail, but the general principle.

But was this first inventor of the application of steam, wiser or more ingenious than those who had gone before him? Not at all. Had he not learned much of them, he never would have succeeded—probably, never would have thought of making the attempt. To be fruitful in invention, it is indispensable to have a *habit* of observation and reflection; and this *habit,* our steam friend acquired, no doubt, from those who, to him, were old fogies. But for the difference in *habit* of observation, why did yankees, almost instantly, discover gold in California, which had been trodden upon, and over-looked by indians and Mexican greasers, for centuries? Gold-mines are not the only mines overlooked in the same way. There are more mines above the Earth's surface than below it. All nature—the whole world, material, moral, and intellectual,—is a mine; and, in Adam's day, it was a wholly unexplored mine. Now, it was the destined work of Adam's race to develope [*sic*], by discoveries, inventions, and improvements, the hidden treasures of this mine. But Adam had nothing to turn his attention to the work. If he should do anything in the way of invention, he had first to invent the art of invention—the *instance* at least, if not the *habit* of observation and reflection. As might be expected he seems not to have been a very observing man at first; for it appears he went about naked a considerable length of time, before he even noticed that obvious fact. But when he did observe it, the observation was not lost upon him; for it immediately led to the first of all inventions, of which we have any direct account—*the fig-leaf apron.*

The inclination to exchange thoughts with one another is probably an original impulse of our nature. If I be in pain I wish to let you know it, and to ask your sympathy and assistance; and my pleasurable emotions also, I wish to communicate to, and share with you. But to carry on such communication, some *instrumentality* is indispensable. Accordingly speech—articulate sounds rattled off from the tongue—was used by our first parents, and even by Adam, before the creation of Eve. He gave names to the animals while she was still a bone in his side; and he broke out quite volubly when she first stood before him, the best present of his maker. From this it would appear that speech was not an invention of man, but rather the direct gift of his Creator. But whether Divine gift, or invention, it is still plain that if a mode of communication had been left to invention, *speech* must have been the first, from the superior adaptation to the end, of the organs of speech, over every other means within the whole range of nature. Of the organs of speech the tongue is the principal; and if we shall test it, we shall find the

May 23, 1982, 1–12 for his argument that Lincoln's different versions of the lecture were part of one single lecture. Nicolay, Herndon, and Brooks are cited in Briggs, *Lincoln's Speeches Reconsidered,* 192, 196. For Lincoln's interest, as president, in weapons, ironclad warships, and other tools of war, see Robert V. Bruce, *Lincoln and the Tools of War* (Indianapolis: Bobbs-Merrill, 1956).

2    "Young America" began as a literary movement led primarily by New York–based editors, such as John L. O'Sullivan (1813–1895) and George Nicholas Sanders (1812–1873), and writers who sought to create an American literature free of European influence. The literary movement was complemented by a similar political component, led by young Democratic politicians such as Stephen A. Douglas, James Knox Polk, and Franklin Pierce, who infused their party with new priorities that diverged from its agrarian and strict constructionist traditions to embrace commercial and territorial expansion, technology, regulation, reform, and international intervention. A recent study of the political history of Young America and its influence on the Democratic Party is Yonatan Eyal, *The Young America Movement and the Transformation of the Democratic Party 1828–1861* (New York: Cambridge University Press, 2007). The literary branch of the movement is covered by Perry Miller, in *The Raven and the Whale: The War of Words and Wits in the Era of Poe and Melville* (New York: Harcourt, Brace and Company, 1956), and Edward L. Widmer, *Young America: The Flowering of Democracy in New York City* (New York: Oxford University Press, 1999).

3    Plato (429–347 BCE), the Greek philosopher.

4    Lincoln cited a passage from Joseph Addison's *Cato: A Tragedy* (London: Printed for J. Tonson, 1713), 5.1.1–3, in which Cato says, "It must be so— Plato, thou reason'st well!—Else whence this pleasing Hope, this fond Desire, this Longing after

Immortality?" Lincoln replaced the word "immortality" with "teritory" [*sic*]. Addison (1672–1719) was an English essayist, poet, and playwright.

5    The term "Manifest Destiny," coined in 1845 by American journalist and editor John L. O'Sullivan, referred to the obligation of the United States to spread republican democracy throughout North America. See O'Sullivan, "Annexation," *Democratic Review* 17 (1845): 5. For a useful study of Manifest Destiny, see Frederick Merk, *Manifest Destiny and Mission in American History: A Reinterpretation* (New York: Alfred A. Knopf, 1963).

6    Noah Webster (1758–1843) was the compiler of the first American dictionary, *An American Dictionary of the English Language,* 2 vols. (New York: S. Converse, 1828).

capacities of the tongue, in the utterance of articulate sounds, absolutely wonderful. You can count from one to one hundred, quite distinctly in about forty seconds. In doing this two hundred and eighty three distinct sounds or syllables are uttered, being seven to each second; and yet there shall be enough difference between every two, to be easily recognized by the ear of the hearer. What other *signs* to represent *things* could possibly be produced so rapidly? or, even, if ready made, could be *arranged* so rapidly to express the sense? *Motions* with the hands, are no adequate substitute. *Marks* for the recognition of the eye—*writing*—although a wonderful auxiliary for speech, is no worthy substitute for it. In addition to the more slow and laborious process of getting up a communication in writing, the materials— pen, ink, and paper—are not always at hand. But one always has his tongue with him, and the breath of his life is the ever-ready material with which it works. Speech, then, by enabling different individuals to interchange thoughts, and thereby to combine their powers of observation and reflection, greatly facilitates useful discoveries and inventions. What one observes, and would himself infer nothing from, he tells to another, and that other at once sees a valuable hint in it. A result is thus reached which neither *alone* would have arrived at.

And this reminds me of what I passed unnoticed before, that the very first invention was a joint operation, Eve having shared with Adam in the getting up of the apron. And, indeed, judging from the fact that sewing has come down to our times as "woman's work" it is very probable she took the leading part; he, perhaps, doing no more than to stand by and thread the needle. That proceeding may be reckoned as the mother of all "Sewing societies"; and the first and most perfect "world's fair" all inventions and all inventors then in the world, being on the spot.

But speech alone, valuable as it ever has been, and is, has not advanced the condition of the world much. This is abundantly evident when we look at the degraded condition of all those tribes of human creatures who have no considerable additional means of communicating thoughts. *Writing*— the art of communicating thoughts to the mind, through the eye—is the great invention of the world. Great in the astonishing range of analysis and combination which necessarily underlies the most crude and general conception of it—great, very great in enabling us to converse with the dead, the absent, and the unborn, at all distances of time and of space; and great, not only in its direct benefits, but greatest help, to all other inventions. Suppose the art, with all conception of it, were this day lost to the world, how long, think you, would it be, before even Young America could get up the letter

A. with any adequate notion of using it to advantage? The precise period at which writing was invented, is not known; but it certainly was as early as the time of Moses; from which we may safely infer that it's [*sic*] inventors were very old fogies.

Webster,[6] at the time of writing his Dictionary, speaks of the English Language as then consisting of seventy or eighty thousand words. If so, the language in which the five books of Moses were written must, at that time, now thirtythree or four hundred years ago, have consisted of at least one quarter as many, or, twenty thousand. When we remember that words are *sounds* merely, we shall conclude that the idea of representing those sounds by *marks,* so that whoever should at any time after see the marks, would understand what sounds they meant, was a bold and ingenius [*sic*] conception, not likely to occur to one man of a million, in the run of a thousand years. And, when it did occur, a distinct mark for each word, giving twenty thousand different marks first to be learned, and afterwards remembered, would follow as the second thought, and would present such a difficulty as

Replica of scale-model boat that Lincoln successfully submitted for a federal patent.

would lead to the conclusion that the whole thing was impracticable. But the *necessity* still would exist; and we may readily suppose that the idea was conceived, and lost, and reproduced, and dropped, and taken up again and again, until at last, the thought of dividing sounds into parts, and making a mark, not to represent a whole sound, but only a part of one, and then of combining these marks, not very many in number, upon the principles of permutation, so as to represent any and all of the whole twenty thousand words, and even any additional number was somehow conceived and pushed into practice. This was the invention of *phoenetic* [sic] writing, as distinguished from the clumsy picture writing of some of the nations. That it was difficult of conception and execution, is apparant [sic], as well by the foregoing reflections, as by the fact that so many tribes of men have come down from Adam's time to ours without ever having possessed it. It's [sic] utility may be conceived, by the reflection that, to *it* we owe everything which distinguishes us from savages. Take it from us, and the Bible, all history, all science, all government, all commerce, and nearly all social intercourse go with it.

The great activity of the tongue, in articulating sounds, has already been mentioned; and it may be of some passing interest to notice the wonderful powers of the *eye*, in conveying ideas to the mind from writing. Take the same example of the numbers from *one* to *one hundred,* written down, and you can run your eye over the list, and be assured that every number is in it, in about one half the time it would require to pronounce the words with the voice; and not only so, but you can, in the same short time, determine whether every word is spelled correctly, by which it is evident that every separate letter, amounting to eight hundred and sixty four, has been recognized, and reported to the mind, within the incredibly short space of twenty seconds, or one third of a minute.

I have already intimated my opinion that in the world's history, certain inventions and discoveries occurred, of peculiar value, on account of their great efficiency in facilitating all other inventions and discoveries. Of these were the arts of writing and of printing—the discovery of America, and the introduction of Patent-laws. The date of the first, as already stated, is unknown; but it certainly was as much as fifteen hundred years before the Christian era; the second—printing—came in 1436, or nearly three thousand years after the first. The others followed more rapidly—the discovery of America in 1492, and the first patent laws in 1624. Though not apposite to my present purpose, it is but justice to the fruitfulness of that period, to mention two other important events—the Lutheran Reformation in 1517, and, still earlier, the invention of negroes, or, of the present mode of using them, in 1434. But, to return to the consideration of printing, it is plain that it is but the *other* half—and in real utility, the *better* half—of writing; and that both together are but the assistants of speech in the communication of thoughts between man and man. When man was possessed of speech alone, the chances of invention, discovery, and improvement, were very limited; but by the introduction of each of these, they were greatly multiplied. When writing was invented, any important observation, likely to lead to a discovery, had at least a chance of being written down, and consequently, a better chance of never being forgotten; and of being seen, and reflected upon, by a much greater number of persons; and thereby the chances of a valuable hint being caught, proportionably augmented. By this means the observation of a single individual might lead to an important invention, years, and even centuries after he was dead. In one word, by means of writing, the seeds of invention were more permanently preserved, and more widely sown. And yet, for the three thousand years during which printing remained undiscovered after writing was in use, it was only a small portion of the people who could write, or read writing; and consequently the field of invention, though much extended, still continued very limited. At length printing came. It gave ten thousand copies of any written matter, quite as cheaply as ten were given before; and consequently a thousand minds were brought into the field where there was but one before. This was a great *gain;* and history shows a great *change* corresponding to it, in point of time. I will venture to consider *it,* the true termination of that period called "the dark ages."[7] Discoveries, inventions, and improvements followed rapidly, and have been increasing their rapidity ever since. The effects could not come, all at once. It required time to bring them out; and they are still coming. The *capacity* to read, could not be multiplied as fast as the *means* of reading. Spelling-books just began to go into the hands of the children; but the teachers were not very numerous, or very competent; so that it is safe to infer they did not advance so speedily as they do now-a-days. It is very probable—almost certain—that the great mass of men, at that time, were utterly unconscious, that their *conditions,* or their *minds* were capable of improvement. They not only looked upon the educated few as superior beings; but they supposed themselves to be naturally incapable of rising to equality. To immancipate [*sic*] the mind from this false and under estimate of itself, is the great task which printing came into the world to perform. It is difficult for us, *now* and *here,* to conceive how strong this slavery of the mind was; and how long it did, of necessity, take, to break it's [*sic*] shackles, and to get

7  Few nineteenth-century politicians understood the relationship between politics and print and the power of the printed word as well as Lincoln. A life-long autodidact, he virtually read his way out of the primitive frontier environment of his youth through a vigorous regimen of self-improvement. Keenly appreciating the role of print in shaping public opinion, Lincoln, from the beginning of his career in both New Salem and Springfield, Illinois, and through his years as president, used print, especially newspapers, to further his own and his party's agenda. See Holzer, *Lincoln and the Power of the Press;* and Thomas A. Horrocks, *Lincoln's Campaign Biographies* (Carbondale: Southern Illinois University Press, 2014).

8    Steamboats and railroads.

9    Lincoln remains the only U.S. president to
hold a patent. When Lincoln was twenty-two years
old, he, along with his stepbrother and a cousin,
was hired by a New Salem, Illinois, merchant in
April 1831 to take a flatboat full of hogs and barrels
of foodstuff from Sangamo Town, Illinois, to New
Orleans. When the vessel was grounded on a
milldam near New Salem, Lincoln devised a
mechanism that caused the boat to tilt and thus
drain out the water, freeing the vessel. See "Message to the People of Sangamo County, March 9,
1832," note 2. This event was undoubtedly recalled
by Lincoln in September 1848 when he was
returning to Springfield, Illinois, from Washington, D.C., via a steamboat through the Great
Lakes. During his trip Lincoln observed another
steamship that had run aground and that loose
planks of wood and empty barrels were used to free
it from a sandbar. Intrigued by the event, Lincoln,
with the assistance of a Springfield mechanic,
constructed a model boat with inflatable air
chambers that would enable the vessel to pass over
sandbars or through shallow water. The model,
accompanied by drawings, was submitted by
Lincoln to the U.S. Patent Office on March 10,
1849. On May 22, 1849, Lincoln was issued patent
number 6,469 for "Improved Method of Lifting
Vessels over Shoals." Lincoln never pursued the
production of such a vessel and thus his invention
was not tested. Emerson, *Lincoln the Inventor*, 2–18.
Lincoln's patent application is in *CW,* 2:32–36. The
original wooden model of his device, deposited at
the Patent Office in Washington, was on display in
its massive new headquarters (later the site of
Lincoln's second inaugural ball) when the
president-elect and his family and staff arrived in

M. I. Wright, *Lincoln's Invention.* Broadside (n.d.). Image of Lincoln's invention in its
display case in the Patent Office in Washington, D.C.

a habit of freedom of thought, established. It is, in this connection, a curious fact that a new country is most favorable—almost necessary—to the immancipation [*sic*] of thought, and the consequent advancement of civilization and the arts. The human family originated as is thought, somewhere in Asia, and have worked their way princip[al]ly Westward. Just now, in civilization, and the arts, the people of Asia are entirely behind those of Europe; those of the East of Europe behind those of the West of it; while we, here in America, *think* we discover, and invent, and improve, faster than any of them. *They* may think this is arrogance; but they can not deny that Russia has called on us to show her how to build steam-boats and railroads—while in the older parts of Asia, they scarcely know that such things as S.Bs & RR.s.[8] exist. In anciently inhabited countries, the dust of ages—a real downright old-fogyism—seems to settle upon, and smother the intellects and energies of man. It is in this view that I have mentioned the discovery of America as an event greatly favoring and facilitating useful discoveries and inventions.

Next came the Patent laws.[9] These began in England in 1624; and, in this country, with the adoption of our constitution. Before then [these?], any man might instantly use what another had invented; so that the inventor had no special advantage from his own invention. The patent system changed this; secured to the inventor, for a limited time, the exclusive use of his invention; and thereby added the fuel of *interest* to the *fire* of genius, in the discovery and production of new and useful things.

the nation's capital for the first swearing-in early in 1861. Lincoln's son Robert visited the Patent Office to see the model in late February. *Philadelphia Inquirer,* February 27, 1861. The model is now preserved in the collection of the Smithsonian Museum of American History.

Iron printing press reportedly owned and used by Illinois abolitionist Elijah Lovejoy.

*Lincoln's extensively reprinted debates with Douglas—not his lecture on discoveries and inventions—made him a widely sought speaker outside of Illinois. When a group of Bostonians invited him to appear in their city, Lincoln declined, but he also established a pattern he would pursue for years, and sent this extraordinary letter to be read aloud by his would-be hosts, in which the rising Republican star made an audacious effort to claim Democratic hero and slaveholder Thomas Jefferson for his own antislavery cause. The recipients of this message were so impressed they also had it reprinted in the Boston press.*

1   Henry L. Pierce (1825–1896) was a Boston businessman and Republican politician. He served as mayor of Boston in 1873 and 1878. He served in the U.S. Congress from 1873 to 1877. "Pierce, Henry L.," Biographical Directory of the United States Congress, http://bioguide.congress.gov/scripts/biodisplay.pl?index=P000335 (accessed January 5, 2015). The letter to Lincoln was cosigned by a committee of five Republicans responsible for organizing the event in honor of Thomas Jefferson's birthday. Cited in *CW*, 3:376n1.

2   According to Lincoln, Democrats were turning their backs on Jefferson's Declaration of Independence because of their growing dependence on the support of Southerners. The Republican Party was now embracing the Declaration, especially its "all men created equal" clause, because it was compatible with its advocacy of free labor and economic opportunity. Allen Guelzo, *Abraham Lincoln: Redeemer President* (Grand Rapids, MI: William B. Eerdmans, 1999), 193–194; Wilentz, "Abraham Lincoln and Jacksonian Democracy," 71–72.

# Letter to Henry L. Pierce and Others on Thomas Jefferson

## April 6, 1859

Messrs. Henry L. Pierce,[1] & others. Springfield, Ills.
Gentlemen April 6. 1859

Your kind note inviting me to attend a Festival in Boston, on the 13th. Inst. in honor of the birth-day of Thomas Jefferson, was duly received. My engagements are such that I can not attend.

Bearing in mind that about seventy years ago, two great political parties were first formed in this country, that Thomas Jefferson was the head of one of them, and Boston the head-quarters of the other, it is both curious and interesting that those supposed to descend politically from the party opposed to Jefferson, should now be celebrating his birth-day in their own original seat of empire, while those claiming political descent from him have nearly ceased to breathe his name everywhere.

Remembering too, that the Jefferson party were formed upon their supposed superior devotion to the *personal* rights of men, holding the rights of *property* to be secondary only, and greatly inferior, and then assuming that the so-called democracy of to-day, are the Jefferson, and their opponents, the anti-Jefferson parties, it will be equally interesting to note how completely the two have changed hands as to the principle upon which they were originally supposed to be divided.

The democracy of to-day holds the *liberty* of one man to be absolutely nothing, when in conflict with another man's right of *property*. Republicans, on the contrary, are for both the *man* and the *dollar;* but in cases of conflict, the man *before* the dollar.[2]

I remember once being much amused at seeing two partially intoxicated men engage in a fight with their great-coats on, which fight, after a long, and rather harmless contest, ended in each having fought himself *out* of his own coat, and *into* that of the other. If the two leading parties of this day are

Abraham Lincoln. Photograph by Samuel Fassett (Chicago, October 4, 1859). Mary Lincoln's favorite pre-presidential portrait of her husband.

really identical with the two in the days of Jefferson and Adams, they have performed about the same feat as the two drunken men.

But soberly, it is now no child's play to save the principles of Jefferson from total overthrow in this nation.

One would start with great confidence that he could convince any sane child that the simpler propositions of Euclid are true; but, nevertheless, he would fail, utterly, with one who should deny the definitions and axioms. The principles of Jefferson are the definitions and axioms of free society. And yet they are denied, and evaded, with no small show of success. One

3   Beginning with his eulogy of Henry Clay in 1852, Lincoln consistently cited the "all men are created equal" clause in the Declaration of Independence as proof of the humanity of African Americans and their natural right to life, liberty, and the pursuit of happiness. In his homage to Clay, Lincoln referred to the increasing number of politicians who were, "for the sake of perpetuating slavery," condemning the clause. Lincoln pointed to Rufus Choate (1799–1859), a Whig senator from Massachusetts, who referred to the Declaration's equality clause as "the glittering and sounding generalities of natural right"; John Pettit, Democratic senator from Indiana, who scorned the Declaration's equality clause as a "self-evident lie"; and "the late John C. Calhoun," who claimed that the passage was the "most false and dangerous of all political errors." Stephen Douglas, in several speeches and in his debates with Lincoln, asserted that Jefferson's clause referred only to white men. See "Eulogy for Henry Clay, July 6, 1852," note 18, and "Speech on the Kansas-Nebraska Act at Peoria, Illinois, October, 16, 1854," note 50, in this volume; Lincoln's remarks in the seventh debate with Douglas, CW, 3:301–302. Choate's remarks were made in an August 9, 1856, letter to the Maine Whig State Central Committee. Samuel Gilman Brown, The Works of Rufus Choate with a Memoir of His Life, 2 vols. (Boston: Little, Brown and Company, 1862), 1:215.

4   Lincoln honored Jefferson for his Declaration of Independence, but he was not a supporter of Jefferson's agrarian, states' rights, and antimanufacturing philosophy, which stood in stark contrast to Whig and Republican beliefs.

dashingly calls them "glittering generalities"; another bluntly calls them "self evident lies"; and still others insidiously argue that they apply only to "superior races."[3]

These expressions, differing in form, are identical in object and effect—the supplanting the principles of free government, and restoring those of classification, caste, and legitimacy. They would delight a convocation of crowned heads, plotting against the people. They are the van-guard—the miners, and sappers—of returning despotism. We must repulse them, or they will subjugate us.

This is a world of compensations; and he who would *be* no slave, must consent to *have* no slave. Those who deny freedom to others, deserve it not for themselves; and, under a just God, can not long retain it.

All honor to Jefferson[4]—to the man who, in the concrete pressure of a struggle for national independence by a single people, had the coolness, forecast, and capacity to introduce into a merely revolutionary document, an abstract truth, applicable to all men and all times, and so to embalm it there, that to-day, and in all coming days, it shall be a rebuke and a stumbling-block to the very harbingers of re-appearing tyrany [*sic*] and oppression.

Your obedient Servant
A. LINCOLN

# Letter to Theodore Canisius on Immigration

## May 17, 1859

*Canisius, a German-born newspaper editor, had invited Lincoln to speak at a Springfield rally against a new law proposed in Massachusetts, requiring immigrants to wait at least two years before being allowed to vote. Perhaps worried that he would offend nativist friends, Lincoln declined to speak, but three days after the rally, under pressure from progressive Republicans (including his law partner William Herndon), he wrote this letter to Canisius, the rally organizer. Later, Canisius convinced Lincoln quietly to provide $500 to enable him to launch a German-language weekly in Springfield.*

Dr. Theodore Canisius[1] Springfield, May 17, 1859

Dear Sir: Your note asking, in behalf of yourself and other german citizens, whether I am for or against the constitutional provision in regard to naturalized citizens, lately adopted by Massachusetts; and whether I am for or against a fusion of the republicans, and other opposition elements, for the canvass of 1860, is received.

Massachusetts is a sovereign and independent state; and it is no privilege of mine to scold her for what she does. Still, if from what she *has done,* an inference is sought to be drawn as to what I *would do,* I may, without impropriety, speak out. I say then, that, as I understand the Massachusetts provision, I am against it's [*sic*] adoption in Illinois, or in any other place, where I have a right to oppose it. Understanding the spirit of our institutions to aim at the *elevation* of men, I am opposed to whatever tends to *degrade* them. I have some little notoriety for commiserating the oppressed condition of the negro; and I should be strangely inconsistent if I could favor any project for curtailing the existing rights of *white men,* even though born in different lands, and speaking different languages from myself.

As to the matter of fusion, I am for it, if it can be had on republican grounds; and I am not for it on any other terms. A fusion on any other terms, would be as foolish as unprincipled. It would lose the whole North, while the common enemy would still carry the whole South. The question of *men* is a different one. There are good patriotic men, and able statesmen, in the South whom I would cheerfully support, if they would now place

[1] Heinrich Theodore Canisius (ca. 1830–?) was born in Prussia and migrated to the United States after the failed European revolutions of 1848. Trained in medicine, he later took up journalism in his adopted country. An ardent antislavery

Theodore Canisius. Carte de visite photograph (1876).

Republican, he founded a Republican German-language newspaper in Alton, Illinois, the *Freie Press,* that lasted little more than a year. Canisius, like other German Americans, was outraged by the Massachusetts constitutional amendment that proposed restricting voting rights for immigrants until they had resided in the state for seven years or had been naturalized for two years. The protest rally he organized took place on May 14, 1859. Canisius did arrange to have Lincoln's letter published in the *Illinois State Journal* on May 18 and in several German-language newspapers. By the end of the month Lincoln had secretly become a publisher, with Canisius, of a new German-language newspaper, the *Illinois Staats-Anzeiger,* with the first issue appearing by July 1859. The paper was intended to promote the Republican cause in general and Lincoln's political ambitions in particular. Lincoln's contract with Canisius is in *CW,* 3:383. Holzer, *Lincoln and the Power of the Press,* 186–191.

*The Propagation Society, More Free than Welcome.* Lithograph (New York: N. Currier, ca. 1855). Anti-Catholic cartoon.

themselves on republican ground. But I am against letting down the republican standard a hair's breadth.

I have written this hastily, but I believe it answers your questions substantially.

Yours truly

A. LINCOLN

# Letter to Jesse W. Fell, Enclosing an Autobiographical Sketch

## December 20, 1859

*For more than a year, even during the senate campaign against Douglas, Lincoln had stubbornly declined to provide autobiographical information that friendly editors hoped to use to compose sympathetic life stories emphasizing his inspiring rise from poverty. Finally, just days before the beginning of the presidential campaign year of 1860, Lincoln composed this brief sketch. Not surprisingly, it was lavishly embellished when it appeared in a Pennsylvania newspaper.*

1 Jesse Wilson Fell (1808–1887) was a Bloomington, Illinois, lawyer, politician, and newspaper editor, and a close associate of Lincoln's. Born in Pennsylvania, Fell was a Whig who became a Republican in the wake of the Kansas-Nebraska firestorm. Impressed by Lincoln's performance in his debates with Douglas, Fell was convinced that Lincoln's future was on the national stage. "Seriously, Lincoln," Fell informed his fellow Republican, "Judge Douglas being so widely known, you are getting a national reputation. . . .

J. W. Fell, Esq[1] Springfield,
My dear Sir: Dec. 20. 1859

Herewith is a little sketch, as you requested. There is not much of it, for the reason, I suppose, that there is not much of me.[2]

If any thing be made out of it, I wish it to be modest, and not to go beyond the materials. If it were thought necessary to incorporate any thing from any of my speeches, I suppose there would be no objection. Of course it must not appear to have been written by myself.

Yours very truly
A. LINCOLN

I was born Feb. 12, 1809, in Hardin County, Kentucky. My parents were both born in Virginia, of undistinguished families—second families, perhaps I should say. My mother, who died in my tenth year, was of a family of the name of Hanks, some of whom now reside in Adams, and others in Macon counties, Illinois. My paternal grandfather, Abraham Lincoln, emigrated from Rockingham County, Virginia, to Kentucky, about 1781 or 2, where, a year or two later, he was killed by indians, not in battle, but by stealth, when [where?] he was laboring to open a farm in the forest. His ancestors, who were quakers, went to Virginia from Berks County, Pennsylvania. An effort to identify them with the New-England family of the same name ended in nothing more definite, than a similarity of Christian names in both families, such as Enoch, Levi, Mordecai, Solomon, Abraham, and the like.

Jesse Wilson Fell. Photograph (n.d.).

Your discussion with Judge Douglas has demonstrated your ability and your devotion to freedom; you have no embarrassing record; you have sprung from the humble walks of life, sharing in its toils and trials; and if only we can get these facts sufficiently before the people, depend on it, there is a chance for you." Willing to assist in disseminating Lincoln's life story, Fell requested an autobiographical sketch to share with Eastern voters, especially those in his native Pennsylvania. Fell's remarks to Lincoln are cited in Guelzo, *Lincoln and Douglas,* 303.

2   After initially putting off Fell's request Lincoln eventually complied, with the understanding that his authorship would remain a secret, a reasonable stipulation in a time when politicians were obliged to eschew an interest in popularity and the appearance of publicly seeking office. Fell wanted to send the sketch to Joseph J. Lewis (1801–1883), a friend and Republican activist in Pennsylvania, who had asked for information on Lincoln for an article that would be circulated among fellow Republicans in the state. On receiving the sketch from Fell, Lewis rewrote and embellished the sparse 606-word piece, which surprisingly ended with 1854 and omitted Lincoln's recent senate campaign and his debates with Douglas, turning it into a 3,000-word biography, which was published in the *Chester County Times* on February 11, 1860. Lewis's biography served as the basis for the first campaign biographies of Lincoln when he became the Republican nominee for president. Horrocks, *Lincoln's Campaign Biographies,* 23–24; Harold K. Sage, "Jesse W. Fell and the Lincoln Autobiography," *Journal of the Abraham Lincoln Association* 3 (1981): 49–59. For Lewis's biography of Lincoln, see *Lincoln's Kalamazoo Address against Extending Slavery. Also His Life, by Joseph J. Lewis* (Detroit: Fine Book Circle, 1941).

Chambers (first name unknown), *The Railsplitter.* Oil on canvas (ca. 1860).

My father, at the death of his father, was but six years of age; and he grew up, litterally [*sic*] without education. He removed from Kentucky to what is now Spencer county, Indiana, in my eighth year. We reached our new home about the time the State came into the Union. It was a wild region, with many bears and other wild animals still in the woods. There I grew up. There were some schools, so called; but no qualification was ever required of a teacher, beyond "*readin, writin, and cipherin,*" to the Rule of Three. If a straggler supposed to understand latin, happened to so-journ in the neighborhood, he was looked upon as a wizzard [*sic*]. There was absolutely nothing to excite ambition for education. Of course when I came of age I did not know much. Still somehow, I could read, write, and cipher to the Rule of Three; but that was all. I have not been to school since. The little advance I now have upon this store of education, I have picked up from time to time under the pressure of necessity.

I was raised to farm work, which I continued till I was twenty two. At twenty one I came to Illinois, and passed the first year in Macon county. Then I got to New-Salem (at that time in Sangamon, now in Menard county), where I remained a year as a sort of Clerk in a store. Then came the Black-Hawk war; and I was elected a Captain of Volunteers—a success which gave me more pleasure than any I have had since. I went on the campaign, was elated, ran for the Legislature the same year (1832) and was beaten—the only time I ever have been beaten by the people. The next, and three succeeding biennial elections, I was elected to the Legislature. I was not a candidate afterwards. During this Legislative period I had studied law, and removed to Springfield to practice it. In 1846 I was once elected to the lower House of Congress. Was not a candidate for re-election. From 1849 to 1854, both inclusive, practiced law more assiduously than ever before. Always a whig in politics, and generally on the whig electoral tickets, making active canvasses. I was losing interest in politics, when the repeal of the Missouri Compromise aroused me again. What I have done since then is pretty well known.

If any personal description of me is thought desirable, it may be said, I am, in height, six feet, four inches, nearly; lean in flesh, weighing, on an average, one hundred and eighty pounds; dark complexion, with coarse black hair, and grey eyes—no other marks or brands recollected.

Yours very truly
A. LINCOLN
Hon. J. W. Fell.

*Lincoln was invited to give this, his very first speech in New York, by a claque of young Republicans opposed to the White House aspirations of their own U.S. senator, William H. Seward, and eager to audition western presidential alternatives. Lincoln wrote his "political lecture" in Springfield, designing it for delivery at abolitionist clergyman Henry Ward Beecher's headquarters, Brooklyn's Plymouth Church—where the original invitation summoned him to speak. Only when he arrived in New York on February 25 did he learn that his lecture would instead be delivered in Peter Cooper's new coeducational college in Manhattan. Lincoln somehow managed to revise his text for a secular audience, pose for a famous Mathew Brady photograph, go shopping, worship at Beecher's church, and visit local antislavery editors—all before dazzling the New York crowd with what has come to be called "the speech that made Lincoln President." Some 1,500 men and women attended his Cooper Union lecture, and a hundred times that number read the text in the next day's papers—transforming Lincoln into an instant celebrity and a viable alternative for the Republican presidential nod. This is the edition Lincoln's hosts prepared for republication in September, but it is punctuated by the interruptions for applause and cheers recorded at Cooper Union by the* New York Herald *in the version it published the following morning.*

1    *The Address of the Hon. Abraham Lincoln, in vindication of the Policy of the Framers of the Constitution and the Principles of the Republican Party, Delivered at Cooper Institute, February 27th, 1860* (New York: George F. Nesbitt & Co., Printers and Stationers, 1860). Lincoln had disposed of the original manuscript for the speech after proofreading a typeset version in the offices of the *New York Tribune* late on the night he appeared at Cooper Union. Shortly after Lincoln won the Republican presidential nomination, and months after the *Tribune* and other Republican newspapers had

# Address at Cooper Union, New York City

## February 27, 1860

Mr. president and fellow citizens of New-York:—[1]

The facts with which I shall deal this evening are mainly old and familiar; nor is there anything new in the general use I shall make of them. If there shall be any novelty, it will be in the mode of presenting the facts, and the inferences and observations following that presentation.

In his speech last autumn, at Columbus, Ohio, as reported in "The New-York Times," Senator Douglas said:

"*Our fathers, when they framed the Government under which we live, understood this question just as well, and even better, than we do now.*"

I fully indorse this, and I adopt it as a text for this discourse. (*Applause*) I so adopt it because it furnishes a precise and an agreed starting point for a discussion between Republicans and that wing of the Democracy headed by Senator Douglas. It simply leaves the inquiry: "*What was the understanding those fathers had of the question mentioned?*" What is the frame of government under which we live?

The answer must be: "The Constitution of the United States." That Constitution consists of the original, framed in 1787, (and under which the present government first went into operation,) and twelve subsequently framed amendments, the first ten of which were framed in 1789.[2]

Who were our fathers that framed the Constitution? I suppose the "thirty-nine" who signed the original instrument may be fairly called our fathers who framed that part of the present Government. It is almost exactly true to say they framed it, and it is altogether true to say they fairly represented the opinion and sentiment of the whole nation at that time. Their names, being familiar to nearly all, and accessible to quite all, need not now be repeated.[3]

Abraham Lincoln. Photograph by Mathew Brady (New York, February 27, 1860). The aspiring presidential candidate posed before the camera hours before delivering his Cooper Union address.

rushed out inexpensive pamphlet reprints, Charles C. Nott (1827–1916) and Cephas Brainerd (1831–1910), members of the Cooper Union's board of control and editors of the original printed version of Lincoln's speech, asked Lincoln to provide his source notes for a new, more formal edition. Though the aspiring presidential candidate admitted he "would be pleased . . . with a more perfect edition" of the oration, he informed Nott: "I did not preserve memoranda of my investigations; and I could not now re-examine, and make notes, without an expenditure of time which I can not bestow on it" (Lincoln to Nott, May 31, 1860, *CW,* 4:58). Undaunted, Nott proceeded to draft footnotes for the proposed new text, and Lincoln "touched them only lightly" before approving them. This text is based on the Nott and Brainerd edition, with the young editors' inconsistent, sometimes quirky source notes repeated here (in quotation marks) as originally published, and in several cases, questioned, corrected, and augmented by the editors of this collection.

2    "The Constitution is attested September 17, 1787. It was ratified by all of the States, excepting North Carolina and Rhode Island, in 1788, and went into operation on the first Wednesday in January, 1789. The first Congress proposed, in 1789, ten articles of amendments, all of which were ratified. Article XI. of the amendments was prepared by the Third Congress, in 1794, and Article XII. by the Eighth Congress, in 1803. Another Article was proposed by the Eleventh Congress, prohibiting *citizens* from receiving titles of nobility, presents or offices, from foreign nations. Although this has been printed as one of the amendments, it was in fact never ratified, being approved by but twelve States. *Vide* ["see"—Eds.] Message of President Monroe, February 4, 1818."

3    "The Convention consisted of *sixty-five* members. Of these, *ten* did not attend the Conven-

tion, and *sixteen* did not sign the Constitution. Of these sixteen, six refused to sign, and published their reasons for so refusing, *viz.* [*videlicit,* "namely"—Eds.] Robert Yates and John Lansing, of New-York; Edmund Randolph and George Mason, of Virginia; Luther Martin, of Maryland, and Elbridge Gerry, of Mass. Alexander Hamilton alone subscribed for New-York, and Rhode Island was not represented in the Convention. The names of the 'thirty-nine,' and the States which they represented are subsequently given."

4  "The cession of territory was authorized by New-York, Feb. 19, 1780; by Virginia, January 2, 1781, and again, (without certain conditions at first imposed,) 'at their sessions, begun on the 20th day of October, 1783;' by Mass., Nov. 13, 1784; by Conn., May___, 1786; by S. Carolina, March 8, 1787; by N. Carolina, Dec.___, 1789; and by Georgia at some time prior to April, 1802.

"The deeds of cession were executed by New-York, March 1, 1781; by Virginia, March 1, 1784; by Mass., April 19, 1785; by Conn., Sept. 13, 1786; by S. Carolina, August 9, 1787; by N. Carolina, Feb. 25, 1790; and by Georgia, April 24, 1802. Five of these grants were therefore made before the adoption of the Constitution, and consummated afterward. The cession of this State contains the express proviso 'that no regulations made, or to be made by Congress, shall tend to emancipate slaves.' The cession of Georgia conveys the Territory subject to the Ordinance of '87, except the provision prohibiting slavery.

"These dates are also interesting in connection with the extraordinary assertions of Chief Justice Taney (19 How, page 434,) that 'the example of Virginia was soon afterwards followed by other States,' and that (p. 436) the power in the Constitution 'to dispose of and make all needed rules and regulations respecting the Territory or other property belonging to the United States,' was

I take these "thirty-nine," for the present, as being "our fathers who framed the Government under which we live."

What is the question which, according to the text, those fathers understood "just as well, and even better than we do now?"

It is this: Does the proper division of local from federal authority, or anything in the Constitution, forbid *our Federal Government* to control as to slavery in *our Federal Territories?*

Upon this, Senator Douglas holds the affirmative, and Republicans the negative. This affirmation and denial form an issue; and this issue—this question—is precisely what the text declares our fathers understood "better than we." (*Cheers*) Let us now inquire whether the "thirty-nine," or any of them, ever acted upon this question; and if they did, how they acted upon it—how they expressed that better understanding?

In 1784, three years before the Constitution—the United States then owning the Northwestern Territory, and no other,[4] the Congress of the Confederation had before them the question of prohibiting slavery in that Territory; and four of the "thirty-nine" who afterward framed the Constitution, were in that Congress, and voted on that question. Of these, Roger Sherman, Thomas Mifflin, and Hugh Williamson voted for the prohibition,[5] thus showing that, in their understanding, no line dividing local from federal authority, nor anything else, properly forbade the Federal Government to control as to slavery in federal territory. The other of the four—James M'Henry—voted against the prohibition, showing that, for some cause, he thought it improper to vote for it.[6]

In 1787, still before the Constitution, but while the Convention was in session framing it, and while the Northwestern Territory still was the only territory owned by the United States, the same question of prohibiting slavery in the territory again came before the Congress of the Confederation; and two more of the "thirty-nine" who afterward signed the Constitution, were in that Congress, and voted on the question. They were William Blount and William Few;[7] and they both voted for the prohibition—thus showing that, in their understanding, no line dividing local from federal authority, nor anything else, properly forbade the Federal Government to control as to slavery in Federal territory. This time the prohibition became a law, being part of what is now well known as the Ordinance of '87.[8]

The question of federal control of slavery in the territories, seems not to have been directly before the Convention which framed the original Constitution; and hence it is not recorded that the "thirty-nine," or any of them,

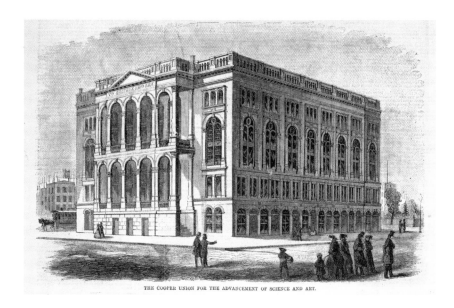

THE COOPER UNION FOR THE ADVANCEMENT OF SCIENCE AND ART.

*Cooper Union.* Engraving (1860). The college building as it looked a few months after Lincoln's speech.

while engaged on that instrument, expressed any opinion on that precise question.[9]

In 1789, by the first Congress which sat under the Constitution, an act was passed to enforce the Ordinance of '87, including the prohibition of slavery in the Northwestern Territory. The bill for this act was reported by one of the "thirty-nine," Thomas Fitzsimmons, then a member of the House of Representatives from Pennsylvania. It went through all its stages without a word of opposition, and finally passed both branches without yeas and nays, which is equivalent to a unanimous passage.[10] (*Cheers*) In this Congress there were sixteen of the thirty-nine fathers who framed the original Constitution. They were John Langdon, Nicholas Gilman, Wm. S. Johnson, Roger Sherman, Robert Morris, Thos. Fitzsimmons, William Few, Abraham Baldwin, Rufus King, William Paterson, George Clymer, Richard Bassett, George Read, Pierce Butler, Daniel Carroll, James Madison.[11]

This shows that, in their understanding, no line dividing local from federal authority, nor anything in the Constitution, properly forbade Congress to prohibit slavery in the federal territory; else both their fidelity to correct principle, and their oath to support the Constitution, would have constrained them to oppose the prohibition.

intended only 'to transfer to the new Government the property then held in common,' 'and has no reference whatever to any Territory or other property, which the new sovereignty might afterwards itself acquire.' On this subject, *vide* Federalist, No. 43, sub. 4 and 5."

5   "Sherman was from Connecticut; Mifflin from Penn.; Williamson from North Carolina, and M'Henry from Maryland."

6   "What Mr. M'Henry's views were, it seems impossible to ascertain. When the Ordinance of '87 was passed he was sitting in the Convention. He was afterward appointed Secretary of War [under Washington, appointed in 1796—Eds.]; yet no record has thus far been discovered of his opinion. Mr. M'Henry also wrote a biography of La Fayette [he had been Lafayette's private secretary—Eds.]. . . .

"Hamilton says of him, in a letter to Washington (*Works*, vol. 6, p. 65): 'M'Henry you know. He would give no strength to the Administration, but he would not disgrace the office; his views are good.'"

7   "William Blount was from North Carolina, and William Few, from Georgia—the two States which afterward ceded their territory to the United States. In addition to these facts the following extract from the speech of Rufus King in the Senate, on the Missouri Bill, shows the entire unanimity with which the Southern States approved the prohibition:—

"'The State of Virginia, which ceded to the United States her claims to this Territory, consented, by her delegates in the old Congress, to this Ordinance. Not only Virginia, but North Carolina, South Carolina, and Georgia, by the unanimous votes of their delegates in the Old Congress, approved of the Ordinance of 1787, by which Slavery is forever abolished in the Territory northwest of the river Ohio. Without the votes of these States the Ordinance could not have been passed; and there is no recollection of an opposition from any of these States to the act of confirmation passed under the actual Constitution.'"

8   The Northwest Ordinance, enacted by the Continental Congress on July 13, 1787, prohibited slavery in territory to the north and west of the Ohio River. See "Eulogy for Henry Clay, July 6, 1852," note 13, in this volume.

9   "It singularly and fortunately happens that one of the 'thirty-nine,' 'while engaged on that instrument,' viz., while advocating its ratification before the Pennsylvania Convention, did express an opinion upon this 'precise question,' which opinion was *never* disputed or doubted, in that or any other Convention, and was accepted by the opponents of the Constitution, as an indisputable fact. This was the celebrated James Wilson, of Pennsylvania. The opinion is as follows:—

"MONDAY, *Dec.* 3, 1787.

"'With respect to the clause restricting Congress from prohibiting the migration or importation of such persons as any one of the States now existing shall think proper to admit, prior to the year 1808: the Hon. gentleman says that this clause is not only dark, but intended to grant to Congress, for that time, the power to admit the importation of slaves. No such thing was intended; but I will tell you what was done, and it gives me high pleasure that so much was done. Under the present Confederation, the States may admit the importation of slaves as long as they please; but by this article, after the year 1808, the Congress will have power to prohibit such importation, notwithstanding the disposition of any State to the contrary. I consider this as laying the foundation for banishing slavery out of this country; and though the period is more distant than I could wish, yet it will produce the same kind, gradual change which was pursued in Pennsylvania. It is with much satisfaction that I view this power in the general government, whereby they may lay an interdiction on this reproachful trade. But an immediate advantage is also obtained; for a tax or duty may be imposed on such importation, not exceeding $10 for each person; and this, sir, operates as a partial prohibition; it was all that could be obtained. I am sorry it was no more; but from this I think there is reason to hope that yet a few years, and it will be prohibited altogether. *And in the* meantime, the new States which are to be formed under the

control of Congress in this particular, and slaves will never be introduced amongst them.'—2 Elliott's Debates, 423.

"It was argued by Patrick Henry in the Convention in Virginia, as follows:

"'May not Congress enact that every black man must fight? Did we not see a little of this in the last war? We were not so hard pushed as to make emancipation general. But acts of Assembly passed, that every slave who would go to the army should be free. Another thing will contribute to bring this event about. Slavery is detested. We feel its fatal effects. We deplore it with all the pity of humanity. Let all these considerations press with full force on the minds of Congress. Let that urbanity which, I trust, will distinguish America, and the necessity of national defence—let all these things operate on their minds, they will search that paper, and see if they have power of manumission. And have they not, sir? Have they not power to provide for the general defence and welfare? Must they not pronounce all slaves free, and will they not be warranted by that power? There is no ambiguous implication, no logical deduction. The paper speaks to the point; they have the power in clear, unequivocal terms, and will clearly and certainly exercise it.'—3 *Elliott's Debates,* 534.

"Edmund Randolph, one of the framers of the Constitution, replied to Mr. Henry, admitting the general force of the argument, but claiming that, because of other provisions, it had no application to the *States* where slavery *then* existed; thus conceding that power to exist in Congress as to all territory belonging to the United States.

"Dr. [David—Eds.] Ramsay, a member of the Convention of South Carolina, in his history of the United States, vol. 3, pages 36, 37, says: 'Under these liberal principles, Congress, in organizing *colonies,* bound themselves to impart to their inhabitants all the privileges of coequal States, as soon as they were capable of enjoying them. In their infancy, *government was administered for them* without any expense. As soon as they should have 60,000 inhabitants, they were authorized to call a convention, and, by common consent, to form their own constitution. This being done, they were entitled to representation in Congress, and every right attached to the original States. These privileges are not confined to any particular country or *complexion.* They are communicable to the emancipated slave, (for in the new State of Ohio, slavery is

Again, George Washington, another of the "thirty-nine," was then President of the United States, and, as such approved and signed the bill; thus completing its validity as a law, and thus showing that, in his understanding, no line dividing local from federal authority, nor anything in the Constitution, forbade the Federal Government, to control as to slavery in federal territory. (*Loud applause*)

No great while after the adoption of the original Constitution, North Carolina ceded to the Federal Government the country now constituting the State of Tennessee; and a few years later Georgia ceded that which now constitutes the States of Mississippi and Alabama. In both deeds of cession it was made a condition by the ceding States that the Federal Government should not prohibit slavery in the ceded country.[12] Besides this, slavery was then actually in the ceded country. Under these circumstances, Congress, on taking charge of these countries, did not absolutely prohibit slavery within them. But they did interfere with it—take control of it—even there, to a certain extent. In 1798, Congress organized the Territory of Mississippi. In the act of organization, they prohibited the bringing of slaves into the Territory, from any place without the United States, by fine, and giving freedom to slaves so brought.[13] This act passed both branches of Congress without yeas and nays. In that Congress were three of the "thirty-nine" who framed the original Constitution. They were John Langdon, George Read and Abraham Baldwin.[14] They all, probably, voted for it. Certainly they would have placed their opposition to it upon record, if, in their understanding, any line dividing local from federal authority, or anything in the Constitution, properly forbade the Federal Government to control as to slavery in federal territory. (*Applause*) In 1803, the Federal Government purchased the Louisiana country. Our former territorial acquisitions came from certain of our own States; but this Louisiana country was acquired from a foreign nation. In 1804, Congress gave a territorial organization to that part of it which now constitutes the State of Louisiana. New Orleans, lying within that part, was an old and comparatively large city. There were other considerable towns and settlements, and slavery was extensively and thoroughly intermingled with the people. Congress did not, in the Territorial Act, prohibit slavery; but they did interfere with it—take control of it—in a more marked and extensive way than they did in the case of Mississippi. The substance of the provision therein made, in relation to slaves, was:

*First.* That no slave should be imported into the territory from foreign parts.

altogether prohibited), to the copper-colored native, and all other human beings who, after a competent residence and degree of civilization, are capable of enjoying the blessings of regular government.'"

10 "The Act of 1789, as reported by the Committee, was received and read Thursday, July 16th. The second reading was on Friday, the 17th, when it was committed to the Committee of the whole house, 'on Monday next.' On Monday, Jul. 20th, it was considered in Committee of the whole, and ordered to a third reading on the following day; on the 21st, it passed the House, and was sent to the Senate. In the Senate it had its first reading on the same day, and was ordered to a second reading the following day, (July 22d,) and on the 4th August it passed, and on the 7th was approved by the President."

11 "The 'sixteen' represented these States:—Langdon and Gilman, New Hampshire; Sherman and Johnson, Connecticut; Morris, Fitzsimmons, and Clymer, Pennsylvania; King, Massachusetts; Paterson, New Jersey; Few and Baldwin, Georgia; Bassett and Read, Delaware; Butler, South Carolina; Carroll, Maryland; and Madison, Virginia." In fact, George Read did not so vote, as he was not a member of Congress at the time; here Lincoln was in error. See Richard Brookhiser, "Abraham Lincoln's Cooper Union Address," *For the People* 16 (Spring 2014): 2.

12 "*Vide* note 4, *ante*" ["see note 4, before"— Eds.].

13 "Chap. 28, S 7, U.S. Statutes, 5th Congress, 2d Session."

14 "Langdon was from New Hampshire, Read from Delaware, and Baldwin from Georgia."

15  "Chap. 38, S. 10, U.S. Statutes, 8th Congress, 1st Session."

16  "Baldwin was from Georgia, and Dayton from New Jersey."

17  "Rufus King, who sat in the old Congress, and also in the Convention, was the representative of Massachusetts, removed to New-York and was sent by that State to the U.S. Senate of the first Congress. Charles Pinckney was in the House, as a representative of South Carolina."

18  "Although Mr. Pinckney opposed the 'slavery prohibition' in 1820, yet his views, with regard to the *powers* of the general government, may be better judged by his actions in the Convention:

"FRIDAY, *June 8th,* 1787.—'Mr. Pinckney moved "that the National Legislature shall have the power of negativing [*sic*] all laws to be passed by the State Legislatures . . . and he considers this as the *corner-stone* of the present system; and hence, the necessity of retrenching the State authorities, in order to preserve the good government of the national council."'—P. 400, *Elliott's Debates.*

"And again, THURSDAY, *August 23d,* 1787, Mr. Pinckney renewed the motion with some modifications.—*P. 1409, Madison Papers.*

"And although Mr. Pinckney, as correctly stated by Mr. Lincoln, 'steadily voted against slavery prohibition, and against all compromises,' he still regarded the passage of the Missouri Compromise as a great triumph of the South, which is apparent from the following letter:

"CONGRESS HALL, March 2d, 1820, 3 o'clock at night.

"DEAR SIR:—I hasten to inform you, that this moment WE have carried the question to admit Missouri, and all Louisiana to the southward of 36°30, free from the restriction of slavery, and give the South, in a short time, an addition of six,

*Second.* That no slave should be carried into it who had been imported into the United States since the first day of May, 1798.

*Third.* That no slave should be carried into it, except by the owner, and for his own use as a settler; the penalty in all the cases being a fine upon the violator of the law, and freedom to the slave.[15] (*Prolonged cheers*)

This act also was passed without yeas and nays. In the Congress which passed it, there were two of the "thirty-nine." They were Abraham Baldwin and Jonathan Dayton.[16] As stated in the case of Mississippi, it is probable they both voted for it. They would not have allowed it to pass without recording their opposition to it, if, in their understanding, it violated either the line properly dividing local from federal authority, or any provision of the Constitution.

In 1819–20, came and passed the Missouri question. Many votes were taken, by yeas and nays, in both branches of Congress, upon the various phases of the general question. Two of the "thirty-nine"—Rufus King and Charles Pinckney—were members of that Congress.[17] Mr. King steadily voted for slavery prohibition and against all compromises, while Mr. Pinckney as steadily voted against slavery prohibition and against all compromises. (*Cheers*) By this, Mr. King showed that, in his understanding, no line dividing local from federal authority, nor anything in the Constitution, was violated by Congress prohibiting slavery in federal territory; while Mr. Pinckney, by his votes, showed that, in his understanding, there was some sufficient reason for opposing such prohibition in that case.[18]

The cases I have mentioned are the only acts of the "thirty-nine," or of any of them, upon the direct issue, which I have been able to discover.

To enumerate the persons who thus acted, as being four in 1784, two in 1787, seventeen in 1789, three in 1798, two in 1804, and two in 1819–20—there would be thirty of them. But this would be counting John Langdon, Roger Sherman, William Few, Rufus King, and George Read each twice, and Abraham Baldwin, three times.[19] (*Applause*) The true number of those of the "thirty-nine" whom I have shown to have acted upon the question, which, by the text, they understood better than we, is twenty-three, leaving sixteen not shown to have acted upon it in any way.[20]

Here, then, we have twenty-three out of our thirty-nine fathers "who framed the government under which we live," who have, upon their official responsibility and their corporal oaths, acted upon the very question which the text affirms they "understood just as well, and even better than we do now"; and twenty-one of them—a clear majority of the whole "thirty-nine"—so acting upon it as to make them guilty of gross political impropriety and willful perjury, if, in their understanding, any proper division be-tween local and federal authority, or anything in the Constitution they had made themselves, and sworn to support, forbade the Federal Government to control as to slavery in the federal territories. (*Cheers*) Thus the twenty-one acted; and, as actions speak louder than words, so actions, under such responsibility, speak still louder.

Two of the twenty-three voted against Congressional prohibition of slav-ery in the federal territories, in the instances in which they acted upon the question. But for what reasons they so voted is not known. They may have done so because they thought a proper division of local from federal author-ity, or some provision or principle of the Constitution, stood in the way; or they may, without any such question, have voted against the prohibition, on what appeared to them to be sufficient grounds of expediency. No one who has sworn to support the Constitution, can conscientiously vote for what he understands to be an unconstitutional measure, however expedi-ent he may think it; but one may and ought to vote against a measure which he deems constitutional, if, at the same time, he deems it inexpedient. It, therefore, would be unsafe to set down even the two who voted against the prohibition, as having done so because, in their understanding, any proper division of local from federal authority, or anything in the Constitution, forbade the Federal Government to control as to slavery in federal terri-tory.[21] (*Laughter and prolonged applause*)

The remaining sixteen of the "thirty-nine," so far as I have discovered, have left no record of their understanding upon the direct question of fed-eral control of slavery in the federal territories. But there is much reason to believe that their understanding upon that question would not have ap-peared different from that of their twenty-three compeers, had it been man-ifested at all.[22]

For the purpose of adhering rigidly to the text, I have purposely omitted whatever understanding may have been manifested by any person, however distinguished, other than the thirty-nine fathers who framed the original Constitution; and, for the same reason, I have also omitted whatever under-standing may have been manifested by any of the "thirty-nine" even, on any other phase of the general question of slavery. If we should look into their acts and declarations on those other phases, as the foreign slave trade, and the morality and policy of slavery generally, it would appear to us that on the direct question of federal control of slavery in federal territories, the sixteen, if they had acted at all, would probably have acted just as the twenty-three did. Among that sixteen were several of the most noted anti-

perhaps eight, members to the Senate of the United States. It is considered here by the slaveholding states, as a great triumph.

"The votes were close—ninety to eighty-six—produced by the seceding and absence of a few moderate men from the North. To the north of 36°30, there is to be, by the present law, restriction; which you will see by the votes, I voted against. But it is at present of no moment; it is a vast tract, uninhabited, only by savages and wild beasts, in which not a foot of the Indian claims to soil is extinguished, and in which, according to the ideas prevalent, no land office will be opened for a great length of time. With respect, your obedient servant,

CHARLES PINCKNEY.

"But conclusive evidence of Mr. Pinckney's views is furnished in the fact, that *he was himself a member of the Committee which reported the Ordinance of '87, and that on every occasion, when it was under the consideration of Congress, he voted against all amendments.—*Jour. Am. Congress, *Sept. 29th,* 1786. *Oct. 4th.* When the ordinance came up for its final passage, Mr. Pinckney was sitting in the Convention, and did not take part in the proceedings of the Congress."

19  Lincoln said "four times," not three, as the press reported the next day, but evidently corrected this error for the final pamphlet. One early campaign biography used the *New York Herald* text, but had Lincoln adding here: "He was a Georgian, too" to "Renewed applause and laughter." Richard Hinton, *The Life and Public Services of Hon. Abraham Lincoln, of Illinois, and Hon. Hannibal Hamlin, of Maine* (Boston: Thayer & Eldridge, 1860), 19.

20  "By reference to notes 4, 6, 10, 13, 15, and 16, it will be seen that, of the twenty-three who acted upon the question of prohibition, twelve were from the present slaveholding States."

21   "*Vide* notes 5 and 17, *ante*."

22   "'The remaining sixteen' were Nathaniel
Gorham, Mass.; Alex. Hamilton, New-York;
William Livingston and David Brearly, New Jersey;
Benjamin Franklin, Jared Ingersoll, James Wilson
and Gouverneur Morris, Penn.; Gunning Brad-
ford, John Dickinson and Jacob Broom, Delaware;
Daniel, of St. Thomas, Jenifer, Maryland; John
Blair, Virginia; Richard Dobbs Spaight, North
Carolina; and John Rutledge and Charles Cotes-
worth Pinckney, South Carolina."

23   "'The only distinction between freedom and
slavery consists in this: in the former state, a man is
governed by the laws to which he has given his
consent, either in person or by his representative;
in the latter, he is governed by the will of another.
In the one case, his life and property are his own;
in the other, they depend upon the pleasure of a
master. It is easy to discern which of the two states
is preferable. No man in his senses can hesitate in
choosing to be free rather than
slave. ****************** Were not the disadvantages of slavery too obvious to stand in need of it, I
might enumerate and describe the tedious train of
calamities inseparable from it. I might show that it
is fatal to religion and morality; that it tends to
debase the mind, and corrupt its noblest springs of
action. I might show that it relaxes the sinews of
industry and clips the wings of commerce, and
works misery and indigence in every shape.'—
Hamilton, *Works,* vol. 2, pp. 3, 9.

"'That you will be pleased to countenance the
restoration of *liberty* to those unhappy *men,* who
alone in this land of freedom, are degraded into
perpetual bondage, and who, amidst the general
joy of surrounding freemen, are groaning in servile
subjection; that you will devise names for
removing this inconsistency from the character of
the American people; that you will promote mercy
and *justice* toward this distressed race; and that you

Lincoln delivering his Cooper Union speech. Drawing (ca. 1860).

slavery men of those times—as Dr. Franklin, Alexander Hamilton and
Gouverneur Morris—while there was not one now known to have been
otherwise, unless it may be John Rutledge, of South Carolina.[23] (*Applause*)

The sum of the whole is, that of our thirty-nine fathers who framed
the original Constitution, twenty-one—a clear majority of the whole—certainly understood that no proper division of local from federal authority,
nor any part of the Constitution, forbade the Federal Government to control slavery in the federal territories; while all the rest probably had the same
understanding. Such, unquestionably, was the understanding of our fathers
who framed the original Constitution; and the text affirms that they understood the question "better than we." (*Laughter and cheers*)

But, so far, I have been considering the understanding of the question
manifested by the framers of the original Constitution. In and by the original instrument, a mode was provided for amending it; and, as I have already
stated, the present frame of "the Government under which we live" consists
of that original, and twelve amendatory articles framed and adopted since.
Those who now insist that federal control of slavery in federal territories violates the Constitution, point us to the provisions which they suppose it

thus violates; and, as I understand, that all fix upon provisions in these amendatory articles, and not in the original instrument. The Supreme Court, in the Dred Scott case, plant themselves upon the fifth amendment, which provides that no person shall be deprived of "life, liberty or property without due process of law"; while Senator Douglas and his peculiar adherents plant themselves upon the tenth amendment, providing that "the powers not delegated to the United States by the Constitution," "are reserved to the States respectively, or to the people."[24]

Now, it so happens that these amendments were framed by the first Congress which sat under the Constitution—the identical Congress which passed the act already mentioned, enforcing the prohibition of slavery in the Northwestern Territory. (*Applause*) Not only was it the same Congress, but they were the identical, same individual men who, at the same session, and at the same time within the session, had under consideration, and in progress toward maturity, these Constitutional amendments, and this act prohibiting slavery in all the territory the nation then owned. The Constitutional amendments were introduced before, and passed after the act enforcing the Ordinance of '87; so that, during the whole pendency of the act to enforce the Ordinance, the Constitutional amendments were also pending.[25]

The seventy-six members of that Congress, including sixteen of the framers of the original Constitution, as before stated, were pre-eminently our fathers who framed that part of "the Government under which we live," which is now claimed as forbidding the Federal Government to control slavery in the federal territories.

Is it not a little presumptuous in any one at this day to affirm that the two things which that Congress deliberately framed, and carried to maturity at the same time, are absolutely inconsistent with each other? And does not such affirmation become impudently absurd when coupled with the other affirmation from the same mouth, that those who did the two things, alleged to be inconsistent, understood whether they really were inconsistent better than we—better than he who affirms that they are inconsistent? (*Applause and great merriment*)

It is surely safe to assume that the thirty-nine framers of the original Constitution, and the seventy-six members of the Congress which framed the amendments thereto, taken together, do certainly include those who may be fairly called "our fathers who framed the Government under which we live."[26] And so assuming, I defy any man to show that any one of them ever, in his whole life, declared that, in his understanding, any proper divi-

will step to the *very verge* of the power vested in you, for discouraging every species of traffic in the persons of our fellow-men'—*Philadelphia, Feb. 3d, 1790, Franklin's Petition to Congress for the Abolition of Slavery.*

"Mr. Gouverneur Morris said:—'He never would concur in upholding domestic slavery. It was a nefarious institution. It was the curse of heaven on the States where it prevailed. * * * The admission of slavery into the representation, when fairly explained, comes to this—that the inhabitant of South Carolina or Georgia, who goes to the coast of Africa, and, in defiance of the most sacred laws of humanity, tears away his fellow-creatures from their dearest connections, and damns them to the most cruel bondage, shall have more votes, in a government instituted for the protection of the rights of mankind, than the citizen of Pennsylvania or New Jersey, who views, with a laudable horror, so nefarious a practice. * * * * * * * He would sooner submit himself to a tax for paying for all the negroes in the United States than saddle posterity with such a constitution'—*Debate on Slave Representation in the Convention—Madison Papers.*"

24 "An eminent jurist (Chancellor Walworth) has said that 'The preamble which was prefixed to these amendments, as adopted by Congress is important to show in what light that body considered them.' (8 *Wend. R.,* p. 100.) It declares that a number of the State Conventions 'having at the time of their adopting the Constitution *expressed a desire,* in order to prevent *misconstruction or abuse of its powers,* that further *declaratory* and restrictive clauses should be added,' resolved &c."

25 "The amendments were proposed by Mr. Madison in the House of Representatives, June 8, 1789. They were adopted by the House, August 24, and some further amendments seem to have been transmitted by the Senate, September 9. The

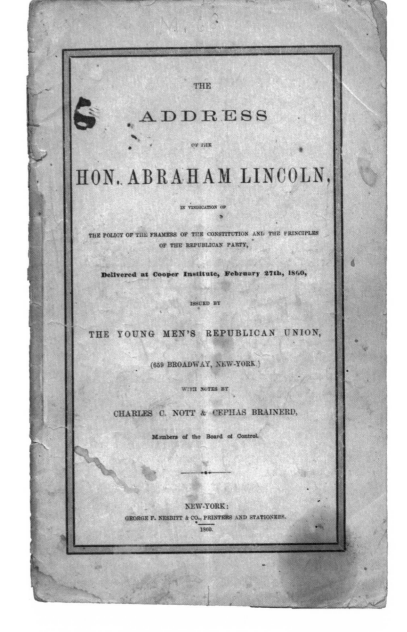

Abraham Lincoln, *The Address of the Hon. Abraham Lincoln . . . Delivered at Cooper Institute, February 27, 1860* (New York: Young Men's Republican Union, 1860). Cover page of the published version of Lincoln's Cooper Union Address.

printed journals of the Senate do not state the time of the final passage, and the message transmitting them to the State Legislatures speaks of them as adopted at the first session, begun on the fourth day of March, 1789. The date of the introduction and passage of the act enforcing the ordinance of '87, will be found at note 10, *ante*."

26  "It is singular that while two of the 'thirty-nine' were in that Congress of 1819, there was but one (besides Mr. King) of the 'seventy-six.' The one was William Smith, of South Carolina. He was then a Senator and, like Mr. Pinckney, occupied extreme Southern ground."

sion of local from federal authority, or any part of the Constitution, forbade the Federal Government to control as to slavery in the federal territories. (*Loud applause*) I go a step further. I defy any one to show that any living man in the whole world ever did, prior to the beginning of the present century, (and I might almost say prior to the beginning of the last half of the present century,) declare that, in his understanding, any proper division of local from federal authority, or any part of the Constitution, forbade the Federal Government to control as to slavery in the federal territories. To those who now so declare, I give, not only "our fathers who framed the Government under which we live," but with them all other living men within the century in which it was framed, among whom to search, and they shall not be able to find the evidence of a single man agreeing with them.

Now, and here, let me guard a little against being misunderstood. I do not mean to say we are bound to follow implicitly in whatever our fathers did. To do so, would be to discard all the lights of current experience—to reject all progress—all improvement. What I do say is, that if we would supplant the opinions and policy of our fathers in any case, we should do so upon evidence so conclusive, and argument so clear, that even their great authority, fairly considered and weighed, cannot stand; and most surely not in a case whereof we ourselves declare they understood the question better than we. (*Laughter*)

If any man at this day sincerely believes that a proper division of local from federal authority, or any part of the Constitution, forbids the Federal Government to control as to slavery in the federal territories, he is right to say so, and to enforce his position by all truthful evidence and fair argument which he can. But he has no right to mislead others, who have less access to history, and less leisure to study it, into the false belief that "our fathers who framed the Government under which we live" were of the same opinion—thus substituting falsehood and deception for truthful evidence and fair argument. (*Applause*) If any man at this day sincerely believes "our fathers who framed the Government under which we live," used and applied principles, in other cases, which ought to have led them to understand that a proper division of local from federal authority or some part of the Constitution, forbids the Federal Government to control as to slavery in the federal territories, he is right to say so. But he should, at the same time, brave the responsibility of declaring that, in his opinion, he understands their principles better than they did themselves; (*Great laughter*) and especially should he not shirk that responsibility by asserting that they "understood the question just as well, and even better, than we do now." (*Applause*)

But enough! *Let all who believe that "our fathers, who framed the Government under which we live, understood this question just as well, and even better, than we do now," speak as they spoke, and act as they acted upon it. This is all Republicans ask—all Republicans desire—in relation to slavery. As those fathers*

27  In this prediction, Lincoln was far too optimistic. Though his name appeared on the ballots of a few Upper South states in November, the Republican ticket received a thrashing from voters, winning only 2 percent of the vote in the region—1 percent in Virginia, and *less* than 1 percent in Lincoln's native Kentucky.

*marked it, so let it be again marked, as an evil not to be extended, but to be tolerated and protected only because of and so far as its actual presence among us makes that toleration and protection a necessity.* (Loud applause) *Let all the guarantees those fathers gave it, be, not grudgingly, but fully and fairly, maintained.* For this Republicans contend, and with this, so far as I know or believe, they will be content. (*Applause*)

And now, if they would listen—as I suppose they will not—I would address a few words to the Southern people. (*Laughter*)

I would say to them:—You consider yourselves a reasonable and a just people; and I consider that in the general qualities of reason and justice you are not inferior to any other people. Still, when you speak of us Republicans, you do so only to denounce us as reptiles, or, at the best, as no better than outlaws. You will grant a hearing to pirates or murderers, but nothing like it to "Black Republicans." (*Laughter*) In all your contentions with one another, each of you deems an unconditional condemnation of "Black Republicanism" as the first thing to be attended to. (*Laughter*) Indeed, such condemnation of us seems to be an indispensable prerequisite—license, so to speak—among you to be admitted or permitted to speak at all. Now, can you, or not, be prevailed upon to pause and to consider whether this is quite just to us, or even to yourselves? Bring forward your charges and specifications, and then be patient long enough to hear us deny or justify.

You say we are sectional. We deny it. (*Loud applause*) That makes an issue; and the burden of proof is upon you. (*Laughter and applause*) You produce your proof; and what is it? Why, that our party has no existence in your section—gets no votes in your section. The fact is substantially true; but does it prove the issue? If it does, then in case we should, without change of principle, begin to get votes in your section, we should thereby cease to be sectional. (*Great merriment*) You cannot escape this conclusion; and yet, are you willing to abide by it? If you are, you will probably soon find that we have ceased to be sectional, for we shall get votes in your section this very year.[27] (*Loud cheers*) You will then begin to discover, as the truth plainly is, that your proof does not touch the issue. The fact that we get no votes in your section, is a fact of your making, and not of ours. And if there be fault in that fact, that fault is primarily yours, and remains until you show that we repel you by some wrong principle or practice. If we do repel you by any wrong principle or practice, the fault is ours; but this brings you to where you ought to have started—to a discussion of the right or wrong of our principle. (*Loud applause*) If our principle, put in practice, would wrong your section for the benefit of ours, or for any other object, then our principle, and we with it, are sectional, and are justly opposed and denounced as such. Meet us, then, on the question of whether our principle, put in practice, would wrong your section; and so meet it as if it were possible that something may be said on our side. (*Laughter*) Do you accept the challenge? No! Then you really believe that the principle which "our fathers who framed the Government under which we live" thought so clearly right as to adopt it, and indorse it again and again, upon their official oaths, is in fact so clearly wrong as to demand your condemnation without a moment's consideration. (*Applause*)

Some of you delight to flaunt in our faces the warning against sectional parties given by Washington in his Farewell Address. Less than eight years before Washington gave that warning, he had, as President of the United States, approved and signed an act of Congress, enforcing the prohibition of slavery in the Northwestern Territory, which act embodied the policy of the Government upon that subject up to and at the very moment he penned that warning; and about one year after he penned it, he wrote La Fayette that he considered that prohibition a wise measure, expressing in the same connection his hope that we should at some time have a confederacy of free States.[28] (*Applause*)

Bearing this in mind, and seeing that sectionalism has since arisen upon this same subject, is that warning a weapon in your hands against us, or in our hands against you? Could Washington himself speak, would he cast the blame of that sectionalism upon us, who sustain his policy, or upon you who repudiate it? (*Applause*) We respect that warning of Washington, and we commend it to you, together with his example pointing to the right application of it. (*Applause*)

But you say you are conservative—eminently conservative—while we are revolutionary, destructive, or something of the sort. What is conservatism? Is it not adherence to the old and tried, against the new and untried? We stick to, contend for, the identical old policy on the point in controversy which was adopted by "our fathers who framed the Government under which we live"; while you with one accord reject, and scout, and spit upon that old policy, and insist upon substituting something new. True, you disagree among yourselves as to what that substitute shall be. You are divided on new propositions and plans, but you are unanimous in rejecting and denouncing the old policy of the fathers. Some of you are for reviving the foreign slave trade; some for a Congressional Slave-Code for the Territories; some for Congress forbidding the Territories to prohibit Slavery within their limits; some for maintaining Slavery in the Territories through the ju-

28 "The following is an extract from the letter referred to:—

"'I agree with you cordially in your views in regard to negro slavery. I have long considered it a most serious evil, both socially and politically, and I should rejoice in any feasible scheme to rid our States of such a burden. The Congress of 1787 adopted an ordinance which prohibits the existence of involuntary servitude in our Northwestern Territory forever. I consider it a wise measure. It meets with the approval and assent of every member from the States more immediately interested in Slave labor. The prevailing opinion in Virginia is against the spread of slavery in our new territories, and I trust we shall have a confederation of free States.'"

Washington's so-called letter to the Marquis de Lafayette, widely reprinted at the time and quoted by many antislavery politicians, was eventually proven to be an invention. It does not exist.

"The following extract from a letter of Washington to Robert Morris, April 12th, 1786, shows how strong were his views, and how clearly he deemed emancipation a subject for legislative enactment:—'I can only say that there is no man living who wishes more sincerely than I do to see a plan adopted for the abolition of it; but there is but one proper and effective mode by which it can be accomplished, and that is, BY LEGISLATIVE AUTHORITY, and that, as far as *my suffrage will go, shall never be wanting.*'"

29 "A Committee of five, consisting of Messrs.
Mason, Davis and Fitch, (Democrats,) and
Collamer and Doolittle, (Republicans,) was
appointed Dec. 14, 1859, by the U.S. Senate, to
investigate the Harper's Ferry affair. That committee was directed, among other things, to inquire:
(1.) 'Whether such invasion and seizure was made
under color of any organization intended to
subvert the government of any of the States of the
Union.' (2.) 'What was the character and extent of
such organization.' (3.) 'And whether any citizens
of the United States, not present, were implicated
therein, or accessory thereto, by contributions of
money, arms, munitions, or otherwise.'

"The majority of the Committee, Messrs.
Mason, Davis, and Fitch, reply to the inquiries as
follows:

"1. 'There will be found in the Appendix, a
copy of the proceedings of a Convention held at
Chatham, Canada, of the Provisional Form of
Government there pretended to have been
instituted, the object of which clearly was to
subvert the government of one or more States, and
of course, to that extent, the government of the
United States.' By reference to the copy of
Proceedings it appears that *nineteen* persons were
present at that Convention, *eight* of whom were
either killed or executed at Charlestown [site of
John Brown's execution—Eds.], and one examined
before the Committee.

"2. 'The character of the military organization
appears, by the commissions issued to certain of
the armed party as captains, lieutenants, &c., a
specimen of which will be found in the Appendix.'

"(These Commissions are signed by John
Brown as Commander-in-Chief, under the
Provisional Government, and by J. H. Kagi as
Secretary.)

"3. 'It does not appear that the contributions
were made with actual knowledge of the use for

diciary; some for the "gur-reat pur-rinciple" (*Laughter*) that "if one man
would enslave another, no third man should object," fantastically called
"Popular Sovereignty"; (*Renewed laughter and applause*) but never a man
among you is in favor of federal prohibition of slavery in federal territories,
according to the practice of "our fathers who framed the Government under
which we live." Not one of all your various plans can show a precedent or an
advocate in the century within which our Government originated. Consider, then, whether your claim of conservatism for yourselves, and your
charge or destructiveness against us, are based on the most clear and stable
foundations.

Again, you say we have made the slavery question more prominent than
it formerly was. We deny it. We admit that it is more prominent, but we
deny that we made it so. It was not we, but you, who discarded the old policy of the fathers. We resisted, and still resist, your innovation; and thence
comes the greater prominence of the question. Would you have that question reduced to its former proportions? Go back to that old policy. What
has been will be again, under the same conditions. If you would have the
peace of the old times, readopt the precepts and policy of the old times.
(*Applause*)

You charge that we stir up insurrections among your slaves. We deny it;
and what is your proof? Harper's Ferry! (*Great laughter*) John Brown!! (*Renewed laughter*) John Brown was no Republican; and you have failed to implicate a single Republican in his Harper's Ferry enterprise. (*Loud applause*)
If any member of our party is guilty in that matter, you know it or you do
not know it. If you do know it, you are inexcusable for not designating the
man and proving the fact. If you do not know it, you are inexcusable for asserting it, and especially for persisting in the assertion after you have tried
and failed to make the proof. (*Great applause*) You need to be told that persisting in a charge which one does not know to be true, is simply malicious
slander.[29] (*Applause*)

Some of you admit that no Republican designedly aided or encouraged
the Harper's Ferry affair, but still insist that our doctrines and declarations
necessarily lead to such results. We do not believe it. We know we hold to
no doctrine, and make no declaration, which were not held to and made by
"our fathers who framed the Government under which we live." (*Applause*)
You never dealt fairly by us in relation to this affair. When it occurred, some
important State elections were near at hand, and you were in evident glee
with the belief that, by charging the blame upon us, you could get an advantage of us in those elections. The elections came, and your expectations

were not quite fulfilled.[30] (*Laughter*) Every Republican man knew that, as to himself at least, your charge was a slander, and he was not much inclined by it to cast his vote in your favor. Republican doctrines and declarations are accompanied with a continual protest against any interference whatever with your slaves, or with you about your slaves. Surely, this does not encourage them to revolt. True, we do, in common with "Our fathers, who framed the Government under which we live," declare our belief that slavery is wrong; (*Applause*) but the slaves do not hear us declare even this. For anything we say or do, the slaves would scarcely know there is a Republican party. I believe they would not, in fact, generally know it but for your misrepresentations of us, in their hearing. In your political contests among yourselves, each faction charges the other with sympathy with Black Republicanism; and then, to give point to the charge, defines Black Republicanism to simply be insurrection, blood and thunder among the slaves. (*Boisterous laughter and applause*)

Slave insurrections are no more common now than they were before the Republican party was organized. What induced the Southampton insurrection, twenty-eight years ago, in which, at least three times as many lives were lost as at Harper's Ferry?[31] You can scarcely stretch your very elastic fancy to the conclusion that Southampton was "got up by Black Republicanism." (*Laughter*) In the present state of things in the United States, I do not think a general, or even a very extensive slave insurrection, is possible. The indispensable concert of action cannot be attained. The slaves have no means of rapid communication; nor can incendiary freemen, black or white, supply it. The explosive materials are everywhere in parcels; but there neither are, nor can be supplied, the indispensable connecting trains.

Much is said by Southern people about the affection of slaves for their masters and mistresses; and a part of it, at least, is true. A plot for an uprising could scarcely be devised and communicated to twenty individuals before some one of them, to save the life of a favorite master or mistress, would divulge it. This is the rule; and the slave revolution in Hayti [*sic*] was not an exception to it, but a case occurring under peculiar circumstances.[32] The gunpowder plot of British history, though not connected with slaves, was more in point. In that case, only about twenty were admitted to the secret; and yet one of them, in his anxiety to save a friend, betrayed the plot to that friend, and, by consequence, averted the calamity. Occasional poisonings from the kitchen, and open or stealthy assassinations in the field, and local revolts extending to a score or so, will continue to occur as the natural results of slavery; but no general insurrection of slaves, as I think, can hap-

which they were designed by Brown, although it does appear that money was freely contributed by those styling themselves the friends of this man Brown, and friends alike of what they styled the cause of freedom, (of which they claimed him to be an especial apostle,) without inquiring as to the way in which the money would be used by him to advance such pretended cause.'

"In concluding the report the majority of the Committee thus characterize the 'invasion': 'It was simply the act of lawless ruffians, under the sanction of no public or political authority—distinguishable only from ordinary felons by the ulterior ends in contemplation by them,' &c."

30 Hinton, *Life and Public Services of Hon. Abraham Lincoln,* 256, added: "You did not sweep New York, and New Jersey, and Wisconsin, and Minnesota, precisely like fire sweeps over the prairie in the high wind. (*Laughter*) You are still drumming at this idea. Go on with it. If you think you can, by slandering a woman, make her love you, or by vilifying a man make him vote with you, go on and try it. (*Boisterous laughter, and prolonged applause*)."

31 "The Southampton insurrection, August, 1831, was induced by the remarkable ability of a slave calling himself General Nat Turner. He led his fellow bondmen to believe that he was acting under the order of Heaven. In proof of this he alleged that the singular appearance of the sun at that time was a divine signal for the commencement of the struggle which would result in the recovery of their freedom. This insurrection resulted in the death of sixty-four white persons, and more than one hundred slaves. The Southampton was the eleventh large insurrection in the Southern States, besides numerous attempts and revolts."

32 "In March, 1790, the General Assembly of France, on the petition of the *free* people of color

in St. Domingo, many of whom were intelligent and wealthy, passed a decree intended to be in their favor, but so ambiguous as to be construed in favor of both the whites and the blacks. The differences growing out of the decree created two parties—the *whites* and the people of color; and some blood was shed. In 1791, the blacks again petitioned, and a decree was passed declaring the colored people citizens, who were born of free parents on both sides. This produced great excitement among the whites, and the two parties armed against each other, and horrible massacres and conflagrations followed. Then the Assembly rescinded this last decree, and like results followed, the blacks being the exasperated parties and the aggressors. Then the decree giving citizenship to the blacks was restored, and commissioners were sent out to keep the peace. The commissioners, unable to sustain themselves, between the two parties, with the troops they had, issued a proclamation that all blacks who were willing to range themselves under the banner of the Republic should be free. As a result a very large proportion of the blacks became in fact free. In 1794, the Conventional Assembly *abolished slavery* throughout the French Colonies. Some years afterward the French government sought, with an army of 60,000 men[,] to reinstate slavery, but were unsuccessful, and then the white planters were driven from the Island."

33  "*Vide* Jefferson's Autobiography, commenced January 6th, 1821. Jefferson's works, vol. 1, p. 49."

34  Italian revolutionary Felice Orsini (1819–1858), head of the Carbonari, tried to assassinate Napoleon III in 1858. The bombs he used were made in Great Britain, igniting much French resentment of "Old England."

35  Lincoln referred to the anti-slavery book by Hinton Rowan Helper, *The Impending Crisis of the South: How to Meet It* (New York: Burdick Brothers, 1857).

pen in this country for a long time. Whoever much fears, or much hopes for such an event, will be alike disappointed.

In the language of Mr. Jefferson, uttered many years ago, "It is still in our power to direct the process of emancipation, and deportation, peaceably, and in such slow degrees, as that the evil will wear off insensibly; and their places be, *pari passu* [at an equal rate]*, filled up by free white laborers. (*Loud applause*) If, on the contrary, it is left to force itself on, human nature must shudder at the prospect held up."[33]

Mr. Jefferson did not mean to say, nor do I, that the power of emancipation is in the Federal Government. He spoke of Virginia; and, as to the power of emancipation, I speak of the slaveholding States only. The Federal Government, however, as we insist, has the power of restraining the extension of the institution—the power to insure that a slave insurrection shall never occur on any American soil which is now free from slavery. (*Applause*)

John Brown's effort was peculiar. It was not a slave insurrection. It was an attempt by white men to get up a revolt among slaves, in which the slaves refused to participate. In fact, it was so absurd that the slaves, with all their ignorance, saw plainly enough it could not succeed. That affair, in its philosophy, corresponds with the many attempts, related in history, at the assassination of kings and emperors. An enthusiast broods over the oppression of a people till he fancies himself commissioned by Heaven to liberate them. He ventures the attempt, which ends in little else than his own execution. Orsini's attempt on Louis Napoleon,[34] and John Brown's attempt at Harper's Ferry were, in their philosophy, precisely the same. The eagerness to cast blame on old England in the one case, and on New England in the other, does not disprove the sameness of the two things.

And how much would it avail you, if you could, by the use of John Brown, Helper's Book[35] and the like, break up the Republican organization? Human action can be modified to some extent, but human nature cannot be changed. There is a judgment and a feeling against slavery in this nation, which cast at least a million and a half of votes. You cannot destroy that judgment and feeling—that sentiment—by breaking up the political organization which rallies around it. You can scarcely scatter and disperse an army which has been formed into order in the face of your heaviest fire; but if you could, how much would you gain by forcing the sentiment which created it out of the peaceful channel of the ballot-box, into some other channel? What would that other channel probably be? Would the number of John Browns be lessened or enlarged by the operation?

But you will break up the Union rather than submit to a denial of your Constitutional rights.[36]

That has a somewhat reckless sound; but it would be palliated, if not fully justified, were we proposing, by the mere force of numbers, to deprive you of some right, plainly written down in the Constitution. But we are proposing no such thing.

When you make these declarations, you have a specific and well-understood allusion to an assumed Constitutional right of yours, to take slaves into the federal territories, and to hold them there as property. But no such right is specifically written in the Constitution. That instrument is literally silent about any such right. We, on the contrary, deny that such a right has any existence in the Constitution, even by implication. (*Applause*)

Your purpose, then, plainly stated, is that you will destroy the Government, unless you be allowed to construe and enforce the Constitution as you please, on all points in dispute between you and us. You will rule or ruin in all events.

This, plainly stated, is your language. Perhaps you will say the Supreme Court has decided the disputed Constitutional question in your favor. Not quite so. But waiving the lawyer's distinction between dictum and decision, the Court have decided the question for you in a sort of way. The Court have substantially said, it is your Constitutional right to take slaves into the federal territories, and to hold them there as property. When I say the decision was made in a sort of way, I mean it was made in a divided Court, by a bare majority of the Judges, and they not quite agreeing with one another in the reasons for making it;[37] that it is so made as that its avowed supporters disagree with one another about its meaning, and that it was mainly based upon a mistaken statement of fact—the statement in the opinion that "the right of property in a slave is distinctly and expressly affirmed in the Constitution."[38]

An inspection of the Constitution will show that the right of property in a slave is not "*distinctly* and *expressly* affirmed" in it. (*Applause*) Bear in mind, the Judges do not pledge their judicial opinion that such right is *impliedly* affirmed in the Constitution; but they pledge their veracity that it is "*distinctly* and *expressly*" affirmed there—"distinctly," that is, not mingled with anything else—"expressly," that is, in words meaning just that, without the aid of any inference, and susceptible of no other meaning.

If they had only pledged their judicial opinion that such right is affirmed in the instrument by implication, it would be open to others to show that neither the word "slave" nor "slavery" is to be found in the Constitution,

36  Six examples of Southern political leaders expressing support for breaking up the Union if a Republican is elected president in 1860 were originally presented in this note. Two examples are offered here:

"'I am not ashamed or afraid publicly to avow, that the election of William H. Seward or Salmon P. Chase, or any such representative of the Republican party, upon a sectional platform, ought to be resisted to the disruption of every tie that binds the Confederacy together. (Applause on the Democratic side of the House.)'—*Mr.* [Jabez L. M.] *Curry, of Alabama* [later in the Confederate army—Eds.], *in the House of Representatives.*

"'Just so sure as the Republican party succeed in electing a sectional man, upon their sectional, anti-slavery platform, breathing destruction and death to the rights of my people, just so sure, in my judgment, the time will have come when the South must and will take an unmistakable and decided action, and then he who dallies is a dastard, and he who doubts is damned! I need not tell what I, as a Southern man, will do. I think I may safely speak for the masses of the people of Georgia—that when that event happens, they, in my judgment, will consider it an overt act, a declaration of war, and meet immediately in convention, to take into consideration the mode and measure of redress. That is my position; and if that be treason to the Government, make the most of it.'—*Mr. Gartell, of Georgia, in the House of Representatives.*"

37  "The Hon. John A. Andrew, of the Boston Bar, made the following analysis of the Dred Scott case in the Massachusetts legislature. Hon. Caleb Cushing was then a member of that body, but did not question its correctness.

"'On the question of possibility of citizenship to one of the Dred Scott color, extraction, and origin, three justices, viz., Taney, Wayne and

Daniels, held the negative. Nelson and Campbell passed over the plea by which the question was raised. Grier agreed with Nelson. Catron said the question was not open. McLean agreed with Catron, but thought the plea bad. Curtis agreed that the question was open, but attacked the plea, met its averments, and decided that a free born colored person, native to any State, is a citizen thereof, by birth, and is therefore a citizen of the Union, and entitled to sue in the Federal Courts.

"'Had a majority of the court directly sustained the plea in abatement, and denied the jurisdiction of the Circuit Court appealed from, then all else they could have said and done would have been done in a cause not theirs to try and not theirs to discuss. In the absence of such majority, one step more was to be taken. And the next step reveals an agreement of six of the Justices, on a point decisive of the cause, and putting an end to all the functions of the court.

"'It is this. Scott was first carried to Rock Island, in the State of Illinois, where he remained about two years, before going with his master to Fort Snelling, in the Territory of Wisconsin. His claim to freedom was rested on the alleged effect of his transition from a slave State, and again into a free territory. If, by his removal to Illinois, he became emancipated from his master, the subsequent continuance of his pilgrimage into the Louisiana purchase could not add to his freedom, nor alter the fact of it. If, by reason of any want or infirmity in the laws of Illinois, or of conformity on his part to their behests, Dred Scott remained a slave while he remained in that State, then—for the sake of learning the effect on him of his territorial residence beyond the Mississippi, and of his marriage and other proceedings there, and the effect of the sojournment and marriage of Harriet, in the same territory, upon herself and her children—it might become needful to advance one other step into the investigation of the law; to inspect the Missouri Compromise, banishing slavery to the south of the line of 36°30 in the Louisiana Purchase.

"'But no exigency of the cause ever demanded or justified that advance; for six of the Justices, including the Chief Justice himself, decided that the *status* of the plaintiff, as free or slave, was dependent, not upon the laws of the State into which he had been, but of the State of Missouri, in which he was at the commencement of the suit. The Chief Justice asserted that "it is now firmly settled by the decision of the highest court in the State, that Scott and his family, on their return were not free, but were, by the laws of Missouri, the property of the defendant." This was the burden of the opinion of Nelson, who declares "the question is one solely depending upon the law of Missouri, and that the federal Court, sitting in the State, and trying the case before us, was bound to follow it." It received the emphatic endorsement of Wayne, whose general concurrence was with the Chief Justice. Grier concurred in set terms with Nelson on all "the questions discussed by him." Campbell says, "The claim of the plaintiff to freedom depends upon the effect to be given to his absence from Missouri, in company with his master in Illinois and Minnesota, *and this effect is to be ascertained by reference to the laws of Missouri.*" Five of the Justices, then, (if no more of them,) regard the law of Missouri as decisive of the plaintiff's rights.'"

38 "'Now, as we have already said in an earlier part of this opinion upon a different point, the right of property in a slave is distinctly and expressly affirmed in the Constitution. The right to traffic in it, *like an ordinary article of merchandise and property,* was guaranteed to the citizens of the United States in every State that might desire it for twenty years.'—*Ch. J. Taney,* 19 *How. U.S.R.,* p. 451. *Vide* language of Mr. Madison, note . . . , as to '*merchandise.*'"

39 "Not only was the right of property *not* intended to be 'distinctly and expressly affirmed in the Constitution'; but the following extract from Mr. Madison demonstrates that the utmost care was taken to avoid so doing:—

"The clause as originally offered [respecting fugitive slaves], read 'If any person LEGALLY bound to service or labor in any of the United States shall escape into another State,' etc., etc. (Vol. 3, p. 1456.) In regard to this, Mr. Madison says, 'The term "*legally*" was struck out, and the words "under the laws thereof," inserted after the word State, in compliance with the wish of some who thought the term "legally" equivocal and favoring the idea that slavery was legal in a moral point of view.'—*Ib.* [*ibidem,* "in the same place"—Eds.], p. 1589."

40 "We subjoin a portion of the history alluded to by Mr. Lincoln. The following extract relates to the provision of the Constitution relative to the slave trade. (Article I, Sec. 9.)

"*25th August,* 1787.—The report of the Committee of eleven being taken up, Gen. [Charles Cotesworth] Pinckney moved to nor the word "property" even, in any connection with language alluding to the things slave, or slavery; (*Applause*) and that wherever in that instrument the slave is alluded to, he is called a "person";—and wherever his master's legal right in relation to him is alluded to, it is spoken of as "service or labor which may be due,"—as a debt payable in service or labor.[39] Also, it would be open to show, by contemporaneous history, that this mode of alluding to slaves and slavery, instead of speaking of them, was employed on purpose to exclude from the Constitution the idea that there could be property in man.

To show all this, is easy and certain.[40]

When this obvious mistake of the Judges shall be brought to their notice, is it not reasonable to expect that they will withdraw the mistaken statement, and reconsider the conclusion based upon it?

And then it is to be remembered that "our fathers, who framed the Government under which we live"—the men who made the Constitution—decided this same Constitutional question in our favor, long ago—decided it without division among themselves, when making the decision; without division among themselves about the meaning of it after it was made, and, so far as any evidence is left, without basing it upon any mistaken statement of facts.

Under all these circumstances, do you really feel yourselves justified to break up this Government, unless such a court decision as yours is, shall be at once submitted to as a conclusive and final rule of political action? But you will not abide the election of a Republican president! In that supposed event, you say, you will destroy the Union; and then, you say, the great crime of having destroyed it will be upon us! (*Laughter*) That is cool. (*Great laughter*) A highwayman holds a pistol to my ear, and mutters through his teeth, "Stand and deliver, or I shall kill you, and then you will be a murderer!" (*Continued laughter*)

To be sure, what the robber demanded of me—my money—was my own; and I had a clear right to keep it; but it was no more my own than my vote is my own; (*"That's so," and applause*) and the threat of death to me, to extort my money, and the threat of destruction to the Union, to extort my vote, can scarcely be distinguished in principle.

A few words now to Republicans. *It is exceedingly desirable that all parts of this great Confederacy shall be at peace, and in harmony, one with another. Let us Republicans do our part to have it so.* ("We will," and applause) *Even though much provoked, let us do nothing through passion and ill temper. Even though the southern people will not so much as listen to us, let us calmly consider their demands, and yield to them if, in our deliberate view of our duty, we pos-*

strike out the words 'the year 1800,' and insert the words 'the year 1808.'

"Mr. Gorham seconded the motion.

"Mr. Madison—Twenty years will produce all the mischief that can be apprehended from the liberty to import slaves. So long a term will be more dishonorable to the American character than to say nothing about it in the Constitution.

\* \* \* \* \* \* \* \* \* \* \* \* \* \* \* \* \* \* \* \* \* \* \* \* \* \* \* \* \* \*

"Mr. Gouverneur Morris was for making the clause read at once—

"'The importation of slaves into North Carolina, South Carolina, and Georgia, shall not be prohibited,' &c.

"This, he said, would be most fair, and would avoid the ambiguity by which, under the power with regard to naturalization the liberty reserved to the States might be defeated. He wished it to be known, also, that this part of the Constitution was a compliance with those States. If the change of language, however, should be objected to by the members from those States, he should not urge it.

"Col. Mason (of Va.,) was not against using the term 'slaves,' but against naming North Carolina, South Carolina, and Georgia, lest it should give offence to the people of those States.

"Mr. Sherman liked a description better than the terms proposed, which had been declined by the old Congress, and were not pleasing to some people.

"Mr. Clymer concurred with Mr. Sherman.

"Mr. Williamson, of North Carolina, said that *both in opinion and practice he was against slavery; but thought it more in favor of humanity, from a view of all circumstances, to let in South Carolina and Georgia, on those terms, than to exclude them from the Union.*

"Mr. Morris withdrew his motion.

"Mr. Dickinson wished the clause to be confined to the States which had not themselves prohibited the importation of slaves, and for that purpose moved to amend the clause so as to read—

"'The importation of slaves into such of the States as shall permit the same, shall not be prohibited by the Legislature of the United States, until the year 1808,' which was disagreed to, *nem. con.* [*nemine contradicente,* "with no one contesting"—Eds.]

"The first part of the report was then agreed to as follows:

"'The migration or importation of such persons as the several states now existing shall think proper to admit, shall not be prohibited by the Legislature prior to the year 1808.'

\* \* \* \* \* \* \* \* \* \* \* \* \* \* \* \* \* \* \* \* \* \* \* \* \* \* \* \* \*

"Mr. Sherman was against the second part, ['but a tax or duty may be imposed on such migration or importation at a rate not exceeding *the average of the duties laid on imports,*'] as acknowledging men to be property by taxing them as such under the character of slaves.

\* \* \* \* \* \* \* \* \* \* \* \* \* \* \* \* \* \* \* \* \* \* \* \* \* \* \* \* \*

"Mr. Madison *thought it wrong to admit in the Constitution the idea that there could be property in men.* The reason of duties did not hold, as slaves *are not, like merchandise,* consumed.

\* \* \* \* \* \* \* \* \* \* \* \* \* \* \* \* \* \* \* \* \* \* \* \* \* \* \* \* \*

"It was finally agreed, *nem. con.* to make the clause read—

"'But a tax or duty may be imposed on such importation, not exceeding *ten dollars* for each PERSON.'—*Madison Papers,* Aug. 25, 1787."

41  "That demand has since been made. Says MR. O'CONOR, counsel for the State of Virginia in

*sibly can.* Judging by all they say and do, and by the subject and nature of their controversy with us, let us determine, if we can, what will satisfy them.

Will they be satisfied if the Territories be unconditionally surrendered to them? We know they will not. In all their present complaints against us, the Territories are scarcely mentioned. Invasions and insurrections are the rage now. Will it satisfy them, if, in the future, we have nothing to do with invasions and insurrections? We know it will not. We so know, because we know we never had anything to do with invasions and insurrections; and yet this total abstaining does not exempt us from the charge and the denunciation. The question recurs, what will satisfy them? Simply this: We must not only let them alone, but we must somehow, convince them that we do let them alone. This, we know by experience, is no easy task. We have been so trying to convince them from the very beginning of our organization, but with no success. In all our platforms and speeches we have constantly protested our purpose to let them alone; but this has had no tendency to convince them. Alike unavailing to convince them, is the fact that they have never detected a man of us in any attempt to disturb them.

These natural, and apparently adequate means all failing, what will convince them? This, and this only: cease to call slavery *wrong,* and join them in calling it *right.* And this must be done thoroughly—done in *acts* as well as in *words.* Silence will not be tolerated—must place ourselves avowedly with them. Senator Douglas' new sedition law must be enacted and enforced, suppressing all declarations that slavery is wrong, whether made in politics, in presses, in pulpits, or in private. We must arrest and return their fugitive slaves with greedy pleasure. We must pull down our Free State constitutions. The whole atmosphere must be disinfected from all taint of opposition to slavery, before they will cease to believe that all their troubles proceed from us.

I am quite aware they do not state their case precisely in this way. Most of them would probably say to us, "Let us alone, *do* nothing to us, and *say* what you please about slavery." But we do let them alone—have never disturbed them—so that, after all, it is what we say, which dissatisfies them. They will continue to accuse us of doing, until we cease saying.

I am also aware they have not, as yet, in terms, demanded the overthrow of our Free-State Constitutions.[41] Yet those Constitutions declare the wrong of slavery, with more solemn emphasis, than do all other sayings against it; and when all these other sayings shall have been silenced, the overthrow of these Constitutions will be demanded, and nothing be left to resist the demand. It is nothing to the contrary, that they do not demand the whole of this just now. Demanding what they do, and for the reason they do, they can voluntarily stop nowhere short of this consummation. Holding, as they do, that slavery is morally right, and socially elevating, they cannot cease to demand a full national recognition of it, as a legal right, and a social blessing.[42] (*Applause*)

Nor can we justifiably withhold this, on any ground save our conviction that slavery is wrong. If slavery is right, all words, acts, laws, and constitutions against it, are themselves wrong, and should be silenced, and swept away. If it is right, we cannot justly object to its nationality—its universality; if it is wrong, they cannot justly insist upon its extension—its enlargement. All they ask, we could readily grant, if we thought slavery right; all we ask, they could as readily grant, if they thought it wrong.[43] Their thinking it right, and our thinking it wrong, is the precise fact upon which depends the whole controversy. Thinking it right, as they do, they are not to blame for desiring its full recognition, as being right; but, thinking it wrong, as we do, can we yield to them? Can we cast our votes with their view, and against our own? In view of our moral, social, and political responsibilities, can we do this? (*"No, no," and applause*)

Wrong as we think slavery is, we can yet afford to let it alone where it is, because that much is due to the necessity arising from its actual presence in the nation; but can we, while our votes will prevent it, allow it to spread into the National Territories, and to overrun us here in these Free States? (*"No, never," and applause. A voice—"Guess not." Laughter*) If our sense of duty forbids this, then let us stand by our duty, fearlessly and effectively. Let us be diverted by none of those sophistical contrivances wherewith we are so industriously plied and belabored—contrivances such as groping for some middle ground between the right and the wrong, vain as the search for a man who should be neither a living man nor a dead man—such as a policy of "don't care" on a question about which all true men do care—such as Union appeals beseeching true Union men to yield to Disunionists, reversing the divine rule, and calling, not the sinners, but the righteous to repentance (*Prolonged cheers and laughter*)—such as invocations to Washington, imploring men to unsay what Washington said, and undo what Washington did.

Neither let us be slandered from our duty by false accusations against us, nor frightened from it by menaces of destruction to the Government nor of dungeons to ourselves. (*Applause*) LET US HAVE FAITH THAT RIGHT MAKES MIGHT, AND IN THAT FAITH, LET US, TO THE END, DARE TO DO OUR DUTY AS WE UNDERSTAND IT. (*Three rousing cheers were given to the orator; the waving of handkerchiefs and hats, and repeated cheers*)[44]

the *Lemon Case,* page 44: 'We claim that under these various provisions of the Federal Constitution, a citizen of Virginia has an immunity against the operation of any law which the State of New-York can enact, whilst he is a stranger and wayfarer, or whilst passing through our territory; and that he has absolute protection for all his domestic rights, and for all his rights of property, which under the laws of the United States, and the laws of his own State, he was entitled to, whilst in his own State. We claim this, and neither more NOR LESS.'

"Throughout the whole of that case, in which the right to pass through New-York with slaves at the pleasure of the slave owners is maintained, it is nowhere contended that the statute is contrary to the Constitution of New-York; but that the statute and Constitution of the State are both contrary to the Constitution of the United States.

"The State of Virginia, not content with the decision of our own courts upon the right claimed by them, is now engaged in carrying this, the Lemon case, to the Supreme Court of the United States, hoping by a decision there, in accordance with the intimations of the Dred Scott case, to overthrow the Constitution of New-York.

"Senator [Robert] Toombs of Georgia [future Confederate secretary of state—Eds.], has claimed in the Senate, that laws of Connecticut, Maine, Massachusetts, Michigan, New Hampshire, Ohio, Rhode Island, Vermont, and Wisconsin, for the exclusion of slavery, conceded to be warranted by the State Constitutions, are contrary to the Constitution of the United States, and has asked for the enactment of laws by the General Government which shall override the laws of those States and the Constitutions which authorize them."

42 Five examples of views claiming that slavery was morally right were presented in this note. Two are offered here:

"'I am satisfied that the mind of the South has

undergone a change to this great extent, that it is now *the almost universal belief* in the South, not only that the condition of African slavery in their midst, is the best condition to which the African race has ever been subjected, *but* that *it has the effect of ennobling both races, the white and the black.'—Senator Mason, of Virginia* [later Confederate envoy to Great Britain—Eds.]

"'I declare again, as I did in reply to the Senator from Wisconsin (Mr. Doolittle,) that, in my opinion, slavery is a great moral, social and political blessing—a blessing to the slave, and a blessing to the master.'—*Mr.* [Albert Gallatin] *Brown* [of Mississippi, later a Confederate officer and Senator—Eds.], *in the Senate, March 6, 1860."*

**43** "It is interesting to observe how two profoundly logical minds, though holding extreme, opposite views, have deduced this common conclusion. Says Mr. O'Conor, the eminent leader of the New-York Bar, and the counsel for the State of Virginia in the Lemon case, in his speech at Cooper Institute, December 19th, 1859:—

"'That is the point to which this great argument must come—Is negro slavery unjust? If it is unjust, it violates the first rule of human conduct—"Render to every man his due." If it is unjust, it violates the law of God which says, "Love thy neighbor as thyself," for that requires that we should perpetuate no injustice. Gentlemen, if it could be maintained that negro slavery was unjust, perhaps I might be prepared—perhaps we all ought to be prepared—to go with that distinguished man to whom allusion is frequently made, and say, "There is a higher law which compels us to trample beneath our feet the Constitution established by our fathers, with all the blessings it secures to our children" [the words of New York senator William H. Seward, by then defeated by Lincoln for the presidential nomination—Eds.]. But I insist—and that is the argument which we must meet, and on which we must come to a conclusion that shall govern our actions in the future selection of representatives in the Congress of the United States—I insist that negro slavery is not unjust.'"

**44** These reactions were published in the February 28, 1860, editions of the *New York Times* and *New York Evening Post*.

# Autobiography Written for John L. Scripps

## [ca. June 1860]

ABRAHAM LINCOLN WAS BORN FEB. 12, 1809, THEN IN HARDIN, NOW in the more recently formed county of Larue, Kentucky.[1] His father, Thomas, & grand-father, Abraham, were born in Rockingham county Virginia, whither their ancestors had come from Berks county Pennsylvania. His lineage has been traced no farther back than this. The family were originally quakers, though in later times they have fallen away from the peculiar habits of that people. The grand-father Abraham, had four brothers—Isaac, Jacob, John & Thomas. So far as known, the descendants of Jacob and John are still in Virginia. Isaac went to a place near where Virginia, North Carolina, and Tennessee, join; and his decendants are in that region. Thomas came to Kentucky, and after many years, died there, whence his decendants went to Missouri. Abraham, grandfather of the subject of this sketch, came to Kentucky, and was killed by indians about the year 1784. He left a widow, three sons and two daughters. The eldest son, Mordecai, remained in Kentucky till late in life, when he removed to Hancock county, Illinois, where soon after he died, and where several of his descendants still reside. The second son, Josiah, removed at an early day to a place on Blue River, now within Harrison [Hancock] county, Indiana; but no recent information of him, or his family, has been obtained. The eldest sister, Mary, married Ralph Crume and some of her descendants are now known to be in Breckenridge county Kentucky. The second sister, Nancy, married William Brumfield, and her family are not known to have left Kentucky, but there is no recent information from them. Thomas, the youngest son, and father of the present subject, by the early death of his father, and very narrow circumstances of his mother, even in childhood was a wandering laboring boy, and grew up litterally [sic] without education. He never did more in the way of writing than to bunglingly sign his own name.[2] Before he was grown, he passed

*Though Lincoln may have truly believed what he had expressed to Jesse Fell months earlier, that there was "not much of me" for a biography of more than a few paragraphs in length, several publishers and the authors they commissioned thought differently. Biographical details of the Republican candidate were in high demand. The autobiographical sketch Lincoln supplied to Chicago newspaper editor John L. Scripps—and shared with other biographers—is twice as long and contains substantially more information than the sparse draft he wrote for Fell. In keeping with tradition, Lincoln, though open to sharing biographical information in private, did not publicly admit to such cooperation. This is the most detailed account Lincoln ever wrote in his life.*

1   John Locke Scripps was a journalist and newspaper editor. A Republican in politics and an associate of Lincoln's, Scripps established the *Chicago Daily Democratic Press,* which later united with the *Chicago Tribune* to form the *Chicago Press and Tribune,* a newspaper that supported Lincoln in his 1858 senate and 1860 presidential campaigns. Scripps most likely wrote—in haste—the first biographical account of Lincoln, appearing in his and several Eastern newspapers on May 19, 1860, the day after Lincoln's nomination for president at the Republican convention in Chicago. Wishing to write a fuller account of Lincoln's life, Scripps requested additional biographical details from the candidate. Lincoln, according to Scripps, was reluctant to cooperate, claiming that "it is a great piece of folly to attempt to make anything out of my early life. It can all be condensed into a single sentence, and that sentence you will find in Gray's Elegy: 'The short and simple annals of the poor.' That's my life, and that's all you or any one else can make of it." Lincoln soon relented, however, and provided Scripps with a longer version, written in the third person, of what he had prepared for Jesse Fell the previous December. With several campaign biographies already on the market, Scripps worked

quickly and drafted a ninety-six-page account of Lincoln's life, expanding on his earlier effort. His manuscript was reduced to sixty pages by Horace Greeley (1811–1872), his New York publisher; owing to significant cuts in the final section, the work ended before the 1858 Lincoln-Douglas debates. Due to time constraints, Scripps reneged on his promise to Lincoln to submit the manuscript to him before publication. He later apologized for the "sadly botched" final section and for not giving Lincoln the opportunity to review the draft. Scripps's *Life of Abraham Lincoln,* published simultaneously by the *Chicago Press and Tribune* and Horace Greeley's *New York Daily Tribune* (as *Tribune Tracts, No. 6*), appeared in mid-July as a thirty-two-page, double-column pamphlet. A second Chicago edition was subsequently issued. Despite assuring the candidate that he had added "nothing that I was not fully authorized to put into it," Scripps embellished the draft, adding details concerning Lincoln's ancestors, parents, and religious upbringing that Lincoln had not mentioned. Moreover, there was at least one portion of the biography that Scripps invented. Without checking with Lincoln, Scripps wrote that Lincoln read *Plutarch's Lives*: "What fields of thought its perusal opened up to the stripling, what hopes were excited in his youthful breast, what worthy models of probity, of justice, of honor, and of devotion to great principles he resolved to pattern after, can readily be imagined by those who are familiar with his subsequent career." He urged Lincoln that if he had not already read the work, he "must read it at once to make my statement good." Scripps's campaign biography was one of the most popular of the sixteen published in 1860, selling more than one million copies. After assuming the presidency, Lincoln appointed Scripps postmaster of Chicago. Scripps, *Life of Abraham Lincoln,* 3. Lincoln's reference to Gray's *Elegy* is cited in Wilson and Davis, *Herndon's Informants,* 57. Scripps's apology

one year as a hired hand with his uncle Isaac on Wata[u]ga, a branch of the Holsteen [Holston] River. Getting back into Kentucky, and having reached his 28th. year, he married Nancy Hanks—mother of the present subject—in the year 1806. She also was born in Virginia; and relatives of hers of the name of Hanks, and of other names, now reside in Coles, in Macon, and in Adams counties, Illinois, and also in Iowa. The present subject has no brother or sister of the whole or half blood. He had a sister,[3] older than himself, who was grown and married, but died many years ago, leaving no child. Also a brother, younger than himself, who died in infancy.[4] Before leaving Kentucky he and his sister were sent for short periods, to A.B.C. schools, the first kept by Zachariah Riney,[5] and the second by Caleb Hazel.[6]

At this time his father resided on Knob-creek, on the road from Bardstown Ky. to Nashville Tenn. at a point three, or three and a half miles South or South-West of Atherton's ferry on the Rolling Fork. From this place he removed to what is now Spencer county Indiana, in the autumn of 1816, A. then being in his eigth [*sic*] year. This removal was partly on account of slavery; but chiefly on account of the difficulty in land titles in Ky. He settled in an unbroken forest; and the clearing away of surplus wood was the great task a head. A. though very young, was large of his age, and had an axe put into his hands at once; and from that till within his twentythird year, he was almost constantly handling that most useful instrument—less, of course, in plowing and harvesting seasons.[7] At this place A. took an early start as a hunter, which was never much improved afterwards. (A few days before the completion of his eigth [*sic*] year, in the absence of his father, a flock of wild turkeys approached the new log-cabin, and A. with a rifle gun, standing inside, shot through a crack, and killed one of them. He has never since pulled a trigger on any larger game.) In the autumn of 1818 his mother died; and a year afterwards his father married Mrs. Sally Johnston, at Elizabeth-Town, Ky—a widow, with three children of her first marriage. She proved a good and kind mother to A. and is still living in Coles Co. Illinois. There were no children of this second marriage. His father's residence continued at the same place in Indiana, till 1830. While here A. went to A.B.C. schools by littles, kept successively by Andrew Crawford,[8]—Sweeney,[9] and Azel W. Dorsey.[10] He does not remember any other. The family of Mr. Dorsey now reside in Schuyler Co. Illinois. A. now thinks that the agregate [*sic*] of all his schooling did not amount to one year. He was never in a college or Academy as a student; and never inside of a college or accademy [*sic*] building till since he had a law-license. What he has in the way of education, he has picked up. After he was twentythree, and had separated from

Abraham Lincoln. Photograph by Alexander Hesler (Springfield, IL, June 3, 1860). One of several photographs taken of Lincoln by Hesler inside the Illinois State Capitol. The candidate liked them, commenting that they expressed "me better than any I've ever seen."

to Lincoln concerning the final section, and his letter to Lincoln regarding *Plutarch's Lives* is cited in Douglas Egerton, *Year of Meteors: Stephen Douglas, Abraham Lincoln, and the Election that Brought on the Civil War* (New York: Bloomsbury Press, 210), 180. Sale figures for Scripps's biography come from Stephen B. Oates, *With Malice toward None: The Life of Abraham Lincoln* (New York: Harper & Row, 1977), 181. For biographical information on Scripps, see Neely, *Lincoln Encyclopedia*, 271. See also Horrocks, *Lincoln's Campaign Biographies*, 54–55; Ernst James Wessen, "Campaign Lives of Abraham Lincoln, 1860," *Papers in Illinois History and Transactions for the Year 1937* (Springfield: Illinois State Historical Society, 1938), 211–213.

2    Historians view Lincoln's denigrating statement about his father as evidence of the strained relationship between father and son. Lincoln resented his father for failing to appreciate his thirst for knowledge. According to contemporary testimony, Lincoln's father believed that all a man required to obtain success in life was physical strength, and that education was a waste of time. Burlingame, *Abraham Lincoln*, 1:10–11.

3    Sarah Lincoln was born in Elizabethtown, Kentucky, in 1807. She married Aaron Grigsby in Indiana on August 2, 1826, and died on January 20, 1828, while giving birth. According to David Donald, Lincoln blamed Sarah's death on the negligence of the Grigsby family in not seeking medical help. Donald, *Lincoln*, 22, 33–34.

4    Thomas Lincoln died in infancy sometime in 1812. Ibid., 23.

5    Zachariah Riney was a Lincoln family friend and a popular teacher. Lincoln respected Riney, a Roman Catholic, highly, especially for not attempting to convert his Protestant students to his faith. Richard Lawrence Miller, *Lincoln and His*

his father, he studied English grammar, imperfectly of course, but so as to speak and write as well as he now does. He studied and nearly mastered the Six-books of Euclid, since he was a member of Congress. He regrets his want of education, and does what he can to supply the want. In his tenth year he was kicked by a horse, and apparently killed for a time. When

*Word: The Early Years: Birth to Illinois Legislature* (Mechanicsburg, PA: Stackpole Books, 2006), 24.

6   Caleb Hazel owned a farm that was located next to the Lincolns'. He taught at a school four or five miles from the Lincoln cabin. Miller, *The Early Years*, 24.

7   By the 1860 presidential campaign, the axe had become an important symbol associated with Lincoln's image. See note 15.

8   Andrew Crawford, a justice of the peace, taught Lincoln in the summer and autumn of 1820. Knowing of young Lincoln's interest in reading, Crawford loaned him a copy of Weems's biography of George Washington, a book that greatly impressed Lincoln. Miller, *The Early Years*, 55.

9   James Swaney. Ibid.

10   Azel W. Dorsey knew the Lincoln family when they lived in Kentucky. In addition to teaching, he was a merchant and a politician. Years later, he recalled Lincoln as a student, commenting on his "diligence and eagerness," and his attire, which included buckskins and a coonskin cap. Ibid.; Dorsey quoted in Burlingame, *Abraham Lincoln*, 1:31.

11   See note 15.

12   John Davis Johnston was the youngest son of Lincoln's stepmother, Sarah Bush Lincoln. See "Letters to Thomas Lincoln and John D. Johnston, December 24, 1848," note 4, in this volume.

13   John Hanks was the first cousin of Lincoln's mother, Nancy Hanks. He lived with the Lincoln family for four years in the 1820s when they resided in Spencer County, Indiana. Wilson and Davis, *Herndon's Informants*, 752.

14   Denton Offutt not only hired Lincoln to take a flatboat of cargo to New Orleans but also brought him to New Salem, Illinois, to clerk in a store and

he was nineteen, still residing in Indiana, he made his first trip upon a flat-boat to New-Orleans. He was a hired hand merely; and he and a son of the owner, without other assistance, made the trip. The nature of part of the cargo-load, as it was called—made it necessary for them to linger and trade along the Sugar coast—and one night they were attacked by seven negroes with intent to kill and rob them. They were hurt some in the melee, but suc-ceeded in driving the negroes from the boat, and then "cut cable" "weighed anchor" and left.

March 1st. 1830—A. having just completed his 21st. year, his father and family, with the families of the two daughters and sons-in-law, of his step-mother, left the old homestead in Indiana, and came to Illinois. Their mode of conveyance was waggons [*sic*] drawn by ox-teams, or A. drove one of the teams. They reached the county of Macon, and stopped there some time within the same month of March. His father and family settled a new place on the North side of the Sangamon river, at the junction of the timber-land and prairie, about ten miles Westerly from Decatur. Here they built a log-cabin, into which they removed, and made sufficient of rails to fence ten acres of ground, fenced and broke the ground, and raised a crop of sow[n] corn upon it the same year. These are, or are supposed to be, the rails about which so much is being said just now, though they are far from being the first, or only rails ever made by A.[11]

The sons-in-law, were temporarily settled at other places in the county. In the autumn all hands were greatly afflicted with augue [*sic*] and fever, to which they had not been used, and by which they were greatly discour-aged—so much so that they determined on leaving the county. They re-mained however, through the succeeding winter, which was the winter of the very celebrated "deep snow" of Illinois. During that winter, A. together with his step-mother's son, John D. Johnston,[12] and John Hanks,[13] yet resid-ing in Macon county, hired themselves to one Denton Offutt,[14] to take a flat boat from Beardstown Illinois to New-Orleans; and for that purpose, were to join him—Offutt—at Springfield, Ills[.,] so soon as the snow should go off. When it did go off which was about the 1st. of March 1831—the county was so flooded, as to make traveling by land impracticable; to obviate which difficulty the[y] purchased a large canoe and came down the Sangamon river in it. This is the time and the manner of A's first entrance into San-gamon County. They found Offutt at Springfield, but learned from him that he had failed in getting a boat at Beardstown. This led to their hiring themselves to him at $12 per month, each; and getting the timber out of the trees and building a boat at old Sangamon Town on the Sangamon river, seven miles N.W. of Springfield, which boat they took to New-Orleans, substantially upon the old contract. It was in connection with this boat that occurred the ludicrous incident of sewing up the hogs eyes. Offutt bought thirty odd large fat live hogs, but found difficulty in driving them from where [he] purchased them to the boat, and thereupon conceived the whim that he could sew up their eyes and drive them where he pleased. No sooner thought of than decided, he put his hands, including A. at the job, which they completed—all but the driving. In their blind condition they could not be driven out of the lot or field they were in. This expedient failing, they were tied and hauled on carts to the boat. It was near the Sangamon River, within what is now Menard county.

During this boat enterprize acquaintance with Offutt, who was previously an entire stranger, he conceved [sic] a liking for A. and believing he could turn him to account, he contracted with him to act as clerk for him, on his return from New-Orleans, in charge of a store and Mill at New-Salem, then in Sangamon, now in Menard county. Hanks had not gone to New-Orleans, but having a family, and being likely to be detained from home longer than at first expected, had turned back from St. Louis. He is the same John Hanks who now engineers the "rail enterprise"[15] at Decatur; and is a first cousin to A's mother. A's father, with his own family & others mentioned, had, in pursuance of their intention, removed from Macon to Coles county. John D. Johnston, the step-mother's son, went to them; and A. stopped indefinitely, and, for the first time, as it were, by himself at New-Salem, before mentioned. This was in July 1831. Here he rapidly made acquaintances and friends. In less than a year Offutt's business was failing—had almost failed,—when the Black-Hawk war of 1832—broke out. A joined a volunteer company, and to his own surprize, was elected captain of it. He says he has not since had any success in life which gave him so much satisfaction. He went the campaign, served near three months, met the ordinary hardships of such an expedition, but was in no battle. He now owns in Iowa, the land upon which his own warrants for this service, were located. Returning from the campaign, and encouraged by his great popularity among his immediate neighbors, he, the same year, ran for the Legislature and was beaten—his own precinct, however, casting it's [sic] votes 277 for and 7, against him. And this too while he was an avowed Clay man, and the precinct the autumn afterwards, giving a majority of 115 to Genl. Jackson over Mr. Clay. This was the only time A was ever beaten on a direct vote of the people. He was now without means and out of business, but was anxious to remain with his friends who had treated him with so much gen-

mill he owned. Donald, *Lincoln,* 38–44. See also "Message to the People of Sangamo County, March 9, 1832," note 2, in this volume.

15  On May 9, 1860, Illinois Republicans met at Decatur to nominate a gubernatorial candidate. Several delegates, including Richard J. Oglesby (1824–1899), a future governor of the state, attended the convention with an additional objective in mind: to secure unanimous support from the state delegation for the nomination of Lincoln at the Republican convention the following week in Chicago. Oglesby was convinced that Lincoln's rise from humble circumstances on the western frontier would resonate with American voters, especially if tied to an attractive image that would generate enthusiasm. Hoping to identify something in Lincoln's background that would lend itself to a captivating image, Oglesby sought out John Hanks, who recalled that three decades earlier he and Lincoln had made many split-rail fences at a place several miles from Decatur. His curiosity aroused, Oglesby asked Hanks days before the convention to show him the split-rail fences. After Hanks took Oglesby to see the fences, the two men brought a pair of split rails to Decatur, storing them in Oglesby's barn. A plan was then devised (with both men taking the credit for the idea) to use the rails at the convention. On the opening day of the convention, Hanks and a friend, at Oglesby's invitation, appeared carrying the two split rails decorated with red, white, and blue streamers and a banner promoting "Abraham Lincoln, the Rail Candidate for President in 1860," causing a sensation among the delegates. The popular image of Lincoln the "Rail Splitter" was born, and was soon embraced enthusiastically by Republicans across the country. Michael S. Green, *Lincoln and the Election of 1860* (Carbondale: Southern Illinois University Press, 2011), 47–50; Wayne C. Temple, "Lincoln's Split Fence Rails," *Journal of the Illinois State Historical Society* 47

(Spring 1954): 20–34; Horrocks, *Lincoln's Campaign Biographies,* 1–3; Harold Holzer, Gabor S. Boritt, and Mark E. Neely Jr., *The Lincoln Image: Abraham Lincoln and the Popular Print* (New York: Charles Scribner's Sons, 1984), chap. 1.

16  Before he received the Rail Splitter sobriquet, Lincoln was called "Honest Abe" by friends, associates, and political supporters. How this term came to be connected with Lincoln is unclear, though it may date back to his New Salem days when in 1832 he entered into a partnership with Willam F. Berry to operate a store. The partners immediately sank into debt, a situation that was exacerbated a year later when they purchased the stock of another store. Berry's heavy drinking led to the termination of the partnership, with Lincoln selling his share to Berry. When the store went out of business, suits were filed against both Berry and Lincoln for unpaid debts. When Berry died, Lincoln assumed all of the store's debt, totaling more than $1,000. Although it took him several years and he was forced to sell most of his personal belongings, Lincoln paid the debt in full. Thomas A. Horrocks, "Abraham Lincoln," in Mathew Manweller, ed., *Chronology of the Presidency,* 4 vols. (Santa Barbara, CA: ABC-Clio, 2012), 2:479.

17  Abel Flint (1765–1825) was the author of *A System of Geometry and Trigonometry, together with a Treatise on Surveying* (Hartford, CT: Lincoln & Gleason, 1804). There were numerous editions of this work.

18  Robert Gibson's book *A Treatise on Practical Surveying* was first published in Dublin, Ireland, in 1739. The first of many American editions was published in Philadelphia in 1785.

19  John Todd Stuart was Lincoln's first law partner (1837–1841). Neely, *Lincoln Encyclopedia,* 292.

20  See "Protest on Slavery in Illinois Legislature, March 3, 1837," in this volume.

erosity, especially as he had nothing elsewhere to go to. He studied what he should do—thought of learning the black-smith trade—thought of trying to study law—rather thought he could not succeed at that without a better education. Before long, strangely enough, a man offered to sell and did sell, to A. and another as poor as himself, an old stock of goods, upon credit. They opened as merchants; and he says that was *the* store. Of course they did nothing but get deeper and deeper in debt. He was appointed Postmaster at New-Salem—the office being too insignificant, to make his politics an objection. The store winked out.[16] The Surveyor of Sangamon, offered to depute to A that portion of his work which was within his part of the county. He accepted, procured a compass and chain, studied Flint,[17] and Gibson[18] a little, and went at it. This procured bread, and kept soul and body together. The election of 1834 came, and he was then elected to the Legislature by the highest vote cast for any candidate. Major John T. Stuart,[19] then in full practice of the law, was also elected. During the canvass, in a private conversation he encouraged A. [to] study law. After the election he borrowed books of Stuart, took them home with him, and went at it in good earnest. He studied with nobody. He still mixed in the surveying to pay board and clothing bills. When the Legislature met, the law books were dropped, but were taken up again at the end of the session. He was re-elected in 1836, 1838, and 1840. In the autumn of 1836 he obtained a law licence, and on April 15, 1837[,] removed to Springfield, and commenced the practice, his old friend, Stuart taking him into partnership. March 3rd. 1837, by a protest entered upon the Ills. House Journal of that date, at pages 817, 818, A. with Dan Stone, another representative of Sangamon, briefly defined his position on the slavery question; and so far as it goes, it was then the same that it is now. The protest is as follows—(Here insert it).[20] In 1838, & 1840 Mr. L's party in the Legislature voted for him as Speaker; but being in the minority, he was not elected. After 1840 he declined a re-election to the Legislature. He was on the Harrison electoral ticket in 1840, and on that of Clay in 1844, and spent much time and labor in both those canvasses. In Nov. 1842 he was married to Mary, daughter of Robert S. Todd, of Lexington, Kentucky. They have three living children, all sons—one born in 1843,[21] one in 1850,[22] and one in 1853.[23] They lost one, who was born in 1846.[24] In 1846, he was elected to the lower House of Congress, and served one term only, commencing in Dec. 1847 and ending with the inauguration [*sic*] of Gen. Taylor, in March 1849. All the battles of the Mexican war had been fought before Mr. L. took his seat in congress, but the American army was still in Mexico, and the treaty of peace was not fully and formally ratified till the June afterwards. Much has been said of his course in Congress in regard to this war. A careful examination of the Journals and Congressional Globe shows, that he voted for all the supply measures which came up, and for all the measures in any way favorable to the officers, soldiers, and their families,[25] who conducted the war through; with this exception that some of these measures passed without yeas and nays, leaving no record as to how particular men voted. The Journals and Globe also show him voting that the war was unnecessarily and unconstitutionally begun by the President of the United States. This is the language of Mr. Ashmun's amendment, for which Mr. L. and nearly or quite all, other whigs of the H. R. voted.

Mr. L's reasons for the opinion expressed by this vote were briefly that the President had sent Genl. Taylor into an inhabited part of the country belonging to Mexico, and not to the U.S. and thereby had provoked the first act of hostility—in fact the commencement of the war; that the place, being the country bordering on the East bank of the Rio Grande, was inhabited by native Mexicans, born there under the Mexican government; and had never submitted to, nor been conquered by Texas, or the U.S. nor transferred to either by treaty—that although Texas claimed the Rio Grande as her boundary, Mexico had never recognized it, the people on the ground had never recognized it, and neither Texas nor the U.S. had ever enforced it—that there was a broad desert between that, and the country over which Texas had actual control—that the country where hostilities commenced, having once belonged to Mexico, must remain so, until it was somehow legally transferred, which had never been done.[26]

Mr. L. thought the act of sending an armed force among the Mexicans, was *unnecessary,* inasmuch as Mexico was in no way molesting, or menacing the U.S. or the people thereof; and that it was *unconstitutional,* because the power of levying war is vested in Congress, and not in the President. He thought the principal motive for the act, was to divert public attention from the surrender of "Fifty-four, forty, or fight" to Great Brittain [*sic*], on the Oregon boundary question.[27]

Mr. L. was not a candidate for re-election. This was determined upon, and declared before he went to Washington, in accordance with an understanding among whig friends, by which Col. Hardin, and Col. Baker had each previously served a single term in the same District.

In 1848, during his term in congress, he advocated Gen. Taylor's nomination for the Presidency, in opposition to all others, and also took an active part for his election, after his nomination—speaking a few times in Maryland, near Washington, several times in Massachusetts, and canvassing quite

21 Robert Todd Lincoln (1843–1926).

22 William Wallace (Willie) Lincoln (1850–1862).

23 Thomas (Tad) Lincoln (1853–1871).

24 Edward (Eddy) Baker Lincoln (1846–1850).

25 Ever sensitive to Democratic charges that he did not support the American troops in the Mexican War, Lincoln made sure that any campaign biography made clear the distinction between his support of the troops and his opposition to the war.

26 See "Speech in Congress against the War with Mexico, January 12, 1848," in this volume.

27 The United States and Great Britain had jointly occupied the Oregon Territory since 1818. When Democrat James Knox Polk ran for president in 1844, he pledged to acquire the entire territory for the United States. "Fifty-Four, Forty, or Fight" became a popular slogan of advocates of this course of action. Once elected president, however, Polk proposed to divide Oregon in half, at the 49th parallel. The British government, after initially rejecting the offer, accepted, and the U.S. Senate ratified the agreement, to the chagrin of many Americans, especially Northerners, who charged the president with backing away from his campaign promise. Sam Hayes, *James K. Polk and the Expansionist Impulse* (New York: Longman, 1995), 116–122, 128–129.

28  On Richard Yates, see "Speech on the Kansas-Nebraska Act at Peoria, Illinois, October 16, 1854," notes 3 and 56, in this volume.

29  See *CW,* 4:68n11. Lincoln's July 23, 1856, speech was reported in the *Galena Weekly North-Western Gazette* three days later, on July 29, in which he was quoted as saying, "The Supreme Court of the United States is the tribunal to decide such questions [restriction of slavery in the territories], and we submit to its decisions." Regarding the 1857 *Dred Scott* decision, Lincoln's advice to Republicans was to obey the decision until they reversed it, which Democrats saw as a contradiction of his remarks at Galena. See his Galena speech in *CW,* 2:353–355.

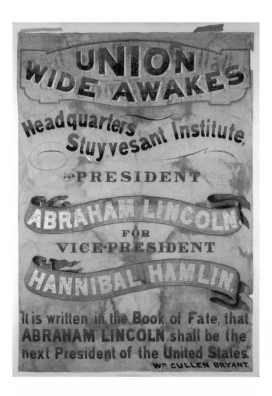

fully his own district in Illinois, which was followed by a majority in the district of over 1500 for Gen. Taylor.

Upon his return from Congress he went to the practice of the law with greater earnestness than ever before. In 1852 he was upon the Scott electoral ticket, and did something in the way of canvassing, but owing to the hopelessness of the cause in Illinois, he did less than in previous presidential canvasses.

In 1854, his profession had almost superseded the thought of politics in his mind, when the repeal of the Missouri compromise aroused him as he had never been before.

In the autumn of that year he took the stump with no broader practical aim or object that [than] to secure, if possible, the re-election of Hon Richard Yates[28] to congress. His speeches at once attracted a more marked attention than they had ever before done. As the canvass proceeded, he was drawn to different parts of the state, outside of Mr. Yates['s] district. He did not abandon the law, but gave his attention, by turns, to that and politics. The State agricultural fair was at Springfield that year, and Douglas was announced to speak there.

In the canvass of 1856, Mr. L. made over fifty speeches, no one of which, so far as he remembers, was put in print. One of them was made at Galena, but Mr. L. has no recollection of any part of it being printed; nor does he remember whether in that speech he said anything about a Supreme court decision. He may have spoken upon that subject; and some of the newspapers may have reported him as saying what is now ascribed to him; but he thinks he could not have expressed himself as represented.[29]

"Union Wide Awakes . . . for President Abraham Lincoln. For Vice-President Hannibal Hamlin." Hand-painted banner (New York, 1860). This campaign piece was created for a New York City Wide-Awake Club to promote the Lincoln-Hamlin ticket.

# Letter to Grace Bedell

## October 19, 1860

*During the final weeks of the 1860 presidential election, Lincoln received a letter from an eleven-year-old girl suggesting he grow a beard because "ladies like whiskers and they would tease their husband's [sic] to vote for you." What influence this letter had on Lincoln's decision to grow facial hair is unclear, though he did grow whiskers soon after his election, and he thanked little Grace for her advice when his inaugural journey brought him to her Chautauqua County, New York, hometown in February 1861.*

1    Grace Bedell (1848–1936) lived in Westfield, New York. Neely, *Lincoln Encyclopedia,* 22. Bedell's letter to Lincoln is in *CW,* 4:130n1.

Private
Miss. Grace Bedell[1] Springfield, Ills.
My dear little Miss. Oct 19. 1860

Your very agreeable letter of the 15th. is received.

I regret the necessity of saying I have no daughters. I have three sons—one seventeen, one nine, and one seven, years of age. They, with their mother, constitute my whole family.

As to the whiskers, having never worn any, do you not think people would call it a piece of silly affection [*sic*] if I were to begin it now?

Your very sincere well-wisher A. LINCOLN.

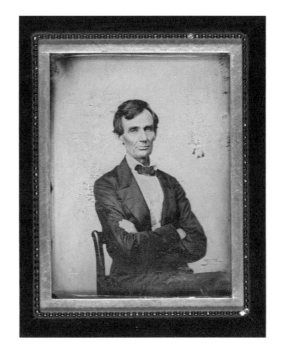

Abraham Lincoln. Photograph by Preston Butler
(Springfield, IL, August 13, 1860).

Abraham Lincoln. Photograph by Samuel G. Alschuler (Chicago, November 25, 1860). First photograph of Lincoln with a beard. Young Grace Bedell may have provided the impetus for Lincoln's decision to grow facial hair.

*National Republican Chart.* Broadside (New York: H. H. Lloyd & Co., 1860). Grace Bedell may have been inspired to write to Lincoln after seeing a copy of this very poster in her upstate New York hometown.

# Letter to Alexander H. Stephens

## December 22, 1860

*Lincoln's onetime fellow Whig congressman Alexander H. Stephens of Georgia urged his state not to secede from the Union. Lincoln appreciated the Georgian's sentiments and wrote to allay Stephens's and his fellow Southerners' fears that his administration would threaten slavery where it already existed. For a time, Lincoln considered offering Stephens a cabinet post, then decided he could not do so.*

1    Alexander H. Stephens (1812–1883) of Georgia served in Congress as a Whig from 1843 to 1859 and stood against secession until Georgia left the Union in 1861, after which he accepted the post of vice president of the Confederate States of America. During his time in Congress, he and Lincoln had been friends and allies, both opposing the Mexican War and supporting Zachary Taylor for the Whig nomination for president in 1848. "Stephens, Alexander H.," Biographical Directory

*For your own eye only.*

Hon. A. H. Stephens[1]—                                    Springfield, Ills.
                                                                        Dec. 22, 1860

My dear Sir

Your obliging answer to my short note is just received, and for which please accept my thanks. I fully appreciate the present peril the country is in, and the weight of responsibility on me.

Do the people of the South really entertain fears that a Republican administration would, *directly,* or *indirectly,* interfere with their slaves, or with them, about their slaves? If they do, I wish to assure you, as once a friend, and still, I hope, not an enemy, that there is no cause for such fears.

The South would be in no more danger in this respect, than it was in the days of Washington. I suppose, however, this does not meet the case. You think slavery is *right* and ought to be extended; while we think it is *wrong* and ought to be restricted. That I suppose is the rub. It certainly is the only substantial difference between us.

Yours very truly
A. LINCOLN

Alexander Stephens. Photograph by Mathew Brady (Washington, DC, ca. 1860s).

of the United States Congress, http://bioguide.
congress.gov/scripts/biodisplay.pl?index=s000854
(accessed January 12, 2015). In February 1865, the
tiny, consumptive Stephens would be part of a
three-man delegation of "peace commissioners"
that met face to face with President Lincoln at
Hampton Roads, Virginia, to propose an armistice
in the Civil War in return for Confederate
independence and abrogation of the Emancipation
Proclamation. Lincoln refused the offer but
generously consented to exchange Stephens's
nephew, a captured Confederate army officer, for
an imprisoned Union officer of a similar rank. *CW*,
8:259.

Abraham Lincoln to Alexander H. Stephens.
Manuscript (December 22, 1860).

*Charleston Mercury Extra . . . The Union Is Dissolved!*
(Charleston, SC: Charleston Mercury, 1860).
Broadside announcing South Carolina's secession
from the Union.

*Sometime in January of the secession winter—South Carolina had seceded from the Union the previous December and six additional Southern states followed her lead in the first weeks of 1861—president-elect Lincoln jotted down his thoughts on the indelible link between the Declaration of Independence, the Constitution, and the Union. The purpose of this draft, whether as a basis for his upcoming inaugural address or as part of another speech, is unknown, for these words never appeared in a Lincoln speech.*

1   Extraordinarily, Lincoln's reference to the metaphor "apple of gold" from Proverbs 25:11 probably came from Alexander Stephens, vice president of the Confederacy and Lincoln's former colleague in Congress. In his reply to Lincoln's letter (see "Letter to Alexander H. Stephens, December 22, 1860"), Stephens suggested that the president-elect would calm the fears of Southerners by issuing a public statement assuring them that his administration would not attempt to abolish slavery, writing, "A word fitly spoken by you now would be like 'apples of gold in pictures of silver.'" Alexander Stephens, *Recollections of Alexander H. Stephens,* ed. Myrta Lockett Avary (New York: Doubleday, Page & Company, 1910), 60.

After Alexander Hesler, "President Elect Abraham Lincoln," *Frank Leslie's Illustrated Newspaper.* Engraving (New York, June 1861). Portrait of Lincoln (incorrectly portrayed as still beardless) surrounded by scenes from his life.

# Fragment on the Constitution and the Union

## [ca. January 1861]

ALL THIS IS NOT THE RESULT OF ACCIDENT. IT HAS A PHILOSOPHICAL cause. Without the Constitution and the Union, we could not have attained the result; but even these, are not the primary cause of our great prosperity. There is something back of these, entwining itself more closely about the human heart. That something, is the principle of "Liberty to all"—the principle that clears the *path* for all—gives *hope* to all—and, by consequence, *enterprize,* and *industry* to all.

The *expression* of that principle, in our Declaration of Independence, was most happy, and fortunate. *Without* this, as well as *with* it, we could have declared our independence of Great Britain; but *without* it, we could not, I think, have secured our free government, and consequent prosperity. No oppressed, people will *fight,* and *endure,* as our fathers did, without the promise of something better, than a mere change of masters.

The assertion of that *principle,* at *that time,* was the word, "fitly spoken" which has proved an "apple of gold" to us. The *Union,* and the *Constitution,* are the *picture* of *silver,* subsequently framed around it. The picture was made, not to *conceal,* or *destroy* the apple; but to *adorn,* and *preserve* it. The *picture* was made *for* the apple—*not* the apple for the picture.[1]

So let us act, that neither *picture,* or *apple* shall ever be blurred, or bruised or broken.

That we may so act, we must study, and understand the points of danger.

# Farewell Address at Springfield, Illinois

## February 11, 1861

MY FRIENDS—NO ONE, NOT IN MY SITUATION, CAN APPRECIATE MY feeling of sadness at this parting. To this place, and the kindness of these people, I owe every thing. Here I have lived a quarter of a century, and have passed from a young to an old man. Here my children have been born, and one is buried. I now[1] leave, not knowing when, or whether ever, I may return, with a task before me greater than that which rested upon Washington. Without the assistance of that Divine Being, who ever attended him, I cannot succeed. With that assistance I cannot fail. Trusting in Him, who can go with me, and remain with you and be every where for good,[2] let us confidently hope that all will yet be well. To His care commending you, as I hope in your prayers you will commend me, I bid you an affectionate farewell.

*On the rainy morning of February 11, 1861, thousands of Lincoln's Springfield friends and neighbors gathered at the town's Great Western depot to see the president-elect off on his inaugural journey to the nation's capital. At 8:00 A.M. Lincoln appeared on the platform of the rear passenger car and delivered an emotional, heartfelt farewell. While newspaper accounts of his actual impromptu remarks suggested a less refined spoken version, the final text of this masterpiece was written and dictated by Lincoln for the press corps traveling with him, almost immediately after the train left the station. Lincoln would never return to Springfield.*

1    Here Lincoln's increasingly rocky handwriting (he was no doubt jolted as the train gained speed) ends and his secretary John Nicolay's writing begins. Cited in *CW,* 4:191n2.

2    Nicolay's handwriting ends; Lincoln resumes writing and completes the text. Ibid., n. 3. For details surrounding the speech, see Harold Holzer, *Lincoln President-Elect: Abraham Lincoln and the Great Secession Winter 1860–1861* (New York: Simon & Schuster, 2008), 295–301.

Abraham Lincoln. Photograph by C. S. German (Springfield, February 9, 1861). The last portrait taken of the president-elect before he left Springfield for the nation's capital.

*More than eight hours after departing Springfield, Illinois, Lincoln's train arrived in Indianapolis, where he would stay the night in the Bates House hotel. Having delivered eight speeches during the first day of his inaugural journey, a tired Lincoln stepped out onto the hotel balcony before a crowd of twenty thousand and delivered a provocative speech that previewed the firm stance he would take against the secession of Southern states in his inaugural address.*

1  Ecclesiastes 3:7.

# Speech at Indianapolis

## February 11, 1861

IT IS NOT POSSIBLE, IN MY JOURNEY TO THE NATIONAL CAPITAL, TO address assemblies like this which may do me the great honor to meet me as you have done, but very briefly. I should be entirely worn out if I were to attempt it. I appear before you now to thank you for this very magnificent welcome which you have given me, and still more for the very generous support which your State recently gave to the political cause of the whole country, and the whole world. (*Applause*) Solomon has said, that there is a time to keep silence.[1] (*Renewed and deafening applause*) ***** We know certain that they mean the same thing while using the same words now, and it perhaps would be as well if they would keep silence.

The words "coercion" and "invasion" are in great use about these days. Suppose we were simply to try if we can, and ascertain what, is the meaning of these words. Let us get, if we can, the exact definitions of these words—not from dictionaries, but from the men who constantly repeat them—what things they mean to express by the words. What, then, is "coercion"? What is "invasion"? Would the marching of an army into South California, for instance, without the consent of her people, and in hostility against them, be coercion or invasion? I very frankly say, I think it would be invasion, and it would be coercion too, if the people of that country were forced to submit. But if the Government, for instance, but simply insists upon holding its own forts, or retaking those forts which belong to it,— (*Cheers*)—or the enforcement of the laws of the United States in the collection of duties upon foreign importations,—(*Renewed cheers*)—or even the withdrawal of the mails from those portions of the country where the mails themselves are habitually violated; would any or all of these things be coercion? Do the lovers of the Union contend that they will resist coercion or invasion of any State, understanding that any or all of these would be coercing or invading a State? If they do, then it occurs to me that the means for the preservation of the Union they so greatly love, in their own estimation, is of a very thin and airy character. (*Applause*) If sick, they would consider the little pills of the homeopathist[2] as already too large for them to swallow. In their view, the Union, as a family relation, would not be anything like a regular marriage at all, but only as a sort of free-love arrangement[3]—(*Laughter*)—to be maintained on what that sect calls passionate attraction. (*Continued laughter*) But, my friends, enough of this.

What is the particular sacredness of a State? I speak not of that position which is given to a State in and by the Constitution of the United States, for that all of us agree to—we abide by; but that position assumed, that a State can carry with it out of the Union that which it holds in sacredness by virtue of its connection with the Union. I am speaking of that assumed right of a State, as a primary principle, that the Constitution should rule all that is less than itself, and ruin all that is bigger than itself. (*Laughter*) But, I ask, wherein does consist that right? If a State, in one instance, and a county in another, should be equal in extent of territory, and equal in the number of people, wherein is that State any better than the county? Can a change of name change the right? By what principle of original right is it that one-fiftieth or one-ninetieth of a great nation, by calling themselves a State, have the right to break up and ruin that nation as a matter of original principle? Now, I ask the question—I am not deciding anything—(*Laughter*)—and with the request that you will think somewhat upon that subject and decide for yourselves, if you choose, when you get ready,—where is the mysterious, original right, from principle, for a certain district of country with inhabitants, by merely being called a State, to play tyrant over all its own citizens, and deny the authority of everything greater than itself.[4] (*Laughter*) I say I am deciding nothing, but simply giving something for you to reflect upon; and, with having said this much, and having declared, in the start, that I will make no long speeches, I thank you again for this magnificent welcome, and bid you an affectionate farewell. (*Cheers*)

2   One who practices homeopathy, a form of medicine based on the administration of very small doses of a remedy that, in larger amounts, would produce symptoms in healthy persons similar to those of the disease being treated.

3   The nineteenth-century free-love movement in the United States was inspired by the views of the French philosopher and socialist Charles Fourier (1772–1837), who believed conventional marriage should be replaced by sexual relationships free from social and legal restraints. Cited in *Lincoln's Selected Writings,* 223n1. See also, John C. Spurlock, *Free Love: Marriage and Middle-Class Radicalism, 1825–1860* (New York: New York University Press, 1987).

4   Lincoln's tough remarks, implying he would take a hard line against secession, delighted the assembled crowd and the Republican press, including the *New York Times,* which endorsed his statements as appropriate for the situation Lincoln would face as president. "Mr. Lincoln maintains the right and the duty of the Government to enforce the laws," asserted the newspaper's editors, as "it is utterly impossible for any President of the United States to take any other view of his duty in this matter." Cited in Holzer, *Lincoln President-Elect,* 310. Democratic newspapers and Southern politicians reacted with shock, anger, and dismay at what they perceived as a confrontational speech. One Virginia congressman responded testily to Lincoln's remarks: "After the recent declaration of war by the President-elect of the United States, I deem it my duty to interpose every obstacle to the tyrannical and military despotism now about to be inaugurated." Cited in James Rawley, *A Lincoln Dialogue* (Lincoln: University of Nebraska Press, 2014), 39. The Democratic *New York Herald* panned the speech for displaying "the obstinacy of an intractable partisan" that threatened to "destroy the hopes of law and order of the North in a wasting civil war." Cited in Burlingame, *Abraham*

*Lincoln,* 2:6. Lincoln spoke the next day in Cincinnati, delivering an address that was more conciliatory to the South than his Indianapolis speech: "We mean to treat you, as near as possibly we can, as Washington, Jefferson, and Madison treated you. We mean to leave you alone, and in no way to interfere with your institution; to abide by all and every compromise of the constitution. . . . We mean to remember that you are as good as we; that there is no difference between us, other than the difference of circumstances." *CW,* 4:199.

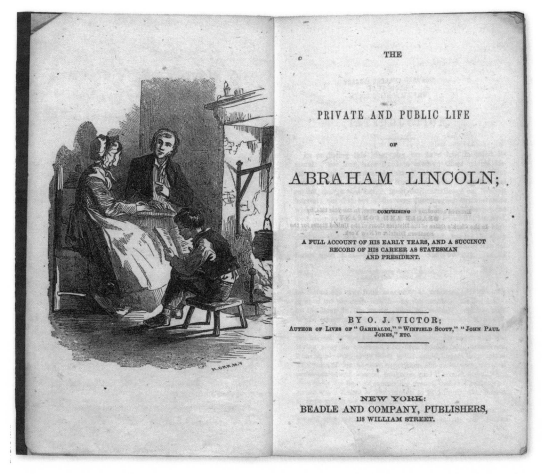

Orville J. Victor, *The Private and Public Life of Abraham Lincoln; Comprising a Full Account of His Early Years, and a Succinct Record of His Career as Statesman and President* (New York: Beadle and Company, 1864). Number 14 in Beadle's Dime Biographical Library series. The cover and frontispiece show the boy Lincoln practicing his reading skills by the light of a hearth fire.

# Address to the New Jersey State Senate, Trenton

## February 21, 1861

*Viewing the preserved Hessian barracks in Trenton, and no doubt inspired by the victory his hero George Washington had won at the battle there during the Revolutionary War, Lincoln in this speech recalled reading as a boy about the victorious exploits of Washington and his underfed and ill-clothed men, and the cause for which they fought. As he had declared in his farewell remarks in Springfield two weeks before, Lincoln believed he faced a struggle greater than that which Washington confronted some eighty years before. Lincoln pledged, with God's help, to preserve the Union and perpetuate freedom and liberty for its people.*

1    Mason Locke Weems (1759–1825) was the author of *The Life of George Washington* (Philadelphia: Joseph Allen, 1800), which was published in many editions.

MR. PRESIDENT AND GENTLEMEN OF THE SENATE OF THE STATE OF NEW-JERSEY: I am very grateful to you for the honorable reception of which I have been the object. I cannot but remember the place that New-Jersey holds in our early history. In the early Revolutionary struggle, few of the States among the old Thirteen had more of the battle-fields of the country within their limits than old New-Jersey. May I be pardoned if, upon this occasion, I mention that away back in my childhood, the earliest days of my being able to read, I got hold of a small book, such a one as few of the younger members have ever seen, "Weem's Life of Washington."[1] I remember all the accounts there given of the battle fields and struggles for the liberties of the country, and none fixed themselves upon my imagination so deeply as the struggle here at Trenton, New-Jersey. The crossing of the river; the contest with the Hessians; the great hardships endured at that time, all fixed themselves on my memory more than any single revolutionary event; and you all know, for you have all been boys, how these early impressions last longer than any others. I recollect thinking then, boy even though I was, that there must have been something more than common that those men struggled for. I am exceedingly anxious that that thing which they struggled for; that something even more than National Independence; that something that held out a great promise to all the people of the world to all time to come; I am exceedingly anxious that this Union, the Constitution, and the liberties of the people shall be perpetuated in accordance with the original idea for which that struggle was made, and I shall be most happy indeed if I shall be an humble instrument in the hands of the Almighty, and of this, his almost chosen people, for perpetuating the object of that great struggle. You give me this reception, as I understand, without distinction of party. I learn that this body is composed of a majority of

Old Hessian Barracks in Trenton, a landmark associated with the Revolutionary War Battle of Trenton.

2    Lincoln was probably referring to the fact that in the 1860 presidential election he lost the popular vote in New Jersey to Northern Democrat Stephen A. Douglas and the other two candidates, Southern Democrat John Breckinridge (1821–1875) and Constitutional Union Party candidate John Bell (1796–1869), having received 58,300 votes to their combined 62,000. He was awarded four of the state's seven electoral votes, however, owing to how New Jersey's Electoral College votes were apportioned; http://www.nj.gov/state/archives/lincoln.html (accessed January 14, 2015).

gentlemen who, in the exercise of their best judgment in the choice of a Chief Magistrate, did not think I was the man.[2] I understand, nevertheless, that they came forward here to greet me as the constitutional President of the United States—as citizens of the United States, to meet the man who, for the time being, is the representative man of the nation, united by a purpose to perpetuate the Union and liberties of the people. As such, I accept this reception more gratefully than I could do did I believe it was tendered to me as an individual.

# Address to the New Jersey General Assembly, Trenton

## February 21, 1861

*Following his eloquent and inspiring address to the New Jersey State Senate, Lincoln immediately appeared before the state's General Assembly and began delivering pedestrian remarks that, for the most part, adhered to his usual practice of thanking his hosts and saying little about how he would address the sectional crisis as president. Near the end of his brief speech, however, Lincoln raised eyebrows as well as cheers when he resorted to provocative language not heard since his Indianapolis speech of ten days earlier.*

MR. SPEAKER AND GENTLEMEN: I HAVE JUST ENJOYED THE honor of a reception by the other branch of this Legislature, and I return to you and them my thanks for the reception which the people of New-Jersey have given, through their chosen representatives, to me, as the representative, for the time being, of the majesty of the people of the United States.[1] I appropriate to myself very little of the demonstrations of respect with which I have been greeted. I think little should be given to any man, but that it should be a manifestation of adherence to the Union and the Constitution. I understand myself to be received here by the representatives of the people of New-Jersey, a majority of whom differ in opinion from those with whom I have acted. This manifestation is therefore to be regarded by me as expressing their devotion to the Union, the Constitution and the liberties of the people. You, Mr. Speaker,[2] have well said that this is a time when the bravest and wisest look with doubt and awe upon the aspect presented by our national affairs. Under these circumstances, you will readily see why I should not speak in detail of the course I shall deem it best to pursue. It is proper that I should avail myself of all the information and all the time at my command, in order that when the time arrives in which I must speak officially, I shall be able to take the ground which I deem the best and safest, and from which I may have no occasion to swerve. I shall endeavor to take the ground I deem most just to the North, the East, the West, the South, and the whole country. I take it, I hope, in good temper—certainly no malice toward any section. I shall do all that may be in my power to promote a peaceful settlement of all our difficulties. The man does not live who is more devoted to peace than I am. (*Cheers*) None who would do more to preserve it. But it may be necessary to put the foot down firmly.[3] (*Here the audience broke out into cheers so loud and long that for some moments it was*

1. When his inaugural train reached Trenton, Lincoln was greeted by a large crowd, estimated at twenty thousand, and a thirty-four-gun artillery salute. Lincoln's secretary John Hay thought the "official display was embarrassingly elaborate" and "rather increased than mitigated the prevalent disorder." Hay cited in Holzer, *Lincoln President-Elect*, 371.

2. Charles Haight (1838–1891), a Democrat, served as speaker of New Jersey's General Assembly from 1861 through 1862. He later served in the U.S. House of Representatives from 1867 to 1871. "Haight, Charles," Biographical Directory of the United States Congress, http://bioguide.congress.gov/scripts/biodisplay.pl?index=H000020 (accessed January 15, 2015).

3. An observer noted that as Lincoln spoke these words, he lifted his boot "slightly" and pressed it "with a quick, but not violent, gesture upon the floor," which unleashed "cheers so loud and long that for some moments it was impossible to hear Mr. L's voice." Cited in Holzer, *Lincoln President-Elect*, 372.

*impossible to hear Mr. L's voice*) He continued: And if I do my duty, and do right, you will sustain me, will you not? (*Loud cheers, and cries of "Yes," "Yes," "We will"*) Received, as I am, by the members of a Legislature the majority of whom do not agree with me in political sentiments, I trust that I may have their assistance in piloting the ship of State through this voyage, surrounded by perils as it is; for, if it should suffer attack now, there will be no pilot ever needed for another voyage.

Gentlemen, I have already spoken longer than I intended, and must beg leave to stop here.

# Speech in Independence Hall, Philadelphia

## February 22, 1861

*Despite being informed the evening before of an assassination attempt awaiting him in Baltimore, Lincoln refused to cut short his planned visit to Philadelphia's historic Independence Hall. Clearly affected by his visit to the "sacred hall" in which the founders had drafted the Declaration of Independence, Lincoln delivered emotional and heartfelt remarks emphasizing his devotion to the Declaration and the principles it embodied. Undoubtedly thinking of the disconcerting news he had received the night before, Lincoln avowed he would rather be "assassinated on this spot" than not try to preserve the nation based on the Declaration's principles. After his speech, Lincoln stepped outside onto a platform erected in front of the hall and, as a crowd of thirty thousand people shared in the emotionally charged early-morning ceremony, hoisted a huge new flag bearing an additional star for the newly admitted state of Kansas.*

MR. CUYLER:[1]—I AM FILLED WITH DEEP EMOTION AT FINDING MY-self standing here in the place where were collected together the wisdom, the patriotism, the devotion to principle, from which sprang the institutions under which we live. You have kindly suggested to me that in my hands is the task of restoring peace to our distracted country. I can say in return, sir, that all the political sentiments I entertain have been drawn, so far as I have been able to draw them, from the sentiments which originated, and were given to the world from this hall in which we stand. I have never had a feeling politically that did not spring from the sentiments embodied in the Declaration of Independence. (*Great cheering*) I have often pondered over the dangers which were incurred by the men who assembled here and adopted that Declaration of Independence—I have pondered over the toils that were endured by the officers and soldiers of the army, who achieved that Independence. (*Applause*) I have often inquired of myself, what great principle or idea it was that kept this Confederacy so long together. It was not the mere matter of the separation of the colonies from the mother land; but something in that Declaration giving liberty, not alone to the people of this country, but hope to the world for all future time. (*Great applause*) It was that which gave promise that in due time the weights should be lifted from the shoulders of all men, and that *all* should have an equal chance. (*Cheers*) This is the sentiment embodied in that Declaration of Independence.

Now, my friends, can this country be saved upon that basis? If it can, I will consider myself one of the happiest men in the world if I can help to save it. If it can't be saved upon that principle, it will be truly awful. But, if this country cannot be saved without giving up that principle—I was about

1    Theodore Cuyler (1819–1876) was a prominent Philadelphia lawyer who served as chief counsel for the Pennsylvania Railroad. In 1860 Cuyler was elected president of Philadelphia's Select Council, a post he held until 1862. Richard F. Miller, ed., *States at War*, vol. 3: *A Reference Guide for Pennsylvania in the Civil War* (Lebanon, NH: University Press of New England, 2014), 321n13.

Enoch Lewis, *Extra Schedule for Special Train, for the Accommodation of the President-Elect, to Be Run from Philadelphia to Harrisburg, on Friday February 22, 1861*. Broadside (Altoona, PA: McCrum and Dern, 1861). Schedule of the special train that took Lincoln from Philadelphia to Harrisburg, Pennsylvania. It turned out that the Harrisburg stop would be the president-elect's last public appearance on his inaugural journey, owing to the discovery the night before of a plot to assassinate him in Baltimore.

Lincoln raising the flag in front of Independence Hall. Photograph by F. DeBourg Richards (Philadelphia, February 22, 1861). The flag raising captured here, occurring on George Washington's birthday, took place in honor of the new star added for the admission of Kansas to the Union.

to say I would rather be assassinated on this spot than to surrender it.[2] (*Applause*)

Now, in my view of the present aspect of affairs, there is no need of bloodshed and war. There is no necessity for it. I am not in favor of such a course, and I may say in advance, there will be no blood shed unless it be forced upon the Government. The Government will not use force unless force is used against it. (*Prolonged applause and cries of "That's the proper sentiment"*)

My friends, this is a wholly unprepared speech. I did not expect to be called upon to say a word when I came here—I supposed I was merely to do something towards raising a flag. I may, therefore, have said something indiscreet, (*Cries of "no, no"*) but I have said nothing but what I am willing to live by, and, in the pleasure of Almighty God, die by.

2   In Philadelphia, Lincoln was informed by detective Allan Pinkerton (1819–1884) that his agents had received credible information concerning a plan to assassinate the president-elect when he arrived in Baltimore on February 23. Taking this information seriously, especially after it was confirmed by Frederick Seward (1830–1915), son of the secretary of state–designate, Lincoln's advisers convinced him to avoid any public appearances in Baltimore. It was decided that Harrisburg, Pennsylvania, would be the site of president-elect's last such event. After Harrisburg, Lincoln returned covertly to Philadelphia, where he boarded a train that traveled to Washington through Baltimore under a shroud of secrecy, arriving unannounced in the nation's capital in the early hours on February 23. Lincoln's clandestine arrival was ridiculed by the Democratic press and caused much embarrassment among Lincoln's supporters. Holzer, *Lincoln President-Elect,* 377–381, 397–403.

*Lincoln drafted this, his most important speech to date, in February 1861, in a room above his brother-in-law's store in Springfield. He was so confident that the manuscript would serve as his reading copy on Inauguration Day that he had it set in type at the office of the local Republican newspaper, the* Illinois State Journal. *In the intervening weeks, the president-elect showed the text to several allies, incorporating many of their proposed changes by hand. William Seward, the incoming secretary of state, suggested a conciliatory closing, which the president-elect ingeniously recrafted into one of his most memorable perorations. By the time he rose to deliver this speech, his typeset text had been so densely altered with handwritten emendations and hand-pasted slips—amounting to twelve dense pages in all—that Lincoln had felt compelled to sketch a small pointing finger to indicate the reading order of his closing lines. Long overshadowed by his more famous second inaugural address, this speech is now justifiably considered one of Lincoln's greatest orations. But in its time, Lincoln's calculated effort to offer an olive branch to slaveholders while holding firm against disunion in the South and slavery extension in the West, failed either to conciliate Southerners or inspire Northern progressives. The* Richmond Enquirer *labeled it the work of a "fanatic," while Frederick Douglass spoke for many liberals (and free African Americans) when he condemned Lincoln for "prostrating himself before the foul and withering curse of slavery."*

1    According to contemporary reports, Lincoln approached the rostrum, slowly unfolded his papers, then removed his spectacles from their case, snapping it shut so briskly that the noise was heard throughout the Capitol plaza. Although one eyewitness testified that the incoming president "could not make a movement, however slight, which did not elicit rounds of applause," another observer on the scene insisted that Lincoln's awkward gestures were greeted with silence, and that when he placed his eyeglasses on his nose,

# First Inaugural Address

## March 4, 1861

FELLOW CITIZENS OF THE UNITED STATES:[1]

In compliance with a custom as old as the government itself, I appear before you to address you briefly, and to take, in your presence, the oath prescribed by the Constitution of the United States, to be taken by the President "before he enters on the execution of his office."

I do not consider it necessary, at present, for me to discuss those matters of administration about which there is no special anxiety, or excitement.

Apprehension seems to exist among the people of the Southern States, that by the accession of a Republican Administration, their property, and their peace, and personal security, are to be endangered. There has never been any reasonable cause for such apprehension. Indeed, the most ample evidence to the contrary has all the while existed, and been open to their inspection. It is found in nearly all the published speeches of him who now addresses you.[2]

I do but quote from one of those speeches when I declare that "I have no purpose, directly or indirectly, to interfere with the institution of slavery in the States where it exists. I believe I have no lawful right to do so, and I have no inclination to do so." Those who nominated and elected me did so with full knowledge that I had made this, and many similar declarations, and had never recanted them. And more than this, they placed in the platform, for my acceptance, and as a law to themselves, and to me, the clear and emphatic resolution which I now read:

"*Resolved,* That the maintenance inviolate of the rights of the States, and especially the right of each State to order and control its own domestic institutions according to its own judgment exclusively, is essential to that balance of power on which the perfection and endurance of our political fabric depend; and we denounce the lawless invasion by armed force of the soil of any State or Territory, no matter under what pretext, as among the gravest of crimes."[3]

I now reiterate these sentiments: and in doing so, I only press upon the public attention the most conclusive evidence of which the case is susceptible, that the property, peace and security of no section are to be in anywise endangered by the now incoming Administration. I add too, that all the protection which, consistently with the Constitution and the laws, can be given, will be cheerfully given to all the States when lawfully demanded, for whatever cause—as cheerfully to one section, as to another.

There is much controversy about the delivering up of fugitives from service or labor. The clause I now read is as plainly written in the Constitution as any other of its provisions:

"No person held to service or labor in one State, under the laws thereof, escaping into another, shall, in consequence of any law or regulation therein, be discharged from such service or labor, but shall be delivered up on claim of the party to whom such service or labor may be due."[4]

It is scarcely questioned that this provision was intended by those who made it, for the reclaiming of what we call fugitive slaves; and the intention of the law-giver is the law.[5] All members of Congress swear their support to the whole Constitution—to this provision as much as to any other. To the proposition, then, that slaves whose cases come within the terms of this clause, "shall be delivered up," their oaths are unanimous. Now, if they would make the effort in good temper, could they not, with nearly equal unanimity, frame and pass a law, by means of which to keep good that unanimous oath?

There is some difference of opinion whether this clause should be enforced by national or by state authority; but surely that difference is not a very material one. If the slave is to be surrendered, it can be of but little consequence to him, or to others, by which authority it is done. And should any one, in any case, be content that his oath shall go unkept, on a merely unsubstantial controversy as to *how* it shall be kept?[6]

Again, in any law upon this subject, ought not all the safeguards of liberty known in civilized and humane jurisprudence to be introduced, so that a free man be not, in any case, surrendered as a slave? And might it not be well, at the same time, to provide by law for the enforcement of that clause

someone in the vast audience shouted, "Look at old goggles!" See Charles Aldrich's recollections in Rufus Rockwell Wilson, ed., *Intimate Memories of Lincoln* (Elmira, NY: Primavera Press, 1945), 345; Stephen Fiske's 1897 recollection published in the *Ladies' Home Journal,* reprinted in Rufus Rockwell Wilson, *Lincoln among His Friends: A Sheaf of Intimate Memories* (Caldwell, ID: Caxton Printers, 1942), 309.

2  During the so-called Secession Winter between election day and the inauguration, Lincoln had steadfastly refused to provide new assurances to the South that he was willing to leave slavery alone where it already existed. Confiding to *New York Times* editor Henry J. Raymond (1820–1869), Lincoln insisted that at one time the fire-eating secessionists were "political fiends." Now, he claimed, "'Party malice' and not 'public good' possesses them entirely, they seek a sign and no sign shall be given them." *CW,* 4:146. The president-elect had steadfastly remained silent on doctrinal points.

3  Party platforms were important—and widely read—in the nineteenth century. Here Lincoln cited a plank from the Republican Party platform that assured the autonomy of the individual states, and reminded Southerners that he and his party were pledged against military action against them.

4  U.S. Constitution, Article IV, Section 2.

5  Lincoln felt he must reaffirm his support, however reluctant, for the Fugitive Slave Law enshrined in the Compromise of 1850. Frederick Douglass was outraged by the declaration, editorializing: "Mr. Lincoln's admission of the constitutional duty of surrendering persons claimed" was "[h]orrible," and worse, expressed "heartily." *Douglass' Monthly,* April 1861.

6  Douglass added: "Aside from the inhuman coldness of the sentiment, it was a weak and inappropriate utterance to such an audience, since

it could neither appease nor check the wild fury of the rebel Slave Power." Ibid.

7    U.S. Constitution, Article IV, Section 2.

8    Lincoln had written, but deleted, "menaced, and so far as it can be on paper, is already effected." *CW,* 4:264n11. Lincoln perhaps hoped against hope that his olive branches would convince the seceding states to reconsider their announced separation from the Union. At least he could point to these sections, and their mild language, as proof that he was offering conciliation (though without conceding such doctrinal issues as the extension of slavery into the West).

9    After opening his speech on a conciliatory note, Lincoln here drew a line in the sand regarding secession. It was, he contended, illegal and unconstitutional.

in the Constitution which guarranties [*sic*] that "The citizens of each State shall be entitled to all previleges [*sic*] and immunities of citizens in the several States?"[7]

I take the official oath to-day, with no mental reservations, and with no purpose to construe the Constitution or laws, by any hypercritical rules. And while I do not choose now to specify particular acts of Congress as proper to be enforced, I do suggest, that it will be much safer for all, both in official and private stations, to conform to, and abide by, all those acts which stand unrepealed, than to violate any of them, trusting to find impunity in having them held to be unconstitutional.

It is seventy-two years since the first inauguration of a President under our national Constitution. During that period fifteen different and greatly distinguished citizens, have, in succession, administered the executive branch of the government. They have conducted it through many perils; and, generally, with great success. Yet, with all this scope for precedent, I now enter upon the same task for the brief constitutional term of four years, under great and peculiar difficulty. A disruption of the Federal Union heretofore only menaced, is now formidably attempted.[8]

I hold, that in contemplation of universal law, and of the Constitution, the Union of these States is perpetual. Perpetuity is implied, if not expressed, in the fundamental law of all national governments. It is safe to assert that no government proper, ever had a provision in its organic law for its own termination. Continue to execute all the express provisions of our national Constitution, and the Union will endure forever—it being impossible to destroy it, except by some action not provided for in the instrument itself.[9]

Again, if the United States be not a government proper, but an association of States in the nature of contract merely, can it, as a contract, be peaceably unmade, by less than all the parties who made it? One party to a contract may violate it—break it, so to speak; but does it not require all to lawfully rescind it?

Descending from these general principles, we find the proposition that, in legal contemplation, the Union is perpetual, confirmed by the history of the Union itself. The Union is much older than the Constitution. It was formed in fact, by the Articles of Association in 1774. It was matured and continued by the Declaration of Independence in 1776. It was further matured and the faith of all the then thirteen States expressly plighted and engaged that it should be perpetual, by the Articles of Confederation in 1778.

And finally, in 1787, one of the declared objects for ordaining and establishing the Constitution, was "*to form a more perfect union.*"

But if destruction of the Union, by one, or by a part only, of the States, be lawfully possible, the Union is *less* perfect than before the Constitution, having lost the vital element of perpetuity.

It follows from these views that no State, upon its own mere motion, can lawfully get out of the Union,—that *resolves* and *ordinances* to that effect are legally void; and that acts of violence, within any State or States, against the authority of the United States, are insurrectionary or revolutionary, according to circumstances.

I therefore consider that, in view of the Constitution and the laws, the Union is unbroken; and, to the extent of my ability, I shall take care, as the Constitution itself expressly enjoins upon me, that the laws of the Union be faithfully executed in all the States. Doing this I deem to be only a simple duty on my part; and I shall perform it, so far as practicable, unless my rightful masters, the American people, shall withhold the requisite means, or, in some authoritative manner, direct the contrary. I trust this will not be regarded as a menace, but only as the declared purpose of the Union that it *will* constitutionally defend, and maintain itself.

In doing this there needs to be no bloodshed or violence; and there shall be none, unless it be forced upon the national authority. The power confided to me, will be used to hold, occupy, and possess the property, and places belonging to the government, and to collect the duties and imposts; but beyond what may be necessary for these objects, there will be no invasion—no using of force against, or among the people anywhere.[10] Where hostility to the United States, in any interior locality, shall be so great and so universal, as to prevent competent resident citizens from holding the Federal offices, there will be no attempt to force obnoxious strangers among the people for that object.[11] While the strict legal right may exist in the government to enforce the exercise of these offices, the attempt to do so would be so irritating, and so nearly impracticable with all, that I deem it better to forego [*sic*], for the time, the uses of such offices. The mails, unless repelled, will continue to be furnished in all parts of the Union. So far as possible, the people everywhere shall have that sense of perfect security which is most favorable to calm thought and reflection. The course here indicated will be followed, unless current events, and experience, shall show a modification, or change, to be proper; and in every case and exigency, my best discretion will be exercised, according to circumstances actually existing, and with a

10  In his original text, Lincoln had been much tougher: "All the power at my disposal will be used to reclaim the public property and places which have fallen." A succession of confidants who were invited to read his original text urged him to tone down what sounded to them like bravado and bellicosity.

11  Here was a major concession by the first Republican president ever elected. Though poised and legally entitled to appoint fellow Republicans to federal posts nationwide (and abroad), Lincoln here offered to withhold such patronage in the South, which boasted so few members of the Republican Party that it was thought there that "obnoxious," antislavery strangers would be sent among them by the incoming administration to take over their post offices and arsenals.

Abraham Lincoln. Photograph by Alexander Gardner for Mathew Brady Gallery (Washington, DC, February 24, 1861). One of several poses taken of the president-elect a day after his arrival in the nation's capital.

view and a hope of a peaceful solution of the national troubles, and the restoration of fraternal sympathies and affections.

That there are persons in one section, or another who seek to destroy the Union at all events, and are glad of any pretext to do it, I will neither affirm or deny; but if there be such, I need address no word to them.[12] To those, however, who really love the Union, may I not speak?

Before entering upon so grave a matter as the destruction of our national fabric, with all its benefits, its memories, and its hopes, would it not be wise to ascertain precisely why we do it? Will you hazard so desperate a step, while there is any possibility that any portion of the ills you fly from, have no real existence? Will you, while the certain ills you fly to, are greater than all the real ones you fly from? Will you risk the commission of so fearful a mistake?

All profess to be content in the Union, if all constitutional rights can be maintained. Is it true, then, that any right, plainly written in the Constitution, has been denied? I think not. Happily the human mind is so constituted, that no party can reach to the audacity of doing this. Think, if you can, of a single instance in which a plainly written provision of the Constitution has ever been denied. If, by the mere force of numbers, a majority should deprive a minority of any clearly written constitutional right, it might, in a moral point of view, justify revolution—certainly would, if such right were a vital one. But such is not our case. All the vital rights of minorities, and of individuals, are so plainly assured to them, by affirmations and negations, guarranties [sic] and prohibitions, in the Constitution, that controversies never arise concerning them. But no organic law can ever be framed with a provision specifically applicable to every question which may occur in practical administration. No foresight can anticipate, nor any document of reasonable length contain express provisions for all possible questions. Shall fugitives from labor be surrendered by national or by State authority? The Constitution does not expressly say. *May* Congress prohibit slavery in the territories? The Constitution does not expressly say. *Must* Congress protect slavery in the territories? The Constitution does not expressly say.

From questions of this class spring all our constitutional controversies, and we divide upon them into majorities and minorities. If the minority will not acquiesce, the majority must, or the government must cease. There is no other alternative; for continuing the government, is acquiescence on one side or the other. If a minority, in such case, will secede rather than acquiesce, they make a precedent which, in turn, will divide and ruin them;

12 Here Lincoln reintroduced a rhetorical device he had used to great effect at Cooper Union a year earlier: prosopopoeia, from the Greek for "masked person"—the art of speaking to unseen audiences. See Harold Holzer, *Lincoln at Cooper Union: The Speech That Made Abraham Lincoln President* (New York: Simon & Schuster, 2004); and Michael C. Leff and Gerald P. Mohrmann, "Lincoln at Cooper Union: A Rhetorical Analysis of the Text," *Quarterly Journal of Speech* 60 (1974): 346–358.

13   When Lincoln delivered his inaugural address, seven Southern states—South Carolina, Mississippi, Florida, Alabama, Georgia, Louisiana, and Texas—had seceded. Those states would soon be joined by Virginia, Arkansas, Tennessee, and North Carolina.

14   In this convoluted passage Lincoln reminded his Republican supporters that he did not feel bound to support the bitterly controversial 1857 *Dred Scott* decision—even as its author, Chief Justice Roger B. Taney, sat right behind him on the Capitol portico, listening to these words, just a few moments from performing his own constitutional duty and administering the presidential oath to his political enemy.

15   Lincoln had made precisely the same point two and a half months earlier in a letter to his onetime Whig congressional colleague Alexander H. Stephens: "You think slavery is *right* and ought to be extended; while we think it is *wrong* and ought to be restricted. . . . It certainly is the only substantial difference between us." See "Letter to Alexander H. Stephens, December 22, 1860," in this volume. Stephens had replied, "widely we may differ politically, yet I trust we both have an earnest desire to preserve and maintain the Union." Stephens to Lincoln, December 30, 1860, *CW,* 4:160. But by the time Lincoln introduced a concept he had once told Stephens was "*For your eyes only,*" the Georgian had endorsed Georgia secession—albeit reluctantly—and, more important, become vice president of the Confederate States of America.

16   U.S. Constitution, Article IV, Section 2.

17   Article I, Section 9, of the Constitution stipulated that Congress could not outlaw the slave trade before 1808. Congress did prohibit the slave trade effective January 1 of that year.

for a minority of their own will secede from them, whenever a majority refuses to be controlled by such minority.[13] For instance, why may not any portion of a new confederacy, a year or two hence, arbitrarily secede again, precisely as portions of the present Union now claim to secede from it. All who cherish disunion sentiments, are now being educated to the exact temper of doing this. Is there such perfect identity of interests among the States to compose a new Union, as to produce harmony only, and prevent renewed secession?

Plainly, the central idea of secession, is the essence of anarchy. A majority, held in restraint by constitutional checks, and limitations, and always changing easily, with deliberate changes of popular opinions and sentiments, is the only true sovereign of a free people. Whoever rejects it, does, of necessity, fly to anarchy or to despotism. Unanimity is impossible; the rule of a minority, as a permanent arrangement, is wholly inadmissable; so that, rejecting the majority principle, anarchy, or despotism in some form, is all that is left.

I do not forget the position assumed by some, that constitutional questions are to be decided by the Supreme Court; nor do I deny that such decisions must be binding in any case, upon the parties to a suit, as to the object of that suit, while they are also entitled to very high respect and consideration, in all paralel [*sic*] cases, by all other departments of the government. And while it is obviously possible that such decision may be erroneous in any given case, still the evil effect following it, being limited to that particular case, with the chance that it may be over-ruled, and never become a precedent for other cases, can better be borne than could the evils of a different practice.[14] At the same time the candid citizen must confess that if the policy of the government, upon vital questions, affecting the whole people, is to be irrevocably fixed by decisions of the Supreme Court, the instant they are made, in ordinary litigation between parties, in personal actions, the people will have ceased, to be their own rulers, having, to that extent, practically resigned their government, into the hands of that eminent tribunal. Nor is there, in this view, any assault upon the court, or the judges. It is a duty, from which they may not shrink, to decide cases properly brought before them; and it is no fault of theirs, if others seek to turn their decisions to political purposes.

One section of our country believes slavery is *right,* and ought to be extended, while the other believes it is *wrong,* and ought not to be extended.[15] This is the only substantial dispute. The fugitive slave clause of the Constitution,[16] and the law for the suppression of the foreign slave trade,[17] are each

Alexander Gardner, Lincoln's first Inaugural on the U.S. Capitol portico. Photograph (Washington, DC, March 4, 1861).

as well enforced, perhaps, as any law can ever be in a community where the moral sense of the people imperfectly supports the law itself. The great body of the people abide by the dry legal obligation in both cases, and a few break over in each. This, I think, cannot be perfectly cured; and it would be worse in both cases *after* the separation of the sections, than before. The foreign slave trade, now imperfectly suppressed, would be ultimately revived without restriction, in one section; while fugitive slaves, now only partially surrendered, would not be surrendered at all, by the other.

Physically speaking, we cannot separate. We cannot remove our respective sections from each other, nor build an impassable wall between them. A husband and wife may be divorced, and go out of the presence, and beyond the reach of each other; but the different parts of our country cannot do this. They cannot but remain face to face; and intercourse, either amicable or hostile, must continue between them. Is it possible then to make that intercourse more advantageous, or more satisfactory, *after* separation

18 Lincoln's onetime law partner Stephen T. Logan was one of the old friends to whom Lincoln showed his inaugural text in advance. Logan later claimed that when he objected to one passage (it could have been this very sentence) as too threatening to the South, Lincoln replied: "The statements express the convictions of duty that the great office I shall endeavor to fill will impose upon me, and if there is patriotism enough in the American people, the Union will be saved; if not, it will go down, and I will go with it." Logan's speech in Springfield after Lincoln's death is quoted in Charles S. Zane, "Lincoln as I Knew Him," *Sunset* 29 (October 1912): 434–435.

than *before?* Can aliens make treaties easier than friends can make laws? Can treaties be more faithfully enforced between aliens, than laws can among friends? Suppose you go to war, you cannot fight always; and when, after much loss on both sides, and no gain on either, you cease fighting, the identical old questions, as to terms of intercourse, are again upon you.[18]

This country, with its institutions, belongs to the people who inhabit it. Whenever they shall grow weary of the existing government, they can exercise their *constitutional* right of amending it, or their *revolutionary* right to dismember, or overthrow it. I can not be ignorant of the fact that many worthy, and patriotic citizens are desirous of having the national constitution amended. While I make no recommendation of amendments, I fully recognize the rightful authority of the people over the whole subject, to be exercised in either of the modes prescribed in the instrument itself; and I should, under existing circumstances, favor, rather than oppose, a fair oppertunity [*sic*] being afforded the people to act upon it.

I will venture to add that, to me, the convention mode seems preferable, in that it allows amendments to originate with the people themselves, instead of only permitting them to take, or reject, propositions, originated by others, not especially chosen for the purpose, and which might not be precisely such, as they would wish to either accept or refuse. I understand a proposed amendment to the Constitution—which amendment, however, I have not seen, has passed Congress, to the effect that the federal government, shall never interfere with the domestic institutions of the States, including that of persons held to service. To avoid misconstruction of what I have said, I depart from my purpose not to speak of particular amendments, so far as to say that, holding such a provision to now be implied constitutional law, I have no objection to its being made express, and irrevocable.

The Chief Magistrate derives all his authority from the people, and they have conferred none upon him to fix terms for the separation of the States. The people themselves can do this also if they choose; but the executive, as such, has nothing to do with it. His duty is to administer the present government, as it came to his hands, and to transmit it, unimpaired by him, to his successor.

Why should there not be a patient confidence in the ultimate justice of the people? Is there any better, or equal hope, in the world? In our present differences, is either party without faith of being in the right? If the Almighty Ruler of nations, with his eternal truth and justice, be on your side of the North, or on yours of the South, that truth, and that justice, will surely prevail, by the judgment of this great tribunal, the American people.

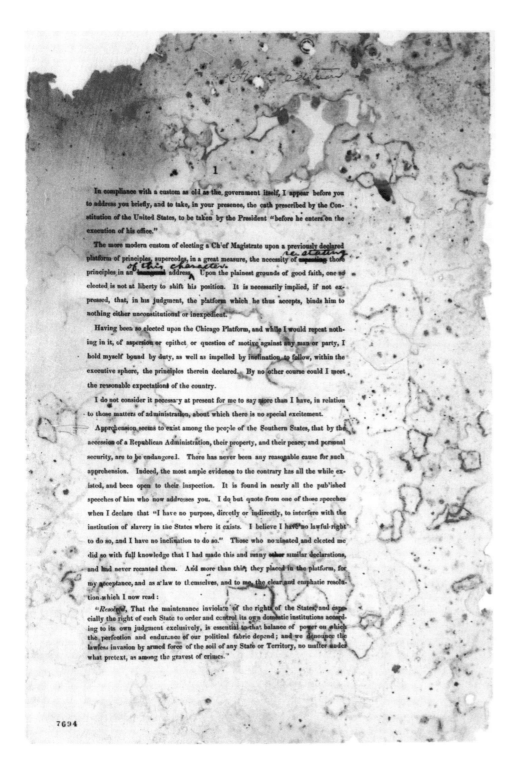

1

In compliance with a custom as old as the government itself, I appear before you to address you briefly, and to take, in your presence, the oath prescribed by the Constitution of the United States, to be taken by the President "before he enters on the execution of his office."

The more modern custom of electing a Chief Magistrate upon a previously declared platform of principles, supercedes, in a great measure, the necessity of ~~repeating~~ *re-stating* those principles in an ~~inaugural~~ address *of this character.* Upon the plainest grounds of good faith, one so elected is not at liberty to shift his position. It is necessarily implied, if not expressed, that, in his judgment, the platform which he thus accepts, binds him to nothing either unconstitutional or inexpedient.

Having been so elected upon the Chicago Platform, and while I would repeat nothing in it, of aspersion or epithet, or question of motive against any man or party, I hold myself bound by duty, as well as impelled by inclination to follow, within the executive sphere, the principles therein declared. By no other course could I meet the reasonable expectations of the country.

I do not consider it necessary at present for me to say more than I have, in relation to those matters of administration, about which there is no special excitement.

Apprehension seems to exist among the people of the Southern States, that by the accession of a Republican Administration, their property, and their peace, and personal security, are to be endangered. There has never been any reasonable cause for such apprehension. Indeed, the most ample evidence to the contrary has all the while existed, and been open to their inspection. It is found in nearly all the published speeches of him who now addresses you. I do but quote from one of those speeches when I declare that "I have no purpose, directly or indirectly, to interfere with the institution of slavery in the States where it exists. I believe I have no lawful right to do so, and I have no inclination to do so." Those who nominated and elected me did so with full knowledge that I had made this and many other similar declarations, and had never recanted them. And more than this, they placed in the platform, for my acceptance, and as a law to themselves, and to me, the clear and emphatic resolution which I now read:

"*Resolved*, That the maintenance inviolate of the rights of the States, and especially the right of each State to order and control its own domestic institutions according to its own judgment exclusively, is essential to that balance of power on which the perfection and endurance of our political fabric depend; and we denounce the lawless invasion by armed force of the soil of any State or Territory, no matter under what pretext, as among the gravest of crimes."

7694

Page from Abraham Lincoln's first inaugural address. Printed proof sheet (Springfield, IL: Privately printed, February 1861). The proof is extensively revised in the hand of Lincoln's secretary, John George Nicolay, 1861.

**19** Lincoln used the cumbersome construct "I shall have" because he had not yet been formally sworn in—he was still a few minutes away from officially assuming the presidency. Under customs that prevailed at the time, inaugural ceremonies were conducted in precisely the reverse order they are staged today: first the inaugural parade, then the inaugural address, and finally the administering of the oath of office.

**20** Lincoln's original ending, which he discarded, was: "*You* can forbear the *assault* upon it [the federal government]; *I* can *not* shrink from the *defense* of it. With *you*, and not with *me*, is the solemn question of 'Shall it be peace, or a sword?'"

**21** This memorable ending was proposed—indeed, drafted—by William H. Seward. Lincoln displayed a brilliant facility for editing when he turned the incoming secretary of state's conciliatory but prosaic conclusion into pure poetry (famously quoted by Barack Obama at his victory speech in Chicago in November 2008). This was Seward's proposed peroration: "I close. We are not we must not be aliens or enemies but fellow countrymen and brethren. Although passion has strained our bonds of affection too hardly they must not, I am sure they will not be broken. The mystic chords which proceeding from so many battle fields and so many patriot graves pass through all the hearts and all the hearths in this broad continent of ours will yet again harmonize in their ancient music when breathed upon by the guardian angel of the nation." Interestingly, Seward had originally drafted "better angel," but crossed those words out; Lincoln must have glimpsed the deletion and rescued it.

By the frame of the government under which we live, this same people have wisely given their public servants but little power for mischief; and have, with equal wisdom, provided for the return of that little to their own hands at very short intervals.

While the people retain their virtue, and vigilence [*sic*], no administration, by any extreme of wickedness or folly, can very seriously injure the government, in the short space of four years.

My countrymen, one and all, think calmly and *well*, upon this whole subject. Nothing valuable can be lost by taking time. If there be an object to *hurry* any of you, in hot haste, to a step which you would never take *deliberately*, that object will be frustrated by taking time; but no good object can be frustrated by it. Such of you as are now dissatisfied, still have the old Constitution unimpaired, and, on the sensitive point, the laws of your own framing under it; while the new administration will have no immediate power, if it would, to change either. If it were admitted that you who are dissatisfied, hold the right side in the dispute, there still is no single good reason for precipitate action. Intelligence, patriotism, Christianity, and a firm reliance on Him, who has never yet forsaken this favored land, are still competent to adjust, in the best way, all our present difficulty.

In *your* hands, my dissatisfied fellow countrymen, and not in *mine*, is the momentous issue of civil war. The government will not assail *you*. *You* can have no conflict, without being yourselves the aggressors. *You* have no oath registered in Heaven to destroy the government, while *I* shall have the most solemn one to "preserve, protect and defend" it.[19]

I am loth to close.[20] We are not enemies, but friends. We must not be enemies. Though passion may have strained, it must not break our bonds of affection. The mystic chords of memory, stretching from every battle-field, and patriot grave, to every living heart and hearthstone, all over this broad land, will yet swell the chorus of the Union, when again touched, as surely they will be, by the better angels of our nature.[21]

# Letter to William H. Seward

## April 1, 1861

*On April 1, Secretary of State Seward submitted "Some Thoughts for the President's consideration," making a blatant attempt to seize power over what he viewed as a rudderless administration. Nor did Seward offer his audacious proposals in strict confidence; he summoned a newspaper ally, Henry Raymond of the New York Times, to rush to Washington to report the impending "coup d'état" firsthand. Lincoln's calm and measured response thoroughly deflated the power grab and so greatly impressed his would-be "prime minister" that Seward never doubted Lincoln's abilities or authority again.*

Hon: W. H. Seward:                    Executive Mansion April 1, 1861

My dear Sir: Since parting with you I have been considering your paper dated this day, and entitled "Some thoughts for the President's consideration."[1] The first proposition in it is, "1st. We are at the end of a month's administration, and yet without a policy, either domestic or foreign."[2]

At the *beginning* of that month, in the inaugural [address], I said "The power confided to me will be used to hold, occupy and possess the property and places belonging to the government, and to collect the duties, and imposts." This had your distinct approval at the time;[3] and, taken in connection with the order I immediately gave General Scott, directing him to employ every means in his power to strengthen and hold the forts, comprises the exact domestic policy you now urge, with the single exception, that it does not propose to abandon Fort Sumpter [*sic*].

Again, I do not perceive how the re-inforcement of Fort Sumpter [*sic*] would be done on a slavery, or party issue, while that of Fort Pickens would be on a more national, and patriotic one.[4]

The news received yesterday in regard to St. Domingo,[5] certainly brings a new item within the range of our foreign policy; but up to that time we have been preparing circulars, and instructions to ministers, and the like, all in perfect harmony, without even a suggestion that we had no foreign policy.

Upon your closing propositions, that "whatever policy we adopt, there must be an energetic prossecution [*sic*] of it"

"For this purpose it must be somebody's business to pursue and direct it incessantly[.]"[6]

1    Seward's long and imperious three-page memorandum was divided between domestic and diplomatic advice, and suggested, among other things, considering a declaration of war against European powers. Historians have stressed Seward's insolence in sending such a presumptuous manifesto, but in fact he and Lincoln agreed on many of the secretary of state's ideas, including Seward's suggestion: *Change the question before the Public from one upon Slavery, or about Slavery* for a question upon *Union* or *Disunion*. In other words, from what would be regarded as a Party question to one of *Patriotism* or *Union*." Original in the Abraham Lincoln Papers, Library of Congress.

2    In obvious collusion with Seward, *New York Times* editor Henry J. Raymond published an April 3 editorial, "Wanted—A Policy," which charged that "our Government has done absolutely nothing, towards carrying the country through the tremendous crisis which is so rapidly and so steadily settling down upon us."

3    Lincoln reminded his secretary of state that he (Seward) had earlier provided extensive suggestions for the inaugural address, and Lincoln had adopted most of them.

4    Seward believed that the administration should make its stand against Confederate attempts to seize federal installations in the South not at

John C. Buttre, *President and Cabinet.* Engraving (New York, 1864). Lincoln with Secretaries Seward, Chase, Stanton, Smith, Blair, Welles, Bates, and Vice President Hamlin.

Artist unknown, after Mathew Brady, *William H. Seward.*
The New York senator was Lincoln's first and only choice to
serve as secretary of state.

Charleston but at remote Fort Pickens in Florida,
arguing that the Buchanan administration had
been far too intent on reinforcing Fort Sumter.

5    On March 16 Spain had launched an effort to
annex its onetime colony San Domingo (now the
Dominican Republic), sending a troop ship from
Cuba and encouraging Spanish colonists to fly its
flag.

6    In perhaps the most incendiary passages in
Seward's memorandum, the secretary had implied
that the president had spent too much time dealing
with "applications for patronage," adding that
"further delay to adopt and prosecute our policies
for both domestic and foreign affairs would not
only bring scandal on the Administration, but
danger upon the country."

7    Seward had ended his astounding memorandum: "But I neither seek to evade nor assume
responsibility." Of course, even the mere idea that
he might have been prepared to "assume responsibility" was unprecedented.

8    The only known copy of this presidential
response remained in Lincoln's White House files.
No copy has ever been found in the Seward papers,
suggesting that, instead of sending such a forceful
repudiation of his chief cabinet officer, the
president summoned him to his office and read or
paraphrased his thoughts in person. If so, it was
the first time, but not the last, that Lincoln let off
steam by writing a harsh letter and then, for fear of
hurting or alienating its intended recipient, filed it
away without sending it.

"Either the President must do it himself, and be all the while active in
it, or"
"Devolve it on some member of his cabinet[.]"[7]
"Once adopted, debates on it must end, and all agree and abide" I remark that if this must be done, *I* must do it. When a general line of policy
is adopted, I apprehend there is no danger of its being changed without
good reason, or continuing to be a subject of unnecessary debate; still, upon
points arising in its progress, I wish, and suppose I am entitled to have the
advice of all the cabinet.[8]

Your Obt. Servt.
A. LINCOLN

*Lincoln signed this order two weeks after the surrender of Fort Sumter, and eight days after anti-Union hooligans in Baltimore attacked soldiers of the Sixth Massachusetts regiment as they tried to change trains en route to Washington to join in the defense of the national capital. The order authorized the suspension of the writ of habeas corpus from Philadelphia to Washington. This action represented the first time Lincoln used the authority he later described as his "war power." Under the terms of the order, the federal army proceeded to arrest pro-Confederate Marylanders, thus preventing state legislators from holding a secession convention and effectively keeping Maryland in the Union.*

1    Lieutenant General Winfield Scott, nearly seventy-five years old when Lincoln became his commander in chief, had served in the military for half a century, distinguishing himself in conflicts as early as the War of 1812 and earning glory in the Mexican-American War. Scott proposed the "Anaconda Plan"—the ingenious proposal for a blockade of Southern ports.

2    The printed edition of the order changed this phrase to "any military line."

3    Printed version added "or shall be."

4    The writ of habeas corpus, designed to protect against unlawful detention, gives defendants the right to appear in court, before a judge.

# Letter to Winfield Scott

## April 27, 1861

To the Commanding General of the Army of the United States:[1]

You are engaged in repressing an insurrection against the laws of the United States. If at any point on or in the vicinity of the military line,[2] which is now[3] used between the City of Philadelphia and the City of Washington, via Perryville, Annapolis City, and Annapolis Junction, you find resistance which renders it necessary to suspend the writ of Habeas Corpus[4] for the public safety, you, personally or through the officer in command at the point where the resistance occurs, are authorized to suspend that writ.

ABRAHAM LINCOLN
April 27 1861

General Winfield Scott. Photograph by Mathew Brady (ca. 1861–1866).

# Letter to Ephraim D. and Phoebe Ellsworth

## May 25, 1861

*On May 24, Colonel Elmer Ephraim Ellsworth—a beloved young Lincoln protégée who had served as one of his bodyguards during the inaugural journey—died of shotgun wounds after hauling down a huge Confederate flag from the roof of an Alexandria hotel across the Potomac from Washington. Ellsworth became an instant martyr in the North: the first Union officer killed in the Civil War. Devastated by his death, Lincoln wrote this achingly tender condolence note to Ellsworth's parents on the same day he afforded the youthful onetime drillmaster a White House funeral.*

To the Father and Mother of Col.  Washington D.C.
Elmer E. Ellsworth:  May 25. 1861
My dear Sir and Madam,

In the untimely loss of your noble son, our affliction here, is scarcely less than your own.[1] So much of promised usefulness to one's country, and of bright hopes for one's self and friends, have rarely been so suddenly dashed, as in his fall. In size, in years, and in youthful appearance, a boy only, his power to command men, was surpassingly great.[2] This power, combined with a fine intellect, an indomitable energy, and a taste altogether military, constituted in him, as seemed to me, the best natural talent, in that department, I ever knew. And yet he was singularly modest and deferential in social intercourse. My acquaintance with him began less than two years ago;[3] yet through the latter half of the intervening period, it was as intimate as the disparity of our ages, and my engrossing engagements, would permit. To me, he appeared to have no indulgences or pastimes; and I never heard him utter a profane, or an intemperate word. What was conclusive of his good heart, he never forgot his parents. The honors he labored for so laudably, and, in the sad end, so gallantly gave his life, he meant for them, no less than for himself.[4]

In the hope that it may be no intrusion upon the sacredness of your sorrow, I have ventured to address you this tribute to the memory of my young friend, and your brave and early fallen child.

May God give you that consolation which is beyond all earthly power. Sincerely your friend in a common affliction—

A. LINCOLN

Ephraim Elmer Ellsworth. Photograph by Mathew Brady (New York, ca. 1860). The young Zouave drillmaster was like a son to the Lincolns.

1    A reporter happened to visit Lincoln shortly after news of Elmer E. Ellsworth's death reached him, and found the President in tears. "I will make no apology . . . for my weakness," Lincoln stammered, "but I knew poor Ellsworth well and held him in great regard." *New York Herald,* May 25, 1861.

2    Before Lincoln took office, Ellsworth (1837–1861) had led a famous peacetime unit, the U.S. Zouave Cadets of Chicago, which specialized in rapid-time drills that dazzled audiences throughout the West. Ellsworth's obituary appeared in the *New York Times* on May 25, 1861.

3    For a time, young Ellsworth studied law at the Lincoln-Herndon legal office in Springfield, Illinois, and grew close to the Lincoln family.

4    Offended by the sight of a sixteen-by-twenty-four-foot enemy flag flying within view of the White House—at least by telescope—Ellsworth marched his brightly uniformed Eleventh New York Fire Zouaves across the Potomac on May 24, determined to tear the banner down. As Ellsworth made his way down the stairs leading from the rooftop of the hotel, clutching the flag, innkeeper James T. Jackson opened fire on him at close range with a shotgun, killing him instantly. Ellsworth became an immediate martyr in the North, and his celebrity was cemented by the publication of countless print portraits and song sheet covers. Mark E. Neely and Harold Holzer, *The Union Image: Popular Prints of the Civil War North* (Chapel Hill: University of North Carolina Press, 2000), 27–31.

Alonzo Chappel, *Death of E. E. Ellsworth.* Oil on canvas (1862). Dramatic depiction of Ellsworth being slain as he descends stairs of the Jackson House hotel.

# Message to Special Session of Congress

## July 4, 1861

*After suspending habeas corpus, calling for 75,000 volunteers, and ordering a blockade of Southern ports—all without the approval of Congress, which was in recess—Lincoln had called a special session on the symbolic date of the Fourth of July. Hoping the House and Senate would ratify the executive actions he had taken to meet the secession emergency, Lincoln sent one of his most brilliant, if somewhat disorganized, messages—filled with quotable lines like, "This is a People's Contest"—and making a forceful case that saving the Union by even the toughest means would guarantee future Americans a "fair chance in the race of life." While most pro-Republican newspapers applauded the substance of the message (the* New York Times *did criticize it as a "painful jumble"), the secessionist Baltimore paper,* The South, *responded by denouncing Lincoln as "the equal, in despotic wickedness, of Nero or any of the other tyrants who have polluted this earth." Within months, the administration shut the latter paper down and arrested its staff for "contributing to unsettle and excite the public mind."*

FELLOW-CITIZENS OF THE SENATE AND HOUSE OF REPRESENTATIVES:[1]

Having been convened on an extraordinary occasion, as authorized by the Constitution, your attention is not called to any ordinary subject of legislation.

At the beginning of the present Presidential term, four months ago, the functions of the Federal Government were found to be generally suspended within the several States of South Carolina, Georgia, Alabama, Mississippi, Louisiana, and Florida, excepting only those of the Post Office Department.[2]

Within these States, all the Forts, Arsenals, Dock-yards, Custom-houses, and the like, including the movable and stationary property in, and about them, had been seized, and were held in open hostility to this Government, excepting only Forts Pickens, Taylor, and Jefferson, on, and near the Florida coast, and Fort Sumter, in Charleston harbor, South Carolina. The Forts thus seized had been put in improved condition; new ones had been built; and armed forces had been organized, and were organizing, all avowedly with the same hostile purpose.[3]

The Forts remaining in the possession of the Federal government, in, and near, these States, were either besieged or menaced by warlike preparations; and especially Fort Sumter was nearly surrounded by well-protected hostile batteries, with guns equal in quality to the best of its own, and outnumbering the latter as perhaps ten to one. A disproportionate share, of the Federal muskets and rifles, had somehow found their way into these States, and had been seized, to be used against the government. Accumulations of the public revenue, lying within them, had been seized for the same object. The Navy was scattered in distant seas; leaving but a very small part of it within the immediate reach of the government. Officers of the Federal

[1]  Lincoln devoted much time to drafting this message, giving it his full attention for several weeks prior to its delivery to Congress. On the night before the message was to be read to Congress, Lincoln read it aloud to Orville Hickman Browning, who thought it was "a most admirable history of our present difficulties, and a conclusive and unanswerable argument against the abominable heresy of secession. It is an able state paper and will fully meet the expectations of the Country." *The Diary of Orville Hickman Browning,* ed. Theodore Calvin Pease and James G. Randall, 2 vols. (Springfield: Trustees of the Illinois State Historical Library, 1925–1933), 1:475. One of Lincoln's secretaries wrote that the president "is engaged in constant thought upon his Message: It will be an exhaustive review of the questions of the hour & of the future." Cited in Burlingame, *Abraham Lincoln,* 2:166. On the same day he sent this message to Capitol Hill, Lincoln joined

General Winfield Scott and the cabinet at a
pavilion outside the White House to review a
procession of 20,000 New York volunteers who
had arrived in the city en route to the seat of war.
Greeting the troops, the commander in chief made
only brief remarks, explaining, "There is a kind of
rule that constrains" presidents from making
statements in public (a tradition he soon abandoned). "I have made a great many poor speeches
in my life," he told the soldiers, "and I feel
considerably relieved now to know that the dignity
of the position in which I have been placed does
not permit me to expose myself any longer" *CW,*
4:441.

2    Lincoln began a litany of updates on recent
federal business, almost in the manner of an
annual address, rather than a special message,
calmly laying out the history of the secession crisis
and the first outbreaks of rebellion to date.

3    One of the seminal questions debated between
North and South at the outset of the rebellion was
that of who owned federal forts—the national
government that had built them, or the states
where they had been built?

4    West Point–educated Major Robert Anderson
(1805–1871), who had commanded the besieged
federal garrison inside Fort Sumter, was, like the
president, a Kentuckian who had once fought in
the Black Hawk War. On May 15, Lincoln had
breveted Anderson to the rank of brigadier general.
After service in his native Kentucky, however,
Anderson took sick and retired in 1863. On April
15, 1865—the day Lincoln died—Anderson
returned to Fort Sumter, now a ruin pummeled
almost into dust by Union gunboats, to preside
over a flag raising there, precisely four years after
his men had hauled the flag down in surrender to
the Confederacy. Thomas Marshall Spaulding,
"Robert Anderson," *American National Biography,*
24 vols. (New York: Oxford University Press, 1999),
1:481–482.

Army and Navy, had resigned in great numbers; and, of those resigning,
a large proportion had taken up arms against the government. Simultaneously, and in connection, with all this, the purpose to sever the Federal
Union, was openly avowed. In accordance with this purpose, an ordinance
had been adopted in each of these States, declaring the States, respectively,
to be separated from the National Union. A formula for instituting a combined government of these states had been promulgated; and this illegal organization, in the character of confederate States was already invoking recognition, aid, and intervention, from Foreign Powers.

Finding this condition of things, and believing it to be an imperative
duty upon the incoming Executive, to prevent, if possible, the consummation of such attempt to destroy the Federal Union, a choice of means to that
end became indispensable. This choice was made; and was declared in the
Inaugural address. The policy chosen looked to the exhaustion of all peaceful measures, before a resort to any stronger ones. It sought only to hold
the public places and property, not already wrested from the Government,
and to collect the revenue; relying for the rest, on time, discussion, and the
ballot-box. It promised a continuance of the mails, at government expense,
to the very people who were resisting the government; and it gave repeated
pledges against any disturbance to any of the people, or any of their rights.
Of all that which a president might constitutionally, and justifiably, do in
such a case, everything was foreborne [*sic*], without which, it was believed
possible to keep the government on foot.

On the 5th of March, (the present incumbent's first full day in office) a
letter of Major Anderson, commanding at Fort Sumter, written on the 28th
of February, and received at the War Department on the 4th of March, was,
by that Department, placed in his hands.[4] This letter expressed the professional opinion of the writer, that re-inforcements could not be thrown into
that Fort within the time for his relief, rendered necessary by the limited
supply of provisions, and with a view of holding possession of the same,
with a force of less than twenty thousand good, and well-disciplined men.
This opinion was concurred in by all the officers of his command; and their
*memoranda* on the subject, were made enclosures of Major Anderson's letter. The whole was immediately laid before Lieutenant General Scott, who
at once concurred with Major Anderson in opinion. On reflection, however, he took full time, consulting with other officers, both of the Army
and the Navy; and, at the end of four days, came reluctantly, but decidedly,
to the same conclusion as before. He also stated at the same time that no
such sufficient force was then at the control of the Government, or could be

*Bombardment of Fort Sumter, Charleston Harbor: 12th & 13th of April 1861.* Lithograph (New York: Currier & Ives, 1861).

raised, and brought to the ground, within the time when the provisions in the Fort would be exhausted. In a purely military point of view, this reduced the duty of the administration, in the case, to the mere matter of getting the garrison safely out of the Fort.

It was believed, however, that to so abandon that position, under the circumstances, would be utterly ruinous; that the *necessity* under which it was to be done, would not be fully understood—that, by many, it would be construed as a part of a *voluntary* policy—that, at home, it would discourage the friends of the Union, embolden its adversaries, and go far to insure to the latter, a recognition abroad—that, in fact, it would be our national

5   The U.S.S. *Sabine* ultimately transferred 115 marines and 86 soldiers to Fort Pickens. Craig L. Symonds, *Lincoln and His Admirals: Abraham Lincoln, the U.S. Navy, and the Civil War* (New York: Oxford University Press, 2008), 31.

6   Francis W. Pickens (1805–1869), served as governor of South Carolina from 1860 to 1862. "Pickens, Francis Wilkinson," Biographical Directory of the United States Congress, http://bioguide.congress.gov/scripts/biodisplay.pl?index=p000321 (accessed February 1, 2015).

7   Lincoln's decision to resupply—but not reinforce—Fort Sumter forced the Confederacy to act the aggressor in starting the war. Just as the president hoped, the attack, when it came, unified Northern public opinion and inspired tens of thousands of citizens to volunteer for military service.

8   Lincoln had drafted some of these passages in the first person but later revised the text.

destruction consummated. This could not be allowed. Starvation was not yet upon the garrison; and ere it would be reached, *Fort Pickens* might be reinforced. This last, would be a clear indication of *policy,* and would better enable the country to accept the evacuation of Fort Sumter, as a military *necessity.* An order was at once directed to be sent for the landing of the troops from the Steamship Brooklyn, into Fort Pickens. This order could not go by land, but must take the longer, and slower route by sea. The first return news from the order was received just one week before the fall of Fort Sumter. The news itself was, that the officer commanding the Sabine, to which vessel the troops had been transferred from the Brooklyn, acting upon some *quasi* armistice of the late administration, (and of the existence of which, the present administration, up to the time the order was despatched, had only too vague and uncertain rumors, to fix attention) had refused to land the troops. To now re-inforce Fort Pickens, before a crisis would be reached at Fort Sumter was impossible[5]—rendered so by the near exhaustion of provisions in the latter-named Fort. In precaution against such a conjuncture, the government had, a few days before, commenced preparing an expedition, as well adapted as might be, to relieve Fort Sumter, which expedition was intended to be ultimately used, or not, according to circumstances. The strongest anticipated case, for using it, was now presented; and it was resolved to send it forward. As had been intended, in this contingency, it was also resolved to notify the Governor of South Carolina,[6] that he might except an attempt would be made to provision the Fort; and that, if the attempt should not be resisted, there would be no effort to throw in men, arms, or ammunition, without further notice, or in case of an attack upon the Fort.[7] This notice was accordingly given; whereupon the Fort was attacked, and bombarded to its fall, without even awaiting the arrival of the provisioning expedition.

It is thus seen that the assault upon, and reduction of, Fort Sumter, was, in no sense, a matter of self defence on the part of the assailants. They well knew that the garrison in the Fort could, by no possibility, commit aggression upon them. They knew—they were expressly notified—that the giving of bread to the few brave and hungry men of the garrison, was all which would on that occasion be attempted, unless themselves, by resisting so much, should provoke more. They knew that this Government desired to keep the garrison in the Fort, not to assail them, but merely to maintain visible possession, and thus to preserve the Union from actual, and immediate dissolution—trusting, as herein-before stated, to time, discussion, and the ballot-box, for final adjustment; and they assailed, and reduced the Fort, for

precisely the reverse object—to drive out the visible authority of the Federal Union, and thus force it to immediate dissolution.

That this was their object, the Executive well understood; and having said to them in the inaugural address, "You can have no conflict without being yourselves the aggressors," he took pains, not only to keep this declaration good, but also to keep the case so free from the power of ingenious sophistry, as that the world should not be able to misunderstand it.[8] By the affair at Fort Sumter, with its surrounding circumstances, that point was reached. Then, and thereby, the assailants of the Government, began the conflict of arms, without a gun in sight, or in expectancy, to return their fire, save only the few in the Fort, sent to that harbor, years before, for their own protection, and still ready to give that protection, in whatever was lawful. In this act, discarding all else, they have forced upon the country, the distinct issue: "Immediate dissolution, or blood."

Thomas Nast, *Study for "Departure of the Seventh Regiment for the War, April 19, 1861."* Oil over graphite on brown paper (New York, ca. 1865–1869). One of the many flags on display to inspire recruits along the parade route depicted in this image was the tattered flag of Fort Sumter. The garrison had fallen to South Carolina troops days before.

9  In fact, Lincoln's proclamations calling for volunteers and ordering a naval blockade were surely the more important factors in provoking Virginia to secede, not jubilation over the capture of Fort Sumter.

And this issue embraces more than the fate of these United States. It presents to the whole family of man, the question, whether a constitutional republic, or a democracy—a government of the people, by the same people—can, or cannot, maintain its territorial integrity, against its own domestic foes. It presents the question, whether discontented individuals, too few in numbers to control administration, according to organic law, in any case, can always, upon the pretences made in this case, or on any other pretences, or arbitrarily, without any pretence, break up their Government, and thus practically put an end to free government upon the earth. It forces us to ask: "Is there, in all republics, this inherent, and fatal weakness?" "Must a government, of necessity, be too *strong* for the liberties of its own people, or too *weak* to maintain its own existence?"

So viewing the issue, no choice was left but to call out the war power of the Government; and so to resist force, employed for its destruction, by force, for its preservation.

The call was made; and the response of the country was most gratifying; surpassing, in unanimity and spirit, the most sanguine expectation. Yet none of the States commonly called Slave states, except Delaware, gave a Regiment through regular State organization. A few regiments have been organized within some others of those states, by individual enterprise, and received into the government service. Of course the seceded States, so called, (and to which Texas had been joined about the time of the inauguration,) gave no troops to the cause of the Union. The border States, so called, were not uniform in their actions; some of them being almost *for* the Union, while in others—as Virginia, North Carolina, Tennessee, and Arkansas—the Union sentiment was nearly repressed, and silenced. The course taken in Virginia was the most remarkable—perhaps the most important. A convention, elected by the people of that State, to consider this very question of disrupting the Federal Union, was in session at the capital of Virginia when Fort Sumter fell. To this body the people had chosen a large majority of *professed* Union men. Almost immediately after the fall of Sumter, many members of that majority went over to the original disunion minority, and, with them, adopted an ordinance for withdrawing the State from the Union. Whether this change was wrought by their great approval of the assault upon Sumter, or their great resentment at the government's resistance to that assault, is not definitely known.⁹ Although they submitted the ordinance, for ratification, to [a] vote of the people, to be taken on a day then somewhat more than a month distant, the convention, and the Legislature, (which was also in session at the same time and place) with leading men of

David Gilmour Blythe, *Lincoln Crushing the Dragon of Rebellion.* Oil on canvas (1862). This painting shows Lincoln lunging at the snarling dragon with a rail splitter's maul, while restrained by a chain tied to a stump and held by an Irishman, representing the antiwar Democrats of New York.

10  Union forces stationed at the armory at Harper's Ferry, Virginia—site of John Brown's 1859 raid—abandoned and burned their building on April 18. Two days later, federal forces burned parts of the Gosport Navy Yard before abandoning that installation, too.

the State, not members of either, immediately commenced acting, as if the State were already out of the Union. They pushed military preparations vigorously forward all over the state. They seized the United States Armory at Harper's Ferry, and the Navy-yard at Gosport, near Norfolk.[10] They received—perhaps invited—into their state, large bodies of troops, with their warlike appointments, from the so-called seceded States. They formally entered into a treaty of temporary alliance, and co-operation with the so-called "Confederate States," and sent members to their Congress at Montgomery. And, finally, they permitted the insurrectionary government to be transferred to their capital at Richmond.

The people of Virginia have thus allowed this giant insurrection to make its nest within her borders; and this government has no choice left but to deal with it, *where* it finds it. And it has the less regret, as the loyal citizens have, in due form, claimed its protection. Those loyal citizens, this government is bound to recognize, and protect, as being Virginia.

The first **Flag of Independence** raised
in the South, by the Citizens of Savannah, Ga. November 8th 1860.
*Dedicated to the Morning News.*

Henry Cleenewercke, *The First Flag of Independence Raised in the South by the Citizens of Savannah, Georgia, November 8, 1860.* Lithograph (Savannah: R. H. Howell, 1860). Within a month of South Carolina's move to secede from the Union, five more Southern states—Mississippi, Florida, Alabama, Louisiana, and Georgia—followed its lead. Eventually eleven states seceded from the Union to form the Confederate States of America. Savannah, pictured here, would fall to General William T. Sherman's troops near Christmas, 1864.

In the border States, so called—in fact, the middle states—there are those who favor a policy which they call "armed neutrality"—that is, an arming of those states to prevent the Union forces passing one way, or the disunion, the other, over their soil. This would be disunion completed. Figuratively speaking, it would be the building of an impassable wall along the line of separation. And yet, not quite an impassable one; for, under the guise of neutrality, it would tie the hands of the Union men, and freely pass supplies from among them, to the insurrectionists, which it could not do as an open enemy. At a stroke, it would take all the trouble off the hands of secession, except only what proceeds from the external blockade. It would do for the disunionists that which, of all things, they most desire—feed them well, and give them disunion without a struggle of their own. It recognizes no fidelity to the Constitution, no obligation to maintain the Union; and while very many who have favored it are, doubtless, loyal citizens, it is, nevertheless, treason in effect.

Recurring to the action of the government, it may be stated that, at first, a call was made for seventy-five thousand militia; and rapidly following this, a proclamation was issued for closing the ports of the insurrectionary districts by proceedings in the nature of Blockade. So far all was believed to be strictly legal. At this point the insurrectionists announced their purpose to enter upon the practice of privateering.

Other calls were made for volunteers, to serve three years, unless sooner discharged; and also for large additions to the regular Army and Navy. These measures, whether strictly legal or not, were ventured upon, under what appeared to be a popular demand, and a public necessity; trusting, then as now, that Congress would readily ratify them. It is believed that nothing has been done beyond the constitutional competency of Congress.[11]

Soon after the first call for militia, it was considered a duty to authorize the Commanding General, in proper cases, according to his discretion, to suspend the privilege of the writ of habeas corpus; or, in other words, to arrest, and detain, without resort to the ordinary processes and forms of law, such individuals as he might deem dangerous to the public safety. This authority has purposely been exercised but very sparingly. Nevertheless, the legality and propriety of what has been done under it, are questioned; and the attention of the country has been called to the proposition that one who is sworn to "take care that the laws be faithfully executed," should not himself violate them. Of course some consideration was given to the questions of power, and propriety, before this matter was acted upon. The whole of the laws which were required to be faithfully executed, were being resisted, and failing of execution, in nearly one-third of the States. Must they be allowed to finally fail of execution, even had it been perfectly clear, that by the use of the means necessary to their execution, some single law, made in such extreme tenderness of the citizen's liberty, that practically, it relieves more of the guilty, than of the innocent, should, to a very limited extent, be violated? To state the question more directly, are all the laws, *but one*, to go unexecuted, and the government itself go to pieces, lest that one be violated?[12] Even in such a case, would not the official oath be broken, if the government should be overthrown, when it was believed that disregarding the single law, would tend to preserve it? But it was not believed that this

11   This constitutional question has been debated ever since the Civil War.

12   This was Lincoln's strongest and most eloquent defense to date of the suspension of the writ of habeas corpus. Lincoln's actions on habeas corpus generated much heated debate in Congress; some of the president's friends and loyal supporters disagreed with his decision, with the result that authorization for executive suspension was withheld until March 3, 1863, with the passage of the Habeas Corpus Act. Mark E. Neely Jr., *The Fate of Liberty: Abraham Lincoln and Civil Liberties* (New York: Oxford University Press, 1991), 68; and Rawley, *A Lincoln Dialogue,* 125.

13 U.S. Constitution, Article I, Section 9.

14 Edward Bates (1793–1869) of Missouri served as attorney general in the Lincoln administration from 1861 to 1864. "Bates, Edward," *Biographical Directory of the United States Congress,* http://bioguide.congress.gov/scripts/biodisplay.pl?index=B000231 (accessed February 1, 2015).

15 Salmon P. Chase served as secretary of the treasury from 1861 to 1864; Simon Cameron (1799–1889) of Pennsylvania served as secretary of war from 1861 to 1862. He was replaced by Edwin M. Stanton (1814–1869) in 1862. Stanton was secretary of war under both Lincoln and his successor, Andrew Johnson (1808–1875), until 1868. Gideon Welles (1802–1878) served as secretary of the navy under Lincoln. He and William H. Seward were the only two members of Lincoln's cabinet to serve throughout Lincoln's entire time as president. "Cameron, Simon," *Biographical Directory of the United States Congress,* http://bioguide.congress.gov/scripts/biodisplay.pl?index=c000068 (accessed February 1, 2015). Biographical sketches of Stanton and Welles can be found in Neely, *Lincoln Encyclopedia,* 287–288, 330–331. See Doris Kearns Goodwin, *Team of Rivals: The Political Genius of Abraham Lincoln* (New York: Simon & Schuster, 2005), for a useful study of Lincoln's cabinet.

16 Here Lincoln finally gets to what modern politicians call his "ask": four hundred thousand more troops and $400 million in funding—plus, crucially, retrospective congressional approval of all of Lincoln's executive initiatives between April and July to recruit and arm troops and suspend civil liberties. The House and Senate responded precisely as the president wished.

question was presented. It was not believed that any law was violated. The provision of the Constitution that "The privilege of the writ of habeas corpus, shall not be suspended unless when, in cases of rebellion or invasion, the public safety may require it,"[13] is equivalent to a provision—is a provision—that such privilege may be suspended when, in cases of rebellion, or invasion, the public safety *does* require it. It was decided that we have a case of rebellion, and that the public safety does require the qualified suspension of the privilege of the writ which was authorized to be made. Now it is insisted that Congress, and not the Executive, is vested with this power. But the Constitution itself, is silent as to which, or who, is to exercise the power; and as the provision was plainly made for a dangerous emergency, it cannot be believed the framers of the instrument intended, that in every case, the danger should run its course, until Congress could be called together; the very assembling of which might be prevented, as was intended in this case, by the rebellion.

No more extended argument is now offered; as an opinion, at some length, will probably be presented by the Attorney General.[14] Whether there shall be any legislation upon the subject, and if any, what, is submitted entirely to the better judgment of Congress.

The forbearance of this government had been so extraordinary, and so long continued, as to lead some foreign nations to shape their action as if they supposed the early destruction of our national Union was probable. While this, on discovery, gave the Executive some concern, he is now happy to say that the sovereignty, and rights of the United States, are now everywhere practically respected by foreign powers; and a general sympathy with the country is manifested throughout the world.

The reports of the Secretaries of the Treasury, War, and the Navy,[15] will give the information in detail deemed necessary, and convenient for your deliberation, and action; while the Executive, and all the Departments, will stand ready to supply omissions, or to communicate new facts, considered important for you to know.

It is now recommended that you give the legal means for making this contest a short, and a decisive one; that you place at the control of the government, for the work, at least four hundred thousand men, and four hundred millions of dollars.[16] That number of men is about one tenth of those of proper ages within the regions where, apparently, *all* are willing to engage; and the sum is less than a twentythird part of the money value owned by the men who seem ready to devote the whole. A debt of six hundred millions of dollars *now,* is a less sum per head, than was the debt of our revolution, when we came out of that struggle; and the money value in the country now, bears even a greater proportion to what it was *then,* than does the population. Surely each man has as strong a motive *now,* to *preserve* our liberties, as each had *then,* to *establish* them.

A right result, at this time, will be worth more to the world, than ten times the men, and ten times the money. The evidence reaching us from the country, leaves no doubt, that the material for the work is abundant; and that it needs only the hand of legislation to give it legal sanction, and the hand of the Executive to give it practical shape and efficiency. One of the greatest perplexities of the government, is to avoid receiving troops faster than it can provide for them. In a word, the people will save their government, if the government itself, will do its part, only indifferently well.[17]

It might seem, at first thought, to be of little difference whether the present movement at the South be called "secession" or "rebellion." The movers, however, well understand the difference. At the beginning, they knew they could never raise their treason to any respectable magnitude, by any name which implies *violation* of law. They knew their people possessed as much of moral sense, as much of devotion to law and order, and as much pride in, and reverence for, the history, and government, of their common country, as any other civilized, and patriotic people. They knew they could make no advancement directly in the teeth of these strong and noble sentiments. Accordingly they commenced by an insidious debauching of the public mind. They invented an ingenious sophism, which, if conceded, was followed by perfectly logical steps, through all the incidents, to the complete destruction of the Union. The sophism itself is, that any state of the Union may, *consistently* with the national Constitution, and therefore *lawfully,* and *peacefully,* withdraw from the Union, without the consent of the Union, or of any other state. The little disguise that the supposed right is to be exercised only for just cause, themselves to be the sole judge of its justice, is too thin to merit any notice.

With rebellion thus sugar-coated,[18] they have been drugging the public mind of their section for more than thirty years; and, until at length, they have brought many good men to a willingness to take up arms against the government the day *after* some assemblage of men have enacted the farcical pretense of taking their State out of the Union, who could have been brought to no such thing the day *before.*

This sophism derives much—perhaps the whole—of its currency, from the assumption, that there is some omnipotent, and sacred supremacy, pertaining to a *State*—to each State of our Federal Union. Our States have

17  From this point forward, the president spoke directly to the public, not to Congress alone—aware that his message would be published in full, and judged, by the press. "Perhaps the most striking feature of President Lincoln's first message to the new Congress," his secretaries and biographers John Nicolay and John Hay accurately remembered, "was his simple and direct appeal to the people to defend their Constitution and Government." Nicolay and Hay, *Abraham Lincoln,* 4:371.

18  The newly appointed U.S. government printer, former journalist John D. Defrees, strongly objected to this colloquialism as undignified and urged Lincoln to rewrite it. In refusing, the president explained: "The time will never come in this country when the people won't know exactly what *sugar-coated* means . . . I think I'll let it go." Roy P. Basler, *A Touchstone for Greatness: Essays, Addresses, and Occasional Pieces about Abraham Lincoln* (Westport, CT: Greenwood Press, 1976), 3, 90; Frank [Francis B.] Carpenter, "Anecdotes and Reminiscences of President Lincoln," in Henry J. Raymond, *The Life and Public Services of Abraham Lincoln* (New York: Derby & Miller, 1865), 758.

19  The Republic of Texas was established as an independent nation when it won its independence from Mexico in 1836. The Republic of Texas became a state in 1845.

neither more, nor less power, than that reserved to them, in the Union, by the Constitution—no one of them ever having been a State *out* of the Union. The original ones passed into the Union even *before* they cast off their British colonial dependence; and the new ones each came into the Union directly from a condition of dependence, excepting Texas. And even Texas, in its temporary independence, was never designated a State.[19] The new ones only took the designation of States, on coming into the Union, while that name was first adopted for the old ones, in, and by, the Declaration of Independence. Therein the "United Colonies" were declared to be "Free and Independent States"; but, even then, the object plainly was not to declare their independence of *one another,* or of the *Union;* but directly the contrary, as their mutual pledge, and their mutual action, before, at the time, and afterwards, abundantly show. The express plighting of faith, by each and all of the original thirteen, in the Articles of Confederation, two years later, that the Union shall be perpetual, is most conclusive. Having never been States, either in substance, or in name, *outside* of the Union, whence this magical omnipotence of "State rights," asserting a claim of power to lawfully destroy the Union itself? Much is said about the "sovereignty" of the States; but the word, even, is not in the national Constitution; nor, as is believed, in any of the State constitutions. What is a "sovereignty," in the political sense of the term? Would it be far wrong to define it "A political community, without a political superior"? Tested by this, no one of our States, except Texas, ever was a sovereignty. And even Texas gave up the character on coming into the Union; by which act, she acknowledged the Constitution of the United States, and the laws and treaties of the United States made in pursuance of the Constitution, to be, for her, the supreme law of the land. The States have their *status* IN the Union, and they have no other *legal status.* If they break from this, they can only do so against law, and by revolution. The Union, and not themselves separately, procured their independence, and their liberty. By conquest, or purchase, the Union gave each of them, whatever of independence, and liberty, it has. The Union is older than any of the States; and, in fact, it created them as States. Originally, some dependent colonies made the Union; and, in turn, the Union threw off their old dependence, for them, and made them States, such as they are. Not one of them ever had a State constitution, independent of the Union. Of course, it is not forgotten that all the new States framed their constitutions, before they entered the Union; nevertheless, dependent upon, and preparatory to, coming into the Union.

Unquestionably the States have the powers, and rights, reserved to them

in, and by the National Constitution; but among these, surely, are not included all conceivable powers, however mischievous, or destructive; but, at
most, such only, as were known in the world, at the time, as governmental powers; and certainly, a power to destroy the government itself, had
never been known as a governmental—as a merely administrative power.
This relative matter of National power, and State rights, as a principle, is no
other than the principle of *generality,* and *locality.* Whatever concerns the
whole, should be confided to the whole—to the general government; while,
whatever concerns *only* the State, should be left exclusively, to the State.
This is all there is of original principle about it. Whether the National Constitution, in defining boundaries between the two, has applied the principle
with exact accuracy, is not to be questioned. We are all bound by that defining, without question.

What is now combatted, is the position that secession is *consistent* with
the Constitution—is *lawful,* and *peaceful.* It is not contended that there is
any express law for it; and nothing should ever be implied as law, which
leads to unjust, or absurd consequences. The nation purchased, with money,
the countries out of which several of these States were formed. Is it just that
they shall go off without leave, and without refunding? The nation paid
very large sums, (in the aggregate, I believe, nearly a hundred millions) to
relieve Florida of the aboriginal tribes. Is it just that she shall now be off
without consent, or without making any return? The nation is now in debt
for money applied to the benefit of these so-called seceding States, in common with the rest. Is it just, either that creditors shall go unpaid, or the remaining States pay the whole? A part of the present national debt was contracted to pay the old debts of Texas. Is it just that she shall leave, and pay
no part of this herself?

Again, if one State may secede, so may another; and when all shall have
seceded, none is left to pay the debts. Is this quite just to creditors? Did we
notify them of this sage view of ours, when we borrowed their money? If we
now recognize this doctrine, by allowing the seceders to go in peace, it is
difficult to see what we can do, if others choose to go, or to extort terms
upon which they will promise to remain.

The seceders insist that our Constitution admits of secession. They have
assumed to make a National Constitution of their own, in which, of necessity, they have either *discarded,* or *retained,* the right of secession, as they
insist, it exists in ours. If they have discarded it, they thereby admit that,
on principle, it ought not to be in ours. If they have retained it, by their
own construction of ours they show that to be consistent they must secede

20 Lincoln never abandoned his belief, "sugar-coated" though it probably was, that a majority of whites in the Confederate states in fact felt loyal to the Union.

from one another, whenever they shall find it the easiest way of settling their debts, or effecting any other selfish, or unjust object. The principle itself is one of disintegration, and upon which no government can possibly endure.

If all the States, save one, should assert the power to *drive* that one out of the Union, it is presumed the whole class of seceder politicians would at once deny the power, and denounce the act as the greatest outrage upon State rights. But suppose that precisely the same act, instead of being called "driving the one out," should be called "the seceding of the others from that one," it would be exactly what the seceders claim to do; unless, indeed, they make the point, that the one, because it is a minority, may rightfully do, what the others, because they are a majority, may not rightfully do. These politicians are subtle, and profound, on the rights of minorities. They are not partial to that power which made the Constitution, and speaks from the preamble, calling itself "We, the People."

It may well be questioned whether there is, to-day, a majority of the legally qualified voters of any State, except perhaps South Carolina, in favor of disunion. There is much reason to believe that the Union men are the majority in many, if not in every other one, of the so-called seceded States.[20] The contrary has not been demonstrated in any one of them. It is ventured to affirm this, even of Virginia and Tennessee; for the result of an election, held in military camps, where the bayonets are all on one side of the question voted upon, can scarcely be considered as demonstrating popular sentiment. At such an election, all that large class who are, at once, *for* the Union, and *against* coercion, would be coerced to vote against the Union.

It may be affirmed, without extravagance, that the free institutions we enjoy, have developed the powers, and improved the condition, of our whole people, beyond any example in the world. Of this we now have a striking, and an impressive illustration. So large an army as the government has now on foot, was never before known, without a soldier in it, but who had taken his place there, of his own free choice. But more than this: there are many single Regiments whose members, one and another, possess full practical knowledge of all the arts, sciences, professions, and whatever else, whether useful or elegant, is known in the world; and there is scarcely one, from which there could not be selected, a President, a Cabinet, a Congress, and perhaps a Court, abundantly competent to administer the government itself. Nor do I say this is not true, also, in the army of our late friends, now adversaries, in this contest; but if it is, so much better the reason why the government, which has conferred such benefits on both them and us, should not be broken up. Whoever, in any section, proposes to abandon such a government, would do well to consider, in deference to what principle it is, that he does it—what better he is likely to get in its stead—whether the substitute will give, or be intended to give, so much of good to the people. There are some foreshadowings on this subject. Our adversaries have adopted some Declarations of Independence; in which, unlike the good old one, penned by Jefferson, they omit the words "all men are created equal." Why? They have adopted a temporary national constitution, in the preamble of which, unlike our good old one, signed by Washington, they omit "We, the People," and substitute "We, the deputies of the sovereign and independent States." Why? Why this deliberate pressing out of view, the rights of men, and the authority of the people?[21]

This is essentially a People's contest.[22] On the side of the Union, it is a struggle for maintaining in the world, that form, and substance of government, whose leading object is, to elevate the condition of men—to lift artificial weights from all shoulders—to clear the paths of laudable pursuit for all—to afford all, an unfettered start, and a fair chance, in the race of life.[23] Yielding to partial, and temporary departures, from necessity, this is the leading object of the government for whose existence we contend.

I am most happy to believe that the plain people understand, and appreciate this. It is worthy of note, that while in this, the government's hour of trial, large numbers of those in the Army and Navy, who have been favored with the offices, have resigned, and proved false to the hand which had pampered them, not one common soldier, or common sailor is known to have deserted his flag.

Great honor is due to those officers who remain true, despite the example of their treacherous associates; but the greatest honor, and most important fact of all, is the unanimous firmness of the common soldiers, and common sailors. To the last man, so far as known, they have successfully resisted the traitorous efforts of those, whose commands, but an hour before, they obeyed as absolute law. This is the patriotic instinct of the plain people. They understand, without an argument, that destroying the government, which was made by Washington, means no good to them.

Our popular government has often been called an experiment. Two points in it, our people have already settled—the successful *establishing,* and the successful *administering* of it. One still remains—its successful *maintenance* against a formidable internal attempt to overthrow it. It is now for them to demonstrate to the world, that those who can fairly carry an election, can also suppress a rebellion—that ballots are the rightful, and peaceful, successors of bullets; and that when ballots have fairly, and constitu-

21 Lincoln referred to the constitution of the Confederate States of America. Marshall L. DeRosa, *The Confederate Constitution of 1861* (Columbia: University of Missouri Press, 1991), appendix.

22 This line has been so frequently and independently quoted that it is usually forgotten that it appeared in this message as a counterpoint to the previously repeated opening lines of the "We the people" preamble to the Constitution. For some reason, Lincoln, a chronic underliner, did not underscore the word "people" here—but no doubt he expected the clerk who read the message aloud in Congress to emphasize that word.

23 In this crucial sentence, Lincoln placed an economic emphasis on resistance to the rebellion: the fight was not just an abstract attempt to save the federal Union but an effort to preserve opportunity for working people.

tionally, decided, there can be no successful appeal, back to bullets; that there can be no successful appeal, except to ballots themselves, at succeeding elections. Such will be a great lesson of peace; teaching men that what they cannot take by an election, neither can they take it by a war—teaching all, the folly of being the beginners of a war.

Lest there be some uneasiness in the minds of candid men, as to what is to be the course of the government, towards the Southern States, *after* the rebellion shall have been suppressed, the Executive deems it proper to say, it will be his purpose then, as ever, to be guided by the Constitution, and the laws; and that he probably will have no different understanding of the powers, and duties of the Federal government, relatively to the rights of the States, and the people, under the Constitution, than that expressed in the inaugural address.

He desires to preserve the government, that it may be administered for all, as it was administered by the men who made it. Loyal citizens everywhere, have the right to claim this of their government; and the government has no right to withhold, or neglect it. It is not perceived that, in giving it, there is any coercion, any conquest, or any subjugation, in any just sense of those terms.

The Constitution provides, and all the States have accepted the provision, that "The United States shall guarantee to every State in this Union a republican form of government."[24] But, if a State may lawfully go out of the Union, having done so, it may also discard the republican form of government; so that to prevent its going out, is an indispensable *means,* to the *end,* of maintaining the guaranty mentioned; and when an end is lawful and obligatory, the indispensable means to it, are also lawful, and obligatory.

It was with the deepest regret that the Executive found the duty of employing the war-power, in defence of the government, forced upon him. He could but perform this duty, or surrender the existence of the government. No compromise, by public servants, could, in this case, be a cure; not that compromises are not often proper, but that no popular government can long survive a marked precedent, that those who carry an election, can only save the government from immediate destruction, by giving up the main point, upon which the people gave the election. The people themselves, and not their servants, can safely reverse their own deliberate decisions. As a private citizen, the Executive could not have consented that these institutions shall perish; much less could he, in betrayal of so vast, and so sacred a trust, as these free people had confided to him. He felt that he had no moral right to shrink; nor even to count the chances of his own life, in what might fol-

*Construction of the U.S. Capitol Dome.* Unmounted stenograph on salted paper (ca. 1860–1863).

low. In full view of his great responsibility, he has, so far, done what he has deemed his duty. You will now, according to your own judgment, perform yours. He sincerely hopes that your views, and your action, may so accord with his, as to assure all faithful citizens, who have been disturbed in their rights, of a certain, and speedy restoration to them, under the Constitution, and the laws.

And having thus chosen our course, without guile, and with pure purpose, let us renew our trust in God, and go forward without fear, and with manly hearts.[25]

ABRAHAM LINCOLN

25 Overall, the response to Lincoln's message was quite positive. The newspaper reporter Henry Villard claimed that no one could be found among "the throng that daily now frequent the hotels and capital," outside of Confederate sympathizers, "who does not heartily endorse the patriotic message of the President." George William Curtis (1824–1892), a columnist for *Harper's Weekly,* once wary of Lincoln's ability to lead the nation, gushingly pronounced Lincoln's message as "the most truly American message ever delivered. Think upon what a millennial year we have fallen when the President of the United States declares officially that this government is founded upon the rights of man! Wonderfully acute, simple, sagacious, and of antique honesty! I can forgive the jokes and the big hands, and the inability to make bows. Some of us who doubted were wrong." Cited in Burlingame, *Abraham Lincoln,* 2:171. Not all were pleased, including Frederick Douglass, who was bitterly disappointed that Lincoln made no mention of slavery. "Any one reading the document with no previous knowledge of the United States," asserted Douglas, "would never dream from anything there written that a slaveholding war [is] waged upon the Government, determined to overthrow it." Political leaders and the press in the border slave states and in the Confederacy denounced the message. Douglas cited in Holzer, *Lincoln and the Power of the Press,* 313–314.

*Frémont had been the first Republican presidential standard-bearer (although unsuccessful) back in 1856. Now, as a newly minted Union general, the onetime "Pathfinder of the West" had decided on his own authority to confiscate the property of Confederate sympathizers within his Missouri military command, including their property in slaves. Lincoln believed that this order was both premature and presumptuous, and that, unless countermanded, it might drive border slave states into the Confederacy. He sent this letter to beseech the ambitious general to acknowledge civilian authority and revoke his order. Frémont refused, and Lincoln was forced to send a more direct command a few days later.*

1   John Charles Frémont, one of the first major generals named by President Lincoln when the war began, was appointed to command the Department of the West, headquartered in Saint Louis, in the hope that the mere presence of the celebrated explorer would cement Union loyalty in Missouri. Although he proved a poor military strategist, Frémont showed himself to be an aggressive administrator. In late August 1861 the general placed his entire department under martial law and began shutting down Democratic newspapers that encouraged secession. In August he moved to emancipate all the slaves under his jurisdiction.

2   Indeed, Lincoln's closest friend, Joshua Speed of Louisville, warned the president that if left standing, the order would "crush out every vestige of a union party in the state." Speed to Lincoln, September 3, 1861, Lincoln Papers, Library of Congress.

3   The Confiscation Act of 1861 allowed for the liberation of slaves owned by Confederates and "employed in hostile service against the Government." Frémont refused to recognize the limits of the federal law, insisting that his order be allowed to apply to all slaves whose owners lived in the territory under his command.

# Letters to General John C. Frémont

## September 2 and September 11, 1861

*Private and confidential.*
Major General Fremont:[1] Washington D.C. Sept. 2, 1861.

My dear Sir: Two points in your proclamation of August 30th give me some anxiety. First, should you shoot a man, according to the proclamation, the Confederates would very certainly shoot our best man in their hands in retaliation; and so, man for man, indefinitely. It is therefore my order that you allow no man to be shot, under the proclamation, without first having my approbation or consent.

Secondly, I think there is great danger that the closing paragraph, in relation to the confiscation of property, and the liberating slaves of traiterous [*sic*] owners, will alarm our Southern Union friends, and turn them against us—perhaps ruin our rather fair prospect for Kentucky.[2] Allow me therefore to ask, that you will as of your own motion, modify that paragraph so as to conform to the *first* and *fourth* sections of the act of Congress, entitled, "An act to confiscate property used for insurrectionary purposes," approved August, 6th, 1861, and a copy of which act I herewith send you.[3] This letter is written in a spirit of caution and not of censure.[4]

I send it by a special messenger, in order that it may certainly and speedily reach you.

Yours very truly
A. LINCOLN

John C. Frémont. Photograph (ca. 1855–1865). Probably taken at the Mathew Brady Gallery, Washington, D.C. Lincoln ordered the general to rescind his emancipation initiatives; the president reserved that right (and opportunity) for himself.

4 General Frémont resisted Lincoln's entreaty that he personally modify his proclamation, and within days his wife, Jessie Benton Frémont, presented herself at the White House bearing letters supporting her husband's position, prompting Lincoln to assure her: "No impression has been made on my mind against the honor or integrity of Gen. Fremont; and I now enter my protest against being understood as acting in any hostility towards him." Lincoln to Mrs. Frémont, September 12, 1861, *CW,* 4:519.

5 Frémont had written Lincoln to insist: "If . . . your better judgment still decides that I am wrong in the article respecting the liberation of slaves, I have to ask that you will openly direct me to make the correction. . . . I acted with full deliberation and . . . the conviction that it was . . . right and necessary. I still think so." Frémont to Lincoln, September 8, 1861, Lincoln Papers, Library of Congress.

6 Lincoln received much editorial and personal advice on how to solve the Frémont controversy, which required the President to placate abolitionists while maintaining tenuous loyalty among border-state slave owners.

7 Frémont obliged and had the president's order printed and distributed.

Copy of letter sent to Gen. Fremont, by special messenger leaving Washington Sep. 3. 1861.

———————

Major General John C. Fremont   Washington, D.C. Sep. 11, 1861.

Sir: Yours of the 8th. in answer to mine of 2nd. Inst. is just received.[5] Assuming that you, upon the ground, could better judge of the necessities of your position than I could at this distance, on seeing your proclamation of August 30th. I perceived no general objection to it.[6] The particular clause, however, in relation to the confiscation of property and the liberation of slaves, appeared to me to be objectionable, in its non-conformity to the Act of Congress passed on the 6th. of August upon the same subjects; and hence I wrote you expressing my wish that that clause should be modified accordingly. Your answer, just received, expresses the preference on your part, that I should make an open order for the modification, which I very cheerfully do. It is therefore ordered that the said clause of said proclamation be so modified, held, and construed, as to conform to, and not to transcend, the provisions on the same subject contained in the act of Congress entitled "An Act to confiscate property used for insurrectionary purposes[,]" Approved, August 6. 1861; and that said act be published at length with this order.[7]

Your Obt. Servt
A. LINCOLN.

Major General David Hunter. Photograph by Mathew Brady Gallery (ca. 1860–1863). In May 1862, General Hunter also issued an emancipation order, which Lincoln overruled.

# From Annual Message to Congress

⬦⬦⬦⬦⬦⬦⬦⬦⬦⬦⬦⬦⬦⬦⬦⬦⬦⬦⬦⬦

## December 3, 1861

*Annual messages of the president were the equivalent of today's State of the Union addresses, but by tradition they were read aloud by a clerk, not the president himself. Lincoln's first "annual message" may be best known because, shockingly, it was published in the press before being delivered to Capitol Hill. Congressional investigators later looked into the scandal but eventually backed off, probably after discovering that Mary Lincoln was likely behind the leak. Much of the message was actually mundane— such as the expected recitation of federal budget and trade statistics—but as usual, Lincoln elevated the genre. He included a stern warning against foreign intervention in America's civil war and reminded Congress that he believed labor superior to capital.*

FELLOW CITIZENS OF THE SENATE AND HOUSE OF REPRESENTATIVES:

In the midst of unprecedented political troubles, we have cause of great gratitude to God for unusual good health, and most abundant harvests.

You will not be surprised to learn that, in the peculiar exigencies of the times, our intercourse with foreign nations has been attended with profound solicitude, chiefly turning upon our own domestic affairs.

A disloyal portion of the American people have, during the whole year, been engaged in an attempt to divide and destroy the Union. A nation which endures factious domestic division, is exposed to disrespect abroad; and one party, if not both, is sure, sooner or later, to invoke foreign intervention.

Nations, thus tempted to interfere, are not always able to resist the counsels of seeming expediency, and ungenerous ambition, although measures adopted under such influences seldom fail to be unfortunate and injurious to those adopting them.

The disloyal citizens of the United States who have offered the ruin of our country, in return for the aid and comfort which they have invoked abroad, have received less patronage and encouragement than they probably expected. If it were just to suppose, as the insurgents have seemed to assume, that foreign nations, in this case, discarding all moral, social, and treaty obligations, would act solely, and selfishly, for the most speedy restoration of commerce, including, especially, the acquisition of cotton, those nations appear, as yet, not to have seen their way to their object more directly, or clearly, through the destruction, than through the preservation, of the Union. If we could dare to believe that foreign nations are actuated by no higher principle than this, I am quite sure a sound argument could be

1 Knowing his message would be reprinted in Europe, Lincoln hoped with this paragraph to tamp down British outrage over the so-called *Trent Affair*—ignited on November 9 when a Union ship on patrol in the waters north of Cuba seized two Confederate emissaries bound for European diplomatic posts aboard the *Trent,* a neutral English mail steamer. But even before the president's conciliatory words could be transported across the Atlantic, Lord Palmerston (1784–1865), the prime minister, predicted that the "masses" in America would "make it impossible for Lincoln and Seward to grant our demands, and we must therefore look forward to war as the probable result." Palmerston cited in Amanda Foreman, *A World on Fire: Britain's Crucial Role in the American Civil War* (New York: Random House, 2010), 183. A possible global conflict was avoided only when Lincoln ordered the Southern diplomats freed around Christmas.

made to show them that they can reach their aim more readily, and easily, by aiding to crush this rebellion, than by giving encouragement to it.[1]

The principal lever relied on by the insurgents for exciting foreign nations to hostility against us, as already intimated, is the embarrassment of commerce. Those nations, however, not improbably, saw from the first, that it was the Union which made as well our foreign, as our domestic, commerce. They can scarcely have failed to perceive that the effort for disunion produces the existing difficulty; and that one strong nation promises more durable peace, and a more extensive, valuable and reliable commerce, than can the same nation broken into hostile fragments.

It is not my purpose to review our discussions with foreign states, because whatever might be their wishes, or dispositions, the integrity of our country, and the stability of our government, mainly depend, not upon them, but on the loyalty, virtue, patriotism, and intelligence of the American people. The correspondence itself, with the usual reservations, is herewith submitted.

I venture to hope it will appear that we have practiced prudence, and liberality towards foreign powers, averting causes of irritation; and, with firmness, maintaining our own rights and honor.

Since, however, it is apparent that here, as in every other state, foreign dangers necessarily attend domestic difficulties, I recommend that adequate and ample measures be adopted for maintaining the public defences on every side. While, under this general recommendation, provision for defending our sea-coast line readily occurs to the mind, I also, in the same connexion, ask the attention of Congress to our great lakes and rivers. It is believed that some fortifications and depots of arms and munitions, with harbor and navigation improvements, all at well selected points upon these, would be of great importance to the national defence and preservation. I ask attention to the views of the Secretary of War, expressed in his report, upon the same general subject.

I deem it of importance that the loyal regions of East Tennessee and western North Carolina should be connected with Kentucky, and other faithful parts of the Union, by railroad. I therefore recommend, as a military measure, that Congress provide for the construction of such road, as speedily as possible. Kentucky, no doubt, will co-operate, and, through her legislature, make the most judicious selection of a line. The northern terminus must connect with some existing railroad; and whether the route shall be from Lexington, or Nicholasville, to the Cumberland Gap; or from Lebanon to the Tennessee line, in the direction of Knoxville; or on some still

U.S. House of Representatives chamber. Photograph (Washington, DC, ca. 1860s). Earliest extant photograph of the recently completed House chamber.

different line, can easily be determined. Kentucky and the general government co-operating, the work can be completed in a very short time; and when done, it will be not only of vast present usefulness, but also a valuable permanent improvement, worth its cost in all the future.[2]

Some treaties, designed chiefly for the interests of commerce, and having no grave political importance, have been negotiated, and will be submitted to the Senate for their consideration.

Although we have failed to induce some of the commercial powers to adopt a desirable melioration of the rigor of maritime war, we have removed all obstructions from the way of this humane reform, except such as are merely of temporary and accidental occurrence.

I invite your attention to the correspondence between her Britannic Majesty's minister accredited to this government, and the Secretary of State, relative to the detention of the British ship Perthshire in June last, by the United States steamer Massachusetts, for a supposed breach of the blockade. As this detention was occasioned by an obvious misapprehension of the facts, and as justice requires that we should commit no belligerent act not founded in strict right, as sanctioned by public law, I recommend that an

2   Not even civil war could diminish Lincoln's lifelong enthusiasm for internal improvements—public works—as a means of creating economic opportunity and connecting people and communities.

3   The *Perthshire* was carrying cotton from Mobile, Alabama, to Great Britain when it was seized by the *U.S.S. Massachusetts* and boarded off of Pensacola, Florida, on June 9, 1861. The vessel was released by the United States because it departed Mobile within the time granted by the Proclamations of Blockade. Cited in *CW,* 5:38n4.

4   In late 1858, the United States and China had agreed that claims against China by American citizens be funded with one-fifth of the duties levied on U.S. ships in Chinese ports. The agreement was apparently too liberal, for it produced a $200,000 surplus in the claims fund, which President James Buchanan had proposed be given to "some benevolent object in which the Chinese may be specially interested"—an idea Lincoln here endorsed. James Buchanan, "Fourth Annual Message," December 3, 1860, in *Works of James Buchanan,* 11:31.

5   The United States officially recognized these countries on June 5, when Lincoln signed a bill that had been authored by Senator Charles Sumner of Massachusetts.

appropriation be made to satisfy the reasonable demand of the owners of the vessel for her detention.[3]

I repeat the recommendation of my predecessor, in his annual message to Congress in December last, in regard to the disposition of the surplus which will probably remain after satisfying the claims of American citizens against China, pursuant to the awards of the commissioners under the act of the 3rd of March, 1859. If, however, it should not be deemed advisable to carry that recommendation into effect, I would suggest that authority be given for investing the principal, over the proceeds of the surplus referred to, in good securities, with a view to the satisfaction of such other just claims of our citizens against China as are not unlikely to arise hereafter in the course of our extensive trade with that Empire.[4]

By the act of the 5th of August last, Congress authorized the President to instruct the commanders of suitable vessels to defend themselves against, and to capture pirates. This authority has been exercised in a single instance only. For the more effectual protection of our extensive and valuable commerce, in the eastern seas especially, it seems to me that it would also be advisable to authorize the commanders of sailing vessels to re-capture any prizes which pirates might make of United States vessels and their cargoes, and the consular courts, now established by law in eastern countries, to adjudicate the cases, in the event that this should not be objected to by the local authorities.

If any good reason exists why we should persevere longer in withholding our recognition of the independence and sovereignty of Hayti and Liberia, I am unable to discern it.[5] Unwilling, however, to inaugurate a novel policy in regard to them without the approbation of Congress, I submit for your consideration the expediency of an appropriation for maintaining a chargé d'affaires near each of those new states. It does not admit of doubt that important commercial advantages might be secured by favorable commercial treaties with them.

The operations of the treasury during the period which has elapsed since your adjournment have been conducted with signal success. The patriotism of the people has placed at the disposal of the government the large means demanded by the public exigencies. Much of the national loan has been taken by citizens of the industrial classes, whose confidence in their country's faith, and zeal for their country's deliverance from present peril, have induced them to contribute to the support of the government the whole of their limited acquisitions. This fact imposes peculiar obligations to economy in disbursement and energy in action.

The revenue from all sources, including loans, for the financial year ending on the 30th June, 1861, was eighty six million, eight hundred and thirty five thousand, nine hundred dollars, and twenty seven cents, ($86,835,900.27,) and the expenditures for the same period, including payments on account of the public debt, were eighty four million, five hundred and seventy eight thousand, eight hundred and thirty four dollars and forty seven cents, ($84,578,834.47;) leaving a balance in the treasury, on the 1st July, of two million, two hundred and fifty seven thousand, sixty five dollars and eighty cents, ($2,257,065.80.) For the first quarter of the financial year, ending on the 30th September, 1861, the receipts from all sources, including the balance of first of July, were $102,532,509.27, and the expenses $98,239,733.09; leaving a balance on the 1st of October, 1861, of $4,292,776.18.[6]

Estimates for the remaining three quarters of the year, and for the financial year 1863, together with his views of ways and means for meeting the demands contemplated by them, will be submitted to Congress by the Secretary of the Treasury. It is gratifying to know that the expenditures made necessary by the rebellion are not beyond the resources of the loyal people, and to believe that the same patriotism which has thus far sustained the government will continue to sustain it till Peace and Union shall again bless the land.

I respectfully refer to the report of the Secretary of War for information respecting the numerical strength of the army, and for recommendations having in view an increase of its efficiency and the well being of the various branches of the service intrusted to his care. It is gratifying to know that the patriotism of the people has proved equal to the occasion, and that the number of troops tendered greatly exceeds the force which Congress authorized me to call into the field.

I refer with pleasure to those portions of his report which make allusion to the creditable degree of discipline already attained by our troops, and to the excellent sanitary condition of the entire army.

The recommendation of the Secretary for an organization of the militia upon a uniform basis, is a subject of vital importance to the future safety of the country, and is commended to the serious attention of Congress.

The large addition to the regular army, in connexion with the defection that has so considerably diminished the number of its officers, gives peculiar importance to his recommendation for increasing the corps of cadets to the greatest capacity of the Military Academy.

By mere omission, I presume, Congress has failed to provide chaplains

6   However dry and enervating these statistical reports might sound to modern Americans accustomed to bravura generalities in State of the Union orations, such accounting was expected of nineteenth-century presidents in their annual messages.

7   Peter Vivian Daniel (1784–1860).

8   John Archibald Campbell (1811–1889) was a Southerner who resigned from the Supreme Court on April 30, 1861, in the wake of the bombardment of Fort Sumter and Lincoln's proclamation of a state of rebellion. *History of the Federal Judiciary,* http://www.fjc.gov/serviet/nGetinfo?jid=361 (accessed February 2, 2015).

9   This marked the first time Lincoln had explained his peculiar reluctance to fill the Supreme Court vacancy left by the resignation of a Southern-born justice who had pledged loyalty to the Confederacy.

for hospitals occupied by volunteers. This subject was brought to my notice, and I was induced to draw up the form of a letter, one copy of which, properly addressed, has been delivered to each of the persons, and at the dates respectively named and stated, in a schedule, containing also the form of the letter, marked A, and herewith transmitted.

These gentlemen, I understand, entered upon the duties designated, at the times respectively stated in the schedule, and have labored faithfully therein ever since. I therefore recommend that they be compensated at the same rate as chaplains in the army. I further suggest that general provision be made for chaplains to serve at hospitals, as well as with regiments.

The report of the Secretary of the Navy presents in detail the operations of that branch of the service, the activity and energy which have characterized its administration, and the results of measures to increase its efficiency and power. Such have been the additions, by construction and purchase, that it may almost be said a navy has been created and brought into service since our difficulties commenced.

Besides blockading our extensive coast, squadrons larger than ever before assembled under our flag have been put afloat and performed deeds which have increased our naval renown.

I would invite special attention to the recommendation of the Secretary for a more perfect organization of the navy by introducing additional grades in the service.

The present organization is defective and unsatisfactory, and the suggestions submitted by the department will, it is believed, if adopted, obviate the difficulties alluded to, promote harmony, and increase the efficiency of the navy.

There are three vacancies on the bench of the Supreme Court—two by the decease of Justices Daniel[7] and McLean, and one by the resignation of Justice Campbell.[8] I have so far forborne making nominations to fill these vacancies for reasons which I will now state. Two of the outgoing judges resided within the States now overrun by revolt; so that if successors were appointed in the same localities, they could not now serve upon their circuits; and many of the most competent men there, probably would not take the personal hazard of accepting to serve, even here, upon the supreme bench. I have been unwilling to throw all the appointments northward, thus disabling myself from doing justice to the south on the return of peace; although I may remark that to transfer to the north one which has heretofore been in the south, would not, with reference to territory and population, be unjust.[9]

During the long and brilliant judicial career of Judge McLean his circuit grew into an empire—altogether too large for any one judge to give the courts therein more than a nominal attendance—rising in population from one million four hundred and seventy-thousand and eighteen, in 1830, to six million one hundred and fifty-one thousand four hundred and five, in 1860.

Besides this, the country generally has outgrown our present judicial system. If uniformity was at all intended, the system requires that all the States shall be accommodated with circuit courts, attended by supreme judges, while, in fact, Wisconsin, Minnesota, Iowa, Kansas, Florida, Texas, California, and Oregon, have never had any such courts. Nor can this well be remedied without a change of the system; because the adding of judges to the Supreme Court, enough for the accommodation of all parts of the country, with circuit courts, would create a court altogether too numerous for a judicial body of any sort. And the evil, if it be one, will increase as new States come into the Union. Circuit courts are useful, or they are not useful. If useful, no State should be denied them; if not useful, no State should have them. Let them be provided for all, or abolished as to all.

Three modifications occur to me, either of which, I think, would be an improvement upon our present system. Let the Supreme Court be of convenient number in every event. Then, first, let the whole country be divided into circuits of convenient size, the supreme judges to serve in a number of them corresponding to their own number, and independent circuit judges be provided for all the rest. Or, secondly, let the supreme judges be relieved from circuit duties, and circuit judges provided for all the circuits. Or, thirdly, dispense with circuit courts altogether, leaving the judicial functions wholly to the district courts and an independent Supreme Court.

I respectfully recommend to the consideration of Congress the present condition of the statute laws, with the hope that Congress will be able to find an easy remedy for many of the inconveniences and evils which constantly embarrass those engaged in the practical administration of them. Since the organization of the government, Congress has enacted some five thousand acts and joint resolutions, which fill more than six thousand closely printed pages, and are scattered through many volumes. Many of these acts have been drawn in haste and without sufficient caution, so that their provisions are often obscure in themselves, or in conflict with each other, or at least so doubtful as to render it very difficult for even the best informed persons to ascertain precisely what the statute law really is.

It seems to me very important that the statute laws should be made as plain and intelligible as possible, and be reduced to as small a compass as may consist with the fullness and precision of the will of the legislature and the perspicuity of its language. This, well done, would, I think, greatly facilitate the labors of those whose duty it is to assist in the administration of the laws, and would be a lasting benefit to the people, by placing before them, in a more accessible and intelligible form, the laws which so deeply concern their interests and their duties.

I am informed by some whose opinions I respect, that all the acts of Congress now in force, and of a permanent and general nature, might be revised and re-written, so as to be embraced in one volume (or at most, two volumes) of ordinary and convenient size. And I respectfully recommend to Congress to consider of the subject, and, if my suggestion be approved, to devise such plan as to their wisdom shall seem most proper for the attainment of the end proposed.

One of the unavoidable consequences of the present insurrection is the entire suppression, in many places, of all the ordinary means of administering civil justice by the officers and in the forms of existing law. This is the case, in whole or in part, in all the insurgent States; and as our armies advance upon and take possession of parts of those States, the practical evil becomes more apparent. There are no courts nor officers to whom the citizens of other States may apply for the enforcement of their lawful claims against citizens of the insurgent States; and there is a vast amount of debt constituting such claims. Some have estimated it as high as two hundred million dollars, due, in large part, from insurgents, in open rebellion, to loyal citizens who are, even now, making great sacrifices in the discharge of their patriotic duty to support the government.

Under these circumstances, I have been urgently solicited to establish, by military power, courts to administer summary justice in such cases. I have thus far declined to do it, not because I had any doubt that the end proposed—the collection of the debts—was just and right in itself, but because I have been unwilling to go beyond the pressure of necessity in the unusual exercise of power. But the powers of Congress I suppose are equal to the anomalous occasion, and therefore I refer the whole matter to Congress, with the hope that a plan may be devised for the administration of justice in all such parts of the insurgent States and Territories as may be under the control of this government, whether by a voluntary return to allegiance and order or by the power of our arms. This, however, is not to be a permanent institution, but a temporary substitute, and to cease as soon as the ordinary courts can be re-established in peace.

It is important that some more convenient means should be provided, if possible, for the adjustment of claims against the government, especially in view of their increased number by reason of the war. It is as much the duty of government to render prompt justice against itself, in favor of citizens, as it is to administer the same, between private individuals. The investigation and adjudication of claims, in their nature belong to the judicial department; besides it is apparent that the attention of Congress, will be more than usually engaged, for some time to come, with great national questions. It was intended, by the organization of the court of claims, mainly to remove this branch of business from the halls of Congress; but while the court has proved to be an effective, and valuable means of investigation, it in great degree fails to effect the object of its creation, for want of power to make its judgments final.

Fully aware of the delicacy, not to say the danger, of the subject, I commend to your careful consideration whether this power of making judgments final, may not properly be given to the court, reserving the right of appeal on questions of law to the Supreme Court, with such other provisions as experience may have shown to be necessary.

. . .

The present insurrection shows, I think, that the extension of this District across the Potomac river, at the time of establishing the capital here, was eminently wise, and consequently that the relinquishment of that portion of it which lies within the State of Virginia was unwise and dangerous. I submit for your consideration the expediency of regaining that part of the District, and the restoration of the original boundaries thereof, through negotiations with the State of Virginia.

The report of the Secretary of the Interior,[10] with the accompanying documents, exhibits the condition of the several branches of the public business pertaining to that department. The depressing influences of the insurrection have been especially felt in the operations of the Patent and General Land Offices. The cash receipts from the sales of public lands during the past year have exceeded the expenses of our land system only about $200,000. The sales have been entirely suspended in the southern States, while the interruptions to the business of the country, and the diversion of large numbers of men from labor to military service, have obstructed settlements in the new States and Territories of the northwest.

. . .

10  Caleb B. Smith (1808–1864) of Indiana served as Lincoln's secretary of the interior from 1861 until 1862, when he resigned for medical reasons. He later became U.S. District Court judge in his home state. "Smith, Caleb B.," Biographical Directory of the United States Congress, http://bioguide. congress.gov/scripts/biodisplay.pl?index=S000519 (accessed February 2, 2015). Smith was succeeded by his assistant secretary John Palmer Usher (1816–1889).

11   Lincoln, on May 15, 1862, approved and signed into law legislation creating the Department of Agriculture. *CW,* 5:46n20.

12   Nathaniel Gordon (ca. 1834–1862), captain of the *Erie,* which carried more than eight hundred slaves from Africa bound for the United States. The *Erie* was captured by the *U.S.S. Mohican* on August 8, 1860. Gordon was convicted in New York City on November 9, 1861, and was hanged on February 7, 1862. He was the only American slave trader who was tried, convicted, and executed for violating the Piracy Act of 1820, which prohibited engaging in the slave trade. Ron Soodalter, *Hanging Captain Gordon: The Life and Trial of an American Slave Trader* (New York: Atria Books, 2006).

The relations of the government with the Indian tribes have been greatly disturbed by the insurrection, especially in the southern superintendency and in that of New Mexico. The Indian country south of Kansas is in the possession of insurgents from Texas and Arkansas. The agents of the United States appointed since the 4th. of March for this superintendency have been unable to reach their posts, while the most of those who were in office before that time have espoused the insurrectionary cause, and assume to exercise the powers of agents by virtue of commissions from the insurrectionists. It has been stated in the public press that a portion of those Indians have been organized as a military force, and are attached to the army of the insurgents. Although the government has no official information upon this subject, letters have been written to the Commissioner of Indian Affairs by several prominent chiefs, giving assurance of their loyalty to the United States, and expressing a wish for the presence of federal troops to protect them. It is believed that upon the repossession of the country by the federal forces the Indians will readily cease all hostile demonstrations, and resume their former relations to the government.

Agriculture, confessedly the largest interest of the nation, has, not a department, nor a bureau, but a clerkship only, assigned to it in the government. While it is fortunate that this great interest is so independent in its nature as to not have demanded and extorted more from the government, I respectfully ask Congress to consider whether something more cannot be given voluntarily with general advantage.[11]

Annual reports exhibiting the condition of our agriculture, commerce, and manufactures would present a fund of information of great practical value to the country. While I make no suggestion as to details, I venture the opinion that an agricultural and statistical bureau might profitably be organized.

The execution of the laws for the suppression of the African slave trade, has been confided to the Department of the Interior. It is a subject of gratulation that the efforts which have been made for the suppression of this inhuman traffic, have been recently attended with unusual success. Five vessels being fitted out for the slave trade have been seized and condemned. Two mates of vessels engaged in the trade, and one person in equipping a vessel as a slaver, have been convicted and subjected to the penalty of fine and imprisonment, and one captain, taken with a cargo of Africans on board his vessel, has been convicted of the highest grade of offence under our laws, the punishment of which is death.[12]

The Territories of Colorado, Dakotah and Nevada, created by the last

Congress, have been organized, and civil administration has been inaugurated therein under auspices especially gratifying, when it is considered that the leaven of treason was found existing in some of these new countries when the federal officers arrived there.

The abundant natural resources of these Territories, with the security and protection afforded by organized government, will doubtless invite to them a large immigration when peace shall restore the business of the country to its accustomed channels. I submit the resolutions of the legislature of Colorado, which evidence the patriotic spirit of the people of the Territory. So far the authority of the United States has been upheld in all the Territories, as it is hoped it will be in the future. I commend their interests and defence to the enlightened and generous care of Congress.

I recommend to the favorable consideration of Congress the interests of the District of Columbia. The insurrection has been the cause of much suffering and sacrifice to its inhabitants, and as they have no representative in Congress, that body should not overlook their just claims upon the government.

At your late session a joint resolution was adopted authorizing the President to take measures for facilitating a proper representation of the industrial interests of the United States at the exhibition of the industry of all nations to be holden at London in the year 1862. I regret to say I have been unable to give personal attention to this subject,—a subject at once so interesting in itself, and so extensively and intimately connected with the material prosperity of the world. Through the Secretaries of State and of the Interior a plan, or system, has been devised, and partly matured, and which will be laid before you.

Under and by virtue of the act of Congress entitled "An act to confiscate property used for insurrectionary purposes," approved August, 6, 1861, the legal claims of certain persons to the labor and service of certain other persons have become forfeited; and numbers of the latter, thus liberated, are already dependent on the United States, and must be provided for in some way. Besides this, it is not impossible that some of the States will pass similar enactments for their own benefit respectively, and by operation of which persons of the same class will be thrown upon them for disposal. In such case I recommend that Congress provide for accepting such persons from such States, according to some mode of valuation, in lieu, *pro tanto*,[13] of direct taxes, or upon some other plan to be agreed on with such States respectively; that such persons, on such acceptance by the general government, be at once deemed free; and that, in any event, steps be taken for colonizing

13   The legal term for "as much as one is able."

14  Five weeks earlier, Lincoln had authorized Secretary of the Interior Smith to enter into a contract with a private developer who proposed mining coal—and colonizing free African Americans—in Central America, on the Isthmus of Chiriquí. *CW,* 4:561.

15  Likely an oblique reference to his recent decision to overturn General John C. Frémont's order emancipating slaves in Missouri—which went beyond federal confiscation laws. See "Letters to John C. Frémont, September 2 and September 11, 1861," in this volume. Congress responded by enacting a new, broader Confiscation Act.

both classes, (or the one first mentioned, if the other shall not be brought into existence,) at some place, or places, in a climate congenial to them. It might be well to consider, too,—whether the free colored people already in the United States could not, so far as individuals may desire, be included in such colonization.[14]

To carry out the plan of colonization may involve the acquiring of territory, and also the appropriation of money beyond that to be expended in the territorial acquisition. Having practiced the acquisition of territory for nearly sixty years, the question of constitutional power to do so is no longer an open one with us. The power was questioned at first by Mr. Jefferson, who, however, in the purchase of Louisiana, yielded his scruples on the plea of great expediency. If it be said that the only legitimate object of acquiring territory is to furnish homes for white men, this measure effects that object; for the emigration of colored men leaves additional room for white men remaining or coming here. Mr. Jefferson, however, placed the importance of procuring Louisiana more on political and commercial grounds than on providing room for population.

On this whole proposition,—including the appropriation of money with the acquisition of territory, does not the expediency amount to absolute necessity—that, without which the government itself cannot be perpetuated? The war continues. In considering the policy to be adopted for suppressing the insurrection, I have been anxious and careful that the inevitable conflict for this purpose shall not degenerate into a violent and remorseless revolutionary struggle. I have, therefore, in every case, thought it proper to keep the integrity of the Union prominent as the primary object of the contest on our part, leaving all questions which are not of vital military importance to the more deliberate action of the legislature.

In the exercise of my best discretion I have adhered to the blockade of the ports held by the insurgents, instead of putting in force, by proclamation, the law of Congress enacted at the late session, for closing those ports.

So, also, obeying the dictates of prudence, as well as the obligations of law, instead of transcending, I have adhered to the act of Congress to confiscate property used for insurrectionary purposes. If a new law upon the same subject shall be proposed, its propriety will be duly considered.[15]

The Union must be preserved, and hence, all indispensable means must be employed. We should not be in haste to determine that radical and extreme measures, which may reach the loyal as well as the disloyal, are indispensable.

The inaugural address at the beginning of the Administration, and the message to Congress at the late special session, were both mainly devoted to the domestic controversy out of which the insurrection and consequent war have sprung. Nothing now occurs to add or subtract, to or from, the principles or general purposes stated and expressed in those documents.

The last ray of hope for preserving the Union peaceably, expired at the assault upon Fort Sumter; and a general review of what has occurred since may not be unprofitable. What was painfully uncertain then, is much better defined and more distinct now; and the progress of events is plainly in the right direction. The insurgents confidently claimed a strong support from north of Mason and Dixon's line; and the friends of the Union were not free from apprehension on the point. This, however, was soon settled definitely and on the right side. South of the line, noble little Delaware led off right from the first. Maryland was made to *seem* against the Union. Our soldiers were assaulted, bridges were burned, and railroads torn up, within her limits; and we were many days, at one time, without the ability to bring a single regiment over her soil to the capital.[16] Now, her bridges and railroads are repaired and open to the government; she already gives seven regiments to the cause of the Union and none to the enemy; and her people, at a regular election, have sustained the Union, by a larger majority, and a larger aggregate vote than they ever before gave to any candidate, or any question. Kentucky, too, for some time in doubt, is now decidedly, and, I think, unchangeably, ranged on the side of the Union. Missouri is comparatively quiet; and I believe cannot again be overrun by the insurrectionists. These three States of Maryland, Kentucky, and Missouri, neither of which would promise a single soldier at first, have now an aggregate of not less than forty thousand in the field, for the Union; while, of their citizens, certainly not more than a third of that number, and they of doubtful whereabouts, and doubtful existence, are in arms against it. After a somewhat bloody struggle of months, winter closes on the Union people of western Virginia, leaving them masters of their own country.

An insurgent force of about fifteen hundred, for months dominating the narrow peninsular region, constituting the counties of Accomac and Northampton, and known as eastern shore of Virginia, together with some contiguous parts of Maryland, have laid down their arms; and the people there have renewed their allegiance to, and accepted the protection of, the old flag. This leaves no armed insurrectionist north of the Potomac, or east of the Chesapeake.

Also we have obtained a footing at each of the isolated points, on the southern coast, of Hatteras, Port Royal, Tybee Island, near Savannah, and

16  In April, Baltimore secessionists had attacked a regiment of Massachusetts soldiers passing through the city en route to the defense of Washington. A few days later, fifty members of Baltimore's Young Men's Christian Association visited the White House to beseech Lincoln to send no further troops through the city. Angered, the president retorted: "There is no Washington in that—no Jackson in that—no manhood nor honor in that," wryly adding: "Our men are not moles, and can't dig under the earth; they are not birds, and can't fly through the air. There is no way but to march across, and that they must do." *CW,* 4:341–342.

17   George B. McClellan (1826–1885) was born
into a prominent Philadelphia family. A graduate
of West Point, McClellan formed the Army of the
Potomac and became very popular with Union
soldiers under his command. Lincoln never
underestimated McClellan's broad popularity in
the early days of the war. Stephen W. Sears, *George
B. McClellan: The Young Napoleon* (New York:
Ticknor & Fields, 1988). The relationship of
Lincoln and McClellan is covered in John C.
Waugh, *Lincoln and McClellan: The Troubled
Partnership between a President and His General*
(New York: Palgrave Macmillan, 2010).

Ship Island; and we likewise have some general accounts of popular movements, in behalf of the Union, in North Carolina and Tennessee.

These things demonstrate that the cause of the Union is advancing
steadily and certainly southward.

Since your last adjournment, Lieutenant General Scott has retired from
the head of the army. During his long life, the nation has not been unmind-
ful of his merit; yet, on calling to mind how faithfully, ably and brilliantly
he has served the country, from a time far back in our history, when few of
the now living had been born, and thenceforward continually, I cannot but
think we are still his debtors. I submit, therefore, for your consideration,
what further mark of recognition is due to him, and to ourselves, as a grateful people.

With the retirement of General Scott came the executive duty of appointing, in his stead, a general-in-chief of the army. It is a fortunate circumstance that neither in council nor country was there, so far as I know,
any difference of opinion as to the proper person to be selected. The retiring
chief repeatedly expressed his judgment in favor of General McClellan for
the position; and in this the nation seemed to give a unanimous concurrence.[17] The designation of General McClellan is therefore in considerable
degree, the selection of the Country as well as of the Executive; and hence
there is better reason to hope there will be given him, the confidence, and
cordial support thus, by fair implication, promised, and without which, he
cannot, with so full efficiency, serve the country.

It has been said that one bad general is better than two good ones; and
the saying is true, if taken to mean no more than that an army is better directed by a single mind, though inferior, than by two superior ones, at variance, and cross-purposes with each other.

And the same is true, in all joint operations wherein those engaged, *can*
have none but a common end in view, and *can* differ only as to the choice of
means. In a storm at sea, no one on board *can* wish the ship to sink; and yet,
not unfrequently, all go down together, because too many will direct, and
no single mind can be allowed to control.

It continues to develop that the insurrection is largely, if not exclusively, a
war upon the first principle of popular government—the rights of the people. Conclusive evidence of this is found in the most grave and maturely
considered public documents, as well as in the general tone of the insurgents. In those documents we find the abridgement of the existing right of
suffrage and the denial to the people of all right to participate in the selection of public officers, except the legislative boldly advocated, with labored

arguments to prove that large control of the people in government, is the source of all political evil. Monarchy itself is sometimes hinted at as a possible refuge from the power of the people.

In my present position, I could scarcely be justified were I to omit raising a warning voice against this approach of returning despotism.

It is not needed, nor fitting here, that a general argument should be made in favor of popular institutions; but there is one point, with its connexions, not so hackneyed as most others, to which I ask a brief attention. It is the effort to place *capital* on an equal footing with, if not above *labor,* in the structure of government. It is assumed that labor is available only in connexion with capital; that nobody labors unless somebody else, owning capital, somehow by the use of it, induces him to labor. This assumed, it is next considered whether it is best that capital shall *hire* laborers, and thus induce them to work by their own consent, or *buy* them, and drive them to it without their consent. Having proceeded so far, it is naturally concluded that all laborers are either *hired* laborers, or what we call slaves. And further it is assumed that whoever is once a hired laborer, is fixed in that condition for life.

Now, there is no such relation between capital and labor as assumed; nor is there any such thing as a free man being fixed for life in the condition of a hired laborer. Both these assumptions are false, and all inferences from them are groundless.

Labor is prior to, and independent of, capital. Capital is only the fruit of labor, and could never have existed if labor had not first existed. Labor is the superior of capital, and deserves much the higher consideration. Capital has its rights, which are as worthy of protection as any other rights. Nor is it denied that there is, and probably always will be, a relation between labor and capital, producing mutual benefits. The error is in assuming that the whole labor of community exists within that relation. A few men own capital, and that few avoid labor themselves, and, with their capital, hire or buy another few to labor for them. A large majority belong to neither class— neither work for others, nor have others working for them. In most of the southern States, a majority of the whole people of all colors are neither slaves nor masters; while in the northern a large majority are neither hirers nor hired. Men with their families—wives, sons, and daughters—work for themselves, on their farms, in their houses, and in their shops, taking the whole product to themselves, and asking no favors of capital on the one hand, nor of hired laborers or slaves on the other. It is not forgotten that a considerable number of persons mingle their own labor with capital—that

18   Response to Lincoln's first annual message was mixed. Those looking for strong statements concerning slavery were disappointed. One congressman bemoaned the fact that Lincoln referred "only incidentally to the subject . . . and indicates no policy whatever for dealing with the momentous question." *New York Evening Post* editor William Cullen Bryant (1794–1878) wrote that, given Lincoln's downplay of the slavery issue, it "will be felt universally that he does not meet either the necessities or the difficulties of the case with sufficient determination." A Washington correspondent denounced the message as "a wet blanket upon the hopes of the ardent anti-slavery party," while abolitionist Lucretia Mott (1793–1880) condemned the president's "proslavery conservatism." Lincoln's remarks concerning colonization provoked outrage among blacks as well as antislavery whites. Frederick Douglass, "bewildered" by Lincoln's "moral blindness," blasted the president as being "as destitute of any anti-slavery principle or feeling" as his predecessor James Buchanan. Quotes cited in Burlingame, *Abraham Lincoln,* 2:232–233, 235.

is, they labor with their own hands, and also buy or hire others to labor for them; but this is only a mixed, and not a distinct class. No principle stated is disturbed by the existence of this mixed class.

Again: as has already been said, there is not, of necessity, any such thing as the free hired laborer being fixed to that condition for life. Many independent men everywhere in these States, a few years back in their lives, were hired laborers. The prudent, penniless beginner in the world, labors for wages awhile, saves a surplus with which to buy tools or land for himself; then labors on his own account another while, and at length hires another new beginner to help him. This is the just, and generous, and prosperous system, which opens the way to all—gives hope to all, and consequent energy, and progress, and improvement of condition to all. No men living are more worthy to be trusted than those who toil up from poverty—none less inclined to take, or touch, aught which they have not honestly earned. Let them beware of surrendering a political power which they already possess, and which, if surrendered, will surely be used to close the door of advancement against such as they, and to fix new disabilities and burdens upon them, till all of liberty shall be lost.

From the first taking of our national census to the last are seventy years; and we find our population at the end of the period eight times as great as it was at the beginning. The increase of those other things which men deem desirable has been even greater. We thus have at one view, what the popular principle applied to government, through the machinery of the States and the Union, has produced in a given time; and also what, if firmly maintained, it promises for the future. There are already among us those, who, if the Union be preserved, will live to see it contain two hundred and fifty millions. The struggle of today, is not altogether for today—it is for a vast future also. With a reliance on Providence, all the more firm and earnest, let us proceed in the great task which events have devolved upon us.[18]

# President's General War Order No. 1

· · ·

## January 27, 1862

· · ·

# Letter to General George B. McClellan

· · ·

## February 3, 1862

*Always alert to symbolism, Lincoln ordered Union general George B. McClellan to commit his idle Army of the Potomac to a major military offensive on Washington's birthday, February 22. McClellan, who had trained his men well but resisted committing them to fight, replied by insisting that a major movement was impossible during the winter. By this time the impatient Lincoln had read a number of books on military strategy and absorbed so much knowledge so quickly that he felt justified in further prodding his reluctant general. A week after McClellan resisted the January 27 order, the commander in chief again wrote to McClellan, this time insisting that he justify his inaction. Neither approach stimulated the general known as "Young Napoleon" into battle.*

### President's General War Order No. 1

Executive Mansion,
President's general} Washington, January 27, 1862.
War Order No. 1 }

Ordered that the 22nd. day of February 1862, be the day for a general movement of the Land and Naval forces of the United States against the insurgent forces.

That especially—

The Army at & about, Fortress Monroe.[1]

The Army of the Potomac.

The Army of Western Virginia

The Army near Munfordsville [*sic*], Ky.

The Army and Flotilla at Cairo.

And a Naval force in the Gulf of Mexico, be ready for a movement on that day.

That all other forces, both Land and Naval, with their respective commanders, obey existing orders, for the time, and be ready to obey additional orders when duly given.[2]

That the Heads of Departments, and especially the Secretaries of War and of the Navy, with all their subordinates; and the General-in-Chief, with

1   Completed nearly three decades before the onset of the Civil War, Fortress Monroe stood at the easternmost point of the Virginia Peninsula, its big guns facing the body of water known as Hampton Roads, where the James River emptied into the Chesapeake Bay.

2   The notion of joint action—the coordination of land and naval forces—was relatively new during the Civil War. In this case, Lincoln's orders were not followed.

*A Great Rush to Join the 36th Regiment New York Volunteers.* Lithographed broadside (New York: Baker & Godwin, ca. 1863). Posters such as this one were displayed in shop windows and on fences and trees to attract volunteers.

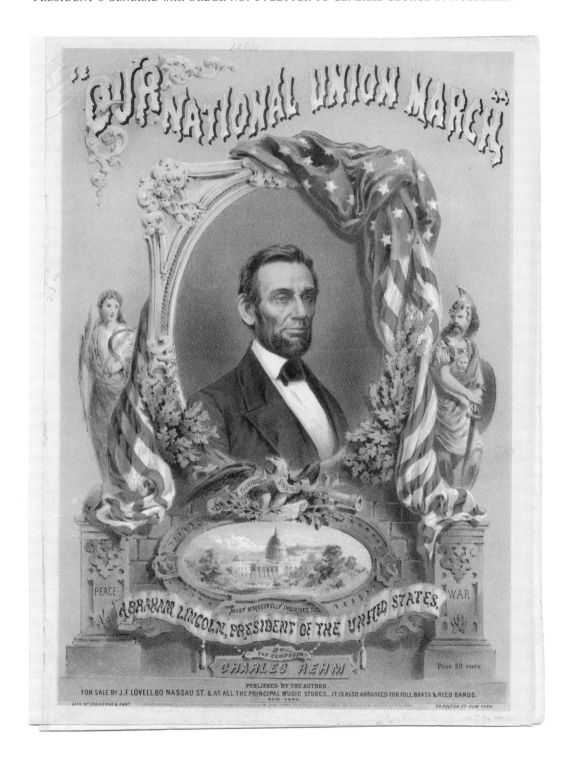

"Our National Union March."
Sheet music (New York: J. F.
Lovel, 1862). Music for a march in
support of the Union cause,
featuring a color-lithograph
portrait of Lincoln.

*Gen'l. Geo. B. McClellan and Staff, before Yorktown, Va., April 1862.* Lithograph (New York: Currier & Ives, 1862).

all other commanders and subordinates, of Land and Naval forces, will severally be held to their strict and full responsibilities, for the prompt execution of this order.

ABRAHAM LINCOLN

Draft of Order sent to Army & Navy Departments respectively this day.

A. LINCOLN

Jan. 27. 1862.

The Secretary of War will enter this Order in his Department, and execute it to the best of his ability. A. LINCOLN

Jan. 27, 1862.

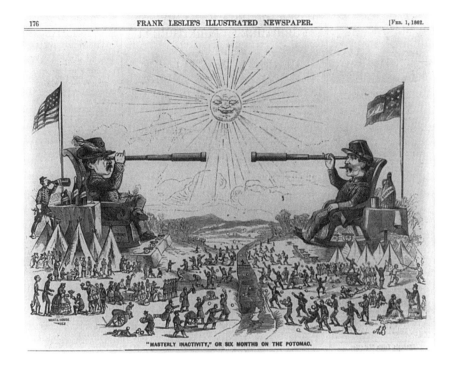

"MASTERLY INACTIVITY," OR SIX MONTHS ON THE POTOMAC.

"Masterly Inactivity, or Six Months on the Potomac," *Frank Leslie's Illustrated Newspaper.* Woodcut engraving (February 1, 1862). This caricature mocks the idleness of Confederate and Union forces on both sides of the Potomac River.

## Letter to George B. McClellan

Executive Mansion,
Major General McClellan[3] Washington, Feb. 3, 1862.

My dear Sir: You and I have distinct, and different plans for a movement of the Army of the Potomac—yours to be down the Chesapeake, up the Rappahannock to Urbana, and across land to the terminus of the Railroad on the York River,—mine to move directly to a point on the Railroad South West of Manassas.[4]

If you will give me satisfactory answers to the following questions, I shall gladly yield my plan to yours.

1st. Does not your plan involve a greatly larger expenditure of *time,* and *money* than mine?

2nd. Wherein is a victory *more certain* by your plan than mine?

3rd. Wherein is a victory *more valuable* by your plan than mine?

4th. In fact, would it not be *less* valuable, in this, that it would break no great line of the enemie's [sic] communications, while mine would?[5]

3   Thirty-five-year-old George Brinton McClellan replaced the aged Winfield Scott as general in chief in November 1861. Summoned to the East to take command of the Army of the Potomac, McClellan proved a brilliant organizer, but was slow to advance his army.

4   It is no wonder that the general was inclined to ignore his commander in chief's recommendation. Less than three months before this letter was written, McClellan had privately described the president as "the *original* gorilla," complaining: "What a specimen to be at the head of our affairs now." McClellan to Mary Ellen McClellan, ca. November 14, 1861, in Stephen W. Sears, ed., *The Civil War Papers of George B. McClellan: Selected Correspondence, 1860–1865* (New York: Ticknor & Fields, 1989), 135.

5   A month after receiving this letter, McClellan finally landed more than one hundred thousand men on the Virginia Peninsula in a campaign to march northwest to capture the Confederate capital of Richmond. Over the next few months,

despite a large advantage in manpower, McClellan got bogged down, and by summer he was facing General Robert E. Lee (1807–1870) in the Seven Days' Battles, after which he withdrew in retreat.

6   McClellan was willing, as he put it, to "stake my life, my reputation" on his plan to advance on Urbana rather than Manassas. "More than that," he added, "I will stake upon it the success of our cause. I hope but little from the attack on Manassas." In the end, "Little Mac" pursued neither option. McClellan to General Henry W. Halleck, ca. February 3, 1862, in Sears, *Civil War Papers of George B. McClellan,* 170.

A DISPATCH FROM LITTLE MACK.
" Still waiting for more reinforcements !!! "

5th. In case of disaster, would not a safe retreat be more difficult by your plan than by mine?[6]

Yours truly

A. LINCOLN

[Memorandum accompanying letter of president to General McClellan, dated February 3, 1862]

1. Suppose the enemy should attack us in force *before* we reach the Ocoquan, what? In view of the possibility of this, might it not be safest to have our entire force to move together from above the Ocoquan.

2. Suppose the enemy, in force, shall dispute the crossing of the Ocoquan, what? In view of this, might it not be safest for us to cross the Ocoquan at Colchester rather than at the village of Ocoquan? This would cost the enemy two miles more of travel to meet us, but would, on the contrary, leave us two miles further from our ultimate destination.

3. Suppose we reach Maple valley without an attack, will we not be attacked there, in force, by the enemy marching by the several roads from Manassas? and if so, what?

*A Dispatch from Little Mack. 'Still waiting for more reinforcements!!!'* Pencil and wash on paper (n.p., 1862). An unidentified artist portrays Lincoln as a frustrated commander in chief dealing with a general who will not fight.

# Message to Congress on Gradual Emancipation

## March 6, 1862

*Deciding the time had come to strike a blow against slavery without, Lincoln calculated, greatly risking further Union disloyalty in the Border States, the president deployed this special message to prod Maryland, Delaware, Kentucky, and Missouri to abandon slavery on their own—gradually, and in return for compensation to slave owners from the federal government. The proposal fell on deaf ears.*

1    There would, in fact, be no "end" to this effort. Four months later Lincoln would send a new emancipation appeal to the Border States.

FELLOW-CITIZENS OF THE SENATE, AND HOUSE OF REPRESENTATIVES,

I recommend the adoption of a Joint Resolution by your honorable bodies which shall be substantially as follows:

"Resolved that the United States ought to co-operate with any state which may adopt gradual abolishment of slavery, giving to such state pecuniary aid, to be used by such state in it's [*sic*] discretion, to compensate for the inconveniences public and private, produced by such change of system."

If the proposition contained in the resolution does not meet the approval of Congress and the country, there is the end;[1] but if it does command such approval, I deem it of importance that the states and people immediately interested, should be at once distinctly notified of the fact, so that they may begin to consider whether to accept or reject it. The federal government would find it's [*sic*] highest interest in such a measure, as one of the most efficient means of self-preservation. The leaders of the existing insurrection entertain the hope that this government will ultimately be forced to acknowledge the independence of some part of the disaffected region, and that all the slave states North of such part will then say "the Union, for which we have struggled, being already gone, we now choose to go with the Southern section." To deprive them of this hope, substantially ends the rebellion; and the initiation of emancipation completely deprives them of it, as to all the states initiating it. The point is not that *all* the states tolerating slavery would very soon, if at all, initiate emancipation; but that, while the offer is equally made to all, the more Northern shall, by such initiation, make it certain to the more Southern, that in no event, will the former ever join the latter, in their proposed confederacy. I say "initiation" because, in my judgment, gradual, and not sudden emancipation, is better for all. In the mere financial, or pecuniary view, any member of Congress, with the

**2**   When the pro-administration *New York Times* unexpectedly editorialized that Lincoln's plan for compensated emancipation was, indeed, too expensive, the president wrote this reply to editor Henry Raymond: "My dear Sir: I am grateful to the New-York Journals, and not less so to the Times than to others, for their kind notices of the late special Message to Congress. Your paper, however, intimates that the proposition, though well-intentioned, must fail on the score of expense. I do hope you will reconsider this. Have you noticed the facts that less than one-half day's cost of this war would pay for all the slaves in Delaware, at four hundred dollars per head?—that eighty-seven days cost of this war would pay for all in Delaware, Maryland, District of Columbia, Kentucky, and Missouri at the same price? Were those states to take the step, do you doubt that unit would shorten the war more than eighty seven days, and thus be an actual saving of expense. Please look at these things, and consider whether there should not be another article in the Times?" Raymond quickly replied that he was out of town when the offending editorial appeared and pointed out to the president that a more supportive commentary had already been published, praising the president's message "*without qualifications or cavil.*" *CW,* 5:152–153. Lincoln collected and filed supportive editorials from several papers.

Edwin Forbes, *Coming into the Lines.* Drawing (ca. 1876). Slaves seek freedom with the Union Army.

census-tables and Treasury-reports before him, can readily see for himself how very soon the current expenditures of this war would purchase, at fair valuation, all the slaves in any named State. Such a proposition, on the part of the general government, sets up no claim of a right, by federal authority, to interfere with slavery within state limits, referring, as it does, the absolute control of the subject, in each case, to the state and it's [*sic*] people, immediately interested. It is proposed as a matter of perfectly free choice with them.

In the annual message last December, I thought fit to say "The Union must be preserved; and hence all indispensable means must be employed." I said this, not hastily, but deliberately. War has been made, and continues to be, an indispensable means to this end. A practical re-acknowledgement of the national authority would render the war unnecessary, and it would at once cease. If, however, resistance continues, the war must also continue; and it is impossible to foresee all the incidents, which may attend and all the ruin which may follow it. Such as may seem indispensable, or may obviously promise great efficiency towards ending the struggle, must and will come.

The proposition now made, though an offer only, I hope it may be esteemed no offence to ask whether the pecuniary consideration tendered would not be of more value to the States and private persons concerned, than are the institution, and property in it, in the present aspect of affairs.[2]

While it is true that the adoption of the proposed resolution would be merely initiatory, and not within itself a practical measure, it is recommended in the hope that it would soon lead to important practical results.[3] In full view of my great responsibility to my God, and to my country, I earnestly beg the attention of Congress and the people to the subject. ABRAHAM LINCOLN

March 6. 1862.

3    In fact, Lincoln's proposal utterly failed to gain traction among stubborn Border State slaveholders—and their elected leaders—who remained unwilling to build on the freedom momentum begun with the passage of emancipation in the District of Columbia, even with the inducement of compensation.

*After several days of suspense and anxiety, Lincoln signed a historic bill ending slavery in Washington, D.C., but added a few caveats and concerns in the memorandum. Nevertheless, Frederick Douglass at once realized the momentous importance of Lincoln's signature on the landmark legislation. "[That] I should live to see the President of the United States deliberately advocating Emancipation," he editorialized, "was more than I ever ventured to hope. . . . A blind man can see where the President's heart is."*

1   The bill, which passed in the Senate (April 3) and the House (April 12) with two-thirds majorities, freed the district's enslaved people at once and authorized the sum of $1 million to compensate their owners (with as much as $300 ultimately awarded for each former slave).

2   As a freshman in Congress, Lincoln had introduced a Washington, D.C., emancipation bill of his own, back in 1849. See "Remarks and Resolution concerning the Abolition of Slavery in the District of Columbia, U.S. House of Representatives, January 10, 1849," in this volume.

3   Lincoln had expressed some concern that the bill called for immediate rather than gradual emancipation, his own preference.

4   The law authorized the payment of $100 to each former slave who chose to leave the country and colonize elsewhere. Lincoln had been a supporter of voluntary colonization for nearly two decades. The District of Columbia Emancipation Act ultimately freed 3,185 enslaved people. (Almost no former slaves chose to leave the country.)

5   Married women.

6   Congress took up the president's recommendations and passed a supplemental bill on July 12.

# Signing Message Accompanying Presidential Approval of D.C. Emancipation

## April 16, 1862

FELLOW CITIZENS OF THE SENATE, AND HOUSE OF REPRESENTATIVES.

The Act entitled "An Act for the release of certain persons held to service, or labor in the District of Columbia" has this day been approved, and signed.[1]

I have never doubted the constitutional authority of congress to abolish slavery in this District; and I have ever desired to see the national capital freed from the institution in some satisfactory way.[2] Hence there has never been, in my mind, any question upon the subject, except the one of expediency, arising in view of all the circumstances.[3] If there be matters within and about this act, which might have taken a course or shape, more satisfactory to my jud[g]ment, I do not attempt to specify them. I am gratified that the two principles of compensation, and colonization, are both recognized, and practically applied in the act.[4]

In the matter of compensation, it is provided that claims may be presented within ninety days from the passage of the act "but not thereafter"; and there is no saving for minors, femes-covert,[5] insane, or absent persons. I presume this is an omission by mere over-sight, and I recommend that it be supplied by an amendatory or supplemental act.[6] ABRAHAM LINCOLN

April 16, 1862.

Rec 16 Apr.          Public 50.

## Thirty-seventh Congress of the United States of America;

At the second Session.

Begun and held at the city of Washington, on Monday, the second day of December, one thousand eight hundred and sixty-one

## AN ACT

For the release of certain persons held to service or labor in the District of Columbia.

**Be it enacted** *by the Senate and House of Representatives of the United States of America in Congress assembled,* **That** all persons held to service or labor within the District of Columbia by reason of African descent are hereby discharged and freed of and from all claim to such service or labor; and from and after the passage of this act neither slavery nor involuntary servitude, except for crime whereof the party shall be duly convicted, shall hereafter exist in said District. Sec. 2. And be it further enacted, That all persons loyal to the United States holding claims to service or labor against persons discharged therefrom by this act may, within ninety days from the passage thereof, but not thereafter present to the Commissioners hereinafter mentioned their respective statements or petitions in writing, verified by oath or affirmation setting forth the names, ages, and personal description of such persons the manner in which said petitioner acquired such claim, and any facts touching the value thereof; and declaring his allegiance to the government of the United States; and that he has not borne arms against the United States during the present rebellion, nor in any way given aid or comfort thereto; Provided, That the oath of the party to the petition shall not be evidence of the facts therein stated. Sec. 3. And be it further enacted, That the President of the United States, with the advice and consent of the Senate, shall appoint three commissioners, residents of the District of Columbia any two of whom shall have power to act, who shall receive the petitions above mentioned, and who shall investigate and determine the validity and value of the claims therein presented, as aforesaid, and appraise and apportion, under the proviso hereto annexed, the value in money of the several claims by them found to be valid; Provided, however, That the entire sum so appraised and apportioned shall not exceed in the aggregate an amount equal to three hundred dollars for each person shown to have been so held by lawful claim:

The D.C. Emancipation Act. Manuscript (April 16, 1862). The law provided for immediate emancipation, compensation to loyal Unionist slaveholders of up to $300 for each slave, and voluntary colonization of former slaves outside of the United States.

*Determined by July to act against slavery on his own terms, Lincoln wrote this appeal to Border State representatives in a final attempt to win their support for gradual, compensated emancipation, accompanied by voluntary colonization. The president hoped for their approval before Congress adjourned for the summer. Lincoln was frank about his political challenges: by countermanding General Hunter's order, he admitted, he had alienated "many whose support the country can not afford to lose." More important, he now put himself on record linking the end of slavery to the "happy future" and "grandeur" of the entire country. But when the Border State representatives caucused on the proposal two days later, they voted overwhelmingly to reject the president's plan.*

1 Lincoln invited all the senators and congressmen from the Border States—Missouri, Kentucky, Maryland, and Delaware—to the White House, where he read this document to them aloud.

2 Congress was not scheduled to reconvene until December.

3 See "Message to Congress on Gradual Emancipation, March 6, 1862," in this volume.

4 Fine points, or formal procedure.

# Appeal to Border State Representatives to Support Compensated Emancipation

## July 12, 1862

GENTLEMEN.[1] AFTER THE ADJOURNMENT OF CONGRESS, NOW VERY near, I shall have no opportunity of seeing you for several months.[2] Believing that you of the border-states hold more power for good than any other equal number of members, I feel it a duty which I can not justifiably waive, to make this appeal to you. I intend no reproach or complaint when I assure you that in my opinion, if you all had voted for the resolution in the gradual emancipation message of last March,[3] the war would now be substantially ended. And the plan therein proposed is yet one of the most potent, and swift means of ending it. Let the states which are in rebellion see, definitely and certainly, that, in no event, will the states you represent ever join their proposed Confederacy, and they can not, much longer maintain the contest. But you can not divest them of their hope to ultimately have you with them so long as you show a determination to perpetuate the institution within your own states. Beat them at elections, as you have overwhelmingly done, and, nothing daunted, they still claim you as their own. You and I know what the lever of their power is. Break that lever before their faces, and they can shake you no more forever.

Most of you have treated me with kindness and consideration; and I trust you will not now think I improperly touch what is exclusively your own, when, for the sake of the whole country I ask[,] "Can you, for your states, do better than to take the course I urge?["] Discarding *punctillio*[4] [*sic*] and maxims adapted to more manageable times, and looking only to the unprecedentedly stern facts of our case, can you do better in any possible even[t]? You prefer that the constitutional relation of the states to the nation shall be practically restored, without disturbance of the institution; and if this were done, my whole duty, in this respect, under the constitution, and my oath of office, would be performed. But it is not done, and we are trying

Samuel Casey of Kentucky. Photograph (1865–1880).

Horace Maynard of Tennessee. Photograph by Julian Vannerson (1859).

to accomplish it by war. The incidents of the war can not be avoided. If the war continue long, as it must, if the object be not sooner attained, the institution in your states will be extinguished by mere friction and abrasion—by the mere incidents of the war. It will be gone, and you will have nothing valuable in lieu of it. Much of it's [sic] value is gone already. How much better for you, and for your people, to take the step which, at once, shortens the war, and secures substantial compensation for that which is sure to be wholly lost in any other event. How much better to thus save the money which else we sink forever in the war. How much better to do it while we can, lest the war ere long render us pecuniarily unable to do it. How much better for you, as seller, and the nation as buyer, to sell out, and buy out, that without which the war could never have been, than to sink both the thing to be sold, and the price of it, in cutting one another's throats.

I do not speak of emancipation *at once,* but of a *decision* at once to emancipate *gradually.* Room in South America for colonization, can be obtained cheaply, and in abundance; and when numbers shall be large enough to be

5    Lincoln referred to the May 9 order issued by Union general David Hunter (1802–1886) that freed all slaves in the states of Georgia, South Carolina, and Florida. Because Hunter had not been "authorized by the Government of the United States to make proclamations declaring the slaves of any State free," Lincoln revoked the order on May 19. *CW,* 5:222–223.

6    This was a novel argument by Lincoln: help me rebut the criticism of those who supported the Hunter proclamation by mounting your own effort to end slavery.

7    Only eight of the twenty-eight Border State representatives consented to link their names with the "happy future" and "grandeur" Lincoln promised if they endorsed his proposal. The majority of the caucus argued in its July 15 reply that the government could not afford to compensate slave owners in their districts, and that any effort to deprive them of their "property," even for compensation, would drive them into loyalty to the Confederacy. That same day, Senator Orville Browning of Illinois visited the White House and found his old friend "weary, care-worn, and troubled," undoubtedly as a result of this painful rejection from the Border State representatives. When the senator expressed concern about Lincoln's health, the president grasped his hand and said: "Browning I must die sometime." Then, as Browning added in his diary entry that day: "I replied 'your fortunes are bound up with those of the Country, and disaster to one would be disaster to the other, and I hope you will do all you can to preserve your health and life.' He looked very sad, and there was a cadence of deep sadness in his voice. We parted I believe both of us with tears in our eyes." *Diary of Orville Hickman Browning,* 1:559–560.

company and encouragement for one another, the freed people will not be so reluctant to go.

I am pressed with a difficulty not yet mentioned—one which threatens division among those who, united are none too strong. An instance of it is known to you. Gen. Hunter is an honest man. He was, and I hope, still is, my friend. I valued him none the less for his agreeing with me in the general wish that all men everywhere, could be free. He proclaimed all men free within certain states, and I repudiated the proclamation.[5] He expected more good, and less harm from the measure, than I could believe would follow. Yet in repudiating it, I gave dissatisfaction, if not offence, to many whose support the country can not afford to lose. And this is not the end of it. The pressure, in this direction, is still upon me, and is increasing. By conceding what I now ask, you can relieve me, and much more, can relieve the country, in this important point.[6] Upon these considerations I have again begged your attention to the message of March last. Before leaving the Capital, consider and discuss it among yourselves. You are patriots and statesmen; and, as such, I pray you, consider this proposition; and, at the least, commend it to the consideration of your states and people. As you would perpetuate popular government for the best people in the world, I beseech you that you do in no wise omit this. Our common country is in great peril, demanding the loftiest views, and boldest action to bring it speedy relief. Once relieved, it's [*sic*] form of government is saved to the world; it's [*sic*] beloved history, and cherished memories, are vindicated; and it's [*sic*] happy future fully assured, and rendered inconceivably grand. To you, more than to any others, the previlege [*sic*] is given, to assure that happiness, and swell that grandeur, and to link your own names therewith forever.[7]

# Address to a Deputation of Freedmen, the White House

## August 14, 1862

THIS AFTERNOON the PRESIDENT of the UNITED STATES gave audience to a Committee of colored men at the White House.[1] They were introduced by the Rev. J. Mitchell, Commissioner of Emigration.[2] E. M. Thomas, the Chairman,[3] remarked that they were there by invitation to hear what the Executive had to say to them. Having all been seated, the President, after a few preliminary observations, informed them that a sum of money had been appropriated by Congress, and placed at his disposition for the purpose of aiding the colonization in some country of the people, or a portion of them, of African descent, thereby making it his duty, as it had for a long time been his inclination, to favor that cause; and why, he asked, should the people of your race be colonized, and where? Why should they leave this country? This is, perhaps, the first question for proper consideration. You and we are different races. We have between us a broader difference than exists between almost any other two races. Whether it is right or wrong I need not discuss, but this physical difference is a great disadvantage to us both, as I think your race suffer very greatly, many of them by living among us, while ours suffer from your presence. In a word we suffer on each side. If this is admitted, it affords a reason at least why we should be separated. You here are freemen I suppose.

A VOICE: Yes, sir.

The President—Perhaps you have long been free, or all your lives. Your race are suffering, in my judgment, the greatest wrong inflicted on any people. But even when you cease to be slaves, you are yet far removed from being placed on an equality with the white race. You are cut off from many of the advantages which the other race enjoy. The aspiration of men is to enjoy equality with the best when free, but on this broad continent, not a single

*When he read this chilling speech aloud to a delegation of free African American visitors—declaring that blacks and whites could never live together in harmony and urging them to consider colonization in Africa or Central America—Lincoln had already drafted a preliminary Emancipation Proclamation. He had read it to his cabinet in July and, at its urging, tabled it until a Union military victory could give its announcement teeth. But he did not reveal those plans to his White House guests on August 14. However insensitive this address may appear to modern eyes, it might be argued that this rhetorical ambush was designed for political reasons, to reach a wider audience: voting-age whites who would soon read it in their newspapers and, convinced that Lincoln did not favor black rights, might come to support emancipation as a nonphilanthropic war measure. The idea that Lincoln intended this disinformation effort as a means of advancing freedom can be gleaned from the fact that he subsequently spent only $38,000 of the $600,000 that Congress appropriated for colonization. Nonetheless, these words have long haunted Lincoln's reputation as a liberator. In another scathing editorial, his increasingly disappointed critic Frederick Douglass condemned what he called Lincoln's "pride of race and blood, his contempt for Negroes and his canting hypocrisy."*

1 Never before had an American president invited a group of free African Americans to the executive mansion. For details of the meeting, see Foner, *The Fiery Trial*, 223–225; Kate Masur, "The African American Delegation to Abraham Lincoln: A Reappraisal," *Civil War History* 56 (June 2010): 117–144. Lincoln was accompanied to the meeting by an Associated Press reporter who transcribed his remarks verbatim for release to the newspapers—a sure indication that the president desired that his sentiments be shared quickly and widely with white readers. With racial prejudice rampant, Lincoln was worried that his forthcoming emancipation order might be criticized for creating

a population of free African Americans eligible to compete with whites for jobs—unless he also advocated their voluntary colonization. The version of the meeting used in *CW* is from the *New York Tribune,* August 15, 1862.

2    James Mitchell (1818–1903), appointed just eleven days earlier as federal commissioner of emigration, was an antislavery, procolonization Methodist minister. He was asked by Lincoln to arrange the meeting at the White House. Foner, *The Fiery Trial,* 223.

3    Edward M. Thomas (?–1863), the leader of the five-member delegation gathered by Mitchell, served as president of the Anglo-American Institute for the Encouragement of Industry and Art. Masur, "The African American Delegation," 130.

4    Joseph Jenkins Roberts (1809–1876) had served from 1848 to 1856 as the first president of Liberia, a nation that had been serving as a homeland for freed African American slaves since 1820. The Virginia-born Roberts had left for Liberia in 1829. In their otherwise unrecorded meeting, Roberts tried to interest Lincoln in designating his country as the principal destination for colonization, but the American president thought the West African outpost too distant from the United States and its shipping routes. This meeting is covered in Benjamin Quarles, *Lincoln and the Negro* (New York: Oxford University Press, 1962), 110–111.

man of your race is made the equal of a single man of ours. Go where you are treated the best, and the ban is still upon you.

I do not propose to discuss this, but to present it as a fact with which we have to deal. I cannot alter it if I would. It is a fact, about which we all think and feel alike, I and you. We look to our condition, owing to the existence of the two races on this continent. I need not recount to you the effects upon white men, growing out of the institution of Slavery. I believe in its general evil effects on the white race. See our present condition—the country engaged in war!—our white men cutting one another's throats, none knowing how far it will extend; and then consider what we know to be the truth. But for your race among us there could not be war, although many men engaged on either side do not care for you one way or the other. Nevertheless, I repeat, without the institution of Slavery and the colored race as a basis, the war could not have an existence.

It is better for us both, therefore, to be separated. I know that there are free men among you, who even if they could better their condition are not as much inclined to go out of the country as those, who being slaves could obtain their freedom on this condition. I suppose one of the principal difficulties in the way of colonization is that the free colored man cannot see that his comfort would be advanced by it. You may believe you can live in Washington or elsewhere in the United States the remainder of your life, perhaps more so than you can in any foreign country, and hence you may come to the conclusion that you have nothing to do with the idea of going to a foreign country. This is (I speak in no unkind sense) an extremely selfish view of the case.

But you ought to do something to help those who are not so fortunate as yourselves. There is an unwillingness on the part of our people, harsh as it may be, for you free colored people to remain with us. Now, if you could give a start to white people, you would open a wide door for many to be made free. If we deal with those who are not free at the beginning, and whose intellects are clouded by Slavery, we have very poor materials to start with. If intelligent colored men, such as are before me, would move in this matter, much might be accomplished. It is exceedingly important that we have men at the beginning capable of thinking as white men, and not those who have been systematically oppressed.

There is much to encourage you. For the sake of your race you should sacrifice something of your present comfort for the purpose of being as grand in that respect as the white people. It is a cheering thought throughout life that something can be done to ameliorate the condition of those

*Monrovia, a Settlement of the American Colonization Society in Libera.* Engraving (1832). Print shows freed slaves from the United States arriving in Monrovia under the sponsorship of the American Colonization Society.

who have been subject to the hard usage of the world. It is difficult to make a man miserable while he feels he is worthy of himself, and claims kindred to the great God who made him. In the American Revolutionary war sacrifices were made by men engaged in it; but they were cheered by the future. Gen. Washington himself endured greater physical hardships than if he had remained a British subject. Yet he was a happy man, because he was engaged in benefiting his race—something for the children of his neighbors, having none of his own.

The colony of Liberia has been in existence a long time. In a certain sense it is a success. The old President of Liberia, Roberts, has just been with me—the first time I ever saw him.[4] He says they have within the bounds of

5    Lincoln soon authorized Kansas senator Samuel C. Pomeroy (1816–1891) to accompany "500 able-bodied negroes" to identify an appropriate spot for colonization somewhere on the Isthmus of Chiriquí in Central America. The Chiriquí Improvement Company had recommended the supposedly coal-rich area in what is now Panama, but coal samples brought back for analysis by the Smithsonian Institution were discovered to be fake. Worse, several countries in the region opposed the immigration of American blacks and three—Costa Rica, Honduras, and Nicaragua—threatened the use of force to keep them from settling on the isthmus. Lincoln later encouraged settlement of Île-à-Vache off the coast of Haiti, but the first colonists to try staking claims on the torrid island found it inhospitable and conducive to disease; survivors of the first expedition eventually returned to the United States.

6    Believed to be from "Hosanna in the Highest" (1839) by Robert Grant (1779–1838). *Lincoln's Selected Writings,* 274n5. Also attributed to J. W. Cunningham (1780–1861) under the title "Christ's Entry into Jerusalem," in *Cyclopaedia of Poetry, Second Series: Embracing Poems Descriptive of the Scenes, Incidents, Persons and Places of the Bible* (New York: Funk & Wagnalls, 577), 97. No one knows whether the delegation of freedmen was familiar with the obscure verse Lincoln quoted at the end of his remarks. Since he was encouraging freedmen to leave the country, it is not surprising he omitted the previous lines of the poem, which refer to "A noble army following fast / His track of pain and woe."

7    Reacting to the widely reprinted transcripts of these remarks, Frederick Douglass published a withering response in the September 1862 issue of *Douglass' Monthly:* "The President of the United States seems to possess an ever increasing passion for making himself appear silly and ridiculous, if nothing worse. . . . In this address, Mr. Lincoln

that colony between 300,000 and 400,000 people, or more than in some of our old States, such as Rhode Island or Delaware, or in some of our newer States, and less than in some of our larger ones. They are not all American colonists, or their descendants. Something less than 12,000 have been sent thither from this country. Many of the original settlers have died, yet, like people elsewhere, their offspring outnumber those deceased.

The question is if the colored people are persuaded to go anywhere, why not there? One reason for an unwillingness to do so is that some of you would rather remain within reach of the country of your nativity. I do not know how much attachment you may have toward our race. It does not strike me that you have the greatest reason to love them. But still you are attached to them at all events.

The place I am thinking about having for a colony is in Central America.[5] It is nearer to us than Liberia—not much more than one-fourth as far as Liberia, and within seven days' run by steamers. Unlike Liberia it is on a great line of travel—it is a highway. The country is a very excellent one for any people, and with great natural resources and advantages, and especially because of the similarity of climate with your native land—thus being suited to your physical condition.

The particular place I have in view is to be a great highway from the Atlantic or Caribbean Sea to the Pacific Ocean, and this particular place has all the advantages for a colony. On both sides there are harbors among the finest in the world. Again, there is evidence of very rich coal mines. A certain amount of coal is valuable in any country, and there may be more than enough for the wants of the country. Why I attach so much importance to coal is, it will afford an opportunity to the inhabitants for immediate employment till they get ready to settle permanently in their homes.

If you take colonists where there is no good landing, there is a bad show; and so where there is nothing to cultivate, and of which to make a farm. But if something is started so that you can get your daily bread as soon as you reach there, it is a great advantage. Coal land is the best thing I know of with which to commence an enterprise.

To return, you have been talked to upon this subject, and told that a speculation is intended by gentlemen, who have an interest in the country, including the coal mines. We have been mistaken all our lives if we do not know whites as well as blacks look to their self-interest. Unless among those deficient of intellect everybody you trade with makes something. You meet with these things here as elsewhere.

If such persons have what will be an advantage to them, the question is whether it cannot be made of advantage to you. You are intelligent, and know that success does not as much depend on external help as on self-reliance. Much, therefore, depends upon yourselves. As to the coal mines, I think I see the means available for your self-reliance.

I shall, if I get a sufficient number of you engaged, have provisions made that you shall not be wronged. If you will engage in the enterprise I will spend some of the money intrusted to me. I am not sure you will succeed. The Government may lose the money, but we cannot succeed unless we try; but we think, with care, we can succeed.

The political affairs in Central America are not in quite as satisfactory condition as I wish. There are contending factions in that quarter; but it is true all the factions are agreed alike on the subject of colonization, and want it, and are more generous than we are here. To your colored race they have no objection. Besides, I would endeavor to have you made equals, and have the best assurance that you should be the equals of the best.

The practical thing I want to ascertain is whether I can get a number of able-bodied men, with their wives and children, who are willing to go, when I present evidence of encouragement and protection. Could I get a hundred tolerably intelligent men, with their wives and children, to "cut their own fodder," so to speak? Can I have fifty? If I could find twenty-five able-bodied men, with a mixture of women and children, good things in the family relation, I think I could make a successful commencement.

I want you to let me know whether this can be done or not. This is the practical part of my wish to see you. These are subjects of very great importance, worthy of a month's study, [instead] of a speech delivered in an hour. I ask you then to consider seriously not pertaining to yourselves merely, nor for your race, and ours, for the present time, but as one of the things, if successfully managed, for the good of mankind—not confined to the present generation, but as

> From age to age descends the lay,
> To millions yet to be,
> Till far its echoes roll away,
> Into eternity.[6]

The above is merely given as the substance of the President's remarks.[7]

The Chairman of the delegation briefly replied that "they would hold a consultation and in a short time give an answer." The President said: "Take your full time—no hurry at all."[8]

The delegation then withdrew.

assumes the language and arguments of an itinerant Colonization lecturer. . . . It does not require any great amount of skill to point out the fallacy and expose the unfairness of the assumption, for by this time every man who has an ounce of brain in his head, no matter to which party he may belong, and even Mr. Lincoln himself, must know quite well that the mere presence of the colored race never could have provoked this horrid and desolating rebellion. . . . A horse thief pleading that the existence of the horse is the apology for his theft or a highway man contending that the money in the traveler's pocket is the sole first cause of his robbery are about as much entitled to respect as is the President's reasoning at this point. No, Mr. President, it is not the innocent horse that makes the horse thief, not the traveler's purse that makes the highway robber, and it is not the presence of the Negro that causes this foul and unnatural war, but the cruel and brutal cupidity of those who wish to possess horses, money and Negroes by means of theft, robbery, and rebellion."

8    Edward M. Thomas replied two days after the visit to inform Lincoln that the delegation had arrived at the White House "entirely hostile to the [colonization] movement until all the advantages were so ably brought to our views by you." Thomas proposed to "confer with leading colored men in Phila[delphia], New York and Boston upon this movement of emigration to the point recommended in your address," and predicted that "our friends and co-laborers for our race in those cities will when the Subject is explained by us to them join heartily in Sustaining Such a movement." Thomas to Lincoln, August 16, 1862, Lincoln Papers, Library of Congress. But Thomas did not speak for all free African Americans, and the voices of those opposed to Lincoln's proposal soon drowned out that of the generous president of the Anglo-American Institute. The president's proposal was overwhelmingly rejected.

*Arguably one of the most famous letters to the editor in American history, this ingenious argument was in one sense a reply to a* New York Tribune *editorial, condemning the administration as "strangely and disastrously remiss" for failing to act against slavery and to recruit freedmen for the Union army. In a broader context, it gave Lincoln his best platform yet for arguing to a wide public that his forthcoming emancipation order, already drafted, would be aimed at saving the Union and nothing else. In fact,* Tribune *editor Horace Greeley already suspected that Lincoln's proclamation was imminent, and he had likely published his editorial so he could reap credit once emancipation was announced. In turn, Lincoln craftily had this letter published first not in the* Tribune *but in a Washington newspaper. By the time it got to Greeley, it had been read—and largely praised—nationwide.*

1  Horace Greeley founded the *New York Tribune* in 1841. By the late 1850s, it was the nation's most widely circulated and most influential antislavery newspaper—and a weekly national edition counted among its readers Illinois politician Abraham Lincoln. Lincoln had long admired Greeley, but the two never became friends or confidants; Greeley was far too unpredictable for the president, as this famous exchange demonstrated. Lincoln's complicated relationship with Greeley is addressed in Gregory A. Borchard, *Abraham Lincoln and Horace Greeley* (Carbondale: Southern Illinois University Press, 2011).

2  Greeley's open letter appeared in the *New York Tribune* on August 20, demanding that the president move against slavery immediately in order to secure the manpower to win the war.

3  Abolitionist leaders were divided in their appraisal of the letter. Wendell Phillips (1811–1884) criticized it as "the most disgraceful document that ever came from the head of a free people," but

# To Horace Greeley

## August 22, 1862

Hon. Horace Greel[e]y:[1]   Executive Mansion,
Dear Sir   Washington, August 22, 1862.

I have just read yours of the 19th. addressed to myself through the New-York Tribune.[2] If there be in it any statements, or assumptions of fact, which I may know to be erroneous, I do not, now and here, controvert them. If there be in it any inferences which I may believe to be falsely drawn, I do not now and here, argue against them. If there be perceptable [*sic*] in it an impatient and dictatorial tone, I waive it in deference to an old friend, whose heart I have always supposed to be right.

As to the policy I "seem to be pursuing" as you say, I have not meant to leave any one in doubt.

I would save the Union. I would save it the shortest way under the Constitution. The sooner the national authority can be restored; the nearer the Union will be "the Union as it was." If there be those who would not save the Union, unless they could at the same time *save* slavery, I do not agree with them. If there be those who would not save the Union unless they could at the same time *destroy* slavery, I do not agree with them. My paramount object in this struggle *is* to save the Union, and is *not* either to save or to destroy slavery. If I could save the Union without freeing *any* slave I would do it, and if I could save it by freeing *all* the slaves I would do it; and if I could save it by freeing some and leaving others alone I would also do that. What I do about slavery, and the colored race, I do because I believe it helps to save the Union; and what I forbear, I forbear because I do *not* believe it would help to save the Union. I shall do *less* whenever I shall believe what I am doing hurts the cause, and I shall do *more* whenever I shall believe doing more will help the cause. I shall try to correct errors when shown

Gerrit Smith (1797–1874) praised it as "sound in doctrine and argument and admirable in style." Quotes from James Oakes, *Freedom National: The Destruction of Slavery in the United States, 1861–1865* (New York: W. W. Norton, 2013), 312–313.

256 FIFTH AVENUE,
NEW YORK.

Horace Greeley. Photograph by Sarony Studio (New York, 1872). Greeley, the editor of the *New York Tribune,* is shown reading his newspaper.

to be errors; and I shall adopt new views so fast as they shall appear to be true views.[3]

I have here stated my purpose according to my view of *official* duty; and I intend no modification of my oft-expressed *personal* wish that all men every where could be free. Yours,

A. LINCOLN

*No one knows precisely when Lincoln wrote this extraordinarily heartfelt rumination on faith, only that it likely reflected his anguish after the Union defeat at the Second Battle of Bull Run on August 29, 1862.*

1   When Union forces prevailed at the Battle of Antietam on September 17, Lincoln revealed to his entire cabinet "that he had made a vow, a covenant, that if God gave us the victory in the approaching battle, he would consider it an indication of Divine will, and that it was his duty to move forward in the cause of emancipation." *Diary of Gideon Welles,* ed. John T. Morse Jr., 3 vols. (Boston: Houghton Mifflin, 1911), 1:143.

# Meditation on the Divine Will

## [September 2, 1862?]

THE WILL OF GOD PREVAILS. IN GREAT CONTESTS EACH PARTY claims to act in accordance with the will of God. Both *may* be, and one *must* be wrong. God can not be *for,* and *against* the same thing at the same time. In the present civil war it is quite possible that God's purpose is something different from the purpose of either party—and yet the human instrumentalities, working just as they do, are of the best adaptation to effect His purpose. I am almost ready to say this is probably true—that God wills this contest, and wills that it shall not end yet. By his mere quiet power, on the minds of the now contestants, He could have either *saved* or *destroyed* the Union without a human contest. Yet the contest began. And having begun He could give the final victory to either side any day. Yet the contest proceeds.[1]

The will of God prevails— In great contests each party claims to act in accordance with the will of God. Both may be, and one must be wrong. God can not be for, and against the same thing at the same time. In the present civil war it is quite possible that God's purpose is something different from the purpose of either party— and yet the human instrumentalities, working just as they do, are of the best adaptation to effect his purpose. I am almost ready to say this is probably true— that God wills this contest, and wills that it shall not end yet— By his mere quiet power, on the minds of the now contestants, He could have either saved or destroyed the Union without a human contest— Yet the contest began— And having begun He could give the final victory to either side any day— Yet the contest proceeds—

Abraham Lincoln, Meditation on the Divine Will. Manuscript (ca. September 1862).

# The Preliminary Emancipation Proclamation

September 22, 1862

*Lincoln read this history-altering document to his cabinet members five days after Union forces triumphed at the Battle of Antietam, telling them he would now brook no opposition to its immediate release. The executive order gave Confederates 100 days' notice to throw down their arms and return to the Union or else forfeit their slaves "then, thenceforward, and forever." Lincoln's hometown Republican paper promptly hailed the thunderbolt act as "the most important and the most memorable of his official career," but not everyone agreed. The Democratic* Chicago Times *charged that the president had "cut loose from the constitution," while the equally hostile* London Times *warned that the "nefarious resolution" would "light up a servile war in the distant homesteads of the South."*

1   Treasury Secretary Salmon Chase recalled that Lincoln summoned the cabinet to the White House at noon, opened the meeting by reading a chapter from a recently received book by humorist Artemus Ward (Charles Farrar Browne [1834–1867]), which the president "seemed to enjoy . . . very much," then "took a graver tone" and read the entire proclamation aloud, "making remarks on the several parts as he went on, and showing that he had fully considered the whole subject, in all the lights under which it had been presented to him." *The Civil War Diaries of Salmon P. Chase*, ed. David Donald (New York: Longmans, Green & Co., 1954), 149, 151. "His mind was fixed, his decision made," remembered Secretary of the Navy Gideon Welles. He recalled Lincoln declaring: "God had decided this question in favor of the slaves." *Diary of Gideon Welles*, 1:143.

2   Lincoln made good on this vow. See "From Annual Message to Congress, December 1, 1862," in this volume.

3   Whether by design or by chance, the January 1 deadline gave the Confederacy exactly 100 days

## By the President of the United States of America
### A Proclamation.

I, Abraham Lincoln, President of the United States of America, and Commander-in-chief of the Army and Navy thereof, do hereby proclaim and declare that hereafter, as heretofore, the war will be prossecuted [*sic*] for the object of practically restoring the constitutional relation between the United States, and each of the states, and the people thereof, in which states that relation is, or may be suspended, or disturbed.[1]

That it is my purpose, upon the next meeting of Congress to again recommend the adoption of a practical measure tendering pecuniary aid to the free acceptance or rejection of all slave-states, so called, the people whereof may not then be in rebellion against the United States, and which states, may then have voluntarily adopted, or thereafter may voluntarily adopt, immediate, or gradual abolishment of slavery within their respective limits; and that the effort to colonize persons of African descent, with their consent, upon this continent, or elsewhere, with the previously obtained consent of the Governments existing there, will be continued.[2]

That on the first day of January in the year of our Lord, one thousand eight hundred and sixty-three,[3] all persons held as slaves within any state, or designated part of a state, the people whereof shall then be in rebellion against the United States shall be then, thenceforward, and forever free;[4] and the executive government of the United States, including the military and naval authority thereof, will recognize and maintain[5] the freedom of such persons, and will do no act or acts to repress such persons, or any of them, in any efforts they may make for their actual freedom.

That the executive will, on the first day of January aforesaid, by proclamation, designate the States, and parts of states, if any, in which the people thereof respectively, shall then be in rebellion against the United States; and the fact that any state, or the people thereof shall, on that day be, in good faith represented in the Congress of the United States, by members chosen thereto, at elections wherein a majority of the qualified voters of such state shall have participated, shall, in the absence of strong countervailing testimony, be deemed conclusive evidence that such state and the people thereof, are not then in rebellion against the United States.

That attention is hereby called to an act of Congress entitled "An act to make an additional Article of War" approved March 13, 1862, and which act is in the words and figure following:

"*Be it enacted by the Senate and House of Representatives of the United States of America in Congress assembled,* That hereafter the following shall be promulgated as an additional article of war for the government of the army of the United States, and shall be obeyed and observed as such:

Article—. All officers or persons in the military or naval service of the United States are prohibited from employing any of the forces under their respective commands for the purpose of returning fugitives from service or labor, who may have escaped from any persons to whom such service or labor is claimed to be due, and any officer who shall be found guilty by a court-martial of violating this article shall be dismissed from the service.

SEC. 2. *And be it further enacted,* That this act shall take effect from and after its passage."[6]

Also to the ninth[7] and tenth sections of an act entitled "An Act to suppress Insurrection, to punish Treason and Rebellion, to seize and confiscate property of rebels, and for other purposes," approved July 17, 1862, and which sections are in the words and figures following:

"SEC. 9. *And be it further enacted,* That all slaves of persons who shall hereafter be engaged in rebellion against the government of the United States, or who shall in any way give aid or comfort thereto, escaping from such persons and taking refuge within the lines of the army; and all slaves captured from such persons or deserted by them and coming under the control of the government of the United States; and all slaves of such persons found *on* (or) being within any place occupied by rebel forces and afterwards occupied by the forces of the United States, shall be deemed captives of war, and shall be forever free of their servitude and not again held as slaves.

SEC. 10. *And be it further enacted,* That no slave escaping into any State, Territory, or the District of Columbia, from any other State, shall be delivered up, or in any way impeded or hindered of his liberty, except for crime,

from September 22 to abandon its rebellion or forfeit its citizens' property in slaves.

4   Lincoln's original draft supposedly did not contain the phrase "forever free." See, for example, Eric Foner, quoting Seward and Chase, in *Forever Free: Abraham Lincoln and American Slavery* (New York: W. W. Norton, 2010), 231. However, this is contradicted by the handwritten proclamation purchased by abolitionist Gerrit Smith after Lincoln donated it to an Albany charity fair, then sold to the New York State Legislature in 1865. Now preserved at the New York State Library in Albany, the draft contains deleted lines and inserts but shows no indication of any rewriting at this point.

5   The words "and maintain" were added later, doubtless at the suggestion of Seward or Chase, perhaps even as the document was being read aloud. *CW,* 5:434n5.

6   For this section, Lincoln clipped and pasted a newspaper or official government printing of the Confiscation Act. Ibid., n. 6.

7   Here Lincoln resumed his handwritten draft, but this word is smudged and, remarkably, bears a vivid fingerprint—undoubtedly Lincoln's—probably left inadvertently when he struggled with the glue pot as he pasted in the above-mentioned insert. For a reproduction, see Robert Weible, Jennifer A. Lemak, and Aaron Noble, *An Irrepressible Conflict: The Empire State in the Civil War* (Albany: State University of New York Press, 2014), 118–119.

Alexander Hay Ritchie, after a painting by Francis B. Carpenter, *The First Reading of the Emancipation Proclamation before the Cabinet*. Engraving (New York: Derby & Miller, 1864). Carpenter's original depicted the moment the proclamation was deferred in July 1862.

or some offence against the laws, unless the person claiming said fugitive shall first make oath that the person to whom the labor or service of such fugitive is alleged to be due is his lawful owner, and has not borne arms against the United States in the present rebellion, nor in any way given aid and comfort thereto; and no person engaged in the military or naval service of the United States shall, under any pretence whatever, assume to decide on the validity of the claim of any person to the service or labor of any other person, or surrender up any such person to the claimant, on pain of being dismissed from the service."[8]

And I do hereby enjoin upon and order all persons engaged in the military and naval service of the United States to observe, obey, and enforce, within their respective spheres of service, the act, and sections above recited.

And the executive will in due time recommend that all citizens of the United States who shall have remained loyal thereto throughout the rebellion, shall (upon the restoration of the constitutional relation between the United States, and their respective states, and people, if that relation shall have been suspended or disturbed) be compensated for all losses by acts of the United States, including the loss of slaves.

---

In witness whereof, I have hereunto set my hand, and caused the seal of the United States to be affixed.

Done at the City of Washington, this twenty second day of September, in the year of our Lord, one thousand eight hundred and sixty two, and of the Independence of the United States, the eighty seventh.[9]

ABRAHAM LINCOLN
By the President:
WILLIAM H. SEWARD, Secretary of State.

8   This section was also pasted in; the original was damaged by the bleeding through of the glue or paste. CW, 5:435n7.

9   "From the date of this proclamation," the *Chicago Tribune* predicted, "begins the history of this Republic as . . . the home of freedom." Cited in Foner, *The Fiery Trial,* 232.

*Somewhat overlooked in the firestorm of reaction that greeted the emancipation announcement only two days earlier, Lincoln's broadest habeas corpus suspension yet revoked liberty just as surely as his September 22 emancipation order widened it. Both executive orders, the president insisted, were necessary to save the Union. With its main purpose being to prevent resistance to volunteering for the army and the militia draft, this proclamation increased the controversial arrests of supposedly disloyal newspaper editors and political opponents. Nonetheless Congress ratified the suspension in March 1863; later that year, in September, Lincoln would issue an even wider suspension order.*

1    Hours after this order was issued, a crowd gathered at the White House to salute Lincoln for issuing the Preliminary Emancipation Proclamation two days before. "I can only trust in God I have made no mistake," Lincoln declared that evening. "It is now for the country and the world to pass judgment on it, and, may be, take action upon it. . . . In my position I am environed with difficulties." *CW,* 5:438.

# Proclamation Suspending the Writ of Habeas Corpus

## September 24, 1862

**By the President of the United States of America: A Proclamation.**

Whereas, it has become necessary to call into service not only volunteers but also portions of the militia of the States by draft in order to suppress the insurrection existing in the United States, and disloyal persons are not adequately restrained by the ordinary processes of law from hindering this measure and from giving aid and comfort in various ways to the insurrection;

Now, therefore, be it ordered, first, that during the existing insurrection and as a necessary measure for suppressing the same, all Rebels and Insurgents, their aiders and abettors within the United States, and all persons discouraging volunteer enlistments, resisting militia drafts, or guilty of any disloyal practice, affording aid and comfort to Rebels against the authority of the United States, shall be subject to martial law and liable to trial and punishment by Courts Martial or Military Commission:

Second. That the Writ of Habeas Corpus is suspended in respect to all persons arrested, or who are now, or hereafter during the rebellion shall be, imprisoned in any fort, camp, arsenal, military prison, or other place of confinement by any military authority or by the sentence of any Court Martial or Military Commission.

In witness whereof, I have hereunto set my hand, and caused the seal of the United States to be affixed.

Done at the City of Washington this twenty fourth day of September,[1] in the year of our Lord one thousand eight hundred and sixty-two, and of the Independence of the United States the 87th.

ABRAHAM LINCOLN

By the President:

WILLIAM H. SEWARD, Secretary of State.

*Behind the Scenes.* Lithograph (1864). Venomous anti-Lincoln cartoon showing Lincoln and his cabinet rehearsing for a production of Shakespeare's *Othello.* Lincoln, playing the title role in blackface, stands at center stage. At right, sitting at a table with a bottle, is an inebriated Secretary of State William Seward, who mutters "Sh-shomethin's matt'r er my little bell: The darned thing won't ring anyway confixit." Seward, who once boasted that he could have someone arrested merely by ringing a bell, was roundly criticized for his arbitrary imprisonment of civilians.

Back in command of the Army of the Potomac for a second tour as its commander, McClellan, who opposed emancipation, dawdled after his costly Antietam victory. Pressed to justify his reluctance to resume fighting, McClellan informed the War Department that he could not advance because his cavalry horses were "fatigued." This is the exasperated Lincoln's mordant reply to the general's latest excuse for his chronic inaction.

# Telegram to General George B. McClellan

## October 24 [25], 1862

Washington City, D.C.
Majr. Genl. McClellan    Oct. 24 [25]. 1862

I have just read your despatch about sore tongued and fatiegued [sic] horses. Will you pardon me for asking what the horses of your army have done since the battle of Antietam that fatigue anything?

A. LINCOLN

General George B. McClellan. Carte de visite, photograph by J. W. Black (Boston, 1864).

*The Commander-in-Chief Conciliating the Soldier's Votes on the Battle Field.* Lithograph (New York, 1864). Anti-Lincoln cartoon by an unknown printmaker, from the 1864 presidential campaign.

President Lincoln at Antietam battlefield. Photograph by Alexander Gardner (1862). This is one of several photographs Gardner made of Lincoln on October 3. Lincoln is standing between Union spy-in-chief Allan G. Pinkerton and General John A. McClernand.

1   The House of Representatives had requested that President Lincoln submit "whatever information he possesses concerning the relations existing between this country and foreign powers." On July 12, 1862, Lincoln complied with the request: "I transmit a report of the Secretary of State upon the subject of the resolution of the House of Representatives of the 9th ultimo." *CW,* 5:319.

2   Lincoln would have to wait until the end of the war for Great Britain and France to withdraw their recognition of the Confederacy as a belligerent.

# From Annual Message to Congress

## December 1, 1862

*Fellow-citizens of the Senate and House of Representatives:*

Since your last annual assembling another year of health and bountiful harvests has passed. And while it has not pleased the Almighty to bless us with a return of peace, we can but press on, guided by the best light He gives us, trusting that in His own good time, and wise way, all will yet be well.

The correspondence touching foreign affairs which has [*sic*] taken place during the last year is herewith submitted, in virtual compliance with a request to that effect, made by the House of Representatives near the close of the last session of Congress.[1]

If the condition of our relations with other nations is less gratifying than it has usually been at former periods, it is certainly more satisfactory than a nation so unhappily distracted as we are, might reasonably have apprehended. In the month of June last there were some grounds to expect that the maritime powers which, at the beginning of our domestic difficulties, so unwisely and unnecessarily, as we think, recognized the insurgents as a belligerent, would soon recede from that position, which has proved only less injurious to themselves, than to our own country. But the temporary reverses which afterwards befell the national arms, and which were exaggerated by our own disloyal citizens abroad have hitherto delayed that act of simple justice.[2]

The civil war, which has so radically changed for the moment, the occupations and habits of the American people, has necessarily disturbed the social condition, and affected very deeply the prosperity of the nations with which we have carried on a commerce that has been steadily increasing throughout a period of half a century. It has, at the same time, excited political ambitions and apprehensions which have produced a profound agita-

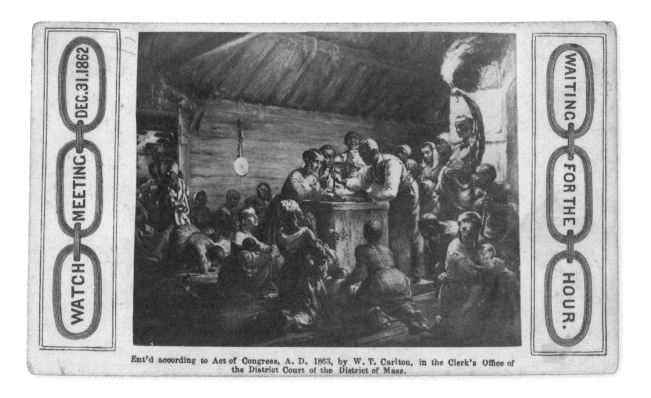

Ent'd according to Act of Congress, A. D. 1863, by W. T. Carlton, in the Clerk's Office of
the District Court of the District of Mass.

tion throughout the civilized world. In this unusual agitation we have for-borne from taking part in any controversy between foreign states, and between parties or factions in such states. We have attempted no propagan-dism, and acknowledged no revolution. But we have left to every nation the exclusive conduct and management of its own affairs. Our struggle has been, of course, contemplated by foreign nations with reference less to its own merits, than to its supposed, and often exaggerated effects and conse-quences resulting to those nations themselves. Nevertheless, complaint on the part of this government, even if it were just, would certainly be unwise.

The treaty with Great Britain for the suppression of the slave trade has been put into operation with a good prospect of complete success. It is an occasion of special pleasure to acknowledge that the execution of it, on the part of Her Majesty's government, has been marked with a jealous respect for the authority of the United States, and the rights of their moral and loyal citizens.

The convention with Hanover for the abolition of the stade dues[3] has been carried into full effect, under the act of Congress for that purpose.

*Watch Meeting, Dec. 31, 1862—Waiting for the Hour.* Cabinet card by Heard and Mosley (Boston, 1863). A group of African Americans anxiously awaiting the stroke of midnight and the anticipated announcement of the Emancipation Proclamation.

3   Tolls levied on ships going up the Elbe River and passing the mouth of the Schwinge River. In March 1862, Congress passed legislation that provided funds to support a treaty by which the tolls were abolished by the king of Hanover in exchange for a lump-sum payment by the United States. Cited in *Lincoln's Selected Writings,* 287n1.

4   On February 4, 1863, Congress passed legislation that awarded $14,309.13 in compensation to
the owners of the *Admiral P. Tordenskiold.* Cited in
*CW,* 5:520n5.

A blockade of three thousand miles of sea-coast could not be established, and vigorously enforced, in a season of great commercial activity like the present, without committing occasional mistakes, and inflicting unintentional injuries upon foreign nations and their subjects.

A civil war occurring in a country where foreigners reside and carry on trade under treaty stipulations, is necessarily fruitful of complaints of the violation of neutral rights. All such collisions tend to excite misapprehensions, and possibly to produce mutual reclamations between nations which have a common interest in preserving peace and friendship. In clear cases of these kinds I have, so far as possible, heard and redressed complaints which have been presented by friendly powers. There is still, however, a large and an augmenting number of doubtful cases upon which the government is unable to agree with the governments whose protection is demanded by the claimants. There are, moreover, many cases in which the United States, or their citizens, suffer wrongs from the naval or military authorities of foreign nations, which the governments of those states are not at once prepared to redress. I have proposed to some of the foreign states, thus interested, mutual conventions to examine and adjust such complaints. This proposition has been made especially to Great Britain, to France, to Spain, and to Prussia. In each case it has been kindly received, but has not yet been formally adopted.

I deem it my duty to recommend an appropriation in behalf of the owners of the Norwegian bark Admiral P. Tordenskiold, which vessel was, in May, 1861, prevented by the commander of the blockading force off Charleston from leaving that port with cargo, notwithstanding a similar privilege had, shortly before, been granted to an English vessel. I have directed the Secretary of State to cause the papers in the case to be communicated to the proper committees.[4]

Applications have been made to me by many free Americans of African descent to favor their emigration, with a view to such colonization as was contemplated in recent acts of Congress. Other parties, at home and abroad—some from interested motives, others upon patriotic considerations, and still others influenced by philanthropic sentiments—have suggested similar measures; while, on the other hand, several of the Spanish-American republics have protested against the sending of such colonies to their respective territories. Under these circumstances, I have declined to move any such colony to any state, without first obtaining the consent of its government, with an agreement on its part to receive and protect such emigrants in all the rights of freemen; and I have, at the same time, offered to

Christian Inger, *Liberty. "Liberty Brings to the Earth Justice and Peace."* Lithograph (Philadelphia, 1864). A pro-Union allegorical print produced for a Philadelphia newspaper.

the several states situated within the tropics, or having colonies there, to negotiate with them, subject to the advice and consent of the Senate, to favor the voluntary emigration of persons of that class to their respective territories, upon conditions which shall be equal, just, and humane. Liberia and Hayti are, as yet, the only countries to which colonists of African descent from here, could go with certainty of being received and adopted as citizens; and I regret to say such persons, contemplating colonization, do not seem so willing to migrate to those countries, as to some others, nor so willing as I think their interest demands. I believe, however, opinion among them, in this respect, is improving; and that, ere long, there will be an augmented, and considerable migration to both these countries, from the United States.

The new commercial treaty between the United States and the Sultan of Turkey has been carried into execution.

A commercial and consular treaty has been negotiated, subject to the Senate's consent, with Liberia; and a similar negotiation is now pending with the republic of Hayti. A considerable improvement of the national commerce is expected to result from these measures.

Our relations with Great Britain, France, Spain, Portugal, Russia, Prussia, Denmark, Sweden, Austria, the Netherlands, Italy, Rome, and the other European states, remain undisturbed. Very favorable relations also continue to be maintained with Turkey, Morocco, China and Japan.

. . .

The Territories of the United States, with unimportant exceptions, have remained undisturbed by the civil war, and they are exhibiting such evidence of prosperity as justifies an expectation that some of them will soon be in a condition to be organized as States, and be constitutionally admitted into the federal Union.

The immense mineral resources of some of those Territories ought to be developed as rapidly as possible. Every step in that direction would have a tendency to improve the revenues of the government, and diminish the burdens of the people. It is worthy of your serious consideration whether some extraordinary measures to promote that end cannot be adopted. The means which suggests itself as most likely to be effective, is a scientific exploration of the mineral regions in those Territories, with a view to the publication of its results at home and in foreign countries—results which cannot fail to be auspicious.

The condition of the finances will claim your most diligent consideration. The vast expenditures incident to the military and naval operations required for the suppression of the rebellion, have hitherto been met with a promptitude, and certainty, unusual in similar circumstances, and the public credit has been fully maintained. The continuance of the war, however, and the increased disbursements made necessary by the augmented forces now in the field, demand your best reflections as to the best modes of providing the necessary revenue, without injury to business and with the least possible burdens upon labor.

. . .

The Indian tribes upon our frontiers have, during the past year, manifested a spirit of insubordination, and, at several points, have engaged in open hostilities against the white settlements in their vicinity. The tribes occupying the Indian country south of Kansas, renounced their allegiance to the United States, and entered into treaties with the insurgents. Those who remained loyal to the United States were driven from the country. The chief of the Cherokees has visited this city for the purpose of restoring the former relations of the tribe with the United States. He alleges that they were constrained, by superior force, to enter into treaties with the insurgents, and that the United States neglected to furnish the protection which their treaty stipulations required.

In the month of August last the Sioux Indians, in Minnesota, attacked the settlements in their vicinity with extreme ferocity, killing, indiscriminately, men, women, and children.[5] This attack was wholly unexpected, and, therefore, no means of defence had been provided. It is estimated that not less than eight hundred persons were killed by the Indians, and a large amount of property was destroyed. How this outbreak was induced is not definitely known, and suspicions, which may be unjust, need not to be stated. Information was received by the Indian bureau, from different sources, about the time hostilities were commenced, that a simultaneous attack was to be made upon the white settlements by all the tribes between the Mississippi river and the Rocky mountains. The State of Minnesota has suffered great injury from this Indian war. A large portion of her territory has been depopulated, and a severe loss has been sustained by the destruction of property. The people of that State manifest much anxiety for the removal of the tribes beyond the limits of the State as a guarantee against future hostilities. The Commissioner of Indian Affairs will furnish full details. I submit for your especial consideration whether our Indian system shall not be remodelled. Many wise and good men have impressed me with the belief that this can be profitably done.

I submit a statement of the proceedings of commissioners, which shows the progress that has been made in the enterprise of constructing the Pacific railroad. And this suggests the earliest completion of this road, and also the favorable action of Congress upon the projects now pending before them for enlarging the capacities of the great canals in New York and Illinois, as being of vital, and rapidly increasing importance to the whole nation, and especially to the vast interior region hereinafter to be noticed at some greater length. I purpose having prepared and laid before you at an early day some interesting and valuable statistical information upon this subject. The military and commercial importance of enlarging the Illinois and Michigan canal, and improving the Illinois river, is presented in the report of Colonel

5  After the Sioux raids in Minnesota described here, Colonel Henry H. Sibley had been ordered to lead the state's militia against the Indians; he took 1,500 Sioux prisoners. Following a trial before a military court, 307 were condemned to death. Before they could be hanged, Lincoln meticulously reviewed each case, and commuted the sentences of all but 39. Later in December, 37 were executed for murder and 1 for rape (the 39th won a last-minute reprieve) in what, despite Lincoln's propensity for clemency, became the largest mass execution in American history. For details of the Sioux uprising and Lincoln's role, see Hank H. Cox, *Lincoln and the Sioux Uprising of 1862* (Nashville, TN: Cumberland House, 2005); Duane Schultz, *Over the Earth I Come: The Great Sioux Uprising of 1862* (New York: St. Martin's Press, 1992); and Burlingame, *Abraham Lincoln*, 2:480–484. On Lincoln's relationship with Native Americans in general, see David A. Nichols, *Lincoln and the Indians: Civil War Policy and Politics* (Columbia: University of Missouri Press, 1978).

6   Lincoln had named as his first commissioner of agriculture a portly onetime Quaker farmer from Pennsylvania named Isaac Newton (1800–1867)—despite his name, "an ignorant, credulous old gentleman," complained Washington journalist Ben: Perley Poore. Yet Newton did hire scientists to advance agricultural research and, what is more, won the confidence of Mary Lincoln by encouraging her into the decidedly unscientific world of spiritualism. Ben: Perley Poore, *Perley's Reminiscences of Sixty Years in the National Metropolis*, 2 vols. (Boston: Hubbard Bros., 1886), 2:124; Boritt, *Lincoln and the Economics of the American Dream*, 216.

7   Ecclesiastes 1:4.

Webster to the Secretary of War, and now transmitted to Congress. I respectfully ask attention to it.

To carry out the provisions of the act of Congress of the 15th of May last, I have caused the Department of Agriculture of the United States to be organized.

The Commissioner[6] informs me that within the period of a few months this department has established an extensive system of correspondence and exchanges, both at home and abroad, which promises to effect highly beneficial results in the development of a correct knowledge of recent improvements in agriculture, in the introduction of new products, and in the collection of the agricultural statistics of the different States.

. . .

On the twenty-second day of September last a proclamation was issued by the Executive, a copy of which is herewith submitted.

In accordance with the purpose expressed in the second paragraph of that paper, I now respectfully recall your attention to what may be called "compensated emancipation."

A nation may be said to consist of its territory, its people, and its laws. The territory is the only part which is of certain durability. "One generation passeth away, and another generation cometh, but the earth abideth forever."[7] It is of the first importance to duly consider, and estimate, this everenduring part. That portion of the earth's surface which is owned and inhabited by the people of the United States, is well adapted to be the home of one national family; and it is not well adapted for two, or more. Its vast extent, and its variety of climate and productions, are of advantage, in this age, for one people, whatever they might have been in former ages. Steam, telegraphs, and intelligence, have brought these, to be an advantageous combination, for one united people.

In the inaugural address I briefly pointed out the total inadequacy of disunion, as a remedy for the differences between the people of the two sections. I did so in language which I cannot improve, and which, therefore, I beg to repeat:

"One section of our country believes slavery is *right,* and ought to be extended, while the other believes it is *wrong,* and ought not to be extended. This is the only substantial dispute. The fugitive slave clause of the Constitution, and the law for the suppression of the foreign slave trade, are each as well enforced, perhaps, as any law can ever be in a community where the moral sense of the people imperfectly supports the law itself. The great body of the people abide by the dry legal obligation in both cases, and a few break over in each. This, I think, cannot be perfectly cured; and it would be worse in both cases *after* the separation of the sections, than before. The foreign slave trade, now imperfectly suppressed, would be ultimately revived without restriction in one section; while fugitive slaves, now only partially surrendered, would not be surrendered at all by the other.

"Physically speaking, we cannot separate. We cannot remove our respective sections from each other, nor build an impassable wall between them. A husband and wife may be divorced, and go out of the presence, and beyond the reach of each other; but the different parts of our country cannot do this. They cannot but remain face to face; and intercourse, either amicable or hostile, must continue between them. Is it possible, then, to make that intercourse more advantageous, or more satisfactory, *after* separation than *before?* Can aliens make treaties, easier than friends can make laws? Can treaties be more faithfully enforced between aliens, than laws can among friends? Suppose you go to war, you cannot fight always; and when, after much loss on both sides, and no gain on either, you cease fighting, the identical old questions, as to terms of intercourse, are again upon you."

There is no line, straight or crooked, suitable for a national boundary, upon which to divide. Trace through, from east to west, upon the line between the free and slave country, and we shall find a little more than one-third of its length are rivers, easy to be crossed, and populated, or soon to be populated, thickly upon both sides; while nearly all its remaining length, are merely surveyor's lines, over which people may walk back and forth without any consciousness of their presence. No part of this line can be made any more difficult to pass, by writing it down on paper, or parchment, as a national boundary. The fact of separation, if it comes, gives up, on the part of the seceding section, the fugitive slave clause, along with all other constitutional obligations upon the section seceded from, while I should expect no treaty stipulation would ever be made to take its place.

But there is another difficulty. The great interior region, bounded east by the Alleghanies [*sic*], north by the British dominions, west by the Rocky mountains, and south by the line along which the culture of corn and cotton meets, and which includes part of Virginia, part of Tennessee, all of Kentucky, Ohio, Indiana, Michigan, Wisconsin, Illinois, Missouri, Kansas,

Iowa, Minnesota and the Territories of Dakota, Nebraska, and part of Colorado, already has above ten millions of people, and will have fifty millions within fifty years, if not prevented by any political folly or mistake. It contains more than one-third of the country owned by the United States—certainly more than one million of square miles. Once half as populous as Massachusetts already is, it would have more than seventy-five millions of people. A glance at the map shows that, territorially speaking, it is the great body of the republic. The other parts are but marginal borders to it, the magnificent region sloping west from the rocky mountains to the Pacific, being the deepest, and also the richest, in undeveloped resources. In the production of provisions, grains, grasses, and all which proceed from them, this great interior region is naturally one of the most important in the world. Ascertain from the statistics the small proportion of the region which has, as yet, been brought into cultivation, and also the large and rapidly increasing amount of its products, and we shall be overwhelmed with the magnitude of the prospect presented. An[d] yet this region has no sea-coast, touches no ocean anywhere. As part of one nation, its people now find, and may forever find, their way to Europe by New York, to South America and Africa by New Orleans, and to Asia by San Francisco. But separate our common country into two nations, as designed by the present rebellion, and every man of this great interior region is thereby cut off from some one or more of these outlets, not, perhaps, by a physical barrier, but by embarrassing and onerous trade regulations.

And this is true, *wherever* a dividing, or boundary line, may be fixed. Place it between the now free and slave country, or place it south of Kentucky, or north of Ohio, and still the truth remains, that none south of it, can trade to any port or place north of it, and none north of it, can trade to any port or place south of it, except upon terms dictated by a government foreign to them. These outlets, east, west, and south, are indispensable to the well-being of the people inhabiting, and to inhabit, this vast interior region. *Which* of the three may be the best, is no proper question. All, are better than either, and all, of right, belong to that people, and to their successors forever. True to themselves, they will not ask *where* a line of separation shall be, but will vow, rather, that there shall be no such line. Nor are the marginal regions less interested in these communications to, and through them, to the great outside world. They too, and each of them, must have access to this Egypt of the West, without paying toll at the crossing of any national boundary.

Our national strife springs not from our permanent part; not from the land we inhabit; not from our national homestead. There is no possible severing of this, but would multiply, and not mitigate, evils among us. In all its adaptations and aptitudes, it demands union, and abhors separation. In fact, it would, ere long, force reunion, however much of blood and treasure the separation might have cost.

Our strife pertains to ourselves—to the passing generations of men; and it can, without convulsion, be hushed forever with the passing of one generation.

In this view, I recommend the adoption of the following resolution and articles amendatory to the Constitution of the United States:[8]

"*Resolved by the Senate and House of Representatives of the United States of America in Congress assembled,* (two thirds of both houses concurring,) That the following articles be proposed to the legislatures (or conventions) of the several States as amendments to the Constitution of the United States, all or any of which articles when ratified by three-fourths of the said legislatures (or conventions) to be valid as part or parts of the said Constitution, viz:

"Article _____.

"Every State, wherein slavery now exists, which shall abolish the same therein, at any time, or times, before the first day of January, in the year of our Lord one thousand and nine hundred,[9] shall receive compensation from the United States as follows, to wit:

"The President of the United States shall deliver to every such State, bonds of the United States, bearing interest at the rate of _____ per cent, per annum, to an amount equal to the aggregate sum of[10] _____ for each slave shown to have been therein, by the eig[h]th census of the United States, said bonds to be delivered to such State by instalments, or in one parcel, at the completion of the abolishment, accordingly as the same shall have been gradual, or at one time, within such State; and interest shall begin to run upon any such bond, only from the proper time of its delivery as aforesaid. Any State having received bonds as aforesaid, and afterwards reintroducing or tolerating slavery therein, shall refund to the United States the bonds so received, or the value thereof, and all interest paid thereon.

"Article _____.

"All slaves who shall have enjoyed actual freedom by the chances of the war, at any time before the end of the rebellion, shall be forever free; but all owners of such, who shall not have been disloyal, shall be compensated for them, at the same rates as is provided for States adopting abolishment of slavery, but in such way, that no slave shall be twice accounted for.

"Article _____.

8  Ironically, Lincoln's proposals for colonization and gradual, compensated emancipation might have become the Thirteenth Amendment to the Constitution had he convinced the House and Senate to pass these resolutions and send them to the states for ratification.

9  This passage marked the only time in his entire canon of writings that Lincoln conceded that American slavery might exist in some form until 1900.

10  Lincoln left the amount blank.

"Congress may appropriate money, and otherwise provide, for colonizing free colored persons, with their own consent, at any place or places
without the United States."

I beg indulgence to discuss these proposed articles at some length. Without slavery the rebellion could never have existed; without slavery it could
not continue.

Among the friends of the Union there is great diversity, of sentiment,
and of policy, in regard to slavery, and the African race amongst us. Some
would perpetuate slavery; some would abolish it suddenly, and without
compensation; some would abolish it gradually, and with compensation;
some would remove the freed people from us, and some would retain them
with us; and there are yet other minor diversities. Because of these diversities, we waste much strength in struggles among ourselves. By mutual concession we should harmonize, and act together. This would be compromise;
but it would be compromise among the friends, and not with the enemies
of the Union. These articles are intended to embody a plan of such mutual
concessions. If the plan shall be adopted, it is assumed that emancipation
will follow, at least, in several of the States.

As to the first article, the main points are: first, the emancipation; secondly, the length of time for consummating it—thirty-seven years; and
thirdly, the compensation.

The emancipation will be unsatisfactory to the advocates of perpetual
slavery; but the length of time should greatly mitigate their dissatisfaction.
The time spares both races from the evils of sudden derangement—in fact,
from the necessity of any derangement—while most of those whose habitual course of thought will be disturbed by the measure will have passed
away before its consummation. They will never see it. Another class will hail
the prospect of emancipation, but will deprecate the length of time. They
will feel that it gives too little to the now living slaves. But it really gives
them much. It saves them from the vagrant destitution which must largely
attend immediate emancipation in localities where their numbers are very
great; and it gives the inspiring assurance that their posterity shall be free
forever. The plan leaves to each State, choosing to act under it, to abolish
slavery now, or at the end of the century, or at any intermediate time, or by
degrees, extending over the whole or any part of the period; and it obliges
no two states to proceed alike. It also provides for compensation, and generally the mode of making it. This, it would seem, must further mitigate the
dissatisfaction of those who favor perpetual slavery, and especially of those
who are to receive the compensation. Doubtless some of those who are to

pay, and not to receive will object. Yet the measure is both just and economical. In a certain sense the liberation of slaves is the destruction of property—property acquired by descent, or by purchase, the same as any other property. It is no less true for having been often said, that the people of the south are not more responsible for the original introduction of this property, than are the people of the north; and when it is remembered how unhesitatingly we all use cotton and sugar, and share the profits of dealing in them, it may not be quite safe to say, that the south has been more responsible than the north for its continuance. If then, for a common object, this property is to be sacrificed is it not just that it be done at a common charge?

And if, with less money, or money more easily paid, we can preserve the benefits of the Union by this means, than we can by the war alone, is it not also economical to do it? Let us consider it then. Let us ascertain the sum we have expended in the war since compensated emancipation was proposed last March, and consider whether, if that measure had been promptly accepted, by even some of the slave States, the same sum would not have done more to close the war, than has been otherwise done. If so the measure would save money, and, in that view, would be a prudent and economical measure. Certainly it is not so easy to pay *something* as it is to pay *nothing;* but it is easier to pay a *large* sum than it is to pay a larger one. And it is easier to pay any sum *when* we are able, than it is to pay it *before* we are able. The war requires large sums, and requires them at once. The aggregate sum necessary for compensated emancipation, of course, would be large. But it would require no ready cash; nor the bonds even, any faster than the emancipation progresses. This might not, and probably would not, close before the end of the thirty-seven years. At that time we shall probably have a hundred millions of people to share the burden, instead of thirty one millions, as now. And not only so, but the increase of our population may be expected to continue for a long time after that period, as rapidly as before; because our territory will not have become full. I do not state this inconsiderately. At the same ratio of increase which we have maintained, on an average, from our first national census, in 1790, until that of 1860, we should, in 1900, have a population of 103,208,415. And why may we not continue that ratio far beyond that period? Our abundant room—our broad national homestead—is our ample resource. Were our territory as limited as are the British Isles, very certainly our population could not expand as stated. Instead of receiving the foreign born, as now, we should be compelled to send part of the native born away. But such is not our condition. We have two millions nine hundred and sixty-three thousand square miles. Europe has

11   In a section of his annual address deleted by the editors of this volume, Lincoln had estimated that the population of the United States would reach 217,186,000 by 1930. In fact, the 1930 U.S. census would count only 122 million Americans. Lincoln had overestimated—perhaps failing to take into account the population loss (in his own and future generations) that would result from war.

three millions and eight hundred thousand, with a population averaging seventy-three and one-third persons to the square mile. Why may not our country, at some time, average as many? Is it less fertile? Has it more waste surface, by mountains, rivers, lakes, deserts, or other causes? Is it inferior to Europe in any natural advantage? If, then, we are, at some time, to be as populous as Europe, how soon? As to when this *may* be, we can judge by the past and the present; as to when it *will* be, if ever, depends much on whether we maintain the Union. Several of our States are already above the average of Europe—seventy three and a third to the square mile. Massachusetts has 157; Rhode Island, 133; Connecticut, 99; New York and New Jersey, each, 80; also two other great States, Pennsylvania and Ohio, are not far below, the former having 63, and the latter 59. The States already above the European average, except New York, have increased in as rapid a ratio, since passing that point, as ever before; while no one of them is equal to some other parts of our country, in natural capacity for sustaining a dense population.

. . .

And we *will* reach this, too, if we do not ourselves relinquish the chance, by the folly and evils of disunion, or by long and exhausting war springing from the only great element of national discord among us.[11] While it cannot be foreseen exactly how much one huge example of secession, breeding lesser ones indefinitely, would retard population, civilization, and prosperity, no one can doubt that the extent of it would be very great and injurious.

The proposed emancipation would shorten the war, perpetuate peace, insure this increase of population, and proportionately the wealth of the country. With these, we should pay all the emancipation would cost, together with our other debt, easier than we should pay our other debt, without it. If we had allowed our old national debt to run at six per cent. per annum, simple interest, from the end of our revolutionary struggle until to day, without paying anything on either principal or interest, each man of us would owe less upon that debt now, than each man owed upon it then; and this because our increase of men, through the whole period, has been greater than six per cent.; has run faster than the interest upon the debt. Thus, time alone relieves a debtor nation, so long as its population increases faster than unpaid interest accumulates on its debt.

This fact would be no excuse for delaying payment of what is justly due; but it shows the great importance of time in this connexion—the great advantage of a policy by which we shall not have to pay until we number a hundred millions, what, by a different policy, we would have to pay now, when we number but thirty one millions. In a word, it shows that a dollar will be much harder to pay for the war, than will be a dollar for emancipation on the proposed plan. And then the latter will cost no blood, no precious life. It will be a saving of both.

As to the second article, I think it would be impracticable to return to bondage the class of persons therein contemplated. Some of them, doubtless, in the property sense, belong to loyal owners; and hence, provision is made in this article for compensating such.

The third article relates to the future of the freed people. It does not oblige, but merely authorizes, Congress to aid in colonizing such as may consent. This ought not to be regarded as objectionable, on the one hand, or on the other, in so much as it comes to nothing, unless by the mutual consent of the people to be deported, and the American voters, through their representatives in Congress.

I cannot make it better known than it already is, that I strongly favor colonization. And yet I wish to say there is an objection urged against free colored persons remaining in the country, which is largely imaginary, if not sometimes malicious.

It is insisted that their presence would injure, and displace white labor and white laborers. If there ever could be a proper time for mere catch arguments, that time surely is not now. In times like the present, men should utter nothing for which they would not willingly be responsible through time and in eternity. Is it true, then, that colored people can displace any more white labor, by being free, than by remaining slaves? If they stay in their old places, they jostle no white laborers; if they leave their old places, they leave them open to white laborers. Logically, there is neither more nor less of it. Emancipation, even without deportation, would probably enhance the wages of white labor, and, very surely, would not reduce them. Thus, the customary amount of labor would still have to be performed; the freed people would surely not do more than their old proportion of it, and very probably, for a time, would do less, leaving an increased part to white laborers, bringing their labor into greater demand, and, consequently, enhancing the wages of it. With deportation, even to a limited extent, enhanced wages to white labor is mathematically certain. Labor is like any other commodity in the market—increase the demand for it, and you increase the price of it. Reduce the supply of black labor, by colonizing the black laborer out of the country, and, by precisely so much, you increase the demand for, and wages of, white labor.

But it is dreaded that the freed people will swarm forth, and cover the whole land? Are they not already in the land? Will liberation make them any more numerous? Equally distributed among the whites of the whole country, and there would be but one colored to seven whites. Could the one, in any way, greatly disturb the seven? There are many communities now, having more than one free colored person, to seven whites; and this, without any apparent consciousness of evil from it. The District of Columbia, and the States of Maryland and Delaware, are all in this condition. The District has more than one free colored to six whites; and yet, in its frequent petitions to Congress, I believe it has never presented the presence of free colored persons as one of its grievances. But why should emancipation south, send the free people north? People, of any color, seldom run, unless there be something to run from. *Heretofore* colored people, to some extent, have fled north from bondage; and *now,* perhaps, from both bondage and destitution. But if gradual emancipation and deportation be adopted, they will have neither to flee from. Their old masters will give them wages at least until new laborers can be procured; and the freed men, in turn, will gladly give their labor for the wages, till new homes can be found for them, in congenial climes, and with people of their own blood and race. This proposition can be trusted on the mutual interests involved. And, in any event, cannot the north decide for itself, whether to receive them?

Again, as practice proves more than theory, in any case, has there been any irruption of colored people northward, because of the abolishment of slavery in this District last spring?

What I have said of the proportion of free colored persons to the whites, in the District, is from the census of 1860, having no reference to persons called contrabands, nor to those made free by the act of Congress abolishing slavery here.

The plan consisting of these articles is recommended, not but that a restoration of the national authority would be accepted without its adoption.

Nor will the war, nor proceedings under the proclamation of September 22, 1862, be stayed because of the *recommendation* of this plan. Its timely *adoption,* I doubt not, would bring restoration and thereby stay both.

And, notwithstanding this plan, the recommendation that Congress provide by law for compensating any State which may adopt emancipation, before this plan shall have been acted upon, is hereby earnestly renewed. Such would be only an advance part of the plan, and the same arguments apply to both.

This plan is recommended as a means, not in exclusion of, but additional to, all others for restoring and preserving the national authority throughout the Union. The subject is presented exclusively in its economical aspect. The plan would, I am confident, secure peace more speedily, and maintain it more permanently, than can be done by force alone; while all it would cost, considering amounts, and manner of payment, and times of payment, would be easier paid than will be the additional cost of the war, if we rely solely upon force. It is much—very much—that it would cost no blood at all.

The plan is proposed as permanent constitutional law. It cannot become such without the concurrence of, first, two-thirds of Congress, and, afterwards, three-fourths of the States.[12] The requisite three-fourths of the States will necessarily include seven of the Slave states. Their concurrence, if obtained, will give assurance of their severally adopting emancipation, at no very distant day, upon the new constitutional terms. This assurance would end the struggle now, and save the Union forever.

I do not forget the gravity which should characterize a paper addressed to the Congress of the nation by the Chief Magistrate of the nation. Nor do I forget that some of you are my seniors, nor that many of you have more experience than I, in the conduct of public affairs. Yet I trust that in view of the great responsibility resting upon me, you will perceive no want of respect to yourselves, in any undue earnestness I may seem to display.

Is it doubted, then, that the plan I propose, if adopted, would shorten the war, and thus lessen its expenditure of money and of blood? Is it doubted that it would restore the national authority and national prosperity, and perpetuate both indefinitely? Is it doubted that we here—Congress and Executive—can secure its adoption? Will not the good people respond to a united, and earnest appeal from us? Can we, can they, by any other means, so certainly, or so speedily, assure these vital objects? We can succeed only by concert. It is not 'can *any* of us *imagine* better?' but 'can we *all* do better?' Object whatsoever is possible, still the question recurs "can we do better?" The dogmas of the quiet past, are inadequate to the stormy present. The occasion is piled high with difficulty, and we must rise with the occasion. As our case is new, so we must think anew, and act anew. We must disenthrall ourselves, and then we shall save our country.

Fellow-citizens, *we* cannot escape history. We of this Congress and this administration, will be remembered in spite of ourselves. No personal significance, or insignificance, can spare one or another of us. The fiery trial through which we pass, will light us down, in honor or dishonor, to the latest generation. We *say* we are for the Union. The world will not forget that

12  U.S. Constitution, Article V.

**13**  The response of the press to Lincoln's second annual address generally followed party lines. Republican newspapers applauded the message. Horace Greeley's *New York Tribune* praised the message's eloquent final passage as containing "sentiments so noble, so forceful, so profoundly true," and noted their appearance was "an immense fact, significant, fruitful, enduring." The pro-administration *New York Times* hailed the message as "concise, clear, and perspicuous." The Democratic press, on the other hand, criticized Lincoln's message. The *Cincinnati Enquirer,* for example, dismissed it as "poor in manner, poorer still in argument," and criticized it for "avoiding the topics for the discussion of which the people looked with the utmost anxiety, and giving prominence to ideas of which they are tired and disgusted." Radicals and African Americans were not pleased with Lincoln's remarks concerning gradual, compensated emancipation and colonization. Regarding the former, the *New York Post* declared that "to free men gradually, or by installments, is like cutting off a dog's tail by inches, to get him used to the pain." The *Weekly Anglo African* proclaimed "As free colored men, we thank Mr. Lincoln for nothing . . . when he asks Congress to provide the expatriation of such of us as may be desirous to leave the country. We are decidedly of the opinion that we will stay." Quotes from the *New York Tribune, Cincinnati Enquirer,* and *New York Post* are cited in Burlingame, *Abraham Lincoln,* 2:440–442. Quotes from the *New York Times* and *Weekly Anglo African* are cited in Holzer, *Lincoln and the Power of the Press,* 413–414.

we say this. We know how to save the Union. The world knows we do know how to save it. We—even *we here*—hold the power, and bear the responsibility. In *giving* freedom to the *slave,* we *assure* freedom to the *free*—honorable alike in what we give, and what we preserve. We shall nobly save, or meanly lose, the last best, hope of earth. Other means may succeed; this could not fail. The way is plain, peaceful, generous, just—a way which, if followed, the world will forever applaud, and God must forever bless.[13]

December 1, 1862.                                        ABRAHAM LINCOLN

# Final Emancipation Proclamation

<hr>

## January 1, 1863

**By the President of the United States of America:**
**A Proclamation.**

Whereas, on the twentysecond day of September, in the year of our Lord one thousand eight hundred and sixty two, a proclamation was issued by the President of the United States,[1] containing, among other things, the following, towit:

"That on the first day of January, in the year of our Lord one thousand eight hundred and sixty-three, all persons held as slaves within any State or designated part of a State, the people whereof shall then be in rebellion against the United States, shall be then, thenceforward, and forever free; and the Executive Government of the United States, including the military and naval authority thereof, will recognize and maintain the freedom of such persons, and will do no act or acts to repress such persons, or any of them, in any efforts they may make for their actual freedom.

"That the Executive will, on the first day of January aforesaid, by proclamation, designate the States and parts of States, if any, in which the people thereof, respectively, shall then be in rebellion against the United States; and the fact that any State, or the people thereof, shall on that day be, in good faith, represented in the Congress of the United States by members chosen thereto at elections wherein a majority of the qualified voters of such State shall have participated, shall, in the absence of strong countervailing testimony, be deemed conclusive evidence that such State, and the people thereof, are not then in rebellion against the United States."

Now, therefore I, Abraham Lincoln, President of the United States, by virtue of the power in me vested as Commander-in-Chief, of the Army and Navy of the United States in time of actual armed rebellion against author-

*Some Americans doubted that Lincoln would summon the courage to make good on his September 22 promise to free slaves in the rebellious states on January 1—especially after the Union army suffered a disastrous defeat at the Battle of Fredericksburg in December, a few weeks before emancipation was to take effect. Anxiety only increased when the president delayed his formal approval of the proclamation for hours on New Year's Day, until an error-free engrossed copy could be created for his signature. Although written in numbingly legalistic language—it was designed primarily to withstand legal challenges—the proclamation eventually inspired decorative reproductions meant for display on parlor walls.*

1    Although African Americans and abolitionists began gathering at churches throughout the North at midnight on January 1, Lincoln did not sign the document at the first stroke of the new year as many had apparently expected or hoped. In fact, when he woke up later that morning, the president declined to sign the official copy of the proclamation prepared by a government scribe because, as he discovered in proofreading, it contained an error in the template paragraph near the end. Lincoln insisted that the final document be perfect, and he ordered that the scroll be entirely recopied. Meanwhile, he hosted the traditional holiday reception in the East Room, spending hours greeting both dignitaries and the general public. As thousands of black and white Americans anxiously awaited word from Washington that emancipation had become legal, Lincoln finally returned to his White House office sometime in the afternoon, where he carefully reread the second attempt at engrossing the official document. Only then did he approve it and sign the scroll. Allen C. Guelzo, *Lincoln's Emancipation Proclamation: The End of Slavery in America* (New York: Simon & Schuster, 2004), 181–183.

Max Rosenthal, *Proclamation of Emancipation*. Broadside (Philadelphia: L. Franklin Smith, 1865). This printed version portrays Lincoln as the central figure in the abolitionist movement. Vignettes adorn each side of the print, contrasting the evils of slavery with the blessings of liberty.

J. W. Watts, *Reading the Emancipation Proclamation.* Engraving (Hartford, CT: S. A. Peters and Co., ca. 1864). This print depicts African Americans listening to a Union soldier read aloud Lincoln's historic executive order.

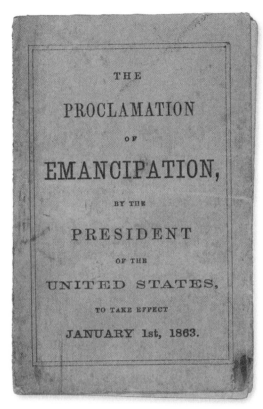

*The Proclamation of Emancipation, by the President of the United States, to Take Effect January 1st, 1863* (Boston: J. M. Forbes, 1863). Miniature reproduction of the Emancipation Proclamation.

ity and government of the United States, and as a fit and necessary war measure for suppressing said rebellion, do, on this first day of January, in the year of our Lord one thousand eight hundred and sixty three, and in accordance with my purpose so to do publicly proclaimed for the full period of one hundred days, from the day first above mentioned, order and designate as the States and parts of States wherein the people thereof respectively, are this day in rebellion against the United States, the following, towit:

Arkansas, Texas, Louisiana, (except the Parishes of St. Bernard, Plaquemines, Jefferson, St. Johns, St. Charles, St. James[,] Ascension, Assumption, Terrebonne, Lafourche, St. Mary, St. Martin, and Orleans, including the City of New-Orleans) Mississippi, Alabama, Florida, Georgia, South-Carolina, North-Carolina, and Virginia, (except the fortyeight counties designated as West Virginia, and also the counties of Berkley, Accomac,

2   Legislation authorizing black recruitment passed in March.

3   "Law and the sword can and will in the end abolish slavery," Frederick Douglass predicted. But he warned that "law and the sword cannot abolish the malignant slaveholding sentiment which has kept the slave system alive in this country during two centuries. . . . The slave having ceased to be the abject slave of a single master, his enemies will endeavor to make him the slave of society at large." *Douglass' Monthly,* January 1863.

4   When Lincoln picked up his pen to sign his name to the official document, according to an account of the period, he "held it a moment, and then removed his hand and dropped the pen. After a little hesitation he again took up the pen and went through the same movement as before. Mr. Lincoln then turned to Mr. Seward, and said:—'I have been shaking hands since nine o'clock this morning, and my right arm is almost paralyzed. If my name ever goes into history it will be for this act, and my whole soul is in it. If my hand trembles when I sign the Proclamation, all who examine the document will hereafter say, "He hesitated."' He then turned to the table, took up the pen again, and slowly wrote that 'Abraham Lincoln' with which the whole world is now familiar. He looked up, smiled, and said: 'That will do.'" Carpenter, *Inner Life of Abraham Lincoln,* 269–270.

Northampton, Elizabeth-City, York, Princess Ann, and Norfolk, including the cities of Norfolk & Portsmouth[)]; and which excepted parts are, for the present, left precisely as if this proclamation were not issued.

And by virtue of the power, and for the purpose aforesaid, I do order and declare that all persons held as slaves within said designated States, and parts of States, are, and henceforward shall be free; and that the Executive government of the United States, including the military and naval authorities thereof, will recognize and maintain the freedom of said persons.

And I hereby enjoin upon the people so declared to be free to abstain from all violence, unless in necessary self-defence; and I recommend to them that, in all cases when allowed, they labor faithfully for reasonable wages.

And I further declare and make known, that such persons of suitable condition, will be received into the armed service of the United States to garrison forts, positions, stations, and other places, and to man vessels of all sorts in said service.[2]

And upon this act, sincerely believed to be an act of justice, warranted by the Constitution, upon military necessity, I invoke the considerate judgment of mankind, and the gracious favor of Almighty God.[3]

In witness whereof, I have hereunto set my hand and caused the seal of the United States to be affixed.

Done at the City of Washington, this first day of January, in the year of our Lord one thousand eight hundred and sixty three, and of the Independence of the United States of America the eighty-seventh.

ABRAHAM LINCOLN[4]
By the President
WILLIAM H. SEWARD, Secretary of State.

# Message to the Workingmen of Manchester, England

## January 19, 1863

Executive Mansion, Washington,
To the workingmen of Manchester: January 19, 1863.

I have the honor to acknowledge the receipt of the address and resolutions which you sent to me on the eve of the new year.[1]

When I came, on the fourth day of March, 1861, through a free and constitutional election, to preside in the government of the United States, the country was found at the verge of civil war. Whatever might have been the cause, or whosoever the fault, one duty paramount to all others was before me, namely, to maintain and preserve at once the Constitution and the integrity of the federal republic. A conscientious purpose to perform this duty is a key to all the measures of administration which have been, and to all which will hereafter be pursued. Under our form of government, and my official oath, I could not depart from this purpose if I would. It is not always in the power of governments to enlarge or restrict the scope of moral results which follow the policies that they may deem it necessary for the public safety, from time to time, to adopt.

I have understood well that the duty of self-preservation rests solely with the American people. But I have at the same time been aware that favor or disfavor of foreign nations might have a material influence in enlarging and prolonging the struggle with disloyal men in which the country is engaged. A fair examination of history has seemed to authorize a belief that the past action and influences of the United States were generally regarded as having been beneficient towards mankind. I have therefore reckoned upon the forbearance of nations. Circumstances, to some of which you kindly allude, induced me especially to expect that if justice and good faith should be practiced by the United States, they would encounter no hostile influence on the part of Great Britain. It is now a pleasant duty to acknowledge the

*It is possible that Great Britain would have extended diplomatic recognition to the Confederacy had it not been for the active opposition of the country's antislavery workingmen. Remarkably, these groups of laborers continued to support the Union even though some were put out of work by the Union blockade's disruption of England's cotton imports. In the end Britain maintained its neutrality, and on the eve of emancipation, Manchester workingmen met to "joyfully honor" Lincoln for believing, with America's founders, that "All men are created free and equal." Lincoln sent this heartfelt reply via Charles Francis Adams, American minister to England.*

1    On January 2, 1863, Charles Francis Adams (1807–1886), U.S. minister to England, forwarded to Secretary of State Seward a letter from Manchester's mayor addressed to President Lincoln, expressing the sentiments of the "working men and others" of that city: "We rejoice in your greatness. . . . We honor your free States, as a singular, happy abode for the working millions. . . . One thing alone has, in the past, lessened our sympathy with your country and our confidence in it; we mean the ascendancy of politicians who not merely maintained negro slavery, but desired to extend and root it more firmly. Since we have discerned, however, that the victory of the free north . . . will strike off the fetters of the slave, you have attracted our warm and earnest sympathy. We joyfully honor you, as the President, and the Congress with you, for the many decisive steps towards practically exemplifying your belief in the words of your great founders, 'All men are created free and equal.'" *CW*, 6:65n1. At their New Year's Eve meeting, one speaker predicted that "the name of Abraham Lincoln" would be "honored and revered by posterity." *New York Times*, January 15, 1863.

PUNCH, OR THE LONDON CHARIVARI.—November 14, 1863.

NEUTRALITY.

Mrs. North. "HOW ABOUT THE *ALABAMA*, YOU WICKED OLD MAN?"
Mrs. South. "WHERE'S MY RAMS? TAKE BACK YOUR PRECIOUS CONSULS—THERE!!!"

John Tenniel, "Neutrality," Engraving published in *Punch* (London, November 14, 1863). John Bull, a symbol of Great Britain, is surrounded by Abraham Lincoln and Jefferson Davis, dressed as women, in a cartoon satirizing Union and Confederate relations with England.

demonstration you have given of your desire that a spirit of peace and amity towards this country may prevail in the councils of your Queen, who is respected and esteemed in your own country only more than she is by the kindred nation which has its home on this side of the Atlantic.

I know and deeply deplore the sufferings which the workingmen at Manchester and in all Europe are called to endure in this crisis. It has been often and studiously represented that the attempt to overthrow this government, which was built upon the foundation of human rights, and to substitute for it one which should rest exclusively on the basis of human slavery, was likely to obtain the favor of Europe. Through the actions of our disloyal citizens the workingmen of Europe have been subjected to a severe trial, for the purpose of forcing their sanction to that attempt. Under these circumstances, I cannot but regard your decisive utterance upon the question as an instance of sublime Christian heroism which has not been surpassed in any age or in any country. It is, indeed, an energetic and reinspiring assurance of the inherent power of truth and of the ultimate and universal triumph of justice, humanity, and freedom. I do not doubt that the sentiments you have expressed will be sustained by your great nation, and, on the other hand, I have no hesitation in assuring you that they will excite admiration, esteem, and the most reciprocal feelings of friendship among the American people. I hail this interchange of sentiment, therefore, as an augury that, whatever else may happen, whatever misfortune may befall your country or my own, the peace and friendship which now exist between the two nations will be, as it shall be my desire to make them, perpetual.

ABRAHAM LINCOLN.

# Letter to General Joseph Hooker

## January 26, 1863

*Exasperated anew by General McClellan's seemingly incurable reluctance to fight, Lincoln had replaced him with General Ambrose Burnside, who soon led Union forces to disastrous defeat at the Battle of Fredericksburg in December 1862. Lincoln's next choice to command the Army of the Potomac was the dashing, supremely confident "Fighting Joe" Hooker, but only one day after appointing him, Lincoln sent this cautionary letter, warning him of the dangers of hubris. "It is a beautiful letter," Hooker nevertheless insisted, "and although I think he was harder on me than I deserved, I will say that I love the man who wrote it." Two months later, Hooker mismanaged the Army of the Potomac into yet another devastating loss at Chancellorsville.*

1 Massachusetts-born General Joseph Hooker (1814–1879) graduated from West Point in 1837. Hooker acquitted himself well in the early years of the Civil War, earning distinction even at Union defeats like the Second Battle of Bull Run. He won the nickname "Fighting Joe" when he fell from a wounded horse into the mud at the 1862 Battle of Williamsburg, and bravely continued fighting. Lincoln admired his aggressiveness, and worried only that Hooker might display too *much* bravado and prove reckless. Hooker remained in the army until 1868, when he suffered a stroke. Walter H. Herbert, *Fighting Joe Hooker* (Indianapolis: Bobbs-Merrill, 1944).

2 Hooker turned apparent victory into ruinous defeat at the Battle of Chancellorsville in May 1863. Lincoln relieved the general and replaced him with George Gordon Meade (1815–1872) even as Confederate forces under Robert E. Lee marched toward Gettysburg.

Major General Hooker:[1]
General.

Executive Mansion,
Washington, January 26, 1863

I have placed you at the head of the Army of the Potomac. Of course I have done this upon what appear to me to be sufficient reasons. And yet I think it best for you to know that there are some things in regard to which, I am not quite satisfied with you. I believe you to be a brave and a skilful soldier, which, of course, I like. I also believe you do not mix politics with your profession, in which you are right. You have confidence in yourself, which is a valuable, if not an indispensable quality. You are ambitious, which, within reasonable bounds, does good rather than harm. But I think that during Gen. Burnside's command of the Army, you have taken counsel of your ambition, and thwarted him as much as you could, in which you did a great wrong to the country, and to a most meritorious and honorable brother officer. I have heard, in such way as to believe it, of your recently saying that both the Army and the Government needed a Dictator. Of course it was not *for* this, but in spite of it, that I have given you the command. Only those generals who gain successes, can set up dictators. What I now ask of you is military success, and I will risk the dictatorship. The government will support you to the utmost of it's [sic] ability, which is neither more nor less than it has done and will do for all commanders. I much fear that the spirit which you have aided to infuse into the Army, of criticising their Commander, and withholding confidence from him, will now turn upon you. I shall assist you as far as I can, to put it down. Neither you, nor Napoleon, if he were alive again, could get any good out of an army, while such a spirit prevails in it.

And now, beware of rashness. Beware of rashness, but with energy, and sleepless vigilance, go forward, and give us victories.[2]

Yours very truly A. LINCOLN

General Joseph Hooker. Photograph by Mathew Brady (ca. 1862).

# Remarks to a Delegation of Indians Visiting the White House

## March 27, 1863

*Lincoln's attitude toward Native Americans was understandably complicated. His grandfather, also named Abraham Lincoln, had been killed by Indians. Years later, the future president joined many of his New Salem, Illinois, friends to fight against the Sauk tribe in the Black Hawk War. When Winfield Scott ran for president in 1852, his fellow Whig Lincoln, in a speech in Peoria on September 17, hailed the general's previous efforts to remove the Cherokee people "from their homes to the west of the Mississippi in such manner as to gain the applause of the great and good of the land" (CW, 2:159). Yet as president, Lincoln intervened to prevent an unwarranted mass execution in Minnesota by reducing the number to be hanged from 303 to 38. And when a delegation of tribal leaders visited the White House five months later, Lincoln formally received them in the East Room. There he shook each chief's hand, pledged to honor prevailing treaties, and offered this charming if somewhat condescending appeal, suggesting that they assure their future survival by turning from hunting to agriculture.*

1    The tribal chiefs present for this ceremony included leaders of the Cheyenne, Kiowa, Arapahoe, Comanche, Apache, and Caddo tribes. *CW,* 6:152n1.

2    The descriptive comments are from the report published in the *Washington Daily Chronicle* on March 28. The story added: "These Indians are fine-looking men. They have all the hard and cruel lines in their faces which we might expect in savages; but they are evidently men of intelligence, and force of character. They were both dignified and cordial in their manner, and listened to every thing with great interest."

3    Joseph Henry (1797–1878), secretary of the Smithsonian Institution.

You have all[1] spoken of the strange sights you see here, among your pale-faced brethren; the very great number of people that you see; the big wigwams; the difference between our people and your own. But you have seen but a very small part of the palefaced people. You may wonder when I tell you that there are people here in this wigwam, now looking at you, who have come from other countries a great deal farther off than you have come.

We pale-faced people think that this world is a great, round ball, and we have people here of the pale-faced family who have come almost from the other side of it to represent their nations here and conduct their friendly intercourse with us, as you now come from your part of the round ball.
*(Here a globe was introduced,[2] and the President, laying his hand upon it, said:)*

One of our learned men will now explain to you our notions about this great ball, and show you where you live.
*(Professor Henry[3] then gave the delegation a detailed and interesting explanation of the formation of the earth, showing how much of it was water and how much was land; and pointing out the countries with which we had intercourse. He also showed them the position of Washington and that of their own country, from which they had come. The President then said:)*

We have people now present from all parts of the globe—here, and here, and here. There is a great difference between this palefaced people and their red brethren, both as to numbers and the way in which they live. We know not whether your own situation is best for your race, but this is what has made the difference in our way of living.

The pale-faced people are numerous and prosperous because they cultivate the earth, produce bread, and depend upon the products of the earth rather than wild game for a subsistence.

LINCOLN RECEVANT LES INDIENS COMANCHES.

This is the chief reason of the difference; but there is another. Although we are now engaged in a great war between one another, we are not, as a race, so much disposed to fight and kill one another as our red brethren.

You have asked for my advice. I really am not capable of advising you whether, in the providence of the Great Spirit, who is the great Father of us all, it is best for you to maintain the habits and customs of your race, or adopt a new mode of life.

I can only say that I can see no way in which your race is to become as numerous and prosperous as the white race except by living as they do, by the cultivation of the earth.[4]

Ferdinand Delannoy, *Lincoln Recevant les Indiens Comanches.* Engraving (Paris, 1863). This print was issued in France, indicating that country's fascination with American Indians.

4   Although Commissioner of Agriculture Isaac Newton recommended the planting of "Indian corn," among other crops, he also counted white settlers' resistance to "the Indians" as one of the great accomplishments of American farmers and farming. Nichols, *Lincoln and the Indians,* 184–185.

5   Bombarded with reports of rampant corruption among federally appointed Indian Affairs agents, but committed first and foremost to the fight to save the Union, Lincoln reportedly told an Episcopal clergyman: "If I get through this war, and I live, *this Indian system shall be reformed.*" Ibid., 141.

It is the object of this Government to be on terms of peace with you, and with all our red brethren. We constantly endeavor to be so. We make treaties with you, and will try to observe them; and if our children should sometimes behave badly, and violate these treaties, it is against our wish.

You know it is not always possible for any father to have his children do precisely as he wishes them to do.

In regard to being sent back to your own country, we have an officer, the Commissioner of Indian Affairs, who will take charge of that matter, and make the necessary arrangements.[5]

*(The President's remarks were received with frequent marks of applause and approbation. "Ugh," "Aha" sounded along the line as the interpreter proceeded, and their countenances gave evident tokens of satisfaction.)*

# Letter to Erastus Corning and Albany, New York, Democrats

## [June 12] 1863

Executive Mansion
Hon. Erastus Corning[1] & others   Washington, [June 12] 1863.
Gentlemen

Your letter of May 19th. inclosing the resolutions of a public meeting held at Albany, N.Y. on the 16th. of the same month, was received several days ago.[2]

The resolutions, as I understand them, are resolvable into two propositions—first, the expression of a purpose to sustain the cause of the Union, to secure peace through victory, and to support the administration in every constitutional, and lawful measure to suppress the rebellion; and secondly, a declaration of censure upon the administration for supposed unconstitutional action such as the making of military arrests.

And, from the two propositions a third is deduced, which is, that the gentlemen composing the meeting are resolved on doing their part to maintain our common government and country, despite the folly or wickedness, as they may conceive, of any administration. This position is eminently patriotic, and as such, I thank the meeting, and congratulate the nation for it. My own purpose is the same; so that the meeting and myself have a common object, and can have no difference, except in the choice of means or measures, for effecting that object.

And here I ought to close this paper, and would close it, if there were no apprehension that more injurious consequences, than any merely personal to myself, might follow the censures systematically cast upon me for doing what, in my view of duty, I could not forbear. The resolutions promise to support me in every constitutional and lawful measure to suppress the rebellion; and I have not knowingly employed, nor shall knowingly employ, any other. But the meeting, by their resolutions, assert and argue, that cer-

*Following the military arrest of the "Copperhead" former Ohio congressman Clement L. Vallandigham for encouraging local men to resist the military draft, Democrats nationwide denounced the Lincoln administration for dictatorially imposing reins on legal dissent. One of the largest protest meetings took place in Albany, New York, chaired by Erastus Corning, who forwarded its manifesto of criticism to the White House. Lincoln weighed his response for weeks, ultimately composing this justly famous defense of temporary presidential power during national emergencies. As usual, Lincoln made sure the lengthy letter was published in the press. While Corning denounced the reply as "a gigantic and monstrous heresy" and a "plea for absolute power," Republicans praised the letter, which soon reappeared in pamphlet form and achieved even wider circulation. Not surprisingly, the antiwar* New York World *complained: "Was anything so extraordinary ever before uttered by the chief magistrate of a free country?"*

1   Erastus Corning (1794–1872), founder of an Albany, New York, political dynasty that dominated the city's politics until the 1980s, was serving his second stint in Congress at the time he chaired the May 1863 protest meeting of local, anti-administration Democrats. Later that year, Corning sought a U.S. Senate seat from New York but failed, then resigned from the House of Representatives. Although he continued his longtime interest in politics, Corning was always primarily a businessman—an iron manufacturer, banking executive, and railroad tycoon. It has been said that metal from his Troy ironworks was used to clad the iron-plated *U.S.S. Monitor.* Another long-standing myth—never definitively proved or disproved—is that after Lincoln delivered his Cooper Union speech in February 1860, Corning, then president of the New York Central Railroad, offered the Illinois politician the post of general counsel to the rail line at the generous annual salary of $10,000. Lincoln is said to have replied

jocularly: "Why, Mr. Corning, what could I do with $10,000 a year? It would ruin my family to have that much income. I don't believe that I had better consider it." Horace Merwin, quoted in John W. Starr, *Lincoln and the Railroads: A Biographical Study* (New York: Dodd, Mead & Co., 1927), 126–130. The story may be exaggerated, but it is safe to say that when Corning sent his resolutions to the White House three years later, he was no stranger to the president. "Corning, Erastus," Biographical Directory of the United States Congress, http://bioguide.congress.gov/scripts/biodisplay.pl?index=C000784 (accessed February 5, 2015).

2    The resolutions adopted by what Corning assured Lincoln was "one of the most respectable [meetings] as to numbers and character, and one of the most earnest in support of the Union, ever held in this city" included a "demand that the Administration shall be true to the Constitution; shall recognize and maintain the rights of States and the liberties of the citizen; shall everywhere, outside the lines of necessary military occupation and the scenes of insurrection, [and] exert all its powers to maintain the supremacy of civil over military law." Lincoln might not have thought such a benign expression of Democratic principles worthy of a long and careful reply, but the Albany resolutions went on: "in view of these principles, we denounce the recent assumption of a military commander to seize and try a citizen of Ohio, Clement L. Vallandigham, for no other reasons than words addressed to a public meeting, in criticism of the course of the Administration, and in condemnation of the military orders of that General. *Resolved,* That this assumption of power by a military tribunal, if successfully asserted, not only abrogates the right of the people to assemble and discuss the affairs of the Government, the liberty of speech and the press, the right of trial by jury, the law of evidence, and the priviledge [sic] of *habeas*

tain military arrests and proceedings following them for which I am ultimately responsible, are unconstitutional. I think they are not. The resolutions quote from the constitution, the definition of treason; and also the limiting safe-guards and guarrantees [sic] therein provided for the citizen, on trials for treason, and on his being held to answer for capital or otherwise infamous crimes, and, in criminal prossecutions [sic], his right to a speedy and public trial by an impartial jury. They proceed to resolve "That these safe-guards of the rights of the citizen against the pretentions of arbitrary power, were intended more *especially* for his protection in times of civil commotion." And, apparently, to demonstrate the proposition, the resolutions proceed "They were secured substantially to the English people, *after* years of protracted civil war, and were adopted into our constitution at the *close* of the revolution." Would not the demonstration have been better, if it could have been truly said that these safe-guards had been adopted, and applied *during* the civil wars and *during* our revolution, instead of *after* the one, and at the close of the other. I too am devotedly for them *after* civil war, and *before* civil war, and at all times "except when, in cases of Rebellion or Invasion, the public Safety may require" their suspension. The resolutions proceed to tell us that these safe-guards "have stood the test of seventysix years of trial, under our republican system, under circumstances which show that while they constitute the foundation of all free government, they are the elements of the enduring stability of the Republic." No one denies that they have so stood the test up to the beginning of the present rebellion if we except a certain matter[3] at New-Orleans hereafter to be mentioned; nor does any one question that they will stand the same test much longer after the rebellion closes. But these provisions of the constitution have no application to the case we have in hand, because the arrests complained of were not made for treason—that is, not for *the* treason defined in the constitution, and upon the conviction of which, the punishment is death—; nor yet were they made to hold persons to answer for any capital, or otherwise infamous crimes; nor were the proceedings following, in any constitutional or legal sense, "criminal prossecutions [sic]." The arrests were made on totally different grounds, and the proceedings following, accorded with the grounds of the arrests. Let us consider the real case with which we are dealing, and apply to it the parts of the constitution plainly made for such cases. [May I be indulged to submit a few general remarks upon the subject of arrests?][4]

Prior to my instalation [sic] here it had been inculcated that any State had a lawful right to secede from the national Union; and that it would be

Clement L. Vallandigham. Photograph
(ca. 1855–1865).

*corpus,* but it strikes a fatal blow at the supremacy
of law, and the authority of the State and Federal
Constitution." Erastus Corning et al. to Lincoln,
May 19, 1863, in Sidney David Brummer, *Political
History of New York State during the Period of the
Civil War* (New York: Columbia University Press,
1911), 310. The group's plainly stated "earnest
support of the Union" made clear that the protest
emanated from War Democrats, not Peace
Democrats—an important distinction, since
Lincoln relied on the former group to support the
administration in putting down the rebellion.

3   The word "occurrence" was substituted here for
the version published in the *New York Tribune* on
June 15, 1863.

4   Included in Lincoln's handwritten draft, but
apparently deleted for the published version. *CW,*
6:263n4.

expedient to exercise the right, whenever the devotees of the doctrine should
fail to elect a President to their own liking. I was elected contrary to their
liking; and accordingly, so far as it was legally possible, they had taken seven
states out of the Union, had seized many of the United States Forts, and had
fired upon the United States' Flag, all before I was inaugurated; and, of
course, before I had done any official act whatever. The rebellion, thus began soon ran into the present civil war; and, in certain respects, it began on
very unequal terms between the parties. The insurgents had been preparing
for it more than thirty years, while the government had taken no steps to
resist them. The former had carefully considered all the means which could
be turned to their account. It undoubtedly was a well pondered reliance
with them that in their own unrestricted effort to destroy Union, constitu-

The great American **WHAT IS IT?** chased by Copperheads.

E. W. T. Nichols, *The Great American WHAT IS IT? Chased by Copperheads.* Lithograph (Boston, 1863). An anti-Lincoln cartoon showing the president and his supporters menaced by giant antiwar "Copperheads."

5   "Raise a squabble" in Lincoln's draft. Ibid., n. 6.

6   A "howl" in the draft. Ibid., n. 7.

tion, and law, all together, the government would, in great degree, be restrained by the same constitution and law, from arresting their progress. Their sympathizers pervaded all departments of the government, and nearly all communities of the people. From this material, under cover of "Liberty of speech" "Liberty of the press" and "*Habeas corpus*" they hoped to keep on foot amongst us a most efficient corps of spies, informers, suppliers [*sic*], and aiders and abettors of their cause in a thousand ways. They knew that in times such as they were inaugurating, by the constitution itself, the "Habeas corpus" might be suspended; but they also knew they had friends who would make a question[5] as to *who* was to suspend it; meanwhile their spies and others might remain at large to help on their cause. Or if, as has happened, the executive should suspend the writ, without ruinous waste of time, instances of arresting innocent persons might occur, as are always likely to occur in such cases; and then a clamor[6] could be raised in regard to this, which might be, at least, of some service to the insurgent cause. It needed no very keen perception to discover this part of the enemies' programme, so soon as by open hostilities their machinery was fairly put in motion. Yet, thoroughly imbued with a reverence for the guarranteed [*sic*] rights of individuals, I was slow to adopt the strong measures, which by degrees I have been forced to regard as being within the exceptions of the constitution, and as indispensable to the public Safety. Nothing is better known to history than that courts of justice are utterly incompetent to such cases. Civil courts are organized chiefly for trials of individuals, or, at most, a few individuals acting in concert; and this in quiet times, and on charges of crimes well defined in the law. Even in times of peace, bands of horse-thieves and robbers frequently grow too numerous and powerful for the ordinary courts of justice. But what comparison, in numbers, have such bands ever borne to the insurgent sympathizers even in many of the loyal states? Again, a jury too frequently have [has] at least one member, more ready to hang the panel than to hang the traitor. And yet again, he who dissuades one man from volunteering, or induces one soldier to desert, weakens the Union cause as much as he who kills a union soldier in battle. Yet this dissuasion, or inducement, may be so conducted as to be no defined crime of which any civil court would take cognizance.

Ours is a case of Rebellion—so called by the resolutions before me—in fact, a clear, flagrant, and gigantic case of Rebellion; and the provision of the constitution that "The previlege [*sic*] of the writ of Habeas Corpus shall not be suspended, unless when in cases of Rebellion or Invasion, the public Safety may require it"[7] is *the* provision which specially applies to our present case. This provision plainly attests the understanding of those who made the constitution that ordinary courts of justice are inadequate to "cases of Rebellion"—attests their purpose that in such cases, men may be held in custody whom the courts acting on ordinary rules, would discharge. Habeas Corpus, does not discharge men who are proved to be guilty of defined crime; and its suspension is allowed by the constitution on purpose that, men may be arrested and held, who can not be proved to be guilty of defined crime, "when, in cases of Rebellion or Invasion the public Safety may require it." This is precisely our present case—a case of Rebellion, wherein the public Safety does require the suspension. Indeed, arrests by process of courts, and arrests in cases of rebellion, do not proceed altogether upon the same basis. The former is directed at the small per centage of ordinary and continuous perpetration of crime; while the latter is directed at sudden and extensive uprisings against the government, which, at most, will succeed or fail, in no great length of time. In the latter case, arrests are made, not so much for what has been done, as for what probably would be done. The latter is more for the preventive, and less for the vindictive, than the former. In such cases the purposes of men are much more easily understood, than

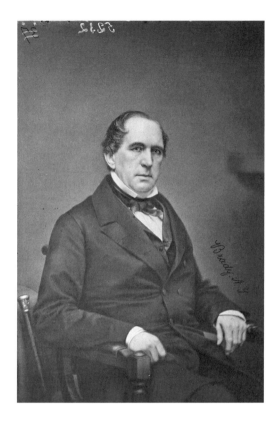

Erastus Corning. Photograph by Mathew Brady (New York, ca. 1855–1865).

7   U.S. Constitution, Article I, Section 9.

8  Among Lincoln's chronic misspellings—many of them in evidence within this document—was his inability to spell the surname of the man who had run against him for president in 1860 as the candidate for the Southern Democrats. After losing the election, Breckinridge, a Kentuckian who had served as vice president of the United States in the Buchanan administration, took a seat in the U.S. Senate but indicated sympathy for secession and was arrested and detained in September. Breckinridge escaped, went south, and became a brigadier general in the Confederate army. The Senate formally expelled him in December. After serving in the final months of the conflict as secretary of war for the Confederate States, the onetime presidential candidate spent three years in exile in Cuba. William C. Davis, *Breckinridge: Statesman, Soldier, Symbol* (Baton Rouge: Louisiana State University Press, 1974).

9  Joseph E. Johnston (1807–1891), John B. Magruder (1807–1871), and Simon B. Buckner (1823–1914) were Confederate generals. William B. Preston (1805–1862) drafted Virginia's ordinance of secession and served in the Confederate Congress. Franklin Buchanan (1800–1874) served as an admiral in the Confederate navy.

10  Former Ohio congressman Clement Laird Vallandigham (1820–1871), an antiwar Democrat representing the Dayton area, had in 1862 lost his bid for a third term in the House of Representatives. He was a leader of the Copperheads, a group of conservative Democrats who believed in a strict construction of the Constitution and opposed the war and various Lincoln administration war measures, including the Emancipation Proclamation. On April 30, 1863, Vallandigham delivered an intentionally provocative speech at a Mount Vernon, Ohio, antidraft rally in which he denounced the war and charged it was being waged "for the freedom of the blacks and the enslavement of the whites." Union troops under the command

in cases of ordinary crime. The man who stands by and says nothing, when the peril of his government is discussed, can not be misunderstood. If not hindered, he is sure to help the enemy. Much more, if he talks ambiguously—talks for his country with "buts" and "ifs" and "ands." Of how little value the constitutional provision I have quoted will be rendered, if arrests shall never be made until defined crimes shall have been committed, may be illustrated by a few notable examples. Gen. John C. Breckienridge,[8] Gen. Robert E. Lee, Gen. Joseph E. Johnston, Gen. John B. Magruder, Gen. William B. Preston, Gen. Simon B. Buckner, and Comodore [*sic*] Buchanan,[9] now occupying the very highest places in the rebel war service, were all within the power of the government since the rebellion began, and were nearly as well known to be traitors then as now. Unquestionably if we had seized and held them, the insurgent cause would be much weaker. But no one of them had then committed any crime defined in the law. Every one of them if arrested would have been discharged on Habeas Corpus, were the writ allowed to operate. In view of these and similar cases, I think the time not unlikely to come when I shall be blamed for having made too few arrests rather than too many.

By the third resolution the meeting indicate their opinion that military arrests may be constitutional in localities where rebellion actually exists; but that such arrests are unconstitutional in localities where rebellion, or insurrection, does not actually exist. They insist that such arrests shall not be made "outside of the lines of necessary military occupation, and the scenes of insurrection[.]" In asmuch [*sic*], however, as the constitution itself makes no such distinction, I am unable to believe that there is any such constitutional distinction. I concede that the class of arrests complained of, can be constitutional only when, in cases of Rebellion or Invasion, the public Safety may require them; and I insist that in such cases, they are constitutional *wherever* the public safety does require them—as well in places to which they may prevent the rebellion extending, as in those where it may be already prevailing—as well where they may restrain mischievous interference with the raising and supplying of armies, to suppress the rebellion, as where the rebellion may actually be—as well where they may restrain the enticing men out of the army, as where they would prevent mutiny in the army—equally constitutional at all places where they will conduce to the public Safety, as against the dangers of Rebellion or Invasion.

Take the particular case mentioned by the meeting. They assert in substance that Mr. Vallandigham[10] was by a military commander, seized and tried "for no other reason than words addressed to a public meeting, in criticism of the course of the administration, and in condemnation of the military orders of that general[.]" Now, if there be no mistake about this—if this assertion is the truth and the whole truth—if there was no other reason for the arrest, then I concede that the arrest was wrong. But the arrest, as I understand, was made for a very different reason. Mr. Vallandigham avows his hostility to the war on the part of the Union; and his arrest was made because he was laboring, with some effect, to prevent the raising of troops, to encourage desertions from the army, and to leave the rebellion without an adequate military force to suppress it. He was not arrested because he was damaging the political prospects of the administration, or the personal interests of the commanding general; but because he was damaging the army, upon the existence, and vigor of which, the life of the nation depends. He was warring upon the military; and this gave the military constitutional jurisdiction to lay hands upon him. If Mr. Vallandigham was not damaging the military power of the country, then his arrest was made on mistake of fact, which I would be glad to correct, on reasonably satisfactory evidence.

I understand the meeting, whose resolutions I am considering, to be in favor of suppressing the rebellion by military force—by armies. Long experience has shown that armies can not be maintained unless desertion shall be punished by the severe penalty of death. The case requires, and the law and the constitution, sanction this punishment. Must I shoot a simple-minded soldier boy who deserts, while I must not touch a hair of a wiley [sic] agitator who induces him to desert? This is none the less injurious when effected by getting a father, or brother, or friend, into a public meeting, and there working upon his feeling, till he is persuaded to write the soldier boy, that he is fighting in a bad cause, for a wicked administration of a contemptable [sic] government, too weak to arrest and punish him if he shall desert. I think that in such a case, to silence the agitator, and save the boy, is not only constitutional, but, withal, a great mercy.[11]

If I be wrong on this question of constitutional power, my error lies in believing that certain proceedings are constitutional when, in cases of rebellion or Invasion, the public Safety requires them, which would not be constitutional when, in absence of rebellion or invasion, the public Safety does not require them—in other words, that the constitution is not in it's [sic] application in all respects the same, in cases of Rebellion or invasion, involving the public Safety, as it is in times of profound peace and public security. The constitution itself makes the distinction; and I can no more be persuaded that the government can constitutionally take no strong measure in time of rebellion, because it can be shown that the same could not be

of General Ambrose Burnside arrested him six days later for inciting treason. Following his trial and conviction, he was ordered imprisoned for the duration of the war, but Lincoln commuted the sentence and had him banished to the Confederacy. A defiant Vallandigham soon made his way to Canada via North Carolina and Bermuda and as an exile there launched a campaign for governor of Ohio. He lost decisively, to Lincoln's immense relief. Frank L. Klement, *The Limits of Dissent: Clement L. Vallandigham and the Civil War* (New York: Fordham University Press, 1998). The best account of the Copperhead movement is Jennifer L. Weber, *Copperheads: The Rise and Fall of Lincoln's Opponents in the North* (New York: Oxford University Press, 2006).

11   In his original draft, Lincoln had added to this famous phrase, and then elected to delete the additional words "and a great merit." *CW,* 6:267n11.

lawfully taken in time of peace, than I can be persuaded that a particular drug is not good medicine for a sick man, because it can be shown to not be good food for a well one. Nor am I able to appreciate the danger, apprehended by the meeting, that the American people will, by means of military arrests during the rebellion, lose the right of public discussion, the liberty of speech and the press, the law of evidence, trial by jury, and Habeas corpus, throughout the indefinite peaceful future which I trust lies before them, any more than I am able to believe that a man could contract so strong an appetite for emetics during temporary illness, as to persist in feeding upon them through the remainder of his healthful life.

In giving the resolutions that earnest consideration which you request of me, I can not overlook the fact that the meeting speak as "Democrats." Nor can I, with full respect for their known intelligence, and the fairly presumed deliberation with which they prepared their resolutions, be permitted to suppose that this occurred by accident, or in any way other than that they preferred to designate themselves "democrats" rather than "American citizens." In this time of national peril I would have preferred to meet you upon a level one step higher than any party platform; because I am sure that from such more elevated position, we could do better battle for the country we all love, than we possibly can from those lower ones, where from the force of habit, the prejudices of the past, and selfish hopes of the future, we are sure to expend much of our ingenuity and strength, in finding fault with, and aiming blows at each other. But since you have denied me this, I will yet be thankful, for the country's sake, that not all democrats have done so. He on whose discretionary judgment Mr. Vallandigham was arrested and tried, is a democrat, having no old party affinity with me; and the judge who rejected the constitutional view expressed in these resolutions, by refusing to discharge Mr. V. on Habeas Corpus, is a democrat of better days than these, having received his judicial mantle at the hands of President Jackson. And still more, of all those democrats who are nobly exposing their lives and shedding their blood on the battle-field, I have learned that many approve the course taken with Mr. V. while I have not heard of a single one condemning it. I can not assert that there are none such.

And the name of President Jackson recalls a bit of pertinent history. After the battle of New-Orleans, and while the fact that the treaty of peace had been concluded, was well known in the city, but before official knowledge of it had arrived, Gen. Jackson still maintained martial, or military law. Now, that it could be said the war was over, the clamor against martial law, which had existed from the first, grew more furious. Among other things a

Mr. Louiallier published a denunciatory newspaper article.[12] Gen. Jackson arrested him. A lawyer by the name of [Pierre L.] Morel procured the U.S. Judge [Dominick A.] Hall to order a writ of Habeas Corpus to release Mr. Louiallier. Gen. Jackson arrested both the lawyer and the judge. A Mr. Hollander[13] ventured to say of some part of the matter that "it was a dirty trick." Gen. Jackson arrested him. When the officer undertook to serve the writ of Habeas Corpus, Gen. Jackson took it from him, and sent him away with a copy. Holding the judge in custody a few days, the general sent him beyond the limits of his encampment, and set him at liberty, with an order to remain till the ratification of peace should be regularly announced, or until the British should have left the Southern coast. A day or two more elapsed, the ratification of the treaty of peace was regularly announced, and the judge and others were fully liberated. A few days more, and the judge called Gen. Jackson into court and fined him a thousand dollars, for having arrested him and the others named. The general paid the fine, and there the matter rested for nearly thirty years, when congress refunded principal and interest.[14] The late Senator Douglas, then in the House of Representatives, took a leading part in the debate, in which the constitutional question was much discussed. I am not prepared to say whom the Journals would show to have voted for the measure.

It may be remarked: First, that we had the same constitution then, as now. Secondly, that we then had a case of Invasion, and that now we have a case of Rebellion, and: Thirdly, that the permanent right of the people to public discussion, the liberty of speech and the press, the trial by jury, the law of evidence, and the Habeas Corpus, suffered no detriment whatever by that conduct of Gen. Jackson, or it's subsequent approval by the American congress.

And yet, let me say that in my own discretion, I do not know whether I would have ordered the arrest of Mr. V. While I can not shift the responsibility from myself, I hold that, as a general rule, the commander in the field is the better judge of the necessity in any particular case. Of course I must practice a general directory and revisory power in the matter.

One of the resolutions expresses the opinion of the meeting that arbitrary arrests will have the effect to divide and distract those who should be united in suppressing the rebellion; and I am specifically called on to discharge Mr. Vallandigham. I regard this as, at least, a fair appeal to me, on the expediency of exercising a constitutional power which I think exists. In response to such appeal I have to say it gave me pain when I learned that Mr. V. had been arrested,—that is, I was pained that there should have

12   Louisiana legislator Louis Louaillier had sent a letter to a New Orleans newspaper protesting General Jackson's allegedly dictatorial control of the city. *Niles' National Register*, January 14, 1843, 312.

13   A New Orleans merchant, first name unknown. *CW,* 6:268n18.

14   By this time, Republican Abraham Lincoln was displaying a portrait of Democrat Andrew Jackson—his old political enemy—in his White House office. This was not the first time Lincoln had cited Jackson as a precedent for strong executive action; he had raised the specter of "Old Hickory" together with "manhood" to defend the right of troops to march through Baltimore after the 1861 riots there. In this instance, Lincoln identifies with *General* Jackson's retaliation against dissent while occupying New Orleans. See Wilentz, "Abraham Lincoln and Jacksonian Democracy."

15   The *New York Tribune* version had "strong" rather than "arbitrary." *CW,* 6:269n20.

16   On June 30, 1863, the Albany committee responded to the president's letter by arguing, in part: "We have carefully considered the grounds on which your pretensions to more than regal authority are claimed to rest; and if we do not misinterpret the misty and clouded forms of expression in which these pretensions are set forth, your meaning is that while the rights of the citizen are protected by the Constitution in time of peace, they are suspended or lost in time of war, or when invasion or rebellion exist." The reply branded Lincoln's argument as "subversive of liberty and law, and quite as certainly tending to the establishment of despotism. Your [You] claim to have found not outside, but within the Constitution, a principle or germ of arbitrary power, which in time of war expands at once into an absolute sovereignty, wielded by one man; so that liberty perishes, or is dependent on his will, his discretion or his caprice. . . . You must permit us to say to you with all due respect, but with the earnestness demanded by the occasion, that the American people will never acquiesce in this decision." Corning to Lincoln, June 30, 1863, Lincoln Papers, Library of Congress, and in *CW,* 6:261n1.

17   Washington editor John Wein Forney (1817–1881) spoke for many pro-Republican journalists when he wrote to Lincoln after initial publication of what became known as his "Corning Letter": "From a full heart let me thank you for your letter to the Albanians. I have almost committed it to memory. God be praised the right word has at last been spoken by the right man, at the right time, and from the right place. It will thrill the whole land." Francis Lieber (1798–1872), an ardent defender of Lincoln's use of executive power in wartime, pledged to see to the publication of 10,000 copies by New York's Loyal Publication Society. Forney to Lincoln, June 14, 1863; Lieber to Lincoln, June 16, 1863, Lincoln Papers, Library of Congress.

seemed to be a necessity for arresting him—and that it will afford me great pleasure to discharge him so soon as I can, by any means, believe the public safety will not suffer by it. I further say, that as the war progress, it appears to me, opinion, and action, which were in great confusion at first, take shape, and fall into more regular channels; so that the necessity for arbitrary[15] dealing with them gradually decreases. I have every reason to desire that it would cease altogether; and far from the least is my regard for the opinions and wishes of those who, like the meeting at Albany, declare their purpose to sustain the government in every constitutional and lawful measure to suppress the rebellion.[16] Still, I must continue to do so much as may seem to be required by the public safety.[17]

A. LINCOLN.

# Response to a Victory Serenade

## July 7, 1863

*On Independence Day two years earlier, Lincoln had been compelled to issue a plea to Congress merely to recognize his authority to wage war against secession. Two years later to the day, the president received word that Robert E. Lee's Confederate army had been driven from Gettysburg, Pennsylvania, and that General Ulysses S. Grant had captured Vicksburg, Mississippi. These twin Union triumphs, east and west, inspired an impromptu serenade on the White House lawn three days later, to which Lincoln, never at his best when speaking extemporaneously, responded with this infelicitous but heartfelt address. It is notable chiefly for the jumbled sentence that begins, "How long ago is it?—eighty odd years," words that presaged Lincoln's more elegiac arrangement of the same opening thought a few months later at Gettysburg.*

FELLOW-CITIZENS: I AM VERY GLAD INDEED TO SEE YOU TO-NIGHT,[1] and yet I will not say I thank you for this call, but I do most sincerely thank Almighty God for the occasion on which you have called. (*Cheers*) How long ago is it?—eighty odd years—since on the Fourth of July for the first time in the history of the world a nation by its representatives, assembled and declared as a self-evident truth that "all men are created equal." (*Cheers*) That was the birthday of the United States of America. Since then the Fourth of July has had several peculiar recognitions. The two most distinguished men in the framing and support of the Declaration were Thomas Jefferson and John Adams—the one having penned it and the other sustained it the most forcibly in debate—the only two of the fifty-five who sustained[2] it being elected President of the United States. Precisely fifty years after they put their hands to the paper it pleased Almighty God to take both from the stage of action. This was indeed an extraordinary and remarkable event in our history. Another President,[3] five years after, was called from this stage of existence on the same day and month of the year; and now, on this last Fourth of July just passed, when we have a gigantic Rebellion, at the bottom of which is an effort to overthrow the principle that all men were[4] created equal, we have the surrender of a most powerful position and army on that very day, *(Cheers)* and not only so, but in a succession of battles in Pennsylvania, near to us, through three days, so rapidly fought that they might be called one great battle on the 1st, 2d and 3d of the month of July; and on the 4th the cohorts of those who opposed the declaration that all men are created equal, "turned tail" and run. (*Long and continued cheers*) Gentlemen, this is a glorious theme, and the occasion for a speech, but I am not prepared to make one worthy of the occasion. I would like to speak in terms of praise due to the many brave officers and soldiers who

1  Lincoln observed the public demonstration—and spoke—from the second-floor window of the White House. *New York Times*, July 8, 1863.

2  In reprinting these impromptu words in their multivolume collection of Lincoln speeches years later, White House secretaries John Nicolay and John Hay recorded this word as "signed." *CW,* 6:320n2.

3  James Monroe.

4  Nicolay and Hay recorded "are." *CW,* 6:320n3.

5   The *New York Herald* and *New York Tribune* heard this word as "There"; the *Times* transcript, which had "These," is logically the correct interpretation.

6   As the *New York Times* reported (July 8, 1864): "At 8 P.M. a crowd assembled in front of the National Hotel, and marched up Pennsylvania Avenue, headed by the Marine Band, to the executive Mansion, serenaded and enthusiastically cheered the President, with repeated cheers for Gens. Grant, Meade, Rosecrans, the Armies of the Union, etc."

have fought in the cause of the Union and liberties of the country from the beginning of the war. These[5] are trying occasions, not only in success, but for the want of success. I dislike to mention the name of one single officer lest I might do wrong to those I might forget. Recent events bring up glorious names, and particularly prominent ones, but these I will not mention. Having said this much, I will now take the music.[6]

# Letter to General Ulysses S. Grant

## July 13, 1863

*In an extraordinarily gracious letter of commendation, Lincoln acknowledged what few other leaders would dare to concede: that General Grant had been right, and his commander in chief wrong, in charting the successful siege of Vicksburg.*

1   Although he was yet to meet his victorious western commander, Lincoln had long defended him against charges that he drank to excess and took too many casualties. "I can't spare this man," Lincoln had told Grant's critics. "He fights." Cited in A. K. McClure, *Lincoln and Men of War-Times: Some Personal Recollections of War and Politics during the Lincoln Administration* (Philadelphia: Times Publishing Co., 1892), 194.

2   Nathaniel P. Banks (1816–1894) was a former governor of Massachusetts and Union general.

Major General Grant                                      Executive Mansion,
My dear General                        Washington, July 13, 1863.

   I do not remember that you and I ever met personally.[1] I write this now as a grateful acknowledgment for the almost inestimable service you have done the country. I wish to say a word further. When you first reached the vicinity of Vicksburg, I thought you should do, what you finally did— march the troops across the neck, run the batteries with the transports, and thus go below; and I never had any faith, except a general hope that you knew better than I, that the Yazoo Pass expedition, and the like, could succeed. When you got below, and took Port-Gibson, Grand Gulf, and vicinity, I thought you should go down the river and join Gen. Banks;[2] and when you turned Northward East of the Big Black, I feared it was a mistake. I now wish to make the personal acknowledgment that you were right, and I was wrong.

Yours very truly
A. LINCOLN

James Fagan, after Ole Peter Hansen Balling, *U.S. Grant in the Trenches before Vicksburg.* Etching (ca. June 5, 1899). General Grant's siege of Vicksburg ended when Confederate forces surrendered on July 4, 1863, one day after Union forces defeated those of General Robert E. Lee at Gettysburg.

*Lincoln was incensed when he learned that the winning commander at Gettysburg had failed to pursue Lee's retreating Confederate army, which eventually escaped into Virginia. Lincoln's disappointment, which may have been unreasonable considering the brutal summer weather and the casualties that exhausted Union forces had endured, was conveyed in this scathing letter. Once he got his anger off his chest, however, Lincoln had second thoughts and in a mature display of forbearance decided not to dispatch it after all. Instead he filed it away, marking it, "To Gen. Meade, never sent, or signed."*

1 Henry Halleck (1815–1872) was general in chief of the Union army.

2 Darius N. Couch (1822–1897) and William Farrar Smith (1824–1903).

3 The day after he drafted this letter, Lincoln disgustedly told his son Robert: "If I had gone up there, I could have whipped them myself." Robert told John Hay that his father "grieved silently but deeply about the escape of Lee." *Inside Lincoln's White House: The Complete Civil War Diary of John Hay*, ed. Michael Burlingame and John R. Turner Ettlinger (Carbondale: Southern Illinois University Press, 1997), 63.

# Letter to General George G. Meade

## July 14, 1863

Major General Meade

Executive Mansion
Washington, July 14, 1863.

I have just seen your despatch to Gen. Halleck,[1] asking to be relieved of your command, because of a supposed censure of mine. I am very—*very*—grateful to you for the magnificient [*sic*] success you gave the cause of the country at Gettysburg; and I am sorry now to be the author of the slightest pain to you. But I was in such deep distress myself that I could not restrain some expression of it. I had been oppressed nearly ever since the battles at Gettysburg, by what appeared to be evidences that yourself, and Gen. [Darius] Couch, and Gen. Smith,[2] were not seeking a collision with the enemy, but were trying to get him across the river without another battle. What these evidences were, if you please, I hope to tell you at some time, when we shall both feel better. The case, summarily stated is this. You fought and beat the enemy at Gettysburg; and, of course, to say the least, his loss was as great as yours. He retreated; and you did not, as it seemed to me, pressingly pursue him; but a flood in the river detained him, till, by slow degrees, you were again upon him. You had at least twenty thousand veteran troops directly with you, and as many more raw ones within supporting distance, all in addition to those who fought with you at Gettysburg; while it was not possible that he had received a single recruit; and yet you stood and let the flood run down, bridges be built, and the enemy move away at his leisure, without attacking him.[3] And Couch and Smith! The latter left Carlisle in time, upon all ordinary calculation, to have aided you in the last battle at Gettysburg; but he did not arrive. At the end of more than ten days, I believe twelve, under constant urging, he reached Hagerstown from Carlisle, which is not an inch over fiftyfive miles, if so much. And Couch's movement was very little different.

General George G. Meade. Photograph by Mathew Brady Gallery (Washington, DC, ca. 1860–1865).

Peter F. Rothermel, *Battle of Gettysburg: Pickett's Charge.* Oil on canvas (1870). This grand and heroic rendering depicts the infantry assault ordered by Robert E. Lee against Union positions on Cemetery Ridge on July 3, 1863, the last day of the Battle of Gettysburg. The charge, led by General George Pickett, was decisively repulsed.

Again, my dear general, I do not believe you appreciate the magnitude of the misfortune involved in Lee's escape. He was within your easy grasp, and to have closed upon him would, in connection with our other late successes, have ended the war. As it is, the war will be prolonged indefinitely. If you could not safely attack Lee last monday, how can you possibly do so South of the river, when you can take with you very few more than two thirds of the force you then had in hand? It would be unreasonable to expect, and I do not expect you can now effect much. Your golden opportunity is gone, and I am distressed immeasureably [*sic*] because of it.

I beg you will not consider this a prossecution [*sic*], or persecution of yourself. As you had learned that I was dissatisfied, I have thought it best to kindly tell you why.[4]

4   Nicolay and Hay wrote of this unsent letter: "It was not an unusual proceeding with him to put upon paper in this way his expressions of dissatisfaction and then to lay them away, rather than wound a deserving public servant by even a merited censure." Nonetheless, the secretaries believed the text "the clearest statement which could be made of the failure to reap the full harvest of the Gettysburg victory." Lincoln was heard to add: "Our army held the war in the hollow of their hand and they would not close it." Nicolay and Hay, *Abraham Lincoln*, 7:278–279.

Edwin Forbes, *Charge of Ewell's Corps at Cemetery Gate*. Oil on canvas (Brooklyn, NY, ca. 1866–1870). This painting depicts fighting on Cemetery Hill at Gettysburg on July 2, with Union troops on the defensive against a charge led by Confederate general Richard Ewell.

1    The following day, the adjutant general's office issued this document as General Orders No. 232.

# Order of Retaliation

## July 30, 1863

Executive Mansion, Washington D.C. July 30. 1863

It is the duty of every government to give protection to its citizens, of whatever class, color, or condition, and especially to those who are duly organized as soldiers in the public service. The law of nations and the usages and customs of war as carried on by civilized powers, permit no distinction as to color in the treatment of prisoners of war as public enemies. To sell or enslave any captured person, on account of his color, and for no offence against the laws of war, is a relapse into barbarism and a crime against the civilization of the age.

The government of the United States will give the same protection to all its soldiers, and if the enemy shall sell or enslave anyone because of his color, the offense shall be punished by retaliation upon the enemy's prisoners in our possession.

It is therefore ordered that for every soldier of the United States killed in violation of the laws of war, a rebel soldier shall be executed; and for every one enslaved by the enemy or sold into slavery, a rebel soldier shall be placed at hard labor on the public works and continued at such labor until the other shall be released and receive the treatment due to a prisoner of war[.][1]

ABRAHAM LINCOLN

[Louis] Kurz & [Alexander] Allison, *Battle of Olustee, Florida, 1864.* Lithograph (Chicago, 1894). Also known as the Battle of Ocean Pond, this engagement included three black Union regiments: the First North Carolina Colored Infantry, the Eighth U.S. Colored Infantry, and the Fifty-Fourth Massachusetts Volunteer Infantry. Despite the courage and valor shown by the black soldiers, the Union army lost the battle on February 20, 1864. After the battle, it was reported that a number of wounded black soldiers were killed on the battlefield by roaming bands of Confederate troops.

*As debates raged over the effort to recruit African Americans to fight for the Union, Lincoln's old Springfield neighbors invited him home to address a "Grand Mass Meeting" there. For a time Lincoln gave serious consideration to making the trip, but in the end he decided, as usual, that he could not leave Washington and should not speak publicly. He determined instead to compose this long, extraordinary message, crafting it as a letter to his friend James C. Conkling, and instructing him to read it "very slowly" at the rally. Lincoln's most impassioned defense of black recruitment was garbled in its first newspaper adaptations but eventually corrected and reprinted widely, to enormous acclaim from Republican editors. The* New York Tribune *commented: "The most consummate rhetorician never used language more put to the purpose." Harriet Beecher Stowe hailed it as a "masterly" product of "a mind both strong and generous."*

1   A onetime mayor of Springfield, James Cook Conkling (1816–1899) had known Lincoln for nearly twenty years and had run as a Lincoln elector in the 1860 presidential race. Conkling was married to Mary Lincoln's good friend, the former Mercy Levering. Neely, *Lincoln Encyclopedia,* 68–69.

2   Conkling had written the president: "The unconditional Union men of all parties in our State are to hold a Grand Mass Meeting at Springfield on the 3rd day of September next. It would be gratifying to the many thousands who will be present on that occasion if you would also meet with them. It is stated in the public papers that you will visit the White Mountains and perhaps you can make it convenient to extend your trip to Illinois. A visit to your old home would not be inappropriate if you can break away from the pressure of public duties. We intend to make the most imposing demonstration that has ever been held in the Northwest. Many of the most distinguished men in the country have been, and

# Address Written for Delivery at Springfield, Illinois, Conveyed as a Letter to James C. Conkling

## August 26, 1863

Hon. James C. Conkling[1]
My Dear Sir.

Executive Mansion,
Washington, August 26, 1863.

Your letter inviting me to attend a mass-meeting of unconditional Union-men, to be held at the Capital of Illinois, on the 3d day of September, has been received.[2]

It would be very agreeable to me, to thus meet my old friends, at my own home; but I can not, just now, be absent from here, so long as a visit there, would require.[3]

The meeting is to be of all those who maintain unconditional devotion to the Union; and I am sure my old political friends will thank me for tendering, as I do, the nation's gratitude to those other noble men, whom no partizan malice, or partizan hope, can make false to the nation's life.[4]

There are those who are dissatisfied with me. To such I would say: You desire peace; and you blame me that we do not have it. But how can we attain it? There are but three conceivable ways. First, to suppress the rebellion by force of arms. This, I am trying to do. Are you for it? If you are, so far we are agreed. If you are not for it, a second way is, to give up the Union. I am against this. Are you for it? If you are, you should say so plainly. If you are not for *force,* nor yet for *dissolution,* there only remains some imaginable *compromise.* I do not believe any compromise, embracing the maintenance of the Union, is now possible. All I learn, leads to a directly opposite belief. The strength of the rebellion, is its military—its army. That army dominates all the country, and all the people, within its range. Any offer of terms made by any man or men within that range, in opposition to that army, is simply nothing for the present; because such man or men, have no power whatever to enforce their side of a compromise, if one were made with them. To illustrate—Suppose refugees from the South, and peace men of

STORMING FORT WAGNER.

Kurz & Allison, *Storming Fort Wagner*. Lithograph (Chicago, 1890). The Fifty-Fourth Massachusetts Regiment, composed of African American soldiers, culminates its famous charge on Battery Wagner in Charleston Harbor, South Carolina, in July 1863.

the North, get together in convention, and frame and proclaim a compromise embracing a restoration of the Union; in what way can that compromise be used to keep Lee's army out of Pennsylvania? Meade's army can keep Lee's army out of Pennsylvania; and, I think, can ultimately drive it out of existence. But no paper compromise, to which the controllers of Lee's army are not agreed, can, at all, affect that army. In an effort at such compromise we should waste time, which the enemy would improve to our disadvantage; and that would be all. A compromise, to be effective, must be made either with those who control the rebel army, or with the people first liberated from the domination of that army, by the success of our own army.

will be invited to attend and I know that nothing could add more to the interest of the occasion than your presence." Conkling to Lincoln, August 14, 1863, Lincoln Papers, Library of Congress. Lincoln did not go on vacation to the White Mountains as reported.

3   "I can not leave now," Lincoln wrote Conkling on August 27. "You are one of the best public readers. Read it very slowly. And now God bless you, and all good Union men." *CW*, 6:414.

4   At this point Lincoln drafted, but later deleted: "Are we degenerate—unworthy sons of noblest sires?" *CW*, 6:406n2.

**COME AND JOIN US BROTHERS.**

PUBLISHED BY THE SUPERVISORY COMMITTEE FOR RECRUITING COLORED REGIMENTS
1210 CHESTNUT ST. PHILADELPHIA.

*Come and Join Us Brothers.* Lithograph (Philadelphia: P. S. Duval, 1863–1865). This recruitment poster was published by the Supervisory Committee for Recruiting Colored Regiments.

Now allow me to assure you, that no word or intimation, from that rebel army, or from any of the men controlling it, in relation to any peace compromise, has ever come to my knowledge or belief. All charges and insinuations to the contrary, are deceptive and groundless. And I promise you, that if any such proposition shall hereafter come, it shall not be rejected, and kept a secret from you. I freely acknowledge myself the servant of the people, according to the bond of service—the United States constitution; and that, as such, I am responsible to them.

But, to be plain, you are dissatisfied with me about the negro. Quite likely there is a difference of opinion between you and myself upon that subject. I certainly wish that all men could be free, while I suppose you do not. Yet I have neither adopted, nor proposed any measure, which is not consistent with even your view, provided you are for the Union. I suggested compensated emancipation; to which you replied you wished not to be taxed to buy negroes. But I had not asked you to be taxed to buy negroes, except in such way, as to save you from greater taxation to save the Union exclusively by other means.

You dislike the emancipation proclamation; and, perhaps, would have it retracted. You say it is unconstitutional—I think differently. I think the constitution invests its commander-in-chief, with the law of war, in time of war. The most that can be said, if so much, is, that slaves are property. Is there—has there ever been—any question that by the law of war, property, both of enemies and friends, may be taken when needed? And is it not needed whenever taking it, helps us, or hurts the enemy? Armies, the world over, destroy enemies' property when they can not use it; and even destroy their own to keep it from the enemy. Civilized belligerents do all in their power to help themselves, or hurt the enemy, except a few things regarded as barbarous or cruel. Among the exceptions are the massacre of vanquished foes, and non-combatants, male and female.

But the proclamation, as law, either is valid, or is not valid. If it is not valid, it needs no retraction. If it is valid, it can not be retracted, any more than the dead can be brought to life. Some of you profess to think its retraction would operate favorably for the Union. Why better *after* the retraction, than *before* the issue? There was more than a year and a half of trial to suppress the rebellion before the proclamation issued, the last one hundred days of which passed under an explicit notice that it was coming, unless averted by those in revolt, returning to their allegiance. The war has certainly progressed as favorably for us, since the issue of the proclamation as before. I know as fully as one can know the opinions of others, that some of the commanders of our armies in the field who have given us our most important successes, believe the emancipation policy, and the use of colored troops, constitute the heaviest blow yet dealt to the rebellion; and that, at least one of those important successes, could not have been achieved when it was, but for the aid of black soldiers. Among the commanders holding these views are some who have never had any affinity with what is called abolitionism, or with republican party politics; but who hold them purely as military opinions. I submit these opinions as being entitled to some

5   The Mississippi River. With the Union victory at Vicksburg, Mississippi, in July, the river was open to commercial shipping.

6   New York, the Empire State.

7   Pennsylvania, the Keystone State.

8   Lincoln's novel term for the Union navy.

weight against the objections, often urged, that emancipation, and arming the blacks, are unwise as military measures, and were not adopted, as such, in good faith.

You say you will not fight to free negroes. Some of them seem willing to fight for you; but, no matter. Fight you, then, exclusively to save the Union. I issued the proclamation on purpose to aid you in saving the Union. Whenever you shall have conquered all resistance to the Union, if I shall urge you to continue fighting, it will be an apt time, then, for you to declare you will not fight to free negroes.

I thought that in your struggle for the Union, to whatever extent the negroes should cease helping the enemy, to that extent it weakened the enemy in his resistance to you. Do you think differently? I thought that whatever negroes can be got to do as soldiers, leaves just so much less for white soldiers to do, in saving the Union. Does it appear otherwise to you? But negroes, like other people, act upon motives. Why should they do any thing for us, if we will do nothing for them? If they stake their lives for us, they must be prompted by the strongest motive—even the promise of freedom. And the promise being made, must be kept.

The signs look better. The Father of Waters[5] again goes unvexed to the sea. Thanks to the great North-West for it. Nor yet wholly to them. Three hundred miles up, they met New-England, Empire,[6] Key-Stone,[7] and Jersey, hewing their way right and left. The Sunny South too, in more colors than one, also lent a hand. On the spot, their part of the history was jotted down in black and white. The job was a great national one; and let none be banned who bore an honorable part in it. And while those who have cleared the great river may well be proud, even that is not all. It is hard to say that anything has been more bravely, and well done, than at Antietam, Murfreesboro, Gettysburg, and on many fields of lesser note. Nor must Uncle Sam's Web-feet be forgotten.[8] At all the watery margins they have been present. Not only on the deep sea, the broad bay, and the rapid river, but also up the narrow muddy bayou, and wherever the ground was a little damp, they have been, and made their tracks. Thanks to all. For the great republic—for the principle it lives by, and keeps alive—for man's vast future,—thanks to all.

Peace does not appear so distant as it did. I hope it will come soon, and come to stay; and so come as to be worth the keeping in all future time. It will then have been proved that, among free men, there can be no successful appeal from the ballot to the bullet; and that they who take such appeal are sure to lose their case, and pay the cost. And then, there will be some black men who can remember that, with silent tongue, and clenched teeth, and steady eye, and well-poised bayonet, they have helped mankind on to this great consummation; while, I fear, there will be some white ones, unable to forget that, with malignant heart, and deceitful speech, they have strove to hinder it.

Still let us not be over-sanguine of a speedy final triumph. Let us be quite sober. Let us diligently apply the means, never doubting that a just God, in his own good time, will give us the rightful result.[9]

Yours very truly
A. LINCOLN

9   Lincoln had refused entreaties from the Associated Press that this message be prepared in advance for publication nationwide immediately after its delivery, and, worried about leaks and misprints, the president also refused to release it in advance himself. As it happened, Conkling proved far less careful, and excerpts from the speech appeared prematurely anyway, and in mangled form. "I am mortified this morning to find the letter to you, botched up, in the Eastern papers, telegraphed from Chicago," an angry Lincoln wrote Conkling on September 3. "How did this happen?" Conkling tried explaining the following day: "In order that the St Louis Chicago and Springfield papers might publish your Letter simultaneously and at the earliest period after the meeting, so as to gratify the intense anxiety which existed with regard to your views, copies were sent to the two former places with strict injunctions not to permit it to be published before the meeting or to make any improper use of it[.] But it appears that a part of it was telegraphed from Chicago to New York contrary to my express directions. . . . I was very much mortified at the occurrence, but hope that no prejudicial results have been experienced as the whole letter was published the next day." When the *Washington Daily Chronicle* also printed the imperfect copy, its editor, John Wein Forney, promised Lincoln he would "republish it, accompanied by a strong editorial endorsement." Indeed, Republican newspapers universally applauded the speech, one of the so-called public letters that Lincoln so ingeniously crafted for public consumption in an era when presidents rarely spoke before the people. Holzer, *Lincoln and the Power of the Press*, 472–473.

514

*The Shakespearean actor Hackett was considered the premier Falstaff interpreter of his day. Apparently aware that Lincoln was a lover of Shakespeare, the thespian wrote him on October 3, 1862, to announce a series of upcoming performances in Washington. On December 14 the president saw Hackett in* Henry IV, Part One *at Ford's Theatre, returning the following night to see* Part Two. *Although he told John Hay, who accompanied him on the second night, that he objected to one of Hackett's readings, Lincoln remained an admirer and struck up a correspondence with the actor, one that promptly got him into trouble with the press.*

1    James Hackett (1800–1871), apparently reluctant to apologize directly for the breach of protocol involved in publicizing the president's letter without permission, instead had written to report his son's regret over the "unwarrantable liberty taken by certain News-paper-Presses inn [*sic*] publishing your kind, sensible & unpretending letter to me of '17 Augt.' Last & more particularly at the Editorial remarks upon & perversion of its subject-matter to antagonistic political purposes, accompanied by satirical abuse in general. . . . I replied that I felt assured that, as a man of the world now and an experienced politician you were not likely to be so thin skinned, and that in my humble opinion such political squibs would probably affect your sensibility about as much as would a charge of mustard seed shot at forty yards distance, fired through a pop-gun barrel at the naturally armed Alligator." Hackett to Lincoln, October 22, 1863, Lincoln Papers, Library of Congress. Lincoln had written the letter in question on August 17, 1863, belatedly acknowledging Hackett's gift of his book of Shakespeare commentaries. In the most extensive comments he had ever shared about his passion for the bard, Lincoln had written: "For one of my age, I have seen very little of the drama. The first presentation of Falstaff I ever saw was yours here, last winter or

# Letter to James H. Hackett

## November 2, 1863

*Private*

James H. Hackett                           Executive Mansion,
My dear Sir:                     Washington, Nov. 2. 1863.

Yours of Oct. 22nd. is received,[1] as also was, in due course, that of Oct. 3rd. I look forward with pleasure to the fulfilment of the promise made in the former.

Give yourself no uneasiness on the subject mentioned in that of the 22nd.

My note to you I certainly did not expect to see in print; yet I have not been much shocked by the newspaper comments upon it. Those comments constitute a fair specimen of what has occurred to me through life. I have endured a great deal of ridicule without much malice; and have received a great deal of kindness, not quite free from ridicule. I am used to it.

Yours truly
A. LINCOLN

Abraham Lincoln. Photograph by Anthony Berger, Mathew Brady Gallery (Washington, DC, February 9, 1864). This profile was later engraved for the Lincoln penny.

spring. Perhaps the best compliment I can pay is to say, as I truly can, I am very anxious to see it again. Some of Shakespeare's plays I have never read; while others I have gone over perhaps as frequently as any unprofessional reader. Among the latter are Lear, Richard Third, Henry Eighth, Hamlet, and especially Macbeth. I think nothing equals Macbeth. It is wonderful. Unlike you gentlemen of the profession, I think the soliloquy in Hamlet commencing 'O, my offence is rank' surpasses that commencing 'To be, or not to be.'" *CW,* 6:392. The September 17, 1863, issue of the *New York Herald* had mocked Lincoln, climaxing with a barbed reference to the "popular astonishment and admiration for [Lincoln's] showing himself to be a dramatic critic of the first order, and the greatest and most profound of the army of Shakespearean commentators."

*One of the many legends long surrounding Lincoln's most cherished address is true: the president was not invited to be the principal speaker at the ceremonies dedicating a national soldiers' cemetery at Gettysburg. That honor went to the celebrated orator Edward Everett. Lincoln was asked only to provide "a few appropriate remarks" (David Wills to Lincoln, November 2, 1863, Lincoln Papers, Library of Congress). But other stubborn myths about the Gettysburg Address are absurd: Lincoln did not dash off his remarks haphazardly, much less on the back of an envelope while aboard the lurching train taking him to Gettysburg; and he certainly did not believe, as his friend Ward Hill Lamon later maintained, that his performance there was a "flat failure." In fact, typical of public and press reaction to almost all of the president's public proclamations and utterances, Republicans praised the speech and Democrats savaged it. Lincoln was surely surprised and delighted when a gracious Everett wrote to him immediately afterward to concede: "I should be glad, if I could flatter myself that I came as near to the central idea of the occasion, in two hours, as you did in two minutes." Lincoln wrote several versions of his speech, five of which survive in manuscript; this is his final copy, written for a Baltimore charity fair in 1864.*

1     Lincoln wrote this final version of the address in March 1864 for reproduction in a book, *Autograph Leaves of Our Country's Authors,* to be sold at the Maryland Sanitary Commission Fair in Baltimore. *CW,* 7:22n33.

2     The phrase "under God" does not appear in the manuscript copy of the address that Lincoln used in delivering his speech. The version transcribed on the scene by Joseph Ignatius Gilbert of the Associated Press did include these words, however, suggesting that the president ad-libbed them on the spot. Martin P. Johnson, *Writing the Gettysburg Address* (Lawrence: University Press of Kansas, 2013), 226–227.

# The Gettysburg Address

## November 19, 1863
## [Final Draft, March 1864]

**Address delivered at the dedication
of the Cemetery at Gettysburg.**[1]

Four score and seven years ago our fathers brought forth on this continent, a new nation, conceived in Liberty, and dedicated to the proposition that all men are created equal.

Now we are engaged in a great civil war, testing whether that nation, or any nation so conceived and so dedicated, can long endure. We are met on a great battle-field of that war. We have come to dedicate a portion of that field, as a final resting place for those who here gave their lives that that nation might live. It is altogether fitting and proper that we should do this.

But, in a larger sense, we can not dedicate—we can not consecrate—we can not hallow—this ground. The brave men, living and dead, who struggled here, have consecrated it, far above our poor power to add or detract. The world will little note, nor long remember what we say here, but it can never forget what they did here. It is for us the living, rather, to be dedicated here to the unfinished work which they who fought here have thus far so nobly advanced. It is rather for us to be here dedicated to the great task remaining before us—that from these honored dead we take increased devotion to that cause for which they gave the last full measure of devotion—that we here highly resolve that these dead shall not have died in vain—that this nation, under God,[2] shall have a new birth of freedom—and that government of the people, by the people, for the people, shall not perish from the earth.

November 19. 1863.         ABRAHAM LINCOLN.

Lincoln on speakers' platform at Gettysburg. Photograph by David Bachrach? (Gettysburg, PA, 1863). This photograph was taken as dignitaries took their places on the platform for the dedication of the soldiers' national cemetery.

*Lincoln's Address at the Dedication of the Gettysburg National Cemetery, November 19, 1863.* Lithograph (Chicago: Sherwood Lithograph Co., c. 1905).

*Lincoln fell ill with smallpox on his way home to Washington from Gettysburg. Bedridden for weeks, he was surely not at his best when compelled to compose his annual message to Congress in early December. If it lacked for eloquence however, the message abounded in determination. Lincoln pledged himself to enforcing the Emancipation Proclamation and again defended the recruitment of African American troops. Lincoln's secretary reported that when this long and mostly prosaic message was read to the Republican-dominated Congress, "Men acted as if the millennium had come." He was no doubt referring to the reaction that greeted the message Lincoln added on the subjects of amnesty and reconstruction.*

1    Lincoln's message was read to a Congress comprising fewer Republicans than were there a year earlier, the result of the 1862 elections. Rumors spread under the newly completed Capitol dome that Democrats were conspiring to gain control of the House of Representatives. Emerson Etheridge, the House clerk, hatched a plot to exclude several Republican congressmen from the roll call and thus place Democrats in power. On hearing of the so-called plot, Lincoln advised members of his party to make sure "all our men" are present; then, he said, "if Mr. Etheridge undertakes revolutionary proceedings . . . let him be carried out on a chip [log], and let our men organize the House." The House clerk attempted to carry out his plan by excluding nineteen names from the roll call, but Republicans, heeding Lincoln's advice, had their men in place and defeated the Democratic maneuver. Lincoln quoted in Rawley, *A Lincoln Dialogue*, 419. The Etheridge plot is covered by Herman Belz, "The Etheridge Conspiracy of 1863: A Projected Conservative Coup," *Journal of Southern History* 36 (1970): 549–567.

2    Rather than summarize the army's military operations over the preceding year and other issues such as prisoner exchange, recruitment of black

# From Annual Message to Congress

## December 8, 1863

FELLOW CITIZENS OF THE SENATE AND HOUSE OF REPRESENTATIVES:[1]
Another year of health, and of sufficiently abundant harvests has passed. For these, and especially for the improved condition of our national affairs, our renewed, and profoundest gratitude to God is due.

We remain in peace and friendship with foreign powers.

The efforts of disloyal citizens of the United States to involve us in foreign wars, to aid an inexcusable insurrection, have been unavailing. Her Britannic Majesty's government, as was justly expected, have exercised their authority to prevent the departure of new hostile expeditions from British ports. The Emperor of France has, by a like proceeding, promptly vindicated the neutrality which he proclaimed at the beginning of the contest. Questions of great intricacy and importance have arisen out of the blockade, and other belligerent operations, between the government and several of the maritime powers, but they have been discussed, and, as far as was possible, accommodated in a spirit of frankness, justice, and mutual good will. It is especially gratifying that our prize courts, by the impartiality of their adjudications, have commanded the respect and confidence of maritime powers.

. . .

The duties devolving on the naval branch of the service during the year,[2] and throughout the whole of this unhappy contest, have been discharged with fidelity and eminent success. The extensive blockade has been constantly increasing in efficiency, as the navy has expanded; yet on so long a line it has so far been impossible to entirely suppress illicit trade. From returns received at the Navy Department, it appears that more than one thousand vessels have been captured since the blockade was instituted, and that the value of prizes already sent in for adjudication amounts to over thirteen millions of dollars.

The naval force of the United States consists at this time of five hundred and eighty-eight vessels, completed and in the course of completion, and of these seventy-five are iron-clad or armored steamers.[3] The events of the war give an increased interest and importance to the navy which will probably extend beyond the war itself.

The armored vessels in our navy completed and in service, or which are under contract and approaching completion, are believed to exceed in number those of any other power. But while these may be relied upon for harbor defence and coast service, others of greater strength and capacity will be necessary for cruising purposes, and to maintain our rightful position on the ocean.

The change that has taken place in naval vessels and naval warfare, since the introduction of steam as a motive-power for ships-of-war, demands either a corresponding change in some of our existing navy yards, or the establishment of new ones, for the construction and necessary repair of modern naval vessels. No inconsiderable embarrassment, delay, and public injury have been experienced from the want of such governmental establishments. The necessity of such a navy yard, so furnished, at some suitable place upon the Atlantic seaboard, has on repeated occasions been brought to the attention of Congress by the Navy Department, and is again presented in the report of the Secretary which accompanies this communication. I think it my duty to invite your special attention to this subject, and also to that of establishing a yard and depot for naval purposes upon one of the western rivers.[4] A naval force has been created on those interior waters, and under many disadvantages, within little more than two years, exceeding in numbers the whole naval force of the country at the commencement of the present administration. Satisfactory and important as have been the performances of the heroic men of the navy at this interesting period, they are scarcely more wonderful than the success of our mechanics and artisans in the production of war vessels which has created a new form of naval power.

Our country has advantages superior to any other nation in our resources of iron and timber, with inexhaustible quantities of fuel in the immediate vicinity of both, and all available and in close proximity to navigable waters. Without the advantage of public works the resources of the nation have been developed and its power displayed in the construction of a navy of such magnitude which has, at the very period of its creation, rendered signal service to the Union.

soldiers, and the organization of the invalid corps, Lincoln submitted a report by the secretary of war.

3 The next sentence replaced this long passage in Lincoln's preliminary draft: "As this government is destined to occupy a leading position among maritime powers it is a primary duty to provide the means and adequate establishments for a navy commensurate with its wants. The improvements which have been made in naval architecture and naval armament, and the services which the new class of vessels have already rendered and are destined hereafter to perform are among the marked events which have their origin in the exigencies of the war and the necessities of the times. Other governments have been making large expenditures for years in experiments with a view to attain naval supremacy, but the condition of the country and the emergencies of the period have stimulated the inventive genius of our countrymen into great activity, and the Navy Department, successfully availing itself of what was useful, has applied with effect the novel principles which modern inventions and improvements have developed." *CW*, 7:43n24.

4 After a long effort by the navy, on June 30, 1864, Congress finally authorized the secretary of the navy to name a commission to choose a site for a new navy yard on the Mississippi River. *CW*, 7:44n25.

5 The next sentence replaced this long passage in Lincoln's preliminary draft: "It is of paramount importance that the naval service, which must always give strength and renown to the Union, should be cherished and sustained. I therefore think it proper to authorize mariners or professional seamen who may enlist under the late call for 300,000 volunteers to enter the naval or army service at their election; and in view of the exactions which may be made upon the maritime communities, if compelled to furnish the full complement of army recruits in addition to those of their citizens who may enter the navy, I [respectfully?] suggest that the townships and states should each be credited on their respective quotas with the number who may hereafter enter the navy. If in the judgment of congress any further legislation be needed to authorize this policy and give it effect, then I recommend such legislative action." *CW,* 7:44n26.

6 Not wishing to upset Radical Republicans, who held different opinions on reconstruction policy, Lincoln deleted from his delivered message the following paragraph that was part of his preliminary draft: "The depredations committed upon American commerce by a class of semi piratical vessels, built, armed and manned abroad, and with no recognized nationality, have naturally excited our countrymen, and sometimes even seemed likely to endanger our friendly relations with other countries. From the protection and assistance extended to them by governments which recognized the insurgents as belligerents and equals, and entitled to all privilieges [sic] of the public national vessels of the United States, these predatory rovers have yet escaped our cruisers, and are capturing and destroying our merchant vessels upon the high seas without sending them in to any port for adjudication. The general policy of nations in the interest of peace and the moral sentiment of mankind are averse to such lawless proceedings.

The increase of the number of seamen in the public service, from seven thousand five hundred men, in the spring of 1861, to about thirty four thousand at the present time has been accomplished without special legislation, or extraordinary bounties to promote that increase. It has been found, however, that the operation of the draft, with the high bounties paid for army recruits, is beginning to affect injuriously the naval service, and will, if not corrected, be likely to impair its efficiency, by detaching seamen from their proper vocation and inducing them to enter the Army.[5] I therefore respectfully suggest that Congress might aid both the army and naval services by a definite provision on this subject, which would at the same time be equitable to the communities more especially interested.

I commend to your consideration the suggestions of the Secretary of the Navy in regard to the policy of fostering and training seamen, and also the education of officers and engineers for the naval service. The Naval Academy is rendering signal service in preparing midshipmen for the highly responsible duties which in after life they will be required to perform. In order that the country should not be deprived of the proper quota of educated officers, for which legal provision has been made at the naval school, the vacancies caused by the neglect or omission to make nominations from the States in insurrection have been filled by the Secretary of the Navy.

The school is now more full and complete than at any former period, and in every respect entitled to the favorable consideration of Congress.[6]

. . .

It has long been a cherished opinion of some of our wisest statesmen that the people of the United States had a higher and more enduring interest in the early settlement and substantial cultivation of the public lands than in the amount of direct revenue to be derived from the sale of them. This opinion has had a controlling influence in shaping legislation upon the subject of our national domain. I may cite, as evidence of this, the liberal measures adopted in reference to actual settlers; the grant to the States of the overflowed lands within their limits in order to their being reclaimed and rendered fit for cultivation; the grants to railway companies of alternate sections of land upon the contemplated lines of their roads which, when completed, will so largely multiply the facilities for reaching our distant possessions. This policy has received its most signal and beneficent illustration in the recent enactment granting homesteads to actual settlers.

Since the first day of January last the before-mentioned quantity of one million four hundred and fifty-six thousand five hundred and fourteen acres

Abraham Lincoln. Photograph by Lewis E. Walker (Washington, DC, ca. 1863).

of land have been taken up under its provisions. This fact and the amount of sales furnish gratifying evidence of increasing settlement upon the public lands, notwithstanding the great struggle in which the energies of the nation have been engaged, and which has required so large a withdrawal of our citizens from their accustomed pursuits. I cordially concur in the recommendation of the Secretary of the Interior suggesting a modification of the act in favor of those engaged in the military and naval service of the United States. I doubt not that Congress will cheerfully adopt such measures as will, without essentially changing the general features of the system, Governments seemed disposed to discountenance the conduct of those who, without a country or port to which they can resort, are depredating on the peaceful commerce of a country with which those governments are in amity. The action recently taken by them indicates a determination to permit no armed vessel with hostile preparation and purpose against our commerce and people to go forth from their shores. These manifestations have, I trust, tranquilized whatever excitement may have at any time existed." *CW,* 7:45n29.

secure to the greatest practicable extent, its benefits to those who have left their homes in the defence of the country in this arduous crisis.

I invite your attention to the views of the Secretary as to the propriety of raising by appropriate legislation a revenue from the mineral lands of the United States.

The measures provided at your last session for the removal of certain Indian tribes have been carried into effect. Sundry treaties have been negotiated which will, in due time, be submitted for the constitutional action of the Senate. They contain stipulations for extinguishing the possessory rights of the Indians to large and valuable tracts of land. It is hoped that the effect of these treaties will result in the establishment of permanent friendly relations with such of these tribes as have been brought into frequent and bloody collision with our outlying settlements and emigrants.

Sound policy and our imperative duty to these wards of the government demand our anxious and constant attention to their material well-being, to their progress in the arts of civilization, and, above all, to that moral training which, under the blessing of Divine Providence, will confer upon them the elevated and sanctifying influences, the hopes and consolation of the Christian faith.

I suggested in my last annual message the propriety of remodelling our Indian system. Subsequent events have satisfied me of its necessity. The details set forth in the report of the Secretary evince the urgent need for immediate legislative action.

I commend the benevolent institutions, established or patronized by the government in this District, to your generous and fostering care.

The attention of Congress, during the last session, was engaged to some extent with a proposition for enlarging the water communication between the Mississippi river and the northeastern seaboard, which proposition, however, failed for the time. Since then, upon a call of the greatest respectability a convention has been held at Chicago upon the same subject, a summary of whose views is contained in a memorial addressed to the President and Congress, and which I now have the honor to lay before you. That this interest is one which, ere long, will force its own way, I do not entertain a doubt, while it is submitted entirely to your wisdom as to what can be done now. Augmented interest is given to this subject by the actual commencement of work upon the Pacific railroad, under auspices so favorable to rapid progress and completion. The enlarged navigation becomes a palpable need to the great road.

I transmit the second annual report of the Commissioner of the Department of Agriculture, asking your attention to the developments in that vital interest of the nation.

When Congress assembled a year ago the war had already lasted nearly twenty months, and there had been many conflicts on both land and sea, with varying results.

The rebellion had been pressed back into reduced limits; yet the tone of public feeling and opinion, at home and abroad, was not satisfactory. With other signs, the popular elections, then just past, indicated uneasiness among ourselves, while amid much that was cold and menacing the kindest words coming from Europe were uttered in accents of pity, that we were too blind to surrender a hopeless cause. Our commerce was suffering greatly by a few armed vessels built upon and furnished from foreign shores, and we were threatened with such additions from the same quarter as would sweep our trade from the sea and raise our blockade. We had failed to elicit from European governments anything hopeful upon this subject. The preliminary emancipation proclamation, issued in September, was running its assigned period to the beginning of the new year. A month later the final proclamation came, including the announcement that colored men of suitable condition would be received into the war service. The policy of emancipation, and of employing black soldiers, gave to the future a new aspect, about which hope, and fear, and doubt contended in uncertain conflict. According to our political system, as a matter of civil administration, the general government had no lawful power to effect emancipation in any State, and for a long time it had been hoped that the rebellion could be suppressed without resorting to it as a military measure. It was all the while deemed possible that the necessity for it might come, and that if it should, the crisis of the contest would then be presented. It came, and as was anticipated, it was followed by dark and doubtful days. Eleven months having now passed, we are permitted to take another review. The rebel borders are pressed still further back, and by the complete opening of the Mississippi the country dominated by the rebellion is divided into distinct parts, with no practical communication between them. Tennessee and Arkansas have been substantially cleared of insurgent control, and influential citizens in each, owners of slaves and advocates of slavery at the beginning of the rebellion, now declare openly for emancipation in their respective States. Of those States not included in the emancipation proclamation, Maryland, and Missouri, neither of which three years ago would tolerate any restraint upon the extension of slavery into new territories, only dispute now as to the best mode of removing it within their own limits.

7   In his preliminary draft, Lincoln wrote the following: "The governments of England and France have prevented war vessels, built on their shores to be used against us, from sailing thence." *CW,* 7:50n37.

8   See "Proclamation of Amnesty and Reconstruction, December 8, 1863," in this volume.

9   U.S. Constitution, Article IV, Section 4.

Of those who were slaves at the beginning of the rebellion, full one hundred thousand are now in the United States military service, about one-half of which number actually bear arms in the ranks; thus giving the double advantage of taking so much labor from the insurgent cause, and supplying the places which otherwise must be filled with so many white men. So far as tested, it is difficult to say they are not as good soldiers as any. No servile insurrection, or tendency to violence or cruelty, has marked the measures of emancipation and arming the blacks. These measures have been much discussed in foreign countries, and contemporary with such discussion the tone of public sentiment there is much improved.[7] At home the same measures have been fully discussed, supported, criticised, and denounced, and the annual elections following are highly encouraging to those whose official duty it is to bear the country through this great trial. Thus we have the new reckoning. The crisis which threatened to divide the friends of the Union is past.

Looking now to the present and future, and with reference to a resumption of the national authority within the States wherein that authority has been suspended, I have thought fit to issue a proclamation, a copy of which is herewith transmitted.[8] On examination of this proclamation it will appear, as is believed, that nothing is attempted beyond what is amply justified by the Constitution. True, the form of an oath is given, but no man is coerced to take it. The man is only promised a pardon in case he voluntarily takes the oath. The Constitution authorizes the Executive to grant or withhold the pardon at his own absolute discretion; and this includes the power to grant on terms, as is fully established by judicial and other authorities.

It is also proffered that if, in any of the States named, a State government shall be, in the mode prescribed, set up, such government shall be recognized and guarantied by the United States, and that under it the State shall, on the constitutional conditions, be protected against invasion and domestic violence. The constitutional obligation of the United States to guaranty to every State in the Union a republican form of government,[9] and to protect the State, in the cases stated, is explicit and full. But why tender the benefits of this provision only to a State government set up in this particular way? This section of the Constitution contemplates a case wherein the element within a State, favorable to republican government, in the Union, may be too feeble for an opposite and hostile element external to, or even within the State; and such are precisely the cases with which we are now dealing.

An attempt to guaranty and protect a revived State government, constructed in whole, or in preponderating part, from the very element against whose hostility and violence it is to be protected, is simply absurd. There must be a test by which to separate the opposing elements, so as to build only from the sound; and that test is a sufficiently liberal one, which accepts as sound whoever will make a sworn recantation of his former unsoundness.

But if it be proper to require, as a test of admission to the political body, an oath of allegiance to the Constitution of the United States, and to the Union under it, why also to the laws and proclamations in regard to slavery? Those laws and proclamations were enacted and put forth for the purpose of aiding in the suppression of the rebellion. To give them their fullest effect, there had to be a pledge for their maintenance. In my judgment they have aided, and will further aid, the cause for which they were intended. To now abandon them would be not only to relinquish a lever of power, but would also be a cruel and an astounding breach of faith. I may add at this point, that while I remain in my present position I shall not attempt to retract or modify the emancipation proclamation; nor shall I return to slavery any person who is free by the terms of that proclamation, or by any of the acts of Congress. For these and other reasons it is thought best that support of these measures shall be included in the oath; and it is believed the Executive may lawfully claim it in return for pardon and restoration of forfeited rights, which he has clear constitutional power to withhold altogether, or grant upon the terms which he shall deem wisest for the public interest. It should be observed, also, that this part of the oath is subject to the modifying and abrogating power of legislation and supreme judicial decision.

The proposed acquiescence of the national Executive in any reasonable temporary State arrangement for the freed people is made with the view of possibly modifying the confusion and destitution which must, at best, attend all classes by a total revolution of labor throughout whole States. It is hoped that the already deeply afflicted people in those States may be somewhat more ready to give up the cause of their affliction, if, to this extent, this vital matter be left to themselves; while no power of the national Executive to prevent an abuse is abridged by the proposition.

The suggestion in the proclamation as to maintaining the political framework of the States on what is called reconstruction, is made in the hope that it may do good without danger of harm. It will save labor and avoid great confusion.[10]

But why any proclamation now upon this subject? This question is beset with the conflicting views that the step might be delayed too long or be taken too soon. In some States the elements for resumption seem ready for

10  Lincoln had composed a longer paragraph in his preliminary draft: "The suggestion in the proclamation, as to maintaining the general old frame-work of the States, on what is called re-construction, is made in the hope that it may do good, without danger of harm. The question whether these States have continued to be States in the Union, or have become territories, out of it, seems to me, in every present aspect, to be of no practical importance. They all have been States in the Union; and all are to be hereafter, as we all propose; and a controversy whether they have ever been out of it, might divide and weaken, but could not enhance our strength, in restoring the proper national and State relations." *CW*, 7:52n40.

11  Predictably, the response of the press to Lincoln's message was along partisan lines. Horace Greeley's *New York Tribune* applauded Lincoln's "wise and generous impulses," while the *Richmond Examiner* condemned the president as "a Yankee monster of inhumanity and falsehood." Cited in Holzer, *Lincoln and the Power of the Press,* 456.

action, but remain inactive, apparently for want of a rallying point—a plan of action. Why shall A adopt the plan of B, rather than B that of A? And if A and B should agree, how can they know but that the general government here will reject their plan? By the proclamation a plan is presented which may be accepted by them as a rallying point, and which they are assured in advance will not be rejected here. This may bring them to act sooner than they otherwise would.

The objections to a premature presentation of a plan by the national Executive consists in the danger of committals on points which could be more safely left to further developments. Care has been taken to so shape the document as to avoid embarrassments from this source. Saying that, on certain terms, certain classes will be pardoned, with rights restored, it is not said that other classes, or other terms, will never be included. Saying that reconstruction will be accepted if presented in a specified way, it is not said it will never be accepted in any other way.

The movements, by State action, for emancipation in several of the States, not included in the emancipation proclamation, are matters of profound gratulation. And while I do not repeat in detail what I have heretofore so earnestly urged upon this subject, my general views and feelings remain unchanged; and I trust that Congress will omit no fair opportunity of aiding these important steps to a great consummation.

In the midst of other cares, however important, we must not lose sight of the fact that the war power is still our main reliance. To that power alone can we look, yet for a time, to give confidence to the people in the contested regions, that the insurgent power will not again overrun them. Until that confidence shall be established, little can be done anywhere for what is called reconstruction. Hence our chiefest care must still be directed to the army and navy, who have thus far borne their harder part so nobly and well. And it may be esteemed fortunate that in giving the greatest efficiency to these indispensable arms, we do also honorably recognize the gallant men, from commander to sentinel, who compose them, and to whom, more than to others, the world must stand indebted for the home of freedom disenthralled, regenerated, enlarged, and perpetuated.[11]

ABRAHAM LINCOLN

# Proclamation of Amnesty and Reconstruction

<hr/>

## December 8, 1863

*Lincoln surprised Congress, and the country, by attaching this draft reconstruction plan to his 1863 annual message, offering generous pardons to loyal Southerners, along with restitution of personal property—"except as to slaves."*

1   U.S. Constitution, Article II, Section 2.

**By the President of the United States of America:**
**A Proclamation.**

Whereas, in and by the Constitution of the United States, it is provided that the President "shall have power to grant reprieves and pardons for offences against the United States, except in cases of impeachment;"[1] and

Whereas a rebellion now exists whereby the loyal State governments of several States have for a long time been subverted, and many persons have committed and are now guilty of treason against the United States; and

Whereas, with reference to said rebellion and treason, laws have been enacted by Congress declaring forfeitures and confiscation of property and liberation of slaves, all upon terms and conditions therein stated, and also declaring that the President was thereby authorized at any time thereafter, by proclamation, to extend to persons who may have participated in the existing rebellion, in any State or part thereof, pardon and amnesty, with such exceptions and at such times and on such conditions as he may deem expedient for the public welfare; and

Whereas the congressional declaration for limited and conditional pardon accords with well-established judicial exposition of the pardoning power; and

Whereas, with reference to said rebellion, the President of the United States has issued several proclamations, with provisions in regard to the liberation of slaves; and

Whereas it is now desired by some persons heretofore engaged in said rebellion to resume their allegiance to the United States, and to reinaugurate loyal State governments within and for their respective States; therefore,

I, Abraham Lincoln, President of the United States, do proclaim, declare, and make known to all persons who have, directly or by implication, partic-ipated in the existing rebellion, except as hereinafter excepted, that a full pardon is hereby granted to them and each of them, with restoration of all rights of property, except as to slaves, and in property cases where rights of third parties shall have intervened, and upon the condition that every such person shall take and subscribe an oath, and thenceforward keep and main-tain said oath inviolate; and which oath shall be registered for permanent preservation, and shall be of the tenor and effect following, to wit:

"I, _____ , do solemnly swear, in presence of Almighty God, that I will henceforth faithfully support, protect and defend the Constitution of the United States, and the union of the States thereunder; and that I will, in like manner, abide by and faithfully support all acts of Congress passed dur-ing the existing rebellion with reference to slaves, so long and so far as not repealed, modified or held void by Congress, or by decision of the Supreme Court; and that I will, in like manner, abide by and faithfully support all proclamations of the President made during the existing rebellion having reference to slaves, so long and so far as not modified or declared void by decision of the Supreme Court. So help me God."

The persons excepted from the benefits of the foregoing provisions are all who are, or shall have been, civil or diplomatic officers or agents of the so-called confederate government; all who have left judicial stations under the United States to aid the rebellion; all who are, or shall have been, military or naval officers of said so-called confederate government above the rank of colonel in the army, or of lieutenant in the navy; all who left seats in the United States Congress to aid the rebellion; all who resigned commissions in the army or navy of the United States, and afterwards aided the rebellion; and all who have engaged in any way in treating colored persons or white persons, in charge of such, otherwise than lawfully as prisoners of war, and which persons may have been found in the United States service, as soldiers, seamen, or in any other capacity.

And I do further proclaim, declare, and make known, that whenever, in any of the States of Arkansas, Texas, Louisiana, Mississippi, Tennessee, Ala-bama, Georgia, Florida, South Carolina, and North Carolina, a number of persons, not less than one-tenth in number of the votes cast in such State at the Presidential election of the year of our Lord one thousand eight hun-dred and sixty, each having taken the oath aforesaid and not having since violated it, and being a qualified voter by the election law of the State exist-ing immediately before the so-called act of secession, and excluding all oth-ers, shall re-establish a State government which shall be republican, and in no wise contravening said oath, such shall be recognized as the true government of the State, and the State shall receive thereunder the benefits of the constitutional provision which declares that "The United States shall guaranty to every State in this union a republican form of government, and shall protect each of them against invasion; and, on application of the legislature, or the executive, (when the legislature cannot be convened,) against domestic violence."

And I do further proclaim, declare, and make known that any provision which may be adopted by such State government in relation to the freed people of such State, which shall recognize and declare their permanent freedom, provide for their education, and which may yet be consistent, as a temporary arrangement, with their present condition as a laboring, landless, and homeless class, will not be objected to by the national Executive. And it is suggested as not improper, that, in constructing a loyal State government in any State, the name of the State, the boundary, the subdivisions, the constitution, and the general code of laws, as before the rebellion, be maintained, subject only to the modifications made necessary by the conditions hereinbefore stated, and such others, if any, not contravening said conditions, and which may be deemed expedient by those framing the new State government.

To avoid misunderstanding, it may be proper to say that this proclamation, so far as it relates to State governments, has no reference to States wherein loyal State governments have all the while been maintained. And for the same reason, it may be proper to further say that whether members sent to Congress from any State shall be admitted to seats, constitutionally rests exclusively with the respective Houses, and not to any extent with the Executive. And still further, that this proclamation is intended to present the people of the States wherein the national authority has been suspended, and loyal State governments have been subverted, a mode in and by which the national authority and loyal State governments may be re-established within said States, or in any of them; and, while the mode presented is the best the Executive can suggest, with his present impressions, it must not be understood that no other possible mode would be acceptable.[2]

Given under my hand at the city, of Washington, the 8th. day of December, A.D. one thousand eight hundred and sixty-three, and of the independence of the United States of America the eighty-eighth.

ABRAHAM LINCOLN
By the President:
    WILLIAM H. SEWARD, Secretary of State.

2    On December 11, the *New York Times* editorialized in approval of the proclamation: "The President's plan avoids all incongruities, and fulfills each cardinal requirement. By preserving the integrity of the States, it secures a Federal restoration, true alike in name and fact. By necessitating an oath of loyalty as a condition precedent to amnesty and pardon and the renewal of civil rights, it deprives unrepentant traitors of the malign use of any civil power, and thus makes the Federal restoration safe. The plan, in principle and application, is perfectly adapted to the exigency, and will be approved by the loyal people." Republicans in general and most Radical Republicans in particular were, for the most part, supportive of Lincoln's amnesty and reconstruction plan. One Radical newspaper, the *Boston Commonwealth,* celebrated Lincoln's "conversion to the radical programme," as he now accepted the premise that "no rebel State shall again be received into the Union as a slave State, or with slavery existing as a political and social element." Not all were as enthusiastic as the *Boston Commonwealth.* Some Radicals, Conservative Republicans, and Democrats objected to various aspects of the plan. The Democratic *Cincinnati Enquirer,* for example, condemned Lincoln's plan "as crude and unconstitutional as it is impolitic." In the end, however, it would be the Radicals who would present the biggest challenge to Lincoln's plan, culminating in the passage of the Wade-Davis Bill, on July 2, 1864, which sought to remove responsibility for reconstruction from the executive to the legislative branch. Lincoln pocket vetoed the legislation, causing extreme indignation among Radicals. Quotes cited in Burlingame, *Abraham Lincoln,* 2:597–599.

*No American president had ever recommended black suffrage until Lincoln wrote this extraordinary letter —urging the newly elected governor of newly Unionized Louisiana to grant voting rights to "some of the colored people" there.*

1    Michael Hahn (1830–1886) was elected governor of the readmitted state of Louisiana on February 22, 1864. Lincoln later appointed him military governor of the state. Hahn supported emancipation but not equal rights for blacks. "Hahn, Michael," Biographical Directory of the United States Congress, http://bioguide.congress. gov/scripts/biodisplay.pl?index=H000019 (accessed February 6, 2015).

2    The new state constitution adopted by the convention in September restricted the elective franchise to whites, but it did not specifically rule out extending voting rights to African Americans later.

# Letter to Louisiana Governor Michael Hahn

## March 13, 1864

*Private*

Hon. Michael Hahn[1]

My dear Sir:

Executive Mansion,
Washington,
March 13. 1864.

I congratulate you on having fixed your name in history as the first-free-state Governor of Louisiana. Now you are about to have a Convention which, among other things, will probably define the elective franchise. I barely suggest for your private consideration, whether some of the colored people may not be let in—as, for instance, the very intelligent, and especially those who have fought gallantly in our ranks. They would probably help, in some trying time to come, to keep the jewel of liberty within the family of freedom. But this is only a suggestion, not to the public, but to you alone.[2]

Yours truly
A. LINCOLN

Abraham Lincoln. Photograph by Anthony Berger, Mathew Brady Gallery (Washington, DC, February 9, 1864).

Abraham Lincoln. Photograph by Anthony Berger, Mathew Brady Gallery (Washington, DC, February 9, 1864). The pose was later engraved for the five-dollar bill.

*Lincoln soon set his sights on increasing Union loyalty in his native Kentucky. On March 26, he met with a small delegation that included newspaper editor Albert Hodges, who told the president that there was "much dissatisfaction" in his state over the "enlistment of slaves." Apparently Lincoln's painstaking justification impressed his visitors, for Hodges requested a written copy so he could publish it in his paper. The resulting letter, in which Lincoln reiterates his intense abhorrence of slavery, is famous for Lincoln's overly modest insistence that he had not controlled events but, rather, that "events have controlled me." It also notably assigned responsibility for emancipation to a higher authority. "God alone," the president insisted, could claim responsibility for the "nation's condition."*

1  Archibald Dixon (1802–1876) was a proslavery former U.S. senator from Kentucky. Thomas Elliott Bramlette (1817–1875) was the governor of Kentucky. He had served as a colonel in the Union army early in the war, but later opposed the recruitment of African Americans. The two men met with Lincoln at the White House on March 26, 1864, to express their concerns about black recruitment. Accompanying Dixon and Bramlette was Albert G. Hodges (1802–1881), editor of Kentucky's pro-Union *Frankfort Commonwealth.* Lincoln talked about the meeting with his friend Orville H. Browning, Republican senator from Illinois, the following week. Browning recalled: "He said when they were discussing the matter he asked them to let him make a little speech to them, which he did and with which they were much pleased. That afternoon Mr Hodges came back to him, and asked him to give him a copy of his remarks to take with him to Ky. He told Mr. Hodges that what he had said was not written, and that he had not then time to commit it to paper— but to go home and he would write him a letter in which he would give, as nearly as he could all that he had said to them orally." *Diary of Orville Hickman Browning,* 2:665.

# Letter to Albert G. Hodges

## April 4, 1864

A. G. Hodges, Esq                                      Executive Mansion,
Frankfort, Ky.                            Washington, April 4, 1864.
My dear Sir:

You ask me to put in writing the substance of what I verbally said the other day, in your presence, to Governor Bramlette and Senator Dixon.[1] It was about as follows:

"I am naturally anti-slavery. If slavery is not wrong, nothing is wrong. I can not remember when I did not so think, and feel. And yet I have never understood that the Presidency conferred upon me an unrestricted right to act officially upon this judgment and feeling. It was in the oath I took that I would, to the best of my ability, preserve, protect, and defend the Constitution of the United States. I could not take the office without taking the oath. Nor was it my view that I might take an oath to get power, and break the oath in using the power. I understood, too, that in ordinary civil administration this oath even forbade me to practically indulge my primary abstract judgment on the moral question of slavery. I had publicly declared this many times, and in many ways. And I aver that, to this day, I have done no official act in mere deference to my abstract judgment and feeling on slavery. I did understand however, that my oath to preserve the constitution to the best of my ability, imposed upon me the duty of preserving, by every indispensable means, that government—that nation—of which that constitution was the organic law. Was it possible to lose the nation, and yet preserve the constitution? By general law life *and* limb must be protected; yet often a limb must be amputated to save a life; but a life is never wisely given to save a limb. I felt that measures, otherwise unconstitutional, might become lawful, by becoming indispensable to the preservation of the constitu-

Edward Herline, *President Lincoln and His Cabinet. Reading of the Emancipation Proclamation.* Lithograph (Philadelphia: D. Hensel & Co. and Goff & Bros., 1866).

tion, through the preservation of the nation. Right or wrong, I assumed this ground, and now avow it. I could not feel that, to the best of my ability, I had even tried to preserve the constitution, if, to save slavery, or any minor matter, I should permit the wreck of government, country, and Constitution all together. When, early in the war, Gen. Fremont attempted military emancipation, I forbade it, because I did not then think it an indispensable necessity. When a little later, Gen. Cameron, then Secretary of War, sug-

2   Lincoln and Browning agreed that there had been "much dissatisfaction" in Kentucky "in regard to the enlistment of slaves as soldiers." But recalling his recent meeting with the Kentucky delegation, the president expressed the belief that "everything had been amicably adjusted between them, and that they had gone home satisfied." The president then read the text aloud to Senator Browning, who called it a "well written and excellent paper." Ibid., 2:665.

3   Lincoln was eager to see this letter published in the *Frankfort Commonwealth*—and elsewhere. When no word of its appearance arrived, he wired Hodges to inquire: "Did you receive my letter?" Hodges quickly assured the president that the message "will be given to the people of Kentucky at the proper time," adding: "I have shown it to some of the prominent Union men here and from other parts of the State . . . and I have met but one as yet who dissents from your reasoning upon the subject of slavery." Referring to the upcoming presidential election later that year, Hodges warned that Democratic papers would make "extraordinary efforts" to defeat him but confidently predicted: "with your name before the people of our State—to use a homely phrase,—'we shall *flax them out handsomely.*'" Lincoln to Hodges, April 22, 1864, *CW*, 7:308; Hodges to Lincoln, April 22, 1864, Lincoln Papers, Library of Congress. In fact, with Governor Bramlette leading the opposition, Lincoln lost Kentucky badly that November, earning just 30 percent of the popular vote and losing the soldiers' votes, counted separately, by more than two to one. William C. Harris, *Lincoln and the Border States: Preserving the Union* (Lawrence: University Press of Kansas, 2011), 245–257.

gested the arming of the blacks, I objected, because I did not yet think it an indispensable necessity. When, still later, Gen. Hunter attempted military emancipation, I again forbade it, because I did not yet think the indispensable necessity had come. When, in March, and May, and July 1862 I made earnest, and successive appeals to the border states to favor compensated emancipation, I believed the indispensable necessity for military emancipation, and arming the blacks would come, unless averted by that measure.[2] They declined the proposition; and I was, in my best judgment, driven to the alternative of either surrendering the Union, and with it, the Constitution, or of laying strong hand upon the colored element. I chose the latter. In choosing it, I hoped for greater gain than loss; but of this, I was not entirely confident. More than a year of trial now shows no loss by it in our foreign relations, none in our home popular sentiment, none in our white military force,—no loss by it any how or any where. On the contrary, it shows a gain of quite a hundred and thirty thousand soldiers, seamen, and laborers. These are palpable facts, about which, as facts, there can be no cavilling. We have the men; and we could not have had them without the measure.

And now let any Union man who complains of the measure, test himself by writing down in one line that he is for subduing the rebellion by force of arms; and in the next, that he is for taking these hundred and thirty thousand men from the Union side, and placing them where they would be but for the measure he condemns. If he can not face his case so stated, it is only because he can not face the truth.["]

I add a word which was not in the verbal conversation. In telling this tale I attempt no compliment to my own sagacity. I claim not to have controlled events, but confess plainly that events have controlled me. Now, at the end of three years struggle the nation's condition is not what either party, or any man devised, or expected. God alone can claim it. Whither it is tending seems plain. If God now wills the removal of a great wrong, and wills also that we of the North as well as you of the South, shall pay fairly for our complicity in that wrong, impartial history will find therein new cause to attest and revere the justice and goodness of God.[3]

Yours truly
A. LINCOLN

# Address at the Maryland Sanitary Commission Fair, Baltimore

## April 18, 1864

LADIES AND GENTLEMEN—CALLING TO MIND THAT WE ARE IN BALTI-more, we can not fail to note that the world moves.[1] Looking upon these many people, assembled here, to serve, as they best may, the soldiers of the Union, it occurs at once that three years ago, the same soldiers could not so much as pass through Baltimore. The change from then till now, is both great, and gratifying. Blessings on the brave men who have wrought the change, and the fair women who strive to reward them for it.[2]

But Baltimore suggests more than could happen within Baltimore. The change within Baltimore is part only of a far wider change.[3] When the war began, three years ago, neither party, nor any man, expected it would last till now. Each looked for the end, in some way, long ere to-day. Neither did any anticipate that domestic slavery would be much affected by the war. But here we are; the war has not ended, and slavery has been much affected—how much needs not now to be recounted. So true is it that man proposes, and God disposes.

But we can see the past, though we may not claim to have directed it; and seeing it, in this case, we feel more hopeful and confident for the future.

The world has never had a good definition of the word liberty, and the American people, just now, are much in want of one. We all declare for liberty; but in using the same *word* we do not all mean the same *thing*. With some the word liberty may mean for each man to do as he pleases with himself, and the product of his labor; while with others the same word may mean for some men to do as they please with other men, and the product of other men's labor. Here are two, not only different, but incompatable [*sic*] things, called by the same name—liberty. And it follows that each of the things is, by the respective parties, called by two different and incompatable [*sic*] names—liberty and tyranny.

*Lincoln made one of his rare presidential speeches at an April 1864 fair organized for the benefit of Union soldiers. These somewhat disorganized remarks do boast Lincoln's justly famous rumination on the "definition of the word liberty." His speech did not include a passage he drafted for the occasion but wisely deleted: a surprisingly bitter recollection that when he had passed through the city en route to his swearing-in back in February 1861, "not one hand reached forth to greet me, not one voice broke the stillness to cheer me." After writing those lines, perhaps Lincoln recalled that his 1861 visit had elicited no welcome because he had passed through the city in secret, and, some said, in disguise.*

1   As he ascended the speaker's platform for the evening ceremony opening the Maryland fair, Lincoln was greeted by the "waving of handkerchiefs and continuous cheers." *Baltimore Sun,* April 20, 1864. Accompanied by Mrs. Lincoln, he later spent two hours touring the lavish displays and booths, at one point offering a kiss to a lady costumed as the old woman who lived in a shoe. *Baltimore American,* April 20, 1864.

2   Lincoln originally planned to open his speech with a long rumination on the icy reception that had awaited him in Baltimore back in February 1861. "Now, three years having past [*sic*]," the president planned to say: "Baltimore marks my coming, and cheers me when I come. Traitorous malice has sought to wrong Baltimore, ascribing to one cause what is justly due to another. . . . I take it to be unquestionable that what happened here three years ago, and what happens here now, was contempt of office then, and is purely appreciation of merit now." Lincoln wisely decided to omit these unusually self-serving remarks. *CW,* 7:303.

3   During this same month, a Maryland state constitutional convention adopted an article banning slavery in the state, which had been excluded from the Emancipation Proclamation

*Buildings of the Great Central Fair, in aid of the U.S. Sanitary Commission, Logan Square, Philadelphia, June 1864.* Lithograph (Philadelphia: P. S. Duval & Son, 1864). The success of sanitary fairs in Chicago, Cincinnati, and Boston encouraged other cities, such as Baltimore and Philadelphia (shown here), to hold their own fairs.

because it did not secede. On November 1, 1864, Maryland officially abolished slavery.

4   The *Baltimore New Era* reported that three thousand "Colored" soldiers marched through the streets that day, "huzzahed on their way to the front by the white population"—although their parade occurred only *after* white troops had marched along the same route first, and separately. Robert W. Schoeberlein, "A Fair to Remember: Maryland Women in Aid of the Union," *Maryland Historical Society Magazine* 90 (Winter 1995): 477. Those troops may have joined the dense crowd to hear the president that evening.

The shepherd drives the wolf from the sheep's throat, for which the sheep thanks the shepherd as a *liberator,* while the wolf denounces him for the same act as the destroyer of liberty, especially as the sheep was a black one. Plainly the sheep and the wolf are not agreed upon a definition of the word liberty; and precisely the same difference prevails to-day among us human creatures, even in the North, and all professing to love liberty. Hence we behold the processes by which thousands are daily passing from under the yoke of bondage, hailed by some as the advance of liberty, and bewailed by others as the destruction of all liberty. Recently, as it seems, the people of Maryland have been doing something to define liberty; and thanks to them that, in what they have done, the wolf's dictionary, has been repudiated.[4]

It is not very becoming for one in my position to make speeches at great length; but there is another subject upon which I feel that I ought to say a word. A painful rumor, true I fear, has reached us of the massacre, by the rebel forces, at Fort Pillow, in the West end of Tennessee, on the Mississippi river, of some three hundred colored soldiers and white officers, who had just been overpowered by their assailants.[5] There seems to be some anxiety in the public mind whether the government is doing it's [*sic*] duty to the colored soldier, and to the service, at this point. At the beginning of the war, and for some time, the use of colored troops was not contemplated; and how the change of purpose was wrought, I will not now take time to explain. Upon a clear conviction of duty I resolved to turn that element of strength to account; and I am responsible for it to the American people, to the christian world, to history, and on my final account to God. Having determined to use the negro as a soldier, there is no way but to give him all the protection given to any other soldier. The difficulty is not in stating the principle, but in practically applying it. It is a mistake to suppose the government is indiffe[re]nt to this matter, or is not doing the best it can in regard to it. We do not to-day *know* that a colored soldier, or white officer commanding colored soldiers, has been massacred by the rebels when made a prisoner. We fear it, believe it, I may say, but we do not *know* it. To take the life of one of their prisoners, on the assumption that they murder ours, when it is short of certainty that they do murder ours, might be too serious, too cruel a mistake. We are having the Fort-Pillow affair thoroughly investigated; and such investigation will probably show conclusively how the truth is. If, after all that has been said, it shall turn out that there has been no massacre at Fort-Pillow, it will be almost safe to say there has been none, and will be none elsewhere. If there has been the massacre of three hundred there, or even the tenth part of three hundred, it will be conclusively proved; and being so proved, the retribution shall as surely come.[6] It will be a matter of grave consideration in what exact course to apply the retribution; but in the supposed case, it must come.

5    On April 12, Confederate forces under General Nathan Bedford Forrest (1821–1877) had overrun Fort Pillow, Tennessee, an earthwork fortification high above the Mississippi River some forty miles north of Memphis. According to the claims of some of the Union survivors, Forrest's forces shot and killed black troops who had already surrendered and thrown down their arms. Confederates insisted that soldiers of the 11th U.S. Colored Troops and the 4th U.S. Colored Light Artillery surrendered but then seized their weapons and tried to resume fighting, resulting in an unusually high casualty rate among them (more than 60 percent). The so-called Fort Pillow Massacre enraged Northerners and became a rallying cry for African American soldiers.

6    Lincoln called members of his cabinet together for a meeting at the White House on May 3 and told them: "It is now quite certain that a large number of our colored soldiers, with their white officers, were, by the rebel force, massacred after they had surrendered, at the recent capture of Fort-Pillow." *CW*, 7:328. Lincoln asked each of his cabinet officers for a written recommendation on the matter of possible reprisals. In the end, the administration did not adopt an official policy of reprisals against Confederate prisoners of war for the Fort Pillow massacre.

*After refusing to sign a recent congressional resolution on reconstruction because, he claimed, it was not presented for his approval until the waning hours of the session, Lincoln issued this proclamation belatedly endorsing the bill and welcoming rebel states to rejoin the Union if they abandoned both slavery and their allegiance to the Confederacy. It was probably no coincidence that the president made his views on reconstruction public as casualties mounted in Grant's stalled effort to destroy Lee's army in Virginia, and also as the presidential election campaign began to heat up.*

1   In response to the president's lenient proposals for reconstruction, the Wade-Davis Bill, passed by Congress on July 2, allowed seceded states to rejoin the Union only if they called a constitutional convention (to be attended only by those who swore allegiance to the Union), agreed to emancipate slaves, and received loyalty pledges from 50 percent of their citizens. When Lincoln killed the bill with a pocket veto, its authors, Ohio senator Benjamin F. Wade (1800–1878) and Maryland representative Henry Winter Davis (1817–1865), responded with a manifesto criticizing Lincoln. The *New York Times* (which published it as a scoop) denounced the manifesto as "a treacherous and malignant attempt to stab a president whom they profess to support" (August 11, 1864).

2   Indefinite adjournment.

3   Lincoln had drafted the following conclusion to this proclamation: "it having been impossible, for want of time, even had the Bill been approved, to nominate Provisional Governors to, and have them confirmed by, the Senate, before it's [sic] adjournment." Attorney General Edward Bates proposed a slightly rewritten version, but the thought was dropped entirely from the official proclamation. *CW,* 7:434n9.

# Proclamation on Reconstruction

## July 8, 1864

**By the President of the United States.**
**A Proclamation.**

Whereas, at the late Session, Congress passed a Bill, "To guarantee to certain States, whose governments have been usurped or overthrown, a republican form of Government," a copy of which is hereunto annexed:[1]

And whereas, the said Bill was presented to the President of the United States, for his approval, less than one hour before the *sine die* adjournment[2] of said Session, and was not signed by him:

And whereas, the said Bill contains, among other things, a plan for restoring the States in rebellion to their proper practical relation in the Union, which plan expresses the sense of Congress upon that subject, and which plan it is now thought fit to lay before the people for their consideration:

Now, therefore, I, Abraham Lincoln, President of the United States, do proclaim, declare, and make known, that, while I am, (as I was in December last, when by proclamation I propounded a plan for restoration) unprepared, by a formal approval of this Bill, to be inflexibly committed to any single plan of restoration; and, while I am also unprepared to declare, that the free-state constitutions and governments, already adopted and installed in Arkansas and Louisiana, shall be set aside and held for nought, thereby repelling and discouraging the loyal citizens who have set up the same, as to further effort; or to declare a constitutional competency in Congress to abolish slavery in States, but am at the same time sincerely hoping and expecting that a constitutional amendment, abolishing slavery throughout the nation, may be adopted, nevertheless, I am fully satisfied with the system for restoration contained in the Bill, as one very proper plan for the loyal people of any State choosing to adopt it; and that I am, and at all times shall

HON. ABRAHAM LINCOLN, President of United States.

be, prepared to give the Executive aid and assistance to any such people, so soon as the military resistance to the United States shall have been suppressed in any such State, and the people thereof shall have sufficiently returned to their obedience to the Constitution and the laws of the United States,—in which cases, military Governors will be appointed, with directions to proceed according to the Bill[.][3]

In testimony whereof, I have hereunto set my hand and caused the Seal of the United States to be affixed.

Done at the City of Washington this eighth day of July, in the year of Our Lord, one thousand eight hundred and sixtyfour, and of the Independence of the United States the eighty-ninth.

ABRAHAM LINCOLN.
By the President:
WILLIAM H. SEWARD, Secretary of State.

Lewis E. Walker, *Hon. Abraham Lincoln, President of the United States*. Stereo photograph (Washington, DC: E. & H. T. Anthony, ca. 1865). Lincoln may have had his hair cut short in preparation for having a life mask taken by sculptor Clark Mills in February 1865. One artist observed that the president's hair stood out "like an oven broom."

# Telegram to General Ulysses S. Grant

## August 17, 1864

*Hearing rumors that the War Department planned to "draw troops" from his ranks to "keep the loyal States in harness" if their citizens resisted the latest draft quotas, Grant had warned that it would then "prove difficult to suppress the rebellion in the disloyal States" (emphasis added). Lincoln reassured Grant with this dispatch.*

*"Cypher"*
Lieut. Gen. Grant                                    Executive Mansion,
City Point, Va.                          Washington, August 17. 1864.

I have seen your despatch expressing your unwillingness to break your hold where you are. Neither am I willing. Hold on with a bull-dog gripe [*sic*], and chew & choke, as much as possible.

A. LINCOLN

*The Old Bulldog on the Right Track.* Lithograph (New York: Currier & Ives, 1864). This cartoon represents the military situation in August 1864, with General Grant, in the form of a bulldog, cornering Confederates Robert E. Lee, Jefferson Davis, and P. G. T. Beauregard in their Richmond doghouse, and Democratic presidential candidate George B. McClellan urging Lincoln to call off his "dog."

*Lincoln did no overt campaigning for a second term as president, refusing several invitations to speak at rallies and mass meetings. But he did impart his feelings about the struggle to save the Union to several Ohio regiments that fortuitously gathered, one after another, at the White House in the summer of 1864. This is one of the best of those impromptu orations— the closest things to campaign speeches that Lincoln delivered in 1864. Widely reprinted in Northern newspapers, these talks served as ample substitutes for stump speeches and kept Lincoln's thoughts before a wide public.*

1    During this same period Lincoln also addressed the soldiers of the 164th and 148th Ohio Regiments, delivering similar messages, all widely published in the press. *CW*, 7:505–506, 528–529.

"This reminds me of a little joke," *Harper's Weekly.* Woodcut engraving (September 17, 1864). Cartoon showing the six foot four Lincoln holding in his palm his much smaller Democratic opponent in the 1864 campaign, George McClellan.

# Speech to the 166th Ohio Regiment

## August 22, 1864

I SUPPOSE YOU ARE GOING HOME TO SEE YOUR FAMILIES AND FRIENDS. For the service you have done in this great struggle in which we are engaged I present you sincere thanks for myself and the country.[1] I almost always feel inclined, when I happen to say anything to soldiers, to impress upon them in a few brief remarks the importance of success in this contest. It is not merely for to-day, but for all time to come that we should perpetuate for our children's children this great and free government, which we have enjoyed all our lives. I beg you to remember this, not merely for my sake, but for yours. I happen temporarily to occupy this big White House. I am a living witness that any one of your children may look to come here as my father's child has. It is in order that each of you may have through this free government which we have enjoyed, an open field and a fair chance for your industry, enterprise and intelligence; that you may all have equal privileges in the race of life, with all its desirable human aspirations. It is for this the struggle should be maintained, that we may not lose our birthright—not only for one, but for two or three years. The nation is worth fighting for, to secure such an inestimable jewel.

# Memorandum on His Likely Defeat

## August 23, 1864

*In the depths of political despair, Lincoln wrote this prediction of his own election loss. Grant's army was stalemated in Virginia with casualties (and criticism) mounting. The powerful newspaper editor Horace Greeley had undermined Lincoln's candidacy with a breakaway peacemaking effort, and now Henry Raymond of the* New York Times, *who also served as chairman of the Republican National Committee, had warned the president of his almost certain defeat. Believing his reelection doomed, Lincoln composed this pledge of cooperation with the incoming Democratic administration, then sealed the memo shut and asked his cabinet officers to sign it sight unseen.*

Executive Mansion
Washington, Aug. 23, 1864.

This morning, as for some days past, it seems exceedingly probable that this Administration will not be re-elected. Then it will be my duty to so co-operate with the President elect, as to save the Union between the election and the inauguration; as he will have secured his election on such ground that he can not possibly save it afterwards.[1]

A. LINCOLN

1    Although many guesses have been offered to explain why Lincoln wrote the memo—among them a secret desire to set up a coalition Unionist transition government between Election and Inauguration Day, after likely Democratic nominee George B. McClellan defeated him—it seems most plausible that Lincoln meant what he said when he opened the document and read it to his cabinet three days after he in fact won the election. He had genuinely hoped to secure McClellan's cooperation, he told the cabinet, to raise enough troops to finish the war before he left office. See Matthew Pinsker, "Seeing Lincoln's Blind Memorandum," in *Lincoln and Leadership: Military, Political, and Religious Decision Making,* ed. Randall M. Miller (New York: Fordham University Press, 2012), 60–77. Reminded that McClellan would likely have agreed but done nothing, his usual practice when commanding the army, Lincoln replied: "At least I should have done my duty and have stood clear before my own conscience." *Inside Lincoln's White House,* 248.

Memorandum concerning his probable failure of reelection. Manuscript (August 23, 1864). Lincoln ordered his cabinet members to sign this document sight unseen.

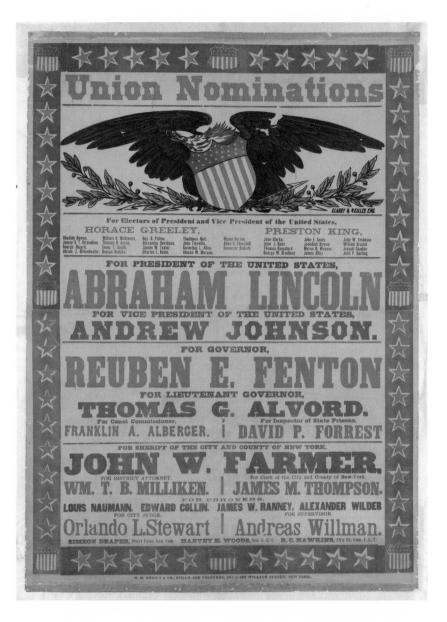

*Union Nominations . . . for President of the United States, Abraham Lincoln, for Vice President of the United States, Andrew Johnson.* Lithograph (New York, 1864). Poster by an unknown printmaker promoting the Union ticket and a list of other candidates in the state of New York.

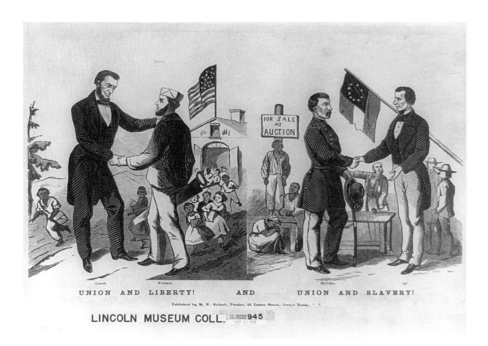

M. W. Siebert, *Union and Liberty! And Union and Slavery!* Lithograph (New York, 1864). Campaign print contrasting the 1864 Republican and Democratic platforms.

Projection of November 1864 election. Manuscript (Washington, DC, October, 1864). Weeks before the 1864 presidential election, Lincoln jotted down his projections concerning its outcome. At the time, Lincoln believed his Democratic rival George McClellan would win New York, Pennsylvania, and his own home state of Illinois (Lincoln ended up winning all three states) in a dead-heat electoral college vote.

*Eliza Gurney and three fellow Quakers had visited and prayed with Lincoln at the White House on a rain-swept autumn day back in 1862. The following year she had written the president, as she put it, to "give thee the assurance of my continued hearty sympathy in all thy heavy burthens and responsibilities and to express . . . the prayer of many thousands whose hearts thou hast gladdened by thy praiseworthy and successful effort 'to burst the bands of wickedness, and let the oppressed go free.'" When Lincoln wrote this belated but heartfelt response, General William Sherman had just taken Atlanta, injecting new energy into the president's moribund campaign for reelection.*

1   Mrs. Gurney (1801–1881) was the widow of English Quaker reformer Joseph J. Gurney (whose family owned the bank that would later become Barclays). She had visited the White House sometime around October 26, 1862—either just before or just after Lincoln wrote his undated thoughts on divine will. See "Meditation on the Divine Will, [September 2, 1862?]," in this volume.

# Letter to Eliza Paul Gurney

## September 4, 1864

Eliza P. Gurney.                                    Executive Mansion,
My esteemed friend.                    Washington, September 4. 1864.

I have not forgotten—probably never shall forget—the very impressive occasion when yourself and friends visited me on a Sabbath forenoon two years ago.[1] Nor has your kind letter, written nearly a year later, ever been forgotten. In all, it has been your purpose to strengthen my reliance on God. I am much indebted to the good christian people of the country for their constant prayers and consolations; and to no one of them, more than to yourself. The purposes of the Almighty are perfect, and must prevail, though we erring mortals may fail to accurately perceive them in advance. We hoped for a happy termination of this terrible war long before this; but God knows best, and has ruled otherwise. We shall yet acknowledge His wisdom and our own error therein. Meanwhile we must work earnestly in the best light He gives us, trusting that so working still conduces to the great ends He ordains. Surely He intends some great good to follow this mighty convulsion, which no mortal could make, and no mortal could stay.

Your people—the Friends—have had, and are having, a very great trial. On principle, and faith, opposed to both war and oppression, they can only practically oppose oppression by war. In this hard dilemma, some have chosen one horn and some the other. For those appealing to me on conscientious grounds, I have done, and shall do, the best I could and can, in my own conscience, under my oath to the law. That you believe this I doubt not; and believing it, I shall still receive, for our country and myself, your earnest prayers to our Father in Heaven.

Your sincere friend
A. LINCOLN.

Paul Wood, *Absolution under Fire.* Oil on canvas (1891). Battered and wounded men of
the Union Irish Brigade take a break during the Battle of Gettysburg and listen to an
inspiring speech by Catholic priest William J. Corby. The prelate asked the men to pray
and to remember the noble cause for which they fought, before he offered the assembled
soldiers, most of whom were Catholic, a collective absolution for their sins.

*Lincoln offered many impromptu remarks from the second-floor window of the White House during his nearly four years as president, but his November 10 speech was of particular importance because it constituted his only victory statement following a triumphant reelection just two days earlier. He addressed an enormous crowd that celebrated his reelection with cheers and music. Lincoln's conciliatory message was important chiefly for its proud defense of the election itself—which some political enemies had predicted he would cancel to maintain his "dictatorial" powers.*

1    In the November 8 election, Lincoln received 55 percent (2,213,665) of the civilian vote to 45 percent (1,802,237) for George McClellan, winning 212 of the 233 electoral votes. Soldiers voted 78 to 22 percent (116,887 to 33,748) for Lincoln, though recent research suggests that Democratic enthusiasm was discouraged or even suppressed in military camps where balloting was held. Jonathan W. White, *Emancipation, the Union, and the Reelection of Abraham Lincoln* (Baton Rouge: Louisiana State University Press), 2014.

2    "Not very graceful," Lincoln modestly admitted later of his speech, "but I am growing old enough not to care much for the manner of doing things." *Inside Lincoln's White House*, 248.

3    Lincoln had appeared in response to the serenade and spoke from his usual perch inside a second-story White House window. A "vast" crowd "filling the entire space within the grounds as far as the eye could reach" greeted Lincoln with "music, the cheers of people, and the roar of cannon" that shook the mansion's windows. Herbert Mitgang, ed., *Washington in Lincoln's Time by Noah Brooks* (New York: Rinehart & Co., 1958), 200.

# Response to a Serenade

## November 10, 1864

It has long been a grave question whether any government, not *too* strong for the liberties of its people, can be strong *enough* to maintain its own existence, in great emergencies.

On this point the present rebellion brought our republic to a severe test; and a presidential election occurring in regular course during the rebellion added not a little to the strain. If the loyal people, *united,* were put to the utmost of their strength by the rebellion, must they not fail when *divided,* and partially paralyzed, by a political war among themselves?

But the election was a necessity.[1]

We can not have free government without elections; and if the rebellion could force us to forego [*sic*], or postpone a national election, it might fairly claim to have already conquered and ruined us. The strife of the election is but human-nature practically applied to the facts of the case.[2] What has occurred in this case, must ever recur in similar cases. Human-nature will not change. In any future great national trial, compared with the men of this, we shall have as weak, and as strong; as silly and as wise; as bad and good. Let us, therefore, study the incidents of this, as philosophy to learn wisdom from, and none of them as wrongs to be revenged.

But the election, along with its incidental, and undesirable strife, has done good too. It has demonstrated that a people's government can sustain a national election, in the midst of a great civil war. Until now it has not been known to the world that this was a possibility. It shows also how *sound,* and how *strong* we still are. It shows that, even among candidates of the same party, he who is most devoted to the Union, and most opposed to treason, can receive most of the people's votes. It shows also, to the extent yet known, that we have more men now, than we had when the war began.

The White House. Photograph (Washington, DC, ca. 1860s). View of the Executive Mansion as it looked during Lincoln's presidency.

Gold is good in its place; but living, brave, patriotic men, are better than gold.

But the rebellion continues; and now that the election is over, may not all, having a common interest, re-unite in a common effort, to save our common country? For my own part I have striven, and shall strive to avoid placing any obstacle in the way. So long as I have been here I have not willingly planted a thorn in any man's bosom.

While I am deeply sensible to the high compliment of a re-election;[3] and duly grateful, as I trust, to Almighty God for having directed my countrymen to a right conclusion, as I think, for their own good, it adds nothing to my satisfaction that any other man may be disappointed or pained by the result.

May I ask those who have not differed with me, to join with me, in this same spirit towards those who have?[4]

And now, let me close by asking three hearty cheers for our brave soldiers and seamen and their gallant and skilful commanders.

4  On Election Day, Lincoln had wistfully remarked to John Hay: "It is a little singular that I who am not a vindictive man, should have always been before the people for election in canvasses marked for their bitterness." *Inside Lincoln's White House,* 243.

Two months before Election Day, Massachusetts governor John A. Andrew asked Lincoln to provide recognition to a Boston widow, five of whose sons had reportedly died fighting for the Union. On November 25, Lydia Bixby received this hand-delivered note from the president, one of the most majestic condolence letters ever composed. The text appeared in a Boston newspaper that evening, and was widely reprinted across the country soon thereafter. Had Lincoln lived longer, the sympathy letter might have proved an embarrassment: as it was later revealed, only two of Mrs. Bixby's sons had died in combat. One had deserted, another had either deserted or become a prisoner of war, and yet another had been honorably discharged. Adding to the mystery surrounding the Bixby case is an ongoing debate about the letter's authenticity. Over the years, scholars have periodically attributed the letter to White House assistant private secretary John Hay, who pasted a clipping of the published transcript into a scrapbook otherwise devoted to his own anonymous wartime journalism. Hay himself both claimed and denied authorship of the letter over the next forty years. Regardless of whether or not Lincoln wrote, dictated, or merely signed the famous note, and whether or not its recipient deserved the approbation, the letter remains one of the most frequently quoted, and widely admired, of all the compositions in the Lincoln canon.

1    No copy of the letter exists in Lincoln's hand, only facsimiles—leading to speculation that Mrs. Bixby, "an ardent Southern sympathizer," according to a descendant, destroyed the original. See, for example, Michael Burlingame, "New Light on the Bixby Letter," *Journal of the Abraham Lincoln Association* 16 (Winter 1995): 59–71.

# Letter to Mrs. Lydia Bixby

## November 21, 1864

Executive Mansion,
Washington, Nov. 21, 1864.

Dear Madam,—I have been shown in the files of the War Department a statement of the Adjutant General of Massachusetts, that you are the mother of five sons who have died gloriously on the field of battle.

I feel how weak and fruitless must be any words of mine which should attempt to beguile you from the grief of a loss so overwhelming. But I cannot refrain from tendering to you the consolation that may be found in the thanks of the Republic they died to save.

I pray that our Heavenly Father may assuage the anguish of your bereavement, and leave you only the cherished memory of the loved and lost, and the solemn pride that must be yours, to have laid so costly a sacrifice upon the altar of Freedom.

Yours, very sincerely and respectfully,

A. LINCOLN.[1]
Mrs. Bixby.

James Hamilton, after Thomas Hovenden, *In the Hands of the Enemy after Gettysburg.* Etching (New York, 1889). The print depicts several wounded Confederate soldiers being cared for in a home in the North.

John Hay. Photograph by Albert Bierstadt (1861).

*Lincoln's fourth and final annual message reiterated the government's determination to eradicate slavery— ideally to nudge passage of a resolution for a constitutional amendment, even though the House had failed by a handful of votes to approve such a measure a few weeks earlier. After offering the required reports on foreign relations, government finance, the state of the armed forces, and proposals for Indian Affairs reforms and railroad construction, Lincoln turned to the issues of war and reunion. The* London Times *found the tenor of the message "decidedly warlike," but if so, it reflected the president's resolve to win the war outright and destroy slavery in the process.*

1   General William Tecumseh Sherman (1820–1891). After capturing Atlanta in early September, Sherman, on November 15, 1864, commenced his daring, devastating, 300-mile-long March to the Sea, perhaps the most famous and widely debated military operation of the entire Civil War. The Union general's army of 62,000 men left conquered Atlanta and headed east through Georgia, largely unsupplied, toward the Atlantic coast. When Lincoln wrote his 1864 annual message a few weeks later, he had heard but few details about Sherman's progress. The general's revolutionary operation—to be accomplished without benefit of supply lines—was designed to lay waste to the South's economic infrastructure and destroy the region's will to resist—in short, as Sherman put it, to "make Georgia howl." Union forces would live off the land ("The army will forage liberally on the country during the march," declared Sherman's official orders), seizing crops, livestock, and "able-bodied . . . Negroes" as needed, while destroying railroad lines, supply depots, and government buildings as opportunities arose. The individual railroad tracks that the army ripped up, burned until soft, and then wrapped around trees became known as "Sherman's Bowties" or "Sherman's Hairpins," signaling his intention not only to disrupt transportation and thus degrade the state's

# From Annual Message to Congress

## December 6, 1864

FELLOW-CITIZENS OF THE SENATE AND HOUSE OF REPRESENTATIVES:
   Again the blessings of health and abundant harvests claim our profoundest gratitude to Almighty God.

. . .

The war continues. Since the last annual message all the important lines and positions then occupied by our forces have been maintained, and our arms have steadily advanced; thus liberating the regions left in rear, so that Missouri, Kentucky, Tennessee and parts of other States have again produced reasonably fair crops.

   The most remarkable feature in the military operations of the year is General Sherman's attempted march of three hundred miles directly through the insurgent region.[1] It tends to show a great increase of our relative strength that our General-in-Chief[2] should feel able to confront and hold in check every active force of the enemy, and yet to detach a well-appointed large army to move on such an expedition. The result not yet being known, conjecture in regard to it is not here indulged.

   Important movements have also occurred during the year to the effect of moulding society for durability in the Union. Although short of complete success, it is much in the right direction, that twelve thousand citizens in each of the States of Arkansas and Louisiana have organized loyal State governments with free constitutions, and are earnestly struggling to maintain and administer them.[3] The movements in the same direction, more extensive, though less definite in Missouri, Kentucky and Tennessee, should not be overlooked. But Maryland presents the example of complete success. Maryland is secure to Liberty and Union for all the future.[4] The genius of rebellion will no more claim Maryland. Like another foul spirit, being driven out, it may seek to tear her, but it will woo her no more.

At the last session of Congress a proposed amendment of the Constitution abolishing slavery throughout the United States, passed the Senate, but failed for lack of the requisite two-thirds vote in the House of Representatives. Although the present is the same Congress, and nearly the same members, and without questioning the wisdom or patriotism of those who stood in opposition, I venture to recommend the reconsideration and passage of the measure at the present session.[5] Of course the abstract question is not changed; but an intervening election shows, almost certainly, that the next Congress will pass the measure if this does not. Hence there is only a question of *time* as to when the proposed amendment will go to the States for their action. And as it is to so go, at all events, may we not agree that the sooner the better? It is not claimed that the election has imposed a duty on members to change their views or their votes, any further than, as an additional element to be considered, their judgment may be affected by it. It is the voice of the people now, for the first time, heard upon the question. In a great national crisis, like ours, unanimity of action among those seeking a common end is very desirable—almost indispensable. And yet no approach to such unanimity is attainable, unless some deference shall be paid to the will of the majority, simply because it is the will of the majority. In this case the common end is the maintenance of the Union; and, among the means to secure that end, such will, through the election, is most clearly declared in favor of such constitutional amendment.

The most reliable indication of public purpose in this country is derived through our popular elections. Judging by the recent canvass and its result, the purpose of the people, within the loyal States, to maintain the integrity of the Union, was never more firm, nor more nearly unanimous, than now. The extraordinary calmness and good order with which the millions of voters met and mingled at the polls, give strong assurance of this. Not only all those who supported the Union ticket, so called, but a great majority of the opposing party also, may be fairly claimed to entertain, and to be actuated by, the same purpose it is an unanswerable argument to this effect, that no candidate for any office whatever, high or low, has ventured to seek votes on the avowal that he was for giving up the Union. There have [*has*] been much impugning of motives, and much heated controversy as to the proper means and best mode of advancing the Union cause; but on the distinct issue of Union or no Union, the politicians have shown their instinctive knowledge

economy but also to demoralize the entire South by desolating the state's midsection and bringing a scorched-earth destructiveness to what until then had been a war only between armies. The Union army encountered little resistance along the way but did perhaps $100 million worth of damage during its twenty-six-day march. Sherman's strategy has been the subject of much heated discussion among historians. Long regarded as a leap into modern warfare, the operation is now considered by some scholars to reflect Sherman's personal regard for the South, where he had once lived—an effort to use the power of his army against inanimate victims rather than armies and men. Certainly this revisionist view has not permeated the South, where Sherman is still widely regarded as the greatest villain of the war. The March to the Sea ended on December 21, when Sherman reached Savannah and occupied the city largely unopposed. He then turned his army north toward the Carolinas. For studies of the campaign, see Lee Kennett, *Marching through Georgia: The Story of Soldiers and Civilians during Sherman's Campaign* (New York: HarperCollins, 1995); Joseph T. Glatthaar, *The March to the Sea and Beyond: Sherman's Troops in the Savannah and Carolina Campaigns* (New York: New York University Press, 1985).

2   General Ulysses S. Grant.

3   Lincoln had proposed, without success, that the states returning to the Union include voting rights for African Americans in their new constitutions.

4   Maryland abolished slavery on November 1, 1864, but did not begin granting the elective franchise to nonwhite men until three years later.

5   The U.S. Senate had passed the resolution sending the Thirteenth Amendment to the states for ratification on April 8, 1864, by an overwhelm-

ing vote of 38 to 6. But when the House voted on May 17, the resolution passed by a narrower margin, 93 to 65, 13 votes short of the two-thirds needed for passage. Having been reelected on a political platform that included a plank calling for passage, Lincoln was determined that the House take up the measure again. On the history of the Thirteenth Amendment, see Michael Vorenberg, *Final Freedom: The Civil War, the Abolition of Slavery, and the Thirteenth Amendment* (New York: Cambridge University Press, 2001).

6  Lincoln won 78 percent of the separately counted soldiers' votes. The soldier vote in the 1864 election is discussed in David E. Long, *The Jewel of Liberty: Abraham Lincoln's Re-election and the End of Slavery* (Mechanicsburg, PA: Stackpole Books, 1994), 255–256; and White, *Emancipation, the Union Army, and the Reelection of Abraham Lincoln.*

that there is no diversity among the people. In affording the people the fair opportunity of showing, one to another and to the world, this firmness and unanimity of purpose, the election has been of vast value to the national cause.

The election has exhibited another fact not less valuable to be known— the fact that we do not approach exhaustion in the most important branch of national resources—that of living men. While it is melancholy to reflect that the war has filled so many graves, and carried mourning to so many hearts, it is some relief to know that, compared with the surviving, the fallen have been so few. While corps, and divisions, and brigades, and regiments have formed, and fought, and dwindled, and gone out of existence, a great majority of the men who composed them are still living. The same is true of the naval service. The election returns prove this.[6] So many voters could not else be found. The States regularly holding elections, both now and four years ago, to wit, California, Connecticut, Delaware, Illinois, Indiana, Iowa, Kentucky, Maine, Maryland, Massachusetts, Michigan, Minnesota, Missouri, New Hampshire, New Jersey, New York, Ohio, Oregon, Pennsylvania, Rhode Island, Vermont, West Virginia, and Wisconsin cast 3.982.011 votes now, against 3.870.222 cast then, showing an aggregate now of 3.982.011. To this is to be added 33.762 cast now in the new States of Kansas and Nevada, which States did not vote in 1860, thus swelling the aggregate to 4.015.773 and the net increase during the three years and a half of war to 145.551. A table is appended showing particulars. To this again should be added the number of all soldiers in the field from Massachusetts, Rhode Island, New Jersey, Delaware, Indiana, Illinois, and California, who, by the laws of those States, could not vote away from their homes, and which number cannot be less than 90.000. Nor yet is this all. The number in organized Territories is triple now what it was four years ago, while thousands, white and black, join us as the national arms press back the insurgent lines. So much is shown, affirmatively and negatively, by the election. It is not material to inquire *how* the increase has been produced, or to show that it would have been *greater* but for the war, which is probably true. The important fact remains demonstrated, that we have *more* men *now* than we had when the war *began;* that we are not exhausted, nor in process of exhaustion; that we are *gaining* strength, and may, if need be, maintain the contest indefinitely. This as to men. Material resources are now more complete and abundant than ever.

The national resources, then, are unexhausted, and, as we believe, inexhaustible. The public purpose to re-establish and maintain the national authority is unchanged, and, as we believe, unchangeable. The manner of continuing the effort remains to choose. On careful consideration of all the evidence accessible it seems to me that no attempt at negotiation with the insurgent leader could result in any good. He would accept nothing short of severance of the Union—precisely what we will not and cannot give. His declarations to this effect are explicit and oft-repeated. He does not attempt to deceive us. He affords us no excuse to deceive ourselves. He cannot voluntarily reaccept the Union; we cannot voluntarily yield it. Between him and us the issue is distinct, simple, and inflexible. It is an issue which can only be tried by war, and decided by victory. If we yield, we are beaten; if the Southern people fail him, he is beaten. Either way, it would be the victory and defeat following war. What is true, however, of him who heads the insurgent cause, is not necessarily true of those who follow. Although he cannot reaccept the Union, they can. Some of them, we know, already desire peace and reunion. The number of such may increase. They can, at any moment, have peace simply by laying down their arms and submitting to the national authority under the Constitution. After so much, the government could not, if it would, maintain war against them. The loyal people would not sustain or allow it. If questions should remain, we would adjust them by the peaceful means of legislation, conference, courts, and votes, operating only in constitutional and lawful channels. Some certain, and other possible, questions are, and would be, beyond the Executive power to adjust; as, for instance, the admission of members into Congress, and whatever might require the appropriation of money. The Executive power itself would be greatly diminished by the cessation of actual war. Pardons and remissions of forfeitures, however, would still be within Executive control. In what spirit and temper this control would be exercised can be fairly judged of by the past.

A year ago general pardon and amnesty, upon specified terms, were offered to all, except certain designated classes; and, it was, at the same time, made known that the excepted classes were still within contemplation of special clemency. During the year many availed themselves of the general provision, and many more would, only that the signs of bad faith in some led to such precautionary measures as rendered the practical process less easy and certain. During the same time also special pardons have been granted to individuals of the excepted classes, and no voluntary application has been denied. Thus, practically, the door has been, for a full year, open to all, except such as were not in condition to make free choice—that is, such as were in custody or under constraint. It is still so open to all. But the time may come—probably will come—when public duty shall demand that it be closed; and that, in lieu, more rigorous measures than heretofore shall be adopted.

In presenting the abandonment of armed resistance to the national authority on the part of the insurgents, as the only indispensable condition to ending the war on the part of the government, I retract nothing heretofore said as to slavery. I repeat the declaration made a year ago, that "while I remain in my present position I shall not attempt to retract or modify the emancipation proclamation, nor shall I return to slavery any person who is free by the terms of that proclamation, or by any of the Acts of Congress." If the people should, by whatever mode or means, make it an Executive duty to re-enslave such persons, another, and not I, must be their instrument to perform it.

In stating a single condition of peace, I mean simply to say that the war will cease on the part of the government, whenever it shall have ceased on the part of those who began it.

December 6, 1864

# Letter to General Ulysses S. Grant

## January 19, 1865

For months, even years, Lincoln's eldest son, Robert, had tried to convince his wary parents that he should be allowed to join the army before the war ended. The president long opposed Bob's enlistment for fear that if he came to any harm, his wife would lose her precarious hold on mental stability—Mary Lincoln had never fully recovered from the loss of their son Willie three years earlier. In mid-January 1865, Lincoln finally found a way to get his son into uniform safely: he asked General Grant to attach him to his personal staff. Grant obliged, as a result of which Captain Robert Lincoln not only entered the service but also got to be on hand for Lee's surrender at Appomattox.

Executive Mansion, Washington,
Jan. 19, 1865.

Lieut. General Grant:

Please read and answer this letter as though I was not President, but only a friend. My son, now in his twenty second year, having graduated at Harvard, wishes to see something of the war before it ends. I do not wish to put him in the ranks, nor yet to give him a commission, to which those who have already served long, are better entitled, and better qualified to hold. Could he, without embarrassment to you, or detriment to the service, go into your Military family with some nominal rank, I, and not the public, furnishing his necessary means?[1] If no, say so without the least hesitation, because I am as anxious, and as deeply interested, that you shall not be encumbered as you can be yourself.

Yours truly
A. LINCOLN

1   There is no evidence that Lincoln made good on his promise to finance his son's military adventure, which lasted less than three months.

Anton Hohenstein, *President Lincoln and His
Family, Respectfully Dedicated to the People of
the United States.* Lithograph (Philadelphia,
1865). This postwar print was one of the first to
show Captain Robert Lincoln in uniform.

[Charles] Kimmel and [Thomas] Forster, *The
Preservers of Our Union.* Lithograph (New
York, 1865). Flanking the portraits of Lincoln
and General Ulysses S. Grant are scenes of
various Union victories.

# Response to a Serenade

## February 1, 1865

*No one made an exact transcript of the president's exultant impromptu remarks in response to a serenade celebrating House passage of the resolution sending the Thirteenth Amendment to the states for ratification. The closest we have to an authentic record of the speech is this transcription published by the* New York Tribune *on February 3. By the time Lincoln offered these comments, his home state of Illinois had already become the first to ratify the constitutional amendment abolishing slavery.*

THE PRESIDENT SAID HE SUPPOSED THE PASSAGE THROUGH CON-gress of the Constitutional amendment for the abolishment of Slavery throughout the United States,[1] was the occasion to which he was indebted for the honor of this call. (*Applause*) The occasion was one of congratulation to the country and to the whole world. But there is a task yet before us—to go forward and consummate by the votes of the States that which Congress so nobly began yesterday.[2] (*Applause and cries—"They will do it," &c.*) He had the honor to inform those present that Illinois had already to-day done the work. (*Applause*) Maryland was about half through; but he felt proud that Illinois was a little ahead.[3] He thought this measure was a very fitting if not an indispensable adjunct to the winding up of the great difficulty. He wished the reunion of all the States perfected and so effected as to remove all causes of disturbance in the future; and to attain this end it was necessary that the original disturbing cause should, if possible, be rooted out. He thought all would bear him witness that he had never shrunk from doing all that he could to eradicate Slavery by issuing an emancipation proclamation. (*Applause*) But that proclamation falls far short of what the amendment will be when fully consummated. A question might be raised whether the proclamation was legally valid.[4] It might be added that it only aided those who came into our lines and that it was inoperative as to those who did not give themselves up, or that it would have no effect upon the children of the slaves born hereafter. In fact it would be urged that it did not meet the evil. But this amendment is a King's cure for all the evils. (*Applause*) It winds the whole thing up. He would repeat that it was the fitting if not indispensable adjunct to the consummation of the great game we are playing. He could not but congratulate all present, himself, the country and the whole world upon this great moral victory.[5]

1   The constitutional amendment endorsed by Congress held: "Neither slavery nor involuntary servitude, except as a punishment for crime whereof the party shall have been duly convicted, shall exist within the United States, or any place subject to their jurisdiction." *CW,* 8:253.

2   On January 31, 1865, to great cheering from the spectator galleries, the House of Representatives passed the resolution (previously passed by the Senate), sending the Thirteenth Amendment to the states for ratification. The final tally in the House vote was 119 to 56. Vorenberg, *Final Freedom,* 207.

3   By the end of February, legislatures in eighteen of the twenty-seven states needed for ratification of the amendment (three-fourths of the states, as required by the Constitution) had voted to support it, and three more states ratified in March and April. Lincoln was dead when the twenty-seventh state, Georgia, ratified the amendment. Ibid., 212–233.

4   Lincoln had long worried that once the war ended, the Emancipation Proclamation would be declared invalid by the civil courts—or at least no longer in effect, stranding hundreds of thousands of enslaved people in legal uncertainty. As journalist James Welling put it: "Nobody was more quick to perceive or more frank to admit the legal weakness and insufficiency of the Emancipation Proclamation than Mr. Lincoln." James Welling,

"The Emancipation Proclamation," *North American Review* 130 (1880): 182. See Guelzo, *Lincoln's Emancipation Proclamation,* 190–191.

5   Lincoln's idea of "congratulating himself" included adding his signature to the resolution submitting the Thirteenth Amendment to the states—although, according to a 1798 Supreme Court decision, presidential approval was not required by the Constitution. The Senate responded by passing a resolution of its own on February 7 stating that "such approval was unnecessary." *CW,* 8:253n1.

Peter Baumgras, *Abraham Lincoln.* Oil on canvas (Washington, DC, 1865). Washington artist Baumgras (1827–1903) began this portrait of Lincoln from memory and photographs shortly after the president's second inauguration. He completed it soon after the assassination.

# Draft of an Unsent Message to Congress Proposing Compensated Emancipation

## February 5, 1865

*Hours after he posed for his final photographic portrait, Lincoln called his cabinet into session at 7:00 P.M. and proposed that this draft Joint Resolution be sent to the House and Senate. It offered $400 million in federal funding to the Confederate and Border States, and readmission to the Union, in exchange for a speedy cessation of hostilities and the abolition of slavery.*

1    Lincoln had long maintained that compensating slave owners in exchange for emancipation would be far less expensive than waging a giant war to achieve the same result, but even his cabinet secretaries apparently believed that recent House passage of the Thirteenth Amendment had already sealed slavery's doom, with no compensation required. Worried that the approaching spring thaw would bring renewed battles, and more death, the president was apparently willing to make one last attempt to use compensated emancipation to end the war.

FELLOW CITIZENS OF THE SENATE, AND HOUSE OF REPRESENTATIVES.

I respectfully recommend that a Joint Resolution, substantially as follows, be adopted so soon as practicable, by your honorable bodies.

"Resolved by the Senate and House of Representatives, of the United States of America in congress assembled: That the President of the United States is hereby empowered, in his discretion, to pay four hundred millions of dollars to the States of Alabama, Arkansas, Delaware, Florida, Georgia, Kentucky, Louisiana, Maryland, Mississippi, Missouri, North Carolina, South Carolina, Tennessee, Texas, Virginia, and West-Virginia, in the manner, and on the conditions following, towit: The payment to be made in six per cent government bonds, and to be distributed among said States *pro rata* on their respective slave populations, as shown by the census of 1860; and no part of said sum to be paid unless all resistance to the national authority shall be abandoned and cease, on or before the first day of April next; and upon such abandonment and ceasing of resistance, one half of said sum to be paid in manner aforesaid, and the remaining half to be paid only upon the amendment of the national constitution recently proposed by congress, becoming valid law, on or before the first day of July next, by the action thereon of the requisite number of States[.]"[1]

The adoption of such resolution is sought with a view to embody it, with other propositions, in a proclamation looking to peace and re-union.

Whereas a Joint Resolution has been adopted by congress in the words following, towit

Now therefore I, Abraham Lincoln, President of the United States, do proclaim, declare, and make known, that on the conditions therein stated, the power conferred on the Executive in and by said Joint Resolution, will be fully exercised; that war will cease, and armies be reduced to a basis of

Abraham Lincoln. Photograph by Alexander Gardner (Washington, DC, February 5, 1865). This last formal studio portrait shows a war-weary president, aged beyond his years by four years of toil and anxiety.

2    When his cabinet rejected the proposal, Lincoln folded the five-page draft, written on lined foolscap paper, and wrote the following endorsement on the back of the final page—misspelling the word "unanimously."

3    Acknowledging the "earnest desire of the President to conciliate and effect peace," Secretary of the Navy Gideon Welles noted that the proposal "did not meet with favor" from the cabinet (Welles included), commenting that "there may be such a thing as so overdoing as to cause a distrust or adverse feeling." *Diary of Gideon Welles*, 2:237–238.

peace; that all political offences will be pardoned; that all property, except slaves, liable to confiscation or forfeiture, will be released therefrom, except in cases of intervening interests of third parties; and that liberality will be recommended to congress upon all points not lying within executive control.

[Endorsement][2]

Feb. 5. 1865

To-day these papers, which explain themselves, were drawn up and submitted to the Cabinet & unanamously [*sic*] disapproved by them.[3] A LINCOLN

# Second Inaugural Address

## March 4, 1865

*Lincoln himself believed that this extraordinary speech, read aloud before a fully integrated crowd of as many as forty thousand standing outside the U.S. Capitol on a dreary late-winter day, would "wear as well as—perhaps better than—any thing I have ever produced," though he admitted that it was not "immediately popular." As he explained to the Albany editor and New York State Republican boss Thurlow Weed: "Men are not flattered by being shown that there has been a difference of purpose between the Almighty and them" (CW, 8:356). Hungry for a compliment, Lincoln beckoned Frederick Douglass to his side at a White House reception following the inauguration, pumped his hand, and told his long-time critic: "There is no man's opinion that I value more than yours: what did you think of it?" "Mr. Lincoln," Douglass replied, "it was a sacred effort"* (Allen Thorndike Rice, Reminiscences of Abraham Lincoln by Distinguished Men of His Time [*New York: North American Publishing, 1860*], *192–193*).

FELLOW COUNTRYMEN:

At this second appearing to take the oath of the presidential office, there is less occasion for an extended address than there was at the first. Then a statement, somewhat in detail, of a course to be pursued, seemed fitting and proper. Now, at the expiration of four years, during which public declarations have been constantly called forth on every point and phase of the great contest which still absorbs the attention, and engrosses the energies of the nation, little that is new could be presented. The progress of our arms, upon which all else chiefly depends, is as well known to the public as to myself; and it is, I trust, reasonably satisfactory and encouraging to all. With high hope for the future, no prediction in regard to it is ventured.

On the occasion corresponding to this four years ago, all thoughts were anxiously directed to an impending civil-war. All dreaded it—all sought to avert it. While the inaugeral [*sic*] address was being delivered from this place, devoted altogether to *saving* the Union without war, insurgent agents were in the city seeking to *destroy* it without war—seeking to dissol[v]e the Union, and divide effects, by negotiation. Both parties deprecated war; but one of them would *make* war rather than let the nation survive; and the other would *accept* war rather than let it perish. And the war came.

One eighth of the whole population were colored slaves, not distributed generally over the Union, but localized in the Southern part of it. These slaves constituted a peculiar and powerful interest. All knew that this interest was, somehow, the cause of the war. To strengthen, perpetuate, and extend this interest was the object for which the insurgents would rend the Union, even by war; while the government claimed no right to do more than to restrict the territorial enlargement of it. Neither party expected for the war, the magnitude, or the duration, which it has already attained. Nei-

Abraham Lincoln delivering second
inaugural address. Photograph by
Alexander Gardner (Washington,
DC, March 4, 1865).

1    Matthew 7:1.
2    Matthew 18:7.

ther anticipated that the *cause* of the conflict might cease with, or even before, the conflict itself should cease. Each looked for an easier triumph, and
a result less fundamental and astounding. Both read the same Bible, and
pray to the same God; and each invokes His aid against the other. It may
seem strange that any men should dare to ask a just God's assistance in
wringing their bread from the sweat of other men's faces; but let us judge
not that we be not judged.[1] The prayers of both could not be answered; that
of neither has been answered fully. The Almighty has His own purposes.
"Woe unto the world because of offences! for it must needs be that offences
come; but woe to that man by whom the offence cometh!"[2] If we shall suppose that American Slavery is one of those offences which, in the providence of God, must needs come, but which, having continued through His
appointed time, He now wills to remove, and that He gives to both North
and South, this terrible war, as the woe due to those by whom the offence
came, shall we discern therein any departure from those divine attributes

*The Inaugural Address of President Lincoln.* Chromolithograph (New York: J. Gibson, ca. 1865).

**3**    From Psalm 19:9. Horace Greeley, editor of the *New York Tribune,* no doubt had this fire-and-brimstone passage of Lincoln's speech in mind when he complained that his second inaugural boasted none of the "politic" and "humane" spirit of his first (March 5, 1865). He editorialized that the speech should have instead featured "manifestations of generosity, clemency, magnanimity." More predictably, the pro-Democrat *New York Herald* sneered that Lincoln's speech, however "glittering," offered "no information as to his future policy," surprisingly echoing Greeley in its lament that "a fresh, unequivocal exhibition of the spirit which impelled the former Inaugural" might have "quickened and deepened the disintegration of the Rebel forces" (March 5, 1865). Alone among the editors of New York's major newspapers, only Henry J. Raymond immediately recognized the greatness of the speech, exulting: "We have a President who will be faithful to the end, let what betide." *New York Times,* March 6, 1865.

which the believers in a Living God always ascribe to Him? Fondly do we hope—fervently do we pray—that this mighty scourge of war may speedily pass away. Yet, if God wills that it continue, until all the wealth piled by the bond-man's two hundred and fifty years of unrequited toil shall be sunk, and until every drop of blood drawn with the lash, shall be paid by another drawn with the sword, as was said three thousand years ago, so still it must be said "the judgments of the Lord, are true and righteous altogether."[3]

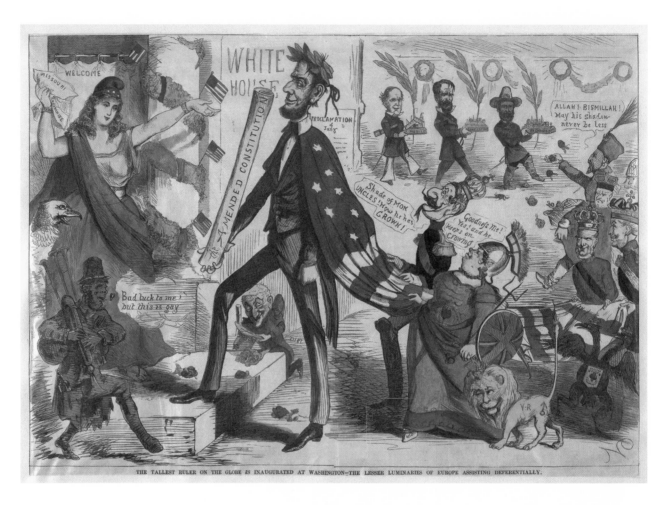

THE TALLEST RULER ON THE GLOBE IS INAUGURATED AT WASHINGTON—THE LESSER LUMINARIES OF EUROPE ASSISTING DEFERENTIALLY.

William Newman, "The tallest ruler on the globe is inaugurated at Washington—the lesser luminaries of Europe assisting deferentially," *Frank Leslie's Budget of Fun.* Woodcut engraving (New York, April 1865). This double-page cartoon depicts Lincoln, carrying an "Amended Constitution," being welcomed back by Columbia for another four years, as several "Lesser Luminaries of Europe" assist with the inauguration.

4   Lincoln read the address on Inauguration Day from a printed copy that contained the entire address within two columns on a single sheet. Ever his own best editor, Lincoln had then crossed out the final two words—"the world"—and revised it brilliantly to the more evocative and harmoniously balanced "all nations." *CW,* 8:333n4.

With malice toward none; with charity for all; with firmness in the right, as God gives us to see the right, let us strive on to finish the work we are in; to bind up the nation's wounds; to care for him who shall have borne the battle, and for his widow, and his orphan—to do all which may achieve and cherish a just, and a lasting peace, among ourselves, and with all nations.[4]

# Speech to the 140th Indiana Regiment, Washington, D.C.

## March 17, 1865

*Lincoln carefully wrote out this speech, unusual for a president who had greeted so many departing and returning regiments extemporaneously during the course of the war. Clearly he wanted to provide an official comment on reports that the Confederacy, its military ranks depleted, was now asking that slaves join its army, in essence to fight for the system that kept them in bondage. Delivered from the balcony of the Washington Hotel at 4:00 P.M., after he presented a captured Confederate battle flag to the governor of Indiana, these were Lincoln's very last recorded comments to men in uniform.*

**[Autograph Draft]**

*Fellow Citizens.* A few words only. I was born in Kentucky, raised in Indiana, reside in Illinois, and now here, it is my duty to care equally for the good people of all the States. I am to-day glad of seeing it in the power of an Indianana [*sic*] regiment to present this captured flag to the good governor of their State. And yet I would not wish to compliment Indiana above other states, remembering that all have done so well. There are but few aspects of this great war on which I have not already expressed my views by speaking or writing. There is one—the recent effort of our erring brethren [*sic*], sometimes so-called, to employ the slaves in their armies. The great question with them has been; "will the negro fight for them?" They ought to know better than we; and, doubtless, do know better than we.[1] I may incidentally remark, however, that having, in my life, heard many arguments,—or strings of words meant to pass for arguments,—intended to show that the negro ought to be a slave, that if he shall now really fight to keep himself a slave, it will be a far better argument why [he] should remain a slave than I have ever before heard. He, perhaps, ought to be a slave, if he desires it ardently enough to fight for it. Or, if one out of four will, for his own freedom, fight to keep the other three in slavery, he ought to be a slave for his selfish meanness. I have always thought that all men should be free; but if any should be slaves it should be first those who desire it for *themselves,* and secondly those who *desire* it for *others.* Whenever [I] hear any one,[2] arguing for slavery I feel a strong impulse to see it tried on him personally.

There is one thing about the negroes fighting for the rebels which we can know as well [as] they can; and that is that they can not, at [the] same time fight in their armies, and stay at home and make bread for them. And this being known and remembered we can have but little concern whether they

[1] With the Confederacy's hopes for military victory fading, its army faced diminishing manpower owing to casualties and increasing desertions. As a result, the Confederate government considered the possibility of enrolling African Americans in the army. In early March the Confederate Congress passed legislation to call up as many as 300,000 black slaves for military duty. This is one of many sarcastic comments in the speech, for Lincoln, aware of the debate within the Confederate government over the use of black soldiers, already well knew that African American troops had shown that they could and would fight for the Union and their freedom. By this time more than 200,000 blacks had served in the federal military, and had suffered a third more casualties than white troops. John David Smith, *Lincoln and the Colored Troops* (Carbondale: Southern Illinois University Press, 2013), 2, 57–58. The decision to accept slaves into the Confederate army is covered in Emory M. Thomas, *The Confederate Nation: 1861–1865* (New York: Harper & Row, 1979), 296–297.

[2] Here Lincoln had originally written "even a preacher" but deleted it. *CW,* 8:361n2.

3   Lincoln may have discarded his written draft
and paraphrased it when speaking, since the
version transcribed (and reprinted) by the *New
York Tribune* and *New York Herald* differs substantially from the handwritten draft. Ibid., n. 1.

become soldiers or not. I am rather in favor of the measure; and would at
any time if I could, have loaned them a vote to carry it. We have to reach
the bottom of the insurgent resources; and that they employ, or seriously
think of employing, the slaves as soldiers, gives us glimpses of the bottom.
Therefore I am glad of what we learn on this subject.[3]

# Address on Reconstruction— Lincoln's Last Speech

## April 11, 1865

*Lincoln returned one final time to his familiar perch in the second-floor window of the White House family quarters to offer these eagerly awaited official comments on reconstruction policy. Again, and this time in public, he endorsed the idea of black suffrage. Just three days after delivering what turned out to be his last public speech, Lincoln fell victim to John Wilkes Booth's fatal shot at Ford's Theatre.*

WE MEET THIS EVENING, NOT IN SORROW, BUT IN GLADNESS OF heart.[1] The evacuation of Petersburg and Richmond, and the surrender of the principal insurgent army, give hope of a righteous and speedy peace whose joyous expression can not be restrained.[2] In the midst of this, however, He, from Whom all blessings flow, must not be forgotten. A call for a national thanksgiving is being prepared, and will be duly promulgated.[3] Nor must those whose harder part gives us the cause of rejoicing, be overlooked. Their honors must not be parcelled out with others. I myself, was near the front, and had the high pleasure of transmitting much of the good news to you; but no part of the honor, for plan or execution, is mine. To Gen. Grant, his skilful officers, and brave men, all belongs. The gallant Navy stood ready, but was not in reach to take active part.

By these recent successes the re-inauguration of the national authority—reconstruction—which has had a large share of thought from the first, is pressed much more closely upon our attention. It is fraught with great difficulty. Unlike the case of a war between independent nations, there is no authorized organ for us to treat with. No one man has authority to give up the rebellion for any other man. We simply must begin with, and mould from, disorganized and discordant elements. Nor is it a small additional embarrassment that we, the loyal people, differ among ourselves as to the mode, manner, and means of reconstruction.

As a general rule, I abstain from reading the reports of attacks upon myself, wishing not to be provoked by that to which I can not properly offer an answer. In spite of this precaution, however, it comes to my knowledge that I am much censured for some supposed agency in setting up, and seeking to sustain, the new State Government of Louisiana. In this I have done just so much as, and no more than, the public knows. In the Annual Message

1  "The night was misty," reported correspondent Noah Brooks, but the illuminated Capitol dome glowed "for miles around. . . . The notable feature of the evening was the President's speech, delivered to an immense throng of people, who, with bands, banners, and loud huzzas, poured around the familiar avenue in front of the mansion. After repeated calls, loud and enthusiastic, the President appeared at the window, the signal for a great outburst. There was something terrible about the enthusiasm with which the beloved Chief Magistrate was received—cheers upon cheers, wave after wave of applause rolled up, the President modestly standing quiet until it was over. The speech was longer and of a different character from what most people had expected, but it was well received, and it showed that the President had shared in and had considered the same anxieties which the people have had as this struggle drew to a close." Philip J. Staudenraus, ed., *Mr. Lincoln's Washington: Selections from the Writings of Noah Brooks, Civil War Correspondent* (New York: Thomas Yoseloff, 1967), 439.

2  Grant's forces had taken Petersburg, Virginia, on April 3. The day before, Confederate troops had abandoned their capital, Richmond. On April 4, Lincoln toured that conquered city in the company of his son Tad (it was the boy's twelfth birthday). Lee surrendered the Army of Northern Virginia to Grant on April 9, unleashing a series of illuminations and serenades in Washington. Appearing to greet one group of serenaders on the evening of April 10, Lincoln declined to offer more than a

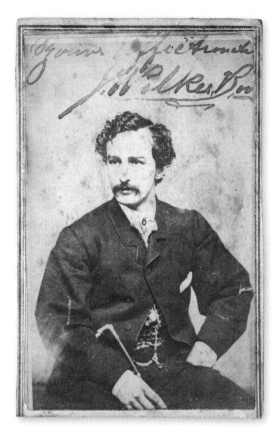

*John Wilkes Booth.* Carte de visite (ca. 1860–1865).

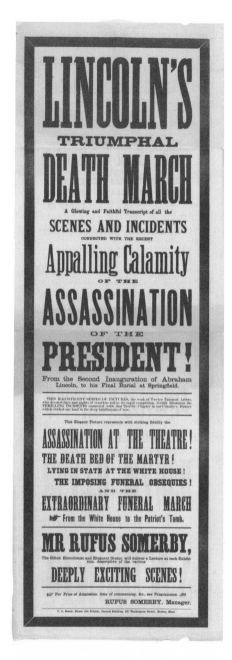

brief impromptu greeting, promising that if "a general demonstration be made to-morrow evening, and it is agreeable, I will endeavor to say something, and not make a mistake, without at least trying carefully to avoid it." *CW,* 8:394. He probably wrote this long April 11 speech in a single day.

3   Lincoln did not live to issue this final proclamation of thanksgiving. He was shot three nights later.

Rufus Somerby, *Lincoln's Triumphal Death March, a Glowing and Faithful Transcript of all the Scenes and Incidents connected with the recent Appalling Calamity of the Assassination of the President!* Broadside (Boston, ca. 1865). Marketed as a "Magnificent Series of Pictures" produced by "Twelve Talented Artists," the series of paintings advertised here was to travel across the country accompanying lectures delivered by the "Gifted Elocutionist and Eloquent Orator" Rufus Somerby.

of Dec. 1863 and accompanying Proclamation, I presented a plan of re-construction (as the phrase goes) which, I promised, if adopted by any State, should be acceptable to, and sustained by, the Executive government of the nation.[4] I distinctly stated that this was not the only plan which might possibly be acceptable; and I also distinctly protested that the Executive claimed no right to say when, or whether members should be admitted to seats in Congress from such States. This plan was, in advance, submitted to the then Cabinet, and distinctly approved by every member of it. One of them suggested that I should then, and in that connection, apply the Emancipation Proclamation to the theretofore excepted parts of Virginia and Louisiana; that I should drop the suggestion about apprenticeship for freed-people, and that I should omit the protest against my own power, in regard to the admission of members to Congress; but even he approved every part and parcel of the plan which has since been employed or touched by the ac-tion of Louisiana. The new constitution of Louisiana, declaring emancipa-tion for the whole State, practically applies the Proclamation to the part previously excepted. It does not adopt apprenticeship for freed-people; and it is silent, as it could not well be otherwise, about the admission of mem-bers to Congress. So that, as it applies to Louisiana, every member of the Cabinet fully approved the plan. The Message went to Congress, and I re-ceived many commendations of the plan, written and verbal; and not a sin-gle objection to it, from any professed emancipationist, came to my knowl-edge, until after the news reached Washington that the people of Louisiana had begun to move in accordance with it. From about July 1862, I had cor-responded with different persons, supposed to be interested, seeking a re-construction of a State government for Louisiana. When the Message of 1863, with the plan before mentioned, reached New-Orleans, Gen. Banks wrote me that he was confident the people, with his military co-operation, would reconstruct, substantially on that plan.[5] I wrote him, and some of them to try it; they tried it, and the result is known. Such only has been my agency in getting up the Louisiana government. As to sustaining it, my promise is out, as before stated. But, as bad promises are better broken than kept, I shall treat this as a bad promise, and break it, whenever I shall be convinced that keeping it is adverse to the public interest. But I have not yet been so convinced.

I have been shown a letter on this subject, supposed to be an able one, in which the writer expresses regret that my mind has not seemed to be defi-nitely fixed on the question whether the seceded States, so called, are in the Union or out of it. It would perhaps, add astonishment to his regret, were

4   See Lincoln's controversial "Proclamation of Amnesty and Reconstruction, December 8, 1863," in this volume. This proposal had required only one-tenth of white voters to declare loyalty to the federal government to qualify seceded states for readmission into the Union and allow them to create new state constitutions.

5   Lincoln was—either consciously or not—con-flating two letters General Nathaniel P. Banks had sent to him, one written before, and one after, the publication of the president's 1863 annual message. Only in the first, sent December 6, did Banks express "a cordial concurrence in your views, and an earnest desire to co-operate in their execution," adding: "From the first I have regarded the reorganization of government here [in Louisiana] as of the highest importance, and I have never failed to advocate everry [sic] where the earliest development of this interest by Congressional elections and by initiatory measures for state organization. . . . Had the organization of a *free* state in Louisiana been committed to me under general instruction only, it would have been complete before this day." Banks to Lincoln, December 6, 1863, Lincoln Papers, Library of Congress. Banks's letter of December 16 was actually quite testy, beginning with the almost insubordinate remark: "It is apparent that you do not view public affairs in this department precisely as they are presented to me and other officers representing your administration." Banks to Lincoln, December 16, 1863, Lincoln Papers, Library of Congress. Lincoln replied on Christmas Eve, insisting that Banks remained "*master . . .* in regard to re-organizing a State government in Louisiana." *CW,* 7:89.

*Latest Photograph of President Lincoln.* Photograph by Henry F. Warren (Washington, DC, March 6, 1865). The last photograph of Abraham Lincoln, taken on the south balcony of the White House.

he to learn that since I have found professed Union men endeavoring to make that question, I have *purposely* forborne any public expression upon it. As [it] appears to me that question has not been, nor yet is, a practically material one, and that any discussion of it, while it thus remains practically immaterial, could have no effect other than the mischievous one of dividing our friends. As yet, whatever it may hereafter become, that question is bad, as the basis of a controversy, and good for nothing at all—a merely pernicious abstraction.[6]

We all agree that the seceded States, so called, are out of their proper practical relation with the Union; and that the sole object of the government, civil and military, in regard to those States is to again get them into that proper practical relation. I believe it is not only possible, but in fact, easier, to do this, without deciding, or even considering, whether these states have even been out of the Union, than with it. Finding themselves safely at home, it would be utterly immaterial whether they had ever been abroad. Let us all join in doing the acts necessary to restoring the proper practical relations between these states and the Union; and each forever after, innocently indulge his own opinion whether, in doing the acts, he brought the States from without, into the Union, or only gave them proper assistance, they never having been out of it.

The amount of constituency, so to speak, on which the new Louisiana government rests, would be more satisfactory to all, if it contained fifty, thirty, or even twenty thousand, instead of only about twelve thousand, as it does. It is also unsatisfactory to some that the elective franchise is not given to the colored man. I would myself prefer that it were now conferred on the very intelligent, and on those who serve our cause as soldiers.[7] Still the question is not whether the Louisiana government, as it stands, is quite all that is desirable. The question is "Will it be wiser to take it as it is, and help to improve it; or to reject, and disperse it?" "Can Louisiana be brought into proper practical relation with the Union *sooner* by *sustaining,* or by *discarding* her new State Government?"

Some twelve thousand voters in the heretofore slave-state of Louisiana have sworn allegiance to the Union, assumed to be the rightful political power of the State, held elections, organized a State government, adopted a free-state constitution, giving the benefit of public schools equally to black and white, and empowering the Legislature to confer the elective franchise upon the colored man. Their Legislature has already voted to ratify the constitutional amendment recently passed by Congress, abolishing slavery throughout the nation. These twelve thousand persons are thus fully committed to the Union, and to perpetual freedom in the state—committed to the very things, and nearly all the things the nation wants—and they ask the nations [*sic*] recognition, and it's [*sic*] assistance to make good their committal. Now, if we reject, and spurn them, we do our utmost to disorganize and disperse them. We in effect say to the white men "You are worth-

6   Newly installed Chief Justice Salmon P. Chase had written a long letter of advice to Lincoln the day the president delivered this speech, strongly urging as a matter of "simplicity, facility & above all, justice," the "reorganization of State Governments under constitutions securing suffrage to all citizens." Chase to Lincoln, April 11, 1865, Lincoln Papers, Library of Congress.

7   Though couched in caveats, this statement marked the first time a sitting American president had ever urged the enfranchisement of African Americans. This was the pronouncement, however mild, that enraged John Wilkes Booth (1838–1865). Reportedly Booth was in the crowd that evening and, hearing the remarks, vowed: "That is the last speech he will ever make." Testimony of Thomas T. Eckert before the House Judiciary Committee, May 30, 1867, cited in Harold Holzer, ed., *President Lincoln Assassinated!!* (New York: Library of America, 2015), 9. According to Clara Harris (1834–1883), the U.S. senator's daughter who accompanied the Lincolns to Ford's Theatre three nights later and witnessed the assassination, Booth had not only heard the oration, but "a less calculating villain might have taken that opportunity for his crime, or the night before, when the White House Alone was brilliantly illuminated, and the figure of the President stood out in full relief to the immense crowd below, who stood in the darkness to listen to his speech. . . . Of course Booth was there, watching his chance. I wonder he did not choose that occasion; but probably he knew a better opportunity would be offered." Clara Harris to "My Dear M——," an unidentified correspondent, April 29, 1865, in ibid., 71–72.

A. Pharazyn, *The Assassination of President Lincoln at Ford's Theatre, Washington, D.C., April 14, 1865.* Lithograph (1865). One of many prints issued in the days and weeks following this tragic event.

8  This was not enough for the chief justice. When he read the text of Lincoln's speech in the newspapers, Chase wrote another letter reiterating his view that Lincoln's proposed reconstruction plan was too lenient to whites, and not helpful enough to blacks in Louisiana. "I know you attach much importance to the admission of Louisiana," wrote the chief justice, "or rather to the recognition of her right to representation in Congress as a loyal State in the Union. If I am not misinformed there is nothing in the way except the indisposition of her Legislature to give satisfactory proof of loyalty by a sufficient guaranty of safety & justice to colored citizens through the extension to loyal colored men of the right of suffrage. Why not, then, as almost every loyal man concurs with you as to the desirableness of that recognition, take the

less, or worse—we will neither help you, nor be helped by you." To the blacks we say "This cup of liberty which these, your old masters, hold to your lips, we will dash from you, and leave you to the chances of gathering the spilled and scattered contents in some vague and undefined when, where, and how." If this course, discouraging and paralyzing both white and black, has any tendency to bring Louisiana into proper practical relations with the Union, I have, so far, been unable to perceive it. If, on the contrary, we recognize, and sustain the new government of Louisiana the converse of all this is made true. We encourage the hearts, and nerve the arms of the twelve thousand to adhere to their work, and argue for it, and proselyte for it, and fight for it, and feed it, and grow it, and ripen it to a complete success. The colored man too, in seeing all united for him, is inspired with vigilance, and energy, and daring, to the same end.[8] Grant that he desires the elective franchise, will he not attain it sooner by saving the already advanced steps toward it, than by running backward over them? Concede that the new government of Louisiana is only to what it should be as the egg

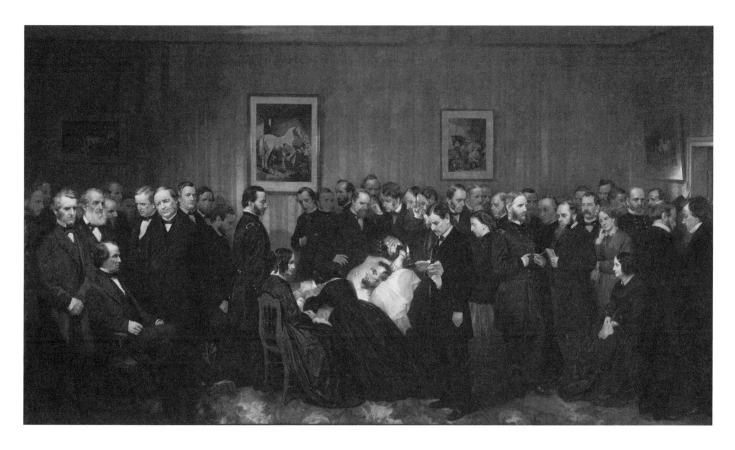

Alonzo Chappel, *Last Hours of Lincoln.* Oil on canvas (1868). Wildly inaccurate, this exaggerated scene of Lincoln's death (which really occurred in a tiny chamber) includes every visitor and physician who attended the dying president during his final nine hours.

is to the fowl, we shall sooner have the fowl by hatching the egg than by smashing it?[9] Again, if we reject Louisiana, we also reject one vote in favor of the proposed amendment to the national constitution. To meet this proposition, it has been argued that no more than three fourths of those States which have not attempted secession are necessary to validly ratify the amendment. I do not commit myself against this, further than to say that such a ratification would be questionable, and sure to be persistently questioned; while a ratification by three fourths of all the States would be unquestioned and unquestionable.

I repeat the question. "Can Louisiana be brought into proper practical relation with the Union *sooner* by *sustaining* or by discarding her new State Government?["]

shortest road to it by causing every proper representation to be made to the Louisiana legislature of the importance of such extension." Chase to Lincoln, April 12, 1865, Lincoln Papers, Library of Congress.

9  Lincoln had drafted—and ultimately deleted— variations on the broken egg metaphor several times during the war. At last he employed it in his final speech, even though it seems as discordant here as it would have sounded in, say, his "paramount object" letter to Horace Greeley on August 22, 1862 (see "To Horace Greeley," in this volume), in which he wrote, then crossed out, the clumsy phrase: "Broken eggs can never be mended, and the more the breaking process proceeds the more will be broken." *CW,* 5:389n2.

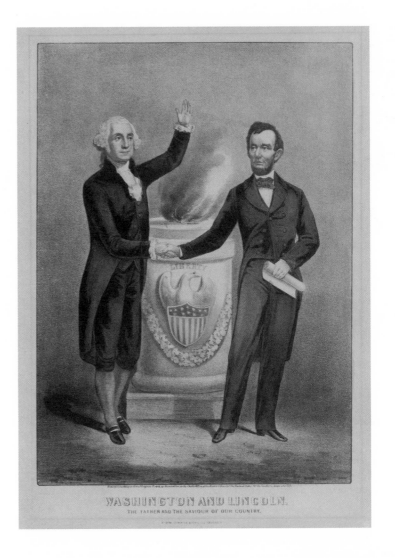

Currier & Ives, *Washington and Lincoln. The Father and Saviour of Our Country.* Lithograph (New York, 1865). After Lincoln's assassination, print publishers began to depict the martyred president as a national saint and linked him with the revered George Washington. This print is one of several examples of the Lincoln-Washington genre.

10  Associated Press bureau chief Lawrence Gobright (1816–1881), who covered the speech, reported that the "repeated cheers" for Lincoln became so vigorous that evening, it "seemed that his tall form had received an additional foot of stature." Lawrence A. Gobright, *Recollections of Men and Things at Washington, during the Third of a Century* (Philadelphia: Claxton, Remsen, & Haffelfinger, 1869), 354. But not all commentators applauded the message. The Democratic *New York World* lamented its "vagueness, indecision, and . . . emptiness." Quoted in Holzer, *Lincoln and the Power of the Press,* 551. Nevertheless, even the *World* recanted its years of criticism when Lincoln died four days after delivering his last public address.

What has been said of Louisiana will apply generally to other States. And yet so great peculiarities pertain to each state; and such important and sudden changes occur in the same state; and, withal, so new and unprecedented is the whole case, that no exclusive, and inflexible plan can safely be prescribed as to details and colatterals [*sic*]. Such [an] exclusive, and inflexible plan, would surely become a new entanglement. Important principles may, and must, be inflexible.

In the present "*situation*" as the phrase goes, it may be my duty to make some new announcement to the people of the South. I am considering, and shall not fail to act, when satisfied that action will be proper.[10]

# Selected Bibliography

### PRIMARY SOURCES

*Abraham Lincoln: Speeches and Writings, 1832–1853: Speeches, Letters, and Miscellaneous Writings: The Lincoln-Douglas Debates.* Edited by Don E. Fehrenbacher. New York: Library of America, 1989.

*Abraham Lincoln: Speeches and Writings, 1859–1865: Speeches, Letters, and Miscellaneous Writings: Presidential Messages and Proclamations.* Edited by Don E. Fehrenbacher. New York: Library of America, 1989.

*The Addresses and Messages of the Presidents of the United States, from 1789 to 1839.* New York: McLean & Taylor, 1839.

*The Civil War Diaries of Salmon P. Chase.* Edited by David Donald. New York: Longmans, Green & Co., 1954.

Clay, Henry. *Speech of the Hon. Henry Clay, before the American Colonization Society, in the Hall of the House of Representatives, January 20, 1827.* Washington, DC, 1827.

*The Collected Works of Abraham Lincoln.* Edited by Roy P. Basler. 9 vols. New Brunswick, NJ: Rutgers University Press, 1953–1955. (Cited as *CW.*)

*Complete Works of Abraham Lincoln.* Edited by John G. Nicolay and John Hay. 12 vols. New York: Francis D. Tandy Company, 1905.

Davis, Rodney O., and Douglas L. Wilson, eds. *The Lincoln-Douglas Debates: The Lincoln Studies Center Edition.* Urbana: Knox College Lincoln Studies Center and University of Illinois Press, 2008.

*Diary of Gideon Welles.* Edited by John T. Morse Jr. 3 vols. Boston: Houghton Mifflin, 1911.

*The Diary of Orville Hickman Browning.* Edited by Theodore Calvin Pease and James G. Randall. 2 vols. Springfield: Trustees of the Illinois State Historical Library, 1925–1933.

Douglas, Stephen A. *Speech of Senator Douglas, of Illinois, against the Admission of Kansas under the Lecompton Constitution.* Washington, DC: Lemuel Towers, 1858.

———. *Remarks of Hon. Stephen A. Douglas, on Kansas, Utah, and the Dred Scott Decision.* Chicago: Daily Times Book and Job Office, 1857.

Ford, Thomas. *A History of Illinois, from Its Commencement as a State in 1818 to 1847.* Chicago: S. C. Griggs, 1854.

Herndon, William H., and Jesse W. Weik. *Herndon's Lincoln.* Edited by Douglas L. Wilson and Rodney O. Davis. Urbana: Knox College Lincoln Studies Center and the University of Illinois Press, 2006.

Holzer, Harold, ed. *The Lincoln-Douglas Debates: The First Complete and Unexpurgated Text.* New York: Fordham University Press, 2004.

*Inside Lincoln's White House: The Complete Diary of John Hay.* Edited by Michael Burlingame and John R. Turner Ettlinger. Carbondale: Southern Illinois University Press, 1997.

*Lincoln's Selected Writings.* Edited by David S. Reynolds. New York: W. W. Norton, 2015.

Nicolay, John G., and John Hay. *Abraham Lincoln: A History.* 10 vols. New York: Century Company, 1890.

*Political Debates between Hon. Abraham Lincoln and Hon. Stephen A. Douglas.* Columbus, OH: Follett, Foster and Company, 1860.

*Political Speeches and Debates of Abraham Lincoln and Stephen A. Douglas 1854–1861.* Chicago: Scott, Foresman & Company, 1896.

Scripps, John Locke. *Life of Abraham Lincoln.* New York: Horace Greeley & Co., 1860.

Wilson, Douglas L., and Rodney O. Davis, eds. *Herndon's Informants: Let-*

*ters, Interviews, and Statements about Abraham Lincoln.* Urbana: University of Illinois Press, 1998.

*The Works of James Buchanan Comprising His Speeches, State Papers, and Private Correspondence.* Edited by John Bassett Moore. 12 vols. New York: Antiquarian Press, 1960.

## Secondary Sources

Angle, Paul M. *"Here I Have Lived": A History of Lincoln's Springfield 1821–1865.* Springfield, IL: Abraham Lincoln Association, 1935.

Barton, William E. *Abraham Lincoln and His Books.* Chicago: Marshall Field and Co., 1920.

Bauer, Jack K. *The Mexican War: 1846–1848.* New York: Macmillan, 1974.

Berkelman, Robert. "Lincoln's Interest in Shakespeare." *Shakespeare Quarterly* 2 (1951): 303–312.

Boas, Norman F. *Abraham Lincoln: Illustrated Biographical Dictionary: Family and Associates, 1809–1861.* Mystic, CT: Seaport Autographs Press, 2009.

Boritt, Gabor S. *Lincoln and the Economics of the American Dream.* Urbana: University of Illinois Press, 1994. First published 1978 by Memphis State University Press.

Bray, Robert. *Reading with Lincoln.* Carbondale: Southern Illinois University Press, 2010.

Briggs, John Channing. *Lincoln's Speeches Reconsidered.* Baltimore: Johns Hopkins University Press, 2005.

Burlingame, Michael. *Abraham Lincoln: A Life.* 2 vols. Baltimore: Johns Hopkins University Press, 2008.

———. "Lincoln Spins the Press." In *Lincoln Reshapes the Presidency,* edited by Charles M. Hubbard, 65–78. Macon, GA: Mercer University Press, 2003.

Campanella, Richard. *Lincoln in New Orleans: The 1828–1831 Flatboat Voyages and Their Place in History.* Lafayette: University of Louisiana at Lafayette Press, 2010.

Carpenter, Francis B. *The Inner Life of Abraham Lincoln: Six Months in the White House.* Boston: Houghton, Osgood and Company, 1880.

Carwardine, Richard J. "Abraham Lincoln and the Fourth Estate: The White House and the Press during the Civil War." *American Nineteenth Century History* 7 (March 2006): 1–27.

Clary, David A. *Eagles and Empire: The United States, Mexico, and the Struggle for a Continent.* New York: Bantam, 2009.

Clinton, Catherine. *Mrs. Lincoln: A Life.* New York: Harper, 2009.

Dirck, Brian. *Lincoln the Lawyer.* Urbana: University of Illinois Press, 2007.

Donald, David Herbert. *Lincoln.* New York: Simon & Schuster, 1995.

———. *Lincoln's Herndon.* New York: Alfred A. Knopf, 1948.

Egerton, Douglas. *Year of Meteors: Stephen Douglas, Abraham Lincoln, and the Election That Brought on the Civil War.* New York: Bloomsbury Press, 2010.

Eisenhower, John D. *So Far from God: The U.S. War with Mexico, 1846–1848.* Norman: University of Oklahoma Press, 2000.

Etcheson, Nicole. *Bleeding Kansas: Contested Liberty in the Civil War Era.* Lawrence: University Press of Kansas, 2004.

Fehrenbacher, Don E. *The Dred Scott Case: Its Significance in American Law and Politics.* New York: Oxford University Press, 1978.

———. *Prelude to Greatness: Lincoln in the 1850s.* Stanford, CA: Stanford University Press, 1962.

Finkelman, Paul. *Slavery and the Founders: Race and Liberty in the Age of Jefferson.* New York: M. E. Sharpe, 1996.

Finkelman, Paul, and Martin J. Hershock, eds. *The Political Lincoln: An Encyclopedia.* Washington, DC: CQ Press, 2009.

Foner, Eric. *The Fiery Trial: Abraham Lincoln and American Slavery.* New York: W. W. Norton, 2010.

———. *Free Soil, Free Labor, Free Men: The Ideology of the Republican Party before the Civil War.* New York: Oxford University Press, 1970.

Fraker, Guy C. *Lincoln's Ladder to the Presidency: The Eighth Judicial Circuit.* Carbondale: Southern Illinois University Press, 2012.

Gates, Henry Louis, Jr., ed. *Lincoln on Race and Slavery.* Princeton, NJ: Princeton University Press, 2009.

Gienapp, William E. *The Origins of the Republican Party, 1852–1856.* New York: Oxford University Press, 1987.

Green, Michael S. *Lincoln and the Election of 1860.* Carbondale: Southern Illinois University Press, 2011.

Greenberg, Amy S. *A Wicked War: Polk, Clay, and Lincoln and the 1846 U.S. Invasion of Mexico.* New York: Alfred A. Knopf, 2012.

Guelzo, Allen C. *Abraham Lincoln: Redeemer President.* Grand Rapids, MI: William B. Eerdmans, 1999.

————. *Lincoln and Douglas: The Debates That Defined America.* New York: Simon & Schuster, 2008.

————. *Lincoln's Emancipation Proclamation: The End of Slavery in America.* New York: Simon & Schuster, 2004.

Holt, Michael F. *The Political Crisis of the 1850s.* New York: John Wiley, 1978.

Holzer, Harold. *Lincoln and the Power of the Press: The War for Public Opinion.* New York: Simon & Schuster, 2014.

————. *Lincoln at Cooper Union: The Speech That Made Abraham Lincoln President.* New York: Simon & Schuster, 2004.

————. *Lincoln President-Elect: Abraham Lincoln and the Great Secession Winter, 1860–1861.* New York: Simon & Schuster, 2008.

Holzer, Harold, Gabor S. Boritt, and Mark E. Neely Jr. *The Lincoln Image: Abraham Lincoln and the Popular Print.* New York: Charles Scribner's Sons, 1984.

Horrocks, Thomas A. *Lincoln's Campaign Biographies.* Carbondale: Southern Illinois University Press, 2014.

————. *President James Buchanan and the Crisis of National Leadership.* New York: Nova Publishing, 2012.

Horrocks, Thomas A., Harold Holzer, and Frank J. Williams, eds., *The Living Lincoln*. Carbondale: Southern Illinois University Press, 2011.

Howe, Daniel Walker. *What Hath God Wrought: The Transformation of America, 1815–1848*. New York: Oxford University Press, 2007.

———. *The Political Culture of the American Whigs*. Chicago: University of Chicago Press, 1979.

Johannsen, Robert W. *Stephen A. Douglas*. 1973. Urbana: University of Illinois Press, 1997.

Kaplan, Fred. *Lincoln: A Biography of a Writer*. New York: Harper, 2008.

Marty, Myron. "Schooling in Lincoln's America and Lincoln's Extraordinary Self-Schooling." In *Lincoln's America 1809–1865*, edited by Joseph R. Fornieri and Sara Vaughn Gabbard, 55–71. Carbondale: Southern Illinois University Press, 2008.

Mearns, David C. "Mr. Lincoln and the Books He Read." In *Three Presidents and Their Books: The Reading of Jefferson, Lincoln, Franklin D. Roosevelt*, edited by Arthur Bestor, David D. Means, and Jonathan Daniels. Urbana: University of Illinois Press, 1955.

Miers, Earl Schenck, ed. *Lincoln Day by Day: A Chronology 1809–1865*. 3 vols. Washington, DC: Lincoln Sesquicentennial Commission, 1960.

Miller, Richard Lawrence. *Lincoln and His World: The Early Years, Birth to Illinois Legislature*. Mechanicsburg, PA: Stackpole Books, 2006.

———. *Lincoln and His World: Prairie Politician, 1834–1842*. Mechanicsburg, PA: Stackpole Books, 2008.

Neely, Mark E., Jr. *The Abraham Lincoln Encyclopedia*. New York: Da Capo Press, 1984.

Nichols, David A. *Lincoln and the Indians: Civil War Policy and Politics*. Columbia: University of Missouri Press, 1978.

Potter, David M. *The Impending Crisis 1848–1861*. New York: Harper & Row, 1976.

Rawley, James A. *A Lincoln Dialogue*. Lincoln: University of Nebraska Press, 2014.

———. *Race and Politics: "Bleeding Kansas" and the Coming of the Civil War.* Lincoln: University of Nebraska Press, 1979.

Remini, Robert V. *Henry Clay: Statesman for the Union.* New York: W. W. Norton, 1991.

Riddle, Donald W. *Congressman Abraham Lincoln.* Urbana: University of Illinois Press, 1957.

Schwartz, Thomas F. "The Springfield Lyceums and Lincoln's 1838 Speech." *Illinois Historical Journal* 83 (Spring 1990): 45–49.

Stamp, Kenneth M. *America in 1857: A Nation on the Brink.* New York: Oxford University Press, 1990.

Steiner, Mark E. *An Honest Calling: The Law Practice of Abraham Lincoln.* De Kalb: Northern Illinois University Press, 2006.

Szasz, Ferenc Morton, and Margaret Connell Szasz. *Lincoln and Religion.* Carbondale: Southern Illinois University Press, 2014.

Temple, Wayne C. *Abraham Lincoln: From Skeptic to Prophet.* Mahomet, IL: Mayhaven Publishing, 1995.

Vorenberg, Michael. *Final Freedom: The Civil War, the Abolition of Slavery, and the Thirteenth Amendment.* New York: Cambridge University Press, 2001.

White, Jonathan W. *Emancipation, the Union, and the Reelection of Abraham Lincoln.* Baton Rouge: Louisiana State University Press, 2014.

White, Ronald C. *A. Lincoln: A Biography.* New York: Random House, 2009.

Wilentz, Sean. "Abraham Lincoln and Jacksonian Democracy." In *Our Lincoln: New Perspectives on Lincoln and His World,* edited by Eric Foner, 62–79. New York: W. W. Norton, 2008.

Wilson, Douglas L. "The Frigate and the Frugal Chariot: Jefferson and Lincoln as Readers." In *Lincoln before Washington: New Perspectives on the Illinois Years,* 3–20. Urbana: University of Illinois Press, 1997.

———. *Honor's Voice: The Transformation of Abraham Lincoln.* New York: Alfred A. Knopf, 1998.

Wilson, Major L. "Lincoln and Van Buren in the Steps of the Fathers: Another Look at the Lyceum Address." In *On Lincoln,* edited by John T. Hubbell, 14–30. Kent, OH: Kent State University Press, 2014.

Zarefsky, David. *Lincoln, Douglas, and Slavery: In the Crucible of Public Debate.* Chicago: University of Chicago Press, 1990.

# Acknowledgments

The editors would like to thank Harvard University Press for the opportunity to work together on this book. We thank our editor at the press, John Kulka, for his ideas, encouragement, understanding, and patience. Christine Thorsteinsson, Hope Stockton, and Julie Ericksen Hagen were extremely helpful when it came to copyediting and assembling illustrations for this volume. We are grateful to the Abraham Lincoln Association for permission to use the texts from *The Collected Works of Abraham Lincoln.*

The following individuals and institutions (and their staffs) deserve our thanks for their assistance in identifying illustrations and granting permission to use them in this volume:

Abraham Lincoln Presidential Library and Museum (Jennifer Ericson and Roberta Fairburn)

American Antiquarian Society

Boston Athenaeum (Patricia M Boulos)

Chicago History Museum (Sarah Yarrito)

Cooper Union Collection (Carol Salomon)

Filson Historical Society (Heather Stone and Aaron L. Rosenblum)

Fine Arts Library, Harvard University

Florida State Archives (N. Adam Watson)

Granger Collection (Ellen Sandberg)

Houghton Library, Harvard University (Heather Cole, Mary Haegert, and Thomas Lingner)

Huntington Library (Anne Blecksmith)

Jack Smith Lincoln Graphics Collection—Indiana Historical Society (Amy C. Vedra and Susan Sutton)

John Hay Library, Brown University (Holly Snyder)

Knox College Library, Galesville IL (MaryJo McAndrew)

Library of Congress (Michelle Wright)

Lilly Library, Indiana (Nile Arena and Zach Downey)

Lincoln Boyhood Home National Memorial (Michael Capps)

Lincoln Financial Foundation Collection, Indiana State Museum (Kisha Tandy)

Lincoln Memorial University, Harrogate TN (Michelle Ganz)

Museum of Fine Arts, Boston (Márta Fodor)

New Castle Historical Society (Cassie Ward)

New-York Historical Society (Robert Delap)

Onondaga Historical Association (Sarah Kozma)

Smithsonian Institution–American History (Debra Hashim)

State Museum of Pennsylvania (Ashley Wolff)

United States Capitol Collection

University of Notre Dame (Rebeka Ceravolo)

U.S. National Archives and Records Administration

Westerville Public Library (Beth Weinhardt)

Widener Library, Harvard University

Finally, we thank our spouses, Edith Holzer and Beth Carroll-Horrocks, for their love, support, and willingness to share (or tolerate) our interest in Abraham Lincoln.

This book is dedicated to the memories of our parents.

# Illustration Credits

*Abraham Lincoln,* oil on canvas, by Thomas Hicks, 1860. Bequest of Oscar B. Cintas, 1959.212, lCHi-66279, Chicago History Museum.  ii

*House in Which Abraham Lincoln Was Born,* silver gelatin photograph mounted on card stock, ca. late 19th century. PO406_623, Jack Smith Lincoln Graphics Collection, Indiana Historical Society.  2

*Sarah Bush Lincoln,* photograph, ca. 1865. Abraham Lincoln Presidential Library & Museum (ALPLM).  3

*The Boyhood of Lincoln (An Evening in a Log Hut),* chromolithograph on wood, by Louis Prang, after a painting by Eastman Johnson (Boston: L. Prang and Co., 1868). Fine Arts Library Special Collections, Harvard University.  4

Abraham Lincoln, exercise book fragment, ca. 1825. fMS Am 1326, Houghton Library, Harvard University.  6

*Lincoln's Schoolhouse in Knob Creek, Kentucky,* photograph, 1932. M151b Lincoln Graphics, John Hay Library, Brown University Library.  7

*Youth of Abraham Lincoln,* intaglio print, engraved by Ernest F. Hubbard, after a painting by Morgan J. Rhees, n.d. PO406_349, Jack Smith Lincoln Graphics Collection, Indiana Historical Society.  7

*Lover of Books and Study,* colored print, by Harriet Putnam, 1900–1910. L3134 Lincoln Graphics, John Hay Library, Brown University Library.  9

*Abraham Lincoln's Residence, Springfield, Illinois, 1860,* hand-colored lithograph, based on a photograph taken by J. A. Whipple, 1860. PO406_335, Jack Smith Lincoln Graphics Collection, Indiana Historical Society.  12

*John Brown Meeting the Slave Mother and Her Child on the Steps of Charlestown Jail on His Way to Execution,* color lithograph by Currier and Ives, after a painting by Louis Ransom, 1863. Chicago History Museum, lCHi-22033. 13

*Abraham Lincoln at His Home in Springfield, Illinois, with a Large Crowd of People Gathered Outside after a Republican Rally, August 8, 1860,* photo-mechanical print, photograph by William Shaw. Reproduction number LC-USZ62-13682, Library of Congress Prints and Photographs Division. 15

*The Republican Banner for 1860,* lithograph, by Currier and Ives (New York: Currier and Ives, 1860). *2008-255, Houghton Library, Harvard University. 16

Title page, *The Life, Speeches, and Public Services of Abram Lincoln* (New York: Rudd and Carleton, 1860). Courtesy The Lilly Library, Indiana University, Bloomington, Indiana. 16

Campaign flag, "For President, Abraham Lincoln—Vice President, Hannibal Hamlin," 1860. B*2007M-43, Houghton Library, Harvard University. 17

"Lincoln and Hamlin," campaign flag, 1860. Lincoln Graphics, John Hay Library, Brown University Library. 17

"Honest Old Abe," song and chorus, words by D. Wentworth, music by a Wide-Awake (Buffalo: Blodgett and Bradford, 1860). LMu 116, Lincoln Sheet Music, John Hay Library, Brown University Library. 18

*The Rail Candidate,* lithograph, by Louis Maurer (New York: Currier and Ives, 1860). PO406_302, Jack Smith Lincoln Graphics Collection, Indiana Historical Society. 19

*A Clean Sweep . . . Lincoln's Elected, and Who's Afraid?* broadside (West Chester, PA: *Chester County Times Extra,* November 7, 1860). Lincoln Broadsides, John Hay Library, Brown University Library. 20

*Ford's Theatre . . . Friday Evening, April 14th, 1865 . . . Our American Cousin* (Washington, DC: H. Polkinhorn and Son, 1865). *2008T-17, Harvard Theatre Collection, Houghton Library, Harvard University. 20

*Muster roll of Capt. Abraham Lincoln's Company of the 4th Regiment of Mounted Volunteers commanded by Brig. Genl. Samuel Whiteside mustered out of service at the mouth of the Fox River,* by Samuel Whiteside, signed by Abraham Lincoln, May 27, 1832. LA 1428, Lincoln Manuscripts, John Hay Library, Brown University Library. 26

*Restored Lincoln-Berry Store, New Salem, Illinois,* photograph, n.d. Lincoln Memorabilia 10-110, courtesy The Lilly Library, Indiana University, Bloomington, Indiana. 27

*Simeon Francis,* photograph, n.d. Abraham Lincoln Presidential Library & Museum (ALPLM). 30

Town plat, survey of Huron, Illinois, by Abraham Lincoln, May 21, 1836. Abraham Lincoln Presidential Library & Museum (ALPLM). 31

*Public Sale of Negroes,* broadside, 1833. Chicago History Museum, lCHi-22002. 33

*Mary S. Owens,* photographic reproduction, n.d. The Alfred Whital Stern Collection of Lincolniana, Library of Congress Rare Book and Special Collections Division. 34

*Attack on the Office of the* Alton Observer *(1837),* lithograph, from Henry Tanner, *Martyrdom of Lovejoy* (Chicago: Fergus Print Co., 1881). Chicago History Museum, lCHi-34910. 37

*Andrew Jackson,* hand-colored lithograph (New York: N. Currier, ca. 1835–1837). Reproduction number LC-DIG-pga-05787, Library of Congress. 38

*King Andrew the First,* lithograph on wove paper (New York? 1833). Reproduction number LC-USZ62-1562, American Cartoon Print Filing Series, Library of Congress Prints and Photographs Division. 39

*Martin Van Buren,* lithograph, by Philip Haas, from a painting by Henry Inman (Washington, DC: P. Haas, ca. 1837). Reproduction number LC-USZ62-7986, Library of Congress. 44

*Orville Hickman Browning,* photograph, n.d. Abraham Lincoln Presidential Library & Museum (ALPLM). 47

*Joshua Fry Speed,* ca. 1830s. The Filson Historical Society, Louisville, KY. 51

*The Drunkard's Progess. From the First Glass to the Grave,* hand-colored lithograph, by N. Currier (New York: N. Currier, 1846). Reproduction number LC-DIG-ppmsca-32719, Library of Congress Prints and Photographs Division. 55

*The Tree of Intemperance,* Color lithograph (New York: N. Currier, 1849). American Antiquarian Society, Worcester, Massachusetts / Bridgeman Images. 57

*Abraham Lincoln Pledges Cleopas Breckenridge to Total Abstinence,* drawing, n.d. Courtesy Westerville Public Library, Westerville, OH. 59

*Joshua Fry Speed and Fanny Henning Speed,* oil on canvas, by George P. A. Healy, ca. 1840s. The Filson Historical Society, Louisville, KY. 63

*James T. Shields,* photograph, n.d. Abraham Lincoln Presidential Library & Museum (ALPLM). 67

*Former Residence of President Lincoln, Birthplace of Robt. Lincoln,* albumen print, photograph by S. M. Fassett, 1865. Reproduction number LC-DIG-ppmsca-19258, Library of Congress Prints and Photographs Division. 68

*Lincoln's Indiana Home,* engraving[?], n.d. Lincoln Boyhood National Memorial. 73

Nancy Hanks Lincoln's gravesite, photograph, n.d. Lincoln Boyhood National Memorial. 76

Bas-relief medallion commemorating centennial of Lincoln's birth, by V. D. Brenner, ca. 1909. LC-USZ62-58312, Library of Congress Prints and Photographs Division. 78

*Abraham Lincoln, Congressman-elect from Illinois,* daguerreotype, by N. H. Shepherd (Springfield, IL, 1846 or 1847). Reproduction number LC-USZC4-2439, Library of Congress Prints and Photographs Division. 79

*Washington. 34, Chamber of Representatives,* lithograph, by Laurent Deroy, after a drawing by Augustus Köllner (New York and Paris: Goupil, Vibert and Co., 1848). Reproduction number LC-USZ62-2907, Library of Congress Prints and Photographs Division. 80

*James Knox Polk,* daguerreotype, by Mathew B. Brady, 1849. Reproduction number LC-USZC4-6742, Library of Congress Prints and Photographs Division. 83

*Mexican News,* engraving, by Alfred Jones, after Richard Caton Woodville, ca. 1853. Reproduction number LC-DIG-pga-03889, Library of Congress Prints and Photographs Division. 86

*The Landing of American Forces under Genl. Scott, at Vera Cruz, March 9th,*

*1847,* hand-colored lithograph, by Nathaniel Currier (New York: N. Currier and Ives, 1847). Reproduction number LC-USZC4-2955, Library of Congress Prints and Photographs Division. 92

*William Henry Herndon,* photograph, n.d. Abraham Lincoln Presidential Library & Museum (ALPLM). 94

*Mary Todd Lincoln,* daguerreotype, by Nicholas H. Shepherd, 1846 or 1847. Reproduction number LC-USZC4-6189, Library of Congress Prints and Photographs Division. 95

*View Looking East down Pennsylvania Avenue…with Carroll Row at Left,* wet collodion glass negative, between 1860 and 1880. Reproduction number LC-DIG-cwpbh-03288, Brady-Handy Photograph Collection, Library of Congress Prints and Photographs Division. 96

*Thomas Lincoln,* photograph, n.d. Photograph courtesy of the Abraham Lincoln Library and Museum of Lincoln Memorial University, Harrogate, Tennessee. 97

*Lincoln Home in Old Salem,* silver gelatin photograph, ca. 1890s. PO406_500, Jack Smith Lincoln Graphics Collection, Indiana Historical Society. 98

*Slave Market of America,* broadside (New York: American Anti-Slavery Society, 1836). Reproduction number LC-DIG-ppmsca-19705, Library of Congress Rare Book and Special Collections Division. 101

*United States Capitol, Washington, D.C., East Front Elevation,* daguerreotype, by John Plumbe, ca. 1846. Reproduction number LC-USZ62-110213, Daguerrotype Collection, Library of Congress Prints and Photographs Division. 103

Abraham Lincoln, *Illinois Central Railroad v. McLean County,* legal brief, February 1854. mssLN 2367, The Huntington Library, San Marino, California. 105

*Lincoln the Circuit Rider,* oil on canvas, by Louis Bonhajo, n.d. Photograph courtesy of the Abraham Lincoln Library and Museum of Lincoln Memorial University, Harrogate, Tennessee. 106

*Zachary Taylor, People's Candidate for President,* lithograph with watercolor, by N. Currier (New York: N. Currier, c. 1848), detail. Reproduction number LC-USZC2-3199, Library of Congress Prints and Photographs Division. 113

*Zachary Taylor,* daguerreotype, by Mathew B. Brady, between 1844 and 1849. Reproduction number LC-USZ62-110067, Library of Congress Prints and Photographs Division. 114

*Henry Clay,* daguerreotype, by Mathew B. Brady, between 1850 and 1852. Reproduction number LC-USZ62-109953, Library of Congress Prints and Photographs Division. 117

*The United States Senate, A.D. 1850,* engraving, by Robert Whitechurch, after a drawing by P. F. Rothermel (Philadelphia: John M. Butler and Alfred Long, ca. 1855). Reproduction number LC-USZC4-1724, Library of Congress Prints and Photographs Division. 121

"Daniel Webster Addressing the Citizens of Boston in Front of the Revere House," *Gleason's Pictorial Drawing Room Companion,* vol. 1, no. 3 (July 19, 1851), p. 37. P198.1F, Widener Library, Harvard University. 130

*American Slave Market,* oil on canvas, by Taylor (first name unknown), 1852. Gift of Miss Ellen N. La Motte, 1954.15, image lCHi-53543, Chicago History Museum. 132

Title page, Harriet Beecher Stowe, *Uncle Tom's Cabin; or, Life among the Lowly* (Boston: John P. Jewett and Company, 1852). Houghton Library, Harvard University. 134

*After the Sale: Slaves Going South from Richmond,* oil on canvas, by Eyre Crowe, 1853. Purchased by the Society, 1957.27, image lCHi-66786, Chicago History Museum. 139

*Abraham Lincoln while Campaigning for the U.S. Senate,* gelatin silver print, by Polycarp. Von Schneidau in Chicago, October 27, 1854. Reproduction number LC-USZ62-10673, Library of Congress Prints and Photographs Division. 147

*Political Chart of the United States,* broadside (Springfield, OH: Rocky Mountain Club, 1856). Chicago History Museum, lCHi-22030. 177

*Millard Fillmore, American Candidate for President of the United States,* woodcut (New York: Baker and Godwin, c. 1856). Reproduction number LC-DIG-pga-03523, Library of Congress Prints and Photographs Division. 186

*Abraham Lincoln,* circular ambrotype, by Anton T. Joslin, 1857. Abraham Lincoln Presidential Library & Museum (ALPLM). 188

*100 Dollars Reward,* broadside, July 6, 1857. Chicago History Museum, ICHi-22008. 190

*Abraham Lincoln,* ambrotype, by Abraham Byers, 1858. Abraham Lincoln Presidential Library & Museum (ALPLM). 202

Title page, Abraham Lincoln, *Speech of Hon. Abram Lincoln, before the Republican State Convention, June 16, 1858* (Sycamore, IL: O. P. Basset, 1858). Courtesy The Lilly Library, Indiana University, Bloomington, Indiana. 210

*Old State House, Springfield, Illinois,* photograph, ca. 1898. Call number HABS ILL, 84-SPRIF, 1–1, view from south-west, Historical American Buildings Survey, Library of Congress Prints and Photographs Division. 213

*Hall of Representatives, Old State House, Springfield, Illinois,* photograph, ca. 1898. Call number HABS ILL, 84-SPRIF, 1–5, Historical American Buildings Survey, Library of Congress Prints and Photographs Division. 217

*Abraham Lincoln,* photograph, 1860. Reproduction number LC-USZ62-7992, Library of Congress Prints and Photographs Division. 221

*Stephen A. Douglas,* photographic print on carte de visite, 1860. Reproduction number LC-USZ62-135560, Library of Congress Prints and Photographs Division. 228

*Lincoln-Douglas Debate,* lantern slide (Chicago: McIntosh Stereopticon Co., ca. 1915). PO406_124,1, Jack Smith Lincoln Graphics Collection, Indiana Historical Society. 230

*Grand Rally of the Lincoln Men of Old Tazewell!* broadside (Pekin, IL, 1858). Abraham Lincoln Presidential Library & Museum (ALPLM). 233

*Stephen A. Douglas,* oil on canvas, by Louis O. Lussier, c. 1855. X.104, image ICHi-62626, Chicago History Museum. 253

Mural commemorating Lincoln-Douglas debate, by Ralph Seymour, 1958. Special Collections and Archives, Knox College Library, Galesburg, Illinois. 254

*Frederick Douglass,* daguerreotype, ca. 1841–1845. Onondaga Historical Association, 321 Montgomery Street, Syracuse, NY, 13202. 268

*Lincoln and Douglas Debate,* oil on canvas, by Robert Marshall Root, 1918. Abraham Lincoln Presidential Library & Museum (ALPLM). 281

*Abraham Lincoln,* photograph by Calvin Jackson in Pittsfield, IL, October 1, 1858. Reproduction number LC-USZ62-16377, Library of Congress Prints and Photographs Division. 285

*The Coles County Court House in Charleston, Ills., in which Lincoln often practiced law and before which he made a short speech in the evening after his fourth joint debate with Douglas, Sept. 18, 1858,* albumen photographic print, between 1860 and 1898? Reproduction number LC-DIG-ppmsca-19197, Library of Congress Prints and Photographs Division. 287

Title page, *Political Debates between Hon. Abraham Lincoln and Hon. Stephen A. Douglas, in the Celebrated Campaign of 1858, in Illinois* (Columbus, OH: Follett, Foster and Company, 1860). Lin 2012.2.2, William Whiting Nolen Collection of Lincolniana, Houghton Library, Harvard University. 293

Replica of Lincoln's Patent Model for a boat, wood, 1978. Accession number 1978.2284, Division of Political History, National Museum of American History, Smithsonian Institution. 315

*Lincoln's Invention,* broadside, by M. I. Wright, n.d. Alfred Whital Stern Collection of Lincolniana, Library of Congress Rare Book and Special Collections Division. 318

Printing press of Elijah Lovejoy, iron, 1837. Purchased by the Society, 1920.894, image lCHi-29035, Chicago History Museum. 319

*Abraham Lincoln,* gelatin silver photographic print, photograph by S. M. Fassett, 1859. Reproduction number LC-USZ62-11492, Library of Congress Print and Photographs Division. 321

*Theodore Canisius,* albumen photographic print on carte de visite, 1876. Reproduction number LC-DIG-ds-03381, Library of Congress Prints and Photographs Department. 323

*The Propagation Society. More Free than Welcome,* lithograph (New York: Nathaniel Currier, 1855). Reproduction number LC-DIG-pga-04985, Library of Congress Prints and Photographs Division. 324

*Jesse Wilson Fell,* photograph, n.d. Abraham Lincoln Presidential Library & Museum (ALPLM). 325

*The Railsplitter,* oil on canvas, by Chambers (first name unknown), ca. 1860.

Gift of Miss Maibelle Heikes Justice, 1917.15, image lCHi-52428, Chicago History Museum.  326

*Abraham Lincoln,* gelatin silver print, photograph by Mathew Brady, February 27, 1860. Reproduction number LC-USZ62-5803, Library of Congress Prints and Photographs Division.  329

*Cooper Union.* 1860. Collection of Harold Holzer.  331

[*Lincoln Delivering His Cooper Union Speech*], drawing, ca. 1860? Courtesy of The Cooper Union Collection.  336

Cover page, Abraham Lincoln, *The Address of the Hon. Abraham Lincoln… Delivered at Cooper Institute, February 27, 1860 . . .* (New York: Young Men's Republican Union, 1860). Alexander L. Sheff Collection, The Cooper Union Archives, Courtesy of The Cooper Union.  338

*Abraham Lincoln,* photograph by Alexander Hesler, Springfield, IL, June 3, 1860. Hesler photographs of Lincoln, page 1, Alfred Whital Stern Collection of Lincolniana, Library of Congress Rare Book and Special Collections Division.  353

*Union Wide Awakes' Campaign Banner,* cloth, New York, 1860. Gift of Mr. James M. Doubleday, Jr., 1973.181, image lCHi-27639, Chicago History Museum.  358

*Abraham Lincoln, Candidate for U.S. President,* ambrotype, by Preston Butler, Springfield, IL, August 13, 1860. Reproduction number LC-DIG-ppmsca-17159, Library of Congress Prints and Photographs Division.  359

*Abraham Lincoln, President-Elect,* gelatin silver print, photograph by Samuel G. Alschuler, Chicago, November 25, 1860. Reproduction number LC-USZ62-15984, Library of Congress Prints and Photographs Division.  360

*National Republican Chart,* broadside (New York: H. H. Lloyd and Co., 1860). 71.2009.081.0559, from the Lincoln Financial Foundation Collection, courtesy of the Allen County Public Library and Indiana State Museum.  360

*Alexander Stephens,* wet collodion glass negative, taken at Mathew Brady's Washington, DC, studio, between 1860 and 1865. Reproduction number LC-DIG-cwpb-04946, Library of Congress Prints and Photographs Division.  361

PO406_661, Jack Smith Lincoln Graphics Collection, Indiana Historical Society. 383

Proof sheets, Abraham Lincoln, [First inaugural address]. [Springfield, IL: Privately printed, January–February, 1861]. Lincoln Collection, Abraham Lincoln, Miscellaneous Papers (84), Houghton Library, Harvard University. 385

*President and Cabinet,* engraving by John C. Buttre (New York, 1864). M34bu.2, Lincoln Graphics, John Hay Library, Brown University Library. 388

William H. Seward. Collection of Harold Holzer. 389

*General Winfield Scott,* albumen print, ca. 1861–1865. Reproduction number LC-DIG-ppmsca-34128, Library of Congress Prints and Photographs Division. 390

*Elmer Ellsworth,* photograph, ca. 1860. Chicago History Museum, lCHi-22165. 391

*Death of E. E. Ellsworth,* painting, by Alonzo Chappel, 1862. Chicago History Museum, lCHi-65208. 392

*Bombardment of Fort Sumter, Charleston Harbor: 12th & 13th of April 1861,* hand-colored lithograph (New York: Currier and Ives, [1861?]). Reproduction number LC-DIG-ppmsca-19520, Library of Congress Prints and Photographs Division. 395

Study for *Departure of the Seventh Regiment for the War, April 19, 1861,* oil over graphite on brown paper, by Thomas Nast, ca. 1865–1869, 22½ x 32¾ inches. Object number 1946.174, gift of George A. Zabriskie, New-York Historical Society. Photography © New-York Historical Society. 397

*Lincoln Crushing the Dragon of Rebellion,* oil on canvas, 18 x 22 in., by David Gilmour Blythe, 1862. Bequest of Martha C. Karolik for the M. and M. Karolik Collection of American Paintings, 48.413, Museum of Fine Arts, Boston. Photograph © 2015 Museum of Fine Arts, Boston. 399

*The First Flag of Independence Raised in the South by the Citizens of Savannah, Georgia, November 8, 1860,* lithograph after a drawing by Henry Cleenewercke (Savannah, GA: R. H. Howell, [1860]). C B6XSa9 Hi.f.1860, Boston Athenæum. 400

*Construction of the U.S. Capitol Dome,* unmounted stereograph on salted paper, ca. 1860–1863. Reproduction number LC-USZ62-56538, Library of Congress Prints and Photographs Division. 409

*John C. Frémont,* wet collodion glass negative, ca.1855–1865. Reproduction number LC-DIG-cwpbh-00792, Brady-Handy Photograph Collection, Library of Congress Prints and Photographs Division. 411

*Maj. Gen. Hunter,* albumen print on carte de visite, photograph by Brady's National Photographic Portrait Galleries, ca. 1860–1863. Reproduction number LC-DIG-ppmsca-32331, Library of Congress Prints and Photographs Division. 412

*Old House of Representatives,* wet collodion glass negative, ca. 1861. Reproduction number LC-DIG-cwpbh-03301, Brady-Handy Photograph Collection, Library of Congress Prints and Photographs Division. 415

*A Great Rush. Cost What It May, the Nation Must Be Saved! 36th Regiment New York Volunteers,* lithographed broadside (New York: Baker and Godwin, ca. 1861–1863). Item no. PR-055-3-148, Civil War Recruiting Posters, New-York Historical Society. Photography © New-York Historical Society. 430

"Our National Union March," sheet music, composed by Charles Rehm, lithography by Shearman and Hart (New York: J. F. Lovell, 1862). LMu 216, Lincoln Sheet Music, John Hay Library, Brown University Library. 431

*Gen'l Geo. B. McClellan and Staff, before Yorktown, Va., April 1862,* lithograph (New York: Currier and Ives, c. 1862). Reproduction number LC-USZC2-2426, Library of Congress Prints and Photographs Division. 432

"Masterly Inactivity, or Six Months on the Potomac," woodcut engraving, by A. B., *Frank Leslie's Illustrated Newspaper,* vol. 13 (February 1, 1862), p. 176. Reproduction number LC-USZ62-82807, Library of Congress Prints and Photographs Division. 433

*A Dispatch from Little Mack. "Still waiting for more reinforcements!!!"* pencil and wash on paper [n.p., 1862]. Abraham Lincoln, Miscellaneous Papers, IV (102), Houghton Library, Harvard University. 434

*Coming into the Lines,* drawing, by Edwin Forbes, c. 1876. Reproduction number LC-DIG-ppmsca-20762, Morgan Collection of Civil War Drawings, Library of Congress Prints and Photographs Division. 436

*The D.C. Emancipation Act of April 16, 1862.* Record Group 11, General Records of the U.S. Government; National Archives and Records Administration, Washington, DC.  439

*Samuel Casey,* wet collodion glass negative, ca. 1865–1880. Reproduction number LC-DIG-cwpbh-04303, Brady-Handy Photograph Collection, Library of Congress Prints and Photographs Division.  441

*Horace Maynard, Representative of Tennessee, Thirty-Fifth Congress,* photograph, by Julian Vannerson (Washington: McClees and Beck, 1859). Reproduction number LC-DIG-ppmsca-26769, Library of Congress Prints and Photographs Division.  441

*Liberia: Freed Slaves,* color engraving, 1832. The Granger Collection, New York.  445

*Horace Greeley,* photograph, 1872, from the Sarony Studio, 256 Fifth Ave., New York. Copy courtesy of the New Castle Historical Society and Horace Greeley House Museum, Chappaqua, New York. Accession # 2013-20. Photo ID # 5096A.  449

Manuscript, Abraham Lincoln, "Meditation on the Divine Will," September, 1862. A39115, Lincoln Manuscripts, John Hay Library, Brown University Library.  451

*First Reading of the Emancipation Proclamation before the Cabinet,* mezzotint, engraved by Alexander Hay Ritchie, after a painting by F. B. Carpenter, 1864. Reproduction number LC-DIG-pga-02502, Library of Congress Prints and Photographs Division.  454

*Behind the Scenes,* lithograph on wove paper, 1864. Reproduction number LC-USZ62-89718, American Cartoon Print Filing Series, Library of Congress Prints and Photographs Division.  457

*General George B. McClellan,* carte de visite (Boston: J. W. Black, 1864). LP4366, Lincoln Graphics, John Hay Library, Brown University Library.  458

*The Commander-in-Chief Conciliating the Soldier's Vote on the Battle Field,* lithograph on wove paper, 1864. Reproduction number LC-USZ62-89731, American Cartoon Print Filing Series, Library of Congress Prints and Photographs Division.  458

*Antietam, Md., Allan Pinkerton, President Lincoln, and Maj. Gen. John A.*

*The Great American What Is It? Chased by Copper-heads,* lithograph, by E. W. T. Nichols (Boston, 1863). Reproduction number LC-DIG-ppmsca-22015, American Cartoon Print Filing Series, Library of Congress Prints and Photographs Division. 492

*Erastus Corning,* wet collodion glass negative, ca. 1855–1865. Reproduction number LC-DIG-cwpbh-02785, Brady-Handy Photograph Collection, Library of Congress Prints and Photographs Division. 493

*U.S. Grant in the Trenches before Vicksburg,* print, [etching by James Fagan after painting by Ole Peter Hansen Balling], c. June 5, 1899. Reproduction number LC-DIG-pga-01223, Library of Congress Prints and Photographs Division. 501

*George G. Meade,* wet collodion glass negative, by Brady National Photographic Art Gallery, ca. 1855–1865. Reproduction number LC-DIG-cwpb-05008, Selected Civil War Photographs Collection, Library of Congress Division of Prints and Photographs. 503

*Battle of Gettysburg: Pickett's Charge,* oil on canvas, by Peter F. Rothermel, 1870. Courtesy of the State Museum of Pennsylvania, Pennsylvania Historical and Museum Commission. 504

*Charge of Ewell's Corps on the Cemetary Gate and Capture of Ricketts Battery,* oil painting, by Edwin Forbes, 1865. Reproduction number LC-DIG-ppmsca-22566, Morgan Collection of Civil War Drawings, Library of Congress Prints and Photographs Division. 505

*Battle of Olustee, Florida, 1864,* lithograph, by Kurz and Allison, 1894. State Archives of Florida. 507

*Storming Fort Wagner,* chromolithograph, by Kurz and Allison (Chicago, 1890). Reproduction number LC-DIG-pga-01949, Library of Congress Prints and Photographs Division. 509

*Come and Join Us Brothers,* lithograph (Philadelphia: P. S. Duval and Son, 1863). Chicago History Museum, lCHi-22051. 510

*Abraham Lincoln* (half-length, right profile), gelatin silver print, photograph by Anthony Berger, Brady National Photographic Art Gallery, February 9, 1864. Reproduction number LC-USZ62-14259, Library of Congress Prints and Photographs Division. 515

Lincoln's Gettysburg Address, Gettysburg, 1863. National Archives. Reproduction number LC-DIG-ds-03106, Library of Congress Prints and Photographs Division. 517

*Lincoln's Address at the Dedication of the Gettysburg National Cemetery, November 19, 1863,* lithograph (Chicago: Sherwood Lithograph Co., ca. 1905). Reproduction number LC-DIG-ppmsca-19926, Library of Congress Prints and Photographs Division. 517

*Abraham Lincoln,* gelatin silver print, photograph by Lewis E. Walker, ca. 1863. Reproduction number LC-USZ62-61374, Library of Congress Prints and Photographs Division. 521

*Abraham Lincoln* (three-quarter length, facing left), gelatin silver print, photograph by Anthony Berger, Brady National Photographic Art Gallery, February 9, 1864. LC-USZ62-13739, Library of Congress Prints and Photographs Division. 530

*Abraham Lincoln* (three-quarter length, facing right), gelatin silver print, photograph by Anthony Berger, Brady National Photographic Art Gallery, February 9, 1864. LC-DIG-ppmsca-19305, Library of Congress Prints and Photographs Division. 531

*President Lincoln and His Cabinet. Reading of the Emancipation Proclamation,* print, [E. Herline], n.d. Reproduction number LC-DIG-pga-01556, Library of Congress Prints and Photographs Division. 533

*Buildings of the Great Sanitary Fair . . . Logan Square, Philadelphia, June 1864,* chromolithograph, drawn by James Queen (Philadelphia: P. S. Duval and Son, 1864). LC-DIG-pga-04061, Library of Congress Prints and Photographs Division. 536

*Hon. Abraham Lincoln, President of the United States,* albumen silver photographic print on stereo card, photograph by Lewis Emory Walker (Washington, DC: E. and H. T. Anthony, 1865). LC-DIG-ppmsca-18958, Library of Congress Prints and Photographs Division. 539

*The Old Bulldog on the Right Track,* lithograph (New York: Currier and Ives, ca. 1864). LC-USZ62-8826, Library of Congress Prints and Photographs Division. 541

"This Reminds Me of a Little Joke," *Harper's Weekly,* [September 17,] 1864, [p. 608]. M175h, Lincoln Graphics, John Hay Library, Brown University Library. 542

Text of the "Blind Memorandum," by Abraham Lincoln, August 23, 1864. Lincoln Papers, Manuscript Division, Library of Congress. 544

*Union Nominations . . . for President of the United States, Abraham Lincoln[.] for Vice President of the United States, Andrew Johnson. . .*, campaign poster (New York, 1864). Pf*AB85.L6384.Z864u, The William Whiting Nolen Collection of Lincolniana, Houghton Library, Harvard University. 544

*Union and Liberty! And the Union and Slavery!* wood engraving (New York: M. W. Siebert, 1864). LC-USZ62-945, American Cartoon Print Filing Series, Library of Congress Prints and Photographs Division. 545

Note written in October 1864, estimating the result in the electoral vote in the coming Presidential election. Abraham Lincoln Collection, New-York Historical Society. Photography © New-York Historical Society. 545

*Absolution under Fire,* oil on canvas, by Paul Wood, 1891. The Snite Museum of Art, University of Notre Dame. 547

*View of the President's Mansion,* stereocard (Washington, D.C.: Bell and Bro., n.d.). OC-0324 from the Lincoln Financial Foundation Collection, courtesy of the Indiana State Museum and Allen County Public Library. 549

*In the Hands of the Enemy after Gettysburg,* lithograph by James Hamilton after a painting by Thomas Hovenden, ca. 1889. LC-DIG-pga-01457, Library of Congress Prints and Photographs Division. 551

*John Hay,* photograph by Bierstadt brothers, 1861. John Hay Library, Brown University Library. 551

*President Lincoln and His Family,* hand-colored lithograph, by Anton Hohenstein (Philadelphia, 1865). PO406_598, Jack Smith Lincoln Graphics Collection, Indiana Historical Society. 558

*The Preservers of Our Union,* lithograph, by Kimmel and Forster, ca. 1865. Abraham Lincoln Presidential Library & Museum (ALPLM). 558

*Abraham Lincoln,* oil on canvas, by Peter Baumgras, 1865. Brown Portrait Number 270, Brown University. 560

*Abraham Lincoln,* gelatin silver print, photograph by Alexander Gardner, February 5, 1865. LC-USZ62-12380, Library of Congress Prints and Photographs Division. 562

*Lincoln's Second Inaugural,* photograph, by Alexander Gardner, March 4, 1865. Reproduction number LC-USA7-16837, Library of Congress Prints and Photographs Division. 564

*The Inaugural Address of President Abraham Lincoln Delivered in the National Capitol, March 4th, 1865,* chromolithograph, brown tint (New York: J. Gibson, c. 1865). Reproduction number LC-DIG-ppmsca-19240, Library of Congress Prints and Photographs Division. 565

*The Tallest Ruler on the Globe Is Inaugurated at Washington—The Lesser Luminaries of Europe Assisting Deferentially,* hand-tinted relief print, by William Newman, double-page spread in *Frank Leslie's Budget of Fun,* April 1865. MS Lincoln 3, Lincoln Collection, Houghton Library, Harvard University. 566

*John Wilkes Booth,* albumen print on carte de visite, ca. 1860–1865. LC-DIG-ppmsca-23892, Library of Congress Prints and Photographs Division. 570

*Lincoln's Triumphal Death March, a Glowing and Faithful Transcript of All the Scenes and Incidents Connected with the Recent Appalling Calamity of the Assassination of the President!* broadside, by Rufus Somerby (Boston: F. A. Searle, [ca. 1865]). PF Cabinet *AB85.L6384.Y865s, Houghton Library, Harvard University. 570

*The Latest Photograph of President Lincoln—Taken on the Balcony at the White House, March 6, 1865,* albumen print, photograph by Henry F. Warren, 1865. Reproduction number LC-DIG-ppmsca-19192, Library of Congress Prints and Photographs Division. 572

A. Pharazyn, *The Assassination of President Lincoln at Ford's Theatre, Washington, on the Night of Friday, April 14, 1865.* Lithograph, Philadelphia, 1865. The Alfred Whital Stern Collection of Lincolniana, Library of Congress. 574

Alonzo Chappel, *Last Hours of Lincoln,* oil on canvas, by Alonzo Chappel, 1868. Purchased by the Society, 1971.177, image lCHi-52425, Chicago History Museum. 575

*Washington and Lincoln. The Father and Savior of Our Country,* hand-colored lithograph, by Currier and Ives, ca. 1865. Reproduction number LC-DIG-pga-05067, Library of Congress Prints and Photographs Division. 576